Systems for Sustainability

People, Organizations, and Environments

Edited by

Frank A. Stowell

De Montfort University
Milton Keynes, United Kingdom

Ray L. Ison
Rosalind Armson
Jacky Holloway

The Open University
Milton Keynes, United Kingdom

Sue Jackson
Steve McRobb

De Montfort University
Milton Keynes, United Kingdom

Plenum Press • New York and London

Systems for Sustainability

People, Organizations,
and Environments

Library of Congress Cataloging-in-Publication Data

Systems for sustainability : people, organisations, and environments /
edited by Frank A. Stowell ... [et al.].
        p.   cm.
    Proceedings of the Fifth International Conference of the United
Kingdom Systems Society on Systems for Sustainability: People,
Organisations, and Environments, held July 7-11, 1997, in Milton
Keynes, U.K.
    Includes bibliographical references and index.
    ISBN 0-306-45615-X
    1. Management information systems--Congresses. 2. System
analysis--Congresses.   I. Stowell, Frank A. II. International
Conference of the United Kingdom Systems Society on Systems for
Sustainability: People, Organisations, and Environments (5th : 1997
: Milton Keynes, England)
    T58.64.S95 1997
    658.4'038--dc21   97-25876
                                                             CIP

Proceedings of the Fifth International Conference of the United Kingdom Systems Society on
Systems for Sustainability: People, Organisations, and Environments,
held July 7–11, 1997, in Milton Keynes, United Kingdom

ISBN 0-306-45615-X

© 1997 Plenum Press, New York
A Division of Plenum Publishing Corporation
233 Spring Street, New York, N. Y. 10013

http://www.plenum.com

Printed in the United States of America

PREFACE

The term "sustainability" has entered the lexicon of many academic disciplines and fields of professional practice, but to date does not appear to have been seriously considered within the systems community unless, perhaps, under other guises. Within the wider community there is no consensus around what sustainability means with some authors identifying 70 to 100 definitions of the term. Some see sustainability as the precise and quantifiable outcomes of biological systems whilst others see it in terms of processes relevant to personal and organizational change with the potential to effect changes in our relationships with out environments. Internationally it has been increasingly used in relation to the term "sustainable development"—a term popularised by the Brundland Commission's report in 1987 entitled "Our Common Future." Despite this diversity of definitions and polarised perception on its utility, unlike many other popular terms, it has not had its time and subsided quietly from our language. It is therefore timely for the systems community to explore the relationship between systems and sustainability in a range of contexts. Participants in this, the 5th International Conference of the United Kingdom Systems Society (UKSS), have been invited to reflect critically on the contribution of systems thinking and action to sustainability—to the sustainability of personal relationships, the organizations in which live and work, and our "natural" environment. Papers explore whether systems thinking has contributed at all and the extent to which the various conceptions of "sustainability" are systemic. In these proceedings these questions are explored in seven themes: systems for environmental sustainability; reflections on systems thinking and practice; learning organizations and systems; critical systems; methodology use and development; information system development; innovation and organization and change management.

Collectively, the papers represent an important contribution to ongoing dialogue about sustainability and systems as a domain of inquiry and practice. Those of you who look to this volume to sharpen the definition(s) of sustainability will be disappointed. As Andrew Campbell (1994) has observed: "attempts to define sustainability miss the point that, like beauty, sustainability is in the eye of the beholder... it is inevitable that assessments of...sustainability are socially constructed, which is why there are so many definitions." The contributed papers represent the perspectives of authors from 17 countries. They provide a contemporary and challenging synthesis of systems scholarship of relevance to practitioners, researchers, policy makers, and any citizens concerned with effecting change which might be described as systemic and sustainable.

This conference and proceedings celebrates a decade of conference achievement by the UKSS. It is a non-profit making professional society committed to the development and promotion of "systems" philosophy, theory, models, concepts and methodologies for improving decision-making and problem-solving for the benefit of organisations and the wider society. Membership currently stands at over 300 people. The Fifth International Conference was co-hosted by The Open University and De Montfort University. De Montfort University is a pioneering and innovative institution and one of Britain's largest universities with around 28,000 students based at four centres. The Open University, which has pioneered supported open learning, is the UK's largest University with over 150,000 students in 1995.

Rosalind Armson
Jacky Holloway
Ray L. Ison
Sue Jackson
Steve McRobb
Frank A. Stowell

REFERENCE

Campbell, A. (1994) Participatory inquiry: beyond research and extension in the sustainability era. Proc. International Symposium on Systems-Oriented Research in Agriculture and Rural Development, Montpellier, France.

ACKNOWLEDGMENTS

Clearly the success of an international conference is because of the efforts and support of a large number of people. Over the last decade the UKSS has held conferences at a number of Universities within the UK and in each case enjoyed a high level of support and encouragement from the staff at those Universities. Judging by the support that we are enjoying from the two host Universities of the 5th International UKSS conference we are pleased to report that this tradition continues to thrive. The committee would like to express their thanks, and the thanks of the United Kingdom Systems Society, to the members of staff at the Open University and De Montfort University for the support and encouragement given by them to the conference. In particular we wish to thank the Vice Chancellors of the hosting institutions Sir John Daniel and Professor Kenneth Barker and also to the Pro-Vice Chancellors Professor Chiddick and Geoff Peters who have given active support for this important event on the UKSS calendar.

The work of the conference committee has been lightened by the unstinting support given by the conference secretariat, Sheila Williamson and Kelly Fabian, who have so ably assisted in the administration and in the preparation of these proceedings.

COMMITTEE

PROGRAMME

Rosalind Armson	Jackie Holloway	Ray Ison
Sue Jackson	Steve McRobb	Frank Stowell

The committee would also like to thank the co-sponsors of this event:

The Greek Systems Society	The Spanish Systems Society
The Italian Systems Society	The Czech Systems Society
The Australian Systems Society	The French System South

INTERNATIONAL ADVISORY COMMITTEE

Hector Rincorn	Gianfranco Minati
Bill Reckmeyer	Evelyne Andreewsky

CONTENTS

Reflections of Systems Thinking and Practice

Learning Organisation and Systems

Critical Systems

Methodology Use and Development

Innovation and Organisations

Change Management

LEARNING TO PERSIST

A Systemic View of Development

Richard Bawden

Centre for Systemic Development
University of Western Sydney Hawkesbury
Richmond NSW 2753 Australia

1. SUSTAINABILISM

Sustainability is a concept which is entirely appropriate to the age which has spawned it. Being as ambiguous, complex, mystical and multi-faceted as it is, it represents a wonderful example of the confusion that comes with what has been termed reflexive modernity (Beck, 1992): This epoch where we must now face up to the "hazards and insecurities induced and introduced by modernisation" and concern ourselves "not just with making nature useful, or with releasing mankind from traditional constraints, but also essentially with problems resulting from techno-economic development itself".

What was to have been our dream, the way which we as a species could escape the almost inevitable tendency towards extinction—a self designed *Homo immortalitus*—is turning out to be a veritable nightmare. Our own great evolutionary endowment, our ability to reason, encouraged us to believe that we could complement inter-generational evolution with intra-generational learning. We reasoned that we could learn how to adapt ourselves to our environments essentially through adapting our environments to us. Yet in this process we have unleashed forces for change on a global scale which we did not foresee, nor seem now able to control. Ironically it has taken science to illustrate its own impacts while also revealing its own inadequacies at dealing with them. Included here is the somewhat paradoxical insight that as a way of learning it is very limited in what it can learn about itself. Even as we come to recognise the limitations of scientific reductionism in dealing with systemic phenomena, including the global ramifications of many technologies, we are also recognising its limitations for self-reflexivity.

The recent emergence of 'sustainabilism', as a new theme for the development agenda, reflects a curious mix of motivations including intellectual arrogance, moral guilt, spiritual imbalance, genuine concern and primeval fear. And not the least of these fears is that perhaps we cannot after all, really ever know what is happening around us, or even more important, what we should be doing about that. Nature has turned out to be much

Systems for Sustainability, edited by Stowell *et al.*
Plenum Press, New York, 1997

more surprising than we at first thought, and included amongst those surprises is the observation that human beings have a second evolutionary endowment, a sense of moral responsibility and obligation, that does not fit well as a focus for scientific inquiry, while
having the capacity to very significantly temper both its processes and outcomes.

Many of these issues are well illustrated by reference to agriculture, where 'sustainabilism' has seriously been on the development agenda for more than a decade, but where
concerns for its non-sustainability have been expressed for almost as long as it has been
practised.

2. THE PROBLEMATIQUE

All farming practices, no matter how minimal, change the very 'nature of things':
Farming is the act of cultivation, and all farmers quite deliberately intervene into the
'natural' pattern to purposefully direct relationships between animals, plants and the
physical environment with which they interact. The nature of these interventions varies
enormously of course, as do the reasons behind them, for farmers do what they do, to fulfil a myriad of purposes. Farming is as much a way of life, as they say, as it is an industry,
and hundreds of millions of people across the world are engaged in it in response to these
multiple motivations. With such a multitude of purposes and outcomes, it is really difficult
to know what precisely it is that anyone would want to sustain especially given the fact
that as it is currently practised, agriculture contains the potential seeds of its own self-destruction in the form those very technologies that were introduced to improve its performance. Science-based technologies are used to amplify production in virtually every part of
the globe with truly global consequences, both positive and negative. And with the globalisation of both its bounty and its risks, has come the realisation that the thinking that has
got us to this stage cannot get us beyond it, to paraphrase Albert Einstein.

An example of a sense of exploration of new ways of thinking about agricultural
sustainability, and some of the confusion inherent in such an endeavour, comes from Gordon Douglass (1984): "Agricultural sustainability", he wrote, "means different things to
different people". He suggested that were at least three quite different approaches here -
three different schools of thought as he called them: (a) the "productivity school" for
whom the primary (exclusive?) focus is the ability to sustain the productivity of farming
enterprises so that the world's ever-growing human population can continue to be fed; (b)
the "stewardship school" where the focus is essentially ecological, in that it conditions the
focus on productivity by placing it within the context of the sustainability of the renewable natural resource base, and (c) the "community school" for which farming is but one
variable in the quest for the "vitality, social organisation and culture of rural life".
Douglass went on to suggest that agriculturists would ideally prefer to ally themselves to a
fourth "school", that of 'responsible agriculture' which represented the synthesis of all of
the other three. However he suggested that commitment to such a position would be extremely difficult given the innate contradictions between protagonists of each of the three
'schools', to say nothing of those who remain uncommitted to the belief that sustainability
has any usefulness at all as a conceptual guide to better agricultures.

Yet herein lies precisely the challenge that agriculturists must face, and by extrapo-
lation, anyone else concerned with 'sustainabilism': To be ultimately responsible, agriculture has to embrace systems which are concurrently productive, self-renewing and
communally beneficial. I want to posit that these can never be designed to be ultimately
sustainable, particularly from the 'outside'. Rather I want to float the proposition that the

only real use of the concept of sustainability is as a focus of concern about their own futures, by systems themselves! In other words, the challenge is to create self-referential
systems which are continually learning how to persist, where this learning will perforce
include learning about the process of learning itself, as well as the impacts of all learning
on the nature of the relationship between the leaner and that which is being learned. This
represents a very significant shift in thinking about the matter of sustainability in agriculture where the emphasis to date has been on how farming systems can be designed in
ways which will allow them to be sustainable into the future; and where the challenge has
been how to accommodate the very different perspectives and worldviews which concurrently prevail within the debate in agriculture.

What I am proposing is that we shift the focus from the quest for sustainable agricultural systems *per se*, to the sustainable quest for systems of inquiry and in exploring that
proposition I need to highlight systemics as philosophy.

3. SYSTEMICS AS PHILOSOPHY

There are three fundamental beliefs that I suggest are the foundations of a systemic
philosophy—or the essence of systemicity if you will: (i) that whole entities are assumed
to have properties different from the sum of their parts (we might say that systemics are
thus grounded in an ontology of holism), (ii) that such properties both reflect and confer a
sense of coherence on to systems which are bounded by knowable conditions (reflecting
particular epistemological stances), and (iii) that the coherence is assumed to reflect 'tensions of difference' of other entities both within the boundary (as subsystems) of specific
systems, and between such systems and the environments (or suprasystems) in which they
'exist'. The host of principles which can be further derived from these fundamental beliefs
provide the basis for systems theories, while these in turn provide the foundations for systems practices.

The relevance of the essence of systemicity to the issue of 'sustainable agriculture'
lies in its application to the notion of different 'systems of inquiry' involved in the discourse about 'better agriculture'. This becomes evident if we re-examine the different
"sustainability schools" presented by Douglass (1984) above. Elsewhere (Bawden, 1995) I
have argued that each of the three positions on sustainability which he identified can be
understood as a reflection of one of three different 'worldviews' each with its own philosophical foundations in ontology and epistemology. Let me pursue these distinctions here,
for they are at the heart of the matter of "learning to persist".

The logic rests in the contention that each of us both views the world and construes
meaning from it, through particular perspectives - worldviews - which are integrations of
intellectual, normative and emotional positions. Worldviews which reflect very different
beliefs about the nature of nature (ontology), or about how nature is known (epistemology), will result in very different interpretations about how nature should be treated! An
ontology of holism, which represents the position that whole entities have properties different from the sum of their parts, is thus contrasted with the ontology of reductionism
which represents its antithesis. Similarly, an epistemology of objectivism, which represents the position that all knowledge must be referential to some objective, unchanging
standard to determine the nature of truth or reality or goodness, is thus contrasted with
(contextual) relativism which represents the antithesis to that.

Imagine an orthogonal matrix composed from these dimensions with the two ontologies representing the opposing poles of the vertical dimension and the two opposing epis-

temologies representing the horizontal. Imagine now the four cells of this matrix as the four panes of a conceptual window on the world through which one both views the world 'beyond' and construes meaning about it, and take this image then to the matter of agricultural sustainability and the different "schools" identified by Douglass (1984).

His "productivity " position reflects a "reductionistic" ontology, while both his "stewardship" and "community" paradigms in contrast, are reflective of an "holistic" ontology. The distinction between these latter two "schools" lies in differences in their epistemologies: "Stewardship" with its ecological emphasis, reflects an epistemology of "objectivism", in other words that knowledge about the "stewardship" of systems can be objectively known. The "community" paradigm for sustainable development, on the other hand, because it embraces issues of ethics, justice, and aesthetics, and a belief that all knowledge is essentially relative to some specific context or other, rather than to only one objective reality, reflects an epistemology of "contextual relativism". Both of these two latter paradigms could be said to be systemic in that they are both centred on systems. In the case of stewardship we have a prevailing worldview of what I have termed "ecocentricity", while the community paradigm reflects an "holonocentric" position (Bawden 1995). I submit that holonocentricity is a most liberting position, for from there, it is easy to construe each of the four "matrix cells" as four sub-systems within a system of inquiry. The coherence of such a system is provided by the substantial tensions of difference which exist between the four sub-systems, reflecting as they do, profoundly different philosophical positions about nature and how it can be known.

4. SYSTEMS OF INQUIRY

In addition to the inherent systemicity of inquiry involving different views, the process of learning also has other opportunities to be systemic: Firstly, the learner and the experience from which he or she is trying to learn, can represent a systemic whole. Secondly, as the context through which anything is learned is influenced profoundly by the worldviews which are held, all inquiry should embrace three "levels" of learning concurrently. Thus even as we go about learning about the matter to hand, we can also be learning about how that is being learned (referred to as meta-learning). Equally, while we are engaged in these two levels of inquiry we can also be learning about the sort of philosophical foundations of worldviews (referred to as epistemic learning) some of which have already been identified, and how they are influencing learning at the other two levels. Finally, as learning is essentially a social act, discourse about changing the way things are done can thus be represented as a multi component system of inquiry of interacting learning individuals. In this manner a complex and dynamic learning system has been created, which at its best will be both self-reflexive and self-regulating: New knowledge is created just as new ways of knowing are created just as new philosophical contexts for knowing are created; with each inter-relating with, and influencing the others. The learning system is constantly using knowledge generated at one level to inform and critique knowledge generated at other levels, just as knowledge being created at one locus (by one individual) in the system, is informing and critiquing knowledge being created at other loci across that system.

The image that emerges is one of a coherent conversation being held across a community of interconnected learning individuals, at three different "levels" concurrently. It is important to recognise that the coherence comes not from consensus, but from dissensus as the source of what I have been calling the "tensions of difference". Learning systems are dynamic and co-adaptive precisely because they deal constantly with their own inherent tensions as well as the tensions that exist between the system and its environment.

And it is precisely because they are self-referential that they can learn how to persist.

Systems of inquiry which focus on better agriculture will thrive on the differences or conflicts between the various worldviews as long as the philosophical boundary conditions of each of those worldviews are drawn into the discourse. "Productivity" is a perfectly legitimate focus for inquiry as long as the reductionism/objectivism boundaries are clarified. So too for "stewardship" and "community" with respect to their particular boundary conditions. Thus to talk critically about productivity as a focus for sustainability is to talk too about the limitations of positivist science to deal with normative issues, and the limitations of utilitarianism as an interpretation of human motivation and action. To talk critically about stewardship as a focus for sustainability is to talk too about the limitations of the reified construct of the eco-system, as well as of notions of balance and equilibrium. To talk critically of community as a focus for sustainability is to address issues of the distortions of communications and the fixity of personal worldviews.

In sum, the quest for persistent forms of agriculture lies with the persistence of our capabilities and competencies to create learning systems from which new ideas for better actions will constantly emerge through discourse. This contrasts with the idea that novel agricultural systems which will persist come what may, can ever be designed.

5. DEDICATION AND ACKNOWLEDGMENTS

This presentation is lovingly and respectfully dedicated to the memory of my late wife Diane, my love for whom perfectly exemplified many of the principles of systemicity and persistence which I have espoused above. I wish also to particularly acknowledge inspirations provided by two of my friends and colleagues, Professors Raymond Ison of the Open University and Laurence Busch of Michigan State University.

6. REFERENCES

Bawden, R.J., 1995, Systemic Development: A Learning Approach to Change, unpublished occasional paper #1 Centre for Systemic Development

Beck, U., 1992, *Risk Society: Towards a New Modernity*, Translation by Mark Ritter, Sage Publications, London

Douglass, G.K., 1984, The Meanings of Agricultural Sustainability, in: *Agricultural Sustainability in a Changing World Order* (G.K. Douglass, ed.), Westview Press, Boulder

2

POLITICS FOR SUSTAINABILITY

Margaret Blunden

The University of Westminster
35 Marylebone Road
London NW1 5LS, England

1. INTRODUCTION

Securing a sustainable future for human societies requires a radical rethink of the nature of political activity. The dominant concept of politics is as problem-solving, an idea derived from a misapplication of the methods of technology, with its undiluted concentration on the immediate desires of the present. This way of thinking has played a major part in creating the distinctive characteristics of the developed world, whose future sustainability, like that of the rest of the planet, is now in doubt.

Sustainability is here defined following Vickers (1983, p. 6) as keeping within critical limits over time the relationships within and between human societies and between human societies and their physical milieu. Stability—similar to but not identical with sustainability—generally has a more political connotation then sustainability and is associated with the maintenance of form or order in human societies over time. The relationship between stability and sustainability raises the question, what are the limits to change, what are the essential parameters which collective political action must retain, beyond what point must deviations from a standard be resisted, if human societies are to avoid destabilisation, to maintain equilibrium into the future. This paper argues that the overwhelming strength of present-mindedness, encouraged among other things by a disfunctional conception of the nature of political activity and of knowledge, makes it difficult even to focus on the question.

2. THE IMPACT OF SCIENCE ON THE CONCEPT OF POLITICS

Sustainability—the maintenance of relationships over time—is a concept which political philosophy and political epistemology, as currently constituted, find difficult to deal with. This is partly because of the impact on political thinking of a misunderstood "epistemology of science" deriving from the particular development of the natural sciences from the Newtonian period onwards.

The prestige attached since the European Enlightenment of the eighteenth century to science and the successes of technology have powerfully affected our capacity to think about, and to manage collectively through the political process, key issues affecting the stability and survivability of modern society. An incomplete understanding of the epistemology of science has been transferred from one field where it has been enormously successful to another where it is not appropriate. Similarly, the transfer of an engineering - type problem solving approach to politics, which has the effect of restricting the focus of concern and value in time and space, has both helped to create modern power holding structures and is in turn powerfully reinforced by them.

Popular understanding of an early period in the development of the scientific method—a way of knowing which is always more than just a technique, as Michael Oakeshott (1991) has reminded us—has conditioned our ways of acquiring knowledge, the focus of our concerns, our ways of acting and our style of acting, thinking and expressing. (Vickers, 1976, p.146) Science has affected our ways of acquiring knowledge by exaggerating the role of analysis and obscuring the importance of the distinct and equally important function of synthesis. The processes of science involve both the imaginative, intuitive leaps of hypothesis formation and the logical, rational acts of hypothesis testing. But the application of science into other areas has in practice transferred only one of these aspects, it has served to emphasise the importance of rational deduction and technique and diminished the importance of the creative, the imaginative and the intuitive. It has encouraged the assumption that form is always something which is discovered rather than, as in the case of human systems, something which is created by the evolution of norms or standards of what ought to be. It has served to create a false, rationalist distinction between the actor and the acted upon, the observer and the observed. Both Vickers and Oakeshott agree that prevailing conceptions of the nature of knowledge are defective. Both argue that the important area of knowledge excluded by the rationalist is tacit knowledge, that which is known but which cannot be precisely described. To Vickers, this means intuitive insight, imagination and sensitivity to form; to Oakeshott it means traditional knowledge, historical inheritance, that which the apprentice absorbs from the master but which cannot explicitly be taught.

The influence of science has been to concentrate our most prestigious human resources on those areas in which the scientific method yields reliable knowledge. Natural science establishes "what is"; it cannot deal with "what ought to be". Its pervasive influence has created a reluctance, discomfort or even embarrasssment about addressing ethical questions which are at the heart of politics. The focus of our intellectual concerns is the practical and the immediate. Other more expansive questions, including human relationships in time and space, are at the margins of serious political concern. The business of science is the creation of new knowledge and its influence, interacting with other factors, has helped to attach intellectual prestige to the discovery of what is new, rather than to the serious consideration of what is old, of what has successfully endured over time. But sustainability involves persistence over time. It means a continuing relationship between the past, the present and the future. The influence of a partial scientific epistemology has led to a relative neglect of the dimension of time, of the creation rather than the discovery of form, of holistic interconnections and interrelations over time and space.

3. TECHNOLOGY, PROBLEM SOLVING, AND RATIONALISM IN POLITICS

Popular understanding of the approach of technologists has had a different but equally profound impact on the theory and practice of politics. What Oakeshott describes as "the approximation of politics to engineering" can otherwise be described as the conception of politics as problem solving. Technology has both altered our conception of the nature of political activity, and greatly complicated its task. Two centuries of unimpeded technological advance have escalated popular expectations of what we can expect the political process to deliver.

Our understanding of the political process as a problem solving technology, put to the service of an endless succession of finite goals, is now so established and unchallenged as to be invisible. Oakeshott's critique of political rationalism centres on its abrupt discontinuities with the past, its present mindedness, and its exaggeration of what is knowable and what is possible. Political rationalists, as defined by Oakeshott, are enemies of the customary or the traditional. The political rationalist wants to begin everything *de novo*. The past is significant only as an encumbrance, never the enjoyment of an inheritance.

> The conduct of affairs, for the Rationalist, is a matter of solving problems...In this activity the character which the Rationalist claims for himself is the character of the engineer, whose mind (it is supposed) is controlled throughout by the appropriate technique and whose first step is to dismiss from his attention everything not directly related to his specific intentions. This assimilation of politics to engineering is, indeed, what may be called the myth of rationalist politics...The politics it inspires may be called the politics of the felt need; for the Rationalist, politics are always charged with the feeling of the moment..That anything should be allowed to stand between a society and the satisfaction of the felt needs at each moment of its history must appear to the Rationalist a piece of mysticism and nonsense..Thus political life is resolved into a succession of crises, each to be surmounted by the application of "reason". Each generation, indeed each administration, should see unrolled before it the blank sheet of infinite possibility. (Oakeshott, 1991, p. 9)

Unfortunate examples of rationalist politics in action, international or domestic, are not hard to call to mind, since they are all around us. Disastrous examples include the Vietnam War, nuclear energy programmes worldwide, and the Soviet irrigation project which dried up the Aral Sea in what is now the independent state of Uzbekistan. Development projects, which by definition are hurried, ahistorical attempts to engineer a path from the "primitive" to the "advanced", illustrate particularly starkly the approach of political rationalism. David Orr has described one such development project, the Bali agricultural project in Indonesia, as a parable for the history of much of the twentieth century. (Orr, 1996, p. 30) It is particularly interesting in this context because it demonstrates how the rationalist politics of problem solving painfully rupture the links between past, present and future.

Between 1978 and 1984 the Asian Development Bank spent $24 million on "improving" agriculture on the island of Bali. The target for improvement—the problem defined for solving—was an ancient agricultural system organized around 173 village co-operatives linked by a network of temples operated by "water priests" devoted to the service of the water goddess Dewi Dann. The new plan required large capital investment in dams and canals and the purchase of pesticides and fertilizers. The objective was to make both the Balinese people and their land productive all the year round. Old practices of fallowing were ended, along with community celebrations and rituals.

The results were catastrophic: agricultural yields declined, pests profilerated, and the coherence of village society began to unravel. "The development experts dismanted a system that had worked well for more than a millenium and replaced it with something that did not work at all." (Orr, 1996, p. 30)

The Bali development, as an example of rationalist politics, and the shortcomings of the problem solving paradigm or goal seeking as applied to politics, illustrates among other things its contempt for the past, its reductionism, and its short termism. In other terms, the Bali project could be described as the misplaced application of a hard systems methodology—a methodology derived from engineering—to a soft, ill-structured problem, to what Peter Checkland calls a "human activity system", in which the meaning which the actors in the situation attach to it are all important. (Checkland,1981) Alternative approaches are not hard to find. A soft systems approach, as developed by Checkland, would explore the variety of meanings which the existing system had for its participants and orchestrate a debate about how to proceed. This would have the advantage of inducing caution, of slowing down the process of innovation, and directing attention to possible unintended consequences of change. A relationship - maintaining approach, following Vickers, would reject problem solving and goal seeking entirely, and concentrate on the maintenance of key relationships, economic, environmental and phenomenological. This might lead to a decision to repair and improve what existed, rather than to destroy and build anew, or even to leave well alone. Either approach is of course more likely to promote sustainable outcomes.

Rationalism in politics—the use of hard systems methodologies in soft, unstructured human activity systems—is the antithesis of sustainability. Sustainability, in all its definitional nuances, involves the maintenance of reliable and acceptable relationships over time. The maintenance of relationships domestically, within states, includes the relationship between freedom and order, between variety and homogeneity. The maintenance of relationships internationally, between states, includes the relationship between national sovereignty and commitment to collective international action. The maintenance of relationships between states and their milieu, in an anthropocentric perspective, includes the relationship between exploitation (meeting present needs) and renewability (meeting future needs). In an ecocentric perspective, it involves maintaining a balance between the needs of the species man and the survivability of ecosystems which have intrinsic value, irrespective of their utility to man.

The foremost critics of politics as short term goal seeking, of applying technological problem solving to the soft, unstructured situations of human governance, have, like Geoffrey Vickers, aimed their criticisms at what we used to call the "western world". But the most stupendous political rationalism in history was Marxist-Leninist, which took for granted the desirability of razing everything which went before and engineering from scratch a new social, economic, political, psychological order on rigid ideological lines. Marx had thoroughly absorbed the capitalist Victorian faith in scientific and technological progress as the means by which human beings could outsmart and master nature. Marx and Engels never doubted instrumental reason, indeed they embraced it with unbounded fervour. (Eckersley, 1992, p. 80) The unquestioned and unquestionable belief in a "scientific" approach to everything has proved far more enduring in Russia than the transitory existence of the Soviet state. Many Russians still appear to believe that, outside science, there is no knowledge. It is not therefore surprising that the Soviet system proved relatively unsustainable among modern political systems, more sustainable than fascism of course, but less sustainable than western democracy. The collapse of the Soviet Union reveals the shortcomings of scientism, of reductionist, cryto-scientific rationalism as well as those of Marxist-Leninism. Problem solving remains, however, deeply rooted both in the successor states and in the west.

Problem solving, with its tight parameters and bounded time frame, has helped to create and is in turn reinforced by the rhythms of modern life, the consultant or the chief executive with the fixed term contract, the three year development project, the politician with five years to impress the electorate before the next election. Problem solving, with its focus on means, not ends, on the solving once and for all of discrete and clearly defined problems, on engineering an optimum path from A to B, on turning one state into another, on the here and now, helps in hundreds of ways to serve individual career objectives. The size and influence of the problem solving constituency makes it extraordinarily to question whether there may be limits to the rate or direction of change. The rationalist approach is embedded in power structures, including universities, whose function, it often appears, is to resist alternative paradigms and world-views.

4. TOWARDS A POLITICS OF SUSTAINABILITY

A politics which focusses on maintaining over time those relationships necessary for sustainability, which avoids the present mindedness of the rationalist, problem-solving approach, is superficially conservative, and profoundly radical. Such a political approach cuts across all major party lines, conservative, liberal, republican, democrat, labour, socialist, in developed countries, with the exception of ecology parties. Sustainable politics ignores the capitalist/socialist divide, the polarisation which has dominated the present generation of political leaders, recognising that in a longer term perspective what capitalism and communism have in common—the rationalist politics of problem solving, and an Enlightenment belief in limitless material progress—is as significant as what divides them. Sustainable politics are a mixture of conservatism and change. The conservative elements are not those normally championed by conservative party policies, which have, in most countries, surrendered entirely to the politics of the immediate felt need. The radical aspects of the agenda are fundamentally epistemological: they involve a reconceptualisation of the nature of political activity. It is perhaps ironical that it is ways of thinking derived from modern science and technology, specifically systems thinking, which are of most help here.

A political approach which maintains relationships, rather than solves problems, has a distinctive attitude towards the past and the future. The more cautious approach towards destroying what is there, the inclination towards evolution, incrementalism and repair rather than revolution, destruction and rebuild, which sustainability calls for, makes common cause with some strands of philosophical, as opposed to practising, conservatism.

Generating a sense of relationship with, and responsibility for, the future, beyond the immediate one or two succeeding generations with whom one coexists, is a more radical matter. There is no precedent for this, no tradition which can be called upon, because it has been less necessary before. It is the relatively new capacity of modern technology to alter the environment far into the future—the physical world, including perhaps the gene pool itself—which requires a different attitude towards and valuation of the relationship between present and the future. What we currently have is a lag between the technological capacity to affect the future and the capacity of human beings to imagine and take responsibility for that future. We do not know to what extent it is possible to extend man's concern to a more distant time horizon. There is at present within orthodox political thinking (again excepting the ecologists) little acknowledgement of a need to attempt it. And any such attempt would quickly collide with the structures of democratic politics, product and promoter of problem solving, which focus so exclusively on responding to the immediate needs of present generations.

An extension of the time horizon necessarily involves an extension of the space horizon. It is hard to think of a technological process impacting on future generations whose effects will be confined within national boundaries. A responsible concern for a sustainable future is incompatible with "national interest" as the measure of all things, the ultimate court of appeal, the stuff of day to day political debate. A first step would be an acknowledgment that national interest is a long term concept, balancing the needs of the present and the future, and that long term national interest so conceived involves an imaginative and thorough rethinking of international policies towards those countries, particularly in the developing world, whose present actions, not less than those of one's own government, will bear so heavily on the future national interest. A second, more radical step, is to acknowledge that national interest, or national sovereignty, cannot however defined be the ultimate criterion by which political action is judged in an interdependent world. There may be circumstances in which not just immediate national interest, but longer term national interest, have to give way before a greater good defined regionally or globally. Global interest, not national interest, becomes the relevant measure.

An equally radical and difficult culture shift, is the necessary retreat from technological over-confidence and unbridled optimism, the belief in limitless human capacity to understand biospherical systems, the assumption of human omnipotence on a global scale, deeply rooted in western culture since the Enlightenment. The distinction constantly reiterated by Geoffrey Vickers, that the power to alter (which mankind undoubtedly has in a high degree) and the power to control over a long timescale (which it does not), is a vital one. His point that the greater the impact on the environment the less predictable the future becomes, is becoming obvious, as "problem solving" itself generates problems faster than subsequent armies of problem solvers can tackle them. The most painful aspect of such a culture shift will undoubtedly be the need collectively to rethink what to expect, what to attempt and what to put up with (Vickers, 1983, p. 49), the implication being that in many dimensions we will in the future have to attempt less and put up with more.

New epistemologies, new ways of thinking, apprehending, and knowing—what the Germans call verstehen as well as wissen—are the most crucial factor in creating a new politics for a sustainable future. The most powerful action, it is said, is a thought. Recent developments in science and technology now hold out new promise, by the familiar processes of transplantation into political thinking. As Robyn Eckersley has pointed out, new scientific discoveries particularly the picture of ecological and subatomic reality that has emerged from new discoveries in biology and physics have made inroads into many assumptions of the Newtonian worldview, including undermining technological optimism, the confident belief that with further scientific research we can rationally manage (ie predict, manipulate and control) all the negative unintended consequences of large-scale human interventions in nature. (Eckersley, 1992, p. 51) Much in modern science tends to discredit the anthropocentric idea that nature is made of up discrete building blocks and that the observer is therefore completely separated from the observed.

But it is systems technology which has generated what Vickers calls "the most powerful conceptual innovation in our culture since the first decade of this century" (Vickers,1976, p. 160), of enormous significance for its potential for exposing the shortcomings of problem solving and challenging the rationalist approach to politics. Whereas the translation of engineering technology into politics has encouraged the short term, the discrete, the reductionist "problem", the translation of systems technology into politics should serve to focus attention on the long term, on the maintenance of relationships and order over time, the essence of systems thinking being the notion of form or order, sustained over time by a self-correcting process. (Vickers, 1983, p. xix) The task of developing a systems epistemology of politics is in its infancy. There is in the literature as yet nothing to compare with the contribution which Vickers made, in the last twenty five years of his life, to thinking through the implications of the systems revolution for the art and practice of human government. Vickers himself identified four key concepts - form, regulation, stability and interdependence - as giving systemic thinking its power and extended relevance in the fields which concerned him, that of "human governance." He identified the importance of stability as the preservation of form (sometimes through enormous changes) over time; he concluded that human organisations, like any others, can only enable if they simultaneously constrain, indeed their capacity to enable depends on their capacity to constrain; and argued that political actors must conceive of themselves as acting not from outside on some system alien to them but from inside more than one system of which they themselves are part. Systemic insight made plain, he argues, that no linear trend, can continue indefinitely, but will ultimately reverse itself, at tremendous cost, unless human intervention takes place earlier to reverse it at a more limited cost. Above all, thinking in systems terms makes clear that stable and sustainable futures depend on conceiving of the business of politics as relationship maintaining, not goal seeking or problem solving.

5. CONCLUSION

A relationship-maintaining perspective shifts the focus of concern, as problem solving does not, to the partnership of present and future, on sustaining a balance between present and future needs and entitlements, according to those norms of the acceptable and unacceptable which it is the business of politics to address. It demands an expansion of the space as well as the time horizon, and moving beyond the concept of national interest. All these processes constrain the immediate demands of the present, they call into question the unquestioned supremacy of responding to immediate felt needs. The obstacles changing our conception of politics from a problem solving to a relationship maintaining activity are enormous. But nothing less is needed if the collective decision making of the political process is to serve the interests of sustainability.

REFERENCES

Checkland, Peter, 1981, *Systems Thinking, Systems Practice,* John Wiley, Chichester.
Eckersly, Robyn, 1992, *Environmentalism and Political Theory*, UCL Press, London.
Oakeshott, Michael, 1991, *Rationalism in Politics and other Essays,* Liberty Press, Indianapolis (first published by Methuen, London, 1962)
Orr, David, 1996, "Slow Knowledge", *Resurgence,* no 179
Vickers, Geoffrey, 1976, unpublished manuscript, copyright Jeanne Vickers (based on 1975 lectures at the University of California, Berkeley)
Vickers, Geoffrey, 1983, *Human Systems are Different,* Harper and Row, London.

3

REQUIREMENTS ANALYSIS FOR INFORMATION SYSTEMS

The QUICKethics Approach

Enid Mumford

Emeritus Professor Manchester Business School
University of Manchester

This paper discusses a participative design method called QUICKethics. QUICK-ETHICS is used to assist the definition of information needs prior to the aquisition of an MIS.

1. WHAT IS QUICKETHICS?

QUICKethics stands for QUality Information from Considered Knowledge. It is the front end of a a systems design methodology called ETHICS - Effective Technical and Human Implementation of Computer based Systems. It involves users in the specification of their information needs and in the redesign of the organizational context that will surround the information system.

QUICKethics has three important design stages. First the analysis and description of information needs. Second, the setting of clear objectives for the design of the new system. These objectives will be both related to improving efficiency and to increasing the job satisfaction and quality of working life of the user group. Third, the redesign of the work organization. This is done to improve the ability of the department or function to operate at high efficiency when achieving its business mission and to enable the new information system to operate as efficiently and effectively as possible. Ideally, this reorganization is carried out before the introduction of the new information system.

QUICKethics will be described in detail later in this paper but first it is important to discuss the advantages of user involvement in the design process and to be clear about what participation means and requires.

2. WHY INVOLVE USERS?

A particularly significant argument today is that expensive systems may fail to work effectively or even to become operational if user participation is not a part of the design

Systems for Sustainability, edited by Stowell *et al.*
Plenum Press, New York, 1997

process. There is now a high degree of risk in not involving users. Frequently users have knowledge that systems designers urgently need. The London Ambulance system failure was apparently influenced by a lack of user involvement. Many of today's users are powerful groups who can be ambivalent about a new information system if they are not involved. This is true of management groups, particularly senior management, many of whom were educated without having contact with computers. Most important, if users are not involved the new system may not be 'relevant' to their information needs. In the author's experience a bad fit between a new system and the requirements of the user is the most frequent cause of user dissatisfaction.

Managers often have to be persuaded to participate. They plead lack of time or claim it is the computer department's responsibility. Once they do get involved, however, they also become committed to the new system and appreciate that they can steer the design process in a direction that will enable them to do a more effective job. The most difficult group to persuade to participate are usually top management.

One of the problems, and also advantages of participation, is that it brings together individuals or groups who may have very different interests. Each interest group is likely to define the problem in a different way and to direct the participation process at different objectives. The challenge for any organization that decides to use participation as a strategy then becomes to create the kinds of structures and processes that will assist all the different stakeholders to obtain some gains from using this approach. These gains will not necessarily be all of the same kind but they should enable each group to say with conviction ' the new system will have clear benefits for us'.

3. PARTICIPATION AS A CONTRIBUTION TO EFFECTIVE INFORMATION SYSTEMS DESIGN

A company creating a participative structure will, for example, have to decide whether to choose direct or indirect forms of participation. Direct participation is when everyone with an interest in the new system wants to exert some influence. This is often true of management or specialist groups. Indirect participation is when influence is exerted through intermediaries. If an indirect approach such as a representative group is chosen as the vehicle for decision making, then attention has to be paid to such matters as ensuring that all interests are represented, to deciding how the members of the participative forum are selected or elected and whether a number of groups at different organizational levels is required.

The process of participation also involves the acquisition of knowledge so that decisions are taken from an informed position. It involves learning, the development of effective working relationships over time, the setting and achieving of goals, and the implementation of solutions.

The design of new information systems is very suitable for a participative approach for the following reasons:

- It usually involves a number of interest groups (management, systems designers, direct users, indirect users, suppliers, customers etc.)
- It requires knowledge and this knowledge is likely to be spread throughout the different interest groups and not be located solely in one.
- The design task is complex and takes time. Participation enables a shared learning process to take place in which each of the interest groups can contribute to the problem solving process.

- The various interest groups are likely to have different values, needs and objectives and these can be brought out into the open, discussed and attempts made to reconcile them as part of the participative process.

Participation involves a process over time and not merely the giving of an opinion at one moment in time. It requires a high commitment from users who may be associated with all aspects of systems development including analysis, design, construction, implementation and evaluation.

Participation in the total design task for a new system would involve the following:

- Participating in the initiation of the project. Agreeing that it shall go ahead.
- Diagnosis and specification of existing problems and needs.
- Setting of organizational and technical objectives.
- Examination of alternative solutions.
- Selection of 'best fit' solution.
- Detailed design of organizational and technical work systems and procedures.
- Implementation of the system.
- Evaluation of the working system.
- Strategies for further development

4. WHY ORGANIZATIONAL REDESIGN SHOULD COME FIRST

Once clear objectives for change have been agreed then, ideally, the change process should begin with organizational redesign or business process improvement. There are two reasons for starting here rather than with technical design. The first is that new technology needs to be associated with an effective, streamlined form of work organization and not with an old system often created to accommodate manual or early computer processes. The second is that it is important for a design group to be very clear about the business mission, objectives, key tasks, critical success factors and major problems of the work area it is concerned with before making major investment decisions in technology.

The methodological framework of QUICKethics is influenced by a cybernetic model developed by Professor Stafford Beer. The work of Beer provides a neat analytical model of a 'viable system' and this, in turn, enables clear simple descriptions of work activities and information needs to be made. A firm, department, or work process can be described as a hierarchy of five levels of activity. Each of these levels must be recognised, designed and managed, and must interact smoothly with the others if work is to proceed at a high level of performance. Figure 1 below shows the five levels in the model.

This viable system model enables those responsible for redesign to examine existing work processes and to set out systematically and comprehensively ideas for an improved system. The next diagram (Figure 2) shows how this can be done.

QUICKethics offers a mix of activities all directed at the elicitation of accurate information. These include a questionnaire, group discussions and the visual build up of information needs through placing individual items of required information on flip charts or a magnetic board.

The questionnaire is given to each manager in the group to complete before the meeting. It begins by asking the manager to describe his or her work mission, key tasks, critical success factors and major problems. These are seen as the **essential elements** of the manager's job. They are also almost certainly the most stable. They will only change fundamentally if the manager experiences major changes of role and function.

A VIABLE SYSTEM

Level 5   CONTROL
Meeting targets and standards

Level 4   DEVELOPMENT
New thinking

Level 3   OPTIMIZATION
Adding value

Level 2   ANTI-OSCILLATION
Preventing and solving problems

Level 1   OPERATIONAL
Day-to-day tasks

[handwritten: triple loop]

Figure 1. VSM - 5 levels.

[handwritten in left margin, vertical: recursive pattern of subsets]

The manager is then asked to describe each of his or her key tasks in detail. This analysis covers the five level cybernetic model, developed by Professor Stafford Beer, shown above. Each of these levels must be handled well individually and interact smoothly with the others if the task is to be carried out at a high level of performance. Finally the manager is asked to state the information needs associated with each level of each key task. He or she is then asked to separate these into quantitative and qualitative and to prioritise them into 'essential', 'desirable' and 'useful'.

[handwritten: Capable of self sustainability]

A VIABLE INFORMATION SYSTEM
(Required information)

[handwritten: connections relationships]

Level 5
Information to monitor performance
(CONTROL)

Level 4
Information to assist creativity
(DEVELOPMENT)

[handwritten: new - innovation, ideas are important !]

Level 3
Information to improve effectiveness
(ADDING VALUE)

[handwritten: market environmental]

[handwritten left margin: It's better to do the right thing wrong / Doing the right thing / Learn from Failure - take risks]

Level 2
Information to improve efficiency
(PREVENTING AND SOLVING PROBLEMS)

[handwritten: factory mgmt / Drucker / making good / horse whips]

[handwritten left margin: Doing things right]

Level 1
Information to assist the performance of day- to -day tasks
(OPERATIONAL)

Figure 2. VSM as a model for redesign.

Some days after completing the questionnaire the managers meet together for two days, discuss their information needs as a group, document these and agree a core information structure that will act as a starting point for implementing the new system. The author has recently used QUICKethics in a Dutch company manufacturing power tools which required computers for shop floor material and machine capacity planning. This will be used as a case study to illustrate the ETHICS approach.

5. A CASE STUDY EXAMPLE

The proposal was to abandon an old and unsatisfactory computer-based material planning system and to substitute more advanced software that would run on a new IBM AS 400 machine that had recently been acquired. Nine managers were involved in the project - two planning managers, three factory production managers, the finance manager, a quality manager and two managers from R and D. The author went through the QUICKethics questionnaire with each manager individually, wrote the interview up and gave the report back to the individual manager so that he could check its accuracy. These interviews had a threefold purpose. First to enable the manager to think clearly and systematically about his role and responsibilities before considering his information needs. Second to enable him to obtain a clear picture of his information needs before meeting his colleagues in a group situation. Third to arouse interest and a sense of ownership in the proposed new system.

One week after the interviews the managers met as a group. As nine is quite a large number for fast decision making the author split them into four groups - Planning, Production, Quality and R and D. Each of these groups was asked to think back to their individual answers the week before and to now agree and prioritise a set of essential information needs. Each list was described and explained by one of the sub-group who had produced it and was discussed by the group as a whole. During the meeting a Board level manager stated what senior management required. This included software that did not need more than 15% customising for the company; that could be implemented safely and without risk - there must be no possibility of plant stoppages, and that was supporting rather than controlling of users.

The last task for the group was to agree a core information system that could act as a starting point for implementation. Everyone present agreed that thus should cover three items. First, Bills of Material. These specified in detail the materials and production steps associated with each product. Second material planning and machine capacity planning should have next priority. These were two critical activities which were essential to the running of the production system.

Finally, it was agreed that the managers, reduced to six in number, should become the user design group for the project.

The author went away and produced a comprehensive report which detailed the core system, the essential information needs of Planning, Production, Quality and R and D, and the detailed information needs of each manager. This last would act as a development guide to be implemented over time once the system became operational.

6. LESSONS LEARNT FROM THE APPLICATION OF QUICKETHICS

One lesson learnt is that participation works and that groups at every level of the company find it useful, satisfying and enjoyable. It produces systems that have a high relevance to user needs and, in the author's experience an absence of perceived relevance is a frequent source of system failure.

A second lesson is that today's systems are so technically and organizationally complex that systems designers have difficulty designing them without help from users. This problem is exacerbated by today's trend to outsource the IT function.

A third lesson is that it is still very difficult to persuade firms to use a participative approach to systems design. There are a number of reasons for this. First, new systems have so much hype associated with them that managers are reluctant to believe there is any risk of system failure. Second, senior managers and systems specialists are often afraid that participation means handing over a degree of control to users. They are reluctant to do this.

A fourth lesson is that participation, like all innovations, requires skill and good management for it to succeed. Firms may not possess these attributes.

7. THE FUTURE DEVELOPMENT OF QUICKETHICS

QUICKethics is well documented but still paper based. Although the formation of user design groups and participative discussions are an essential part of the method, these do not all necessarily need to take place in face-to-face situations. Research in the United States on the structure and management of electronic discussions can provide guidance on how the method could be developed to encompass groups who cannot physically meet. The author hopes to develop appropriate software to facilitate discussion processes over networks.

QUICKethics usually works smoothly, is enjoyed as a social process and produces fast and excellent results. Nevertheless it is not widely used in the UK. Its considerable use in the Netherlands is due to the author at one time being associated with a Dutch software company and to the interest and use of the approach by a Dutch Consultancy specialising in the management of change. There are now many books on QUICKethics and ETHICS and a number of training courses provided by the author. The stimulation of a more general use appears to require more than this.

RELEVANT BOOKS

Mumford, E. 1995, *Effective systems design and requirements analysis*. Macmillan.

Mumford, E. 1996, *Systems design: ethical tools for ethical change*. Macmillan.

Mumford, E and Beekman, G-J, 1994, *Tools for change: and progress: a socio-technical approach to business process reengineering,* CSG Publications.

Mumford, E. 1993, *Designing human systems for health care*, Eight Associates.

Mumford, E and MacDonald, B, 1989, *XSEL's Progress: the continuing journey of an expert system,* Wiley, Chichester.

Mumford, E., 1983, *Designing human systems for new technology,* Manchester Business School.

Nunamaker et al., 1992, 'Electronic meeting systems to support information systems analysis and design' in Cotterman and Senn (eds.) *Challenge and strategies for research in system development*, Wiley, Chichester .

Trist, E. and Murray, H. 1993, *The social engagement of social science: a Tavistock anthology, Vol. 2 the socio-technical perspective.* University of Pennsylvania Press.

4

USING SYSTEMS FOR SUSTAINABILITY IN THE CONTEXT OF AGENDA 21

Christine Blackmore

Systems Department
The Open University
Walton Hall, Milton Keynes, MK7 6AA

1. INTRODUCTION

Sustainability and sustainable development are terms that mean different things to different people. They are considered by some people to be rather vague ideals with implications we have yet to understand, while other people have used these concepts to identify their systems of interest and to develop clear plans of action with achievable goals. This paper will consider some of the thinking and action for sustainability and sustainable development that have taken place in the context of *Agenda 21,* the huge international agenda for environment and development which emerged from the United Nations Conference for Environment and Development (UNCED), also known as the Earth Summit, which was held in Rio de Janeiro in 1992 (Quarrie 1992). In particular, it will consider the extent to which systems ideas and techniques have been used by the groups of people involved.

Progress towards implementation of Agenda 21 will be reviewed in a special session of the UN General Assembly in 1997, so it is timely to reflect critically on the processes different groups have gone through to work out where the boundaries of their systems of interest and activity lie. It is widely recognised that environmental, social, and economic dimensions need to be brought together to address issues of environment and development, which are interconnected. But what does this mean in practice?

2. WHICH GROUPS OF PEOPLE ARE INVOLVED?

Since 1992 many different groups around the world have been working out both their thinking and actions for Agenda 21 at different levels—local, national and international. These groups include those that were formally recognised in the Agenda 21 process - Governments and international bodies such as the United Nations and representatives of nine 'major groups' who became the main focuses of Agenda 21 activities. These were:

Systems for Sustainability, edited by Stowell *et al.*
Plenum Press, New York, 1997

women; children and youth; indigenous people and their communities; non-governmental organisations; local authorities; workers and their trade unions; business and industry; the scientific and technological community; and farmers.

Other groups besides those that are formally recognised have also begun to identify with Agenda 21. One example I will consider in more detail later on in this paper is 'the education community'. Groups have also formed at a local level to develop 'Local Agenda 21'. In many cases these groups are facilitated by local authorities but their membership cuts across all the major groups.

3. WHAT HAS BEEN DONE?

All the groups of people mentioned above have, to some degree, gone through the process of identifying areas of shared interest and concern with a view to working out what actions they and others can take. Some examples are:

1. In several parts of the UK, including Milton Keynes, techniques such as brainstorming and visioning have been used in Local Agenda 21 workshops to work out participants' shared systems of interest and agenda for action.
2. Task groups and round tables from non-governmental organisations have been facilitated by the United Nations Environment and Development UK Committee to work out their actions relating to issues such as health, poverty, forests and education in the context of Agenda 21.
3. The UK's Department of the Environment has hosted and facilitated numerous meetings in preparation for and following Rio's Earth Summit. They have sent out many draft documents for consultation that have been amended in the light of comments received. This process may not sound very systemic but the UK's Government, particularly the Department of the Environment, has developed a mature relationship with many NGOs in considering actions for Agenda 21. They can differ but still keep talking. There is widespread recognition that many of Agenda 21's objectives for sustainability and sustainable development cannot be achieved by Governments alone. For example, Clayton and Radcliffe (1996) discuss the roles of government, industry, business directors and managers, planners, individuals and communities, and educators in moving towards the goal of sustainability.

4. USING SYSTEMS TO FACILITATE LINKS BETWEEN DIFFERENT AGENDAS?

It is difficult to say to what extent systems ideas and techniques have been used in these activities. Overtly, probably very little. However, there has certainly been recognition that there are many systems that are relevant to the Agenda 21 process. O'Riordan (1995) considered links between environmental and social agendas in the UK. He pointed out that environmental groups were devising joint approaches with poverty, welfare and justice organisations but that there was no effective linkage between social and environmental agendas at the governmental level. Non-governmental organisations that have focused on environmental and social issues separately are subsystems of the larger system of organisations that are now focusing on issues of sustainable development, highlighted by

Agenda 21. Separate Government departments are also sub-systems of the Government system that deals with issues of sustainable development & Agenda 21.

Perhaps one of the reasons why NGOs have made more progress on linking environmental and social agendas is that there has been more recognition in those organisations of the need for facilitation of the sub-systems at a higher level in the system hierarchy? The example from the education community that I will explain in more detail later on in this paper is a case in point. A facilitator with an interest in education for sustainable development invited people with perspectives from environmental education and development education to work out their agenda together. In some ways the system of 'education for sustainable development' is at a higher level of the systems hierarchy than the systems of 'environmental education' and 'development education' (though these 'sub-systems' do not fall entirely within the system of education for sustainable development.). It was a lot easier for someone from the education for sustainable development system to facilitate this process than it would have been from environmental education or development education.

In the case of the UK Government, a great deal has been done for Agenda 21 by the Department of the Environment and they have certainly tried to involve other Government departments. The need for many Government departments, not just environmental departments, to get involved was noted in Agenda 21 but it is easier said than done. Perhaps more progress would be made towards linking different agendas and involving other Government departments in Agenda 21 if a facilitator from another level of the hierarchy of the Government's Agenda 21 system could invite departments to work out their thinking and actions together, rather than it falling to one Government Department to invite others at the same level? Similar observations have been made about the need for a facilitator from a higher level of the system hierarchy than an individual department, in the contexts of 'cross-curricular greening' activity in universities and schools, and where companies are implementing environmental policies across all areas of its operations. (Blackmore 1994).

5. SYSTEMS AND EDUCATION FOR SUSTAINABILITY

One area where the role of systems thinking has been overtly recognised in relation to Agenda 21 is in the context of education for sustainability. For example the following extract comes from the 1996 report of the U.S. President's Council for Sustainable Development:

> "The principles underlying education for sustainability include, but are not limited to, strong core academics, understanding the relationships between disciplines, systems thinking, lifelong learning, hands-on experiential learning, community-based learning, technology, partnerships, family involvement, and personal responsibility."

Increasingly, systems thinking is also becoming a part of environmental and development curricula in Higher Education, for example in Open University courses (Blackmore & Ison, 1995) and in WWF/South Bank University's Environmental and Development Education Masters' programme.

In addition, concepts such as 'holism', 'interdisciplinarity', 'multiple perspectives' and 'worldviews' are very familiar to and well understood by many people working in environmental and development education and they are a common part of the language of papers published in journals such as 'Environmental Education Research'. Some writers in this area use many systems concepts, for example Smyth (1995).

I will finish this paper with a more detailed example of how a group of people from the UK, involved in Agenda 21, used a systemic approach to work out their system of interest and agenda for action. They did not use a formal systems methodology but I refer to it a systemic approach because from the outset of their activities there was an awareness of process and context of the discussions and decision making, and recognition of the need for facilitation to draw out multiple partial perspectives on the whole system of 'education for sustainability', a system of interest they defined together rather than separately. There was a general feeling that no one individual knew what needed to be done and by whom, but there was a willingness to find out. Development of concepts informed actions and vice versa. There was also an open-ness to developing something different from the 'sum of the parts' by bringing perspectives together.

6. AN EXAMPLE OF A SYSTEMIC APPROACH FOR SUSTAINABILITY FROM THE UK EDUCATION COMMUNITY

My perspective on this example is that of an individual involved in the process throughout. While this is my own summary of events and the group process and hence some of the views expressed and any errors in the account are my own, I would like to fully acknowledge that I have drawn points about the work being done from conversations with others in the group and from other documentation (Sterling/EDET Group, 1992; UNED-UK/Education for Sustainability Forum, 1995; Harvey, 1995; Smyth, Blackmore & Harvey, 1996).

Well before the Rio conference in 1990, UNEP-UK, which was hosted by the London-based International Institute for Environment and Development, ran a series of events to involve people in the process of defining Agenda 21. One of their early workshops focused on education. Participants came from a range of organisations, primarily from those involved in either environmental education or development education, which up to that time had tended to work out their activities separately rather than together. Understandings of environmental education and development education vary and a wide range of perspectives were represented that spanned environmental, economic and social concerns. There was considerable enthusiasm for the focus on education in the context of Agenda 21 and a group followed up the activity started in the workshop. It became known as the Environmental and Development Education and Training (EDET) group which began to discuss and define the system of interest of 'Education for Sustainability' and to bring together a series of case studies. A publication called 'Good Earthkeeping' (Sterling/EDET Group, 1992) was produced as a result of this activity and was sent as a contribution from the UK to the Earth Summit.

After the Rio conference the EDET group found a need to continue, partly to participate as a group in ECOED, a major conference and curriculum fayre which was held in Toronto in October 1992, which followed up from the Earth Summit and focused entirely on education and communication for environment and development. The group became the 'Education for Sustainability Forum' and the UK's Council for Environmental Education and Development Education Associations, represented by their respective Directors, were central participant organisations. Following the Earth Summit, the new organisation UNED-UK, hosted by the United Nations Association, was formed as a focal point for UN Environment Programme (UNEP) and UN Development Programme (UNDP) activities in the UK. Their activities also began to turn towards education and together with the Education for Sustainability Forum a Task Group was established. The group of people concerned by this stage were all from the UK, mainly from non-governmental organisations and academia. Together, they worked out between them what education for sustainability meant to them and what it meant for their own activities. With help from a facilitating organisation, the United Nations Environment and Development UK Committee (UNED-UK), they also organised themselves to participate in the formal Agenda 21 review process. A document called 'Strengthening the role of the education community in support of sustainable development' (UNED-UK/Education for Sustainability Forum 1995) was prepared, to promote the involvement of the 'educational community' in Agenda 21 through:

- Development of a new programme called Education 21, to be modelled on Local Agenda 21 programmes and built on existing educational activities.
- Recognition of the educational community as a tenth 'major group' in the context of Agenda 21.

Representatives from the group went to the fourth session of the Commission for Sustainable Development in New York in April 1996 to help raise the profile of education in the Agenda 21 process and are now working with people from other countries with similar interests. The group is also working at a national level and making progress in terms of involving more people from the education community in various workshops and discussions. ('The education community' is understood to be the broad group of people who are involved in guiding the learning of others in both formal and non-formal contexts. This includes teachers, lecturers, education officers in non-governmental and community-based organisations, journalists and broadcasters, members of parents' associations and many more.)

It is recognised that 'education for sustainability' had other dimensions besides environmental education and development education—for example, the concept attracted people whose primary interests were basic education, education for peace, global education or citizenship education. At the Commission for Sustainable Development, it also became clear that 'education for sustainability' was considered a 'Northern perspective' as delegates from 'the South' identified more with the concept of 'Education for Sustainable Development' than 'Education for Sustainability'. This ongoing process of reconsidering the system of interest has meant that the boundaries have changed many times. This activity in itself has made a lot of people consider and clarify their actions and recommendations. It has not meant that all parties now subscribe to 'education for sustainability' or 'education for sustainable development' rather than say environmental education or development education. In some cases, the concept has proved too broad and unfocused without the appeal of 'environment' or 'development' and they have returned to their original areas of interest with renewed conviction.

The evolution of both the thinking and the actions of the UNED-UK/ESF Task Group is continuing. There is a lot more that could be said about this example, much of it has been written down (Harvey 1995; Smyth, Blackmore & Harvey 1996). However, my main reason for including it was not to look at all details of what has been done but to illustrate that there are groups of people who are using systemic approaches for decision making in the context of sustainability and Agenda 21, even if they are not overtly using systems concepts and techniques. Perhaps if other systems concepts, approaches, techniques and methodologies were more accessible in terms of language, they would be used by many more of the groups of people who are focusing on Agenda 21?

REFERENCES

Blackmore, C., 1994, *Taking Responsibility - promoting sustainable practice through Higher Education Curricula: Science and Technology*, Council for Environmental Education and WWF with Pluto Press: London.

Blackmore C & Ison R.L, 1995, Learning how to use a systems approach for sustainability. Conference paper for the Greening of Higher Education Council conference, London, 11–13 September 1995

Clayton, A.M.H. and Radcliffe, N.J., 1996, *Sustainability: a systems approach,* Earthscan, London.

Harvey, T., 1995, An education 21 programme: orienting environmental education towards sustainable development and capacity building for Rio. *The Environmentalist,* **15** (3): 202–210.

O'Riordan, T., 1995, Linking the environmental and social agendas. *The Environmentalist,* **15** (3): 233–239.

Quarrie J (ed) 1992, *Earth Summit '92: The United Nations Conference on Environment and Development. Rio de Janeiro 1992.* The Regency Press, London.

Smyth, J., Blackmore, C. & Harvey, T. Promoting Education at CSD4 Connections Newsletter, UNED-UK, London.

Smyth, J., 1995, Environment and education: a view of the changing scene. *Environmental Education Research* **1**(1): 3–20.

Sterling/EDET Group 1992 *Good Earthkeeping: education, training and awareness for a sustainable future, Environmental and Development Education and Training Group*, UNEP-UK, London.

The President's Council for Sustainable Development 1996 *Sustainable America: A New Consensus for Prosperity, Opportunity and a Healthy Environment for the Future,* U.S. Government Printing Office, Washington.

UNED - UK/Education for Sustainability Forum Paper, 1995, Strengthening the role of the education community in support of sustainable development, UNED-UK, London.

5

COPING WITH ENVIRONMENTAL UNCERTAINTY BY SOCIAL LEARNING

The Case of Agricultural Biotechnology Regulation in Europe

Susan Carr and Les Levidow

Systems Department
Faculty of Technology
The Open University
Milton Keynes MK7 6AA, United Kingdom

1. INTRODUCTION

The safety regulation of agricultural biotechnology has proved difficult for European harmonisation. Under the Deliberate Release Directive, EEC 90/220, genetically modified organisms (GMOs) must undergo a Europe-wide procedure to obtain market approval. Applications for approval have led to lengthy disputes, which have revealed strong differences among member states despite the supposedly common regulatory framework.

The delays caused by the disputes have strengthened the calls from some industry lobby groups and politicians for deregulation, or at least a more rigorously scientific and standardised basis for decisions. A more constructive approach would be to explore the underlying reasons for the differences, and to learn from each others experience and perceptions, as a way to enhance understanding of the environmental uncertainties - in other words, to encourage social learning.

This paper discusses the links between social learning and systems theory. It argues that social-environmental learning is particularly vital, since environmental issues often involve fundamental differences in perceptions and values, which give rise to social conflicts. It discusses how the use of structured analysis, such as critical systems heuristics, might be used to reveal the normative assumptions that lie behind the disputes, making them more amenable to resolution by negotiation. It concludes that, in the long term, better informed, more democratic and thus more sustainable decisions about the regulation of agricultural biotechnology will be achieved by encouraging the expression of different perceptions rather than by demanding increased harmonization.

Systems for Sustainability, edited by Stowell *et al.*
Plenum Press, New York, 1997

2. SOCIAL LEARNING AND SYSTEMS THEORY

The concept of social learning has similar theoretical roots to that of organisational learning, which evolved as a way of thinking about how organisations learn to respond and adapt to complex, uncertain and rapidly changing situations. Social learning extends the use of the concept beyond organisations to include communities and society at large. Social-environmental learning extends the concept to the ways in which communities and society must learn to take account of the planet's biophysical limits.

Underpinning all three concepts (organisational, social and social-environmental learning) is the idea that people have different appreciations of situations based on their differing experiences, beliefs and worldviews. In the face of complex and uncertain situations, individuals need to learn to work collaboratively, pooling their knowledge and experience, and they need to be open to other people's perspectives. For example, Wynne (1992) describes social learning as recognising the conditional nature of one's own knowledge, and the implicit assumptions and commitments that constitute it, and at the same time acknowledging the legitimacy of other sources of knowledge, organised in other forms, and borne by other social actors.

Finger and Verlaan (1995) define social-environmental learning as collective and collaborative learning that links the biophysical to the social, cultural and political, the local to the global, and action to reflection and research. They suggest that this new system of learning needs to be joint, co-operative, vertical, horizontal and interdisciplinary, that it needs to be based on an ethic of accommodation rather than control of nature, and that it must function within the realities of the globe's biophysical limits and socio-cultural diversity.

Perhaps one of the most comprehensive explanations of the way in which the concept of social learning links with systems theory is that given by Bawden (1995). Bawden uses the term critical learning systems to encompass this type of learning, which has its origins in cybernetics and in Argyris and Schon's (1978) notion of double-loop learning. Whereas single-loop learning results in small adjustments to maintain stability and keep performance within organisational norms, double-loop learning involves major transformations in the way the organisation operates as a result of a re-assessment and re-structuring of norms.

As one way of distinguishing among the different perspectives that people bring to bear on problematic situations, Bawden uses the two bi-polar dimensions of reductionism and holism, and objectivism and subjectivism, to construct a grid. This produces four cells, which he labels technocentric, egocentric, ecocentric and holonocentric. These he equates to four distinct paradigms. The technocentric perspective combines reductionism with objectivism; the real world can be revealed by studying its component parts, that is by rational reductionist inquiry. The egocentric perspective combines reductionism with subjectivism, recognising that our feelings unavoidably affect our decisions. The ecocentric perspective combines holism with a reliance on objectivity (as in hard systems methodology). The holonocentric perspective combines holism with subjectivism, that is it combines a concern with the whole relationship between a community and its environment, with a concern to take account of the opinions and perspectives of the range of stakeholders involved (as in soft systems methodology). Bawden suggests that it is only when one is comfortable with the holonocentric paradigm can one appreciate the complementary nature of all four of the paradigms. With this appreciation, one can then begin to create learning systems by facilitating interaction between the different paradigms, thus encouraging the emergence of new insights.

Given the uncertainties about the environmental and social impact of agricultural biotechnology, and the disputes surrounding the risk-assessment procedure in Europe, this an area where the concept of social-environmental learning is likely to be particularly relevant. In the next section we examine the background to the disputes, which we have described in greater detail in Levidow and Carr (1996) and Levidow, Carr, von Schomberg and Wield (1996).

3. AGRICULTURAL BIOTECHNOLOGY REGULATION IN EUROPE

In response to controversy about GMO releases in the 1980s, the European Community (as it was then called) enacted two directives, one on the contained use (EEC 90/219) and one on the deliberate release (EEC 90/220) of genetically modified organisms. These provided a Europe-wide regulatory framework that was intended to reassure critics of biotechnology that their concerns were being addressed, while allowing the industry to move ahead cautiously.

The directive on deliberate release requires companies and researchers to provide advance notice of any intended release and to provide evidence, in the form of a risk assessment, that the release will not be harmful. Approval is granted on a case-by-case and step-by-step basis. This means that each different combination of crop and genetic modification has to be assessed separately. Applications for commercial release can only be considered once more contained releases in glasshouses and field trials have been approved and the resulting releases have not given any cause for concern.

To oversee the notification and approval system, each member state is required to designate a 'competent authority'. After the competent authority of one member state has considered an application for commercial release and decided to recommend approval, other member states have the opportunity to respond to the recommendation. Objections are discussed at a formal meeting of all the competent authorities and ultimately resolved by a qualified majority vote if necessary.

Although the Deliberate Release Directive has established a common basis for GMO regulation, it has left scope for flexible interpretation by member states in its implementation. In particular, it has left open the choice of the competent authority and its safety advisers. As a result, member states vary as to whether the lead is taken by a ministry of agriculture, environment, health or some combination of these, for example. They also vary as to whether or not they have a formally constituted advisory body, and in the range of expertise included among the advisors. In addition, they vary as to how widely and thoroughly they consult with other interested or affected parties, such as non-governmental organisations and the general public.

Not surprisingly, this has led to considerable differences of opinion among competent authorities about the relevant risks and uncertainties that need to be assessed. For example, in France the Ministry of Agriculture is the competent authority, whose advisory committee is made up predominantly of molecular biologists. It sees the risks of GMOs as resulting mainly from genetic imprecision, implying that if the precise genetic make-up of the modified organism is known, then any risks are known too.

In the UK, the lead authority is the Department of the Environment, whose advisory committee is broadly-based in that it includes ecologists, an agronomist, a token environmentalist and a farmer, as well as industrialists and more specialised scientists. Risk assessment considers the possible direct effect of GMOs on the agricultural and non-agricultural environment, including changes in farming practice as a result of the availability of GMOs. But it considers the indirect, or secondary, effect of the development of herbicide-tolerant weeds as unproblematic if they can be controlled with existing herbicides.

In Denmark, where there has been fierce public controversy about biotechnology, and a long tradition of developing policy by consensus, regulators hear the views of universities, independent researchers, industry, non-governmental organisations and other interested groups. For each release notification, Parliament participates with the Ministry of the Environment in the value judgement, taking into account the comments from the public consultation. The regulatory procedure considers broad ranging impacts, including the secondary effects and long-term implications for weed-control options.

The resulting differences among member states in the risks and uncertainties that they consider to be relevant have resulted in disagreements among competent authorities. There have been lengthy delays in decisions at the EU-wide level, especially those concerning commercial releases. There has been considerable pressure on member states from the European Commission and from some members of the biotechnology industry for greater harmonisation, and even for deregulation.

In policy documents on biotechnology published since the enactment of the Deliberate Release Directive, the European Commission has been at pains to emphasise the need to enhance industrial competitiveness, and has made a clear distinction between safety regulation and the value-laden issues surrounding biotechnology, thus implying that risk assessment is free from value judgements. The Commission has urged regulators to avoid impeding the biotechnology industry by ensuring that the regulatory requirements are 'commensurate with the identified risks', thus implying that the risks are readily and consensually identifiable.

Such pressures put regulators on the defensive, making them less willing to acknowledge openly the practical difficulties and disagreements, in order to present their risk assessments as objective and soundly science-based. As a result, political pressures threaten to weaken the precautionary nature of the regulations and to restrict opportunities for addressing some of the wider social concerns. They run counter to all the principles of social-environmental learning.

Forcing decisions to a vote, rather than addressing the underlying reasons for differences of opinion, leaves many issues unresolved, which may surface again with greater force later. By narrowing the scope of the risks and uncertainties that are considered, regulators make risk assessment simpler but pre-empt important issues for environmental policy. They also jeopardise public trust in safety regulation.

In the concluding section, we consider how regulators and their advisors, as well as their critics, might be encouraged to adopt a more critically reflective and open-minded approach.

4. TOOLS AND TECHNIQUES TO AID SOCIAL LEARNING

As Wynne (1992) and Bawden (1995) have both suggested, before individuals can undertake social learning they first have to accept the conditionality and partiality of their own knowledge. This is likely to be most difficult for those who operate predominantly within a technocentric paradigm, as exemplified by the French competent authority. Although the joint meetings of the competent authorities from different member states may lead to some critical self-reflection, this potential is limited by the institutional framework already established in each country.

One way of encouraging social learning might be for the European Commission to require a broad range of expertise to be included by each member state among its regulators and their advisors, including environmentalists and informed members of the public. Another way might be to make use of 'holonocentric' facilitators at regulators' meetings. Yet another might be to encourage regulators and their advisors to make use of formal tools and techniques such as critical systems heuristics (Ulrich, 1993) to explore and explain their own value judgements, thus making them more open to public scrutiny and discussion.

Critical systems heuristics involves a checklist of 12 questions, which relate to those involved in decisions (the client, the decision taker, and the designer) and those affected but not involved (who Ulrich refers to as witnesses). The questions concern the design's value basis (for example, who is/ought to be the client, what is/ought to be its purpose, what is/ought to be its measure of success), the design's basis of power (for example, who controls the necessary means and resources, what lies/ought to lie beyond that power's control), the design's basis of knowledge (for example, what are/ought to be the sources of expertise that contribute the necessary information and know-how) and the design's basis of legitimation (for example, what are/ought to be the sources of legitimacy concerning those affected but not involved).

While the adoption of such approaches may seem unlikely given the pressures for harmonisation and deregulation, a number of factors may force a reappraisal of the situation. Disagreements among competent authorities may intensify as applications for commercial release increase and outstanding differences remain unresolved. Some member states may refuse to allow commercial releases in their country if they have been outvoted at EU-level. Potential impacts are likely to become more difficult to anticipate as multiple types of release occur. Consumers (farmers and the general public) may avoid purchasing genetically modified products if they feel their concerns have not been adequately addressed. Commercial use may result in undesirable effects whose acceptability and statutory relevance is disputed.

Given the uncertainties involved, it would be better to exploit to the full the cultural diversity and range of perspectives on biotechnology that exist within the European Union and to learn from them. As Renn (1995) has said, 'Diversity is the strength of Europe, not its weakness or problem'.

REFERENCES

Argyris, C., and Schon, D. A., 1978, *Organizational Learning: A Theory of Action Perspective*, Addison Wesley, Reading, Massachusetts.

Bawden, R., 1995, *Systemic Development: A Learning Approach to Change, Occasional Paper 1*, Centre for Systemic Development, University of Western Sydney, Hawkesbury.

Finger, M., and Verlaan, P., 1995, Learning our way out: a conceptual framework for social-environmental learning, *World Development* 23:503–513.

Levidow, L., and Carr, S., 1996, Special issue on biotechnology risk regulation in Europe, *Science and Public Policy* 23:133–200.

Levidow, L., Carr, S., von Schomberg, R., and Wield, D., 1996, Bounding the risk assessment of a herbicide-tolerant crop, in: *Coping with Deliberate Release: The Limits of Risk Assessment*, (Ad van Dommelen, ed.), pp. 81–102, International Centre for Human and Public Affairs, Tilburg, The Netherlands.

Renn, O., 1995, Styles of using scientific expertise: a comparative framework, *Science and Public Policy* 22:147–156.

Ulrich, W., 1993, Some difficulties of ecological thinking, considered from a critical systems perspective: a plea for critical holism, *Systems Practice* 6:583–611.

Wynne, B., 1992, Risk and social learning: reification to engagement, in: *Social Theories of Risk* (S. Krimsky and D. Golding, eds.), pp. 275–297, Praeger, Westport, Connecticut.

6

PUTTING SUSTAINABILITY INTO PRACTICE IN AGRICULTURAL RESEARCH FOR DEVELOPMENT

P. G. Cox,[1] N. D. MacLeod,[2] and A. D. Shulman[3]

[1]International Crops Research Institute for the Semi-Arid Tropics
Patancheru, Andhra Pradesh 502 324, India
[2]CSIRO Tropical Agriculture
St Lucia, Qld 4067, Australia
[3]Communication Research Institute of Australia
Hackett, ACT 2602, Australia

1. THE MEANINGS OF SUSTAINABILITY

Within scientists' research practices for improving agricultural resource management, their use of concepts of sustainability remains problematic. Sustainability means different things to different people, and in different contexts; it is ambiguous (Allen, 1993; MacLeod and Taylor, 1993, 1994) and contentious (Ison and Humphreys, 1993; Penman, 1994). Linguistic and communication analyses are providing convincing evidence that meanings of sustainability emerge from within the human communication environment (Penman, 1994; Shulman, 1996a,b). They argue that this environment is dynamic and, to a large extent, indeterminate. Penman (1994, in press) and Shulman (1996a; also, Shulman and Martinek, in press) have taken this further, suggesting that good scientist-constituent communication practices need to acknowledge that, because the situation is unique for each participant in time and space, differences in meanings will be the norm. Good negotiation uses this indeterminacy to open up possibilities for examining the adequacy of specific sustainability concepts in use.

With few exceptions, agricultural researchers fail to acknowledge this indeterminacy and can be seen to act as if sustainability is either a goal-prescribing concept or a system-describing concept (e.g. Thompson, 1992), both of which are deterministic. The former might be encapsulated as a normative or ideological management approach to agricultural practice, such as that relating to low-input agriculture or organic farming. Hansen (1996) has argued that this goal-prescribing approach, while offering some value for consolidating concerns and motivating changes in attitudes towards resource uses, has been of comparatively limited value for guiding those changes in human behaviour which ultimately underpin a shift towards sustainable (or persistent) agricultural systems. Rather, he endorses the use of sustainability as a system-describing concept within which scientists seek to determine the capacity of a system (such as an agricultural production system) to meet certain goals or to focus on system properties or levels. Both the goal-prescribing and the system-describing concepts of sustainability see sustainability to be about setting or achieving levels, especially of biophysical system variates. While there is considerable variation in meaning within these broad use-categories, they both imply that a sustainable system is one that 'persists' (Costanza and Patton, 1995). But what persists, for how long, when and how we are meant to assess its persistence, and why we might want something to persist anyway are all confusing questions.

In this paper, we review an example set of economic studies concerned with measures of total factor productivity, and other studies concerned with discounting future values, that illustrate Hansen's system property or level approach. We suggest that many of the arguments about improving practices have not been productive because of their failure both to recognise the indeterminacy of meanings and to engage in practices which open up some possible avenues for improvement. We bring in a second perspective, a 'quality process' approach, which recognises and builds within the indeterminacy of the meanings of sustainability to improve agricultural research for development in a manner consistent with open systems concepts of quality improvement and organisational learning.

2. DIFFICULTIES WITH PRESENT DETERMINISTIC APPROACHES

While recognising weaknesses in the system-describing approach, Hansen (1996) argues that it provides more scope for guiding change if this is based on finding property characterisations that are literal, system-oriented, quantitative, predictive, stochastic and diagnostic. Examples of scientists taking this approach can be found in the research of economists (e.g. Lynam and Herdt, 1988; Barnett, Payne and Steiner, 1995) who construct sustainability as non-declining total factor productivity. This logic has led to a proliferation of 'indicators of sustainability' (e.g. Milon and Shogren, 1995; Ayres, 1996) intended largely to measure the performance of a biological system in terms of its ability to endure either by specifying levels of physically measurable quantities to be maintained (e.g. soil nitrogen or pollution-free water), or the ratio of different quantities combined in various ways (productivity or efficiency measures).

Total factor productivity is defined as the total value of all output from the system over one cycle divided by the total value of all inputs. A system with a non-zero trend in this ratio is taken to be sustainable. But, as Monteith (1990) points out, the total value of all inputs will often be an arbitrary quantity with diverse components the relative values of which are hard to measure. In an attempt to address this, Monteith provides a 'logic table of sustainability' that is based on four possible combinations of total input/output relativities. However, this would seem to be of questionable value because it cannot address the indeterminate and common cases where both outputs and inputs are increasing - a situation of particular interest when knowledge inputs are valued and included in the analysis, as we believe they should be. In any case, defining sustainability in terms of continuing total factor productivity has yet to be demonstrated as a better approach for bringing about change than traditional investment appraisal models (Beckerman, 1995; Alston, Norton, and Pardey, 1995). Even if there were little contention with this approach, it appears in use to limit the possible ways of constructively addressing sustainability.

A parallel argument of utility can be advanced with economists who have entered the sustainability debate seeking to find optimal allocations of resources between present and future consumptive uses, whilst maintaining the integrity of the resource stock (whether natural or artificial, and depending on whether sustainability is 'strong' or 'weak'). The contribution that this work is making towards putting sustainability into practice can be questioned, in part, because of the non-ending debate as to the appropriateness of both traditional and modified discounting procedures being applied to address such issues (Price, 1993). For example, academic debate which treated sustainability as a quantifiable and predictable system property has tied itself in knots trying to figure out how to satisfy the simultaneous requirements of investment appraisal (discounting future money values of flows of services from exploitation of resource stocks in order to allocate those resources most efficiently) and a commitment to maintaining levels of resource stocks in perpetuity. Attempts to resolve this issue using modified discounting schemes (e.g. Kula, 1994; Rabl, 1996) to correct for the more obvious errors of traditional discounting procedures (depending on what is being discounted and how far in the future the required persistence is projected) confound the dilemma.

Discounting procedures appear essential to ration limited current resources to activities where the pay-off, in terms of efficiency or welfare gains, is greatest, but also seem to many to give the wrong answers (e.g. Van Dieren, 1995). Nevertheless, such procedures are increasingly used to prioritise resource allocation to agricultural research for development where issues of sustainability are severe (Alston et al., 1995; Kelley, Ryan, and Patel, 1995). The question of future values, the prices of future resources to which discounting may be applied, remains. In any case, although the use of discounting can provide an inter-temporal model, this procedure does not recognise nor build on the dynamics of the innovation process through which future changes are achieved. It is essentially a static representation of a distribution through time, but not of the dynamics of change. In essence, none of these researchers appears to recognise the dynamic indeterminacy of the 'fixed' definitions they operate from; nor do they appear to know how to learn from the shifting of definitions which is inherent within their dialogues.

Much of the problem can be attributed to such approaches adhering to determinate system viewpoints which will very likely poorly meet the goals of the indeterminate human systems in which agriculture and R&D are enmeshed (Conway, 1987; Harrington, 1992). If sustainable resource use practices are to be sought through analytical frameworks that are appropriate to closed deterministic systems, the sustainability debate is then trapped because it fails to recognise the open indeterminate nature of human systems, either by subjugating them to an imputed imperative of natural systems (as in deep ecology) or by the imposition of a closed deterministic model of human wants and needs which fails to recognise the agency of both future generations and of ourselves.

3. SUSTAINABILITY AS A PROCESS IMPROVEMENT TOOL

Re-constructing sustainability as *process* can be construed as minimising the problems, such as the temporal impasse associated with discounting, because it relates to the way in which individuals and organisations learn in a continual present. It does this, not by modifying the way in which the future is discounted (second-guessing what the future wants, or what the appropriate discount rate for different bundles of goods or different time periods is), nor by using an atemporal ruse such as a Rawlsian 'veil of ignorance' model (Penn, 1990). Both these ways assume, and hence reinforce, the conservative maintenance of closed systems. Sustainability as a system property (sustainability-as-levels) restricts what can be achieved by its insistence on seeing the world as a closed deterministic system.

This alternative process approach does not negate closed-system research. Rather, it asks scientists to examine what might be possible in bringing about better agricultural practices if they construed their target-setting and system-level activities as *punctuations* within human discourse (MacLeod and Shulman, in press). Sustainability-as-process operates with an open non-deterministic human activity system, not closing down opportunities but seeking them out, creating them and building on them. Sustainability re-constructed in this sense refers to how we continually learn to manage in an open indeterminate world. It is about what we can do to make a difference, here and now. What we do now does depend on what we want the future to be like because our conception of the future is part of our present. And what the future will be like does depend on what we do now because the future is continuously invented out of the present. But the future is not pre-specified or hard-coded by the present.

By improving the processes by which we learn our way into the future, we improve the present and the future simultaneously. The main focus of the sustainability debate, from this perspective, is to do with the way we go about agricultural research for development: about the way we go about making change happen and the kinds of changes we try to bring about, and not the pre-specification of environmental or production targets which now become secondary.

4. SUSTAINABILITY AS A QUALITY PROCESS

There are parallels between sustainability re-constructed as process and the idea of quality as this is now understood in business theory and practice (e.g. Kelada, 1996). Parton (1996) points out that the terms, *quality*, *quality assurance* and *quality improvement*, are usually greeted with hostility by scientists. His comparison of quality improvement and quality assurance is instructive. Quality assurance appears to be aligned with a retrospective, externally-directed, reactive, event-based inspection approach which sees quality as a separate activity associated with solving problems. Quality improvement (total quality management, or TQM) is an approach which is prospective, internally-directed, proactive, researcher-focused and involves many people. It sees quality as an integral activity with a focus on improving process. Clearly, if we are to equate sustainability-as-process with the notion of quality, it is with quality improvement not quality assurance.

This emphasis on the concept of sustainability as a descriptor of a quality process through which desirable outcomes can be achieved has much in common with Norgaard's (1995) call for new metaphors to survive by. Norgaard points out some of the limits to the metaphor of limits - in particular, that other understandings produce quite different insights. This fits very well with the notion of a learning organisation. By emphasising learning rather than control as a paradigm for sustainability, we open up opportunities for doing things differently. To some degree, this will require reengineering (Kelada, 1996) of the ways in which agricultural research for development is done. As pointed out by Cox et al. (1996), business process reengineering can be applied to agricultural research for development just as to any other business process. Although reengineering does not provide a recipe for organisational change, the metaphors of modern business culture—the learning organisation (Senge, 1990; Leonard-Barton, 1995)—do provide off-the-shelf process tools that we can build on immediately.

We propose that the search for indicators of sustainability needs to be re-directed towards the establishment of what constitutes good practice in research. Good R&D practice (MacLeod and Shulman, in press; Shulman and Martinek, in press) recognises the limited stability of meanings of sustainability levels and properties in dialogues amongst scientists and their constituents. It strategically uses these temporary punctuated equilibrium states of understanding as part of an ongoing process of action and reflection. Specifying sustainability-as-levels may contribute to the way in which this continual re-negotiation is managed, but by itself leads to temporal paradox as evidenced by the discounting debate and the notion of non-declining total factor productivity. Sustainability-as-levels fails to recognise, and build on, the agency of human actors, both present and future. Sustainability-as 'a quality continual learning process' attempts to do this. Sustainability, construed in this way, is about quality in professional practice and ways of achieving quality outcomes. It is about putting sustainability into practice in agricultural research for development.

REFERENCES

Allen, P. (ed.), 1993, *Food for the Future. Conditions and Contradictions of Sustainability*, Wiley, New York.

Alston, J.M., Norton, G.W., and Pardey, P.G., 1995, *Science Under Scarcity: Principles and Practice for Agricultural Research Evaluation and Priority Setting*, Cornell University Press, Ithaca.

Ayres, R.U., 1996, Statistical measures of unsustainability, *Ecological Economics* **16**:239–255.

Barnett, V., Payne, R., and Steiner, R. (eds.), 1995, *Agricultural Sustainability: Economic, Environmental and Statistical Considerations*, Wiley, Chichester.

Beckerman, W., 1995, *Small is Stupid. Blowing the Whistle on the Greens*, Duckworth, London.

Conway, G.R., 1987, The properties of agroecosystems, *Agricultural Systems* **24**:95–117.

Costanza, R., and Patten, B.C., 1995, Defining and predicting sustainability, *Ecological Economics* **15**:193–196.

Cox, P.G., MacLeod, N.D., Ridge, P.E., and Shulman, A.D., 1996, Reengineering agricultural R,D&E to support management decision-making: problems and prospects, *Proc. 8th Aust. Agronomy Conf., University of Southern Queensland, Toowoomba, Queensland (30 Jan - 2 Feb 1996)*, Aust. Soc. of Agronomy, Carlton, pp. 168–171.

Hansen, J.W., 1996, Is agricultural sustainability a useful concept?, *Agricultural Systems* **50**:117–43.

Harrington, L.W., 1992, Measuring sustainability: issues and alternatives, *J. for Farming Systems Research-Extension* **3**(1):1–20.

Ison, R., and Humphreys, C., 1993, Evaluation of 'Sustainable Beef Productions Systems in Central Queensland' Project, Dept of Crop Sciences, University of Sydney.

Kelada, J.N., 1996, *Integrating Reengineering with Total Quality*, ASQC Quality Press, Milwaukee.

Kelley, T.G., Ryan, J.G., and Patel, B.K., 1995, Applied participatory priority setting in international agricultural research: making trade-offs transparent and explicit, *Agricultural Systems* **49**:177–216.

Kula, E., 1994, *Economics of Natural Resources, the Environment and Politics*. 2nd ed., Chapman & Hall, London.

Leonard-Barton, D., 1995, *Wellsprings of Knowledge: Building and Sustaining the Sources of Innovation*, Harvard Business School Press, Boston.

Lynam, J.K., and Herdt, R.W., 1988, Sense and sustainability: sustainability as an objective in international agricultural research, Paper for CIP-Rockefeller Foundation Conference on Farmers and Food Systems, Lima, Peru.

MacLeod, N.D., and Taylor, J.A., 1993, Sustainable grazing practices in Queensland, *Australian Farm Manager* **3**(6):6–9.

MacLeod, N.D., and Taylor, J.A., 1994, Perceptions of beef cattle producers and scientists relating to sustainable land use issues and their implications for technology transfer, *The Rangeland Journal* **16**:238–253.

Macleod, N.D., and Shulman, A.D., Bridging the output-outcome gap in sustainability R&D - a fifth generation R&D punctuated arena model, *Proc. 5th International UKSS Conference (7 - 11 July, 1997)*, United Kingdom Systems Society, Milton Keynes, in press.

Milon, J.W., and Shogren, J.F. (eds.), 1995, Integrating Economic and Ecological Indicators: Practical Methods for Environmental Policy Analysis, Praeger Press, Westport.

Monteith, J.L., 1990, Can sustainability be quantified? *Indian Journal of Dryland Agricultural Research and Development* **5**(1/2):1–15.

Norgaard, R.B., 1995, Metaphors we might survive by, *Ecological Economics* **15**:129–131.

Parton, K. A., 1996, Quality, quality assurance and quality improvement in agronomic research, *Proc. 8th Aust. Agronomy Conf., University of Southern Queensland, Toowoomba, Queensland (30 Jan - 2 Feb 1996)*, Aust. Soc. of Agron., Carlton, pp. 43–46.

Penman, R., 1994, Environmental matters and communication challenges, *Aust, J. of Communication* **21**(3):26–39.

Penman, R., The researcher in communication: the primary research position, in: *Context and Communication Behavior* (J. Owen, ed.), Context Press, Reno, in press.

Penn, J., 1990, Towards an ecologically-based society: a Rawlsian perspective, *Ecological Economics* **2**:225–242.

Price, C., 1993, *Time, Discounting and Value*, Blackwell, Oxford.

Rabl, A., 1996, Discounting of long-term costs: What would future generations prefer us to do? *Ecological Economics* **17**:137–145.

Senge, P.M., 1990, *The Fifth Discipline: the Art and Practice of the Learning Organization*, Doubleday, New York.

Shulman, A.D., 1996a, Communicating science: opportunities and constraints for a scientist, in: *Science Communication* (D. Sless, ed.), pp. 55–68, Communication Research Press, Canberra.

Shulman, A.D., 1996b, Putting group information technology in its place: communication and good work group performance, in: *Handbook of Organisation Studies* (S.R. Clegg, C. Handy, and W. Nord, eds.), pp. 357 - 374, Sage Publications, Newbury Park.

Shulman, A. D., and Martinek, T., Managing institutional collaboration in catchment systems research, in: *Farming Action: Catchment Reaction* (J. Williams, ed.), CSIRO, Canberra, in press.

Thompson, P.B., 1992, The varieties of sustainability, *Agric, Human Values* **9**(3):11–19.

Van Dieren, W., 1995, *Taking Nature into Account: A Report to the Club of Rome*, Springer-Verlag, New York.

7

PROLETKU'LT, REVOLUTION, AND TEKTOLOGY

Systemness as a Factor of Sustainability

Peter Dudley and Simona Pustylnik

Centre for Systems Studies
University of Hull

> For the bright day when man will grope blindly no more
> But will see how his task must be done;
> If he chooses the path that leads straight to the core
> He and life can then fuse into one.
> —*Bogdanov, 1984c*

If systems theory as a whole is to make a contribution to the understanding of the world it must be in the area of what Bogdanov (1996) called the "transfer of methods", what would today more readily be recognized as Bertalanffy's (1968) "isomorphisms". In addressing issues of sustainability, therefore, it is advantageous to look beyond the narrow confines of "ecological" models to lessons that have been learned in other fields.

Bogdanov, probably best known to western systems theorists as a result of Gorelik's translation of the "Essays in Tektology" (Bogdanov, 1984) and a small number of analytical works (e.g. Gorelik, 1975, 1987; Sochor, 1988; Zeleny, 1988), was also a social theorist and committed Marxist.

This paper explores the relevance of his conviction that a sociopolitical revolution could not succeed without a corresponding cultural revolution. Our contention is that, as a systems theorist, Bogdanov envisaged the Bolshevik revolution as a sustainable system and attempted to create the conditions of its sustainability.

In Filosofija Zhivogo Opyta (1913) (The Philosophy of Living Experience, Bogdanov, 1920) his last major work prior to the Tektology, *organizational science* appeared as a universal science which, unlike the absolute global formula of Laplace, would for the first time "create real global formulae" capable of mastering "any collection of given elements of the world process in a planned way" (Bogdanov, 1920). The idea that all is organization, and that the laws of organization, the laws according to which any organizational complex is formed and develops, are the same for all objects, led Bogdanov to the conclusion that the world consists entirely in processes of organization and de-or-

Systems for Sustainability, edited by Stowell *et al.*
Plenum Press, New York, 1997

ganization (Bogdanov, 1996 and 1989). The universe "displays an infinitely unfolding canvas of forms, of different types and levels of organizedness" (Bogdanov, 1996 and 1989).

It was characteristic of Russian scientific thought that scientific research was always closely intertwined with the search for social utopia. Thus Marxism and systems thinking find in each other a point of intersection - the idea of *organization*. The re-organization of society was, for Marxists, the "key to progress". Following the revolution of 1917 many theories for the creation of a new society and a new science were proposed, all of which shared a common theme— re-organization. Furthermore this re-organization was to be *rational*, both the Bolsheviks and systems theory propose the possibility of the rational design of complex wholes.

Systems theory was first evidenced in Russia in the form of Bogdanov's *Universal Organizational Science, Tektology* (1913–1922). Bogdanov was ahead of his time in proposing a completely new branch of knowledge—the science of organization—a science of the most general laws of the of universe. Only with the acceptance of Bertalanffy's General System Theory and the cybernetics of Ashby and Wiener in Russia was it discovered that the essence of their ideas had been in existence for several decades in Tektology, and Bogdanov's pioneering role in the field of systems science began to be recognized.

It is easy to see in Tektology a reflection of the general aspiration of Bogdanov's epoch for the removal of the contradictions inherent in the development of the specialized sciences, and, by extension his critique of bourgeois society and culture. "Ingineer Menni" (1912/13), Bogdanov's science fiction novel about a future communist civilisation on Mars, reflected all his innermost philosophical and social aspirations, in it one of the characters says:

> " ...modern science is such that even the chosen few who gained access to it master only a small part of it, a single speciality...Modem science is just like the society that created it: powerful but splintered...Because of this fragmentation the individual branches of science have developed separately and lost all vital connection with each other...Each branch has its special language which is the privilege *of the initiated* and serves to exclude everyone else" (Bogdanov, 1984b).

For Bogdanov Marx was "the great forerunner of organizational science", but to what degree was Bogdanov a Marxist? He was attracted to Marx' thinking—as were many Russian thinkers—by the idea of practically changing the world. In Tektology the unity of the world "is not *discovered but created* in an active organizational manner..." Tektology is to achieve the *"Practical mastery"* of organizational forms and methods (Bogdanov, 1996 and 1989)—its formulae of the world are "practical formulae" And it is aimed, primarily, at organizing society *practically and expediently* .

According to Bogdanov, the science of the obsolescent bourgeois social organization shared its problems and, as such, could not be used to solve the *integrative* problems of the *whole world* task—the "triple faceted organization—of things, of people and of ideas... the real organization of mankind into a unified collective" (Bogdanov, 1996 and 1989).

However, Bogdanov intended not the *scientific socialism* of Marx, but the *socialism of science* - Tektology - this science would join all people into single collective for the carrying out of the global task—the construction of a new harmonic social organization. In this sense Tektology appears as a *general human science*.

In "Engineer Menni" (Bogdanov, 1984b) one of Bogdanov's characters asks, "How many times do we have to simply believe?...what can we do so that we ourselves can *know* and *see* and not constantly believe?" Bogdanov's answer is that Tektology, as the socialism of science will bring the gathering *of man as personality,* which is fragmented in specialisation, and then scientific knowledge will be the property not of one, but of all. In one of his earlier works, *" Sobiranie cheloveka"* 1904, ("The Gathering of man", Bogdanov, 1990), Bogdanov formulated the task which denoted for him the change from "man-fraction to man whole" - this notion appears as a leitmotif through all his works.

Tektology was to achieve the harmony of the world through the science of organization: a *"scientific and…integral* concept of "man" "(Bogdanov, 1984a). In the words of *Engineer Menni* it would "fuse them into a single intelligent organism… man fully aware of himself as an element of the real *labouring* whole" (Bogdanov, 1984b). In Tektology Marxist practical directedness joins with the innermost aspiration of Russian philosophy: it is a science which would gather man and nature into one construction.

Undaunted by the intellectual isolation caused by the split with Lenin, Bogdanov allied himself with Gorky and Lunacharsky to found the "High Social-Democratic School" (ibid) and later the group "Vperyod" ("Forward") to promote his ideas of the necessity of a proletarian culture to the success of a proletarian revolution. Although his ideas were to be rejected out of hand, as a result of Lenin's treatment of Empiriomonizm, the notion of proletarian culture was a theme he was to return to following the 1917 revolution, in the form of the *Proletku'lt.*

Another passage from *Ingineer Menni,* more reminiscent of Lyotard's *Postmodern Condition* than a turn of the century socialist, extends the theme of the domination of the *excluded* by the *knowledgeable* when one of the characters states that

> "Thus far science is the weapon of our enemy. We will triumph when have made it our weapon…Scraps and crumbs of knowledge are not what is needed to arrive at an intelligent solution to the most important and complicated problems of life … modern science is such that even the chosen few who gained access to it master only a small part of it, a single speciality … Modem science is just like the society that created it: powerful but splintered…Because of this fragmentation the individual branches of science have developed separately and lost all vital connection with each other…Each branch has its special language which is the privilege *of the initiated* and serves to exclude everyone else" (Bogdanov, 1984).

This demonstrates Bogdanov's commitment to the democratization of *knowledge* and this commitment was to be made concrete through "the creation of a workers' encyclopedia, the organization of workers' universities, the development of proletarian art, etc." (cf. Sadovsky and Kelle, 1996)

Bogdanov's consistent application of systemic principles led him to the conclusion that the "rational transformation" of society necessitates more than the simplistic assumption (of the Bolsheviks) of the sufficiency of the Leninist-Marxist revolution. The simple replacement of the aristocratic or bourgeois powerful without a reconstruction of the cultural conditions of proletarian life would, inevitably, lead to the failure of any attempt at social reform. In order for a truly proletarian revolution to succeed *it was necessary for the proletarian to create and maintain a proletarian culture.* In this way Bogdanov is confronting the conditions of the sustainability of the revolution in systemic terms - long term sustainability becomes a function of the system's interaction with, and adaptedness to, its environment.

REFERENCES

Bertalanffy, L., von, 1968, General System Theory: Foundations, Development, Applications, George Braziller, New York.

Bogdanov, A. A., 1920, Filosofija zhivogo opyta (The Philosophy of Living Experience), Moscow.

Bogdanov, A. A., 1984a, Red Star, Red Star: The First Bolshevik Utopia (C. Rougle trans., L.R. Graham and R. Stites eds.), Indiana University Press, Bloomington.

Bogdanov, A. A., 1984b, Ingineeer Menni, Red Star: The First Bolshevik Utopia (C. Rougle trans., L.R. Graham and R. Stites eds.), Indiana University Press, Bloomington.

Bogdanov, A. A., 1984c, A Martian Stranded on Earth, Red Star: The First Bolshevik Utopia (C. Rougle trans., L.R. Graham and R. Stites eds.), Indiana University Press, Bloomington.

Bogdanov, A. A., 1989, Tektologija: Vseobshchaja organizatsionaja nauka (Tektology: The Universal Organizational Science), Ekonomika, Moscow. Book 1 and 2.

Bogdanov, A. A., 1990, Sobiranie cheloveka (Gathering of Man) // Bogdanov, Voprosy Sotsialisma (Questions of Socialism), pp. 28–46, Moscow.

Bogdanov, A. A., 1996, Bogdanov's Tektology (P. Dudley, ed.), Centre for Systems Studies Press, Hull.

Gorelik, G., 1975, Principal Ideas of Bogdanov's "Tektology:" The Universal Science of Organization, General Systems, XX, pp. 3–13.

Gorelik, G., 1987, Bogdanov's Tektologia, General Systems Theory, and Cybernetics, Cybernetics and Systems: An International Journal, 18, pp. 157–175.

Sochor, Z.A., 1988, Revolution and Culture: The Bogdanov–Lenin Controversy, Cornell University Press, London.

Zeleny, M., 1988, Tectology, General systems: An International Journal, vol. 14, pp. 331 - 343.

8

THE INTEGRATION OF SYSTEMIC AND SCIENTIFIC THINKING IN THE DEVELOPMENT OF AN INNOVATIVE PROCESS FOR ENVIRONMENTAL MANAGEMENT

James Frederickson[1] and Norah Frederickson[2]

[1]Systems Department
Open University
Milton Keynes, England
[2]Psychology Department
University College
London, England

1. INTRODUCTION

The growing debate on issues such as maintaining biological diversity and escalating environmental degradation have highlighted the need for systemic approaches to environmental management. For example, Ulrich (1993) proposes the concept of critical holism as being useful in the debate about designs or applications in the field of ecological thinking. Here, critical systems heuristics has been used to develop a number of boundary judgements which can be used to address the value, power and knowledge bases of particular designs, as well as their basis of legitimisation. Grumbine (1994) has argued that the concept of ecosystem management is an approach which offers a fundamental reframing of how humans work with nature because it 'integrates scientific knowledge of ecological relationships within a complex sociopolitical and values framework toward the general goal of protecting native ecosystem integrity over the long term'. A number of themes underlie the concept such as the need for environmental managers to seek connections between all levels of the biodiversity hierarchy, to work across ecological and administrative boundaries and to conserve viable populations which also includes the reintroduction of species. Importantly he identifies adaptive management, where management is considered to be a learning process, as a theme and highlights the dominant role that human values play in ecosystem management goals.

The research featured in this paper took place within the framework of applying systems thinking to a real world environmental problem situation and led to the development of an innovative biotechnology-based process. The starting point was an exploratory, sci-

Systems for Sustainability, edited by Stowell *et al.*
Plenum Press, New York, 1997

entific research project which confirmed the feasibility of culturing selected earthworm species for applications in environmental management. However, it was not clear how to transform this basic scientific idea into a viable technique. A process of innovation was begun and a re-analysis of the problem situation using Soft Systems Methodology (Checkland, 1981; Checkland and Scholes, 1990) was undertaken, involving a client group as participants in the learning process.

2. BACKGROUND

The Biosystems Research Group at the Open University was keen to build on its expertise in culturing selected earthworm species by focusing on applications in sustainable land restoration. The importance of earthworms in the processes of soil formation and in the creation and maintenance of soil fertility is now well established. Equally, earthworms can be vital components in the food chain for a diverse range of animals. Hence large earthworm populations are often considered to be an essential element in sustainable ecosystems. This recognition has led to many attempts to introduce earthworms into newly reclaimed or derelict land as a means of enhancing the sustainability of the land restoration process (Curry, 1988).

However, current methods of introducing earthworms have been criticised and a number of factors have been identified which have prevented the practice from being adopted more widely. Currently, the large number of earthworms that are required are obtained by first harvesting them from donor sites, which is laborious and often creates severe environmental damage. Equally the process of introducing the earthworms into degraded sites is highly dependent on skilled personnel, making it expensive and elitist. Many researchers have suggested using biotechnology-based techniques to culture selected earthworm species as a means of overcoming these barriers. Little research had been undertaken on culturing true soil-dwelling species and some researchers did not consider this to be possible.

An initial three year programme of scientific inquiry undertaken by the Biosystems Research Group confirmed that selected soil-dwelling earthworms could be cultured on a large scale using standard biotechnology-based techniques. A press release was issued informing the world of our scientific 'breakthrough' but despite our interest in the topic, we expected little response. The response was overwhelming, bringing with it considerable media coverage and including several offers of possible projects. Flushed with success we contracted to undertake a large earthworm introduction project for one of the UK's major landfill operators who were having problems restoring and revegetating a number of their sites due to the hostile nature of the soil and site conditions. After initial discussions with the company it became clear that although we had developed a new method of supplying earthworms we had no clear idea how to introduce them into the soil or keep them alive in the process. We had overcome one of the environmental problems associated with traditional methods by reducing possible donor site damage but had not properly addressed the problem situation.

3. A PROCESS FOR HOLISTIC INNOVATION

There seemed to be a need to transform the basic method of culturing earthworms into some form of novel process that was capable of being utilized and managed by a wide range of operatives. In the commercial world, the process of developing new products and processes, also known as innovation, is often stylised into a linear sequence of stages which embrace a variety of different tasks and functions. In practice, of course, the process is much more complex than this and often there is backtracking and feedback between activities giving rise to a much more iterative approach. While 'many large companies have adopted more concurrent approaches to innovation, Henry, Massey and Wield (1995) have highlighted the ubiquity of the linear model over a wide range of industries. They point out, however, that with this model it is all too easy to isolate the research and development function by over-emphasising the role of scientific and technological activities. It was agreed that we were about to embark on a process of environmental innovation and that we needed to take a systems perspective, but how?

The relationship between scientific and systems thinking has previously been considered in a range of fields (Checkland, 1981; Checkland, 1995), including educational psychology (Frederickson, 1990a). This latter field has also provided rich illustrations of the 'Mode 2' use of Soft Systems Methodology (Frederickson, 1990b; Howell, 1991) which focuses on, 'learning one's way to purposeful improvement in problem situations' (Checkland and Scholes, 1990). These were both important issues in the present study on innovation.

One practical, marketing-based approach to new product development takes the sequence: idea generation, idea screening, product concept development and testing, marketing strategy development, business analysis, product development, market testing and commercialisation (Kotler, 1984). In terms of this model, it was clear that we were only at the initial stage of having generated a basic idea. We now needed to turn the generic idea into a detailed product concept or range of concepts which hopefully addressed a broad range of social, ecological and organisational aspects rather than just focusing on technical and marketing issues. The use of Soft Systems Methodology (SSM) as described below facilitated this necessary re-conceptualisation at this stage in the development of the innovation—from a linear, interventionist 'application' of basic scientific research to a creative, interactionist process of adaptation and learning.

3.1. Appreciating the Problem Situation

Familiarisation with the problem situation was gained through several interviews with the Commercial Director, the Site Manager and the Restoration Contractor. On-site observations and informal discussions with workers were carried out and company documents were consulted. The learning achieved is summarised in Figure 1, from which a number of important themes emerged. Among those selected for further exploration were the following.

Site restoration, although regarded as an important public relations issue, was seen as peripheral to the core business of the company to the extent that the work was subcontracted. Differences between the company staff and the subcontractors in both status and 'culture' limited the extent to which feedback from problems encountered in restoration could impact on the operation and final preparation of the site.

A mis-match was revealed between the skills of restoration workers and those required to restore land by introducing earthworms using current techniques. If current techniques were employed specialist consultants would be required. This proved a crucial stimulus in re-defining the nature of the project—from 'the pilot application in a commercial context of a scientific discovery' to 'the development with commercial partners of an applicable implementation of a scientific discovery'.

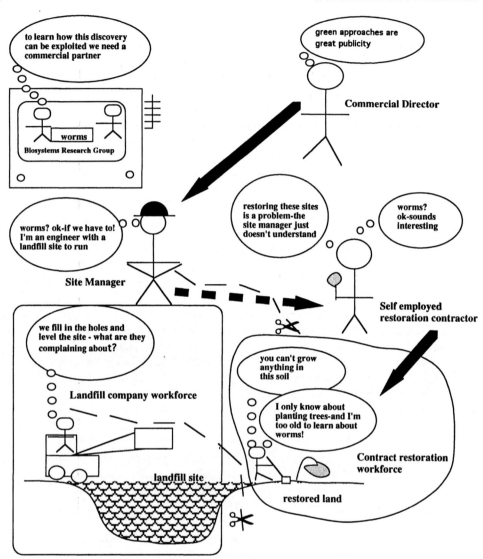

Figure 1. A rich picture of the problem situation in the project landfill site.

3.2. Choosing Relevant Systems and Building Models

Among the potentially relevant systems which were developed to the model building stage were: A system to train landfill operatives in 'worm handling' skills and A system to learn how our scientific discovery could best be 'exploited'. Work on the former served to illustrate it's complete impracticality, while work on the latter led to a number of useful insights which are referred to in the conclusions to this paper. Figure 2 shows the most influential root definition and model from this phase of work, relating to the primary task system, 'to enhance the sustainability of restored land in supporting plant growth through increasing the number of beneficial earthworms in it'.

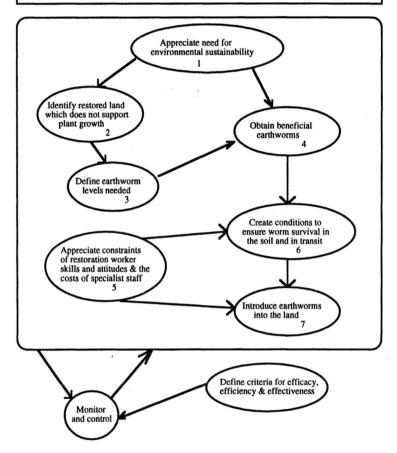

Root Definition
A Commercial Director owned system, staffed by restoration workers which, notwithstanding the worker's skills and attitudes, the costs of specialist staff and the hostile environmental conditions in the soil and in transit, increases the number of beneficial earthworms in the soil to the levels deemed necessary in order to ensure that the company's restored land is able to support plant growth in the sustainable way required for positive public relations.

Figure 2. A root definition and conceptual model used in the systems project.

3.3. Comparing Models with Reality

A comparison between the conceptual model in Figure 2 and what appeared to be happening in the problem situation indicated substantial congruence in steps one to four of the model. Hence the desirability of environmental sustainability was appreciated both in the way in which restored land was targetted and in the importance ascribed to obtaining earthworms in a way which does not involve the denuding of donor sites.

However when steps five to seven of the model were examined it became apparent that there was very little mapping between the model and the real situation. Little was actually done to create the conditions necessary for survival, this being a task requiring specialist knowledge, not possessed by the restoration operatives. Because of the influence of step 5 on the outcome of both subsequent steps, it was decided to examine what actions to improve the problem situation might result from a proper appreciation of the constraints listed. Contract restoration workers saw part of their job as 'planting container grown shrubs and trees.' This involved extracting a soil plug of the correct size, introducing the containerised plant into the hole, slitting and removing the plastic container without damaging its contents followed by back-filling and firming the surrounding soil. With this in mind a reiteration through earlier stages of the methodology suggested a new issue-based system which might be relevant to effecting improvement in the problem situation—'a system to produce container grown worms'. Thus a novel product concept was derived which we would never in our wildest dreams have developed without the participative learning process in which we had engaged.

The idea of the restoration workers purchasing containers of soil containing selected earthworms and planting them using exactly the same method as they used to plant trees, not only met the requirements of step 5 and eliminated the need for expensive specialists but also introduced the earthworms into the land (step 7) thereby creating the conditions which made their survival more likely (step 6). It was in addition appreciated that the other condition specified in step 6, relating to the survival of the worms in transit could be addressed by transporting them to the site in the containers. Further elaboration of 'a system to produce container grown worms' suggested that the potential damage and trauma associated with 'bagging up' the worms could best be avoided by following through the container grown tree analogy and breeding worms in the containers.

Ironically the next stage in this project, which had set out to learn how to apply a scientific discovery, involved a further programme of basic scientific research designed to discover whether and under what conditions it was possible to breed worms in relatively small containers in the substantial numbers required for soil reclamation.

3.4. Outcomes

The successful outcome of the programme of scientific research has been reported elsewhere (Butt, Frederickson and Morris, 1995). The new, improved process, the Earthworm Inoculation Unit (EIU) Technique, also appeared to be a success as regular monitoring of the site has shown a continued rise in earthworm population levels. The process was short-listed for the Prince of Wales Award for Innovation and was subsequently awarded a British Patent, GB2 240 456B. At the time of writing this paper, negotiations to license and exploit the process are being conducted. Clearly there is a need to continue to develop and refine the concept and SSM could make a significant contribution to this. The extent to which the process is adopted either in the UK or overseas and makes a significant contribution to sustainable ecosystem management remains to be seen.

4. CONCLUSIONS

Perhaps the most interesting aspect of the project was the application of a systemic method of enquiry (SSM) to a key stage in the process of innovation. Not only did this afford the opportunity to learn how to generate appropriate, alternative visions from a basic product idea, it also provided a framework for their integration. Arising from this research, it would seem that the use of SSM could be particularly relevant to the development of so called 'green products', where it is vitally important to develop product concepts based on a battery of complex human and environmental considerations as well as commercial criteria. One other obvious conclusion from this work is the need to introduce SSM into the innovation process as early as possible and certainly before undertaking the very costly stages of developing and testing prototype products. However, it is important to appreciate that with many genuinely new technological ideas, there is also a need to address the scientific feasibility of generic ideas and concepts during the early stages of development. Learning to integrate scientific and systemic approaches in the development of socially useful and environmentally benign products will be a difficult but also a rewarding challenge.

REFERENCES

Butt, K. R., Frederickson, J. and Morris, R. M., 1995, An earthworm cultivation and soil-inoculation technique for land restoration, *Ecological Engineering* **4**:1–9.

Checkland, P. B. and Scholes, J., 1990, *Soft Systems Methodology in Action*, Wiley, London.

Checkland, P. B., 1981, *Systems Thinking, Systems Practice*, Wiley, London.

Checkland, P. B., 1995, Model validation in systems practice. *Systems Research* **12**(1):47–54.

Curry, J. P., 1988, The ecology of earthworms in reclaimed soils and their influence on soil fertility, in: *Earthworms in Waste and Environmental Management* (C. A. Edwards and E. F. Neuhauser, eds), pp. 251–261, SPB Academic, The Hauge.

Frederickson, N., 1990a, Systems approaches in educational psychology, *Journal of Applied Systems Analysis* **17**:3–20.

Frederickson, N. (ed.), 1990b, *Soft Systems Methodology: Practical Applications in Work with Schools*, Educational Psychology Publishing, London.

Grumbine, E. R., 1994, What is Ecosystem Management? *Conservation biology* **8**(1):27–38.

Henry, N., Massey, D. and Wield, D., 1995, Along the road: R&D, society and space, *Research Policy* **24**:707–726.

Howell, S., 1991, Methodology on paper and methodology in use: New expositions of soft systems methodology, *Journal of Applied Systems Analysis* **18**:87–90.

Kotler, P., 1984, *Marketing Management: analysis, planning and control*, Prentice-Hall International, inc., London.

Ulrich, W., 1993, Some difficulties of ecological thinking, considered from a critical systems perspective: a plea for critical holism, *Systems Practice* **6**:583–611.

9

THE PRACTICAL USE OF SYSTEMS METHODOLOGIES IN ENVIRONMENTAL MANAGEMENT

W. E. Hutchinson

Edith Cowan University
Churchlands Campus
Pearson Street
Perth, Western Australia 6024

1. INTRODUCTION

For the last two decades systems methodologies have largely been the domain of academics (Ellis, 1995). Their use in practical problem solving has been chiefly restricted to the areas of organisational restructuring or information systems design. Complex, systemic social, and environmental problems have, at best, only been treated at a theoretical level. Yet systems methodologies, when stripped of constraints put there by over zealous theoreticians, have huge potential in these fields.

This paper examines the use of these methodologies (based around Flood and Jackson's (1991) concept of Total Systems Intervention - TSI) in practical, environmental problem situations. The examples used will cover "large" problems (catchment management) to the more local (implementing an organisation's environmental management programme). Environmental conflicts are still often handled in a linear, "win-lose" mode, and overcoming this is where systems methodologies can make their greatest contribution.

2. THE SYSTEMIC NATURE OF ENVIRONMENTAL PROBLEMS

At almost any level you choose, environmental problems can be viewed as complex (see Flood and Jackson, 1991 for a definition of complex). For broad problems such as catchment management, there are numerous, problematic, technical dilemmas such as water quality, land degradation, economic viability, and habitat preservation. Human interests are also diverse, and sometimes antagonistic, such as farmers vying for water entitlements, industries seeking pollution rights, conservationists attempting to halt ecologically detrimental projects, and landowners trying to maximise economic gain from their property. Figure 1 is a diagrammatic representation of a root definition (see Check-

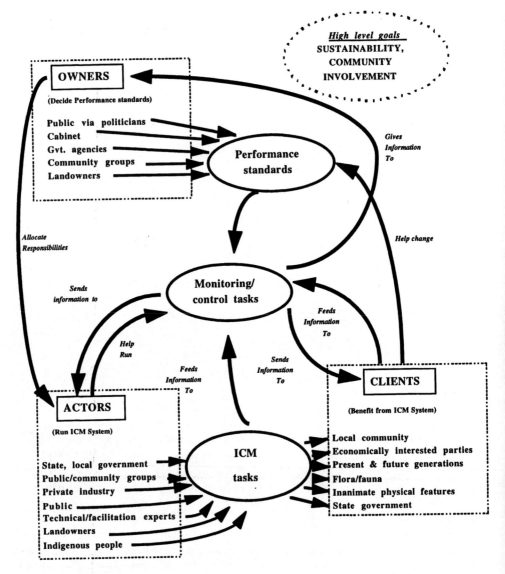

Figure 1. A diagrammatic root definition for Integrated Catchment Management (ICM) in Western Australia.

land, 1981) for an integrated catchment management problem in Western Australia, and shows the variety of interests in the problem. This diversity of interest and values makes the viewing of the problem as "coercive" essential for the development of any meaningful, long term solution.

Whilst catchment management is an inter-organisational problem, a single organisation has also to be environmentally aware in the contemporary world. The release of the ISO 14000 series of standards, for environmental management systems (EMS) and audits, in early 1996 has stimulated some organisations to develop programmes for their implementation. Figure 2 shows a data model developed by the author to demonstrate the information needs of an EMS. This model is displayed to show the pervasiveness of an EMS. It cuts across all the elements in the organisation and requires a change of work practice

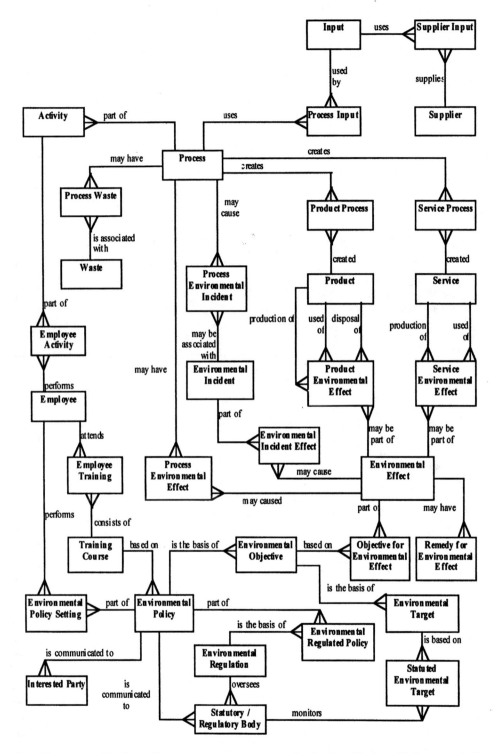

Figure 2. A data model of an environmental management system showing how ubiquitous it is in an organisation.

from almost everyone involved. As an EMS requires proactivity and cooperation within the organisation, it would probably meet some resistance (or at least, disagreement over its value and place). The problem could be viewed as pluralist, and sometimes coercive (Flood and Jackson, 1991).

3. COLLECTING DATA FOR PROBLEM SOLVING

The broader inter-organisational problems are best thought of as coercive, as numerous economic interests and value systems are at work. Collecting the data in a group environment where mutual understanding and learning can take place (Checkland and Scholes, 1991) might be a little optimistic. The requirement in this circumstance is to collect data to find a mutually beneficial solution. A possible way is to collect the data required to build a root definition and hence conceptual models as required in Soft Systems Methodology. One approach is to use Ulrich's twelve questions (Ulrich, 1991) of 'what is' and 'what ought' to be in the desired system. The use of these incisive questions will collect data required to supply such factors as the desired clients, actors, transformations, and constraints of the system plus numerous other insights such as power differentials. This is an elitist approach but it is difficult to see an alternative in these situations.

The intra-organisational problem can use much more group oriented approaches. The aim here is not just to collect data, but to facilitate individual and organisational learning. Soft Systems Methodology (Checkland and Scholes, 1991) provides an appropriate tool for this process. Also, Viable Systems Diagnosis (Beer, 1985) is useful for investigating the organisational needs and weaknesses when implementing a structure for an EMS.

The approach to data collection is very much determined by the analyst's view of the type of problem to be confronted. Many technical specialists approach environmental problems as simple unitary scientific problems and are surprised when their findings produce conflict. Others use the same methodology regardless of the problem type. It is posited here that although any view can be taken by the analyst and valid results obtained, it is more successful to approach environmental problems as complex/ coercive, or pluralist for long lasting and less contentious results to be obtained. One of the major problems with contemporary environmental management is that although great emphasis is put on public participation in an issue (which implies a complex/pluralist approach), the problem is often predefined by the controlling agency (government or private) making it a simple/unitary approach. That is, the public can only comment on a predefined system; in other words, the boundaries have been defined and the agenda set.

4. FLEXIBLE METHODOLOGY USAGE

As TSI advocates reflective use of methodologies, and is itself a meta-methodology, it is proposed that TSI also be used flexibly. The major aim of a system's investigation is to produce useful outcomes, and perhaps individual and organisational learning. The emphasis is on output not methodological "purity". Critical systems theory offers a base from which to evaluate the analyst's approach (Jackson, 1991). The insistence on some theoreticians to adhere rigidly to the structure of a methodology has stifled the use of many powerful ideas. Paradoxically, the rigidity of this approach is very much akin to linear rather than systemic thought. Each investigation is unique and therefore requires a different approach. This puts a large burden on the analyst as the approach will determine the outputs, but, if executed in a reflective and knowledgeable way, can produce useful results. It is the analyst who must be sensitive to the situation. In situations where power is a large factor, the analyst can rarely do anything fundamental about that problem except to recognise and attempt to design a more equitable solution. Ironically, if the analyst can influence power then (s)he has power, and therefore, may be a part of the problem.

Environmental problems are frequently beset by powerful, antagonistic participants. Finding systemic solutions, which are effective and inclusive, can be very difficult. There is a temptation to treat them all as simple and unitary (viewed from the perspective of the most powerful player, or the analyst's employer), as the analyst is overawed by the seeming intransigence of the protagonists. The simplistic solution is often shrouded in scientific rationalism, but is really an admission that technical problems are easier to solve than those involving groups with differing perspectives. In these situations falling back on fixed, rigid procedures is also attempted. This is done to give the appearance of "fairness" as written rules are followed to the letter. It is a bureaucrat's perception of justice, but does not encourage long term, ecologically sound solutions.

There is a great need in environmental management to start producing systemic solutions rather than those which reflect contemporary fads or power structures. The proactive use of critical systems methodologies, when stripped of their more idealistic components, would greatly add to the skills of decision makers. It gives them some tools with which they can achieve the outcomes they often desire. Often, however, the obscurity of the ideas seem to make them irrelevant to people who do not have time to delve into the deep, philosophical content of each methodology. It should be the responsibility of theoreticians to make the methodologies accessible to these people, and not just to stay in the realm of those who are concerned about structure rather than utility.

The choice of a methodology (or part of a methodology) should be determined by a thoughtful analyst with the realisation of the consequences and limitations of using that methodology.

5. CONCLUSION

This brief paper has attempted to show the complex nature (see figures 1 and 2) of environmental problems at both the organisational and social levels. Their systemic nature requires the use of systems methodologies in a creative and flexible manner. This creative use of methodologies must be accompanied by a knowledge of the paradigms of each, but should be output driven. In coercive situations, there is a dire and immediate need to make techniques available to practitioners to enable them to cope with an ever increasing demand on environmental services. Contemporary systems thinking has been around for a half a century, and has provided an effective means of describing environmental problems. The next stage should be to provide mechanisms for producing solutions to these dilemmas.

REFERENCES

Beer, S., 1985, *Diagnosing the System for Organisations*, Wiley, Chichester.
Checkland, P.B., 1981, *Systems Thinking, Systems Practice*, Wiley, Chichester.
Ellis, R.K., 1995, The association of systems thinking with the practice of management, in: *Systems for the Future: Proceedings of the Australian Systems Conference*, (W.Hutchinson, S.Metcalf, C Standing, and M Williams, eds.), pp. 17–22, Edith Cowan University, Perth.

Flood, R.L., and Jackson, M.C., 1991, *Creative Problem Solving*, Wiley, Chichester.

Jackson, M.C., 1991, Five commitments of critical systems thinking, in: *Systems Thinking in Europe*, (M.C. Jackson, ed.), pp. 61–71, Plenum Press, New York.

Ulrich, W., 1993, Some difficulties of ecological thinking, considered from a critical systems perspective: a plea for critical holism, *Systems Practice*, **6**(6):583–611.

10

SUSTAINABILITY AND SYSTEMS THINKING

The Coevolution of Communities and Technological Infrastructures

Paul Jeffrey, Roger Seaton, and Mark Lemon

International Ecotechnology Research Centre
Cranfield University
Cranfield, Beds, MK43 0AL

1. TECHNOLOGY AND SUSTAINABLE DEVELOPMENT

Unchecked technological development in general is at least partly responsible for some of the undesirable and survival threatening phenomena observed today. Problems of pollution, over-production, resource (and capital) concentration, restricted product lifecycles, and lack of social control, have all been attributed to 'technology'. However, whilst there is general consensus regarding the role of technology in creating the problem, there are diverse attitudes towards its future contribution (the debate between the various positions is extensively developed by Gillot and Kumar, 1995).

Two particular features of contributions on technological futures within the sustainable development literature which restrict the scope of debate. The first of these restrictions concerns the perceived nature of 'the problem'. Queries concerning the identification of a desirable and positive role for technology within sustainable societies has been dominated by issues of how much technology rather than what type of technology. The second restriction has been an emphasis on environmental issues, resulting in a prescriptive movement which espouses a 'greening' of the economy. It is the contention of this paper that a significant aspect of the contribution of certain types of utility technologies to sustainable societies' has been largely ignored.

Sustainability is promoted by adaptive change; a concept rarely, if ever, addressed in the literature on technological options for sustainable development. If technologies are to make a genuine contribution to the achievement of sustainable communities, the pertinent focus of attention should be on the design, operation, and management of adaptive technologies and technological systems. The planning of long term technological infrastructures concerns the development of planning methods and implementation strategies designed to ensure consistency in technological system performance over changing operating conditions. In particular, the design of resilient, adaptive technologies and technological systems will enhance the sustainability of our communities and economies under conditions of change.

Within the context of designing and managing sustainable communities, planners require an understanding of the interactions between the macroscopic dynamics of the regional or urban system and its component sub-systems. One major feature of this interaction is the way in which utilities' infrastructure and technology can be designed to allow for flexibility and adaptivity of urban built form as urban systems evolve under conditions of uncertainty.

2. RESILIENCE AND TECHNOLOGICAL SYSTEMS– A 'SYSTEMIC' PERSPECTIVE

Several bodies of literature engage in a debate about resilience and adaptivity, typical representative texts coming from Pielou (1975), Holland (1975), Pye (1978), Shakun (1981), and more recently, Jeffrey (1996). Translating the concepts of adaptivity from their roots in evolutionary and systems theory into the subject area of technological systems, we can readily identify analogous processes and structures. A resilient technological system will possess both options for alternative modes of operation (flexibility), and the ability to exploit these alternatives (adaptivity). The central components of resilience in technological terms might include; modular technology design, diversity of technology configurations, diversity of technology types, scale independent technology designs, and adaptive infrastructures.

Technology design can enhance the resilience of a utility system by ensuring that options for future action are not restricted by current attributes. In addition there will be a series of qualitative features of the technology which may be dictated by considerations of resilience from a different perspective (i.e. environmental, economic etc.). The type of design considerations which will enhance resilience may include the use of a modular design approach which would enable the potential for re-utilisation of components in other system types either during the proposed life-cycle of the plant or post decommissioning. Generally, this ensures that the life-cycles of specific items of plant and their constituent elements are not necessarily identical, thereby engendering an element of modularity. Scale considerations are also an important factor in determining the resilience of a technological system and are closely linked to network attributes. It is erroneous to assume that by scale issues is meant a preference for *small* scale applications. The relevant issue is rather the extent to which appropriate scale is dependent upon technology type and other factors. Life-cycle properties can also influence the resilience of a system as the interactions between different component, sub system and system life-cycles creates opportunities for change and adaptation. The design of network attributes will also have a significant effect on the resilience of a technological system, both spatially and structurally.

Two additional issues require attention. Firstly, it should be noted that the key concepts that have been reflected on in this and the foregoing sections are concerned with **attributes** (general qualities of system or sub-system behaviour) rather than **states** (measures of specific system performance parameters). This is worth some further discussion. The difference between these two phenomena has particular relevance within the context of planning methodologies, where a focus on system states has been allied with a mechanistic approach to problem solving, whereas a focus on system attributes has been associated with an evolutionary approach which is in turn more suitable for the study of emergent phenomena. For example, Allen argues that conventional approaches to modelling systems operate by identifying the components of the system and the interactions between them, and expressing these as a set of causal relationships, to give a mechanical representation of the system (Allen, 1995). However, the predictions generated by such a model can only be true as long as the qualitative structure of the system remains unchanged.

The second issue concerns the nature of the relationships between various attributes. In particular, the hierarchical structure of the relationships between various attributes dictates their influence on overall system performance. This point recognised by Checkland, who identifies 'emergence' as one of the fundamental ideas of systems thinking, stating that:

> "It is the concept of organised complexity which became the subject matter of the new discipline 'systems'; and the general model of organised complexity is that there exists a hierarchy of levels of organisations, each more complex than the one below, a level being characterised by emergent properties which do not exist at the lower level" (Checkland, 1981).

For example, the benefit of a diversified set of electricity generating technologies (each owned by a separate operator) is not of benefit to the operators of individual technologies but to the customers of the industry as a whole. Generically, diversity of individual behaviour does not further the interests of the individual but of the group; ecologists would recognise this as the tension between individual species and community survival.

3. URBAN WATER SUPPLY INFRASTRUCTURES

A central feature of much recent research into water recycling / reuse technologies has been the focus on small scale applications. For example, the use of household scale sandfilters has been suggested (Glücklich, 1995), and physical filter / membrane systems for recycling domestic bath / shower water have also been proposed (Murrer and Bateman, 1996; Till, Judd and McLoughlin 1995). Of particular significance, advances in recycling systems based on biological aerated filter (BAF), molecular oxygen-dosed membrane bioreactor (MOD-MBR) and ultrafiltration (UF) based membrane bioreactor techniques have been reported (Pankhania, Semmens and Stephenson, 1994) and are currently under test in both the UK and elsewhere.

The implications of these types of technologies for water supply and recycling networks are primarily to do with the development of evaluation methods. Given a set of recycling technologies such as that described above, we can begin to see how an appropriate analysis methodology for designing a water supply / recycling infrastructure for an urban area might be constructed. The following issues will form the basis for such a methodology.

3.1. Flexibility: Temporality and Uncertainty

Issues about specific processing technology units can be explored through calculating the cost and performance envelopes of a set of technologies under conditions of uncertain input costs, demand levels and quality over sustained periods of time. In design terms, flexibility is promoted by providing a technology function and performance envelope which goes beyond immediate or anticipated needs. Individual technologies will typically exhibit modularity, long life-cycles, and resilient operating efficiencies over changing throughput volumes and qualities. The beneficial use (application) of such technologies in terms of providing support for a changing community is dependent upon the nature of the network within which they are embedded.

3.2. Adaptability: System Configurations and Cost/Performance Trade-Offs

Exploiting a stock of flexible technologies involves providing a suitable infrastructure or network which translates flexibility into adaptivity. These issues can be addressed by considering water recycling technologies within the wider infrastuctural system of catchment, processing, delivery and disposal as part of an evolving logistical system and investigating how different technologies perform. The nature of the network in terms of its spatial arrangement, level of connectedness, directionality, functional potential, and capacity for expansion will not only determine its value as a source of adaptivity but will also set an agenda for technology design.

3.3. Scale, Hierarchy, and Complexity

It is necessary to formally identify how the water system can be introduced as an interactive sub-system into wider urban system models. The way in which such water supply (and disposal) systems will consist of different technologies at different spatial scales (building, street, community, district, city) and hierarchies, all of which have some economic, physical and social dynamic, is part of a wider research agenda into sustainable cities as complex, dynamic and evolving systems.

The utility of wastewater recycling technologies in terms of their contribution to infrastructure resilience derives from their qualitative role in the network. The readiness with which they can be utilised at various scales of application (for example) is of equal, if not greater, significance as their cost effectiveness. The pertinent questions are concerned with issues such as technology type and location, rather than solely cost and performance.

4. COEVOLUTION OF TECHNOLOGY AND SOCIETY

The ability of our societies to adapt in a sustainable way depends, in part, upon the coevolution of communities with those utilities which deliver fundamentally important services and products such as water, waste disposal, energy, telecommunications and transport. The development of models of communities as complex self organising systems shows that the spatial dynamics of a sustainable community would be likely to give rise to substantial changes over time in the patterns and nature of utility demand (consumption 'footprints'). Indeed, changes in technologies, social priorities, spatial and temporal demand and supply patterns may, in time, necessitate major modifications to the configuration and operation of the system. The concept of technological systems which can provide sustainable resource provision is closely associated with issues of technology flexibility, change, and socio-economic policy, and to associated issues of Demand Side Management (DSM) (Guy and Marvin, 1995).

The emphasis on attributes over states can be seen as the application of some key distinctions made by a number of prominent theorists. In particular, distinctions have been drawn between causal/mechanistic approaches to issue analysis and evolutionary approaches which allow for the existence of emergent properties. The roots of this distinction go back as far as John Stuart Mill, who, in considering the processes of causation and induction, also distinguishes between combinations of causes whose joint effect is the sum of their separate effects, and those where the combination of several causes leads to effects which are qualitatively different (Mill, 1875). To these ideas of causation and qualitative change, with their implicit time dimension, Morgan adds the concepts of hierarchy and process (Morgan, 1993). Morgan is concerned with the evolution of more complex structures from simpler ones. Although at each level, the components may be characterised as "things" which take part in "processes, he argues that what is "new" at each new level of the hierarchy is the ways in which the components of the previous level relate to each other. These observations suggest that the management of emergent phenomena has to be directed at a different level from that at which the effect is observed.

Any arbitrarily defined spatial zone (city, region, state etc.) can be seen as a complex system which evolves over time. Research into the dynamics which underlie such evolution has characterised city and regional economies as the compound result of different activities that to some extent fit together and need each-other; a process of coevolution which is typical of many complex systems. Information relating to the coupled development through time of communities and the technological infrastructures which sustain their most basic needs (food, shelter, warmth etc.), can be identified from a variety of disciplinary sources (e.g. History, Anthropology, Sociology, Engineering, Economics). However, interdisciplinary analyses focused on policy relevant output are now required to convert what is a disparate knowledge base into a focused, coherent understanding of socio-technical issues. Through such an agenda, the resultant understanding of the **coevolution** of society and technology, at the very least in terms of their spatial and temporal dependencies, will enhance our ability to plan (though not necessarily control) a sustainable future.

ACKNOWLEDGMENTS

The authors would like to acknowledge the support of both the EU (project code EV5V-0486 on Environmental Perception) and the EPSRC (Grant ref GR/L04870 on Recycling Technologies for Sustainable Cities)

REFERENCES

Allen, P.M., 1995, Self-organising spatial models; Integrated scenarios of regional development, *Conf. on scenario development for regional planning in eastern China. Shanghai. Oct. 1995.*

Checkland, P., 1981, *Systems Thinking Systems Practice*, Wiley, Chichester.

Gillot, J., and Kumar, M., 1995. *Science and the Retreat from Reason*, The Merlin Press, London.

Glücklich, D., 1995, Water and the environment: Solutions with decentralised wastewater treatment. *2nd International Conference on Ecological Engineering for Wastewater Treatment. Wädenswil, Switzerland. 1995.*

Guy, S., and Marvin, S., 1995, Reconfiguring urban networks: the emergence of demand side management in the UK, *J. Urb. Tech.* **2**: 45–58.

Holland, J., 1975, *Adaptation in Natural and Artificial Systems*, University of Michigan Press, Ann Arbor, USA.

Jeffrey, P., 1996, The use of evolutionary analogies to investigate issues of sustainability: Putting a human face on survival, *Futures* **28**: 173–187.

Mill, J. S.,1875, *A System of Logic*, 9th Ed. Longman, London.

Morgan, L. C., 1993, *The Emergence of Novelty*, Williams & Norgate, London.

Murrer, J., and Bateman, G., 1996, Grey water treatment and reuse. *Institute of Chemical Engineers conference on water recycling: technical and social implications.* London. March 1996.

Pankhania, M., Semmens, M. J., and Stephenson, T., 1994, Hollow fibre bioreactor for wastewater treatment using bubbleless membrane aeration, *Water Research* **28:** 2233–2236.

Pielou, E.C., 1975, *Ecological Diversity.* John Wiley and Sons, New York.

Pye, R., 1978, A formal decision theoretic approach to flexibility and robustness. *J. Op. Res. Soc.,* **29:** 215–227.

Shakun, M.F., 1981, Policy making and meaning as design of purposeful systems. *Int. J. Gen. Sys.,* **7:** 235–251.

Till, S., Judd, S.J., and McLoughlin, R., 1995, Crossflow microfiltration of secondary sewage effluent using extruded polymeric membranes, *Proc. 1995 Inst. Chem. Engs. Research Event*, pp219–221.

11

SUSTAINABLE INTERVENTION

Systems Thinking for Chinese Environmental Management

Wei Hua Jin

Centre for Systems Research
Lincoln School of Management
Lincoln University Campus
University of Lincolnshire and Humberside
Lincoln, LN6 7TS, United Kingdom

1. INTRODUCTION

Since Deng's reforms in 1978, China has made some impressive progress in economic development, which saw GDP growing at an average rate of 9% annually in recent years. However, the efforts to remove people from poverty and more modernization for the country have brought about a significant damaging impact upon the natural environment. The almost annual floods in the 1990s may be due to such an impact. In particular uncontrolled deforestation along the major rivers and lack of attention and investment in the rebuilding of river banks are some of the major causes identified by some experts.

China itself is fully aware of the serious challenge being faced in the issue of environmental management in the coming century. Urban pollution is getting worse, and expanding into the countryside. The environmental problems facing China today have become a hindrance to further economic development. The challenge to achieve successful environmental management can affect the survival and development of the nation as a whole.

The Fourth National Environmental Protection Conference of China pinpointed the following areas for improvement in the environmental management processes:

- consolidate the environmental law system;
- improve environmental monitoring and management processes;
- make technological advance as a key to further progress;
- increase environmental investment;
- develop environmental education programs ("Protecting the environment," 1996).

These appear to be a sound basis in the attempt to carry out the World Conservation Strategy (1980) calling for all countries to aim at sustainable development. It is the implementation of these strategies which will be crucial to the success of China's environmental management. We use Western systems thinking to design an environmental auditing system which will contribute to safeguarding the implementation of such a strategy.

2. SYSTEMS THINKING FOR ENVIRONMENTAL MANAGEMENT

It is necessary to consider the feasibility of applying systems thinking in environmental management. Systems thinking is presently represented by different strands advocating different perspectives and methodologies. However, all strands of systems thinking are built upon the fundamental concept of 'holism'. And the meaning attached to the word 'holism' varies from taking account of all relevant aspects of the whole system while modeling by hard approaches to reflecting continually on the inevitable lack of comprehensiveness in our systems designs in Ulrich's 'Critical Systems Heuristics' (Jackson, 1991).

Therefore, it is appropriate to justify that a holistic perspective is useful to the management of environmental issues. Firstly, in social planning, it is necessary to take account of all relevant aspects of our society, rather than dwelling on the pursuit of prosperity and modernization, regardless of the cost to the natural environment. Clearly the holistic approach requires us to consider our natural environment as well as ourselves as parts of the whole system. Secondly, it is necessary to make people aware of the environmental issues and their significance to a common future. In that case, the management of the environment would become the responsibility of all rather than only a limited number of environmental protection agencies.

However, as Ulrich (1993) points out, we have to ask how holistic we can really be when we pursue our well-intended plans to protect the natural environment while fighting for our survival, particularly in the developing countries such as China.

In fact, we can find that Ulrich's question is particularly useful in countries where Marxism and socialism prevailed up till the end of the 'cold war'. The ecological disasters in Socialist Eastern Europe show us that an advocated holism has not brought the intended results, as we now see the Soviet Union and its satellites treated the environment as recklessly as Western capitalist countries, despite a considerable amount of (seldom enforced) environmental legislation (Taylor, 1992).

We must learn that without critical reflection, we may never be aware of how holistic we can be in reality, let alone how useful the holism of the systems approach can be to the management of complex environmental issues. Therefore, we propose that the Critical Systems Approach can be used to assist the Chinese environmental management process, through the establishment of a systems-based environmental auditing system to compliment existing Chinese environmental management systems.

3. CHINESE ENVIRONMENTAL MANAGEMENT TODAY

It is necessary to briefly describe today's Chinese environmental management and its dilemmas (Ellis, Jin and Warren, 1996). China has made it a national policy to maintain sustained economic growth while protecting the environment (Qu & Li, 1994) by establishing four environmental laws via environmental legislation and environmental standards. It also has 1363 environment monitoring organizations with 16,000 staff all over the country (Zhang, 1994).

Despite all the efforts and progress during recent years, China has become one of the few countries in the world where water shortage is a major problem due to pollution of the major rivers in the modernization process. River pollution has become a serious hazard to health and hindering further development of the economy ("Protecting the environment," 1996). With worsening urban pollution and river pollution, this seems to suggest that the management of industrial pollution has not been as successful as it was intended. The sustainable development of China will depend to a large degree on the control of industrial pollution in the modernization process. This emphasizes why we are investigating the plausibility and the need for a systems-based environmental auditing system in manufacturing industry to compliment the existing management systems.

4. ENVIRONMENTAL AUDITS

There are two types of environmental audits, one external and one internal. The external environmental audits may be defined as audits undertaken by local authorities, public institutions, commerce and industry in order to assess the overall impact of organizations on the environment. Audits are undertaken on a regular cycle, usually annually or biannually. These audits take consideration of such factors as procurement policy, impacts on local air, water and land quality, land use policy, energy and transport policies, risks and emergencies and waste policy. When audits are undertaken in the industrial sector, it is also very important to include 'life cycle analysis' of raw materials, products and wastes (Taylor, 1992).

The internal environmental audits may be defined as audits to provide information on the efficient functioning of relevant plant and other facilities, while making sure that management and the entire organizational structure of the company are serving the goals of environmental protection. Internal audits assist decision processes at all levels. Internal audits may involve systematic regular assessments of internal environmental measures at all levels. The aim of internal environmental audits is to ensure that environmental protection receives as much attention as other operational areas, and that activities and products of a company are evaluated in terms of ecology, and that potential risks are detected and eliminated as soon as possible (Hopfenbeck, 1992).

If we combine the two definitions to provide a composite definition, it can be seen that there is a fit with the systems commitment to holism. In other words, such audits would be able to complement existing management processes by including environmental issues as part of the overall process of modeling and planning and result in a comprehensive involvement of all relevant stakeholders. This reinforces our recommendation to add a systems element to environmental audits.

5. SYSTEMS THINKING FOR ENVIRONMENTAL AUDITS

Ulrich has already questioned the validity of 'the fashionable call for "holistic" or "systems" thinking in ecological issues.' According to Ulrich, we have to remind ourselves that holism or systems thinking may give us 'a false pretension to superior knowledge and understanding (Ulrich, 1993).' It is exactly this kind of insight which enables us to realize that Critical Systems Thinking is necessary to address the challenges posed by the need for effective environmental management. Without critical awareness and reflections, we would be simply replacing the existing reductionist strategies with some unrealizable idealist approaches with incomprehensible contents, exemplified by the failure of the former communist blocks. There was Marxist Utopia at the heart of those communist governments, but they did not know how to get to the Utopia. What happened was that those governments often made a real mess of it by trying to hide the fact of their own ignorance and inability. This Marxist legacy has to be dealt with properly in all the transforming economies including China.

6. CONCLUSION

In today's world of fashion and fads, there will be many who would argue why don't we use the popular management techniques (the so-called management fads) such as TQM, BPR and others for environmental audits. They would question why we should use systems thinking for management science for environmental audits. Fortunately for us systems thinkers, this question has been well answered by Jackson (1995) in his paper 'Beyond the Fads: Systems Thinking for Managers'. Only systems thinking with its long and careful research tradition, and particularly Critical Systems Thinking with its commitments to pluralism and emancipation would be able to guide our sustainable intervention into a complex and coercive problem situation of China. In the next paper, we shall devote our attention to identify the problem context faced by Chinese environmental management, using Jackson's System of Systems Methodologies (Jackson, 1991). To be specific, our next stage will be devoted to identify/develop the right systems methodology for sustainable intervention in the Chinese context, for which we welcome the wisdom from fellow systems thinkers and practitioners.

REFERENCES

Ellis, R.K., Jin, W.H., and Warren, L, 1996, The feasibility of an environmental auditing system for Chinese manufacturing industry: A systemic approach, in: *Information, Intelligence and Systems* (paper collection) for 1996 IEEE International Conference on Systems, Man and Cybernetics (Tsinghua University, ed.), pp. 3015–3020, Wanguoxueshu Publisher, Beijing.

Hopfenbeck, W., 1993, *The Green Management Revolution*, Prentice Hall International (UK) Ltd., Hertfordshire.

Flood, R.L., and Jackson, M.C. (eds.), 1991, *Creative Problem Solving*, John Wiley & Sons, Chichester.

Jackson, M.C., 1991, *Systems Methodology for the Management Sciences*, Plenum Press, New York and London.

Jackson, M.C., 1995, Beyond the fads: Systems thinking for managers, *Systems Research,* **12**: 25–42, John Wiley & Sons Ltd., Chichester.

Liu, C.H., and Zhang, M.S (eds.), 1994, *Environmental Management* (in Chinese), China Environmental Science Publisher, Beijing.

Midgley, G., 1995, *Mixing Methods: Developing Systemic Intervention* (working paper), The University of Hull, Hull.

Morgan, G., 1986, *Images of Organization*, Sage Publications, Inc., California.

Nisbet, E.G., 1991, *Leaving Eden*, Cambridge University Press, USA.

Protecting the environment for sustainable development (in Chinese). (1996, July 18). *People's Daily (Overseas Edition),* p. 1.

Qu, G.P., and Li, J.C., 1994, *Population and the Environment in China*, Paul Chapman.

Taylor, A., 1992, *Choosing Our Future*, Routledge, London.

Ulrich, W., 1993, Some difficulties of ecological thinking, considered from a critical systems perspective: A plea for critical holism, *Systems Practice,* **6**: 583–611.

Ulrich, W., 1996, *A Primer to Critical Systems Heuristics for Action Researchers* (working paper), The University of Hull, Hull.

Zhang, S.M., 1994, The Current Status of China's Environmental Management, in: *Environmental Management and Techniques* (in Chinese, Quan, Ou, and Cheng, eds.), pp. 7–12, China Environmental Science Publisher, Beijing.

12

SUSTAINABLE TRANSPORT DEVELOPMENT IN DEVELOPING COUNTRIES

Using Systemic Thinking and a Global Perspective

C. Jotin Khisty

Civil Engineering Department
Illinois Institute of Technology
Chicago, Illinois 60616-3793

1. INTRODUCTION AND OBJECTIVES

The all-encompassing issue for transport professionals in the closing years of this century is sustainability and its links with economic growth, consumption, and the environment, and there can hardly be any understanding of their mutual growth other than global and systemic, particularly with respect to the developing world. The reason for this is that in comparison to the developed world, the need for transport systems improvement in the developing world is much more intense, with motorized transport (MT) estimated to increase by more than 100 percent in the next ten years (World Bank, 1986). What is most alarming is that a majority of transport policy-makers in developing countries believe that a higher rate of MT is vital for economic development, at the expense of non-motorized transport (NMT). This trend is changing more and more cities in the developing world into unlivable precincts, with horrendous problems of traffic congestion, safety, and environmental damage. Governments in these countries are facing serious challenges to keep people and goods moving, with no relief in sight. The objectives of this paper are: to describe the nature of sustainable transport systems, to briefly outline the transport modes and their characteristics, to spell out the new transport paradigm, and to suggest the more critical strategies for sustainability.

2. SUSTAINABLE TRANSPORT SYSTEMS

Sustainable systems, in general, are those that can function in the foreseeable future without collapse or depletion of the resource base on which they depend. Such systems usually achieve robustness through diversification, decentralization, interconnection, interdependence, and high degrees of system specialization in order to utilize resources effi-

Systems for Sustainability, edited by Stowell *et al.*
Plenum Press, New York, 1997

ciently. The existing transport paradigm in use on a global basis seeks to maximize transport capacity, travel speed, and mobility. On the other hand, the new paradigm seeks to maximize efficiency in overall resource utilization. In fact, the most efficient and sustainable transport systems are ones that display great modal diversity, offering the opportunity for selection of the most efficient mode or combination of modes to meet different functional and qualitative demands for the movement of people and goods, through the greater use of NMT, such as bicycles, carts, rickshaws, and other non-polluting, non-resource-intensive low-cost means of transport (Replogle, 1991). Also, since landuse patterns and transport networks are interdependent, the most efficient and robust forms of organizing city form is by planning transport networks that minimize aggregate trip-lengths. Such landuse patterns and the circulatory system depending on them would minimize the level of energy and resources consumption, while reducing pollution, total fixed and maintenance cost of the infrastructure, the vehicles that use them, thus ensuring that overall sustainability is maintained.

3. TRANSPORT MODES AND THEIR CHARACTERISTICS

A comparison of some of the principal modes of travel available in developed and developing countries conducted by Bouladon (1968) and more recently by Khisty (1993), based on time (T), speed (v), and distance covered (d) is as follows: $T = 6.6d^{0.30}$ and $d = 0.43v^{1.42}$ for developed; $T = 19.74d^{0.36}$ and $d = 0.22v^{1.48}$ for developing. Naturally, the transport modal hierarchy in the developing world is radically different from that found in the developed world, for several reasons, but basically because of the value of time and the economic level at which the country operates. The most striking conclusion from this comparison is that while the "limiting distance" of the walking mode in developed countries is 0.4 km (0.25 mi), the corresponding figure for developing countries is 2 km (1.25 mi). A similar limiting distance for the bicycle mode is 1.5 km and 9 km.

In many cities of the developing world NMT accounts for a significant proportion of all vehicle trips and contributes in many ways to the achievement of regional goals such as job creation, lowering air pollution, and sustainable development. MT and NMT have different operating characteristics such as travel speeds and passenger carrying capacity and these differences are best demonstrated via Figure 1. While MT can run faster and cover longer distances as compared to NMT, the latter are more efficient and occupy less space than single or multiple occupant automobiles. A proper combination of MT and NMT can truly lead to a balanced transport system (Kuranami, Bell and Winston, 1994).

4. TOWARDS A NEW PARADIGM FOR SUSTAINABLE DEVELOPMENT

The widespread use of NMT such as bicycles, rickshaws, and walking is often associated erroneously with a low level of economic development. In fact, planners working for developing countries often recommend that the transport system of the USA ought to be adopted as a model by third world countries. Nothing could be farther from the truth. For instance, Replogle (1991) categorically says that the automobile dominated transport system in USA has induced sprawled and inefficient landuse patterns, forcing people to travel longer distances to meet daily needs, leading to distorted low-density landuse patterns which, in turn, has forced people to travel longer distances to meet daily needs.

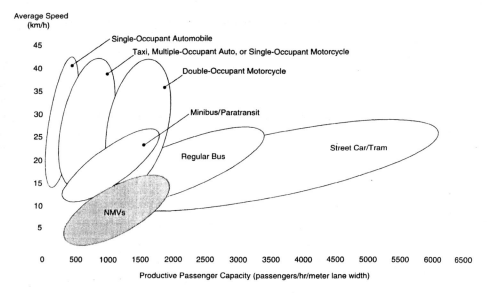

Figure 1. Productive passenger capacities of non-motorized and motorized transport (source: Kuranami, C., Bell, D.D., and Winston, B.P., 1994).

Mean while NMT, far from being a symbol of economic backwardness, is more a symbol of a bundle of modes that is able to meet passenger needs in the most cost effective and sustainable way. Ironically, despite these findings, policy makers in developing countries focus on encouraging MT.

Shimazaki, Hokao, and Mohamed (1994) have recently recorded their findings regarding the modal choice comparison of city dwellers in Asian countries. They use a graphical model as shown in Figure 2, indicating low-cost mode-usage, public transport usage, and private car usage, on the three sides of a triangle. This big triangle is further divided into four smaller equilateral triangles, representing low-cost modes, public transport, private car, and showing pairwise combinations of the first three types. The figure shows the pattern of change in modal choice that is likely to occur with improved economic development. The general pattern that emerges from this figure is that countries begin with low-cost modes, especially nonmotorized modes, to mixed (low-cost and public transport) modes, and then eventually, as the economy continues to improve, the tendency is to progressively adopt higher and higher percentages of MT, displacing NMT. This is unfortunate. Indeed, the optimum situation would be for a country to embrace a proper blend of modes resulting in a balanced transport system, thus ensuring a sustainable transport system.

5. SOME SPECIFIC STRATEGIES

Some of the more vital strategies, from among scores that have been proposed, are briefly addressed below:

- Since it is well known that person-miles traveled or ton-miles of goods moved grows geometrically as the city size increases (Zahavi, 1976), combined with the fact that more trips are made by MT as city size grows larger, resulting in propor-

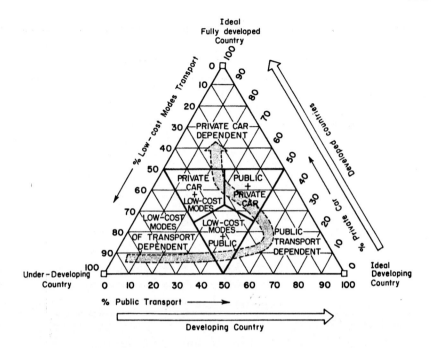

Figure 2. Pattern of change in modal choice (source: Shimazaki, T., Hokao, K., and Mohamed, S., 1994).

tionally higher operating costs, one of the best ways of containing city size is to relocate housing close to the place of work (Maunder, 1981). Proper zoning strategies, avoiding single-function zones, also reduce long trips, save energy, and reduce adverse environmental impacts. Mixed residential, commercial, and low-polluting industrial development have shown improvement in mobility and accessibility to employment opportunities particularly for low-income households which rely solely on NMT.

- The fact that a large proportion of the population in developing countries can at best only afford NMT underlines the need for providing such facilities on a priority basis (Herbert, 1979). Well-planned NMT facilities provide access to jobs, economize on the cost of distributing essential commodities, facilitate access to basic urban services and help social interaction, increase the land suitability for settlement by the poor, and allocate landuse to reduce average trip lengths to the very minimum.

- Because each transport mode has its own growth potential and dynamics, depending upon the physical, institutional, and market system, the key to effective urban transport particularly in developing countries is flexibility. For example the most striking feature in Asian cities is the variety of transport modes - vehicles with two, three, and four wheels, that supplement and complement pedestrian travel, from helicaks and cycle rickshaws to tuk-tuks, and auto-rickshaws, offering a range of innovative technological sophistication.

- A systemic comparison of NMT and MT particularly for application in developing countries has seldom been done. Whitelegg (1993) has provided an example of one such comparison between the "social" speed of a bicycle and a compact-sized car. Social speed takes into consideration the time that individuals spend earning the money needed to cover the cost of that mode. When this time is accounted for, actual time savings afforded by a car becomes considerably reduced; additionally when external environmental costs are factored in, the average social speed for a bicycle is better than for a car.

- Strange as it may seem our knowledge of the total or full cost of different modes of travel is rather limited. For example, public policy has for some reason not encouraged consideration of social costs of transport modes. It is only recently that road pricing schemes have been given serious thought for reducing traffic congestion. However, these schemes are taking only the commuter's travel time into consideration to the exclusion of all other social costs, such as excessive fuel consumption, air and noise pollution, and an increase in the probability of accidents (Khisty and Kaftanski, 1988). For instance, the social cost per mile of automobile traffic congestion on a stretch of urban freeway in Seattle, Washington is estimated to be $ 0.60.

- Using an efficient sustainable transport system means making each system user pay at least the full marginal cost of his or her trip. At the present time users of transport networks pay only a fraction of these costs, and what is even more serious is that these costs are not equitably allocated between different mode users of the system, resulting in external costs that have grown out of control in probably all countries of the world, and more so in developing countries.

- A limited amount of experience has been gained about how people will use telecommunication systems, currently available, as a substitute for transport. The general feeling is that new technology will have a tremendous effect on transport systems throughout the world. Substitution of working at home rather than in the conventional office setting, gaining education through the electronic media in place of face-to-face classroom teaching, and the rampant use of the electronic media for the movement of messages has already benefitted a fair proportion of the industrial and developing world, through communication satellites, fiber optics, and computerized information systems. This progress is not surprising considering that transport systems are indeed a subset of communication systems. How efficiently and how soon can the telecommunication substitution for physical travel be made, resulting in reducing actual trip-making, saving energy, cutting down on pollution and accidents, has been undertaken by several researchers globally and their initial forecasts sound most promising (Khisty, 1990).

- Educating the public in developed and developing countries, particularly the younger generation, on the imperativeness of balancing economic development with future impacts on the environment, is absolutely essential.

6. CONCLUDING REMARKS

The sustainable development paradigm with respect to transport described in this paper, along with the relevant strategies, represents an emerging potent force that can best be dealt with from a systemic perspective in the form of an international movement. Realizing the efficacy of sustainable transport on a global basis will surely need marshalling the political will, technological capabilities, and the societal commitment of every country, developed or developing.

REFERENCES

Bouladon, G., 1968, The transport gaps, *Ekistics*, 25: 6–10.

Herbert, J. D., 1979, *Urban Development in the Third World: Policy Guidelines*, Praeger Publishers, New York.

Khisty, C. J., 1990, *Transportation Engineering: An Introduction*, Prentice-Hall, Englewood Cliffs, N.J.

Khisty, C. J., 1993, Transportation in developing countries: Obvious problems, possible solutions, *Transport Res. Rec.* 1396, National Academy Press, **1993**:44–49.

Khisty, C. J., and Kaftanski, P. J., 1988, The social cost of congestion during peak hours, 3rd IRF Middle-East Regional Conference, *International Road Federation*, Washington, D.C.

Kuranami, C., Bell, D. D., and Winston, B. P., 1994, Planning for non-motorized vehicles, The Wheel Extended, *The Toyota Qty. Rev.* 90:11–16.

Maunder, D., 1981, Household and travel characteristics in two residential areas in New Delhi, India, *TRRL Supplement Report 673*, Crowthorne, U.K.

Replogle, M. A., 1991, Sustainable transportation strategies for third-world development, *Transport Res. Rec.* 1294, National Academy Press, **1991**:1–8.

Shimazaki, T., Hokao, K., and Mohamed, S., 1994, Comparative study of transportation modal choice in Asian countries, *Transport Res. Rec.* 1441, National Academy Press, **1994**:71–83.

Whitelegg, J., 1993, *Transport for a Sustainble Future*, Belhaven Press, London, U.K.

World Bank, 1996, *Urban Transport Policy Study*, The World Bank, Washington, D.C.

Zahavi, Y., 1976, Travel characteristics in Cities of Developing and Developed Countries, Staff Working Paper 230, *The World Bank*, Washington, D.C.

13

THE ASSESSMENT AND MANAGEMENT OF WILDLIFE AREAS

What Can Systems Offer?

Andrew Lane and Sue Oreszczyn

Systems Department
Open University
Milton Keynes, MK7 6AA, United Kingdom

1. INTRODUCTION

There are various systems approaches to tackling decision making, but all systems thinking and analysis is predicated on the concept of holism rather than reductionism. This concept is not unknown in biology. Indeed, it was the study of biological systems that led to the recognition of the significance of this way of viewing complex issues:

> 'Biology is an 'unrestricted' science...and its phenomena are of a complexity which has severely tested scientific method. Biologists, in fact, have been among the pioneers in establishing ways of thinking in terms of wholes, and it was a biologist, Ludwig von Bertalanffy, who suggested generalising this thinking to refer to any kind of whole, not simply to biological systems.' (Checkland, 1981).

Such complexity is amply demonstrated by the management of wildlife areas. Wildlife areas are very diverse; in the types of wildlife they contain, in the processes that shape them, in where they are located and in the scale at which they are viewed. They are also perceived very differently by those with direct and indirect relationships with them. Farmers, planners, policy makers, the rural and urban public, professional ecologists and conservation organisations each have potentially different world views.

Although complexity is often recognised as a feature of wildlife areas, any assessment of their value and prescriptions for management are usually based on a narrow, reductionist framework, involving either just wildlife or people but rarely both. Indeed, despite the quote above there has been little application of systems ideas to such human activity systems. This paper attempts to show how systems ideas may help provide a broader, synthetic approach. In particular, we draw on the idea that holistic thinking brings together multiple views to identify future options (Open University, 1996).

Systems for Sustainability, edited by Stowell *et al.*
Plenum Press, New York, 1997

2. EVALUATING WILDLIFE AREAS

The assessment of wildlife areas is problematic in terms of the scale and criteria chosen. Various sophisticated schemes and methods are used to assess wildlife areas (Usher, 1986; Goldsmith, 1991) but they often concentrate on well bounded, important sites, and are usually assessed by trained professionals. For instance, the assessment of wildlife areas in the UK has, to date, principally focused on the selection of biological Sites of Special Scientific Interest (SSSIs) or similar designations by the relevant nature conservation agencies, to provide a *national* network of prime sites rather than identify the management needs at a *local* level in the wider countryside. Furthermore, although striving to be objective, many of the authors of such schemes recognise that they are not truly objective, but invariably either contain hidden value judgements or overt but largely unused subjective assessments. The criteria for SSSI designation continue to be based on those defined by Ratcliffe (1977) namely the physical and biological criteria of size, diversity, naturalness, rarity, fragility and typicalness as *primary* criteria, and the human related criteria of recorded history, potential value and intrinsic appeal as *secondary* criteria.

Much of this approach is underpinned by the worldview that wild areas equate with wilderness and are hence largely untouched by humans. However, when looking at fragmented habitats in the wider countryside, we are actually dealing with a highly managed cultural landscape (Naveh, 1995) which is the product of human intervention. We need to understand not just how wildlife areas function but also the forces shaping them. Naveh (1995) notes that cultural aspects cannot be treated as 'external disturbance factors'. Positivistic approaches to assessing wildlife areas as part of a wider landscape which fail to consider the human dimension are, therefore, inappropriate.

A systems approach should consider:

1. The system of interest that is being assessed. Should we draw the boundary around a lower level of description e.g. a single habitat, or a higher level e.g. a mosaic of habitats set in a wider landscape? If wildlife is the dominant interest, then many people often just consider the species a single site contains (particularly those which are rare and colourful), rather than the dynamics of populations and communities within a given area (including the less wildlife friendly areas). Where the boundary is drawn will also depend on the perspectives taken.
2. The participants or stakeholders involved and the views they take. A major issue is the degree of influence the participants or stakeholders have on the activities of others. For instance, who decides what is the purpose of the system and which criteria to measure it by? Is the decision maker the problem owners (farmers?), the analysts (professionals?), the system owners (the public?) or all of them? Furthermore, is the purpose of the system to be the designation of important wildlife sites, the distribution of grants, the informing of planning decisions, or the enforcement of management plans or a combination of these?

Work at the Open University is aimed at producing profiles of 'habitats' that are based on a range of criteria rather than a single criterion. The work has involved various participants in devising assessment criteria that can be used by amateur as well as professional workers, and that incorporate different perspectives. The focus is on habitats in the wider urban and rural countryside, rather than habitats in professionally managed and monitored nature reserves. This work is exemplified by two different types of wildlife areas in the UK.

3. WILDLIFE CORRIDORS IN URBAN AREAS

'Wildlife corridors' is a concept that is being used to describe linear areas that link up important, fragmented wildlife areas. They can be wildlife sites in their own right and may also enable the movement of some species between sites. They may be semi-natural in origin, for example rivers, or artificial, such as canals. As part of a project in Milton Keynes that started in 1994 we have helped identify two levels of description or scales of corridor based on the idea that they create networks of habitats (Lane, Wheeler and Oreszczyn, 1995):

- Major, larger corridors which contain a variety of habitats and are usually connected to important wildlife sites. They may be important at a regional scale, often crossing administrative boundaries e.g. road verges and railway lines.
- Local, small, corridors usually of a single habitat type which help to form an intricate network branching off from major corridors e.g. hedgerows and gardens.

As the project was being funded by a variety of participants (Commission for New Towns, Buckinghamshire County Council, Milton Keynes Borough Council, Milton Keynes Parks Trust, English Nature) and the objective was to use it for planning and management purposes, it was decided that the higher level of description was the one to focus on.

We empirically devised an assessment profile partly based on the most popularly used criteria of those proposed by Ratcliffe (1977), but also including recreational and community value, and landscape value. This profile adopted an approach used in a scheme piloted in a training project (Tait, Lane and Carr, 1988) where each criterion was split up into a 4-point star rating scale.

A sample corridor was used for testing the criteria and rating system with several volunteers, and the criteria subsequently refined through several iterations before being applied to various corridors within Milton Keynes. As major corridors can vary greatly along their length, they were divided into units of assessment to achieve more accurate assessments. Each unit of assessment is approximately the same size but is mainly classified as a reasonably coherent geographical unit when looked at on a map or in the field. This profile gives an informative picture on the quality of the characteristics which make up a corridor unit, highlighting strengths and weaknesses. They allow either a composite profile of a whole corridor or a comparison between units within the same corridor to be made (Table 1).

Although this scheme has proved useful there are still many questions surrounding the choice of criteria, their ease of use by amateurs, its widespread applicability and the appropriate assessment unit to use. In particular, although many professionals and amateurs have been used to test the scheme, there has not been any significant involvement of the stakeholders beyond those mentioned here in agreeing to the criteria proposed.

4. HEDGEROWS IN RURAL AREAS

Research on hedgerows and hedgerow management has largely focused on (i) the wildlife aspects of hedgerows, largely ignoring the people part of the system and (ii) the individual hedge scale (the local corridors mentioned above) rather than the landscape scale. There is therefore a need to redraw the boundary to include the complex human factors which have largely been placed outside the system. This project, which began in 1995, attempts to examine hedgerows and their value to people in the landscape rather than as individual components. The project is investigating the cultural dimensions of

Table 1. Examples of assessment profiles of wildlife corridors in Milton Keynes

Criterion	Corridor unit number		
	Unit 1	Unit 2	Unit 3
Naturalness			
Age	****	**	**
Provenance	***	**	***
Diversity			
Habitat number	****	****	****
Habitat proportions	**	*	*
Other greenspace	***	*	**
Rarity			
Habitat rarity	**	*	*
Species rarity	NK	NK	NK
Size and extent			
Corridor unit area	****	****	****
Linearity	****	****	****
Corridor unit connectivity	**	***	***
Habitat connectivity	****	***	**
Habitat continuity	***	*	**
Corridor unit continuity	****	***	**
Recreational and community			
Availability of information	*	*	*
Number of facilities	***	****	****
Proximity to residential area	****	****	***

*Low value; ****High value; NK: Not known.

hedged landscapes through the collection and exploration of different stakeholder perspectives and by examining ways of bringing different stakeholder perspectives together.

Participation in research or management projects by non-specialists may take many forms, ranging from passive participation - where research is carried out on people who then have no share in the information extracted, to self-mobilisation - where people take action independent of external research organisations. Research suggests that complex environmental projects are more likely to succeed if a more active or interactive participatory approach is taken, whereby local people rather than just the institutions are involved in the work (Woodhill and Roling, 1993; Pretty, 1994; Grimble, Chan, Aglionby, and Quan, 1995).

Hedgerows have been chosen for this project because firstly, they are the product of human intervention in the landscape and are valued for many different reasons, e.g. wildlife value, historical, visual, and cultural value. Secondly, they are being lost mainly through lack of management. Management decisions involve many different stakeholders, each with their own perspectives, for example, policy makers through the grants made available, planners through new legislation on the protection of hedgerows and the conservation organisations who campaign and complain about changes in the landscape, etc. Finally, hedgerows function at different scales within the landscape—at the individual hedge scale, farm scale and landscape scale, and decisions occurring at one scale will have implications for the others.

5. DESIGNING FUTURE LANDSCAPES

Much of the work outlined above is aimed at assessing wildlife areas and giving pointers to appropriate management options. However, the adoption of management practices will depend upon the nature of the encouragement and advice being given. In some cases land managers will adopt practices resonant with their own views but many are only influenced by financial reward or legal penalties. Grant aid and legal designations have often been used to encourage the maintenance and recreation of wildlife areas in the wider countryside and at the same time encouraging public access. However, less consideration is given to the impact of these individual developments on the overall landscape, and lay people have little or no say in how grant aid might be apportioned. What is now required is an iterative, participative process based in communities, that looks forward rather than simply trying to conserve the status quo, and which considers not only the consequences of peoples actions but also the actions themselves.

REFERENCES

Checkland, P.B., 1981, *Systems Thinking, Systems Practice*, John Wiley, London.

Goldsmith, F.B., (ed.), 1991, *Monitoring for Conservation and Ecology*, Chapman and Hall, London.

Grimble, R., Chan, M., Aglionby, J., and Quan, J., 1995, *Trees and Trade-offs: A stakeholder approach to natural resource management*. International Institute for Environment and Development Gatekeeper Series No.SA52.

Lane, A., Wheeler, N., and Oreszczyn, S., 1995, Poster on Criteria for assessing and profiling wildlife corridors, British Ecological Society Winter Meeting, 19–21 December 1995, University of Sheffield.

Naveh, Z., 1995, Interactions of landscapes and cultures, *Landscape and Urban Planning* **32**: 43–54.

Open University, 1996, Working with Systems Block 1, Teaching text for a second level course, Open University, Milton Keynes.

Pretty, J., 1994 Alternative Systems of Inquiry for a Sustainable Agriculture. *ids bulletin.***25**: no. 2. Institute of Development Studies at the University of Sussex.

Ratcliffe, D.A., (ed.), 1977, *A Nature Conservation Review* Vols. 1 & 2, Cambridge University Press, Cambridge.

Tait, J., Lane, A. and Carr, S., 1988, *Practical Conservation: Site Assessment and Management Planning*, Hodder and Stoughton, London.

Usher, M.B. (ed.), 1986, *Wildlife Conservation Evaluation*. Chapman & Hall, London.

Woodhill, J. and Roling, N., 1993, The Second Wing of the Eagle: The human dimension in learning our way to more sustainable futures. MIMEO, University of Western Sydney -Hawkesbury, Australia & Wageningen Agricultural University, Holland.

14

EMERGENT PRACTICE IN AGRICULTURAL RESEARCH

Using Metaphors and Dialogue to Create a Space for Understandings

David McClintock,[1] Stephany Kersten,[2] and Ray Ison[1]

[1]Systems Department
The Open University
Milton Keynes, MK7 6AA
[2]BP 284
Maroua, Cameroon

1. INTRODUCTION

Creating a space for understandings to emerge can be contrasted with research approaches that try to *change* understandings. This contrast is illustrated by a distinction between researching *with* people and researching *for* people (or *on* people). Researching *with* people can address issues of social as well as ecological sustainability, as this approach involves relationships between people and their environment at its core.

In this paper, we describe three important elements of researching with people:

1. an explicit consideration of the position of the researcher;
2. emergent practice; and
3. using metaphors and dialogue to create a space for understandings to emerge.

Our traditions are within agricultural research. We draw on some case studies based on our educational, research and practical experiences gained in the UK, Australia, the Netherlands, and sub-Saharan Africa.

2. WHY SAY 'EMERGING RESEARCH PRACTICE'?

Our concern is with research practice. Within systems, researchers and practitioners have appeared to conflate methodology (M) with 'research approach' or method: what researchers do based on their theoretical framework (F) to examine some area of application

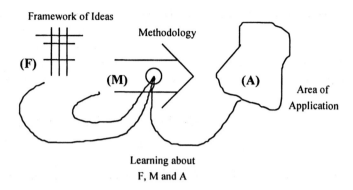

Figure 1. Checkland's FMA diagram (source: Checkland 1991).

(A) (Figure 1). This treats M as an application of ideas in a certain context, and does not consider how context informs both F and M. Further, the researcher or practitioner is assumed to exist separately from the context A. One consequence of viewing M as a research approach is an emphasis on developing self-contained packages, called 'methodologies'.

Instead of a fixed, prescriptive and context-free methodology, we prefer to talk of emergent practice (M) which emerges from the theoretical framework (F) *and* the research context (A). To explicitly consider the position of the researcher/practitioner, we need to modify research context (A) by incorporating a research*er* context (Rc) (see Figure 2). This includes the epistemological underpinnings and the traditions from which the research arises, the interests of the researcher, and the institutional settings for the research. Research*er* context will inform the research context. Potential topics for the research, and people involved also contribute to the research context (A).

Our interests (Rc) are in systems, agricultural research, and in creating a space where understandings can emerge. This space is limited by a number of assumptions in agricultural research that arise from a transfer of technology (ToT) paradigm: i) a detached researcher; ii) knowledge as a commodity; iii) communication as a transfer of information; and iv) a separation between *doing* research and *using* research. Research has

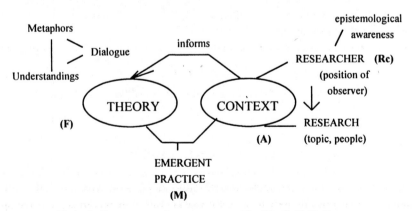

Figure 2. Emergent practice: a response to Checkland's FMA diagram.

been conducted as if its results can be transferred to farmers who will then implement it (see Chambers and Ghildyal 1985; Russell and Ison 1993; Kersten 1995). That is, the research tries to *change* understandings and actions. However, involving people in the research as 'co-researchers', and trying to create a space for understandings, necessitates talking instead of emergent research practice.

3. OUR FRAMEWORK OF IDEAS (F): METAPHORS, DIALOGUE, AND UNDERSTANDINGS

We have found inspiration in concepts of metaphors and dialogue when thinking about 'creating a space for understandings to emerge'. Lakoff and Johnson (1980: 3) demonstrate how "...metaphor is pervasive in everyday life, not just in language but in thought and action". Metaphors, as *ways of seeing,* can be seen to structure our understandings. Metaphors "have entailments through which they highlight and make coherent certain aspects of our experience" (Lakoff and Johnson, 1980: 156; see McClintock and Ison, 1994a). 'Bringing-forth', based on Heidegger's writings, can explain how metaphors are created by a distinction rather than 'exist' independently of distinction. Once a metaphor is created, then we can look at its entailments in a particular context. A framework of 'what aspects are revealed and concealed by a particular metaphor' is used to explore entailments of a number of metaphors.

We follow Isaacs' (1993: 25) description of dialogue: "...the word dialogue comes from two Greek roots, 'dia' and 'logos', suggesting 'meaning flowing through'." Isaacs suggests an initial working definition of "...a sustained collective inquiry into the processes, assumptions, and certainties that compose everyday experience." This then "...allows new possibilities to emerge" (Isaacs, 1993: 26). Dialogue can be contrasted with debate (*to beat down*). Debate implies that one understanding takes priority over another, and that present understandings need to be defended. Instead, we are interested in exploring differences in understandings. Systems research also appears to be interested in differences in understanding, as shown by reference to 'multiple perspectives', and the arbitrariness of 'boundaries'. Engaging in dialogue enables this exploration as well as leading to new understandings. As researchers, we can act to enhance or inhibit processes of dialogue by the way we create an environment for discussion. A non-threatening environment that includes open invitations to participate and relationship building, is a prerequisite for dialogue to emerge. Our attention moves to facilitating that process.

Dialogue and metaphors can enhance attempts to create a space for understandings to emerge. Engaging in dialogue can reveal different metaphors which structure our understandings. That is, different metaphors can lead to different understandings, and these can be revealed through dialogue. Metaphors, and distinctions around metaphors, also provide a trigger for dialogue *about* different metaphors. A relationship between metaphors, dialogue and understandings (our F) is shown in the top left hand portion of Figure 2.

4. OUR EMERGENT PRACTICE

Exploring understandings and creating space for change requires an intense interactions between people. There are no magic formulas or methods for doing this, as practice is informed by research context: that is, by the people with whom we are trying to research with. We have used 'open-ended' methods to build relationships with people, with each step informing the next. These methods include: participant-observation, semi-structured interviewing and 'metaphor' and 'dialogue' workshops. Within these methods, we have used techniques such as diagramming and matrix-ranking.

We use these methods and techniques in order to build relationships, rather than to 'extract' information about the research context. In addition, we have reported back our understandings and interpretations to co-researchers in the form of reports, cartoons, booklets and audio-tapes. This gave the opportunity for co-researchers to amend and learn from our interpretations: to continue the dialogue.

These methods and techniques have a number of common features:

1. they are intensive in terms of researcher time and resources;
2. invitations to be co-researchers are accepted;
3. they involve 'active listening' to people's stories and understandings. A researcher shows interest, asks questions and is aware of their body language. However, it also involves giving a chance for people to articulate and explore their understandings by creating a non-threatening atmosphere; and
4. they involve reflecting on 'role(s) of the researcher', and taking responsibility for research action.

These methods and activities depend on a suitable researcher context and research context. One of the most obvious factors is whether institutional settings will allow people to have the time to engage in methods and techniques such as these. Building relationships and creating space for understandings to emerge seems to invoke intense interactions over a period of time.

5. CASE STUDIES

We offer three case studies in the UK and Australia, which have contributed to our emerging practice. One concentrates on metaphors, the second on dialogue, and the third on facilitating research on issues of concern.

Future countrysides in the UK was the context for the first case study. Countrysides involve 'multiple stakeholders'. One of the main activities within UK countrysides is farming, but many activities and stakeholders are apparent. A starting assumption was that different sorts of countrysides could emerge from different ways of working with people (McClintock and Ison, 1994). This PhD project developed notions of metaphors and how they might facilitate researching with people. Metaphors of countrysides were brought-forth and explored in terms of what aspects were revealed and concealed, which in turn can lead to different understandings. Three examples of these metaphors were: countrysides-as-a tapestry, countrysides-as-meanings, and countrysides-as-polarised. Some 'metaphor workshops' confirmed that it was coherent to talk of 'engaging in dialogue with metaphors as a focus'. Efforts were also made to clarify what it might mean to talk about changing the metaphors that we use.

The second case study proposed that creating a 'dynamic' dialogue on vegetation management in western NSW, Australia, was a positive alternative to the traditional 'static' debate on whether these rangelands had been degraded or not. A 100 years old debate between researchers and pastoralists showed polarised views and cycles of blame and counter-blame. There appeared no appreciation by those involved in this 'debate' of the 'multiple realities' of the different actors. Moving from 'degradation' to 'vegetation management' was a way of breaking this debate, with the various actors becoming *partners* in managing the rangelands. Emphasis could move to how to create a non-threatening environment where different perspectives could be listened to and respected. This research looked at creating space for dialogue to emerge between researchers, advisors and pastoralists. Factors that enhance or inhibit this process were established (see Kersten, 1995). Some of these factors have been discussed under 'building relationships'.

The third research experience was a project looking at facilitating a community of Australian pastoralists to undertake research on their issues of concern. The project was funded by a government body that was concerned with the lack of implementation, or adoption, of research results. The project, Community Approaches to Rangelands Research, worked from assumptions that pastoralists *could* conduct research if it was on issues that concern them. Research did not have to be a property of research institutions, rather it entailed a process of finding out and taking action on the issues of concern. This project consolidated including a position of the researcher and researching *with* people (see Russell and Ison 1993; Ison 1993).

6. CONCLUSIONS

The three case studies demonstrate aspects of our emerging research practice. We are concerned with ways of researching *with* people, and in creating a space for understandings to emerge. Metaphors and dialogue can enhance attempts to create such a space.

Research practice can not be determined in isolation from the context. We have proposed that practice emerges from our theory *and* research context. In addition, we have explained how a consideration of the position of the researcher modifies research context, by including a research*er* context.

A consideration of emergent practice, and of creating a space for understandings to emerge, may enable 'co-researchers' to take part in a research dialogue on social and ecological sustainability.

REFERENCES

Chambers, R., and Ghildyal, B.P., 1985, Agricultural research for resource poor farmers: the farmer-first-and-last model, *Agricultural Administration* **20**: 1–30

Checkland, P., 1991, From framework through experience to learning: the essential nature of action research, in: *Information Systems Research: Contemporary Approaches and Emergent Traditions*, (Nissen, H., Klein, H., and Hirscheim, R., eds), Elsevier, Amsterdam

Issacs, W., 1993, Taking flight: dialogue, collective thinking and organisational learning, *Organisational Dynamics* **22**: 24–39

Ison, R. L., 1993, Changing community attitudes, *Rangelands Journal* **15**(1): 154–166

Kersten, S., 1995, In search of dialogue: vegetation management in western NSW, Australia, unpublished PhD Thesis, Department of Crop Sciences, University of Sydney, Australia

McClintock, D., and Ison, R., 1994, Revealing and concealing metaphors for a systemic agriculture, in: *Proc. International Symposium on Systems-Oriented Research in Agriculture and Rural Development*, Montpellier, France, November: 212–216

Russell, D., and Ison, R., 1993, The research-development relationship in rangelands: an opportunity for contextual science, in: *Proc. IVth International Rangeland Congress*, Montpellier, France, April 1991: 1047–54

15

MOVEMENT AND SUSTAINABILITY

Other Ways of Thinking about Environments

Ingrid Molderez

Limburg University
Faculty of Applied Economic Sciences
Universitaire Campus
3590 Diepenbeek, Belgium

1. THE FALLACY OF DEFINITION

When reading different sources in relation to sustainability, it is easy to become confused about the term and its definition. Think of "a sustainable growth rate" in finance, Michael Porter's "sustainable competitive advantage" and "the sustainable use of natural resources" in environmental jargon. The concept of sustainability is one about which there is little agreement within literature although it is recognised that an economic and an ecological element play an important role in its conceptualisation. Most of the time these elements are perceived as divided, as separated, in which the economic one functions as internal and at the inside whereas the ecological one remains external and at the outside. Between the two there is a *boundary* that does not allow *pollution*. Instead, regarding the inside as the outside and vice versa (cf. Cooper, 1990) emphasizes the boundary that structures them. A boundary, or that which *binds* together, mainly stresses the need for each other. Boundaries shape the different elements which implies that the elements themselves need each other in order to exist. The idea that all these elements are only parts of a larger system is the thin red line that binds this paper.

Sustainability is still seen as an ideal phase one has to strive for, as something *out* there, disconnected from everything. Sustainability is often considered as a final ending, as something one can reach after going through different stages. But that suggests that one can have something like a finished or end product in the development of society. Sustainability has obtained the status of an objective, of a goal to reach. This implies that one overlooks the meaning of sustainability as *being on the road*, as *moving*, whilst encountering facilitating or hindering elements. Sustainability cannot be seen in isolation. It is above all a process and something that never stops. *The idea of something out* there can be compared with Maslow's (1954) self-actualisation. Considering self-actualisation as the *ultimate* point to reach has been criticized for only stressing the goal instead of the process that was necessary to move towards that particular position. The latter is more central in the Aristotelian concept *entelechy*, i.e. the endowment that realizes or gives expression to potential. Entelechy could give the impression that we are predestined and that the *end* is known beforehand. The end is inherent in the system, but that does not imply that the future of the system is fixed. It is comparable with death that can be seen as the end of human life, but there is more. When a child is born, death is already present, yet life is still waiting to be lived. While an end is also a goal, an objective, a purpose or simply a finishing of a process, seeing an end in a much broader way allows it to be an integral part of the system. Finishing stresses a particular moment in time, the chronological end, the last point. But the end is also *open*, not only in the sense of an *open end*, like at the *end* of a book when the reader can add to the story. The openness of an end emphasizes the completion, the process, or the possibility to add during the story.

2. SYSTEM VERSUS/WITH ENVIRONMENT

Sustainability refers to dilemma. It is not clear what has to be sustained or kept in continuance: economy or ecology (cf. Redclift, 1992: 395–397). From within a radically *green* perspective the natural resources need to be preserved. According to economic viewpoints the present and future levels of production and consumption should be sustained. Sustainability functions more or less like a chameleon because its content can be changed according to the people who are using it. In this respect sustainability reminds us of Heidegger's (1959) idea of the word. The word is used as a streetcar; anybody can jump on and ride along for as long as s/he likes. But on the other hand it is not so strange that a word can have different and opposing meanings. Derrida's (1981) analysis of the Greek word *pharmakon*, which is central in Plato's dialogue *Phaedrus*, is interesting in this respect. Whilst translators have been struggling for a very long time with the translation of *pharmakon* by: "choosing to render the word sometimes by *remedy* and sometimes by *poison*, they thereby have consistently decided what in Plato remained undecidable" (Derrida, 1981: xxiv-xxv). Derrida makes it clear that we do not have to choose one *or* the other according to context, but that it is both one *and* the other. Derrida's analysis emphasizes that poison and cure can exist together and even require each other to be able to exist. The same also applies to sustainability which in itself makes it rather undecidable what needs to be sustained. Drawing on Derrida, ecology does not need to be excluded from economy and vice versa. An interpretation of "sustainable yield" in forest management emphasizes that to be able to earn one's money on a continual basis in forestry, which is a reference to *economy*, one has to make sure not to abuse the resources in the long run, which is connected to *ecology*. This mutual interdependence is not earth-shaking and efforts have been made to include it in definitions about sustainability. The "International Association of Scientific Experts in Tourism" for example, describes sustainability as trying to create harmony between economic and ecological interests. The definition seems to be an admirable effort to bring *opposing* elements together. It still invites questions, like "Is this harmony a movement from divisions to unity?" and "Are economic and ecological interests really so different?".

Economy and ecology are distinguished as if a unity has been split before and must become one again, like a movement from divisions to unity or from parts to a whole. One keeps on dividing, separating and fragmenting, although there is continuous search for unity, for wholeness (cf. Bohm, 1985). Bohm makes the link between *whole* and *health*. *Health* is based on the Anglo-Saxon *hale* which means *whole* or *to be healthy is to be whole. Whole* also has the same root as *holy* which indicates that: "man has always sensed that wholeness or integrity is an absolute necessity to make life worth living" (Bohm, 1985: 3). The idea of creating a unity is in itself a desire for wholeness, but this whole is a fragmented one, or as Cooper (1983: 215) explains: "Wholeness continually tries to reconstitute itself against an equally continuous force of differentiation." Parts and wholes are seen as *tensions* (cf. Strathern, 1992: 180) which hold incompatible things together (Haraway, 1990). According to Strathern (quoted by Cooper and Law, 1995: 245): "Things hold together, but only as working compatibilities and certainly not as pure, unitary wholes." Wholeness might be perceived as a jigsaw puzzle formed by different, but neatly fitting pieces. This rather mechanic approach insinuates that a unity can be constructed from single parts and deconstructed again. Cooper and Law (1995: 245) refer to Gleick to state that: "parts do not unproblematically turn into larger wholes" and use Gleick's example of the two pieces of a broken cup that: "can never be rejoined, even though they appear to fit together at some gross scale". This idea of unifying is also impossible because what has been broken once can be fixed, but will still show the lines of separation. The wholeness one is searching for, should not be seen as all-encompassing which leads to suffocation. This wholeness is open, rather than closed. It fits within the openness of an *end* that was discussed earlier in this paper. Wholeness is different from the totalitarian of a *totality*: "A totality can be mastered, dominated, controlled; it can be grasped and possessed; it can be fixed and secured; it can be known with certainty; it is absolutely complete. A whole has its own completeness, but this completeness remains open. A sonata, a painting, a photograph, a sunset, a summer shower, a conversation, an individual's psychoanalysis, a gesture: each of these has a beginning and an end, a certain unity, coherence and completeness. Yet this wholeness does not preclude their continuity, and they are open to further enrichment or development, to different completions" (Levin, 1988: 79). This idea of wholeness fits into the way harmony can be perceived. Harmony immediately relates to an interplay of sounds, to notes of music combined together in a pleasanty sounding way. Harmony presupposes a connection, a joining of different and opposing elements, like the arrow or the lyre (cf. Heraclitus). The different parts are not enforced to work together, but their play is characterised by an understanding for differences. In this way harmony is comparable to dialogue and when there is an on-going dialogue there can be, *in the end*, neither discord nor disconnection.

Aiming for harmony between the economic and ecological interests gives the impression that it is possible to make a separation between inclusion and exclusion, between inside and outside. Within this approach of being able to separate, everything that is included within economic interests cannot be part of ecological ones. Perceiving *economy* as inside and *ecology* as outside, is made explicit in the common use of *environment* as synonymous with *ecology*. Both are seen as outside, but such a conclusion can only be reached by somebody who is standing apart, in the sense of being apathetic or without any commitment. Observing is an act of *objectification*, of turning into an *object*, of separation. Only the one who is observing and who is not involved can see the demarcation lines, while those who are being observed do not notice them. This idea is implicit in the definition of *environment* as: "that which environs; the objects or the region surrounding anything" whereby *to environ* stands for: "to form a ring round, to surround, to encircle", but also "to include, to take in" (cf. *The Oxford English Dictionary*). So, the environment is surrounding something whilst this *something* can also be included in or be part of the environment. Nevertheless, by giving more details, like: "The environment are the conditions under which any person or thing lives or is developed, or the sum-total of influences which modify and determine the development of life or character" and "Environmentalism is a theory of the primary influence of the environment on the development of a person or group", the *Oxford English Dictionary* subscribes to the dominant meaning of system theory. Especially within systemic approaches in social sciences (cf. Lawrence and Lorsch, 1967) the distinction between a system and its environment is emphasized (cf. Cooper, 1990; Cooper and Law, 1995). Although a difference can be made between a closed and an open system there is still a boundary between the two (cf. Cooper, 1990). Within system theory nowadays it is *the system* that has a relationship with the *environment* and the system has usurped the border. What seems to be certain, is that somebody or something must be in the centre, or must be within the borderlines to be able to be surrounded. And who or what is included in the centre is not without significance since: "the centre displaces power from its peripheral sources in order to augment its own power which enables the centre to dominate its world" (Cooper, 1992: 268). This reading of environment fits in a *top-down approach* (cf. Rotman, 1994). Somebody is sitting on the top and is looking down on everything that surrounds him. Derrida (in Cooper, 1989: 482) calls this *logocentrism* since: "it centres human experience around the concept of an original *logos* or presupposed metaphysical structure (e.g. mind, soul, reason) that validates and gives meaning to human activities....The centre not only orients, balances and organises the structure, but above all it serves to limit excessive *play* in the structure."

Derrida's idea of the *de-centred*, the *non-logocentric* therefore has a lot of implications for the way environment and also ecology are seen. In this respect it helps to refer to *milieu* which is often used as an equivalence for environment or ecology, especially on the Continent. Milieu stresses more the environment as a *whole and unbroken movement*. *Milieu* is composed of *mi*, which stems from the Latin *medius*, and *lieu*. *Medius* is the same as *medium* which makes the environment a *medium*, a *middle* and even a *mediating term*. Mi-lieu is being *in the middle of the route* that goes from A to B. This again corresponds with the broader idea of *end*. To be able to reach B, we have to be in the middle of, in the midst of. Milieu, or that which is in the midst of us, i.e. at the core of life, also fits within a *bottom-up approach* (cf. Rotman, 1994). Everything starts from the bottom or there where the action is. And when one is part of the action it becomes difficult to disentangle the different elements. If one goes back to the etymological roots of *economy* and *ecology* then the two so-called separated environments even turn into a *muddle* which makes it difficult to distinguish between the two. Economy and ecology both refer to the same *eco* or *oikos* in Greek, which is *house* or *dwelling*. House is a place where one is at home and underlines the idea of community, of warmth. The *eco* of ecology/economy comes closer to the eco of *Ec(h)o and Narcissus*, the Greek myth about Narcissus who rejected the affections of the nymph Echo, who eventually wasted away until only her voice remained. According to Cooper (1983: 202) this Greek myth allegorizes the significance of the Other: "As punishment for his inability to love others, the gods made Narcissus fall in love with his own reflection, which paradoxically he both possessed and yet could not possess. Narcissus rejected the live-giving structure of the outside society, mediated by other people. We know ourselves only through the echo of the Other." In other words, the echo—the ecology, and the environment—is not something different from ourselves, but more a reflection of ourselves.

3. DIFFERENT WAYS OF THINKING

This paper has been an attempt to break through a functionalist approach: "Parts...are not made independently and then assembled as in a machine, but arise as a result of interactions *with* [this word is preferred to Goodwin's within] its wider environment" (Goodwin, 1994: 183). In the most general way the paper has been *touching* a way towards *ecological thinking*. *Ecology* goes beyond the common concern for an environmentally friendly way of behaving and organising. As has been discussed, the concept *ecology* conceals that we are part of the environment. Ecology refers to the Greek *oikos* or home or *la demeure* (in French). The root *meure* comes from *mourir* or *to die*. In this respect *ecology* implies that we have to die a little, not in the literal sense, but in a metaphorical way to make ourselves less important or to *de-centre* ourselves. 'No man is an island', but is instead connected with the world.

A part only has meaning in its relation with other parts. In this way systems are the temporary result of relationships, of different creating processes. From this position of rest, heterogeneous processes that are moving and shaping will continue to give form. Each part has an intrinsic value and meaning and is important in the whole process. This approach of perceiving the human's role in the world fits within the earlier distinction between top-down, or "we are *within* the environment", and bottom-up approach, or "we are *with* the environment". Movement can therefore be interpreted in two different ways: move*ment*, to stress the result or *end* (cf. '-ent') of an action, and *move*ment to stress the happening itself. Within the former it is a movement from one definite location to another one while the process of creating has been ignored. It gives primacy to: "a reality that pre-exists, independently of observation and that consists of static, discrete and identifiable *things*" (Chia, 1996: 33). In the second definition of movement an entity is seen as a result or an effect of different processes rather than assuming that it is something given by nature (cf. Cooper and Law, 1995; Chia, 1996). This distinction is everything but new and goes back to two modes of thought that existed already before Socrates (4th-5th century before Christ) (cf. Chia, 1996: 34–35). While Heraclitus emphasized the primacy of flux and transformation, his successor Parmenides insisted upon the permanent and unchangeable nature of reality. In our own time, these ideas have been dealt with in great detail by Whitehead (1929). The distinction still exists and has been given different labels by different authors, as *strong and weak thinking* by Vattimo (1988), *the already* and *the un-ready* by Cooper (1993), *being* and *becoming* by Chia (1995, 1996), *distal* and *proximal* by Cooper and Law (1995). Choosing is again not at stake. If *being and becoming* are taken as an example, it is not either being or becoming, but both becoming and being in which being can be seen as a temporary result of becoming. *Being* is therefore always part of *be*-coming or *becoming* is *being* that is *coming*. Distal and proximal thinking are interesting ways of labelling the difference because the pivotal word is *joining* to a central point. Although the point of joining can be far (cf. distal) or near (cf. proximal) it is still a joining or it shows that there is still some link, some connection with something, with each other.

REFERENCES

Bertalanffy von L., 1971, *General System Theory*, Allen Lane, London.

Bohm D., 1985, *Wholeness and the Implicate Order*, Ark, London.

Chia R., 1995, From modern to postmodern organizational analysis, *Organization Studies*, **16**(4):579–604.

Chia R., 1996, The problem of reflexivity in organizational research: Towards a postmodern science of organization, *Organization*, **3**(1):31–59.

Cooper R., 1983, The other. A model of human structuring, in: *Beyond Method: A Study of Social Science Research Strategies*, (G. Morgan, ed.,), pp. 202–218, Sage, California.

Cooper R., 1989, Modernism, post modernism and organizational analysis 3 : The contribution of Jacques Derrida', *Organization Studies*, **10**(4):479–502.

Cooper R., 1990, Organization/disorganization, in: *The Theory and Philosophy of Organisations* (J. HASSARD and D. PYM, eds.,), pp. 167–197, Routledge, London.

Cooper R., 1993, Technologies of representation, in: *Tracing the Semiotic Boundaries of Politics*, (P. AHONEN, ed.), pp. 279–312, Mouton de Gruyter, Berlin, New York.

Cooper R. and Law J., 1995, Organisation: distal and proximal views, *Research in the Sociology of Organizations*, Volume 13, pp. 237–274, JAI Press, Greenwich, Connecticut.

Derrida J., 1981, *Dissemination*, [Translated and with an Introduction and Additional Notes by Barbara Johnson], The Athlone Press, London.

Goodwin B., 1995, *How the Leopard Changed its Spots*, Phoenix Giant, London.

Haraway D., 1990, A manifesto for cyborgs: Science, technology and socialist feminism in the 1980's, in: *Feminism/Postmodernism*, (L. Nicholson, ed.), pp. 190–233, Routledge, New York and London.

Heidegger M., 1959, *Introduction to Metaphysics*, Yale University Press, New Haven.

Lawrence P.R. and Lorsch J.W., 1967, *Organization and Environment: Managing Differentiation and Integration*, Graduate School of Business Administration, Harvard University, Boston.

Lefebvre E., 1986, *Elements of Human Organising. A Phenomenology of Person and Situation*, University of Lancaster, Department of Behaviour in Organisations, PhD Dissertation.

Levin D.M., 1988, *The Opening of Vision*, Routledge, New York, London.

Maslow A.H., 1954, *Motivation and Personality*, Harper & Row Publishers, New York, London.

Redclift M., 1992, The meaning of sustainable development, *Geoforum*, **23**(3):395–403.

Rotman B., 1994, Exuberant materiality - De-minding the store, *Configurations*, **2**:257–274.

Strathern M., 1991, *Partial Connections*, Rowman & Littlefield Publishers, Maryland.

Strathern M., 1992, No nature, no culture: the Hagen case, in: *Nature, Culture and Gender*, (C. Maccormack and M. Strathern, eds.,), pp. 174- 222, Cambridge University Press: Cambridge.

Vattimo G., 1988, *The End of Modernity. Nihilism and Hermeneutics in Post-modern Culture*, Polity Press, Cambridge.

Whitehead A.N., 1929, *Process and Reality*, Macmillan, New York.

16

THE TECHNOLOGY OF SUSTAINABLE AGRICULTURAL SYSTEMS

R. M. Morris

Systems Department
Open University, United Kingdom

1. INTRODUCTION

The sustainability of agricultural systems as the source of almost all food materials is essential for the continuance of human society. The ability of agriculture to meet the food demands of an increasing population has been questioned since 1800 (Malthus,1803), on the assumption that technical improvements must ultimately encounter some fundamental biochemical limits. Despite this, the history of World, and European production since the 1940s has shown steady but continuous improvement, with no sign of a slackening in the rate of increase (Open University, 1987).

Thermodynamically, the ultimate limit is imposed by the energy input from the sun and the biochemical efficiency of conversion of this into useable products. The maximum efficiency achievable is unknown, but must be much less than 100%. In practice, threats to sustainability arise well below these theoretical limits. They can occur for technical, economic or socio-political reasons, or the systemic interactions among these factors (Tait, 1996). This paper attempts to identify the major threats, and to evaluate potential responses to them.

2. TECHNICAL THREATS

Food production depends on the use of both renewable resources, such as solar energy and water, and non-renewable resources such as fossil fuels, synthesised fertilisers and various effect chemicals. It also depends on the maintenance of appropriate conditions for plant and animal growth (Open University 1996). These conditions include climatic and soil factors, and the extent of attack by disease and pest organisms. Current production methods could become unsustainable if conditions move outside defined ranges, or if the rates at which resources can be obtained are restricted. For renewable resources, rates of renewal could change, and the absolute amount of non-renewable resources is finite, so both these could affect sustainability. More immediately, the capture of solar energy for food production depends on the apropriate display of a healthy plant canopy, which depends on the conditions affecting plant growth. There is thus considerable interaction among the various factors, which has to be controlled by the agriculturalist.

Solar income is probably secure over geological timescales, but the rate of renewal of water supplies depends on the hydrological cycle which may be disrupted by climate change (Rosenzweig and Parry, 1994). The chief non-renewable resources needed are the plant nutrients, phosphate and potassium, and fossil fuels. Leach (1976) and others have highlighted that a major use of fossil fuels is to make available the potentially renewable nutrient resource, nitrogen. Under current conditions, the reserves of both phosphate and potassium appear to be non-limiting, (Open University, 1996) and in the longer term, much of these could be re-cycled. Fossil fuels are more problematical, but the total direct and indirect consumption by agriculture is relatively small compared to other industrial and domestic uses (Open University, 1996). For the foreseeable future, adjustments between uses should maintain fossil fuel supply to agriculture.

Maintenance of appropriate conditions for plant growth may be more difficult. Global warming will certainly change climatic conditions, but the net effects of this are difficult to predict (Rosenzweig and Parry, 1994). In the UK, there has been relatively little disquiet over soil conditions, (Agricultural Advisory Council, 1976) which affect both the availability of nutrient resources and the incidence of erosion, but current data (Morgan, 1986; Douglas, 1990) suggest a much less optimistic picture. Atmospheric pollutants have varied effects. Depletion of the ozone layer leading to increased levels of ultraviolet radiation reaching ground level, may affect yields in some temperate crops (Wellburn, Paul and Mehlhorn, 1994), while recent reductions in sulphur deposition require increased use of sulphur containing fertilisers. There are complex interactions between pollutants and disease causing organisms, which are not clearly understood, but diseases and pests provide a potentially serious threat. The genetic base of the major Developed World crops is relatively narrow, with 50% of the UK wheat area sown to two varieties in 1995 (Home Grown Cereals Authority, 1996). The loss of indigenous crop varieties through commercial and ecological pressures reduces the available variety for future breeding programmes. Rates of emergence of new strains of pathogens are high, and the probability of catastrophic breakdown of disease resistance in one or more of the popular crop varieties is certainly not zero. The development of resistance to herbicides among weed species is already well documented (Moss and Rubin, 1993). The new technology of genetic engineering offers a partial response to pests and pathogens, and could dramatically increase yields, but could potentially also give rise to new weed or pest forms (Crawley, Halls, Rees, Kohn and Buxton, 1993).

It appears that with the possible exception of catastrophic disease or pest outbreaks, correct application of the current knowledge base to operations within the farm could avoid most of the technical threats to the sustainability of agricultural production in the Developed World. Geophysical effects such as climate change and stratospheric ozone depletion could be severe but may be amenable at least to amelioration using current knowledge. However, the way this knowledge is used depends critically on economic and socio-political factors.

3. ECONOMIC FACTORS

Economically, agriculture has some unique and paradoxical features. The industry is subject to variable product yields, and to cyclical or unstable prices for commodities.

Farmers have traditionally been weak sellers faced with a smaller number of powerful buyers (Ritson, 1977). Historically, the terms of trade for agriculture against the rest of industry have almost continuously worsened. Given the importance of food supply, government intervention to support agricultural production has been almost universal. Yet farmers and their representatives are among the strongest advocates of the "free market". The response of many farmers to declining prices has been paradoxically, to increase production at least in the short term, and adopt more advanced technology in the medium term. There has also been a reduction in the numbers obtaining a livelihood from agriculture (Central Statistical Office). None of these trends is sustainable should historic economic pressures continue.

The economic environment of agriculture is determined partly by the political strength of the industry, but also by public perception of it.

4. SOCIO-POLITICAL FACTORS

The strength or otherwise of the agricultural lobby has been a matter of debate for many years. However, it appears that the very idea of "sustainability" and the concerns for "the environment" associated with this, may produce pressures for change. These could lead to a more sustainable industry, but the way in which the forces are exerted will be crucial.

Silent Spring (Carson, 1965) was one of the first books to draw attention to some undesirable outputs from agriculture. These included various pollutants, changes in the landscape and in access to it. A succession of authors has taken up the same theme, (for example, Bowers and Cheshire, 1983; Conway and Pretty, 1991) and there has been increasing public pressure for changes or restrictions to agricultural practice. Some restrictions have gained legal force, as in measures designed to limit inputs of nitrate to drinking water from agricultural land. (Commission of the European Community, 1988) Codes of practice for the use and disposal of manures and agricultural chemicals have also been drawn up, to minimise the possibility of off-farm pollution from these (Ministry of Agriculture, Fisheries and Food, 1990). These restrictions appear to have been accepted more or less grudgingly by the agricultural industry, but pressures for more far-reaching change persist. There is evidence that some of the more obvious farmland birds have declined in the UK as a result of changes in agricultural practice (Wilson, Evans, Grynderup Poulsen and Evans 1995). Other landscape changes such as the removal of hedges and replacement of mixed farming with more specialised units have led to unfavourable comment from the more concerned sectors of the public. Recently, the emergence of Bovine Spongiform Encephalopathy and the inept manner in which its control has been approached has intensified pressure for change. The size of the concerned minority calling for change is not clear, and surveys suggest it may be only around 10% of the UK population (Brown, 1992) but the industry and its advisors have found themselves forced to address these concerns. In this sense at least, current technology may not be sustainable, because socio-political pressure will not allow it to continue.

5. POSSIBLE RESPONSES

There appears to be no *a priori* reason why the technical threats to sustainability in the medium term cannot be countered by appropriate use of existing or new technology, although the possibility of catastrophe is always present. However, one of the commonest calls is for agriculture to return to an updated version of practices of an earlier era in the form of organic farming. Research into this is still relatively undeveloped, but present methods of organic production are unlikely to be able to provide current, or anticipated food requirements within the UK or the world. Within Europe as an isolated unit, organic methods might just be feasible, but current methods suffer fundamentally from the need to grow crops suitable only for animal feed on a significant proportion of the cultivable land. This limits the efficiency of the food chain (Morris, 1982) and it also requires that there should be demand for the products of those animals.

Approaches which may be more viable are represented by the LEAF (Drummond, 1992) and LIFE (Jordan, 1993) programmes in the UK. These assume that current or developing technologies can have low impacts on the environment if appropriately used. This is plausible, but requires examination in the context of the whole farm system. Better design and control of machinery for pesticide application could provide unambigous benefits in terms of drift and overapplication, as could new techniques for the management of livestock manures, (Cumby, 1992). New pesticide formulations, deliberately designed to require less active ingredient per hectare, and with reduced environmental impact per unit of ingredient should also be beneficial, but only if rates of usage are appropriate. A reduction in the perceived environmental impact of a given formulation could encourage more widespread use, thereby negating any gains.

Information technology offers the opportunity of more precise control of agricultural processes, (Blackmore, Wheeler, Morris and Morris, 1995) but also provides a typical case of the uncertainty of environmental benefit. Yield monitors and Global Positioning Systems can provide detailed spatial information about crop yields (Blackmore *et al*, 1995). Percentage variation in yield across fields has been shown to be surprisingly large. A farmer using this technology could respond to this variation in one of several ways. Accepting that some areas are inherently lower yielding, it might be economically sensible to reduce inputs to those areas, and accept an overall yield reduction in return for a decrease in costs. Alternatively, areas with low current yields could receive increased inputs, to achieve maximum yields, but with the risk of increases in polluting outputs of surplus nutrients or pesticides. A technology which allows more precise process control will only improve environmental performance and sustainability if used appropriately. The way in which the technology is used depends crucially on the economic position and attitudes of the farmer (Carr and Tait, 1991). Exposing these attitudinal factors and ensuring that appropriate weight is given to environmental and sustainability criteria in the decision making process of the farmer are both essential to the question of sustainability. This can only be achieved using a systems approach.

REFERENCES

Agricultural Advisory Council, 1970, *Modern Farming and the Soil,* HMSO, London

Blackmore, B. S., Wheeler, P. N. Morris, J. Morris, R. M., and Jones, R. J. A., 1995, The role of precision farming in sustainable agriculture: a European perspective. in: P. C. Robert, R. H. Rust, and W. E. Larson, eds, *Site-Specific Management for Agricultural Systems,* ASA, CSSA and SSSA, Madison

Bowers, J. K. and Cheshire, P., 1983, *Agriculture, the Countryside and Land Use. An economic critique,* Methuen, London

Brown, A., ed, 1992., *The UK Environment.* HMSO, London

Carr, S. and Tait, E. J., 1991, Differences in the attitudes of farmers and conservationists and their implications, *Journal of Environmental Management,* **32**: 281–294

Carson, R., 1965, *Silent Spring* Penguin Books, Harmondsworth, UK

Central Statistical Office, various years, *Annual Abstract of Statistics*. HMSO, London

Commission of the European Community, 1988, Directive EC/337/EEC

Conway, G. R. and Pretty, J. 1991, *Unwelcome Harvest,* Earthscan, London.

Crawley, M. J., Halls, R. S. Rees, M., Kohn, D., and Buxton, J., 1993, Ecology of transgenic oilseed rape in natual habitats, *Nature*, **323**: 620–622

Cumby, T. R., 1992, *Expert Systems to Tackle Intensive Livestock Pollution,* Journal of Agricultural Science (Cambridge), **118**: 397

Douglas, I., 1990, Sediment transfer and siltation. In: *The earth as transformed by human action*, ed Turner, B. L. Cambridge University Press, Cambridge UK

Drummond, C. J., 1993, A self-assessment approach to environmental audit and chemical use as a managment tool. *Proceedings of the British Crop Protection Council Conference*, 1993, 8B-2 115–1124

Home Grown Cereals Authority, 1996, Final UK cereal seed certifications. *Weekly Digest* **23**: 14, 1–3 HGCA, London.

Jordan, V., 1993, Integrated farming systems research. The LIFE project - future developments, *ARIA Newsletter*, 1993, AFRC Institute of Arable Crops Research, 20–21

Leach, G., 1976, *Energy and Food Production,* IPC Science and Technology Press, Guildford, UK.

Malthus, T. R. 1803, *An Essay on the Principles of Population,* 2nd ed. J.Johnson, London.

Ministry of Agriculture, Fisheries and Food, 1990, *Pesticides - code of practice for the safe use of pesticides on farms and holdings*, MAFF Publications.

Morgan, R. P. C., 1986, *Soil Erosion and Conservation*. Longman Scientific and Technical, Harlow, UK

Morris, R. M, 1980, Feed conversion efficiency and the efficiency of the UK food chain. *Agricultural Systems* 5 267–78

Moss, S. R., and Rubin, B., 1993, Herbicide resistant weeds: a worldwide perspective, *Journal of Agricultural Science*, Cambridge, **120**: 141–148

Open University, 1987, *Food in the World: Unit 1, T247 Food Production Systems*, Open University Press, Milton Keynes

Open University, 1996, *Food: Block 5, T102 Living with Technology*, Open University Press, Milton Keynes

Ritson, C., 1977, *Agricultural Economics: Principles and Policy,* Crosby Lockwood Staples, London

Rosenzweig, C. and Parry, M. L., 1994, Potential impact of climate-change on world food-supply, Nature, **367**: 133–138

Tait, J., 1996, Sustainable development in agriculture - the need for a systemic approach, *Culture and Agriculture*, (in press)

Wellburn, A. R., Paul, N. D. and Mehlhorn, H. 1994, The relative implications of ozone formation both in the stratosphere and the troposphere. *Proceedings of the Royal Society of Edinburgh, Section B - Biological Sciences*, **102**: 33–47

Wilson, J., Evans, A., Grynderup Poulsen, J. and Evans, J. 1995 Wasteland or oasis? The use of setaside by breeding and wintering birds. *British Wildlife* **6**: 214–223

17

SUSTAINABILITY AND VIABILITY

Neil Stewart and Gerard Lewis

Manchester Business School
Booth St. West
Manchester, M 15 6PB, United Kingdom

1. FOUNDATIONS

In this short paper, it is not possible to explore in full detail all the arguments which build the foundations for our research. Only very general descriptions of the phenomena involved, backed-up by broad indications of the relevant literature, can be given. This is especially the case as the topic of this paper—Global Sustainability—is a vast subject.

The research on which this paper is based, is built upon three foundations. These are (1) that human society confronts an ecological crisis which threatens its well being and perhaps its survival in the coming decades, (2) that sustainable systems can be found by which the human race can survive or at least mitigate the worst effects of this crisis, and (3) that systems-thinking can inform individuals and policy makers as they grope towards the rather nebulous concept of sustainability. Indeed it is our firm belief that an ecological crisis in itself defines the need for a systems approach to solutions.

1.1. Global Crisis

In the last 200 years, and dramatically in the most recent decades, the impact of human activities on the ecosystems of the world has become overwhelming. It is almost now not possible to think of a natural world - it is a world constructed and conditioned by the impact which humanity has made upon it. The human touch is everywhere.

In some ways, humanity has done well for itself. It has raised the material standard of living and quality of life certainly for a fifth of the world's population in the developed world. However there are now quite clear signs that the biosphere's ecological systems are showing signs of distress. There is a very large literature on this ecological crisis, the perceptions of which have, in turn, fostered social and political activism at local and global levels as people try to limit the most damaging aspects of material progress.

Nevertheless, the increasing pressure which human society places upon natural resources, both as raw materials to feed our consumption or as sinks in which to place our wastes, does appear to be endemic in our societies. Highly consumptive lifestyles continue to develop and the developing world, not surprisingly, wants a share of the action. In the

Systems for Sustainability, edited by Stowell *et al.*
Plenum Press, New York, 1997

words of Gandhi, *"If it took England the exploitation of half the globe to be what it is to-day, how many globes will it take India?"*. We only have one globe.

1.2. Sustainability

The report *Our Common Future* produced by the World Commission on Environment and Development (1987), now often called the Brundtland Report, brought the word "sustainability" to the fore as a concept by which we could start to understand and find solutions for our ecological crisis. The United Nations Conference in Rio in 1992 was a global attempt to confront the challenges of sustainability. There are now many worthy groups of people in all parts of the globe who are trying to put actions in place which will create a sustainable human system on the globe, some stimulated by the Agenda 21 agreements at Rio.

While the authors do not wish to decry many of these well-meaning endeavours, from a systems-thinking perspective much of what happens is reductionist in the extreme. Well-meaning companies may set out with the intention of greening their activities but find, rightly or wrongly, major constraints on what they can do based upon the society in which they operate.

Consider the growth of the motor car. It is unquestionably true that motor car manufacturers have made improvements both in fuel efficiency and in reducing the emissions which their products pump into the environment. However most governments, even in the West, base all their projections and planning on a doubling of traffic in the next few decades; no fundamental re-thinking of transport policy to make it sustainable occurs in the real world. Even some decline in the rate of growth of the motor industry is regarded as economic disaster in our societies and any government which tolerated a policy of encouraging reductions in motor car production, would face electoral disaster.

1.3. Viability

The third foundation for this research is based upon the concepts of systems-thinking, and in particular the Viable System Model ("VSM") of Stafford Beer (Beer, 1979; 1981; 1985). Two of the concepts of the VSM seemed to us researchers to be particularly powerful in informing the debate about sustainability. Firstly, there is the notion of viable systems being contained within each other - the concept of "recursion". Part of Beer's development of the model and of recursion is the principle that viable systems within a recursive set must be cohesive if the system as a whole is to be viable. This is the "Law of Cohesion".

The VSM is consistent with the very ecological principle that the only way to secure the future of the human race is by actively looking after other parts of the natural system to which it belongs. Thus the related concepts of recursion and viability would seem to be consistent with our concerns about an ecology in crisis.

The second concept of value to this study is that viable systems contain a set of sub-systems within each level of recursion, which must be effective if a system is to be viable. These are the well-known "Systems 1–5" of the VSM (Beer 1985). For each level of recursion, there are a set of subsystems which manage the day-to-day, another set which manage the future and a set of communication processes (in the form of a homeostat) by which the future and present are brought into harmony. Practitioners of the VSM will perhaps excuse this gross oversimplification but the purpose of this paper is not to describe the VSM in detail, but rather to describe its use.

The starting point for our research has been to use the VSM to inform the debate about sustainability. One of the authors (GL) has designed a questionnaire based upon this model and, using it, has carried out structured interviews with eight companies who have achieved recognition for their environmental leadership, in an attempt to devise a better understanding of possible ways ahead.

2. THE RESEARCH

The research questionnaire based upon the VSM focused on the following question: *"How does an organisation "manage" its environmental performance in order to minimize its vulnerability to environmental liabilities and to contribute more effectively to a sustainable society?"* The answer to the question "how?" in practice seems firmly to be rooted in the development of so-called environmental management systems such as British Standard BS7750 and, more importantly in the future, the International Standard ISO14001.

Although these standards are by no means widespread yet, better companies have embraced them as a way of managing their impact on the environment. It seems very likely that such management systems will increase in importance in the future, not just as a tool for internal control, but also as an article of trade - companies will insist on a management standard from their suppliers and perhaps also, in very vulnerable areas of business, from their customers.

When the research then looked into the development of corporate environmental practice behind the development of such management standards, four quite clear conclusions arose.

1. The Companies which are recognised to have a leadership position in environmental practice were overwhelmingly preoccupied with the control of operations. Environmental management was about the specific impacts they have on the environment, coupled with a concern for indirect effects from their customers and suppliers, and was driven heavily by a need to stay on the right side of developing legislation.

2. These firms had a narrow view of what environment is, partly because of their preoccupation with operational issues. Thus such concepts as resource stewardship and stakeholders were not found to have a great meaning to the companies we surveyed.

3. Again related to the above, there was very little strategic planning, scenario planning or similar radar activities related to sustainability; the interviews showed relatively little development of core-competence in understanding the really long-term strategic issues related to environment. We found very little environmentally related research and development and very few mechanisms in place to allocate long-term development resources for environmentally related programmes.

4. Where environmental issues were clearly identified in formation of policy, this was often in a defensive sense of providing for costs and capital for future environmental duties, rather than as a contribution to a more sustainable company in any radical sense.

We have come to see the process of implementing environmental management systems in companies as part of the culture of focusing on operational issues. However, proponents of such systems would undoubtedly argue that control of operations is but a first step to building a more broadly-based strategic capability.

In the terms of the VSM, what was found was that environmental management seen from the corporate level in the majority of companies which were interviewed, was about control of the operational systems of the company. In the language of the VSM, we might say that, at a corporate level, subsystems 1, 2 and 3 were in place. However we found that subsystems 4 and 5—which are concerned with understanding future possible scenarios and feeding these into strategic planning—were much less well developed. The all-important subsystem 5 was dominated with issues related to subsystem 3.

3. TWO COMPANIES

One of the authors (NDS) has been very directly concerned with development of environmental management systems in a medium-sized healthcare company with a strong commitment to community involvement. We have also looked at a steel-making company which is similarly concerned to be an active and responsible member of its community. Neither company was part of the initial sample of eight companies in the research mentioned above. We looked at these two companies in more depth in order to get a better understanding of the nature of subsystem 4.

The steel-making company is a particularly interesting example. The company is based in a town in the North of England which for decades has been synonymous with the making of steel. This industry is concerned with energy intensive, large-scale production and the company was part of a whole geographical area devoted in the past to the different activities within this one industry. In the turbulent times of the early 1980's, heavy industry was hit particularly hard by the recession and much of the steel making capacity in this part of the world disappeared. The result initially was dereliction on a large scale. A determined attempt by the community followed, led by a newly-formed regional Development Company, to improve this old locality. This resulted in the building of one of the largest retail parks in the UK, smaller parks with fast-food facilities and related changes to the local infrastructure. The steel mill, for instance, now finds itself with a modern urban tramway running next to its premises.

From the earliest days, the company participated actively and fully in the radical change in its neighbourhood which was being brought about. In doing this it was supported fully by its (now) majority owner, an international corporation which is well known for its leadership on environmental issues. Thus the company had not just to clean-up its act in various ways; it had to be ultra sensitive to the needs of its new type of neighbours. It saw this, undoubtedly correctly, as a vital item in its "licence to operate".

This is an interesting example of subsystem 4 in that it is concrete and down-to-earth. The changes to which the company was required to adjust by its stakeholders was not a nebulous and uncertain concept like sustainability. It was the quite positive and clear leadership of community to create a better physical environment, the dynamics of which might be difficult to achieve technically for the company but which were quite clear. The company intends to survive in its present neighbourhood for many decades, but to do so it has had to develop an acute sensitivity to the developing needs of its neighbours (as stakeholders).

For the Company in the healthcare industry, the issues are much less clear. It is far from easy to understand how a more sustainable world would impact on its business. It is not a major polluter and its environmental impacts are small compared to, say, those of a chemicals manufacturing company. Nevertheless the company has made decisions within its environmental programme to move to recycled board in packaging its products, to remove such products as PVC from its packaging, to align itself with best practice in its transport policies and has undertaken a range of other measures which show its commitment to contributing to a better future, but which are hardly revolutionary.

4. CONCLUSION

The research which we are undertaking is ongoing. We will be exploring further how companies can take a strategic view of sustainability and incorporate such thinking into their policies, using the VSM to inform our research.

The VSM gives a way of thinking about these issues and specifically indicates that (1) companies which wish to be sustainable need to be in harmony with the world about them (a loose restatement of the "Law of Cohesion"), and (2) need to have systems in place which explore possible scenarios for their future in a more resource-constrained world. Through these activities and the operation of all the subsystems of the VSM, they should then put into practice activities today which are compatible with this. In short they should have an active subsystem 4.

In the case of the steel company, in the one important respect of being a good neighbour, as it intends to continue its business indefinitely on its current site, it can clearly link its licence to operate to the specific desires of an important stakeholder.

This does not imply that it is clear on all aspects of its future because, in a sustainable world, steel making in both quantity and character might well change dramatically over the coming decades. Nevertheless, as a metaphor for a sustainable world, being a good neighbour in this sense is a very interesting one. It is also an especially valuable one as manufacturing industry tends to have very long lead times which are always intrinsic in capital-intensive activity. Thus such a business needs to know that it can invest in expensive fixed assets with confidence about the future.

Nevertheless the metaphor does have an apparent limitation; the world does not have a Development Company and the extent to which national and regional governments fulfill this role is highly debatable. Yet environmental impacts are often subject to substantial scientific *uncertainty*, both in understanding of current phenomena and in the ability to create new solutions, and society makes *choices* about which impacts it is prepared to tolerate at any time and which it wishes to avoid. Thus many societies tolerate traffic but boycott phosphates in detergents, for example.

While governments, through their regulators, might be seen as the vehicle by which such choices are made, the extent to which decisions have been made in the context of creating a more sustainable world, seems very small. Any choices made by governments appear to be so constrained by lobbyists and other vested interests, and limited by the need to maintain short-term economic performance, that they fail to reflect the future needs of society as a whole. Thus any major change which the healthcare Company might make now in the interests of future sustainability could turn out to be quite misguided as society has not made many firm choices (and, of course the underlying science and technology may change).

The VSM would suggest two outcomes to these reflections. These appear to be mutually conflicting but both contain a gem of the truth. Firstly, it is essential for the well-being of the human race in the future that it builds institutions through which sustainable policies both national and international can be developed and made effective. However, if we believe that this will be very difficult to achieve by the very nature of our governance, especially in areas of high scientific uncertainty, and the UK's BSE/CJD crisis would appear to be an excellent example of this, then alternative strategies for business are essential.

The only strategy for a system in the VSM, if higher level systems fail to give clear and committed leadership, is to position itself for high uncertainty. This it can only do by being very alert to all potential developments and evaluating their influence on its activities, while retaining the maximum flexibility in all its operations. This must be the essence of subsystem 4 for companies.

REFERENCES

Beer, S., (1979), *"The Heart of Enterprise"*, Wiley, Chichester, UK.
Beer, S., (1981),, *"Brain of the Firm"*, Wiley, Chichester, UK, 2nd ed.
Beer, S., (!985), *"Diagnosing the Systems for Organizations"*, Wiley, Chichester, UK.

18

THE INVISIBLE PRACTITIONER OR THE HOLISTIC PRACTITIONER?

The Problem Helper in the Problem Situation

R. Armson

Systems Department
The Open University
Walton Hall, Milton Keynes, MK7 6AA

1. INTRODUCTION

Very little attention has been given in Systems literature to the *experience* of Systems practice, despite the Systems community's collective espousal of reflection and learning cycles. It is too often assumed that, alone of all the participants in the problem situation, the systems practitioner has a clear agenda. This means that the systems practitioner has usually, until very recently, been invisible in models of the problem situation.

This paper reflects on my own experiences of Systems practice and invites others to share their experiences of problem helping. I identify some ways in which the Systems practitioner becomes a part of the problem situation and suggest ways to minimise negative effects and develop practices that are sustainable for the practitioner.

I start by assuming that the systems practitioner brings to the problem situation some natural talent for problem helping - and some aptitude for systems thinking. I also assume that talent is not unitary: that there are many ways of being a good systems practitioner. Being good in some ways means being less good in others. Similarly, the practitioner will prefer some approaches to others. These are often, but not necessarily, those she is good at.

I make an ethical judgement that the practitioner has a responsibility to improve and refine her practice. This means that no engagement is complete without asking questions such as: what actually helped this situation, after I intervened?; could the end have been achieved more efficiently and painlessly? (this has to include the uncomfortable question of whether the problem might have improved more effectively without me); were there any negative outcomes that could have been avoided?; did I provide for unintended consequences?

I also assume that the practitioner must respect and not exploit the client. The practitioner has a professional obligation to avoid adding to the client's problem. This may

Systems for Sustainability, edited by Stowell *et al.*
Plenum Press, New York, 1997

seem obvious but it is possible to exploit the client and the problem situation unconsciously. But it is also impossible for the practitioner to be objective about her own performance. For this reason, evaluation has to be a process of emotional as well as rational engagement with the experience of problem-helping. A check-list of rational criteria will serve to reinforce deficiencies in performance rather than suggesting areas for exploration and development.

I have started by stating my assumptions because these are important issues for all Systems practitioners, whatever their theoretical position. I am writing here from experience in the consultancy context, mostly to teams in the helping professions but increasingly in the area of one-to-one support for professional people engaged in leadership or organisational change.

Because this is about *engaged* reflection, I have compromised between a rational-objective presentation of the practitioner experience and a personal, and thus less generalisable, exploration. I use the word 'she' to make visible the person-hood of the practitioner—a matter easily overlooked by using the more impersonal 'he'.

2. PRACTITIONER AND CLIENT IN THE PROBLEM SITUATION

The problem situation will, at the very least, expose the practitioner to an experience of elusive complexities, ambiguities and uncertainties. Other complicating factors emerge from the relationship with the client and from the practitioner's own psyche. The client, others in the problem situation; and the practitioner; bring expectations, experience and entanglements to their mutual relationship.

2.1. The Client

The client brings to the relationship hopes and expectations of the practitioner's ability to solve his problem. The client also brings a sense of 'having a problem' and a wish to make that problem go away—nobody who likes having a problem engages a consultant. Others in the problem situation may bring the same but may also bring cynicism, suspicion and even hostility. Both client and others are likely to have some perception of the practitioner's expertise, based on reputation, past experience and reports which may, or may not, reflect the reality of the practitioner's capacity to have an improving influence on the problem situation. Schön (1983) characterises this as the 'traditional contract', made between the client and the 'expert' and contrasts it with the 'reflective contract' between the client and the 'reflective practitioner'. It can be hard to escape having an asymmetrical contract in which the client thinks he's getting one thing while the practitioner knows he's getting something else. It then becomes important to make sure that the final outcome is satisfactory to the client and preferably better than he thought he was going to get.

Experience suggests that whatever else is present, realistic expectations are probably not, at least initially. Often clients will try and make the practitioner into a mummy-figure who will 'make it better' or—in the case of the male practitioner—a hero who will 'see the problem off'. At the very least, a sense of expectation will have been created and attempts to address the problem will have been suspended between the decision to bring in a consultant and her arrival.

In practice, one of the most effective ways of addressing this issue is to get the client to complete a problem-improving task very quickly. This will demonstrate to the client that participation in, and ownership of, the problem-managing process can be rewarding and may make real the verbal assent to the practitioner's problem-helping role rather than the hoped-for problem-removal role. The client's high expectations can be used as a means of mobilising the client's commitment to dealing with the problem. People will often take a great deal on trust if they believe the practitioner to be an expert. However there are dangers inherent in allowing this asymmetry to continue long. Even when the client accepts his own responsibility for problem-handling, the perception of the practitioner's 'expertise' may be displaced to some other quality that the practitioner brings to the relationship—sometimes even onto the ability to discuss alternatives to traditional models of engagement.

2.2. The Practitioner's Professional Self

2.2.1. Preferences. Most approaches will very quickly deliver some interim result that pleases a client. This is not to say that there is nothing to chose between approaches but it is clear that a practitioner will function particularly well using approaches that she finds congenial. Identifying that congeniality is an important part of organising experience into learning but it carries a particular obligation for the systems practitioner. A predisposition to one approach or group of approaches is also a decision against other approaches and against the insights that might be generated by them. It is thus a potential trap into a particular view of a problem, especially when one's "predisposition set" matches that of the client group in some way.

2.2.2. Counter-Transference. Counter-transference is a broad term and covers all the baggage that a practitioner brings to a situation that might distort the problem-solving process. These distortions will always be present and all the more problematic for being un-acknowledged. There are two characteristic types.

In the first, the helper is sucked into the client's perception of the problem situation and shares their feelings of stuckness and frustration. While this makes progress difficult, it can also improve the practitioner's understanding of the problem situation and of the surrounding concerns of the client and of others. It may also eventually allow a more satisfactory conclusion to the engagement, since the practitioner will have experienced the points at which the client feels most concerned or constrained.

The second type of counter-transference is where the practitioner buys into the role that the client wants her to adopt. If, for example, the practitioner adopts the mummy role the client wishes from her, then she is likely to avoid proposing difficult or challenging routes to problem-resolution in order to avoid upsetting the client. For the practitioner, 'adopting a nurturing stance' then becomes an excuse for colluding in the client's problem.

Counter-transference may not be problematic if the possibility of its presence is acknowledged and its possible forms recognised. Counter-transference is often signalled by a radical departure from normal practice or methodology or by a perception that this problem is an exception from the norm in some way. It may also be signalled by procrastination about making phone-calls or appointments or writing letters; by uncharacteristic failures of punctuality or by an over-conscientiousness about these matters. It can also manifest as an over-assertiveness in proposing interpretations or as a sudden increase or decrease in interest level (as does erotic interest in one of the people involved).

The only way forward when counter-transference gets in the way is to address it by exploring its meaning and disentangling it from the problem situation.

2.2.3. Motivations. The wish to engage in consultancy arises from an individual's history and aptitudes and is more than the simple application of an acquired skill. A desire to help, to engage in problems outside her own immediate sphere, to be intellectually stimulated, to be well thought of and well paid are all powerful motivations for engaging in problem helping. Guy (1987) distinguishes between functional and dysfunctional motivations.

Functional motivations, for systems practitioners, might include a willingness to engage creatively with problems, an ability to engage with people, an interest in the domain of application and a facility with systems thinking.

Dysfunctional motivations are unlikely to be completely absent. They become dysfunctional in the client-helper relationship when they are unacknowledged (by the practitioner) and remain un-addressed. Problem helping may, for example, be a displacement activity by which the practitioner avoids her own problems. [It is interesting to note that practitioner *teams,* even academic Systems Departments, are as likely to be affected in this sense as individual practitioners.] Systems practice also offers the possibility of immersion in a social and professional milieu which can compensate the practitioner for her failure to engage with people on her own account. Problem helping can attract 'control freaks' who seek a sense of omniscience or omnipotence. It can also attract those who need to be needed, who feed on other people's problems. Problem-helping also provides opportunities for conscious or unconscious mischief-making, by inducing clients to undertake courses of action the practitioner wouldn't dare risk themselves. This is, in some senses at least, unlikely to happen in systems practice. Systems has a theoretical foundation that doesn't seem to lend itself to this last sort of abuse.

2.2.4. The Abuse of Power. Aptitude, acquired skill and experience all put the problem-helper in a powerful position. An inequality of power arises whenever one has something that the other needs and cannot manage without—an inequality that may be reciprocal. The client has money that the practitioner may not be able to do without. However, I cannot take responsibility for the client's exercise of power over the consultancy funds, except to make sure I don't get ripped off. How does the practitioner avoid unconscious abuse of her power advantage in the problem situation? Power is also conferred not just by, for example, the different epistemologies of the practitioner but also by the practitioner's awareness that epistemology is an issue. The extent to which these powers are realised depends on the practitioner, the client and the circumstances. Although power is in many senses given to the practitioner by the client, the scope for abuse is there. Any inequity of power can be magnified by the practitioner's use of unfamiliar language. This is especially a trap in systems language which can be understood, or abusively meant, to represent a 'more real' view of the world.

2.3. For Her Personal Self

The practitioner brings with her a range of unexpressed desires, motives and ethical considerations. This touches, at the deepest level, the sources of meaning for the practitioner and the consequent ethical positions she is likely to derive from them. Questions that arise from this include 'how far am I prepared to compromise in undertaking work for particular clients?' Such compromise is inevitable in a pluralistic context and the practitioner needs to recognise that differing priority given to ethical issues may affect her commitment.

3. ACCOUNTING FOR THE PRACTITIONER IN THE PROBLEM SITUATION

3.1. What the Practitioner Can and Cannot Do

At the very least the client is entitled to expect that the practitioner has some technical competence to undertake the task. But skill must also be supplemented by integrity, honesty and dedication - the client is entitled to expect the practitioner to use her best endeavours to improve the problem situation. The client is also entitled to some genuine respect. It is extremely hard to do good work where one feels, for whatever reason, dismissive or rejecting of the client's difficulties.

What the client is not entitled to expect is that the practitioner will supply all the effort and motivation for handling the problem—'Come back when you've solved it'. This doesn't often happen in my experience. The client, in engaging a systems consultant, has some idea of what systems work entails. This may not be true of all those in the problem situation and one might have to negotiate psychological contracts with each one of them.

All three parties need to negotiate in advance, or agree to ongoing discussions, about how completion of the task is to be recognised. Many forms of helping through Systems involve the client in formulating the plan of action. At this point in a well-conducted encounter the client is sufficiently empowered to generate original and effective approaches to the problem situation—and the practitioner must summon up all the humility at her command. It can feel like rejection if she has invested a great deal of commitment and, even though she may know that this empowerment is the best of all outcomes, it is still hard to yield credit.

3.2. The Professional Obligations of the Practitioner

The process of on-going training and updating together with the practice of critical reflection, serve as an important challenge to the practitioner to explore and extend her capacities.

The discussion in Section 2 above means that the practitioner has obligations to increase her level of self-awareness; to work towards resolution of personal issues that may interfere with the process of problem-helping; to be aware of her personal limitations; to be sufficiently aware of other approaches; to be aware of why she is good at some approaches and not others; and to be prepared and willing to refer on where others might be better able to help.

In particular the practitioner has to be aware of any counter-transferences that are present. The following are a useful set of checks (after Bernstein and Bernstein, 1980).

1. Do I require sympathy and/or friendliness from the client and am I consequently too sympathetic and/or friendly with the client?
2. Do I need to feel important/needed so that I prevent the client becoming independent?
3. Do I need to be liked so much that I get upset by challenges or scepticism from the client or others in the problem situation?
4. Am I being over or under optimistic in my dealings with the client? Why?
5. Do I give uncalled-for advice? (Do I preach what I don't practice?)..Do I talk too much?
6. Am I trying to impress with my own knowledge?

It is extremely difficult to be totally honest in answering these questions—and even more difficult to explore the implications of positive answers on one's own. The practitioner also has an obligation, to herself as well as to the client and others in the problem situation, to consider ethical dilemmas that arise and make conscious decisions about their resolution. She has to cultivate humility, compassion, modesty and self-knowledge.

4. MODELS FOR ADDRESSING THE ROLE OF THE PRACTITIONER IN THE PROBLEM SITUATION

4.1. Supervision

The practice of regular review meetings with a peer practitioner is built into the codes of practice of many professionals, particularly those in the helping professions. Supervision by-passes the helper's internal security which makes counter-transference invisible and protects self-esteem. Supervision is not simply supportive advice. It is a meta-inquiry into the relationship between practitioner and problem situation. It provides an opportunity for structured reflection and learning-from-experience

4.2. Reflection in Action

Schön (1983) has drawn attention to the practices of reflection-in-action that characterise the reflective practitioner. Reflection forms part of the loop that reinforces good practice but without challenge it can just reinforce current perceptions and progressively discard challenges that appear not to fit the practices the practitioner has evolved.

4.3. A Methodology that Includes the Practitioner?

These reflections provide a means for the individual practitioner to begin to engage with the complexity of being a real person in a problem-helping role. A next step would be the inclusion of processes within systems methodologies which specifically represent the role of the practitioner *as a component of the problem situation*.

REFERENCES

Bernstein, L. and Bernstein, R.S., 1980, *Interviewing: a guide for health professionals*, Appleton-Century-Crofts, New York.
Guy, J.D., 1987, *The Personal Life of the Psychotherapist*, Wiley, New York.
Schön D. A., 1982, *The Reflective Practitioner*, Basic Books, USA.

19

OCCUPATIONAL THERAPY

A Profession Sustained through Systems Science

Martin Booy and Gail Boniface

Department of Occupational Therapy Education
University of Wales College of Medicine
Cardiff, United Kingdom

1. A PROFESSION IDENTIFIED

Occupational Therapy first emerged with a separate identity from Medicine and Nursing as the "advancement of occupation as a therapeutic measure, the study of the effects of occupation upon the human being, and the dissemination of scientific knowledge of this subject" (American National Society for the Promotion of Occupational Therapy, 1917). It gained legal recognition in the UK as a profession supplementary to medicine in 1960 when granted state registered status along with seven other health care professions including physiotherapy. Despite such medically oriented classification, contemporary occupational therapy as practised in the 1990s has a largely humanistic and holistic, theoretical, philosophical base originally described by Mary Reilly in 1962 as a belief that the individual "through the use of his hands as they are energised by his mind and will, can influence the state of his own health"(Reilly,1962 p2.) Thus, occupational therapists encourage a client's ownership and management of his real world situation. Occupational therapists also believe that humans *need* to carry out occupations or, as Reilly (1969) describes it, engage in "occupational behaviour". Viewed holistically, occupations are the activities engaged in to fill our lifetime, the classification we ascribe to them (work, leisure or self care), their meaning to us and their social significance and cultural meaning.

To support such a philosophical base, it is necessary for the profession to identify what occupational behaviour is of significance to its client, as it is the patient/client view of their own real world and *their* priorities which should be of paramount concern. Thus in actively encouraging the client's participation in his therapy, the Occupational Therapist can present an alternative perspective to client/patient assessment and intervention to the more reductionist diagnosis-led medical mode adopted by other health-care professionals.

Whilst they accept that the individual *can* influence his health adversely, occupational therapists believe that they can help him to influence his health in a positive way. The instrument of that influence being, in Reilly's (1980) words, "his hands" or in the more general view of occupational therapists, the tasks, activities and occupations he engages in. Occupational Therapists believe that individuals, regardless of illness or disability, *need* to carry out occupations. i.e. not jobs *per se* but ..."units of activity which are classified and named by the culture according to the purposes they serve in enabling people to meet environmental challenges successfully".(Yerxa, 1993, p5.)

2. THE NEED FOR SUSTAINABILITY

As far back as 1917, it appears that occupational therapy was seeking a more holistic, process-oriented way of defining its identity. However, such a conceptual model and accompanying theoretical base was not to emerge until the early to mid 1980s. The reason, according to Shannon (1977) being the "derailment" of occupational therapy into a reductionist 'siding' by its association with rehabilitative medicine and most significantly its biomechanical approach.

This reductionism has been exacerbated by the organisation of health and social care services through client groupings such as physical impairment or mental illness. Such a split conflicts with the 'weltanschauung' of occupational therapy in which client engagement in occupations requires both physical and psychological ability, or an environment which enables the individual to overcome physical or psychological *disability.* Hence the dilemma for occupational therapy pictured in Figure 1.

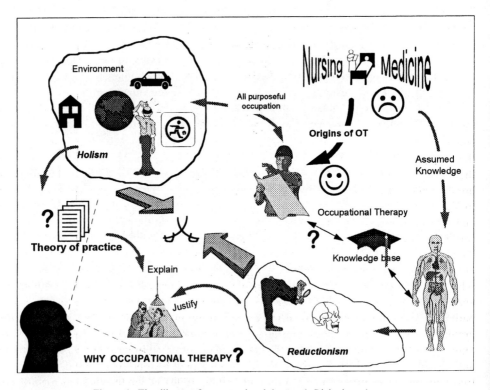

Figure 1. The dilemma for occupational therapy (a Rich picture).

3. A SYSTEMS VIEW OF HUMAN OCCUPATION

Through consideration of General Systems Theory (von Bertalanffy, 1962), and building on Reilly's earlier work (1969), Gary Kielhofner (1980) led the development of a well publicised model of occupational therapy, designed to provide therapists with a conceptual framework, based on theory, which they could use in practice. Though others (Fidler and Fidler, 1961; Mosey, 1981; Reed and Sanderson, 1993) have also sought to develop conceptual frameworks or models for occupational therapy, Kielhofner's work is most noticeable for its recognition of both systemic and systematic thinking.

In attempting a logical description of the holistic nature of the profession, Kielhofner's view of systems thinking "allows us to grapple with the problem of this organised complexity" (Kielhofner, 1995, p9.) in striving to "build a systems view of human occupation",(Kielhofner, 1995, p.10). The individual is viewed as an open system acting occupationally within his environment, from which three subsystems of *volition*, *habituation* and *performance* emerge, reflecting a three dimensional perspective uniquely based on the individual's occupational behaviour rather than the component parts of that behaviour. Thus, Kielhofner (1985,1995) encouraged the profession to utilise its biological, psychological and sociological knowledge, through consideration of how an individual organised his occupations, his motivation for carrying them out and most importantly, the interrelationships of the three subsystems and the individual's environment.

In promoting a systemic understanding of occupations, models of practice therefore enable occupational therapists to both structure their own intervention and explain their view of a client's problems, strengths and needs to other members of the health and social care team. Through iteration of the theory/practice loop, occupational therapy continues to develop conceptual models to help it explain its otherwise nebulous holistic philosophy.

4. THE PROCESS OF OCCUPATIONAL THERAPY

Occupational therapy has always been a practice-led profession and tends to develop its theory based on its practice rather than the other way round. Hence the move to influence practice through conceptual modelling. However, in searching for an 'occupational-therapy profession-owned' knowledge base to support the uniqueness of occupational therapy intervention in the current health-care climate, a need was recognised to reconfigure the way occupational therapists acquire underpinning scientific knowledge. According to Yerxa (1993), Bohannan and Yerxa first described 'occupational science' in 1987, as a new process-oriented focus for researching what occupational behaviour *does*, rather describing constituent parts such as sensori-motor, perceptual and psychological skill. To date, most curricular design for the professional training of occupational therapists depends on the traditional teaching of a core of basic medical and social science. Such methods can encourage a reductionist view of normality, illness and disability, and a disease approach to intervention which reinforces the medical dominance of health care. For occupational therapy to sustain its own unique contribution and identity, its educational programmes should reflect both a problem-solving process supported by an integrated knowledge base (Booy and Wilby, 1994). That opportunity to change was seized by the authors' own department in 1991 with the development of a problem-based, student-centred undergraduate programme (Booy and Wilby, 1994) generated through a SSM core analysis. (Checkland, 1985). Figure 2 refers.

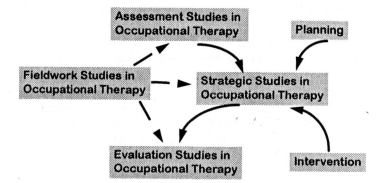

Figure 2. A curriculum design for occupational therapy education.

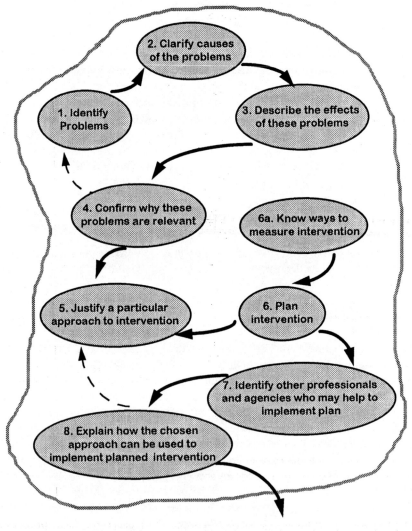

Figure 3. A problem-based study stategy for occupational therapy students to learn intervention planning.

Subsequently, a Study Strategy (or methodology), "cast as a process of enquiry" (Checkland and Schole, 1990, p277) has been developed for use by students to structure their own learning. Through its eight stages, the strategy encourages students to take an overview of the client, his occupations and his environment, in order to investigate and eventually decide on the issues which need addressing. Unlike hard systems "goal directed" (Checkland, 1985 p.149) thinking, students have discovered they often have no definable goal to reach, but rather their task is to identify such goals, that is to say, define the problem to be solved *with the client*. The strategy (Figure 3). is multifaceted and logical, encouraging students to define and redefine problems as they gather more facts and basic science knowledge. The ultimate aim of the strategy being to enable students to strive towards Checkland's definition of an effective systems thinker who can work "simultaneously at different levels of detail, on several stages"(Checkland 1985 p.163)

5. SUSTAINABILITY

In conclusion, occupational therapists quickly felt comfortable with systems theory due to the holistic nature of both the theory and the profession. They began to be able to identify their own practice/theory loop. Wherein they had begun by borrowing other people's theory, through the logical investigation of their own process of practice they have developed new theory - occupational science. The internalisation of systems thinking into the profession is enabling occupational therapy educators to build new curricula models which underpin the process of client-based problem solving. Hence systems science can be seen to be sustaining the philosophy, structure and process of occupational therapy.

REFERENCES

Booy M.J., Wilby P.K.,1994, Do people do what they say they do ?: A paradigm for Occupational Therapy education. In: *Abstracts of the 11th Congress of the World Federation of Occupational Therapists* pp31, World Federation of Occupational Therapists, London

Checkland P., 1985, *Systems Thinking, Systems Practice*, John Wiley and Sons, Chichester.

Checkland P., Scholes J.,1990, *Soft Systems Methodology in Action*, John Wiley and Sons, Chichester.

Fidler G., Fidler J., 1963, *Occupational Therapy*, Macmillan, Toronto.

Kielhofner G., 1995, *A Model of Human Occupation: Theory and Application* , 2nd ed.,Williams and Wilkins, Baltimore.

Kielhofner G., Burke J, 1985, *A Model of Human Occupation: Theory and Application*, Williams and Wilkins, Baltimore.

Kielhofner G., Burke J., 1980, A Model of Human Occupation: Part One, *American Journal of Occupational Therapy* 34, 572–581

Mosey A.C., 1981, Occupational Therapy: Configuration of a Profession, Raven Press, New York.

National Society for the Promotion of Occupational Therapy , 1917, *The Constitution* , Sheppard Hospital Press, Baltimore.

Open Systems Group, 1981, *Systems Behaviour*, 3rd ed., Harper and Row, London.

Reed K.L., Sanderson S., 1992, *Concepts of Occupational Therapy,* 3rd ed., Williams and Wilkins, Baltimore.

Reilly M., 1962, Occupational Therapy can be one of the great ideas of 20th Century medicine. *American Journal of Occupational Therapy* 16 1–9

Reilly M.,1969, The Educational Process, *American Journal of Occupational Therapy* 20, 221–225

Shannon P.,1977, The Derailment of Occupational Therapy. *American Journal of Occupational Therapy* 31 No 4 229–234.

Von Bertalanffy L.,1962, General Systems Theory - a Critical Review, in: *Systems Behaviour*, 3rd ed. Open Systems Group, Harper and Rowe, London. 1981.

Yerxa E., 1993, Occupational Science: a new source of power for participation in Occupational Therapy, *Occupational Science: Australia* April 1993 Vol 1 No 1, 3–10.

20

IF SYSTEM THINKERS ARE ALL SO SMART, WHY AIN'T WE RICH?

Peter Crossley

School of Business and Applied Science
King Alfred's College
Winchester, Hants, United Kingdom, SO22 4NR
Tel: 01962 827472; Fax: 01962 827506; E-Mail: peterc@virgo.wkac.ac.uk

1. INTRODUCTION

If the pace of global change is such that core corporate identity is ephemeral (along with its structure and products), how can we measure longevity? Yet even if the organisation dies, all the systems, sub-systems and individuals (Churchman, 1968) that sustained it so long and so evidently successfully (i.e., its culture, leader selection, product quality) may somehow still exist, even if the parts have absorbed or emerged into new realities. If we could explain this metamorphosis more clearly, and help stakeholders prosper in the process, we would be rich!

2. BACKGROUND

Classical management theorists (Fayol, 1916) listed management functions as Planning, Organising, Directing and Controlling within a formal hierarchical organisational structure. They told us that the resources which managers control in order to achieve organisational objectives are the 4 M's - Men [sic], Machines, Materials and Money (Shafritz and Ott, 1987).

Now, a hundred years later, we systems thinkers know a lot more about what sustains organisations. It's really a 'mess' (Ackoff, 1986), a black box (Flood and Jackson, 1991), or as Joe Kelly suggested at the 1996 BAM Conference at Aston University, 'an existential garbage can filled with competing anarchies'!

Systems consultants march into client offices, armed with a frighteningly complex diagram such as the 'Viable Systems Model' (Beer, 1985; Harnden and Leonard, 1994) or the 'Formal System Model' (Fortune, 1995) and begin the good work of generating much light (and some heat) by describing the (obviously) inappropriate recursive sub-systems. A little multi-looping analysis (Balle, 1994) quickly exposes the absurdity of the client's naive misunderstanding of what may be causing dysfunctional outputs and the implementation contract is half sold.

You quickly and cleverly zero in on the missing or sick part and recommend precise surgery which will turn the company around overnight. But then do you ever get that sinking feeling that they really don't want to know?

3. LOOKING INWARD

Clearly this holistic but introspective approach has accomplished a great deal (even if we are the only ones who truly know it). After all, our focus on the interrelationships of the system components has now given us the 'learning organisation' (Agyris, 1992; Garratt, 1987; Pedler *et al*, 1991; Senge, 1990; Starkey, 1996). Here we advise 'empowerment' of the front line managers by (more than anything else) allowing them to use information-system tools that give them a fighting chance to see what the hell is really going on around them! Assuming Theory Y and Z (Huczynski, 1996) holds up in this situation, the Centre can rely on the beleaguered troops to use their initiative to try to save themselves and hopefully, thereby, the company.

Now the Wizard of Oz/Big Brother Execs at the top of Fayol's 'hierarchy' don't need to proselytise the threats of impending dangers (trust us - would we lie to you?), or the importance of opportunistic thrusts forward. The 'men' on the organisation periphery can see the burning deck themselves! (Peters, 1987) It's not so amazing that such a clear view of the chaotic (Nilson, 1995) and frightening reality of the riskiness of business conditions today succeeds in galvanising the workers to action. It's even possible that individual survival instincts accelerate emerging team structures (Peters, 1991); we will hang apart if we don't hang together! In any case, unless we are totally fatalistic, the business risks need to be considered and managed by contingency planning (Boyadjian and Warren, 1987; Chicken, 1996; Chorafas, 1995; Davis, 1995; Dyson, 1990; Jennings and Watam, 1994).

4. LOOKING OUTWARD

Our paper's discussion of sustainability is more interested in looking outside the formal organisations boundaries. What happens to the '4M's' when part or all of an organisation apparently ceases to exist? Now this can get spooky because we are reflecting on the transformation of the component systems to the world beyond the organisation as we knew it! This analysis is essential if we are to consider the concept of corporate 'longevity'. Consider, for example the metaphor 'autopoesis' - the organisation is deeply programmed to recreate and maintain itself (Foss in Espejo and Harnden, 1989) - and that every cell in our body changes every few years.

If we take the 4M's as the tangible 'value', of the company, how do we measure it? The latest accountancy discussion papers indicate we still can't sort this out. Evidently, balance sheets are a poor description of the wealth of the enterprise, even if the auditors do sign 'true and fair' (Blake, 1995; Lewis and Pendrill, 1996). Can 'value' ever be lost or destroyed? Or does it simply move from my pocket to yours? In every financial transaction, there's a winner and loser—'adebeo' and 'credito' (Pacioli in *Summa de Arithmetica, Geometria, Proportioni et Proportionalita,* 1494).

Is the sustainability of growth a myth? Do we really care if companies live on and on?

Do we really want them to? Sustainability, longevity, expected lifespan, are all about the future, the constant quest for immortality (De Geus in Caulkin, 1995; Bogan and English, 1994) and Sustained Competitive Advantage (Montgomery and Porter, 1979). Life is good. Thou shalt not kill. But who are the main beneficiaries? Stake-holders? We suggest that that it is the self-serving members of the organisational system who are primarily driven by the social imperative. Humans group to create emergent arenas for social satisfaction (McGill and Beaty, 1992). And once we get together and build a hugely complex structural web of interrelationships, we sure are reluctant to quit, even if the original purpose of the enterprise is not so well understood (DeBono, 1993). Is this why the Christian Church has lasted two thousand years? We will soon see another millennium through without Armageddon, but still we wait (and pray) for mercy on the inevitable Judgement Day.

The pious truisms directed at protecting ecological systems also reinforce the trendy biological metaphors of our systems approach to modelling the world. Perhaps we begin to believe that the models are reality—the VSM becomes viable in its own right.

We may summarise our thoughts with three questions; each needs answering in much more depth than permitted here:

1. Are we inexorably shifting to special purpose enterprises, designed to deliver ephemeral products (Drucker, 1993) and to exploit fleeting -now you see it, now you don't - market opportunities?
2. Do today's mega-companies want even more market share? Will Microsoft grow and grow until every man, woman, and child has a commission generating PC on their desks? God knows what they do with them (besides bang out papers like this!).
3. Do we have a world oversupply of capital (money) which makes the never-ending goal seeking focus on increased return on capital (McLaney, 1994) another existentialist absurdity?

5. CONCLUSION

We have questioned the value of sustainability and longevity of Western organisations and wonder where are the limits to our consumerism. We fear the concentration of so much economic power in the hands of so few and wonder where are the constraints on their emergent world hegemonies. Mature companies may be rejuvenated into dynamic new providers of value (Baden-Fuller and Stopford, 1992) but hopefully their contribution of value-added will go beyond the social vested interests of the organisational insiders (Mitroff and Linstone, 1993).

So this paper isn't primarily concerned with the obvious contribution of systems thinking on sustaining organisational viability and longevity. The process works well although (we believe) the inherent complexity has meant that the world-at-large has been slow to offer commercial opportunities for application or implementation. The unanswered challenge is to explain and predict how value and wealth emerges in new systems - and that's why we ain't rich...yet.

REFERENCES

Ackoff, R. (1986) *Management In Small Doses*, Wiley, Chichester.
Agyris, C. (1992) *On Organisational Learning*, Blackwell, Oxford.

Baden-Fuller C. and Stopford J. (1992) *Rejuvenating the Mature Business: The Competitive Challenge*, Routledge, London.

Balle, M. (1994) *Managing With Systems Thinking: Making Dynamics Work For You In Business Decision Making*, Mcgraw-Hill, Maidenhead.

Beer, S. (1985) *Diagnosing the System for Organisations*, Wiley, Chichester.

Blake, J. (1995) *Accounting Standards (5th Ed)*, Pitman, London.

Bogan, C. and English, M. (1994) *Benchmarking For Best Practices: Winning Through Innovative Adaptation*, Mcgraw-Hill, London.

Boyadjian, H. and Warren, J. (1987*) Risks; Reading Corporate Signals*, Wiley, Chichester.

Caulkin, S. (May, 1995) 'The Pursuit of Immortality', *Management Today*.

Chicken, J. C. (1996) *Risk Handbook*, International Thompson, London.

Chorafas, D. N. (1995) *Financial Models and Simulation*, Macmillan, Basingstoke.

Churchman, C. West (1968) *The Systems Approach*, Dell, New York.

Davis, E. P. (1995) *Debt, Financial Fragility and Systemic Risk*, Clarendon Press, Oxford.

DeBono, E. (1993) *Going Beyond Competition*, HarperCollins, London.

Drucker, P. (1993) *Post-capitalist Society*, Butterworth-Heinemann, Oxford.

Dyson, R. (1990) *Strategic Planning: Models And Analytical Techniques*, Wiley, Chichester.

Espejo, R. and Harnden, R. (eds) (1989) *The Viable System Model, Interpretation and Application of Stafford Beer's VSM*, Ch 6 by Foss, F. A. 'The Organisation of a Fortress Factory', Wiley, Chichester.

Fayol, H. (1949 from 1916 French edn) *General and Industrial Administration*, Pitman, London.

Flood, R. and Jackson, M. (1991) *Creative Problem Solving: Total Systems Intervention*, Wiley, Chichester.

Fortune, J. and Peters, G. (1995) *Learning From Failure: The Systems Approach*, Wiley, Chichester.

Garratt, B. (1987) *The Learning Organization: And The Need For Directors Who Think*, Gower, Aldershot.

Harnden, R. and Leonard, A. (1994) *How Many Grapes Went Into The Wine: Stafford Beer On The Art Of Holistic Management*, Wiley, Chichester.

Huczynski, A. A. (1996) *Management Gurus*, Routledge, London.

Jennings, D. and Watam, S. (1994) *Decision Making: An Integrated Approach*, Pitman, London.

Kelly, J. (1996) 'Existential Systems Thinking' paper presented to BAM Conference , Aston University, Birmingham.

Lewis, R. and Pendrill, D. (1996) *Advanced Financial Accounting*, 5th edn, Pitman, London.

Mcgill, I. and Beaty, L. (1992- 2nd Ed 1995) *Action Learning: A Guide For Professional, Management, And Educational Development*, Kogan Page, London.

Mclaney, E. J. (1994) *Business Finance For Decision Makers (2nd Ed.)*, Pitman, London.

Mitroff, I. and Linstone, H. (1993) *The Unbounded Mind: Breaking The Chains Of Traditional Business Thinking*, Oxford University Press, Oxford.

Montgomery, C. and Porter, M., (eds.) (1979) *Strategy: Seeking And Securing Competitive Advantage*, Harvard Business Review, Boston.

Nilson, T. H. (1995) *Chaos Marketing: How To Win In A Turbulent World*, Mcgraw-Hill, London.

Pedler M., Burgoyne J., Boydell T. (1991) *The Learning Company*, McGraw-Hill, Maidenhead.

Peters, Edgar, E. (1991*) Chaos And Order In The Capital Markets: A New View Of Cycles, Prices And Market Volatility*, Wiley, Chichester.

Peters, T. (1987) *Thriving On Chaos*, Pan, London.

Senge, P. (1990) *The Fifth Discipline: The Art And Practice Of The Learning Organization*, Century Business, London.

Shafritz, J. M. and Ott, S. J. (1987) *Classics Of Organisation Theory*, Wadworth, Belmont.

Starkey, K. (ed.) (1996) *How Organizations Learn*, International Thomson Business Press, London.

21

SUSTAINABILITY OF SYSTEMS THINKING AND PRACTICE IN ORGANISATIONS

J. P. Drinan

University of Newcastle
Australia

1. INTRODUCTION

The perils of being ignorant of the world's complexity are evident throughout human history, and never more so than in this last century. A good example lies in the uncontrolled logging allowed by governments in pursuit of jobs and tax revenues, but which ignore the huge costs incurred in extinction of species, erosion of soil, landslides and destruction of villages and their people, fouling and sedimentation of water bodies, mass exodus to overpopulated cities, and hunger for food, shelter and mental and spiritual peace. The very frequency of situations like these emphasises the necessity of seeing organisms and organisations in ways which envisage as many of the consequences of their internal and external interrelationships as possible, so as to permit non-damaging and beneficial interventions, and preparation for amelioration of unavoidable, undesirable effects. Currently entrenched ways do not offer that hope.

The arrival of the notion of "systems" some thirty years or so ago was like turning up a lamp which had, for about 300 years, been close to extinction under the mass of achievements wrought through the dominant reductionist worldview of Western science. Success in applying these views hid the fact that all such changes generate all sorts of consequences, beneficial and otherwise. Gradual recognition of these refuelled the lamp and reilluminated the connectedness and wholeness of things - revealing again that every thing is the consequence of interrelationships among its parts, each of which is the result of the play among its own parts, and so *ad infinitem.*

Most systems thinkers recognise complementarity in systems and reductionist approaches, but view things—organisms and organisations—as wholes. They recognise that: every entity or issue is perceived differently and usefully by each observer or actor according to their prior experience and current circumstances; it is defined and constantly changing through complex interrelationships among component parts, and between the entity and the external world; these relationships and parts must be appreciated if the true nature of the entity or issue is to be identified; appropriate strategies for intervention must be designed and tested in anticipation of flow-on effects; outcomes must be used as bases for further improvement; and, in most cases, it will be best managed by groups of involved people.

The benefits of systems thinking and practice have now been argued through these last thirty years, often with respect to sustainability in environmental, social, economic, and personal terms. But is systems thinking and practice itself sustainable? Despite the many claims of the success of systems approaches as paths to organisational and personal change, the author's experience suggests that the approach is quite difficult to embed and sustain in organisations. In a search for sustainable systems thinking and practice, the paper explores some possible reasons why systems thinking and practice may be eroded in institutions in which it has been introduced, on the fundamental understanding that its introduction constitutes a change process. Out of this, some measures emerge which may be used to advantage in nurturing growth of the desired approach.

2. INHERENT RESISTANCE TO CHANGE

There is no part of the Universe in which change is not continuous, and it is vain for people to hope that they can live and work in organisations where they may be shielded from it. Despite this, in every organisation there is inherent resistance to change, the strength of which depends on the degree of satisfaction its members feel about the organisation. This satisfaction is underpinned by an apparently human desire to avoid disturbance, and is proportional to the extent to which the organisation meets or does not meet the varied needs of its members. Within the organisation, power groups have empires and individuals have egos, both of which depend on the status quo being maintained, and they will use all means to preserve it. Elsewhere, there are other groups and individuals who aspire to the same power and status, perhaps by emulating, perhaps by surpassing and often by neutralising the current holders. Elsewhere, again, there are others who do not lean either way and will go with the prevailing groups and individuals. The balance of power may ebb and flow, but will always be drawn in the direction of the status quo unless overwhelmed by alternative powers.

3. PERVASIVENESS OF SYSTEMS APPROACHES

Resistance to incorporation of systems approaches may be greater if the proponents always behave systemically. Their constant perception of the organisation and its subunits as complex systems will lead them to probe with discomfiting questions everywhere: e.g. "what and why are we really trying to do?", "what are the real issues underlying the apparent ones?", "have we checked that we have the full range of available options for improving the problematical situations?", and so on. Moreover, organisational arrangements in systems-oriented organisations are often vague, fluid and democratic, because they tend to be arranged around projects which change internally and are eventually superseded, with concurrent rearrangement of project teams. These challenges to convention, if followed through, are not only uncomfortable: they can be seen as subversive because they constantly question all aspects of the organisation. Unless there are powerful patrons above, the disturbers are inevitably silenced.

On the other hand, while full-blooded use of systems approaches may generate opposition because of their inherent pervasiveness, failure to practice what is preached can be equally devastating. If systems approaches are segregated to particular aspects of the enterprise, and do not pervade the rest, the contradictions will become evident and destructive, and the systemists will be unlikely to be able to resist the internal strains so created.

4. CHALLENGE TO PREVAILING PARADIGMS

Systems ideas draw very strong opposition from established disciplines which are strongly committed to reductionist perspectives, and have built considerable power and prestige on them. They have strong grounds for concern when others begin to question their approach, because it casts doubt on the validity of what they hold good and true, and creates competition for the resources they largely control. There is, thus, an explosive mix of challenge to matters of status, belief and access to material goods and services. Clearly, no group in such an environment is likely to rest until the contest appears to be won by one or, ideally, resolved in a mutually beneficial arrangement.

5. OBSCURE LANGUAGE

The language of systems is often vague and difficult to those outside "the club", thereby exacerbating conflict. To some extent this appears unavoidable in the same way that every discipline develops its own vocabulary to express ideas that only those steeped in the discipline can understand: as ideas are explored, existing words become inadequate to express developing understandings, and new metaphors and words emerge which are outside common understanding. The word "systems" is a case in point: it now has so many meanings that it is virtually meaningless without context. The resultant vagueness engenders new expressions such as "holons" (Checkland (1981). However, despite these problems, there is much that could be done to make systems ideas more accessible and attractive, particularly when the real world offers so many transparent examples of the nature of systems, and the penalties of ignoring it.

6. INTELLECTUAL CONFLICT AND AMBIGUITY

Communication takes on added importance when the dilemmas and apparent contradictions within systems thought begin to surface. For example, consider what have become fundamental principles of systems thought, much of it in common with the post-modernists/constructivists in disciplines such as language, history, sociology and education. Systems are held to exist only in the mind of the beholder, and each beholder is claimed to see things differently, according to their own prior experience and present circumstances. Thus, they construct their own understanding and each such view is considered to be valid. The profound implications of this argument can be that there is no absolute reality, and that each person has no basis for meaning outside what they create from their own perceptions and beliefs. Furthermore, the argument can be extended to negate those perceptions and beliefs and, of course, any moral standpoint they might take. The impact of this argument on people with firm religious convictions can be disturbing, as on those who contemplate society, but it also erodes the bases on which scientists operate! The absurdity of the contradiction this poses to the apparent reality of our shared experience can lead to the discrediting of systems thought, unless it is acknowledged that it is possible to have different and apparently opposed but defensible ideas existing in some sort of complementary relationship.

7. UNCERTAIN GOALS AND OUTCOMES

Application of systems approaches often generates accusations of failure or ineffectiveness. A central element of the application of systems thinking is admission of diverse possible outcomes as a consequence of the complexity of the focus system. Thus, at the commissioning of a task, it is accepted that the starting point is to question the task: what is it, and why? what are the related factors? what is the real task? Consequently, not only is it not possible to predict the results: it is usually not possible to predict the nature of the real problem(s) which will emerge from the process. The presenting problem and the real problem are often very different, though related and, in the process of understanding, unexpected issues will probably emerge which become significant matters for investigation and resolution. This is one of the strengths of a systems approach, but it becomes another impediment to its influence if care is not taken to involve those affected by it throughout, and to publicise the criteria for success as they emerge. It is particularly important if the work has been commissioned by people who have little understanding of the approach, and who have expectations of clearly defined, technical outcomes.

8. LEADERSHIP, COMMUNICATION, AND ENERGY

In the face of all these difficulties, a high standard of leadership is needed. Change agents are necessarily leaders, though not necessarily the only ones. To introduce change, they have to appreciate the internal dynamics of the organisation, and the environment in which it operates. They must build and maintain alliances with those who seek better ways, articulate a vision which resonates with them, and convert or neutralise those who act to protect the status quo. Gaining access to resources is crucial but difficult, because their scarcity means that they inevitably become the ground for competition with the dominant interest groups.

Systems approaches seem to have flourished in places where a convinced, articulate and energetic leader has been able to attract people disenchanted with the status quo, or people who can see new opportunities for betterment. While ever that leader remains committed to and energised for the task, high production and productivity persist in a ferment of creativity. Conversely, as the leader tires—through constantly having to project and defend the approach, frustration in getting ideas and people to work, encouraging and supporting staff, other distractions and age—and is not replaced, corporate energy declines, teams disintegrate, innovation ceases, and people and approaches regress to the old, non-controversial ways. Other leaders must be in the wings to take over before the danger signals appear.

All this implies that a particular person carries the main burden of leadership, and it is argued that this is utterly crucial for change and sustenance. It is evident that people appear to cohere and work effectively in common cause only where there are shared beliefs and aspirations and a particular leader who can represent, encourage, energise and, even, admonish them. A consistent focal point of energy and wisdom is needed to which others may look when uncertain, discouraged or tired. Practice also suggests, however, that there are leaders for different phases of an organisation's or venture's life. The qualities of the initiator-leader do not often appear to be those of the maintainer-leader, the former often becoming bored once the excitement of the main innovation has passed, although this may be remedied by wise delegation and creation of an environment in which innovation is constant.

Experience demonstrates that representation is a principal responsibility of leaders. In doing so, they need all-round vision, because others apart from the team must also be taken on the journey of change. Superiors and other key people in the institution must be persuaded of its merits and their support obtained, while the community in general also has to be informed about what is happening and the reasons for doing so. Any new venture is bound to elicit opposition, so every opportunity has to be taken to inform everyone, and prevent misinformation from those who feel most threatened by the approach. If support or, at least, acceptance is not gained from those in power, the venture will fail. If the venture attracts suspicion or opposition from the community in general, it again will be discredited and fail.

9. HUMAN CAPABILITY

Obviously, a key concern for staff development has to be identification and grooming of potential new leaders, so that a leadership vacuum is not permitted at any time. However, all people involved in change processes need continuous development and encouragement. Perhaps the most effective form of staff development is that which people achieve when working on a common and meaningful project together, especially if the project is something new and exciting. Building and using a new approach to dealing with the world and its challenges is such a project, and is akin to a journey during which the travellers learn from each new experience along the way. Most of those who walk the path develop shared perceptions, convictions, language and practices which are often difficult for others to appreciate, so creating flow-on problems unless they are anticipated and managed.

A new challenge arises when the travellers inevitably move to journeys in other institutions and are replaced by new staff who have not shared the learning experiences. Such new staff may, quite genuinely, declare their support for the approach, but will often be found to have little real appreciation of it. If strenuous efforts are not made to fully initiate these people into the approach, they will have no alternative but to practice as their prior experience leads them - perhaps in a contrary manner - and facilitate disintegration of the project. Even when every effort is made to familiarise new people with the approach, it has to be remembered that they have not been on The Long March and will have different perspectives on what has to be done. If time and care are taken, however, not only may those people become strong proponents, but their fresh perspectives can be harnessed well in the evolution of the approach, because such are vital if stagnation is to be avoided.

10. CONCLUSIONS

This paper is based on the belief that the adoption of systems approaches is crucial to the resolution of the complex problems of this complex world. Systems approaches are seen to be consistent with the nature of organisms and organisations, thereby giving them great power, yet they appear to be very fragile when introduced into organisations. It is important to recognise such introduction as a change process, and use that understanding in its management so that systems approaches are embedded and maintained in the organisation. Where this has not happened, it is argued that key determinants of failure appear to be inadequate understanding of the nature of resistance to change, the particular challenges posed by introduction of systems ideas into reductionist cultures, use of unnecessarily obscure language, failure to recognise the intellectual and moral challenges posed to some by systems philosophy, the unpredictability and uncertainty of outcomes of systems approaches, and failures of leadership and development of human capability. Leadership is absolutely central to avoiding these pitfalls.

REFERENCES

Checkland, P.,1981, *Systems Thinking, Systems Practice,* Wiley, Chichester.

22

MODERN ACADEMIC MYTHS

Joyce Fortune and John Hughes

The Systems Department
Faculty of Technology
The Open University
Walton Hall, Milton Keynes, MK7 6AA

1. INTRODUCTION

A set of basic assumptions appears to underlie much current research and teaching using systems thinking. But although these assumptions are frequently deployed to support theories, arguments and debate, it is difficult to detect or establish the empirical evidence or observations that justify them. This lack of evidence is worrying. As Burrell and Morgan (1979) point out, 'In order to understand alternative points of view it is important that a theorist be fully aware of the assumptions upon which his own perspective is based.'

Through repetition, these assumptions have gained credence, and have almost become part of the fabric of the subject area. As components of the conventional wisdom they appear to have ceased to be challenged and the questions that should have surrounded their original adoption have never been asked. These academic myths include:

1. technology is out of control;
2. the rate of change is accelerating;
3. complexity is increasing;
4. sustainable development is the only way forward.

In this short paper just two of these will be examined. The first example will illustrate the use of an established myth—complexity is increasing—by looking at the ways it was used in papers presented to the last UKSS Conference. The second - sustainable development is the only way forward - will trace the development of a new myth.

2. COMPLEXITY IS INCREASING

The index to the volume of papers from the last UKSS Conference (Ellis, Gregory, Mears-Young and Ragsdell, 1995) contains a number of entries under the heading 'complexity'. This is hardly surprising. As Paton (1995) points out, systems thinking and the notion of complexity are closely bound together: 'complexity can only adequately be grasped through the employment of systems concepts.' Jayaratna (1994) makes a similar point: 'all [systems] methodologies are complexity-reducing mechanisms.'

When the entries under 'complexity' are consulted it soon becomes obvious that they fall into two distinct categories: those that are examining the notion itself; and those that are using the existence of complexity as a *raison d'être* for the ideas they are putting forward. Closer examination reveals another interesting distinction that tends to hold true elsewhere in the systems literature. Those writing about complexity attempt to define it, to look for ways it can be quantified, to identify its sources, and so on. For example, Ashby (1956) proposes *variety*, meaning the number of distinguishable elements in a system, or by extension, the number of possible systemic states that can be exhibited, as a measure of systemic complexity. Casti (1979) considers that complexity has two facets: the structure of the irreducible subsystem components and the manner in which the components are connected. Connectivity and structure together provide static complexity and the time behaviour of the system provides dynamic complexity. Flood and Jackson (1991) group problem contexts according to two dimensions, systems and participants, with the former referring to 'relative complexity in terms of the "system" or "systems" that make up the problem situation'. They describe complex "systems" as having the following characteristics: a large number of elements; many interactions between the elements; attributes of the elements are not predetermined; they are probabilistic in their behaviour; the "system" evolves over time; "sub-systems" are purposeful and generate their own goals; the "system" is subject to behavioural influences; the "system" is largely open to the environment. Complex problem contexts are said to 'contain relatively "complex systems" manifesting "difficult" problems'.

Agyeman (1995) quotes Waldrop's description of complexity as a representation of the zone 'at the edge of chaos...where the components of a system never quite lock into place, and yet never quite dissolve into turbulence either (1993).' Reyes (1995) defines the complexity of a situation as 'the number of distinctions we can make on it' either by 'observing the interactions of actors constituting the organisation' or by 'participating in these interactions as actors ourselves'. Warfield (1995) postulates a scale of situational complexity on which any given situation can be positioned; situations at the lower end of the scale are ones that are 'commonly dealt with by individuals' whilst those at the upper end 'require teams working together in a designed environment with designed processes'.

The literature about complexity does not, however, concern itself with whether the overall level of complexity aggregated across all situations is increasing, decreasing, or staying the same. This is complete contrast with the papers that use complexity to justify their proposals or theories. They all claim, without citing any evidence, that complexity is increasing. Johannessen (1995), for example, asserts that 'increased turbulence and complexity will require a completely new form of management.' Marshall (1995) talks of 'increasing system complexity' and the problems it will bring for the design, management and maintenance of systems whilst Hammer (1995) refers to the 'exponential increase' in complexity. Gill (1995), who speaks of managers having to deal with 'escalating complexity', does at least give examples of the escalating complexity: 'continuously changing customer preferences, accelerating technological innovation, global competition, [and] a rapidly shifting political and social scene'.

We would suggest, however, that if the definitions of complexity cited above are accepted, Gill's examples are not of complexity but of change. Change brings greater uncertainty and makes forecasting, decision making, planning and the like more tricky, but it does not necessarily make the situations in which they are being undertaken more complex. Through the use of new technology and the development of more sophisticated methods the amount of complexity that is taken on board has undoubtedly increased in many settings, but that is not evidence that the amount of complexity itself has increased. Indeed, it can be argued that some situations have become less complex. The reduction in size of many organizations' supplier bases is a good example. In 1991 Bankers Trust adopted a policy of selecting fewer suppliers through a process of competitive tendering and reduced the number of suppliers it dealt with from 6000 to 2000 (Coles, 1994). Between the mid-eighties and the mid-nineties Ford in Europe more than halved its number of suppliers. Harmonization of standards across the EU is another example.

Because no explanation and no supporting evidence is given, it is impossible to know the basis of the claims that complexity is increasing. Perhaps authors are not heeding Flood and Jackson's warning: 'We will have to be careful not to be fooled by either superficial simplicity or superficial complexity. For example, if we consider an aeroplane that has many parts and interrelations we might mistakenly label this complex. Mistaken it would be, because characteristically such technological realisations are operated according to "well-defined" laws of behaviour and are not evolutionary, and on these grounds should be labelled relatively simple.'

3. SUSTAINABLE DEVELOPMENT IS THE ONLY WAY FORWARD

Concern over the ability of the earth to support the demands made by population and economic activity is not new. As Malthus (1798) famously put it '...the power of population is indefinitely greater than the power in the earth to produce subsidence for man.' This essentially pessimistic view of the human condition has been repeated more recently and with no less influence. In the late 1960s a group of concerned scientists, business leaders and public officials formed the Club of Rome and commissioned the influential *Limits to Growth*. Published in 1972, the central thesis of this 'report' (Meadows, Meadows, Randers and Behrens) was that economic growth cannot continue at the rate that has been achieved over the past 200 years. This viewpoint was complemented by three other contemporary concerns.

The idea that change was occurring too rapidly for human beings to cope with began to gain widespread currency at about the same time. In 1970, Alvin Toffler published an article titled 'Futureshock', in the American magazine *Playboy*. Toffler argued: 'In the three short decades between now [1970] and the turn of the next millennium, millions of psychologically normal people will experience an abrupt collision with the future. Affluent, educated citizens of the world's technically advanced nations, they will fall victim to tomorrow's most menacing malady: the disease of change. Unable to keep up with the supercharged pace of change, brought to the edge of breakdown by incessant demands to adapt to novelty, many will plunge into future shock. For them the future will have arrived too soon.'

The origins of the problems of 'change' were mostly to be found in technology which was seen as a 'great engine, a mighty accelerator' of change with knowledge as its 'fuel'. From being viewed as the '...mainspring of economic and social progress over the past centuries and [...] our chief source of increasing affluence' (Cairncross, 1971), technology was seen as an evil to be tamed before it threatened the very existence of its creator - humankind. Like Malthusian pessimism, the theme of technology out of control can be traced back to social and economic changes taking place at the end of the eighteenth and beginning of the nineteenth centuries and the publication of Mary Shelley's allegoric

Frankenstein (1818). The theme was developed by other authors but the British commentator Dickson (1974) concluded, 'Whatever one feels about these earlier critiques, the current attack on technology is too serious and profound to be dismissed as a transient phenomenon.'

One of the main crimes of which technology stood indicted was widespread, irreversible damage to the environment. Problems associated with the intensive use of artificial fertiliser and pesticides, when combined with monocultural agribusiness, were highlighted and achieved wide acceptance through publication of books such as Rachel Carson's *The Silent Spring* (1965). The adverse effects of large-scale industry were exposed' in Schumacher's *Small is Beautiful* (1973). Pleas were made for the development of alternative technologies which would be 'non-polluting, cheap, and labour intensive, non-exploitive of natural resources, incapable of being misused, compatible with local cultures, understandable by all, functional in a non-centralist context, richly connected with existing forms of knowledge and non-alienating.' (Clarke, 1973.)

The result of these four interconnected issue themes—limits to development and progress, unacceptable pace of change, technology out of control, and environment under threat—was the development of a mind-set which either wanted to halt development, and consequently the destruction of the environment, or, in some cases, reverse it and adopt Arcadian social and economic arrangements. (See, for example, Schumacher, 1973.)

Understandably, calls that 'enough is enough', made predominantly by white, western, middle-class intellectuals and political activists, were viewed in a different light by the leaders of nations that were struggling to achieve a reasonable standard of living for their citizens. In 1972, at a UN Conference on Human Development in Stockholm, the interests of the two groups came into conflict. '...environmentalists had presented development as a threat to the environment while Third World developmentalists, led by Indira Gandhi, had responded by criticising environmentalists as a threat to development.' (Mitcham, 1995.)

The change from a restrictive viewpoint that aimed to halt development to one in which development was conditionally acceptable came through the publication of the *World Conservation Strategy* (1980) by the International Union for the Conservation of Nature and Natural Resources, *Our Common Future* (1987) by the World Commission on Environment and Development and *Agenda 21*, the outcome of the 1992 summit held in Rio de Janeiro. The idea of 'sustainable development' was popularised through the second of these and reinforced through the third.

The central idea in *Our Common Future* is that sustainable development will 'meet the needs of the future without compromising the ability of future generations to meet their own needs.' The report was a compromise between the needs of developing nations and environmental and social activists. It recognised that 'the concept of sustainable development does imply limits—not absolute limits but limitations imposed by the present state of technology and social organization on environmental resources and by the ability of the biosphere to absorb the effects of human activities. But technology and social organization can both be managed and improved to make way for a new era of economic growth.'

The concept of sustainability has gained wide currency in a short time. It is, however, an empty concept, lacking firm substance and containing embedded ideological positions that are, under the best interpretation, condescending and paternalistic. Fundamentally, it embodies the idea that although the developed nations systematically plundered and destroyed natural resources and ecosystems to achieve fast economic growth and to ameliorate poor social conditions, they now realise it was wrong and intend to prevent currently developing nations from doing the same. Certainly the developing nations are to be allowed to achieve progress, but only at a rate the developed nations will find acceptable.

Thus, an underlying assumption of sustainability is that the process of development has to be managed in the name of the common good and on behalf of future generations. To achieve this aim, more government policies and actions are needed. Furthermore, this simple, though not uncontentious, idea has subsequently been elaborated to include other aspects of social and political life. For example, the Canadian International Development Agency's Framework for Social Development (1996) contains the categories of political, social and cultural sustainability in addition to environmental and economic sustainability. In short, 'sustainable' has become a magic word that can be attached to other topics so as to lend legitimacy to other agendas, but the concept still begs many important questions. Without answers to these, its use in policy and as a basis for action is severely hampered.

4. CONCLUSION

The purpose of this paper has not been to argue whether complexity is increasing or sustainable development is the only way forward. The issue is whether assumptions, such as those discussed, are being used to underpin theories, arguments and debate in a manner that lacks rigour and detracts from the development of systems as a serious academic and practical subject.

Are we in danger of basing our work on myths rather than reality?

REFERENCES

Agyeman, S., 1995, Learning to love and leave Ackoff, in Ellis, K., Gregory, A., Mears-Young, B. R. and Ragsdell, G., *Critical Issues in Systems Theory and Practice*, Plenum, New York.

Ashby, W. R., 1956, *Introduction to Cybernetics*, Chapman & Hall, London.

Burrell, G. and Morgan, G., 1979, *Sociological Paradigms and Organizational Analysis*, Gower, Aldershot.

Carson, R., 1965, *The Silent Spring*, Penguin, Harmondsworth.

Cairncross, A., 1971, Presidential address to the British Association for the Advancement of Science, September.

Casti, J. L., 1979, *Connectivity, Complexity and Catastrophe in Large Scale Systems*, Wiley, Chichester.

Clarke, R., 1973, The pressing need for alternative technology, *Impact of Science on Society*, **23**(4).

Coles, M., 1994, Inept buying that costs millions, *Independent on Sunday*, 6 March.

Dickson, D., 1974, *Alternative Technology and the Politics of Technical Change*, Fontana, London.

Ellis, K., Gregory, A., Mears-Young, B. R. and Ragsdell, G., 1995, *Critical Issues in Systems Theory and Practice*, Plenum, New York.

Flood, R. L. and Jackson, M. C., 1991, *Creative Problem Solving*, Wiley, Chichester.

Gill, A., 1995, A life-line for those abandoning check-list management, in Ellis, K., Gregory, A., Mears-Young, B. R. and Ragsdell, G., *Critical Issues in Systems Theory and Practice*, Plenum, New York.

Hammer, K., 1995, Comparing the criticised concepts of 're-engineering the corporation' with a systems structure for organisational change, in Ellis, K., Gregory, A., Mears-Young, B. R. and Ragsdell, G., *Critical Issues in Systems Theory and Practice*, Plenum, New York.

Jayaratna, N., 1994, *Understanding and Evaluating Methodologies*, McGraw-Hill, London.

Johannessen, J., 1995, Creative management, in Ellis, K., Gregory, A., Mears-Young, B. R. and Ragsdell, G., *Critical Issues in Systems Theory and Practice*, Plenum, New York.

Malthus, T. R., 1798, *An Essay on the Principle of Population as it Affects the Future Improvement of Society*, reprinted with notes, 1965, Bonar, J., New York.

Marshall, G., 1995, Management systems for evolving networks, in Ellis, K., Gregory, A., Mears-Young, B. R. and Ragsdell, G., *Critical Issues in Systems Theory and Practice*, Plenum, New York.

Meadows, D. H., Meadows, D. L., Randers, J. and Behrens, W. W., 1972, *The Limits to Growth: A report for the Club of Rome's Project on the Predicament of Mankind*, Universe Books, New York.

Mitcham, C., 1995, The concept of sustainable development: its origins and ambivalence, *Technology in Society*, 17(3):311–26.

Reyes, A., 1995, A theoretical framework for the development of a social accounting system, in Ellis, K., Gregory, A., Mears-Young, B. R. and Ragsdell, G., *Critical Issues in Systems Theory and Practice*, Plenum, New York.

Schumacher, E. F., 1973, *Small is Beautiful*, Blond & Briggs.

Shelley, M. W., 1818, reprinted 1994, *Frankenstein or The Modern Prometheus*, Oxford University Press.

Toffler, A., 1970, Futureshock, *Playboy*, December.

Waldrop, M. M., 1993, *Complexity: The Emerging Science at the Edge of Chaos*, Viking, London.

Wargrave, J. N., 1995, Demands imposed on systems science by complexity, in Ellis, K., Gregory, A., Mears-Young, B. R. and Ragsdell, G., *Critical Issues in Systems Theory and Practice*, Plenum, New York.

World Commission on Environment and Development, 1987, *Our Common Future*, Oxford University Press, New York.

23

IN WHAT SENSE DO SYSTEMS EXIST?

Martin Frické

School of Information
1515 E. First Street
The University of Arizona
Tucson, Arizona 85719
Email: fricke@ccit.arizona.edu

Naive realists suppose that the world presents as it is, carved up into items and properties completely independent of human-kind. The problem with this is that many of the apparent properties—like that of being a pendulum, for instance—have a highly theoretical and intellectual content provided by humans. In contrast, naive idealists suppose that we individually or collectively, perhaps with the help of a God or Gods, construct the external world out of our ideas or perceptions. The problem here lies with there being too much of an intellectual contribution from us (or the Gods). We simply cannot wish things into existence, nor give them, by mere desire, the properties that we would like. We are just part of the natural world, not the creators of it.

A suitable middle ground is provided by arguing that we employ a conceptual scheme to approach the world. Properties are taken to be procedures, which can, in effect, be run or evaluated to see whether they apply to particular items (Oddie, 1986; Tichy, 1988). Whether they do or not, with empirical properties, is for the world itself to determine. So, we invent or devise or adopt the notion of, for example, being a pendulum, but whether anything in the world is or is not a pendulum is not up to us, that part is contributed by the world itself. Suppose that we look for a pendulum in the world, and find one, say x. If our conceptual scheme were altered to a new scheme which no longer had the concept of pendulum, our means of finding x via the notion of pendulum would no longer be available; however, the individual x, that we formerly found by means of this property, would presumably still exist (not only that, it would still exist unchanged). Change of scheme does not causally change the world; what it changes is how we classify and identify individuals. (This stands exactly counter to the influential passage of Kuhn in which he tells us that when Galileo devised the notion of pendulum, the world itself changed (Kuhn, 1962 p.119).)

With the conceptual schemes that we do in fact use, many items in the world stand in part-whole or component-whole relationships. There are two obvious candidates to provide a theoretical underpinning to a hierarchical ontology of this kind: set theory, using the member relation, and mereology, using the part-of relation (Simons, 1987). Set theory,

Systems for Sustainability, edited by Stowell *et al.*
Plenum Press, New York, 1997

although widely used in systems theory, seems to be unsuitable for the purpose. Sets are abstract objects not existing in space and time; so, for example, if an account of the human body theorized that the body was a system qua set, with cells as its members, that would straight away mean that our bodies were outside of space and time, which some might consider an extreme viewpoint.

Bunt (1987) has provided the re-assurance of a full axiomatization, and semantics, for generalized mereological theory. With that backdrop, we can proceed informally. Mereology is based on the 'part-of (-or-equal-to)' relation. Then... x is part of x (reflexivity); if x is part of y and y part of z, then x is part of z (transitivity); two wholes are equal if, and only if, they are parts of each other. If a part does not itself have any parts, other than itself, it is an atom. (Some formulations can permit an empty part, with consequent readjustment of the definitions.) A part not identical to the whole is a proper part; and two parts (or wholes) that have a part in common overlap. Then there is the question of composing parts. Say we start with three parts and consider the mereological whole formed of these parts; this whole or merge or sum or union or fusion has these three parts as parts and further any other part that it has overlaps one of the original three parts. There is an identity of composition between the whole and the parts which compose it. Say I have a bicycle, which, as simplicity would have it, consists of two atomic wheels and an atomic frame. How many things do I have? One, three, or four (two wheels plus a frame plus my bicycle)? Four can never be the appropriate answer. My bicycle just surely is the fusion of its parts.

Parts can have properties, and so too can wholes. Properties of the parts are often not properties of the whole—the wheels of my bicycle are round, yet the bicycle itself is not round. Properties of a kind or type possessed by wholes which are not possessed by proper parts of those wholes are emergent properties. For example, my bicycle has the property of being a convenient means of transport and yet neither its wheels nor its frame can themselves ever be convenient means of transport. Are there, or might there be, identity, composition, or reduction relations between properties of the whole and properties of the parts? Properties should be conceived of as functions; and relations, such as identity, among properties can be conceived of in terms of relations among those functions. Especially interesting are empirical relations among the properties, constrained to worlds structurally similar to our own. That is, our world has certain structural features, being governed by particular laws of gravity, quantum electrodynamics, and the like; given these, do certain micro properties assure or explain certain macro properties? For example, glass is transparent—maybe this comes about solely because of certain properties of its molecules together with the scientific laws; if so, there is reduction or explanation of the macro by the micro. And science has achieved exactly this kind of reduction in the case of many emergent properties. Whether such a reduction can be done for all interesting emergent properties is an empirical question—essentially one for science to attempt to answer.

The reduction relationships between micro and macro properties is a synchronic one, attempting to connect properties of the simple whole with properties of a complex of its parts. But diachronic relationships between properties are also important. We want to explain, to understand, and to predict. With explanation comes intellectual enlightenment and understanding, and with prediction comes control, design, and engineering. In some cases, it may be that explanatory laws connect properties of the parts through time; that is, they govern the time development of the parts. In some cases, it may be that explanatory laws connect properties of the whole through time. And there may or may not be reduction or irreducible emergent properties. There are many possibilities. It may be that causal laws cover the properties of the parts, and that some properties of the whole are reducible to these properties; in which case, explanation and prediction of the properties of the whole can be done via the properties of the parts. But this, the reductionist ideal, is not the only way things might be. Which possibilities obtain in actual cases is for us to find out.

Which brings us to systems... the term 'system', or the devised concept of system, is merely a convenient abbreviation or concept to denote certain kinds of non-atomic wholes—ones that lend themselves to having the explanation and prediction of the time development of their interesting emergent properties made at the macro level. With systems, sometimes these properties are irreducible (or how to reduce them is not known, or pragmatically or mathematically difficult); and also, often the parts act in harmony or co-operate, by exchange of information, to produce the behaviour of the whole.

Cooperation, connection, or assembly in its wider sense, is crucial for systems. From the point of view of mereology, whether the three parts of my bicycle lie separately on the floor or whether they are bolted one to another is irrelevant. The fusion of the parts covers both these cases. But when the parts are assembled, other emergent properties appear (like 'being a convenient means of transport'). Being assembled is itself a property of the whole, and it leads to or brings about other properties of the whole. Assembly, in cases like bicycles, amounts to the appropriate physical contiguity. But for systems this is not necessary. An installation of remote sensing equipment might locate a sensor in the Antarctic and a receptor in New Zealand... providing these communicate suitably a whole composed of these parts might have interesting emergent properties. Systems, then, need to be assembled to the degree of having their parts working together.

Are there systems? Certainly there are. Any air conditioner is a system. Its components exist, and this assures us that the whole exists, and the whole meets the conditions for being a system. And air conditioners exist in the world. Observable systems are just a twentieth century analogue of pendulums. But we can go beyond naturalistic observable systems.

Humans are just one kind of animal, with certain sensory abilities. We can observe many items. However, there may be other things not immediately available to us through our sensory window. There may be non-observables, or theoretical items, like atoms or radio waves. Using rough brush strokes, there are two views about non-observable items: realism and instrumentalism. Realists ascribe to at least some non-observable items exactly the same reality as the observable items: so, there are, or might be, atoms, and cells and genes, and these theoretical entities are just as real as tables and trees. Instrumentalists, in contrast, suggest that the theoretical entities of science are mere convenient fictions, or instruments, useful for theorizing about observable reality; so, for example, there are tables and trees, but there are no atoms and genes, except as fictions (Duhem, 1906). Instrumentalism is implausible on account of its anthropocentrism. Why should the world be built to suit us and our senses? Further, we have extended what we can observe by means of scientific instruments—many formerly unobservable entities can now be observed. Surely, genes and cells, for example, have not just acquired a reality because our instruments have improved. Realism about non-observable entities is the better choice to make. And there are the techniques of scientific method to underly the ascription of existence to theoretical entities. Knowledge given by the wider scientific method is fallible or conjectural knowledge... we have to be humble, we always might be mistaken. And this fallibility fits neatly with a choice, already made in this essay, of what we might call 'externality of reference'. The empirical entities that we talk about, and the properties that we ascribe to them, are external to ourselves. This is plain common sense realism; and it needs to be coupled with fallibilism to provide a strong and coherent position.

Realism is also consistent with the occasional use in physical theories of models or ideal items like perfect spheres or frictionless planes (and, of course, there are no perfect spheres or frictionless planes in the world). Assumptions are needed to connect the ideal with the real. Sad to say, there is a widespread literature which describes the conjuncts of theories and simplifying assumptions as being 'false' or 'unreal' (Friedman, 1953), whereas, in fact, they are usually true (or 'real') (Musgrave, 1981).

There are also properties of a non-naturalistic kind, which can be ascribed even to natural physical objects. That a particular sculpture is a religious icon supervenes on the sculpture's physical form, yet it also requires a substantial social component. And there seem to be socially constructed things in the world, as well as socially constructed properties. Consider, for example, agreements or contracts. Agreements exist. An agreement is a social construct; it is given existence by observance of the appropriate conventions and may well have its existence removed by suitable application of other conventions. Agreements are one example of many exosomatic structures, created by individuals or groups of individuals, which have a life of their own.

Are there systems using theoretical or even, more extremely, socially constructed entities? Certainly... say my stock broker and I reach an agreement about investing an average of $500 a month on the stock market with the purpose of producing a lump sum for retirement; she invests the monthly payment as she thinks fit, and informs me monthly of the state of the fund and of the market; I use her information together with my beliefs about cost averaging and value averaging, and other strategies that I may learn of, to decide how much to invest each month and I inform her of this sum. This retirement plan is a system—a human activity system based on social constructs—and it exists (or might exist, or, indeed, would exist if I could stir myself into action).

What has been expressed here thus far stands against the full might of established lore in current systems theory. Klir tells us '...*systems do not exist in the real world independent of the human mind.*' (Klir, 1991, p.12. Italics in the original.) and that this is the 'predominant view in systems science' (Klir, 1991, p.13). And Checkland writes of '...the canard that human activity systems exist in the real world...' (Checkland, 1995, p.53). And similar views are common, almost universal, in the primary and secondary sources (Wilson, 1990, pp. 27–8; Flood,R.L. and Carson, 1988, p. xvii; Cavalier, 1994, p. 265).

Klir hold his views for two reasons (Klir, 1991). The first is based on the problem of individuation. Take the air-conditioner. Why draw a line around it and consider it as a single individual system? It, or its components, may be part of a climate control system, which is, in turn, part of a building utility system, which is in turn... Both flat and hierarchical relations abound. But, practicing systems theorists actually do want to put a line around, say, air-conditioners. And, since this line is not naturally in the world, it must be in their heads. So, systems are mental constructs, not real things. This argument is unsound. First, any entity is going to bear relations to items outside itself, and these do not make it any the less of a whole entity. Second, an individual item can be, at one and the same time, a part or component of several different composites. A brick, for example, can be part of a wall or of a building containing that wall (or of a city block, or of a district, or of a city...). Both the wall and the building exist in the world; which one we choose to individuate on a particular occasion depends on our focus of interest. The second is an appeal to von Glasersfeld's constructivism... roughly, Klir takes from von Glasersfeld that everything is a mental construction and that therefore systems are mental constructions. Klir misunderstands von Glasersfeld for von Glasersfeld's theory is epistemology not ontology—it concerns ways of knowing, not what exists in the world (von Glaserfeld, 1995). The earlier work of von Glasersfeld lends itself to misinterpretation - he paraphrases Vico

'The human mind can *know* only *what the human mind has made*' (von Glaserfeld, 1991, p. 231). This seems implausible (I know that 2 + 2 = 4 but I did not make either the numbers or the function of addition). The later work of von Glasersfeld is a combination of evolutionary epistemology by way of Popperian conjectures and refutations, Piaget constructivism about observables, and instrumentalism about theoretical entities. Understood as philosophy, much of this is contentious (perhaps like all philosophy). Understood as an empirical cognitive theory in the tradition of Piaget, it seems to have been refuted by experiment (Reyna and Brainerd, 1995).

Checkland has a hybrid view. Hard systems can exist, but 'soft' human activity systems do not. His main argument is this. Our theories are free intellectual constructions; the best physical theories pass reproducible tests and thus we may suppose that reality is as they describe it to be and in particular that the entities that they posit exist; however, even the best theory about a human activity system, dealing, as it does, with nebulous, nefarious, conscious and wilful humans with perceptions and weltanschauung, can never be honed sufficiently to face and withstand reproducible tests, and thus we can never be justified in supposing that reality is as the theory describes it to be and consequently the entities postulated by theories of human activity systems are mere mental constructs (Checkland,1981, pp. 247–9). Checkland is right that our theories are free intellectual constructions. But it does not follow from this that the entitites invoked are mere mental constructs without external reference. (To suppose so is to commit a 'gem' (Stove, 1995).) The lack of reproducibility of tests, if indeed there always is such a lack, merely means that we are missing positive reasons in particular cases. But we should just take realism as the default.

Checkland and followers pinpoint the exact weakness in the traditional uses of systems theory in organizational design. Traditionally the goal of a system is taken as a given, but in practice deciding what the goal should be is by far the most onerous part of the designer's problem. Their remedy is an exploratory semi-phenomenological heuristic. Fine, but at the end of the day, when they have worked their consultancy insights, should not the organization, or parts of it, have goals, and real, existing, systems? The instrumentalism of the Soft Systems Methodologists (SSM) gives them the awkwardness of demarcating real from instrumental. A corporation presumably really makes a profit or loss, really has a workforce that can really be on strike, really has materials arriving for processing, really has satisfied clients... yet it, or parts of it, so SSM say, are definitely not systems for these aspects only can be 'regarded' as being systems (see, as a typical example, Lewis (1994) p. 35). Why not just make everything real?

Why does this question of existence matter? It matters primarily at a methodological level. Realism is more fruitful than instrumentalism (an issue that cannot be explored here). And it matters for the discipline of systems theory and its practitioners. It would be pragmatically aberrant, if not plain ludicrous, for systems theorists to publish research papers on systems, and accept money for consulting about systems, while maintaining that systems do not exist.

REFERENCES

Bunt, H.C., 1985, *Mass Terms and Model-Theoretic Semantics*, Cambridge University Press, Cambridge.

Cavalier, S. A., 1994, 'Soft' Systems Thinking: A Pre-Condition for Organizational Learning, *Human Systems Management*, 13:259–267.

Checkland, P. B., 1981, *Systems Thinking, Systems Practice*, Wiley, New York.

Checkland, P. B., 1995, Model Validation in Soft Systems Practice, *Systems Research*, 12(1):47–54.

Duhem, P., 1906, *La Théorie Physique:Son Objet, Sa Structure,* Translated as Wiener, P.P. (tr.), 1962, The Aim and Structure of Physical Theory, Atheneum, New York.

Glasersfeld, Ernst von, 1991, An Exposition of Constructivism: Why Some Like It Radical, in: *Facets of Systems Science,* (G.J.Klir, ed.), pp. 229–238, Plenum Press, New York and London.

Glasersfeld, Ernst von, 1995, *Radical Constructivism: a way of knowing and learning.* , Falmer Press, London and Washington.

Flood, R. L., and Carson, E. R., 1988, *Dealing with Complexity,* Plenum Press, New York and London.

Friedman, M., 1953, The Methodology of Positive Economics, in: *Essays In Positive Economics,* (M. Friedman, ed.), pp. 3–43, University of Chicago Press, Chicago.

Klir, G. J., (ed.), 1991, *Facets of Systems Science,* Plenum Press, New York and London.

Kuhn, T.S., 1962, *The Structure of Scientific Revolutions,* University of Chicago Press, Chicago.

Lewis, P.J., 1994, *Information-Systems Development,* Pittman, London.

Musgrave, A., 1981, 'Unreal Assumptions' in Economic Theory: The F-Twist Untwisted, *Kyklos,* **34:**377–387.

Oddie, G. J., 1986, *Likeness To Truth,* D.Reidel, Boston.

Reyna V.F. and C.J. Brainerd, 1995, Fuzzy-Trace Theory: An Interim Synthesis, *Learning and Individual Differences* 7(1):1–74.

Simons, P., 1987, *Parts: A study in ontology,* Clarendon,Oxford.

Stove, D., 1991, Idealism: a Victorian Horror-story (Part two) in: *The Plato Cult and other Philosophical Follies,* (D. Stove, ed.), pp.135–178, Blackwell, Oxford.

Tichy, P., 1988, *The Foundations of Frege's Logic,* Walter de Gruyter, Berlin

Wilson, B., 1990, 2nd ed., *Systems: Concepts, Methodologies and Applications,* John Wiley, Chichester.

24

SYSTEMIC APPROACHES AND CONTINGENT ACTIONS IN CONSULTANCY INTERVENTION

John Hassall

University of Wolverhampton
Management Research Centre
Shropshire Campus
Shifnal Road, Priorslee, Telford TF2 9NT

1. INTRODUCTION

When we attempt to employ systems approaches to confront real organisational problems, it becomes clear that a significant barrier to systemic intervention is the contingent nature of much action in these organisations. Because the actors (professionals, managers and consultants) are situated within a constraining cultural environment, they adopt action strategies which are reactive to this environment and which relate to normative assumptions about it (Dudley and Hassall, 1995 and 1996). Action and reaction to particular events in the immediate environment is a natural coping strategy. Doing "what we usually do" has the advantage of reducing the thinking and reaction time whilst ensuring survival. In this paper the term "contingent" is used for just those actions which arise from a developed repertoire based upon specific stimuli received from the environment.

It is clear that under this definition much organisational action is contingent since rules, norms and behaviours will have developed to ensure that the organisation persists in reasonable equilibrium with its environment. The individual actors in the organisation must in turn find an equilibrium position of their own and will develop their behaviours within the internal environment they face. Nothing in this is particularly new, Beer (1979 and 1985) has shown how organisational stability can emerge through the spontaneous development of mechanisms for coping with the variety that exists in the world. All that is being proposed is that, behind the amplifiers and attentuators of variety which appear within all organisational space, are people whose behaviours depend upon the contingent circumstances in which they find themselves.

Systems thinking emerges as an attempt to allow complex organisations and situations to be treated as systemic wholes. Teleology intrudes, seeking to see organisations and sub-organisations as purposeful systems. Following from this, developments in systems thinking have been aimed at providing sufficient analysis to allow prescriptive action. The assumption is that such action is more likely to bring about an improvement in a problem situation if it draws upon a systemic analysis. But how, given the contingent nature of much human action, is it possible to move towards an effective framework for systemically derived interventions?

2. CONTINGENCY OF HUMAN ACTION

Situated human action, it has been argued (action within a particular organisation or problem context), is usually contingent in nature. That behaviours and systemic identities may emerge in contingent ways has been recognised. For example Beer (1985) has memorably stated that "The purpose of a system is what it does", seeming to reflect the point that systems may emerge from interactions with their environment and may express themselves in ways that were not intended by their designers. Also, Checkland (1981) in the original form of Soft Systems Methodology refers to "desirable and feasible" actions in the problem situation; one reading of feasibility being related to contingencies in the environment.

Support for the contingent nature of actions leading to the emergence of organised repertoires of behaviour is also found in psychology and biology. In the case of psychology, transactional analysis in psychotherapy is developed from considerations of programmed responses to specific stimuli (eg. Berne, 1964). In biology, the developed evolutionary theories of Dawkins (1988), make clear how adaptations in successive generations are selectively favoured by means of environmental filtering. In the biological case it is even possible to see the main "active" principle in evolution arising from the environment rather than the organism.

Returning to the behaviour of individuals in organisations or problem contexts we can say that the environment will in most cases be determined outwith that context of the individual actor or system, and in a way that is detached and (possibly) inaccessible to the actor or the environment. Of course, systems theory and methodologies for systemic intervention address this by recognising the importance of boundaries; and re-framing is an art practised by all successful change agents (Handy, 1991). But in many practice situations, choice of frame is not an option.

3. SOME ILLUSTRATIVE EXAMPLES

The hope of systemic intervention is that we can provide some process that is *essentially* prescriptive for solving real problems. This means that all approaches, whether they seek to be diagnostic, creative, critical, critically reflective, emancipatory, or otherwise have the intention of determining actions (Beckford, 1995; Checkland and Scholes, 1990; Flood 1996; Dudley and Hassall, 1996). This often fails in practice. For example:

1. An organisation seeks to provide training in new information technology to staff. It is clear from a systemic view of the problem that traditional training courses have failed in the past and are likely to fail in future. However, the behavioural repertoire within the organisation is biased towards the provision of traditional courses; moreover such courses are less expensive and likely to create less disruption to the working environment. The environment strongly re-enforces a contingent decision to proceed with traditional courses. (Source: ongoing consultancy case).

2. A small company faces the prospect of becoming insolvent. It is clear that only a drastic restructuring can avert the immediate danger; however, there are a number of clear systemic and systematic issues which also need addressing to improve performance in the medium to long term. The Managing Director agrees to, and carries out, the immediate major re-structuring, (essentially a contingent decision, the environment gave no choice). Actions based upon longer term systemic analysis remain uncompleted. (Dudley and Hassall, 1996).

3. One of the major factors leading to deforestation in certain parts of India is the demand for firewood. People can see the effect of using trees for fuel and have sympathy for the systemic requirement to preserve the environment, but their *present* actions are contingent on the need to survive. (Source: conversation between the author and S.K.Tiwari, Naturalist, Bandhavgarh National Park, India, 1996).

Systems theorists may argue that when the right boundaries are drawn all these problem situations are amenable to solution, and so they are. But the actors in each case may have little or no access to the environment which enfolds them and constrains their ability to act systemically.

4. INTEGRATING SYSTEMIC AND CONTINGENT ACTION FRAMES

It is suggested both from research and much practice that an appropriate systemic view and analysis can provide a prescription for effective action, if only the systemic view can be made accessible to the putative actors. If this difficulty is to be overcome it may be by making more explicit the separation between contingent action *now* and the development of an environment which can *in future* result in actions which are systemically desirable. The issue of time is an important one because it is unlikely that actors will continue long with actions which lead to strong negative feedback from their environment, however systemically desirable these may be longer term.

The above reading of the situation leads to the idea of separating the frames of reference for action in intervention to make explicit the differing timescales upon which they become effective. Thus the contingent reference frame is concerned with providing assistance towards understanding the *current* environment and the actions required to cope with it. The systemic reference frame is concerned with influencing the *creation* of the *future environment*; (by definition therefore, creating the future contingent reference frame).

How is this future contingent reference frame created? Theories of the learning cycle, including those of Kolb (1984) and Revans (1982) make clear the importance of reflection and abstraction resulting from action and experimentation in the world. A useful summary discussion of these ideas can be found in Weinstein (1995). The ideas and models developed from reflection and abstraction result in further experimentation and action. It is proposed that systemic intervention must be towards affecting the development of these ideas and models so that they allow progress towards a *future* environment and thus a future contingent reference frame within which systemically desirable actions can emerge.

5. CONCLUSIONS—APPLICATION TO CONSULTANCY

A possible way ahead for consultancy is to make *explicit* two types of active intervention as;

Systemic: Mainly taking an educative stance and seeking to affect the development of future environments conducive to actions which have been determined by appropriate analysis to be systemically desirable.

Contingent: Dealing with improvement of current actions within the given environment.

An exploration of this approach focused upon theory building is being undertaken through case studies of consultancy (from which the first two examples in section 3 above are taken). The intention is to develop a way in which consultancy interventions can be introduced through using the above typology, thus making it easier to avoid outcomes where sound systemic analysis is followed by merely contingent action.

REFERENCES

Beckford, J.L.W., 1995, Towards a Participative Methodology for Viable System Diagnosis, *Systemist*, Vol. 17(3) Aug 1995, ByWord Publications, Fareham, UK.

Beer, S., 1979, *The Heart of Enterprise*, Wiley, Chichester, UK.

Beer, S., 1985, *Diagnosing the System For Organisations*, Wiley, Chichester, UK.

Berne, E., 1964, *Games People Play*, Grove Press, New York, USA.

Checkland, P., 1981, *Systems Thinking, Systems Practice*, Wiley, Chichester, UK.

Checkland, P., Scholes, J., 1990, *Soft Systems Methodology in Action*, Wiley, Chichester, UK.

Dawkings, R., 1988, *The Blind Watchmaker*, Penguin, London, UK.

Dudley, P., Hassall, J.C., 1995, Systemic Refocusing Strategy, An Emancipatory Approach To Intervention, in: *Critical Issues in Systems Theory and Practice*, (K.Ellis, A.Gregory, B.R.Mears-Young, G.Ragsdell, eds.), pp 465–478, Plenum, London, UK.

Dudley, P., Hassall, J.C., 1996, Applying Systemic Refocusing Strategy to Information Systems Innovation, in: *Technology Management in a Changing World*, (R.M.Mason, L.A.Lefebvre, T.M.Khalil, eds.), pp 41–50, Elsevier Advanced Technology, Oxford, UK.

Flood, R.L., 1996, Total Systems Intervention: Local Systemic Intervention, *Research Memorandun No. 13*, Centre for Systems Studies, Hull, UK.

Handy, C., 1991, *Waiting For The Mountain To Move*, Hutchinson, London, UK.

Kolb, D., 1984, *Experiential Learning*, Prentice Hall, Englewood Cliffs N.J, USA.

Revans, R, 1982, *The Origins and Growth of Action Learning*, Chartwell Bratt, UK.

Weinstein, K., 1995, *Action Learning A journey in Discovery and Development*, HarperCollins, London, UK.

25

MODELLING THE PROCESS OF DECIDING IN REAL WORLD PROBLEMS

Athena Marouda-Chatjoulis[1] and Patrick Humphreys[2]

[1]University of Thessaly
Volos, Greece
[2]London School of Economics and Political Science
London, United Kingdom

1. INTRODUCTION

Initially, modelling of the decision process was based on the comparison and the establishment of the preference ordering of the various options of a decision problem in terms of utilities and values (Keeney & Raiffa, 1976; von Winterfeldt and Edwards, 1986). This approach was soon questioned by a number of researchers (Berkeley and Humphreys, 1982; Christensen-Szalanski, 1984), since it relied on the assumptions that the decision making task can be represented in only one correct way, and that the model used constrains the answers to the decision task. This criticism was also supported by a number of studies on intuitive decision making in laboratory experiments, as well as in experiments on real problems in which a normative model has been followed (Tversky & Kahnemann, 1974; Vari et al., 1978). It was found that in structuring 'real-life problems', the personal factors of the problem owner, as well as the social constrains relevant to the problem situation, are very determinative and allow for the consideration of the differences between people in handling a decision problem (Humphreys and Berkeley, 1982; Larichev, 1982; Marouda-Chatjoulis, 1995).

In the meantime, the parallel development of systems thinking and soft system methodologies provided an alternative way of looking at the problem solving, as an integrated whole (Ackoff, 1974; Bertalanffy, 1968; Checkland, 1981; Churchman, 1971; Emery, 1969; Luckmann, 1978). As the problem scope of systems applications increased, soft systems thinking was developed to cope with 'soft problems' in which the objectives are difficult to be defined, and deal with "people and their perceptions, values and interests" (Jackson, 1991). The idea of subjectivity became central in 'soft systems thinking', and in the modelling of the decision making process. It implies that ill-defined problems have to be regarded as problems which allow for different perceptions of reality (Ackoff and Emery, 1974; Jackson, 1989). Systems thinking and soft systems methodologies provided a way of modelling real world (ill-defined) problems as a process through the use of a number of stages (Ackoff, 1981; Brightman, 1978; Checkland, 1981; Churchman, 1979; de Bono, 1970; Janis & Mann, 1977; Mason & Mitroff, 1981; Newell & Simon, 1964; Phillips, 1984; Schein, 1969). Central idea to these models is how the individual deals with the sequence of a number of stages which he or she has to follow in order to reduce uncertainty and increase structure (and thus to transform an ill-defined problem into a well-defined one).

It appears from the above, that in modelling the process of deciding, experience on the development and application of system thinking and decision theory, established the need for structuring the problem prior to choice and made it clear that, different individuals faced with the "same" problem could view it from different perspectives and therefore can have different problem structures. In this paper a process model and methodology, which takes into account the above considerations is presented. The model has been developed in order to represent the decision making process of a real problem, that of career decision making (Marouda-Chatjoulis, 1995). For the creation of the model, elements of decision theory, systems thinking and soft systems methodologies were used. In fact the model, in its procedural schema, is a particular, focused refinement of soft-system methodology. It combines the generic phases of the process of problem solving, i.e. Exploration, Structuring and Evaluation, with the possibilities of the different representations of problem situation and problem solving. It is proposed to represent the career decision making process and it is created for the career decision making problem. The model, which is both descriptive and prescriptive in nature, is designed to help the counsellor to understand what is involved in the decision process, and to identify what are the needs of the client at each particular stage of the process.

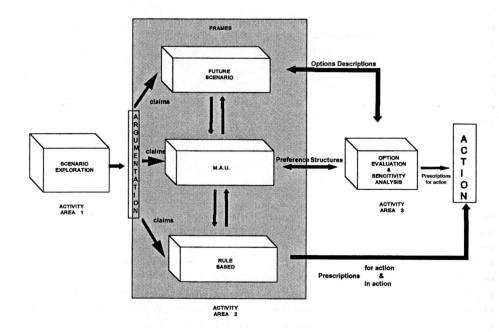

Figure 1. The career decision making process model.

2. THE PROCESS MODEL OF CAREER DECISION MAKING

Figure 1 shows the process model of career decision making. The model consists of three main activity areas, interconnected by pathways which link these areas, and the elements in each area, to demonstrate the processes individuals go through in the investigation of their career problems.

The model has been developed on the results and the findings of a research conducted among young people age 16–20 years old (Marouda-Chatjoulis, 1995). The research investigated career decision making by addressing how individuals represent the knowledge of their career problem, and how, on the basis of this representation, aid can be provided to them. The assumptions used were a) that career decision making is a dynamic process containing the characteristics of personal decision making in real life situations; b) it is relevant to the social context of decision implementation and to the individual's "small world", which define his subjective knowledge representation of the decision situation; c) that the decision making is based on the subjective meaning representation of the decision situation of each decision maker, who uses different ways of representing his career problem. These assumptions were used to define the elements of the model which prescribe the methodology and the counselling procedure followed.

To identify the different ways of problem representation used by the individuals, the *five levels of knowledge representation* developed by Humphreys and Berkeley (1983) were incorporated in the model. According to them, decision problems have to be examined in terms of how they are handled in a 'top to bottom' analysis in five levels of problem knowledge representation. They also suggest that problem situations are seen individually by each stakeholder in different ways, and that each stakeholder is likely to believe that the way he views the problem is the only correct way to see it. Thus, to solve a problem, one needs to increase the structure of the problem and reduce the discretion within it (e.g. by reducing the discretion among different representations of the problem) until a single immediate action can be processed. The operations involved in the various levels are qualitative different and define the way the decision problem is going to be represented, structured and solved. The results of the operations involved at higher levels constrain the way operations are carried out at lower levels. The framework of the five levels of knowledge representation was used to define the operations related to the career decision making process and involved in the three activity areas of the process model for career decision making.

2.1. Activity Area 1 (A1): Scenario Exploration

Activity area 1 refers to the activities involved in the exploration of the problem and the formulation of initial scenarios for the solution of the problem. It corresponds to Level 5 (the problem exploration) and Level 4 (the problem definition) areas of the five levels framework. The exploration of the problem is defined from the exploration of the individual's small world which predispose the material one is willing or able to retrieve in order to think or talk about his problem (Savage, 1954). The elaboration of the scenarios results in the specification of the boundaries in which the individual can express his problem, and identify the relevant structures necessary for the solution of his problem. Of course this is idiosyncratic. Thus the same problem can be expressed in different ways according to the structure and the kind of language the individual uses to represent his problem. Exploration and elaboration of scenarios is facilitated through guidance, by giving to the individual the appropriate information about his problem and by precipitating arguments and claims concerning the way the individual wants to proceed to solve it.

The individual exists Activity area 1, when he is able to make claims in his arguments about the possible alternative ways he takes to achieve his goal and solve his problem. Consequently, the individual's argumentation stands as the bridge from the A1 to the A2 area. The individual can only enter A2 if he is able to form arguments about his problem.

2.2. Activity Area 2 (A2): Option Formation

Activity area 2 refers to problem structuring activities, and corresponds to the Level 3 operations of the five Levels framework. It addresses the formulation of the alternative options which represent the individual's preferred solutions for the problem. This is achieved through the structuring and framing of the individual's claims about the solution of his problem into identifiable frames. In the research conducted for the creation of the present model, it was found that people were using more than one ways to represent their career problem (Marouda-Chatjoulis, 1995). In particular three different frames were identified as the language partitions used by the individuals to collectively represent their career problem, i.e. Multi Attribute Utility frame, Future Scenario frame, Rule based frame. Thus, first, the individuals were representing their problem by identifying different alternative solutions and establishing them through different criteria; second, they were making scenarios about their future, talking about the various contingencies related to their actions; and third, they were basing their alternative solutions on a number of beliefs or principles they felt obliged to follow. These three ways of representations, have been considered as necessary elements of the process of career decision making, for the definition of the way the individual wants to proceed to the solution of his problem, and have been incorporated in the process model for career decision making.

The individual can be considered as operating effectively A2, when he is able to formulate his thoughts in any of the above frames. The links and the pathways that exist in this area show that there is an interplay in the way these three frames can be used by the individual when he is talking about his career problem. By developing a structure within a Future Scenario frame, the individual is formulating descriptions of his options. These were identified as the link in the pathway the individual will take to move to the next activity area for the evaluation of these options. By developing structure in a MAU frame, he formulates preference structures which again can lead towards activity area 3. If the individual is expressing his problem in a rule based frame, them there is no need for structure, since rules by themselves give prescriptions which lead straight to action.

2.3. Activity Area 3 (A3): Option Evaluation

Activity area 3 refers to the problem evaluation activities. It corresponds to Level 2 (problem evaluation) and Level 1 (problem solution) operations. It involves the necessary operations (answer to "what if questions"; sensitivity analysis) for the evaluation of the alternative solutions to the problem, for the formation of an order of preference for the various alternatives and for the extraction of the output of what is the best alternative for the problem solution.

The results of the activities of this area were found to prescribe action to take place. These prescriptions constitute the pathways which move the individual towards taking action and solving his problem. If the individual, after evaluating his career options, is not satisfied with them, he has the option of going back to the previous activity area. he can do this either through the pathway of option description, so that he can reformulate and re-structure his problem in a future scenario frame, or through the pathway of preference structure so that he can restructure his problem in a MAU frame. On the other hand, hav-ing decided on his most desirable solution, if he is still not satisfied and is still unable to take any action, then the model allows him to go back to activity area 1 and reconsider his problem.

3. CONCLUSION

The Process Model for career decision making is proposed as being both structural and dynamic, showing what is essential for the problem resolution (main areas of concern, elements, activities) and how this has to be done, i.e. the processes needing to be accom-plished for the transition from one area to another towards the solution of the problem. There are two distinctive features of the model: First, it is based on the individual's sub-jective perception and representation of the decision problem. By subjective meaning rep-resentation, we are referring to the individual's intuitive way of proceeding towards a solution of his problem. This subjective representation specifies how the decision process varies according to the characteristics of the decision maker, the context of the decision and the type of the decision involved. It suggests also that, for the solution of the problem, there is no single, correct way, but rather, several possible paths; these paths are derived from different perceptions of the problem by each individual and lead to different pre-scriptions for action. The above suggests that, for the investigation of a decision problem the context of the decision, within which the individual's representations are formed, has to be taken into consideration. This view supports the idea that, the appropriate research question should focus in finding what a good prescriptive procedure should be in the par-ticular context of the decision, and not to find the correct way which can describe how to make a decision (Watson, 1992).

As described above, the model in the present study has been developed for applica-tion in the career decision making context. Further research is needed to validate the use of the model in other settings. In addition, although the choice of the three frames identi-fied as the semantic representative units for the representation of the career problem, is supported substantially in the development of the model, further research might needed to investigate the possibility of assigning additional types of frames for different problematic situations. The second feature of the model is that it is a process model, involving certain activities and operations, through which a person progresses in making and carrying out decisions. The activity areas do not represent static stages but 'progressive passages' in which the individual moves. It is possible to enter the model at any point of the decision process, moving forward and looping back to previous areas of problem exploration ac-cording to needs. Progress in any area of the decision process depends on the completion of the objectives involved in this area. If the objectives of one activity area are not satis-fied, the individual is expected to experience difficulties in the next area and should go back. Failing to do so, may result in a state of confusion and dissatisfaction to the point where he may withdraw from the process, leaving the problem unresolved.

The process model of career decision making provides a general procedural schema which could capture how the problem is constrained, how is represented and how is in-tended. It can describe how the individual represents his problem, as well as how he is moving while he is proceeding to the solution of his problem and to action. It can also prescribe the rules for an effective movement through the process, and shows the ways that the counsellor can intervene and help the individual in this movement.

REFERENCES

Ackoff, R.L., 1981, The Art and Science of Mess Managment, *Interfaces* **11**(1):20–26.

Ackoff, R.L., and Emery, F., 1974, *On purposeful systems*, Aldine-Atherton, Chicago.

Berkeley, D., and Humphreys, P., 1982, Structuring decision problems and the bias Heuristic, *Acta Psychologica* **20**:210–252.

Bertalanffy, L.von, 1968, *General System Theory*, Braziller, New York.

Brightman, H.J., 1978, Differences in ill-structured problem solving along the Organizational Hierarchy, *Decision Science* **9**:1–18.

Checkland, P., 1981, *Systems Thinking, Systems Practice*, Wiley and Sons, Chichester.

Christensen-Szalanski, J.J., 1984, Problem solving Strategies: A selection mechanism, some implications, and some data, *Organizational Behavior and Human Performance* **22**:307–323.

Churchman, C. W., 1971, *The Design of Inquiring Systems*, Basic Books, New York.

de Bono, E., 1970, *Lateral Thinking: A Textbook of Creativity*, Allen Lane, London.

Emery, F.E. (ed.,), 1969, *Systems Thinking*, Penguin Books, Harmondsworth.

Humphreys, P.,and Berkeley, D., 1983, Problem solving calculi and levels of knowledge representation in decision making, in: *Decision Making Under Uncertainty* (P.W. Scholz, eds.), pp.121–157, Elsevier Science Publishers B.V., North-Holland.

Jackson, M.C., 1991, *Systems methodology for the Management Sciences*, Plenum, New York.

Jackson, M.C., 1989, Future Prospects in Systems Thinking, in *Systems prospects: The Next Ten Years of System Research*,(R.L. Flood, M.C. Jckson, and P. Keys, eds)., Plenum Press, New York.

Janis, I.L. and Mann, L., 1977, *Decision Making: A psychological analysis of conflict, choice, and commitment*, The Free Press, New York.

Kenney, R., and Raiffa, H., 1976, *Decisions with Multiple Objectives: Preferences and Value Tradeoffs*, John Wiley and Sons, New York.

Larichev,O.I., 1984, Psychological validation of decision methods, *Journal of Applied System Analysis* **11**:37–46.

Marouda-Chatjoulis, A., 1995, *The Process of Representation and Development of Knowledge in Career Decision Making and Counselling*, Unpublished Ph.D. thesis, University of London.

Mason, R.O., and Mitroff,I.I., 1981, *Challenging Strategic Planning Assumptions*, Wiley and Sons, New York.

Newell, A., and Simon, H.A., 1972, *Human problem solving*, Prentice-Hall, Englewood Cliffs, N.J.

Phillips, L.D., 1984, A Theory of Requisite Decision Models, *Acta Psychologica* **56**:29–48.

Savage, L., 1972, *The Foundations of Statistics*, 2nd ed., Dover Publications, New York.

Tversky, A., and Kahnemann, D. (1974). Judgment under uncertainty:heuristics and biases. Science, 185.

von Winterfeldt., and Ward Edwards, 1986, *Decision analysis and behavioral research*, Cambridge University Press, New York.

Watson, S.R., 1992, The presumptions of prescription, *Acta Psychologica*, **80**:7–31.

26

DOING RESEARCH IN THE SOCIAL DOMAIN

Concepts and Criteria

Martha Vahl

Lincoln University Campus
Lincoln School of Management
Centre for Systems Research
Brayford Pool, Lincoln LN6 7TS United Kingdom

1. INTRODUCTION

Any professional activity worth its name will have developed criteria and concepts that help to guarantee the quality of its products (see Stevens, Schade, Chalk, and Slevin, 1993, p. 6, concerning health care professionals). Interestingly this stage does not seem to have been realised yet for systems professionals in the social domain. Not only early workers have been worried (Ackoff, 1981; Beer, 1985; Checkland, 1981), but also more recent ones (Checkland, 1992; De Zeeuw, 1995; Van der Zouwen, 1996).

Various indicators of professional maturity have been formulated. Firstly, some distinctive concepts should be available to convey experience among the professionals. Secondly, it should be possible to recognise successful and non-successful applications. Thirdly, evaluations should exist of precisely defined experimental cases. Fourthly, there should be results of research to indicate what principles and theories are supported by what observations.

The collective of systems professionals seems to be lacking in terms of all such indicators. At least three activities seem to be required to change this situation: a program of research on what criteria to use; a series of evaluation studies; a process of defining and checking on professional qualifications. None of these tasks can be skipped (Anderson, 1996). They are especially relevant given the (post-) modern insight that clients have a right to expect quality in whatever is offered to them.

2. EXAMPLES

On all three activities important deficiencies have been pointed out. No decisive verdict seems to have been reached yet over important professional issues such as 'covering

Systems for Sustainability, edited by Stowell *et al.*
Plenum Press, New York, 1997

up' one's expertise (Taket, 1994), or using methods 'obliquely' to realise aims that clients are not supposed to be aware of (Midgley, 1995). There also is a lack of consensus regarding the extent to which one should respect clients' personal interests when invited to serve their professional interests (Ulrich, 1989).

Furthermore, one may point to a lack of distinctive notions to convey professional experiences. A thorough analysis of this situation is presented in Flood and Jackson (1991). The authors aim to identify the assumptions underlying various systems methodologies, and to integrate these through more general notions. This seems to meet with some difficulties still, however: one can find many alternative proposals (Ellis, Gregory, Mears-Young, and Ragsdell, 1995).

Similar concerns exist concerning the lack of evaluation studies.[*] This pertains to their *technical quality*—the extent to which they are effective, independent of the enthusiasm they create among clients (Broekstra, 1997; Checkland, 1992), or of the support individuals such as CEO's provide—as well as to their *social quality*—that is the extent to which they contribute to a general enthusiasm and an opening up of possibilities (Warfield, 1995; Brown, 1996).

Given the early popularity of the 'systems approach' (Mintzberg, 1979; p. 459), one might have expected a more mature type of systems profession. There seem to be at least two circumstances that mitigate this kind of criticism, however. Firstly, the area of management is one where good business may be based on solid products but also on—any—beliefs (Broekstra, 1995; Angell and Smithson, 1991). Secondly, the area of systems research provides an excuse (Mitroff and Churchman, 1992).

This is not to say that there is something wrong with the notion of system. There is, however, an amazing variety of opinions as to what its study consists of—ranging from claims to treat 'systems' as 'objects' as in physics (Waelchli, 1992; Casti, 1979), to claims that 'systems' bring conceptual order in what researchers do (Checkland, 1995). Such variety may simply indicate a healthy state of growth—but also a lack of clarity as to what should be considered a good systems study.

3. OBSERVATION

In this paper I aim to consider this lack of clarity, contending that systems research lacks sufficient awareness that good practice needs good observations—in contrast to research in general. The professional criteria of the latter have been scrutinised extensively (Popper, 1972; Lakatos, 1970; Latour, 1987). The difference between the two kinds of research is of concern here. I first consider the notion of 'good' observations in non-systems research, making use of introductory texts on research.

According to these texts, the aim is to identify what observations belong together so they can be combined. It is this identification that requires an epistemological interpretation, not observation itself (Hammersley, 1995). Improvement means that observations become 'objective' (without research people might continue to see different things, dependent on their inclinations). It results in (tested) theories that provide 'knowledge about the world or parts of it' (Stevens et al., 1993, p. 13).

---

[*] This is not to say that there is a lack of reports or testimonies. The literature abounds with descriptions of 'examples'. Such descriptions should not be confused with evaluations, however: in the latter one would expect not only indications as to what A (methods) lead to what B (effects), but also to what extent not-A still might lead to B, etc.

When improving on observations one may wish to know the extent of one's success. Notions like 'reliability' have been introduced to do so (the degree to which repeated observations are assigned consistently to the same category; Bryman, 1988), 'validity' (the extent to which improved observations relate to some observed 'object' (Hammersley, 1995)), and 'transferability' (the degree to which new instances of the 'object' can be induced, and improved observations generalised).

The notion of an 'object' does not just refer to 'things' in reality as sometimes is thought. Although 'things' do allow for recognition of repeated observations, one must be able to generalise over all 'things' that are sufficiently similar to lead to the same improved observations. Different disciplines may thus identify different 'objects' given the same 'things'. Chemistry may study instances of the 'object' H_2O, while physics may look at (watery) 'things' as an 'object' with mass.

It usually requires much effort to identify a suitable 'object' (involving the identification of control groups, of subjects, etc.). It thus appears useful to consider a more general reason for observations to belong together. I call this reason 'stories'. These suggest to people what to see as belonging together. Disciplinary 'objects' like H_2O become special cases. They constitute 'observed stories'. The notion of a 'story' may help to elucidate what should constitute 'good' system observations.

4. 'GOOD' SYSTEMS OBSERVATIONS

The reason to look for 'objects' is that they allow for improving observation, independent of what the results will be used for. In the social domain no such 'objects' have been found yet (even though there is an abundance of 'things'). This has stimulated a search for alternatives. An example is statistics. To improve on the observation of probabilities a 'story' has been defined which requires relative frequencies to stabilise asymptotically in 'infinite' sequences (Hacking, 1965).

In contrast, systems research can be said to prefer the notion of 'system' as its observational 'story'. The researcher choose a system, for example, to decide which observations in a 'rich picture' belong together (Checkland, 1995). In practical applications it has been proposed to use 'root definitions', from which to derive 'conceptual models' (Tsouvalis and Checkland, 1996). The models' implementation should help make visible what supports increased levels of action of the system.

The process of practical application is not seen as research, although ongoing reflection on this process has been interpreted as such (Checkland and Scholes, 1990). This explains the lack of criteria that indicate the degree to which observation and its improvement have been successful—although some rules of expediency have been formulated, for example to stop making a 'rich picture'. More explicitly, the choice of the 'conceptual model' has to be 'defensible' (Checkland, 1995; p. 53).

What still appears needed, therefore, are criteria in systems research that are analogous to the notions of reliability, validity and generalisability. They should help to identify the degree to which improved observations still are independent of their use. This kind of improvement seems seldomly realised. Even though obviously in the right direction, a notion like 'defensibility' may be misleading. It allows one to defend an improvement because it is successful in some form of use.

To define such criteria requires one to distinguish strictly between the roles of the researcher and of the user of research results (even though in practice both roles may be fulfilled by the same person at the same time). This allows the researcher to report independently on the degree to which observations have been improved. Observations that are deemed sufficient then can be used by the user—who still may have professional reasons to define what is 'sufficient'.

Given this distinction the three notions can be defined as follows. The notion of 're-liability' is analogous to: will repeated telling of the 'story' each time lead to the same choice of what observations belong together? This implies that the (systems) story achieves some level of 'addressability'. Secondly, the notion of 'validity' is to be read as: will the 'story' allow the improved observation to be communicated to users? The answer indicates some degree of 'communicability'.

Thirdly, if it proves possible for users to understand what the improved observations are and what their independent use implies, one may say that the result achieves 'convin-cibiliy' (or phrased negatively, 'defensibility'): will those who have to use the results, or have to experience their use, resist such use? 'Convincible' results indicate the degree of support to two functions, therefore: the 'systems story' should identify what belongs to-gether and allows for improving observations, as well as under what constraints their use will be independent of the improvement.

5. IMPROVING PROFESSIONALISM

The social domain is quite special. It does not allow for professionalism as in tech-nology. The most unfortunate situation one may think of is one where the 'story' that identifies what observations belong together is the same as what structures the use of the improved observations. In this case the results of research can not be independent of their use. This kind of situation seems identical to the occurrence of an ideology: one sees only what one believes to see, or is forced to see.

In this situation one may expect a tendency to resist new observations, resulting in low addressability and low communicability. If people allow themselves to be convinced, however, they are addressable. This obviously need not imply that communicability is high. To improve on this type of situation, one has to find an approach that helps those that choose to use it, and do not raise resistance from those who do not.

At present the 'story' on which systems professionals base themselves often seem to mingle with the way the results of using the story are treated, as happens. As exemplified in the literature, few applications seem to lead to the liberating effect one is aiming for (Taket and White, 1994). This implies low quality in the results of research, that is low levels of addressability, communicability and convincibility, and, hence, insufficient qual-ity for the results to be used.

This suggests that systems researchers should pay more attention to identifying what levels have been achieved on these criteria—in order to allow professionals for a choice of what they deem 'sufficient'. It is interesting to note, in this context, that the work of Axel-rod (1984) exemplifies such research. This author explores the Prisoner's Dilemma, the rules of which function as a 'story'. The author proves able to identify what increases ad-dressability, communicability and convincibility.

What is needed is a 'story' that extends the dilemma to an 'infinite' game (Carse, 1986): it has to be repeated without it being known what the final move is. This results in increased co-operation. Without this extension one always needs an external 'commis-sioner' who hires a professional, thereby providing the latter with 'authority'. Such 'authority' implies low 'convincibility' as well as low 'addressability' and thus a low level of participation (Bryman, 1988).

6. CONCLUSION

This paper presents some arguments to the effect that systems professionalism itself is in need of improvement. The lack of quality seems due to a lack of clarity concerning notions analogous to reliability, validity and transferability. In this paper I derive a definition of the notions needed. It involves participation not only of commissioners and researchers, but especially of the individual clients who will experience the use of the results of the research effort (Vahl, 1994).

REFERENCES

Ackoff, R., L., 1981, *Creating the Corporate Future*, Wiley, New York.
Anderson, P. W., 1996, They think it's all over, *Times Higher* (September 27), p. 20.
Angell, I.O., and Smithson, S., 1991, *Information Systems Management, Opportunities and Risk*, MacMillan, London.
Axelrod, R., 1984, *The Evolution of Co-operation*, Basic Books, New York.
Beer, S., 1985, *Diagnosing the System for Organisations*, Wiley, Chichester.
Broekstra, G., 1997, Organisations are closed systems, *Systemica* **11** (in press).
Brown, D., 1996, The 'essences' of the fifth discipline: or where does Senge stand to view the world?, *Systems Research* **13**(2): 91–107.
Bryman, A., 1988, *Quantity and Quality in Social Research*, Routledge, London.
Carse, J.P., 1986, *Finite and Infinite Games. A Vision of life as Play and Possibility,* Penguin Books, Middlesex.
Casti, J., 1979, *Connectivity, Complexity and Catastrophe in Large-Scale Systems*, Wiley, New York.
Checkland, P., 1981, *Systems Thinking, Systems Practice*, Wiley, Chichester.
Checkland, P., 1992, Systems and scholarship: the need to do better, *J. Opl Res. Soc.* 43(11): 1023–1030.
Checkland, P., 1995, Model validation in soft systems practice, *Systems Research* 12(1): 47–55.
Checkland, P. and Scholes, J., 1990, *Soft Systems Methodology in Action*, Wiley, Chichester.
Ellis, K., Gregory, A., Mears-Young, B.R., Ragsdell, G., eds., 1995, *Critical Issues in Systems Theory and Practice*, Plenum Press, New York.
Flood, R.L., and Jackson, M.C., 1991, *Creative Problem Solving*. Wiley, Chichester.
Hacking, I., 1965, *Logic of Statistical Inference*, Cambridge University Press, Cambridge.
Hammersley, M., 1995, *Principles of Social and Educational Research*, Open University, Walton Hill.
Lakatos, I., 1970, Falsification and the methodology of scientific research programs, in: *Criticism and the Growth of Knowledge*, (I. Lakatos, and A. Musgrave, A., eds.), p. 91–196, Cambridge University Press, Cambridge.
Latour, B., 1987, *Science in Action*, Open University Press, Milton Keynes.
Midgley, G., 1995, Mixing methods: developing systemic intervention. Research memorandum no. 9, Centre for Systems Studies, University of Hull.
Mintzberg, H., 1979, *The Structuring of Organizations*. Prentice Hall, Englewood Cliffs.
Mitroff, I., and Churchman, C.W., A manifesto for the systems sciences: outrage over the state of science, *General Systems Bulletin* **XXII**(1): 7–10.
Popper, K.R., 1972, *Objective Knowledge*, Clarendon Press, Oxford.
Silverman, D., 1993, *Interpreting Qualitative Data*, Sage, London.
Stevens, P.J.M., Schade, A., Chalk, B., and Slevin, O., 1993, *Understanding Research. A Scientific Approach for Health Care Professionals*, Campion Press, Edinburgh.
Taket, A., 1994, Undercover agency?–ethics, responsibility and the practice of OR, *J. Opl Res. Soc.* **45**: 123–132.
Taket, A., and White, L., 1994, Doing Community Operational Research with Multicultural Groups, *Omega, Intl. J. Mgmt. Sci.* **22**(6): 579–588.
Tsouvalis, C., and Checkland, P., 1996, Reflecting on SSM: the dividing line between 'real world' and 'systems thinking world', Working Paper nr 3 Centre for Systems and Information Sciences, University of Humberside.
Ulrich, W., 1989, Critical heuristics for social systems design, in: *Operational Research and the Social Sciences*, (Jackson, M.C., Keys, P., Cropper, S.A., eds.), p. 79–89, Plenum Press, New York.
Vahl, M., 1994, Improving mental health services in Calderdale, Report of the Centre for Systems Studies, University of Hull.
Waelchli, F., 1992, Eleven Theses of General Systems Theory, *Systems Research* **9**(4): 3–8.

Warfield, J., 1995, Spreadthink: explaining ineffective groups, *Systems Research* **12**(1): 5–15.

Zeeuw, G. de, 1995, Values, science and the quest for demarcation. *Systems Research* **12**(1): 15–25.

Zouwen, J. van der, 1996, Methodological problems with the empirical testability of sociocybernetic theories, unpublished paper presented at the 10th International Congress on Cybernetics and Systems in Bucharest (August 1996).

27

VIRTUAL SELF, VIRTUAL MIND, VIRTUAL WORLD: SUSTAINABLE FUTURE?

Elizabeth White

Texas Instruments
14222 North Dallas Parkway
#2098, Dallas, Texas 75240
Telephone: (972) 917-7078; Fax: (972)917-7179
e-mail:zzil@msg.ti.com

HOMO SAPIENS I

My hypothesis is that it is the emergent capacity for self-referencing in *Homo sapiens* that concurrently opened the potential for the emergence of "mind." The paradox is that it is, perhaps, these same highly evolved neural structuring mechanisms that allowed the emergence of self-referencing that, perhaps, lethally, constrain our ability to see beyond our own, personal, emergent, virtual world (White, 1992, pp. 58–60, 62–63).

I contend that it is the constraints inherent in these neural structuring mechanisms, evolved over eons from far simpler structuring mechanisms shared by other biological entities, mechanisms that allowed us to capture the concept of a virtual object now labeled "self"—and thus to gain an emerging capacity to see "self" "in relation to" other entities, virtual and concrete, and thus to begin to see and to build a virtual world (a software world) called "mind," that constrain us from seeing beyond the patterns of our own virtual worlds to the larger patterns our species as a whole is laying down in the concrete world.

This is true because inherent in these neural structuring mechanisms—in my own work I refer to these neural capturing/re-triggering mechanisms as Sensate Linking Mechanism Phenomenon (White, 1992)—is the capture of the emotional or affect component, critical for consistency in behavior orientation as *Homo sapiens'* behavior evolved to be less and less driven by genetic factors.

The affect component of these neural structure constellations, each containing the whole detail of specific experiences, ensures that each of our experiences of our personal world will be "felt" to be real, to be "the real world," in fact, we strongly tend to experience the whole of our own "real" world as the same as, as *identical* to, the whole of the concrete world. Thus, the emergent potential that we, as individuals, may be functionally blind in the largest sense to the concrete realities of the real world. Recent neural research

Systems for Sustainability, edited by Stowell *et al.*
Plenum Press, New York, 1997

supports my hypothetical Sensate Linking Mechanism Phenomenon, in particular the work of Joseph LeDoux (1996) on neural architecture.

Also, from Dennett, (1991, pp. 183–4) "...the plastic brain is capable of reorganizing itself adaptively...the process by which the brain does this is almost certainly a mechanical process...This is the first new medium of evolution: post-natal design fixing in individual brains...this capability, itself a product of genetic evolution...gives the organisms who have it an edge over their hard-wired cousins who cannot redesign themselves..."

From Ornstein, (1991, p.147) "These studies of the origins of decisions to act show...An unconscious decision center may decide to initiate an action, there is a period of time during which the conscious self can choose to stop the action..." On page 279 Ornstein says, "...it is an understanding of our mental system that may well provide the clues to those who wish to effect changes...it is clear that unless we understand our roots in ancestral worlds and...how our adaptations cling inappropriately now, we have no hope of changing. There will be no future for life unless we can take our own minds into our own hands and change in an appropriate direction."

I suggest a viable possibility exists of learning how we can use our virtual minds to design a concrete and sustainable future. In the concluding comments of *The Structure of Sociological Theory* (1991) Turner says, "...to the extent that the gap between micro and macro can be partially bridged, the analysis of the content of micro encounters and, then, an analysis of how they are aggregated and organized into the various meso-structures from which even larger macrostructures are built constitute a reasonable strategy for trying to link the micro and macro realms...Other perspectives have come, at least implicitly, to the same conclusion...my favorite approach...is to view each realm as a ...constraint on the other and then conceptualize how micro constrains macro, and vice versa. That is, how do the processes of face-to-face interaction constrain what is possible and viable in organizing populations of actors, and conversely, how does the existence of macrostructures constrain face-to-face interaction? These kinds of questions have been addressed occasionally...but none is well developed...What is needed, I believe, are more systematic efforts to model just how micro and macro processes set parameters for each other."

In *A Theory of Social Interaction* (1988) Turner concludes, "The goal of this book has been to change the nature of theoretical dialogue, to move away from philosophical questions...and toward figuring out what people actually do during interaction. Moreover, I hope that my eclecticism will also be emulated...we need to be more tolerant of, and receptive to ideas in what are usually considered incompatible approaches. Taken together these processes go a long way in isolating the key processes (author's note: neural structuring/re-triggering processes, White, 1992) involved in human interaction."

Fritjof Capra writing in the preface to *The Turning Point—Science, Society, and the Rising Culture* (1983, p.15) says, "What we need then is—a new vision of reality, a fundamental change in our thoughts, perceptions, and values. The beginnings of this change, of the shift from the mechanistic to the holistic conception of reality, are already visible in all fields...This new vision includes the emerging systems view of life, mind, consciousness and evolution..." From page 233, "Explicit reference to human attitudes, values, and life styles in future economic thought will make this new science profoundly humanistic. It will deal with human aspirations and potentialities, and will integrate them into the underlying matrix of the global ecosystem. Such an approach will transcend by far anything attempted in today's sciences, in its ultimate nature it will be scientific and spiritual at the same time."

Peter Drucker in *The New Realities, In Government and Politics/ In Economics and Business/ In Society and World View,* writes, " Almost a century ago, in the 1890's configuration (Gestalt) psychology first realized that we perceive...In governmental and business planning we increasingly talk of 'scenarios' in which a perception is the starting point. And, of course, any 'ecology' is perception rather than analysis. In an ecology, the 'whole' has to be seen and understood, and the 'parts' exist only in contemplation of the whole...Since Descartes, the accent has been on the conceptual. Increasingly we will balance the conceptual and perceptual. Indeed, the new realities with which this book deals are **configurations** and as such call for perception as much as for analysis: the dynamic disequilibrium of the new pluralisms...this book attempts as much to make us **see** as it attempts to make us **think**," (see proposed model, White, 1992, pp. 91–92).

Drucker states in the book's final paragraph, "...contemporary philosophers no longer focus on Kant's concerns. They deal with configurations—with signs and symbols, with patterns, with myth, with language. They deal with perception. Thus the shift from the mechanical to the biological universe will eventually require a new philosophical synthesis..."(see description Twin Corollary Theory, White, 1992, pp. 27–41).

Ilya Prigogine writing with Isabelle Stengers in *Order Out of Chaos,* 1984, says, speaking of Whitehead, p.95, "Thus for Whitehead the task of philosophy was to reconcile permanence and change, to conceive of things as processes, to demonstrate that becoming forms entities, individual identities that are born and die...he demonstrated the connection between a philosophy of *relation*—no element of nature is a permanent support for changing relations; each receives its identity from its relations with others—and a philosophy of *innovating becoming.*"

The Image, Knowledge in Life and Society is an extended essay written in 1956 by Kenneth Boulding in which he attempts a beginning for a unifying view of human behavior though seeking to understand the mechanisms governing individual perception, i.e. "the image."

He writes, "Although eiconics (his term for this proposed new discipline) as an abstract discipline falls firmly within the subculture of science...because no part of the image is really independent of any other part...It leads in the direction of a broad, eclectic, organic, yet humble epistemology looking for processes of organization rather than specific tests of validity and finding these processes in many areas of life and experience: in art, religion, and in the common experiences of daily life, as well as in science...It emphasizes communication and feedback as the great sources for orderly and organized growth; thus linking hands with both cybernetics and semantics. Most of all, perhaps, it brings the actor into the act... It represents, I hope, one small step toward the unknown goal of human history," p. 175.

Boulding mentions art as one of many sources in the search for a larger understanding of how perception influences our march into human history. The emergence of art, a minimum of twenty thousand years prior to the emergence of agriculture, is of possibly key significance to the evolutionary sequence in the emerging phenomenon of self-referencing/mind because the emergence of "art" may be fundamentally related to *Homo sapiens'* capacity 1.) to recognize patterns, 2.) to have perspective, 3.) to begin to be able to purposefully *choose* to recreate familiar patterns—first on a cave wall, later on a space of ground, and 4.) to, eventually, purposefully choose to create "new" patterns, of DNA, for example, or of a sustainable future.

The key I believe is in understanding how the mechanisms of neural structuring that allowed *Homo sapiens* the emergent capacity for self-referencing and mind, now constrain our ability to see beyond our own individual perceptual, virtual worlds—built of our own experience. These neural structuring/re-triggering mechanisms constrain our ability to see the larger patterns our species as a whole is generating, and lead us to fail to understand that to the degree our virtual world contains inaccurate information, now that our behavior impacts our biosphere at the meta level, to that extent do we threaten our own sustainable future.

REFERENCES

Boulding, K. E., 1956, *The Image, Knowledge in Life and Society*, University of Michigan Press, Ann Arbor Michigan.
Capra, F., 1983, *The Turning Point—Science, Society, and the Rising Culture*, Bantam, New York.
Dennett, D. C., 1991, *Consciousness Explained*, Little, Brown, and Company, Boston.
Drucker, P., 1990, *The New Realities, In Government and Politics/ In Economics and Business/ In Society and World View*, Harper & Roe, New York.
Ornstein, R., 1991, *The Evolution of the Way We Think, of Darwin, Freud, and Cranial Fire—The Origins of the Way We Think*, Prentice Hall, New York.
LeDoux, J.,1996, *The Emotional Brain: The Mysterious underpinnings of Emotionl Life,* Simon & Schuster, New York.
Prigogine, I., Stengers, I., 1984, *Order Out of Chaos*, Bantam, New York.
Turner, J. H., 1988, *A Theory of Social Interaction*, Stanford University Press, Stanford, California.
Turner, J. H., 1991, *The Structure of Sociological Theory*, Wadsworth Publishing Co., Belmont, California.
White, E., 1992, *Toward a General Model of Human Behavioral Systems*, Doctoral Thesis, UMI, Ann Arbor, MI.

28

CRITICAL THEORY, CARL JUNG, AND SYMBO-CONSTRUCTION IN SOFT SYSTEMS RICH PICTURES

A Seminar for Reflective Practitioners

Mark Campbell Williams

Business Faculty, Management Information Systems School
Edith Cowan University
Phone: (09) 273 8523; Fax: (09) 273 8754
Email: m.williams@cowan.edu.au

1. INTRODUCTION

SSM uses a technique of drawing pictorial metaphors termed 'rich pictures', to serve as aids in investigating 'ill-defined, real-world' problems (Hicks, 1994; Standing and Campbell Williams, 1993). Rich pictures often incorporate symbols or cartoon-like representations to point to key factors in the systems under investigation and to give a sense of the richness which seems to occur in most human situations. As I reported in an earlier paper (Campbell Williams, 1995b), I extend the idea of rich pictures to give pictorial metaphors. Although all metaphors have their limitations and can be confusing, I consider that they help me to convey the rich allusiveness, symbolism and sense of complexity in many human situations.

Hicks (1994, p. 235) commends rich pictures as being suitable for showing patterns, arrangements, connections and relationships in a way that often allows others to see a perspective of the whole, to gain a 'feel' of the overall shape of complex situations. According to Hicks, pictures, rather than written descriptions, are not only often more concise and easier to share with others, but also more clearly show vital links and interactions that may give rise to unexpected or unintentional consequences. The question I pose in this paper is whether or not rich pictures can be viewed in a similar manner to dream symbols, thus allowing the systems practitioner to be aware of unconscious agendas going on in the people and groups with whom s/he is consulting.

2. INSIGHTS FROM CRITICAL SOCIAL THEORY

From the late 1930s onwards, critical theorists have used and defended psychological foundations and the whole approach of being attentive to "the language of the unconscious" (Adorno cited in Held, 1980, p. 110). A fundamental tenet of critical theory is that both the rational and the irrational susceptibilities of the human condition need to be addressed in serious study (Adorno and Horkheimer, 1990; Marcuse, 1969; Held, 1980, p. 119).

Osborne (1992) uses metaphorical language to stress the importance of understanding the importance of psychoanalytic elements to critical theory: "the Frankfurt School felt they needed a wedding between Marx and Freud" (p. 35). Indeed, Habermas (1990) mentions that an inspiration for the work of the Frankfurt School was that "as early as the twenties, Western Marxism entered into a symbiosis with Freudian metapsychology" (p. 5). I think it important to point out that, even though I review the work of some critical theorists to introduce, and give some warrant for my attention to the unconscious, I do not use a Freudian psychoanalytic framework. Rather, I use a Jungian analytical psychological framework which, although acknowledging Freud's seminal insights, has its own discourse. Thus, I do not explicitly employ the insights or methods of the discourse of Freudian psychoanalysis. Rather than entering a Freudian psychoanalytic discourse, my interest in the unconscious is within the discourse about self-development understood from Jungian perspectives.

2.1. Jurgen Habermas

Habermas commends self-reflection as able to bring unconscious agendas to consciousness "in a manner rich in consequences" (1974, p. 23). Habermas states in a recent essay (1992) that Freud was able to "discover a new continent". What is this continent other than the continent of the unconscious? And how is the unconscious made rich in consequences through self-reflection?

There are inherent psychological and communitarian elements in Habermas' understanding of life-worlds, which includes the pre-rational aspects of unconscious knowing and communicating. For Habermas, self-reflection and a bringing to consciousness that which was unconscious is crucial to the individual as well as the group. More importantly than some other influences in the development of his theory, Habermas explains: "I have considered psychoanalysis, despite all the dire predictions, as something to be taken seriously" (Dews, 1986, p. 150). In his book *Knowledge and Human Interests* (1972, Chap. 10), he devotes a whole chapter to "Self-Reflection as Science: Freud's Psychoanalytic Critique of Meaning". Although he has not developed this early 1960's work on Freud's metapsychology (Dews, 1986, p. 165), Habermas looks to psychoanalysis as a model and a method for critical reflexivity and communicative action approaching an ideal speech situation (Young, 1989, p. 36). As Habermas (1971) states: "Psychoanalysis ... is a tangible example of a science employing methodological self-reflection. The birth of psychoanalysis opens up the possibility of arriving at the dimension that positivism closed off, and of doing so in a methodological manner that arises out of the logic of inquiry." (p. 214)

Habermas sees psychoanalysis as a model for the way in which the critical social theorist can act and, in general, the way that communicative action could proceed (Held, 1980, pp. 317–324). This exemplifies the *self-reflection* part of the reflective process which supplements *rational reconstruction,* a more objective reflection on the limits and constraints to knowledge. This process is similar to Bruner's understanding of human *reflexivity* "our capacity to turn around on the past and alter the present in its light, or to alter the past in the light of the present" (Bruner, 1990, p.109).

3. A JUNGIAN PSYCHOLOGICAL FRAMEWORK

Jung asserted that Freud, "by evaluating dreams as the most important source of information concerning the unconscious" (1989, p. 169) and by demonstrating empirically the presence of an unconscious psyche, made foundational insights in many important areas. In both his empirical research and his theory building, Jung relied on Freud's work (Segaller and Berger, 1989, p. 74).

However, Jung (1989) soon moved beyond what he called Freud's doctrinaire "monotony of interpretation" (pp. 152,153) of dream symbols as determined almost solely by sexual motives. Jung emphasised what Freud only partially admitted in his later work - that dreams are more than just heavily disguised recollections and fantasies dealing primarily with repressed deep emotional and infantile sexual reactions from early childhood (O'Connor, 1993, p. 161). The dream events are imaginary but are evoked by real events in the dreamer's life and relate to real needs. Some classes of dreams can re-enact traumatic recent events which would suggest a psychological attempt in fantasy to come to terms with reality (Bullock and Woodings, 1983). Moreover, Jung asserts that most dreams give messages from the unconscious in as graphic a way as possible for consciousness to take heed. As Jung (1989) says in *Memories, Dreams, Reflections*: "I was never able to agree with Freud that the dream is a *facade* behind which its meaning lies hidden - a meaning already known but maliciously, so to speak, withheld from consciousness. To me dreams are a part of nature, which harbours no intention to deceive, but expresses something as best it can." (p. 161)

For Jung, the character of most dreams reveals vital inner forces or psychological energies of the personality in the interface between consciousness and the unconscious (Sanford, 1989, p. 126). Jung accepted, but moved beyond, Freud's somewhat negative perspective to understand a creative and communicative function in unconscious symbolic communication. This is especially so in the way the unconscious uses dream symbols to communicate with the conscious mind. Different from Freud's problem-oriented dream work approach, Jung saw a creative function within the unconscious. While Freud saw the unconscious as a region of the mind where consciousness dumped unwanted impressions and memories, Jung viewed the unconscious as an autonomous second psychic centre with its own mysterious authority, capable of its own processes and communication with consciousness (Monick, 1987, p. 23). His focus was less on the psychological maturation problems (which is also encountered in dreams), being more on the development of mature individuals with their aims, aspirations and racial/cultural historical contexts giving potential meaning and dignity. Ultimately, Jung understood dream symbols as part of the interplay between psychological energies in the conscious and the unconscious, as part the human journey of finding a meaningful place in a purposeful universe.

4. EXAMPLE FROM MY TEACHING PRACTICE

From 1991 to 1993 I was involved in the teaching reform of a university business computing course. The essence of the reform was to encourage *open discourse* (a form of *communicative rationality*) by introducing teaching and learning strategies such as group work, a dialogical communication process in the tutorials and mass lectures, and making students keep personal learning journals. In such a manner, the basic idea of the reform was to encourage communication and discourse about the meaning and purpose and wider societal implications of business computing in addition to the narrowly technical aspects.

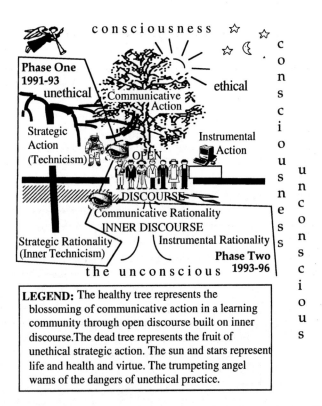

LEGEND: The healthy tree represents the blossoming of communicative action in a learning community through open discourse built on inner discourse. The dead tree represents the fruit of unethical strategic action. The sun and stars represent life and health and virtue. The trumpeting angel warns of the dangers of unethical practice.

Figure 1. Pictorial metaphor showing key elements and the phases of my research: the ethically flawed first phase, from 1991 to 1993, is represented by the 'dead tree' on the upper left of the diagram; the heuristic second stage, from 1993 to 1996, is represented by the 'rising to light' of virtue through inner discourse.

The first phase of my research, from 1991 to 1993, was an interpretive qualitative investigation with the implicit hypothesis that the teaching strategies would encourage communicative rationality and balance the dominating instrumental rationality. Ironically, in 1993, I came to understand that I had succumbed to a form of unbalanced and inappropriate instrumental rationality (a *strategic rationality)* in my conduct of the research in the sense that I had forcibly imposed the teaching strategies on the students and tutors and had not followed due ethical procedures. Thus, during the second stage of my research from 1993 to 1996, I conducted a heuristic and psychologically-oriented self-study (Moustakas, 1990) with the question "what was the underlying reasons for the ethical shortcomings of my flawed investigation of 1991 to 1993, and how could I address this?". As part of this heuristic research, I endeavoured to address my strategic rationality by engaging in an analytical psychological inner *discourse* as part of being a *reflexive practitioner*. Figure 1 gives a pictorial metaphor for the research process.

Depicted in Figure 1, the group of people in the middle of the picture represents the university business computing classes. The spaceman hanging in the dead tree represents my image of myself as teacher-learner-researcher in *Phase One* of my research, investigating open discourse and technicism in the classes of 1991 to 1993. The focus of my research in this phase is represented by the 'eye' next to the spaceman, and is directed only towards the outer dimension of technicism and open discourse in the computing classes. My heuristic research of 1993 to 1996, represented by the *Phase Two* area in the picture, illustrates the 'eye' of my research as observing both the inner and outer aspects of technicism and open discourse. The spaceman does have a space suit to keep him alive, but is cut off from others, from the sun and stars and earth and tree of life. He is under the warning of the avenging angel that unethical behaviour leads to undesirable consequences. The computer on the table represents an image of the way in which technology can be used a part of a legitimate instrumental action to assist in ethical human activity resulting from communicative action.

The question is whether or not this rich picture pictorial metaphor can be viewed as containing symbolic elements that can be interpreted in a Jungian framework as if it were a dream image. For the first time I now look a my picture from this perspective. What do I see? What is at the centre of the picture (an indicator of the unconscious central concern)? - a group of people in unity with the word 'discourse' or is it the 'mess' just above and obscuring the word 'open'? What is in the upper part of the picture (that which is in consciousness)? - an angel, a half sun, and moon and stars and the word 'consciousness'. What is in the lower regions of the picture (that which is in the unconscious) - is it a rectangle with the heading 'legend' or is it a funnel on top of the word 'unconscious' that is soon blocked by words and by a clutter of lines with only a picture of an eye allowing access to the upper regions? What does all this mean? Could it mean that I am still in the middle of my reflective practice but wholeness is being blocked by clutter and words? I need to talk this over with a group of colleagues—what better group than at the UKSS seminar that I will give in July 1997? I will report on the groups' response to these questions in a following paper.

REFERENCES

Adorno, T., and Horkheimer, M., (1992), *The dialectic of enlightenment,* Verso, London.

Barry, D., (1996), Artful Inquiry: A Symbolic Constructivist Framework for Social Science Research, *Qualitative Inquiry* 2(4):411–438.

Barry, D., (1994), Making the Invisible Visible: Using Analogically-based Methods to Surface Unconscious Processes in Organizations, *Organizational Development Journal* 12(4): 37–48.

Bruner, J., (1990), *Acts of meaning,* Harvard University Press, Cambridge, Mass.

Campbell Williams, M., (1995), *Using Soft Systems Rich Pictures in University Teaching-Learning,* Proceeding of the Teaching and Learning in Higher Education Forum, February, 1995, Edith Cowan University, Western Australia.

Dews, P., (Ed.), (1986). *Habermas: Autonomy and solidarity,* Verso, London.

Dieckman, E. (1993). A procedural check for researcher bias in an ethnographic report. *Research in Education,* 50(11), pp. 1–4.

Habermas, J., (1971), *Towards a rational society,* Heinemann, London.

Habermas, J., (1972), *Knowledge and human interests,* Heinemann, London.

Habermas, J., (1974), *Theory and Practice.* London: Heinemann.

Habermas, J., (1992), *Postmetaphysical thinking,* Polity Press, Cambridge.

Held, D. (1980). *Introduction to critical theory*, Polity Press, Cambridge.

Hicks, M., (1991). *Problem Solving in Business and Management.* Chapman and Hall: London.

Johnson, R. A., (1986), *Inner Work: Using dreams and active imagination for personal growth,* HarperCollins, New York.

Jung, C. G., (1989), *Memories, dreams, reflections,* Random House, New York.

Marcuse, H., (1969), *Eros and civilisation,* Allen Lane the Penguin Press, London. '

Monick, E., (1987), *Phallos: sacred image of the masculine,* Inner City Books, Toronto

Moustakas, C., (1990), *Heuristic research: Design, methodology and applications,* Sage Publications, Newbury Park.

O'Conner, P., (1993),*The inner man: Men, myth and dreams,* Pan Mcmillan, Sydney.

Osborne, R., (1992), *Philosophy for beginners,* Writers and Readers Publishing, NY.

Sanford, J., (1989), *Dreams: God's forgotten language,* Harper and Row, New York.

Segaller, S., and Berger, M., (1989), *Jung: The wisdom of the dream,* Weidenfeld and Nicholson, London.

Standing, C., and Campbell-Williams, M., (1993), *Methodogical pluralism in a rapidly changing IT environment,* Conference Proceedings of the International Federation of Information Processing Professionals Conference, August 1993, Parmelia Hotel, Perth, Western Australia.

Young, R., (1989), *A critical theory of education: Habermas and our children's future,* Harvester Wheatsheaf, Hertfordshire, U.K.

29

WHERE IS THE OBSERVER IN IT STRATEGY AND SYSTEMS?

Steve Armstrong[1] and Aidan Ward[2]

[1]Computing Department
Faculty of Maths and Computing
The Open University
Milton Keynes, England MK7 6AA
Tel: +44 1908 654056, Fax: +44 1908 652140
email: s.armstrong@open.ac.uk
[2]Antelope Partnership
9 Underhill Road
East Dulwich, London, SE22 0AH
Tel: +44 181-299-1399, email: antelope@antelope.win-uk.net

1. INTRODUCTION

Systems thinking has placed much stress on where the observer is relative to the observed system. In business organisations technical systems are usually held to be an objective domain which the IT strategist can deal with on the basis of his observations and his budgets: he is outside the system.

We propose that sustainable organisations must recognise the ways in which the IT strategist is part of the systems he plans. We interpret our data to show that organisations progressively dismantle the ability of individual members to ask the questions that count in finding survival strategies. IT systems are heavily implicated in the closing of organisational borders to important elements of learning.

We use results from complexity theory to form models of co-evolving organisations in competition and co-operation with each other. These models form the context for understanding the nature of sustainable strategies of all kinds and of IT strategies in particular. The importance of failure and crisis in continued learning and adaptation is connected to the concept of emergent strategy. Sustainability is in tension with operational stability.

Our case study data shows three important results:

1. IT Strategies can be maladaptive and require major crises to realign them
2. Changing the awareness of the planners changes the nature of the competition
3. The meanings of IT systems and IT strategies undergo rapid shifts

Systems for Sustainability, edited by Stowell *et al.*
Plenum Press, New York, 1997

From these results we show how to model observer effects on strategy development and how to assess which factors an organisation's strategy must be sensitive to. We show how alternative, skunkworks developments lay the foundations for major changes in strategic direction by responding to these factors.

Our research agenda is to map the sorts of interventions that can move IT strategies to more creative places with ways of managing the trauma.

2. LEGITIMATE AND SHADOW SYSTEMS

A focus on organisational sustainability requires some precision in describing what is sustained. All organisations have both a legitimate system for doing work and a shadow system which enables organisation members to circumvent the legitimate system to get their work done or to meet needs not provided for by the legitimate system (Stacey, 1996a).

2.1. Strategic Routes to Change

The legitimate system has a function in perpetuating the edifice of the organisation, as distinct from the organisation as an embodied process for meeting the needs of customers. A crisis will occur if the legitimate system is unable to track the changes in the market place. Either the owners of the legitimate system will initiate radical change (revitalisation) or de facto solutions will be adopted from the shadow system (renaissance). Each one of these "grand paths" for change can counter-invent the other (McWhinney, 1992); witness the fashions on the Internet.

2.2. The Role of IT in Change

If only because of its cost and its connections with the control functions of the legitimate system, IT tends to reinforce the legitimate system. Although IT has been consistently painted as a force for and a route to change in organisations, that change has typically been in automating and making efficient the existing business processes, i.e. consolidating the legitimate system. The fashion for business process re-engineering (BPR), with IT as a core, is a management "revitalisation" response to the legacy, but has to be seen as a process not as a solution (Armstrong, 1994).

2.3. Predictable Crises

The predictable effect of heavy investment in the legitimate system is that it is less able to track change and respond, which opens the system to more likely and larger crises; chaos is not far away (Prigogine and Stengers, 1985). BPR will lead to the need for more radical BPR.

3. SYSTEMS, BOUNDARIES, AND MEANINGS

The descriptions of our case studies below are already a problem because they are described as being "out there": the observer is outside the system. In both cases consultancy was being supplied to the organisations by one of the authors, who became a part of the dynamics (Boxer, 1991). It is now possible to ask about the strategic meanings of the dynamics, from the inside, and what sort of interventions affect them.

3.1. Dismantling the Ability to Ask Questions

A seemingly universal feature of organisations is that they progressively dismantle the ability of their members to ask crucial questions (Hinshelwood, 1994). Part of the meaning of organisational cultures is the set of issues that get taken up as assumptions: questioning these assumptions, for instance continued market leadership or the competence of the parent company, is taken as disloyalty and may result in ostracising or expulsion. From an individual perspective, the crucial questions cannot be formed in the mind, the mental space cannot be supported for the issues to be examined. There is emotional pain and threat in even looking at them.

This threshold of needing to overcome cultural prohibitions is the root of the need for revolutionary change rather than continued evolution and learning. The nature of IT systems is to reinforce, with economic arguments, the pre-existing tendency not to ask the questions that count. It is common for organisations to view IT opportunities as threats.

3.2. Multiple System Membership and Shifts in Meaning

On the face of it, self-organising shadow systems and an inability to ask questions are not compatible observations. In practice, there are overlapping groups of people in organisations, with each group exhibiting these effects. It may be as difficult for the members of a "skunkworks" development team to acknowledge the business logic of management attempts to curtail their work as for business managers to admit the potential of the work.

The implications of these dynamics are that what it is acceptable to think, and the meanings attached to particular policies and strategies do not change gradually but suffer sea changes following the fortunes of the groups competing for changes in meaning. In the security case study below the meaning of the existing IT strategy changed radically in the course of an hour's meeting, although the "runes" were there to be read from the start. Therein lies a difficulty, we find that meanings undergo refinement through negotiation for specific business requirements: "The more important the meaning is, the more likely things will go wrong" (Stamper, 1987).

3.3. Making Sustainable Sense

The focus for talking sustainable sense in an organisation about its IT strategy has to be an understanding of who the stakeholders are and what meanings the policies in the strategy are capable of having for them. If this sounds straightforward if lengthy, it must be remembered that the chronicler is always a stakeholder as well and must reflect inwardly as well as consulting with others in order to comprehend the full range of meanings. There will undoubtedly be resistance to certain meanings, there is always an unacceptable group of "outsiders".

Our interpretation of sustainability is the ability to maintain some sort of useful continuity or persistence through succeeding episodes of revolutionary change. What might this mean for IT strategies? Paradoxically, sustainable sense is available only by the ability to support parallel inconsistent or contradictory threads of meaning and development. There has to be scope for plural views expressed in plural, concrete strategies and someone, somehow, has to balance the cost of inconsistency with the cost of the legitimate system coming to dominate. The process of diversification and building consistent meanings across the organisation must remain a process. Innovation must be stimulated and harmonisation insisted on.

4. COMPETITION AND COLLABORATION

Modern organisations are typically in intense competition with their rivals but also engage in collaborative ventures with them. Rather than analyse the competitive position of an organisation as a basis for strategy formation, the dynamic response of the system of competitors to a given initiative must be assessed.

4.1. Dynamics of Strategic Choice

In making strategic choices organisations are attempting to address some future uncertainty. In IT strategy formation, they need to predict the future course of technology innovation and standardisation, as well as understand future business requirements. All these issues depend on the judgements made by other organisations, leading to feverish speculation.

Both competition for an edge in the market and collaboration to try and create stability are important strategic moves. Despite the effort put into planning, much strategy is emergent in the sense that ways of operating are created in the shadow system before the need for them is recognised by the legitimate system. With IT systems this can be a disaster, because a system created on a shoestring could then have a prominent role to play in the legitimate system.

4.2. Stakeholders and "Licence to Operate"

The context for work is always a set of stakeholders both inside and external to the organisation. Licence to Operate is a concept that without being perceived as contributing to something greater than their own preservation, organisations fail to prosper. Customer service is suddenly much more than a route to competitive advantage, it is an acknowledgement of a debt to the wider community.

Stakeholder analysis shows the web of concerns that must be dealt with to arrive at a viable path forward. The IT strategist will be a stakeholder in other people's webs. Change and strategic choice are interventions in these webs. Since each individual stakeholder is a member of the legitimate and shadow systems, both systems are important to consider. Consequently, a climate of fairness is a precondition on the path to effective change, which requires a new consistency from the leaders of change (Novelli, 1995).

5. CASE STUDIES

5.1. A Security-Based Strategy

This study concerns a new business set up to service a new part of the insurance market by an established insurance company. The new company bought an ancient mainframe package to run their business on during the start-up phase, valuing the tried, tested and low outlay aspects of this choice. Having established a market share they looked to strategy in two directions, their need for alliances with service providers in their insurance sector and their need to move their systems basis forwards which was already a problem with their instant legacy system.

The parent company was invited to provide consultancy support in developing a business and IT strategy and came up with a conventional three layer open systems strategy with a migration plan for moving existing systems into that architecture. The business strategy was explicit in terms of sales targets but vague around the nature of alliances. When the time came to implement a major system to support business development, the work was out-sourced to a vendor who would produce a system according to the IT strategic architecture. As the price was high, senior managers approached the parent company for advice on cheaper options.

In the meantime the parent company's development area had become so bureaucratic and moribund that it could not deliver systems at all, and a saviour had stepped forward with a technology fix solution that was capable of turning out solutions. So the advice given to the new business was to use this new technology, overturning all the business and architectural logic that had been built up. The vendor was dismissed and internal development began. The technology basis for business alliances disappeared in a stroke.

The need of both organisations to close themselves from the world, to prefer internal orthodoxy, no matter how inconsistent, to learning and growth stands out clearly. The actual strategy was one of political security. In contrast the parent company reached a crisis point where emergent strategy was accepted.

5.2. A Family-Based Strategy

The second case study is a high technology start up company in a sector experiencing phenomenal growth. The company grew from a core of six people to several hundred in five years. They make a product that has become a market leader in a specialist technical area and have used it as a passport to alliances with major industry players to produce investment stakes in ventures around the world.

The original software product was grown by technical experts in the application field and expanded rapidly according to demand from customers for additional features. It now consists of in excess of half a million lines of poorly structured code.

Four years ago this was recognised as an issue, and a group was started to redevelop the core of the product to make it more extensible. The redevelopment never achieved critical mass as the commercial imperatives to enhance the existing product kept enlarging the size and the seriousness of the task.

Another tack was taken two years ago when an attempt was made to improve the software development process to allow control to be taken of the product evolution. The same fate occurred on this project: the difficulty of meeting client demands and responding to commercial opportunities in the short term meant that investment in engineering discipline never reached critical mass. Investment in tools, training, consultancy, could scarcely have been higher but did not impact the emergent strategy except as distractors from the underlying business situation.

A third, potential avenue is a new company to do the development, formed by the key players. At the same time major investors have been found for what was a private company. The pattern that is dominating here is of the family group, where attachment to the family power structure is far more important than achieving a customer focused business process. A business crisis is looming which is forcing major structural adjustments to overcome the family loyalties: one of the available adjustments is to set up a new family!

6. INTERPRETATION OF CASE STUDIES

In both studies the IT strategy was dominated by shadow system issues that could not be dealt with effectively in the legitimate system. The official strategies could not be made operational. These emergent strategies were repressive of changes that were important to sustainability, and in that sense were maladaptive to the medium term concerns of the organisations. It requires a strong organisational process to mediate an effective strategy. The official strategy of the parent company in the first study was grossly maladaptive, even dysfunctional.

In the second study, the emergent strategy was fuelled by a perceived thirst for new features on the part of clients, competition is on the basis of the feature list. That awareness is being changed by a refusal of some clients to upgrade their systems and some problematic external audits. The organisation is in the process of changing its competitive stance.

The meaning of the official strategy in the first study suddenly changed from being in line with safe advice from the parent company to being a dangerously exposed expensive adventure. The dependency on the parent meant that questions about constancy of advice could not be asked. Similarly the strategy in the second study was actually cyclic in pushing for reform and then falling back on familial loyalties. Meanings were deliberately made complex in order to paper over the inconsistencies.

7. CONCLUSIONS

7.1. Shadow Side IT

IT departments are one of the last bastions of the view that issues can and should be resolved logically prior to investment. Development methodologies now acknowledge change and the need for rapid and low cost pushes, but they do not acknowledge their own role in the internal generation of multiple meanings.

7.2. Modelling the Stakeholder Map

The first step is to acknowledge and chart the map of stakeholders and their interests. This map describes what is possible and what will be regarded as a success, always a useful thing to know. The growth and success of the organisation is the fruitful interaction of the stakeholders, taking place over a wider range of issues and based upon a strong perspective on justice.

Strategy is a dynamic issue, not just because of external changes. Strategy and IT strategy must support the internal debates and the preservation of differing meanings as part of the "gene pool" of the organisation.

7.3. Detecting Emergent Direction

Organisations are both self-organising and in need of central control, in a tension governed by the environment and the members. Moving emergent direction from the shadow system into the legitimate system is a tricky business and demands early adjustment of the legitimate system to the new directions (Stacey, 1996b). This implies that the legitimate system is the source of authority, but not the source of life for the organisation, because of its incomplete coverage.

7.4. Managing Trauma

It is becoming commonplace to talk about the need to make mistakes. Here we stress that the nature of organisations is to generate a need for traumatic adjustments. The trauma is unavoidable given the nature of people's commitment to organisations and interventions will be designed to produce the trauma as part of a change: some BPR is a deliberate attempt to shake things up.

Avoidance or suppression of the issues is likely to be far more traumatic than an acknowledgement of the extent to which change is required and the depth to which people's previous assumptions and commitments are in need of revision. It is wiser to manage the trauma than avoid it. The dynamic of avoidance is a driver towards authoritarian legitimate systems which turns their members into interchangeable and dispensable objects. How many IT strategists can: maintain separate and inconsistent strategies; link them to separate and inconsistent business strategies; balance the interests of stakeholders and engage constructively in the very debate that makes the job so difficult? Sustainability means that the quality of the process is far more important than individual decisions and outcomes.

REFERENCES

Armstrong, S. and Ward, W. A., 1994, I've found the will. Now, what does it mean?, at: IEE Colloquium on Legacy Systems; barriers to business process re-engineering, London.

Boxer, P. and V. Kenny, V., 1991, The economy of discourses, *Human Systems Management,* **9**(4):205–224.

Hinshelwood, R. D., 1994, Attacks on the reflective space. Containing primitive emotional states, in: *Ring of Fire, primitive affects and object relations in group psychotherapy* (V. L. Schermer and M. Pines, eds.), pp86–106, Routledge, London.

McWhinney, W., 1992, *Paths of change*, Sage Publications, Newbury Park.

Novelli, L., Kirkman, B. L. and Shapiro, D. L., 1995, Effective implementation of organisational change, in: *Trends in Organisational Behaviour*, Volume 2 (C. L. Cooper and D. M. Rousseau, eds.), pp.15–36, Wiley, Chichester.

Prigogine, I. and Stengers, I., 1985, *Order out of chaos*, Flamingo, London.

Stacey, R. D., 1996, *Complexity and Creativity in Organisations*, Barret-Koehle, New York.

Stacey, R. D., 1996, 2nd ed, *Strategic Management and Organisational Dynamics*, Pitman, London.

Stamper, R., 1987, Semantics, in: *Critical issues in information systems research* (R. A. Boland and R.A. Hirschheim, eds.), pp.43–78, Wiley, Chichester.

30

A SYSTEMS VIEW OF TEACHING AND LEARNING

Technological Potential and Sustainable, Supported Open Learning

Simon Bell and Andrew Lane

Systems Department, Technology Faculty
Open University
Milton Keynes, MK7 6AA

1. INTRODUCTION – TEACHING AND LEARNING

The central theme of this paper is the current interest amongst educational institutions in moving from teaching to learning as their main paradigm and the implications which technology media have for unravelling the debate and influencing the resulting practice (for example see *Active Learning: Using the Internet for Teaching*, Number 2, July, 1995). A second theme is how we use language, metaphor and models to describe systems for teaching and learning and what is the role of technology in relation to these systems and vice versa. The final theme is that of moving from an analysis of individual technologies, to a synthesis of the educational ideas into a sustainable system. The movement towards learning and away from teaching is consistent with some of the long-standing traditions of education, particularly involving adults. Interestingly, this educational model should be conducive to the needs of students who are largely self-motivating and self-selecting in their absorption of educational products—a potential definition of the United Kingdom Open University student. In fact this is remarkably in line with the sentiments of the Open University's first Chancellor, Lord Crowther, who said that the OU is: Open as to people, Open as to places, Open as to methods, and Open as to ideas. The models set out in this section will be used as points of reference and comparison in the sections which follow. We will also develop our analysis in the light of three 'virtuous goals for education' ~ connectivity, co-operation, and creativity.

Systems for Sustainability, edited by Stowell *et al.*
Plenum Press, New York, 1997

2. CONVENTIONAL TEACHING

By the conventional paradigm for teaching we mean the traditional face to face teaching system. In terms of a systems view, conventional teaching can be seen as a series of discrete, hierarchically arranged sub-systems with a linear view of knowledge transfer from teacher to student. This is of course a generalisation but it is instructive in typifying the benefits and problems arising:

- Core benefits ~ the system can be seen as being 'humanised' with potential for close co-operation between teacher and student, support staff and student, student and student, etc. If properly designed, this multiple relationship or 'multiplex' system provides an excellent environment for effective feedback and support through monitoring, evaluation and assessment (Bell and Lane, 1996).
- Core problems ~ the system is idiosyncratic, being highly dependent upon individual 'style'. This extends to such issues as variability and quality of content, changes dependent upon the vagaries of individual lecturer's preferences, the ephemeral aspects of some courseware, and students becoming reliant on the teacher's views.

To finish this section we would like to suggest some metaphors to express the nature of the conventional teaching paradigm. We make use of metaphors here in order to provide images which offer humour and insight. The main value for them in the context of this paper is to make comparison with other educational systems. In developing our metaphoric comparison we consider the conventional education system against our three 'virtuous goals for education' - connectivity, co-operation, and creativity.

3. THE DISTANCE TEACHING MODEL

The distance teaching model is characterised by the production and delivery of specially designed courseware, particularly print materials. This material encapsulates the knowledge of the teacher into a (hopefully) accessible format for the learner. A systems view of this distance model also shows a series of discrete sub-systems, but arranged sequentially rather than hierarchically in terms of the communications and relationships between the participants.

- Core benefits ~ the system is not dependent upon individual style. There is non-variability of content and reduced problems of ephemeral materials as courses are produced to an 'industrial standard' and open to wider scrutiny and 'market testing'.

Table 1. Three Cs and metaphors in conventional education

Three Cs	Metaphors for the conventional education system
Connectivity	The Dorset countryside of patchwork fields (Variable, sustainable and interesting but lacking the machine efficiencies of the level landscapes of, for example, East Anglia).
Co-operation	The Pink Panther (A loner, brilliant but by good fortune, constantly on the verge of chaos)
Creativity	The 'art and crafts' movement in architecture. Middle class, middle England. Vernacular, homely and based upon a long-standing tradition.

Table 2. Three Cs and metaphors in distance education

Three Cs	Metaphors for the distance education system
Connectivity	Kansas wheat prairie. Highly connected in terms of technologies and ownership but lacking diversity and ecological richness
Co-operation	Chinese cultural revolution. Massive and obvious co-operation but enforced by systems of control which were too inflexible to allow individuality.
Creativity	Model T Ford. Creative inspiration in design but trapped in a treadmill production process

- Core problems ~ sometimes distance can be de-humanising in this system, with little room for co-operation between teacher and student, the two sides of the learning system or between student and student in a collegiate or community sense. The relationship between the greater number of participants are also largely single interest ones; and there is a poor environment for feedback and joint learning due to severe time delays (Bell and Lane, 1996).

Again, we have suggested some metaphors to describe the distance teaching model of education set against our 3 C's.

4. NEED FOR SUPPORTED OPEN LEARNING

The Open University has always tried to maximise the support to its students and prefers to use the term 'supported open learning' rather than 'distance teaching' (Rumble, 1989). Even so the scope for direct support between participants is limited while it is usually a single interest relationship. The Open University is therefore seeking to develop this 'supported open learning' and so move the distance teaching paradigm into a new era. Indeed we are seeking to make technologies the media whereby we can move on the educational debate and draw out the strengths of the two models we have discussed in overview so far. The authors believe that in the convergence of the two models we will find the emergence of themes for a new paradigm of supported open learning. Such a convergence, facilitated by technology, might provide higher education with advantages through linked benefits whilst avoiding the potential for the two sets of problems. To return to the analysis using extreme metaphors that we developed in sections 2 and 3, in this section we want to move on to synthesis. We developed these extremes from anecdote and common experience. The purpose of the current section is to develop the notions of combined virtues and achievable educational benefits. Taken in this format the two sets of metaphors can be seen as depicting extremes and generally un-likeable views if related to the process of higher education. Table 3 attempts to find the point of synthesis by drawing out the evident questions if we try to put the two models together.

5. TECHNOLOGY AND SUPPORTED OPEN LEARNING

In this section we put some technological flesh on the theoretic bones for supported open learning set out in section 4. Our focus is on the word 'supported', in fact possibly the best phrase is 'media-supported'. In discussing media we refer to at least three forms:

- Connective, electronic media working over a distance (phones, fax, Internet and e-mail).

Table 3. A model of convergence?

Three Cs	The convergence model
Connectivity	Sustainable via diversity of participants and use of technology to increase relationships?
Co-operation	Industrial levels of material of a standard quality delivered in an individualistic and personal manner?
Creativity	Familiar but challenging, unthreatening but dynamic?

- Co-operative, work-share media (groupware such as Lotus Notes but also linked suites of software such as Microsoft Word running via Microsoft Mail on Internet).
- Creative media (multi-media tools such as Macromind Director).

The core of the three and the most vital aspect is the electronic communication medium. It is via this medium that the others come into effective use. We focus on this medium in what follows. When addressing the issue of electronic media, the current centre of interest in Internet products is the World Wide Web (WWW). Sangster (1995:7) has argued: "WWW has the potential to alter permanently the way in which academics teach and students learn". Although Sangster adds little to demonstrate how this is possible, Pickering (1995) has added a useful critique. Relating his thinking primarily to Illich's (1970) notions concerning the need to deschool society. Pickering sets this out as meaning " In Deschooling Society Ivan Illich sought to expose the oppressive side of formal education as it had come to function in the context of the developed nations of the west around the 1960s. He felt that with the technological resources education could become learning rather than teaching. The resources he required but could not find at that time were very much like what the Internet either does or may very soon come to offer". (1995:9), he develops two models of learning which conform in a generalisable manner to those which we have set out as being 'conventional' and 'supported open learning'. In conventional terms Pickering reviews the learning process as having four features:

- Those to be educated ~ generally speaking the young.
- Those who educate ~ generally speaking older people.
- Skills and knowledge itself.
- Practices that facilitate learning and the achievement of educational objectives.

In the educational paradigm Pickering offers, these fourfold principles can be reformulated as follows:

- Who are to be educated? This question envisages a response which is broadening from the young to the old.
- Who will educate? The response which Pickering comes up with is the "Internetuals". These are informal groups of teachers/ learners ~ "fellow browsers in the cybernetic library", the co-learners (1995:10).
- Skills and knowledge. Pickering argues that the "net-base" will be the curriculum to be organised by the learner.
- Practices that facilitate learning and the achievement of educational objectives. With distance learning media there is no going to school ~ the net is the library and the classroom.

In de-schooling society great freedoms are possible and Pickering does go on to set a counter argument in which it can be argued that this utopian model might just apply to white, male, individuals in the west. Of course we are only in the early stages of understanding the barriers involved in the use of the Internet ~ from getting lost to cultural, geographic and economic boundaries to learning.

Building on the positive aspects of Pickering's thinking, the single feature of greatest importance to the authors is the potential empowerment of the learner to develop multiple relationships between co-learners (students, tutors and academics) beyond individual courses, programmes, faculties and disciplines. With so much of the world's information already in a digital format and with access to distance media, technology invites research collaboration and 'the nomadic workplace', where place of work is not of importance but, critically, working relationships are. This is a point also made strongly by Brown and Duguid (1996), where they argue that a university environment should:

- "Enable students to engage in open learning, exploration and knowledge creation.
- Simultaneously, to provide the resources to help them work in both distal and local communities.
- Offer them the means to earn exchangeable, equivalent credentials for work done in class, on-line, or through hand-on experience"

How does the challenge of the Brown and Duguid vision relate to the questions set out in Table 3? The first question was: Sustainable via diversity and technology? This was specifically related to the matter of *connectivity*. In our supported open learning model we are seeking to make effective use of the Internet facilities to bring learners and teachers together. Current experience at the Open University is reflected in the development of the technology course T102 *Living with Technology* where the FirstClass electronic mail system is being used by over 4,000 students.

The second question was: Industrial levels of standard quality delivered in an individualistic and personal manner? Related to *co-operation*, this question is approached in terms of the responsiveness of the learning system to provide a high quality educational product where (at a location of the student's choice), when (providing flexibility over the time of study) and in (the media format) which is most accessible to the learner. These have been long-term policy goals of the Open University since its foundation (see Footnote 1). Technology facilitation means that the University is trying to improve the 'personal' approach via a range of strategies, e.g. course T102 providing students with modem access to conferencing and mail systems; course THD204 *IT and Society*, providing CDROMs of library material as well as conferencing and mail systems; the Knowledge Media Institute at the Open University working on the 'Virtual Summer School' (where students participate from home rather than attending a residential campus). All these items help the student to enter the multiple interest relationships evident within a conventional University atmosphere and collegiate culture whilst remaining in their homes.

The third question was: Familiar and challenging, unthreatening and dynamic? This arose most specifically in the context of *creativity*. True multimedia in terms of learning material delivery is linked here to effective student practice with an emphasis on a community of learners supporting each other. In this sense the individual creativity of the teacher is rapidly and directly involved with students rather than being once or twice removed and delayed. Developments in terms of the Open University's electronic conferencing systems again provide opportunities for this question to be responded to effectively (Jennison, 1996).

An aspect of the system which we have not discussed is that of contemplative reflection (the fourth C). Contemplative reflection on the impact of such technologies and systems on learning processes provides the authors with an interesting comparison with the consumerist (a negative C?) view of educational products where little thought is given to such impact, and which sadly characterises much of current educational planning. The aim of this paper has been to stimulate some of that contemplative reflection.

REFERENCES

Bell, S. and Lane, A. (1996) From Teaching to Learning: Technological Potential and Sustainable, Supported Open Learning. International Workshop on Europe and the Developing World in the Globalised Information Society, 17–19 October 1996, Maastricht, 30 pps.

Brown, J. S. and P. Duguid (1996). Space for the Chattering Classes. *Times Higher Education Supplement: Multimedia Features*, 10/5/96, pps iv-vi, London, Times Newspapers.

Illich, I. (1970). *Deschooling Society*, Calder and Boyars, London.

Jennison, K. (1996). COSY takes the distance out of distance learning: the computer-mediated student campus, Unpublished report, Open University, London region.

Pickering, J. (1995). Teaching on the Internet is learning. *Active Learning: Using the Internet for Teaching*, Number 2, pps 9–13.

Rumble, G. (1989). "'Open Learning', 'Distance Learning', and the Misuse of language." *Open Learning* 4(2): 28–36.

Sangster, A. (1995). "World Wide Web - what can it do for education?" *Active Learning: Using the Internet for Teaching*, Number 2: pps 3–8.

31

FREEING LIFELONG LEARNING SYSTEMS FROM TEACHING SYSTEMS THINKING

Death to Pedagogy?

Sylvia M. Brown

Open University Business School
Milton Keynes, MK7 6AA, United Kingdom

1. INTRODUCTION

Forms of state-provided education increasingly are questioned. Concerns are not confined to need for adaptation to changing economic and demographic circumstances; change proposals to address alleged inadequacies of education systems also attract criticism. Education is possibly the most salient current political issue in Europe (Tuckett, 1996), as it is elsewhere, for example in South Africa. This paper cites some of the factors combining to place pressure on both Adult Education (A.E.) and Higher Education (H.E.) in U.K. before sampling pessimistic and optimistic views of their consequences, particularly for knowledge acquisition and concept attainment. Whilst this paper is based on U.K. experiences, it is hoped that colleagues in other countries will take up some of the issues raised in a debate on what can be retained, what needs to be changed and what invented. It is hoped that some old ideas will be "de-railed" sufficiently to allow thought to proceed on new tracks - or off the tracks.

2. PESSIMISTIC SCENARIOS FOR HIGHER AND ADULT EDUCATION IN THE 21ST CENTURY

Current pressures on Higher and Adult Education, when projected, may produce dismal future scenarios. For example, Keep (1992) and Ranson (1993) express concerns about a strengthening "marketization" thesis (that market forces can solve all perceived deficiencies of the public sector) that has resulted in undue emphasis on the measurable. Some writers fear increased authoritarian control, others the potentially censoring effect of student power on the curriculum. Some of the pressures are mapped below.

Scott (1993) projects current U.K. policies into a discussion of the 21st century university in pragmatic terms. On this view, a two-tier, divisive, teaching versus research sys-

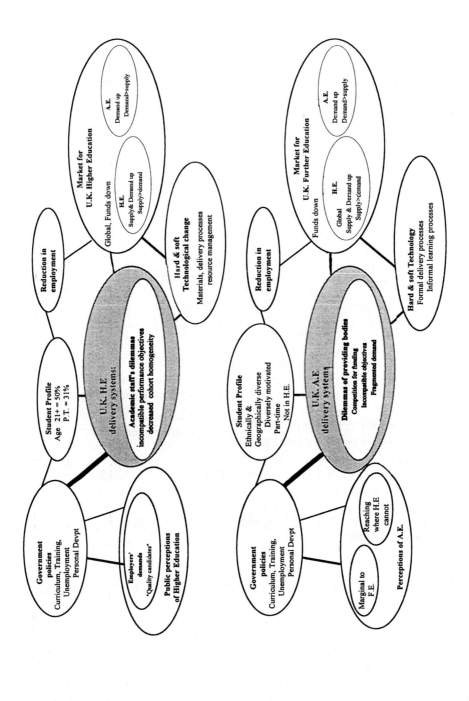

Figure 1. Some pressures on U.K. higher and adult education.

tem will emerge, with "massification" of the former. A larger percentage of the U.K. adult population with access to H.E is not democratic good news, however, but totalitarian bad news. Very large teaching institutions with larger cohorts will provide fewer, standardized modules. "Bidding up" and reduced employment will accelerate "Credentialization", legitimating current U.K. political ideology for the whole education system to become "hard-wired into wealth creation", reified in The National Curriculum and NVQs and resulting in loss of both educational integrity and the Great Traditions, including the scientific tradition.

Is this too black a view? Students will, after all, be able to "pick & mix" course elements and use customised learning materials to make the most of reduced time-on-task and their Student Charters may defend them against easily measurable shortfalls such as non-return of grades.

It could be worse. Non-vocational courses probably will be loan-funded and since vocational development "should" be the employer's responsibility, the increasing pool of unemployed can be denied access altogether. Face-to-face delivery systems could suffer very badly. At the limit, massive cohorts could be issued with materials and instructions, told to teach each other (but not trained to do so); lecturers would lecture (individual tutorial support already has almost disappeared). Active "Effort after meaning" would give way to passive input-to-memory. Assessment would be mechanical, e.g. by multiple-choice, and would be of short-term retention of "what had been taught". No one would be interested in "what had been learned". Qualifications would abound, huge amounts of money would have been spent and *no-one would know whether anyone emerging from the system had been educated*. This is "System1" education - a process to increase the national stock of qualifications. (Brown 1993)

Positive efficiency relationships of benefit to the state, to industry or to the individual are unlikely, i.e. between effort in and value out. Known to be necessary conditions for learning but likely to be missing from a "massified" teaching system are learning how to learn, active, experiential learning, appropriate feedback loops (amongst other Mastery Learning System elements) and contextualization to produce knowledge and understanding. Comprehension (of materials to be learned) depends on abilities to draw inferences and form hypotheses based on prior knowledge. (e.g. Anderson & Ortony, 1975; Block, 1971, Kolb, 1993, Schank & Abelson, 1977). However, finding out individual students' starting-points and "building bridges" would be logistically impossible and whilst pre-tests (especially if also mechanical) may address "concept mastery" (recall when cued) but do not tap "concept ownership" (ability to extrapolate to new applications/situations). What has been retained from what has been taught may be only "inert knowledge", (Bereiter, 1984 Bransford; 1989) not "learning with understanding". (Gardner, 1991; Perkins, 1992)

Peer teaching could assist, *if* supplemented by "expert" feedback, (Chiesi et al 1979, Brown 1993) but the requisite number of experts is unlikely, given the 'Bad eclecticism' of modern curricula (e.g. Youngman, 1986), whereby principles from different disciplines are combined into various "metatheories", depending on local and contextual needs rather than their coherence. (Mackie, 1981, Squires, 1982). Bad eclecticism and lack of prior knowledge combine to place a huge "de-bugging" load on the student trying to form an information processing strategy for admitting some of the material to memory; unsure of what is most important and how to cope with counter-intuitive concepts, rates of processing go down and comprehension failure up (Brown, 1978).

Apart from the potential ineffectiveness of such teaching systems, among other possible adverse consequences of a "massification" model is coerciveness. The controlling nature of teaching systems has been debated by radical thinkers from before Freire to David Deutsch and will not be discussed here but important to note is that belief in "The Pedagogic Fallacy" ("Teaching causes learning") may gain strength as teaching systems become further removed from learning systems under the twin banners of massification and vocationalisation.

3. A PESSIMISTIC VIEW OF THE ROLE OF PEDAGOGY, ITS AIMS, METAPHORS, AND SKILLS

The nineteenth century pegagogic tradition can be regarded as an aberration. Earlier, the Socratic method had assumed latent cognitive abilities; medieval studies aimed to develop the spiritual and intellectual powers of candidates e.g. how to deduce and induce, how to argue. Educere took precedence over educare. Granted, there was not then so much text available to be read thoughtfully and knowledge was not as compartmentalised into "Subjects".

An assumption of post-medieval pedagogy was that all learners need the help of subject-teachers. On no account must novices be let loose *in* a knowledge domain - undigested, direct knowledge is too terrible for most mortals; the territory where it is found is too vast and they might lose their way. Students' become dependent as autonomous use of skills and strategies atrophies. The following figure depicts the nineteenth century traditional didactic approach to pedagogy to which "massification" might have to resort, for logistical reasons.

4. PESSIMISTIC SCENARIOS FOR ADULT EDUCATION IN THE 21ST CENTURY

In U.K., Adult Education formerly was in the liberal, humanistic tradition of lifelong learning systems for personal growth and enhanced life-chances, i.e. very close to System 3 education. Currently, at policy level, needs of lifelong learners (in this context U.K. adult learners and part-time students) are marginalised in an H.E./A.E. system modelled for school leavers on undergraduate courses (Tuckett, 1996); learning to enjoy learning has been sacrificed even at primary school level in favour of drills for the Na-

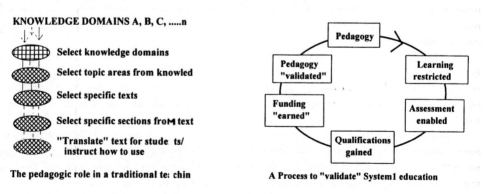

Figure 2. The role of pedagogy in 'System1' education.

tional Curriculum, (Hyland, 1994); non-vocational learning has been stigmatised as a parasitic drain on resources more properly devoted to "the skills crisis" (Lawlor, 1988). Local Authorities' responsibilities for A.E. compete for funding with other local services; the prevailing ethos is that adult learners, not Government, should pay for anything not resembling vocational training, for which employers should pay. All this could result in entrepreneur- and/or learner-organised A.E. provision only for the most advantaged learners, i.e. those that need it least. It is questionable how espoused aims for a lifelong learning system might be served under such conditions, depending on whom and what you think it is for - Ulrich's boundary questions (1987) are pertinent. Various interpretations of "lifelong learning systems" appear in the literature. A popular political version is "Recurrent Education", for which read "Career Updating"; re-skilling is implied more often than skill refreshment. There are exceptions; in Scandinavia and South Africa, for example, the rhetoric of equal opportunities, redress for earlier deprivation of access and personal growth still is heard more frequently than in U.K. (Edwards et al 1996, NCHE 1996). Given the accelerating pace of social change, the changing structure of organisations, reduced employment and growing emphasis on the flexible, increasingly peripatetic "knowledge worker", it is surprising that more attention is not being paid to individuals' learning needs. It would be naive to suppose that the current U.K. political juggernaut might be turned easily, given the weight of inertial myth behind it, so the question for those interested in wide access to quality higher education becomes either how to develop additional system options or how to "work the system"; are there any grounds for optimism?

5. A MORE OPTIMISTIC VIEW

"Lifelong learning" need not be equated to regular work-skills up-dating; business corporations already are sponsoring personal development programmes with no obvious, immediate, direct payoff. Undoubtedly, electronics and telecommunications have created unprecedented freedoms of access to knowledge, including thoughts and perspectives as well as data. The much maligned television has increased vocabularies as well as general knowledge among passive learners; electronic opportunities for active learners are extensive. An important point is that the greater proportion of all human learning is not formal, didactic education and that newer media can enable the many forms that learning takes. These include incidental learning (having one's memory impinged upon unconsciously until some stimulus prompts recall of that which one was not aware one knew) and informal learning (for example a child "helping" its mother) as well as auto-didacticism - ultimately autonomous acquisition of fittedness to teach oneself.

Whilst "experts" usually are needed if learning-with-understanding is to take place in a formal system (Chiesi et al 1979), traditional "sieving and channelling" are inappropriate means to offer the active, adult learner who has learned how to learn - at least once past the learning to learn phase. How, therefore, might appropriate facilitation be provided for the 21st century?

Some multi-media delivery systems have remained with the "sieve" model but there are also technological attempts to liberalise education, e.g. to present a knowledge domain as an "adult play-pen" (Harnden and Stringer, 1993). Domain elements, held on CD Rom, are linked by multiple pathways and the learner is free to explore - but only inside the "pen". However, the domain and the risk could be extended, even to the electronic Galaxy. What the learner then needs is a survival kit. In it are a set of maps, a compass, the address of a consul and/or a local custodian, i.e. means to know the domain exists, the location of the domain in relation to others, means of access, means to explore, someone to explain the local mores, get the voyager out of jail and safely home and *a native speaker of the language to explain what s/he has found.*

This creates two main roles for facilitators. The first is as trainer in survival and need not be domain-specific; the second is as domain expert, in this version much more highly expert than most tutors currently are. Learners would pass their deconstructions of what they had found within the domain through feedback loops allowing comparison with those of the expert and those of other learners. Dialogues would replace monologues. The learner would set and pursue the learning agenda. S/he can decide to travel or stay at home at any point throughout a lifetime of learning.

Also possible is guided, 'System2' education for concept ownership, (e.g. "A process to produce owners of transferable concepts and principles"). Orienteering might be a good metaphor for the educational elements in vocational versions of System2 (supplemented by training and competence assessment, whereby learners must pass through certain checkpoints but are free to choose routes. Domain custodians would need to set the checkpoints, supply the maps and compasses. Accrediting bodies would collaborate with appropriate custodians and/or might be such. Custodians as facilitators would need to reside in their domain in order to become and remain expert but they would also need to travel around their domain and the Galaxy as learners.

Radicals can applaud this model as less coercive, liberals as enabling fully realised people, academics as allowing pursuit of domain obsessions, learners and the body politic as allowing them fuller civil rights; the answers to most of Ulrich's boundary questions might become " the learners should choose". Systems persons might like the system because it can be both viable and self-sustaining. Teachers and Departments of Education might seize the moment gratefully or be enraged at the loss of their enterprise, depending on their commitment to either learning or teaching systems. Resistance to change might be encountered but it could become "sidelined" as the system evolved inexorably anyway.

Governments with reactionary and/or totalitarian ideologies might be less enthused; this system has the potential to escape state control entirely, which is why Anarchists might approve. There might be tax-reduction opportunities; since there could be free, global market competition amongst providers and the whole state education provision could become reduced to the basic literacy/numeracy, "learning how to learn" and "survival skills" elements, hence financial transactions could be transferred to learners and facilitating entities. Distanced as it can be, even "massification" is enabled with less reduction in educational integrity than in the pessimistic model above. Of the two political extremes, free market competition may be a greater threat to equality of educational opportunity than totalitarian control but the chief limiting factors are practical ones, e.g. access to hardware and training support.

There has been no space to discuss the profound implications for assessment and accreditation systems; whilst they are traditional elements in any teaching system, not only their processes but the need for their very existence is questionable as elements in some versions of a viable, sustainable lifelong learning system in a largely unwaged society.

No answers are offered or recommendations made here; much thought, development and examination of feasible possibilities is needed before coherent new education policies and systems to support them can emerge but these tasks need not (and will not?) delay the emerging potential. What this paper has attempted to do is to float an idea, that of a paradigm-shift, and to stimulate amongst stakeholders in education systems both optimism and problem-solving activity, including more radical scenario writing.

REFERENCES

Anderson, R.C., and Ortony, A., 1975, On putting apples into bottles: A problem of polysemy *Cognitive Psychology* **7**, 167–180.

Bereiter, C., 1984, 'How to keep thinking skills from going the way of all frills'. *Educational Leadership* **42**75–77.

Block, J.H., (ed.), 1971, *Mastery Learning; Theory & Practice* Holt, Rinehart & Winston Inc. NY

Bransford, J.D., Stein, B. S., Shelton, T.S. and Owings, R.A., 1981 'Cognition and Adaptation: The importance of learning to learn' in J Harvey (ed.) Cognition, *Social Behaviour and the environmant*, Hillsdale NJ: Lawrence Earlbaum Associates.

Brown, A.L., 1978, 'Advances in learning and instruction', *Educational Researcher* **23** (8) 4–12.

Brown, S.M., 1993, 'Teaching 'Behavioural Science' to Business Undergraduates: Delivery of Qualifications or Enabling Concept Mastery?' unpublished PhD Thesis.

Chiesi, H.L., Spilich, G.J., and Voss, J.F., 1979, 'Acquisition of domain related information in relation to high and low domain knowledge', *Journal of verbal learning and verbal behaviour* ch 181, pp 257–274.

Edwards, R., Hanson, A., and Raggatt, P., 1996, *Boundaries of Adult Learning* London & N.Y. Routledge/OU Press

Gardner, H., 1991, *The unschooled mind*, N.Y. Basic Books.

Harnden, R.J., and Stringer, R., 1993, 'Theseus - A model for global connectivity" in Stowell F et al 1993 (eds.) *Systems Science. Addressing Global Issues* NY & London, Plenum.

NCHE, 1996, *A Framework for Transformation* The Research and Mangement Agency, South Africa

Hyland, T., 1994, *Competence, Education and NVQs* London & N.Y, Cassell Education.

Keep, E., 1992, 'Schools in the marketplace? - Some problems with private sector models' in Wallace G (ed.) *Local Management of Schools: Research and Experience.* Clevedon: Multilingual Matters.

Kolb, D., 1993 'The Process of Experiential Learning' in Thorpe M. et al (eds.) *Culture and Processes of Adult Learning* London: Routledge/O.U. Press.

Lawlor, S., 1988, *Away with LEAs* London: Centre for Policy Studies.

Mackie, K., 1981, 'The application of learning theory adult education to adult teaching', Nottingham:Dept. of Education, Univ. of Nottingham.

Perkins, D., 1992, *Smart Schools: Better thinking and larning for every child.* N.Y: The Free Press.

Ranson, S., 1993, 'Markets or Democracy for Education?' *British Journal of Educational Studies* **41** 333–51.

Scott, P., 1993 'The idea of the university in the 21st century: a British Perspective' *British Journal of Educational Studies* **41** 4–25.

Schank, R.C., and Abelson., R.P., 1977, 'Scripts, plans goals and understanding', Lawrence Erlbaum.

Squires, G., 1982, 'The analysis of teaching' *Newland Paper 8*, Hull: Dept of Adult and Continuing Education, Univ. of Hull.

Tuckett, A., 1996, 'Scrambled eggs: social policy and adult learning' in Raggatt et al (ibid).

Ulrich,W., 1987, 'Critical heuristics of social systems design' *European Jnl. of Operational Research* **31** 276–283.

Youngman, F., 1986, *Adult education and socialist pedagogy,* London:Croom Helm.

32

EVALUATING A LEARNING ORGANISATIONS INITIATIVE

In Search of New Approaches

Sylvia M. Brown

Open University Business School
Milton Keynes, MK7 6AA, United Kingdom

1. INTRODUCTION

During organisational change, whilst practitioners legitimately may resist undue problemetization and argue for "just getting on with it", the research role is to try to understand processes and outcomes and to interpret how and why these occurred. The inherent ambiguities of the Learning Organisations (L.O.) concept (e.g. Brown 1996) will not be discussed here. This paper shares some of the conceptual dilemmas and practical difficulties associated with attempting to evaluate a "Learning Organisations" change initiative in a large and complex organisation.

2. LEARNING ORGANISATIONS THEORY

Some dilemmas are theoretical: what conceptual base was espoused by the interventionist, what did the client understand, what should underpin the evaluation work and how should the evaluating researcher proceed if they are all different? Four main groups of L.O. "Theorists" can be identified:- "Evangelists", like Senge himself (concept-focused, mostly American), "Philosopher-Clerics" (like the Learning Organisations group at the Open University, trying to interpret the Holy Writ), "Bandwagonners" (e.g. academics seeing a new market niche and publishing under a new label, whether they a) understand the concepts or b) have anything to say or not) and "Practitioners" (a miscellany including drowning Human Resources people grasping at the latest straw, academics struggling to get operational axioms out of dogma and consultants along the usual range from honest brokers to charlatans.) It is unsurprising that grasp of and/or acceptance of the original Senge concepts (1990) varies, given the wide range of perspectives.

Systems for Sustainability, edited by Stowell *et al.*
Plenum Press, New York, 1997

3. LEARNING ORGANISATIONS PRACTICE

In addition to a range of conceptual viewpoints upon which design of an intervention might be based, approaches to operationalisation also vary. Public accounts of interventions labelled "Learning Organisation" describe very different approaches and foci of attention (e.g. Economist Conference, 1996). The concept may be seen variously as new or no more than a cynical new marketing label for old products. A collection of change processes may be subsumed to a "Learning Organisations" programme or L.O. can be one plank in a raft labelled something else. Change may be driven through vigorously or "seeds" planted and nurtured. The common trigger is business necessity, linked to de-layering, re-skilling for new hard and soft technology and "more for less". At the executive team level, introduction of a programme called "Learning Organisation" often is taken as sufficient justification for claiming that the enterprise is one.

At one end of the spectrum are initiatives that could equally well fly the banner of TQM, BPR, Customer Focus, Team Building, Empowerment or Training Strategy; these tend to be somewhat shorter term and survival focused. For example, large numbers of new entrants to the fast food market caused McDonalds to move from a product-led to a customer-oriented business strategy in order to remain competitive. The change process was dominated by setting up systems to gather, transmit and respond quickly to customer information. This generated organisational training needs, which were met. The focus was not and is not upon, e.g., Personal Mastery in terms of individual growth and employability but upon organisational efficiency. No pejorative judgements are implied here; McDonalds is hugely successful and is not alone in its equation of "learning" with "training". However, it is doubtful whether Senge or any of his group at M.I.T. would recognise all, if any, of the five disciplines in action.

At the other extreme are long-term programmes where it is recognised that new processes in a new culture require personal, as well as organisational "journeys". Leaders of the L.O. intervention at ICL, for example, whilst acknowledging the business necessity honestly, also recognise that transitions may be difficult, even painful, and that people need help and support, both to begin and along the way, i.e. that training and learning opportunities are not enough.

For those coming to Learning Organisations concepts for the first time, it is important to realise that their first contact, perhaps via an article in a popular journal or at a conference, may be unrepresentative of either the field of practice or the original concepts.

4. LEARNING ABOUT A PARTICULAR LEARNING ORGANISATION INITIATIVE

At the enterprise under review, L.O. was one initiative amongst many introduced by a charismatic CEO with a number of objectives, ranging from obtaining lucrative contracts to culture-change. His conception of the L.O.s programme was still the subject of research at the time of writing but actions taken suggested creation of small islands of entropy that would grow, permeate the organisation and become self-sustaining. The consultant (also a charismatic, somewhat messianic figure) "gave permission" for personal responsibility for organisational problems and opportunities and "sowed seeds". The evaluators were not the change agents, hence, it was hoped, less likely to be biased towards a particular conclusion. The sanctioning executives were, in any case, concerned to avoid criteria connoting "success" or "failure"; there were also resource constraints, hence the design had to be "quick and dirty". For practical reasons, the work was split into two phases. The first took place as the consultancy contract of the change facilitator was running out, the second approximately one year later. Between these two phases the CEO was replaced by a new incumbent whose strategy development method was "design and implement" and whose personal style was less high-profile. Each approach (and each managerial style) had its supporters within the enterprize; for example, whilst the H.R. director supported the first CEO's permeation approach conscientiously, he found an implementation-evaluation model easier to conceptualize, as did the continuing deputy CEO.

5. ELUSIVENESS OF "WHAT WE REALLY WANT TO KNOW" IN A L.O. EVALUATION

The executive wanted to know if the initiative had been worth it. Rigour is difficult in any studies of complex, dynamic organisations; where the conceptual base itself is "fuzzy", as is the case with "Learning Organisation", the difficulty is amplified, for example in terms of operationalisation of "What we really want to know". A major element in the intervention had been creation of a "diagonal slice" team of "Networkers", who, it was hoped, would influence others. Their facilitator claimed to have avoided the language of L.O.s (also seen at ICL as an hazard) and that there was no attempt to teach participants L.O.s concepts but to learn by doing - "...give them a tool to use that will lead to new ways of thinking" (Senge 1994). Use of the L.Os language register was but a weakly valid option as an evaluation measure, therefore.

During the first phase, we thought we wanted to know about "permeation". The metaphor that suggested itself was a spreading inkstain; how far had the stain spread? At the second phase we expected in addition to be interested in "stickability" - had the "inkstain" faded, changed colour or become permanent? What would be our best evidence of either of these is not obvious, e.g. what counts as Personal Mastery - new ways of doing or new ways of perceiving what is already done? Should we focus on a very small, particular aspect, such as the nature of the invitation to "join the L.O.s dance"? Should we test some of Senge's hypotheses, on the importance of "preparing the soil, developing the seeds", for example? (Senge et al 1994, p.39) What might we do with those hypotheses like "Practising a new discipline is different from emulating a model" (Senge 1990, p.11) - what would count as differentiating evidence ?

6. COMPLEX SITUATIONS, SIMPLISTIC METHODS

The "inkstain" metaphor proved unworkable at Phase 1 but "imprint" remained viable at Phase 2. At Phase 1, "Spread throughout the organisation" had sounded as if it might be amenable to simple techniques like questionnaires - what networkers' work practices have changed and how many subsequently have evolved in their vicinity, for example? To what causal chains, over what period, are these changes attributed? We considered surveying each networker and the colleagues interfacing with his/her role set. Boundary questions were not easily resolved, however. The organisation being researched is not *an* organisation but several. The day-time and night-time organisations are different; there are at least four distinct occupational groupings, each with sub-sections and each with its own dominant culture. Some staff "live" in the organisation; others work and are paid there but "belong" to other enterprises. The governance and management systems are separable but linked; each organisation and each system draws membership from different groups. In the case of governance these represent stakeholdings; in the case of management they represent functions and organisational hierarchical levels, at least overtly. Management and reporting structures were in transition from professional functional to service delivery groupings. Even mapping the organisation to select a valid sample proved impossible in the timescale.

The relationship between "What we want to know" and "What we could find out" also generated research issues. What is the relationship between benefits accruing to networking per se (Arias 1995) and organisational learning? Networking is, essentially, informal, hence outside normal organisational control systems: bureaucratise it in order to measure its costs and benefits (e.g. Kidd 1994) and it ceases to qualify as networking. Many staff "wear different hats" but does that mean different perspectives? Major methodological questions arising are, "When someone participates in research, of what systems are the data they provide evidence?" and "How much of what sort of change "counts" as evidence of an evolving L.O.?"

Variables were inextricably mixed since the L.O.s initiative was only one in a stream of change measures; since some of them took place concurrently, what effects were attributable to what causes? "Scientific" methods appeared too crude to cope with such complexity and amorphousness but are other forms of research any less problematic?

If "...the learning organisation exists principally as a vision in our collective experience and imagination" (Senge 1994), neither implementation or evaluation implications are clear. Is evidence of "shared vision" evidence of a learning organisation? Is not some transfer into performance improvement the whole point? At what system levels should this be evaluated?

Practices vary. Closed loop training systems entail and enable validation and evaluation—did the trainees "get" skills and principles, could they transfer them to the workplace, did the enterprise benefit, how did the workers feel? Mobil North Sea desired performance improvement as a function of a "volunteerist" culture; by consultation, a detailed route map for change was translated into training systems entailing extensive measurement. More common are unsupported assertions of connection between change initiatives and improved organisational performance. Of course de-layering, downsizing and "empowerment" can improve productivity whether connected to L.O. ideas or not.

One way to attempt (or avoid getting to grips with) "Learning Organisation" building has been by training hopefully, as an act of faith; the more pessimistic assert that organisational benefits of training and development are unmeasurable anyway. The "permeation" model we favoured does not lend itself well to conventional training validation and evaluation methods since for these outcome measures must be operationalised and pre-determined and the transformation process designed to produce them. (This is true even if processes are targeted rather than content). Had the training that had, indeed, taken place, been "closed loop", our difficulties would have been merely technical and logistical; "hopeful training", however, is open-loop. Here was a nice "bind"; either what we wanted to know was unmeasurable in principle or it was unmeasurable in practice.

A "strategic design and implementation" approach, however, also has its problems. In addition to "Hawthorne Effect", top-down imposition can generate the dependency and perceptions of powerlessness that are antithetical to L.O. principles. It cannot be assumed, however, that this antithesis "kills off" all L.O "infection". For example, Personal Mastery might be an adaptive strategy to be added to Goffman's list or a form of re-framing; either of these can reduce the probability of organisational learning.

What also of Action Research, from its earliest forms (Lewin 1946) to versions for various professions and purposes - "A.R for...", (e.g.Cunningham 1993, Hart & Bond

1995)? What of its Participative offspring, Collaborative Enquiry and related approaches? Leaving aside the sloppy thinking, unhelpfully hyperbolic style and appalling English of some authors in this field, since these methods collapse change process and evaluation of it into the intervention, their adoption would place us in another "bind", this time in relation to our terms of reference as evaluators of the outcomes of someone else's facilitation; we were *not*, in any but the most trivial sense, co-authors of relationships, in Reason's language (1993) but intended to be "in and out" with as little disturbance as possible. Whilst maintaining a reflective journal (Kemmis & McTaggart 1988) has utility, this might just be a situation where "detachment" and "objectivity" should be attempted, albeit critically and with due awareness both of the highly political nature of our activity and of the risk of being perceived as "Apostles" of "the Messiah", bringing comfort to the faithful. Neither is the current vogue for "stories" and "learning histories" (Roth & Kleiner 1996) obviously more useful. "To help an organisation become better aware of its own learning efforts" is another homily inducing the, "O.K. but what do we do Monday morning?" reaction noted by Senge himself. (1994). Costly and long-winded to obtain, capable of multiple deconstructions, without conclusions or recommendations their utility is dependent on receptiveness of the organisational culture, degree of shared vision, time and inclination of the recipients to work out how to use the material. They might be seen by the cynical as processes "...to keep consultants in work for ever" or "...to produce readable, rather than rigorous, research reports".

How best to record and analyse ideographic data and how to ensure these are valid raise issues dealt with by any good research methods textbook; interview notes are experimenter-biased and their data impovished, audio recording can be threatening, produce garbled transcriptions (expensively) and rich but too voluminous material. Grounded Theory (Strauss 1987) would not suffice; a bridge would be needed between its, self-generated data categories and L.O.s concepts.

7. WHAT WE DID (FOR BETTER OR WORSE)

Phase 1 included collection of a time-sample of documents (e.g. business plans and annual reports) so that objectives and rhetoric could be compared. Pre-design, informal interviews obtained information from a small, opportunity-sample taken from various organisational levels. Although focused on the elements included in the initiative, unavoidably, individual views of the initiative were expressed, pre-empting some of what Phase 1 had hoped to achieve. Meetings were attended and notes taken by two observers.

Phase 2 re-visited those from the original sample who were still employed within the enterprize, attempted to track key figures to their new employment and acquired a small number of other participants who wished to air their views. Personal Mastery, Shared Vision and Systems Thinking were deemed most amenable to research but it was hoped that insights into Mental Models and Team Learning might emerge to some extent. We were anxious to avoid leading our respondents, however, so decided to search data for evidence of the five disciplines rather than use them as the basis for design. Problems inherent in data-driven research models have been mentioned above; Cognitive maps are a useful compromise and this was the method chosen for the greater part of the Phase 2; it is not claimed that this was the only or the best choice.

At the time of writing, Phase 2 data collection was proceeding and the remaining, single researcher was encountering difficulties in dealing with "bereavement" following the departure of the interventionist but was encouraged by the data-quality emerging.

8. CONCLUSION

The intention here has not been to insist on the impossibility of doing this kind of research but to surface some research issues that should not be glossed over, much as Ulrich (1987) did when formulating his Boundary Questions, and to seek insightful solutions. The value of doing this is perceived to include assessing both academic and consultancy claims more critically and to suggest areas of possible research into research methods that are appropriate to newer forms both of organisation and interventions in these. It might also encourage L.O. (and other) interventionists to resist some of the more gross research errors; this may entail telling the client, "I'm sorry, but in your complex organisation there is a limit to what is discoverable cost-effectively by means available currently and what I can find out is not, actually, quite what you want to know."

REFERENCES

Arias, J.T.C., 1995, "Do networks really foster innovation?"*Management Decision* Vol33,**9** 52–56.

Brown, D., 1996, "The "Essences" of the Fifth Discipline: or where does Senge stand to view the world?"*Systems Research*Vol.13,**2**, 91–107.

Cunningham, J., Barton, 1993, *Action Research and Organisational Development*, Connecticut, Praeger

Economist Conference, 20th September, 1996, London.

Hart, A.E., and Bond, M., 1995, *Action Research for Health and Social Care: A Guide to Practice* O.U. Press Buckingham.

Kemmis, S., and McTaggart, R., 1988, *The Action Research Reader*, Deakin Univ. Press, Australia.

Kidd, T., 1994, *Managing Business Networks*, Kogan Page, London.

Lewin, K., 1946, "Action Research and Minority Problems"in *Resolving Social Conflicts,* Lewin G.W. (ed) N.Y. Harper & Bros.

Reason, P., 1994, "Co-operative Enquiry, Participatory Action Research and Action Inquiry: three approaches to participative enquiry", in *Handbook of Qualitative Research,* N.K. Denzin & Y.S. Lincoln (eds.) London, Sage.

Roth, G., and Kleiner, A., 1995, "Learning Histories: "Assessing" the Learning Organisation"*The Systems Thinker* Vol 6,**4**,31–33, Pegasus Comms, Cambridge, Mass.

Senge, P., 1990, *The Fifth Discipline* USA, Doubleday.

Senge, P.M., Kleiner, A., Roberts, C., Ross R.B., and Smith B.J., 1994, *The Learning Organisation Fieldbook*, Nicholas Brealey, G.B.

Strauss, A., 1987, *Qualitative Analysis for Social Scientists* Cambs Univ. Press. N.Y.

Ulrich, W., 1987, "Critical Heuristics of Social Systems Design" *European Jnl. of Operational Research* ch31:pp 276–283.

33

DESIGNING SUSTAINABLE SPORTING ORGANISATIONS

John Davies

Victoria University of Wellington
New Zealand

1. INTRODUCTION

The Viable Systems framework of Stafford Beer (1979, 1981, 1985) is well regarded as being capable of providing valuable insights to organisational effectiveness and guidance for organisational design (Brocklesby, Cummings and Davies, 1995; Espejo, 1989; Jackson, 1989). The variety of organisations and activities to which VSM thinking has been applied is considerable, spanning for example, the organisation of ancient Athens (Cummings and Brocklesby, 1993), national government (Beer, 1989), strategic planning (Brocklesby and Cummings, 1996), information systems strategy (Schumann, 1990), project management (Britton and Parker, 1993), training and tourist organisations (Britton and McCallion, 1989; Flood and Zambuni, 1990). Whilst the work of Cummings and Brocklesby (1993) was historical and interpretive, the other works reflected case studies of attempted intervention. This paper, like Cummings and Brocklesby, is also interpretive, in that it seeks to use the Viable Systems framework to assess the rationale underpinning, and the characteristics of, the recent restructuring of a national sports organisation, New Zealand Cricket (NZC).

In early 1995, following an 'informal' meeting of a broad cross-section of individuals interested in the well-being of cricket in New Zealand, the Board of NZC engaged an eight person panel, who in turn appointed the Boston Consulting Group as partners, to review the constitution, structure and organisation of NZC and to come forward with appropriate recommendations of organisational forms and management structures that would best serve the sport. Following extensive research and a rapid process of consultation, within and without cricket, the panel reported within three months (NZC Review Committee / The Boston Consulting Group, 1995). The recommendations were accepted immediately by the Board, as worthy of implementation; the constitution was changed at the next General Meeting, and implemention was well under way with the appointment of a new CEO, before the year ended. Whilst the writer was but an interested bystander during the review process, involvement in similar design exercises and experience with the VSM has made it possible to gain insights about the approach taken. This paper seeks to examine whether, as a consequence of the rapid changes, NZC can be regarded as having the characteristics of a viable, sustainable system.

2. THE VSM

A full description of the VSM can be obtained from Beer's major works. A skeletal outline of the VSM is given here, and a corresponding diagrammatic representation is shown in Figure 1. Beer conceptualises all viable systems as sharing a network of commu-

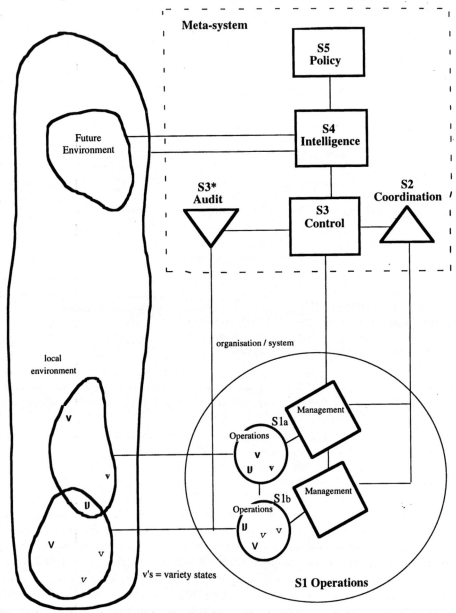

Figure 1. Beer's VSM.

nication channels bonding five complementary sub-systems. The sub-systems, whose effective functioning and communication links are necessary to any system's viability or survival, comprise - an operational system, S1, of autonomous operational units that act out the very identity and purpose of the overall system, and a meta-system comprising four other sub-systemic functions: S2 - effecting overall coordination of the autonomous units; S3 - operational planning, monitoring, control and audit functions relating to the autonomous units; S4 - intelligence and strategy development serving the whole organisation's future ; and S5 - the creation and promulgation of identity, vision, direction, purpose and mission, throughout the organisation and its wider environment. The 'lines' in the VSM diagram represent essential two-way communication channels designed to convey requisite 'hard' and 'soft' information between the sub-systems, and necessarily with the wider environment. As such, the system is better able to match current, and anticipate future requirements for survival.

3. THE REVIEW AND ANALYSIS

A summary of findings that arise from the analysis, results and recommendations of the NZC Review is shown in Appendices 1 and 2. Appendix 1 shows a stylistic VSM representation of NZC as it was in mid 1995, with a corresponding list of systemic features and flaws, identified by the review. Similarly, Appendix 2 shows the systemic/cybernetic interpretations and effects of critical recommendations. The major features of the analysis are briefly discussed below.

S5

Any successful analysis and design using the VSM is predicated on the analysts/designers recognising or creating an appropriate identity, vision and purpose for the organisation. It is noteworthy that the reviewers were able to articulate a clear vision that has gained immediate and enthusiastic acceptance for directing the future of NZC. A prior inability to commit to, and to convey purpose, has been linked to the inbred parochial election process for a large NZC Board of 13 Members. To establish identity and create vision, is now clearly established as a Board S5 responsibility. The vision encompasses being regarded as a strong competitor in the international arena; seeing cricket as the leading summer participation sport in the domestic arena; receiving a high level of public and family interest and support; and being respected for sound and credible governance and management of the game. This vision and purpose are accordingly reflected in the identification of S1 units in the VSM representations (Apps 1 and 2).

S5-S4-S3 Meta-System

The rhetorical questions of whether, if we were able to design an organisation from scratch, it would resemble the organisation we now see (Beer, 1985), or whether the organisational structures have become 'millstones' around the corporate neck (Brocklesby et al, 1995) have pertinence for NZC. Its Board membership, just like that of many volunteer based organisations, have been surrogate planners, administrators and performed a multitude of tasks. Not only have role ambiguity and multiple role conflict been manifest within the meta-system, but Board Members have also been involved in S1 operations, as well as in S3 operational planning . The prior existence of 7 'management' and a further 9 cricket sub-committees of the Board, suggests an extensive involvement of Board Members in operational and planning matters, and provides an indication of how morale-sapping confusion amongst staff about lines of responsibility, reporting and authority, has arisen. Role confusion, role and work overload, may have diverted Board Members from the necessary S5 systemic function of creating purpose and giving direction. Recommendations for a smaller, independently selected Board having specific S5 obligations of choosing direction and deciding on strategy, should do much to remove these systemic weaknesses. Similarly, the management of communications and relationships with key stakeholders, provincial associations, on the one hand, and sponsors, on the other hand, will become clearer and more effective, once any implied unintended responsibility associated with sub-committee membership is removed. The retention of just 3 subcommittees, relating to S5 policy issues and determination, removes Board Members from operational matters, and clarifies staff responsibilities for S4 strategy development, communications, S3 operational planning.

Particular attention is given in the NZC Review to the development and implementation of effective communications strategies. In VSM terms, the systemic impact spans the S4 intelligence and strategy development function, the S3* monitoring/audit function and S2 coordination; the strengthened communication channels are graphically highlighted in Figure 3. The emphasis placed on communication and communication channels is in keeping with traditional VSM thinking. However, it is not limited to consideration of typical formal coordinating mechanisms like fixture schedules, personnel policies, contract templates, peformance and budget targets. The introduction of regular information meetings, bi-annually between the Chair of the Board and Provincial Association chairpersons, and quarterly between the CEO and Association CEOs, provide the opportunity not just to give information and to spread 'the word', but to share information, to build shared vision, and to get 'buy-in'. The setting for these meetings also contributes to a more informal 'management by walking around' S3* monitoring and auditing function, and opens up a possible algedonic filter to 'the top'. In a similar vein, the distribution of draft business plans and budgets to stakeholders for comment before adoption, is meant to convey an ethos of openness and a clear signal that information and ideas don't just flow one way, but that involvement and collaborative input is expected.

S1

Given the fast changing global and local environment which national sports organisations now face, for example, increasing global and national markets for professional cricketers, coaches and administrators, increasing commercialism, merchandising/sponsorship opportunities, it is imperative that the panel's recommendations take effect, so that S1 operations have the autonomy to act quickly, still working within S2 policy guidlines and still being true to the S5 derived identity and ethos of the system, but without the frequent delays and uncertainty created by the involvement of committtees.

4. CONCLUSION

As Schwaninger (1990) has suggested, assessing the effectiveness of an organisation by the level of its profits is similar to drawing conclusions about what season it is by measuring the temperature. Assessing the success of the reorganisation of NZC solely by the victories of its test team would be similarly inappropriate. This paper has established the reorganisation of NZC has been successful in as much as NZC can be regarded as having developed more of the characteristics of a viable, sustainable system.

REFERENCES

NZC Review Committee / The Boston Consulting Group, *A Path to Superior Performance*, 1995

Beer, S., 1979, *The Heart of the Enterprise*, Wiley, Chichester.

Beer, S., 1981, *Brain of the Firm (2nd Edn)*, Wiley, Chichester.

Beer, S., 1985, *Designing the System for Organisation*, Wiley, Chichester.

Brocklesby, J. Cummings, S. and Davies, J., Demystifying the Viable Sytsem Model as a Tool for Organisational Analysis, *Asia Pacific Journal of Operational Research*, **25**(1), 65–86

Espejo, R., 1989, The VSM Revisited, in:*The Viable Systems Model - Interpretations and Applications of the VSM*, (R. Espejo and R. Harnden, eds), pp 77–100, Wiley, Chichester

Jackson, M. C., 1989, Evaluating the Managerial Significance of the VSM, in:*The Viable Systems Model - Interpretations and Applications of the VSM*, (R. Espejo and R. Harnden, eds), pp 77–100, Wiley, Chichester

Cummings, S., and Brocklesby, 1993, The Classical System - Insights into what made Periclean Athens great, *Systems Practice*, **6** (4), 335–357

Beer, S., 1989, Mational government: disseminated regulation in real time, or How to run a country', in: *The Viable Systems Model - Interpretations and Applications of the VSM*, (R. Espejo and R. Harnden, eds), pp 333–360, Wiley, Chichester

Brocklesby, J., and Cummings, S., 1996, Designing a Viable Organisation Structure, *Long Range Planning*, **29** (1): 49–57

Schuhmann, W., 1990, Strategy for information systems in the film division of Hoechst AG, *Sytems Practice*, **3** (3): 265–287.

Britton, G. A., and Parker J., 1993, An Explication of the Viable Systems Model for Project Management, *Sytems Practice*, **6** (1): 21–51.

Britton and McCallion, 1990, Application of the VSM to the trade training network in New Zealand, in: *The Viable Systems Model - Interpretations and Applications of the VSM*, (R. Espejo and R. Harnden, eds), pp 145–174, Wiley, Chichester

Flood, R. L., and Zambuni, S. A., 1990, Viable Systems Diagnosis. 1. Application with a Major Tourism Services Group,*Sytems Practice*, **3** (3): 225–248.

Schwaninger, M., 1990, Embodiments of Organisational Fitness: The Viable Systems Model (VSM) as a Guide, *Sytems Practice*, **3** (3): 225–248.

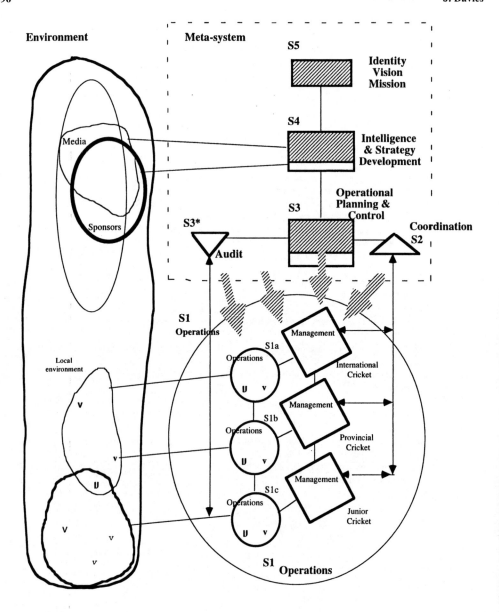

All lines represent two-way flows   ///////////// = Board Member Involvement

v's = variety states, relating to different parts of the
environment impinging on the different sub-systems

Appendix 1. A VSM representation of NZ Cricket, prior to reorganisation in 1995.

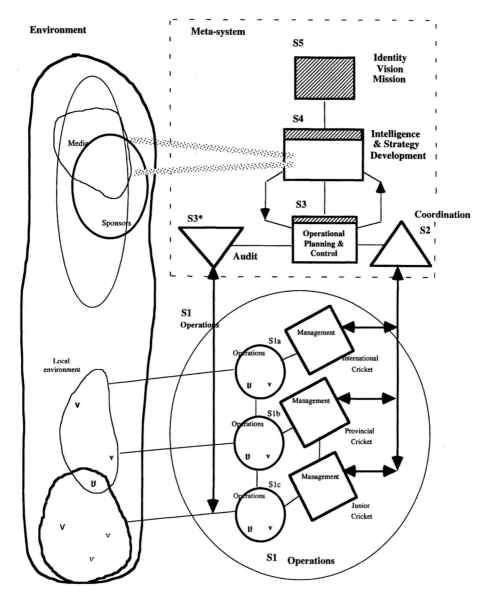

All lines represent two-way flows   ///////////, = Board Member Involvement

v's = variety states, relating to different parts of the
environment impinging on the different sub-systems

Appendix 2. A VSM representation of NZ Cricket, following reorganisation in 1995.

34

LIFE-LONG LEARNING OK! BUT TO WHAT FUTURE LEARNING AGENDA?

Gordon Dyer

Open University
12 Hills Road
Cambridge, CB2 1PF, United Kingdom

1. INTRODUCTION

"Life-long learning" is at the forefront of the current educational debate, but invariably the driving assumption is the need for individuals to continuously develop their technical skills to maintain employability in the context of rapid technological change. Underpinning this is a current paradigm that education should develop independence and competitive capacity in individuals, with the norm expectation that they will generate a net contribution to the economy against a background of a competitive environment. However, the International Systems Institute (ISI), argue that this has led to an underconceptualisation of the purpose of education, and contributed to social decline. The ISI, often called the "social system design community", propose that within future systems of human development and learning, a new learning agenda must be developed aimed at equipping individuals and communities with the capacity to co-design and co-create their future (see Banathy, 1991). This learning agenda will require a new underpinning paradigm which also stresses on individuals the need to recognise their interdependence with others and with their environment.

The UK Government's pre-occupation with higher education is with quality and cost-effectiveness, and "fitness for academic award"; the same values have caused it to sponsor vocational qualifications as a measure of "fitness for employment". Neither government or universities seem to accept that they have a major role in developing citizenship and ethical behaviour, and in developing the recognition of interdependence as a crucially important aspect in the building of a cohesive society. These issues are a key concern as we move into the 21st Century, and face an increasing and disturbing rate of social change and unrest (see Banathy, 1996).

This paper provides some first thoughts on a learning agenda to include: "fitness for life" - defined as the fitness for designing and creating an appropriate life for self, and with others, and with the environment; the strategies for introducing this; and the types of underpinning knowledge and understanding, and core skills required, which would facilitate this.

Systems for Sustainability, edited by Stowell *et al.*
Plenum Press, New York, 1997

2. A CASE STUDY OF UK HIGHER EDUCATION

The UK Higher Education Quality Council (HEQC) is exploring the academic standards of higher education (HE) and the means by which these are to be stated and assured. The examination has recently focused on the concept of "graduateness" and on what generic attributes are attributed by the award of a UK first degree. Graduateness is under scrutiny for a number of reasons, not least because the rapid increase in the scale and cost of higher education demands that its activities are more transparent and more publicly accountable. The HEQC research has revealed a variety of views and approaches to graduateness. An HEQC report (Wright, 1996) identifies that much of the consideration of graduateness has been influenced by earlier work in the USA quoting:

- Bowen (1977) and Allen (1988) who suggest the following as important:
  - cognitive learning (verbal skills, quantitative skills, substantive knowledge, rationality, intellectual tolerance, aesthetic sensibility, creativeness, wisdom and life-long learning)
  - emotional and moral development (personal self-discovery, psychological well-being, human understanding, values and morals and religious interests [defined as, serious and thoughtful exploration of purpose, value and meaning])
  - practical competence (most of the goals already listed plus, future orientation, adaptability, leadership, citizenship, discovery and encouragement of talent, advancement of social welfare, and the avoidance of negative outcomes of society)
- Alverno women's college in Milwaukee.

The Alverno approach is that over her 4 year programme each student develops eight abilities: communication, analysis, problem solving, valuing in a decision-making context, interaction, global perspectives, effective citizenship and aesthetic response. This is apparently done by requiring that a student's overall programme (which is drawn from familiar disciplines and professional areas such as physics, English literature, business administration and nursing) enables her to acquire these abilities.

The HEQC report provides no evidence on whether the Bowen/Allen goals are ever guaranteed in graduate outcomes in any USA university, and this seems most unlikely. But the Bowen/Allen and Alverno goals provide valuable pointers for a new effort by ISI towards a possible vision of an appropriate learning agenda. The HEQC report confirms that the attributes expected of graduates in the UK tend to give less weight to overall personal development and to social purpose. This, the report suggests, is due to differences of history, to the longer tradition of a mass education in the USA, and to the tendency for higher education in the UK to concentrate on single-Honours programmes in contrast to major/minor combinations and liberal arts curricula in the USA.

3. LEARNING AGENDA GAP

Whatever the reason, in the UK HE sector the gap between the current, and what ISI sees as the future essential learning agenda is very wide indeed, as the following analysis demonstrates. There are at least 3 domains of consideration that we can use to evaluate the quality of higher education provision: fitness for award; fitness for employment; and fitness for life (defined above).

3.1. Fitness for Award

The fitness for award domain contains the UK Government interest in defining quality nationally at HE institutions. The issue for Government is very simple, can a given class of degree across the university sector represent a common output? And, if so, are there a set of core abilities and skills which can be ascribed to the holders of certificates, diplomas, degrees, and master's degrees etc.? If standards across universities cannot be compared how can the quality of the provision be determined and funding arrangements be rationally based?

The primary values that government would have associated with university (and all other forms of formal education for that matter) is based on the development of independence, to produce thinkers and doers that will contribute to the economy and not be dependent on it. Neither government or universities seem to accept that they have a significant role in developing citizenship and ethical behaviour, or in developing the recognition of interdependence as a crucially important aspect in the building of a cohesive society. But these issues should be a key concern as we move into the 21st century, and face an increasing and disturbing rate of social change and possible unrest. Both government and universities are encouraging or preparing graduates for life-long learning but in terms of maintaining their technical knowledge and employability.

Despite the expansion in the HE provision, the sector is still designed for an "intellectual elite" and is not assumed to have a role of serving society. Given this background, it is not surprising that universities are self-serving in terms of the academic topics they teach, the research they undertake, and the degrees they award.

3.2. Fitness for Employment

The fitness for employment domain reflects the development of a system of National Vocational Qualifications (NVQs) in the UK. This sets out to confirm individual vocational or work-based competences, and to link these awards to 5 discrete levels of achievement (from roughly those which might be expected of a teenage school leaver, to someone with work experience at post-graduate level [Level 5]). The NVQ system is related not solely to what individuals know (as confirmed by controlled examination), but what they can demonstrate through evidence of work-based competence. The UK Government has sponsored this as a form of learning agenda with a rationale based on catching up with international competitors who have a "better trained work-force". Thus the government is locked to an instrumental vision of skills development.

This whole area has been the cause of considerable conflict both within the educational system, and between the educational system and government. UK Universities are both suspicious and fearful of arrangements for awards which are not under their jurisdiction and control. Despite attempts to build bridging links between the two systems of awards - the academic and the vocational - the HE sector remains critical of the NVQ system. Notwithstanding this, the government has specified national training targets which are based on the combination and equivalence of academic awards and NVQs.

This debate does not contribute to the solution of the major issues that face society. However, what could be important is that the vocational awards system contains a number of core skills, now to be called "key skills" (Dearing, 1996), which are seen to be relevant to anyone in employment. Some of these key skills seem to map onto, and might be adaptable to the future skill requirements for social systems design, namely:

- Communication
- Personal skills—working with others
- Personal skills—improving own learning and performance

As with NVQs, these key skills are specified at five levels of attainment. What is crucial is that the communication key skills requires not only the competence in individuals to put their own points in a relevant and suitable way, but also the competence to listen actively, to create opportunities for others to contribute and to make contributions which carry the discussion forward. These skills are those which social system designers would see as essential to effective design conversations.

3.3. Fitness for Life

The HEQC report shows there are very few learning agendas being consciously developed in UK universities which are related to "fitness for life" - or, as I define it, the fitness for designing and creating an appropriate life for self, and with others, and with the environment. The role of the education system in needing to contribute to this is barely recognised. This brings us to the change in culture and a new set of assumptions which would be required within government, universities and society to bring about this change, and to a re-visioning of the life-long learning agenda.

We would appear to have three strategic options to bring about a recognition of the need for change so that new systems of learning and human development come into place:

1. to introduce the fitness for life considerations into the university system (and other levels of the education system)
2. to retain fitness for life as a separate entity which is developed through the family, community and social agencies
3. a combination of (1) and (2).

Either approach poses some difficulty of how the achievement of fitness for life would/could/should be assessed.

4. NEW LEARNING AGENDA

A logical approach to developing a new learning agenda would be to develop a clear view of:

- the underpinning knowledge and understanding required, and
- the skills which are required

in order to satisfactorily perform the two areas of systems design practice of co-designing and co-creating. It is also important to achieve the correct balance between the development of any particular discipline skills and those of systems design. We also need to consider how the acquisition of knowledge, skills and competences of systems design are to be assessed.

4.1. Underpinning Knowledge and Understanding

Candidate topics for inclusion are:

- the Earth's natural environment and its resources, the concerns and issues

- inappropriate/appropriate use of technology
- aspects of social and human sciences
- systems design purposes (Banathy, 1991)
- systems design tools, including: imaging techniques and idea generation; "Family" Declaration of Interdependence, and "Family" Bill of Rights and Responsibilities (Dyer, 1995); evolutionary guidance systems (Banathy, 1989); and conversation design (Dyer, 1996)
- ethical understanding
- intellectual tolerance
- aesthetic sensibility
- creativity
- wisdom and life-long learning.

Assessment of achievement would be by traditional methods, including examination.

4.2. Core Skills

The candidates are:

- communication skills
- conversation skills
- working with others
- improving learning and own performance
- adaptability
- leadership and citizenship
- skill to seek, to discover and encourage talent
- advancement of social welfare and avoidance of negative outcomes of society

Assessment of achievement would be by part exam and part competency based via portfolio

4.3. Practice of Co-Designing and Co-Creating

There is little point in having a development and learning agenda unless one can measure achievements in some way. A learning agenda which includes the practice of systems design raises some very interesting questions. Thus:

- How would we measure development towards "fitness for practice" and success in this domain?
- In what context would we attempt to measure: individual or group? within the education system or within the social system?
- If within the education system how would we assess individual practice in the K-12 Grade range?
- Assuming evidence of practice is required at graduate level, how would we assess graduateness on this dimension?

We have few existing examples of award systems in this arena. The Duke of Edinburgh Award Scheme is partly applicable. If assessment is to be outside the education system, this implies that it should be left to the family, community or society to do this. but what would this mean? There are very few examples of measures of contribution to society and those which do exist tend to be somewhat archaic, e.g. Royal Honours, awards of civic freedom and honorary degrees.

5. CONCLUSION

An outline set of areas of underpinning knowledge, understanding and key skills are proposed as part of a learning agenda aimed at developing individual and community ability to design and create appropriate lives and social systems for themselves. These, or developments of them, should be introduced and integrated within educational programmes. The challenge is to achieve the right balance between a curriculum stream which is intended to develop within individuals a recognition of their interdependence with others and with the environment, and the primary curriculum stream for any given discipline. It is this form of combined agenda which should be the basis of life-long learning, and not a narrow agenda which focuses on employability. Also problematic, is the issue of assessment of achievement within this combined form of learning agenda, particularly in the practice of co-creating and co-designing of social systems. The proposals represent a change of culture for educationalists, and are key areas of ISI research and activity.

REFERENCES

Allen, M., 1988, *The goals of universities*, SRHE/OU Press, Milton Keynes.

Banathy, B.H., 1989, Design: a journey to create the future: a map of the journey, A paper presented at the first Pacific Rim Fuschl conversation, Asilomar, California, USA.

Banathy, B.H., 1991, *Systems design of education: a journey to create the future*, Educational Technology Publications, Englewood Cliffs, New Jersey, USA.

Banathy, B.H., 1996, *Designing Social Systems in a Changing World*, Plenum, New York.

Bowen, H., 1977, *Investment in Learning*, Jossey-Bass, San Francisco, California, USA.

Dearing, Sir Ron., 1966, Review of Qualifications for 16–19 Year Olds, Department of Education and Employment.

Dyer, G.C., 1995, A Family Declaration of Interdependence: a methodology for systems design within a small social unit, *Systems Research*, **12** (3): 201–208.

Dyer, G.C., 1996, Enthalpy as a metaphor for the chemistry of conversations, *Systems Research*, 13 (2): 145–157.

Wright, P., 1996, What are graduates: clarifying the attributes of graduateness, A Discussion Paper from the UK Higher Education Quality Council.

35

CHARTING CHANGE—THE USE OF SYSTEMS CONCEPTS IN DISTANCE LEARNING BASED MANAGEMENT EDUCATION ACROSS EUROPE

Eion Farmer and Jacky Holloway

Open University Business School
Walton Hall
Milton Keynes MK7 6AA, England

1. INTRODUCTION

The Open University (OU) Systems Group have been presenting distance learning based management courses, which include a large element of systems ideas and concepts, for more than twenty years in the undergraduate programme. Since 1983 the Open University Business School (OUBS) has introduced and developed many of these ideas in their three levels of management development courses – the Professional Certificate in Management for new or aspiring managers, the Professional Diploma for middle managers, and the MBA aimed at senior managers.

Many thousands of OU students in the UK and across Western and, more recently, Eastern Europe, have been introduced to systems ideas and concepts in these courses but little information is available on whether or how management students use them in their 'real worlds' outside the academic boundaries of these courses. All OU courses are evaluated regularly and independently of the Faculties presenting them, by the OU Institute of Educational Technology. Whilst these evaluations yield some information on course content, they focus more on delivery methods and teaching techniques, providing a comparative view of the quality standards being achieved. Much 'information' on the use of systems ideas and concepts is anecdotal—often reported in an unstructured manner from tutorial groups and residential schools which students attend. Not surprisingly, varying messages emerge depending on who reports and the context of the feedback. Many students and tutors report very favourably on the learning experience of residential schools where they have the opportunity to 'practice and apply', with 'like minded' peer students, managers and experienced tutors, concepts and ideas to which they have been introduced in their courses. In reality, very little structured data has been collected on whether systems ideas and concepts are actually used beyond the environment of course work, and what constraints apply to those attempting to use them.

Systems for Sustainability, edited by Stowell *et al.*
Plenum Press, New York, 1997

This paper attempts to start remedying that situation, examining both historical data on the way courses have been developed and presented to an ever-widening base of 'management' students across Europe, and data from a recent student survey. These more structured data have been used to determine which concepts and ideas both managers and non-managers use, and how useful they find them.

2. BRINGING SYSTEMS IDEAS TO MANAGERS – THE OU WAY

The OU distance teaching approach has been highly successful over the last 25+ years and various courses employing systems ideas have used it to the full. The prime teaching tool is the Course Unit consisting of written text with figures and in-text activities, supported by audio and video material which has lent itself well to systems techniques such as diagramming. Course units have been described as 'tutorials in print' and traditional methods of face to face tuition are limited with tutorials once a month at most, generally as participative group events facilitated by tutors rather than conventional lectures. Thus the opportunity to practice diagramming skills and use systems thinking and concepts in applying methodologies such as Checkland's Soft Systems approach and Organisational Development (OD) or the Hard Systems approach and Systems Intervention Strategy (SIS) with peer groups is limited. The use of videos (T245 1994, B751 1994) to demonstrate techniques such as diagramming and modelling has proved very effective in ensuring that a consistent teaching approach is achieved both at a distance and at Residential Schools.

Undergraduate courses have consistently attracted over 1000 students per annum. OUBS courses developed using the systems ideas from these courses attract similar numbers. Basic diagramming techniques and the notion of considering organisations as systems have been introduced in the Certificate courses. They have been developed further in the Diploma where the one of the School's earliest courses, *Planning and Managing Change*, has been revised and expanded as *Managing Development and Change* (B751 1994). In parallel the 'fast track' (mostly graduate entry) management students on the MBA Stage 1 have been introduced to a similar suite of systems ideas and concepts. Students moving on to Stage 2 of the MBA from either this direct entry Stage 1 or the Diploma route have had considerable exposure to these ideas and methodologies. Indeed a number of Diploma students chose to use hard or soft systems approaches including SIS and OD for their projects.

Systems ideas and concepts are taught at a fairly theoretical level and then applied, in depth, to work-based scenarios. Further development is facilitated by getting students to apply them to their own organisations in their Tutor Marked Assignments (TMAs). This has proved an effective way of gaining acceptance by the students, and in some cases by their organisations, since immediate benefits have been demonstrated in certain applications especially where major change is being embarked upon and the management students have appropriate responsibilities and status to carry them through.

While the majority of OUBS students are practising managers (88% in the survey reported here), it was assumed that the percentage of managers on the undergraduate courses was small (10–15%). However this survey has indicated that the numbers of managers being introduced to systems ideas as OU undergraduates may be considerably greater (52% of the 75 respondents from a population of approximately 200 classifying themselves as managers). These managers may not be expected to apply the concepts directly to their work but will consider their use in a range of real world situations.

3. THE USE OF SYSTEMS APPROACHES BY MANAGERS

Progressive introduction of systems ideas throughout OUBS Certificate, Diploma and MBA Stage 1 ensures that management students have a sound grounding in these ideas and their application by the time they finish the Diploma and/or enter Stage 2 of the MBA. At this level the *Creative Management* (B882 1990) and the *Performance Measurement and Evaluation* (B889 1994) electives make significant use of the concepts and approaches and students often use the hard and soft methodologies in the *Business Research Project* (B886 1990). Whilst different course teams are responsible for each course, progressive introduction helps to ensure a reasonable degree of consistency in presentation and use of the concepts and ideas. For example the diagramming introduced in Certificate and Diploma is very similar to that introduced in the MBA Stage 1. However, the application of the systems ideas and concepts varies from course to course depending on the perspectives of that course. For example *Managing Development and Change* will view organisations from a structural and cultural perspective, with these facets depicted as components of a Systems Map. The complementary Diploma course *Managing Resources for the Market* (B752 1995) tends to consider resources such as finance and information as the components of the maps they use. Thus students are successively encouraged to view all perspectives systemically and holistically; individual courses use systems ideas to look holistically at scenarios and examine the systemic nature of interconnections and the influences of components.

The fundamental formula for this 'systems approach', as it is taught in the OUBS, is a four-part definition of a system:

- a system is a set of components connected together in an organised way
- the components are affected by being in the system and the behaviour of the system is changed if any of them leave it
- this organised assembly of components does something
- this assembly of components has been defined by someone as being of particular interest

This definition has been found to be usable by most management students and translates into an acceptable form in most European languages.

This study is aimed at getting a first quantitative feel for the use of systems ideas in management practice. The data were collected by a self-reporting questionnaire which interrogated 'Frequency of use' and 'Usefulness' of a range of Systems ideas and concepts drawn from the Systems and OUBS Courses. The survey focused on two distinct groups:

1. Undergraduate OU Systems students (studying courses T245 and T247) at Systems Summer School in the University of York – 75 respondents out of a possible 200
2. OUBS management students on the Managing Development and Change Diploma course on weekend Residential Schools at various sites across Europe – 136 respondents from approximately 500 population (including 10 from Bulgarian students currently studying the course in English).

Initial analysis suggests the most frequently used ideas are: Difficulties and Messes, Systems Maps and Boundaries, Influence Diagrams, Input-Output Diagrams, Control Model, Multiple Causation and Force Field Analysis. These are all rated as 'quite useful' by 35% of the users, and Systems Maps , Input-Output Diagrams and the Control Model are rated as 'essential' by 17% of the users. The Hard and Soft Systems methodologies are rated at a lower frequency of use i.e. 'monthly' or 'occasionally' rather than 'daily' – not surprisingly in view of their complex nature and time consuming application; but they were rated as 'essential' by 15% of the respondents and 'quite useful' by another 27%. Similarly OD is rated as 'essential' by 12.5% and 'quite useful' by a further 18.3%, but is only used 'occasionally' by most of them—possibly due to the protracted nature of managing 'people dominated' change scenarios.

Certain functional areas appear to find systems ideas more useful than others. For example, the 'usefulness' of Systems Maps was rated overall as 'essential' or 'quite useful' by 49% of all respondents. At the functional level this rating varied from 40–45% for Manufacturing, Operations, HR and Finance, to 53–57% for Marketing, Administrative and Engineering respondents. Level of management also appears to have influence on the application and usefulness of systems approaches. The percentage of managers in each level rating Systems Maps for instance as 'essential' or 'quite useful' was: Senior 39%; Middle 46%; Junior 48%; and Non-managers 57%.

The main constraints on using systems ideas and concepts appear to fall into three categories: i) lack of experience with their use, ii) lack of opportunity in the job role, iii) resistance from colleagues who do not understand the ideas and concepts

Accepting the small percentage of non-UK/EU respondents in the survey (<10%), there appears to be no significant difference in their use of the ideas and concepts. However earlier research (Farmer, Kornyei and Thompson, 1992) suggested that in Hungary the OD ideas of groups and group work were not popular and the presentation of the *Planning and Managing Change* course, using systems ideas, was breaking new ground and required a cultural readjustment. It is planned to follow this up in a later study.

4. BRIDGING THE CULTURAL DIVIDE

Sharing management concepts and approaches across Europe is becoming increasingly important as the former Eastern Bloc countries become more open. OUBS expansion into Europe aims to meet this need. As well as international diversity our student body includes managers from a very wide range of organisations in the commercial and not-for-profit sectors, and all management disciplines. This heterogeneity provides us with diverse cultures which can prove challenging when designing management education materials.

We can look at the challenge of diversity in at least two ways . Firstly, the differing cultures and subcultures within organisations based on either hierarchical layers such as managers/non-managers, or by disciplines such as engineers, marketeers, accountants etc. Secondly at the level of national cultures. This survey facilitates classification from the first perspective and the example in Section 3 above, using data on just one of the 15 concepts examined, suggests noticeable differences.

Consideration of the second perspective on international cultural differences is only possible at a limited level since the percentage of non-EU respondents was quite small (<10%). However it is felt that this group is sufficiently large to be considered as a pilot study and guide for future research. Since 1990 OUBS has been introducing courses into Central and Eastern European (CEEG) countries including Hungary, the Czech and Slovak Republics, Bulgaria, Romania and Russia. With the help of the Know How Fund, Certificate and Diploma courses have been introduced in English to groups of trainee tutors, translated and presented in the local languages. This has ensured that cultural problems with ideas and concepts have been tackled at the outset and relevant local case studies and examples substituted for the original UK examples in courses. The predominantly systems based course *Planning and Managing Change* first introduced into Hungary and Slovakia in 1992, has been superceded by the updated course *Managing Development and Change* in all five CEEG countries. Initial analysis suggests that the Control Model and Force Field Analysis are the most frequently used tools, rated between 'essential' and 'quite useful' by Bulgarian respondents. Constraints are similar to EU respondents including lack of confidence and resistance from colleagues. However, free response answers suggest that these respondents see good opportunities to use systems approaches in their emerging economies.

From a pedagogic perspective the understanding and application of systems ideas and concepts by management students in these countries, measured from the performance on their Tutor Marked assignments which they submit during the courses, compares favourably with UK groups studying the course at the same time. Exam results for non-EU students taking the courses in English (as second language), have consistently been slightly lower (5–10 marks), mainly because of having to handle unseen case studies and use dictionaries to translate questions during the exam. Accepting this constraint, the use of concepts has generally been similar to EU/UK cohorts. The numbers of CEEG students studying these courses in local languages should continue to grow steadily from the current 250 per annum, providing opportunities for more detailed future research.

Building on this success in the CEEG countries, OUBS are now introducing the Certificate in Ethiopia in English and the Diploma will follow in 1997. A small cohort of government officials has successfully completed the OUBS MBA in Ethiopia and acceptance of the systems ideas and concepts in that programme bodes well for their acceptance by Certificate and Diploma students there. Similarly the MBA has been introduced into Hong Kong via the Open Learning Institute and the Diploma is planned for Singapore. These programmes are seen as long term ventures in CEEG countries, Ethiopia and South East Asia, with 'localisation' using local case material and examples providing a sound base for the sustainability of the use of systems ideas and concepts in these countries. Many of the management students and tutors who have completed the systems-based courses are in senior posts in their countries. It is anticipated that considerable 'top down' penetration in the application and use of these ideas should be evident and this will be followed up on a long term basis.

5. SUMMARY AND CONCLUSIONS

Based on this survey of distance learning students across Eastern and Western Europe, we conclude at this stage that:

1. Systems ideas and concepts presented and used in OU systems courses and OUBS management courses are proving useful for both managers and non managers

2. frequency of use and usefulness appear to be affected by factors including: knowledge and experience of the user; awareness of colleagues; position/role of user; and organisational culture in which the user operates—but more analysis and research is needed to draw any usable conclusions

3. Distance Learning has provided an opportunity for practising managers to learn about the ideas but time to implement them is clearly a problem for many respondents—especially the use of methodologies such as SIS and OD

4. there is some evidence that respondents recognise the 'systems approach' as 'the way they normally think', but that concepts and tools introduced through these

courses provide a more structured framework for them to analyse their own approaches

5. there is also evidence that once 'hooked' on the systems approach respondents use it avidly—e.g. the 17+ % that classified the Systems Map and the Control Model as 'essential'. This suggests that sustained use of systems ideas can follow achievement of a firm grounding in them.

Quo Vadis? It is planned to follow up the cohort from this first survey on an annual basis if possible—facilitated by the high number of respondents agreeing to participate in a follow-up (90%). A database of 'systems users' will be assembled and updated regularly to examine trends. This will enable focusing on why some ideas and concepts are used/useful and others not, allowing consideration of ways to improve the introduction of these ideas and facilitation of their use. There is also an opportunity to test out their acceptance in specific corporate cultures since several groups of corporate users will be taking the Diploma courses in the next year.

Clearly this study has only examined the tip of an iceberg but the relatively crude instrument used illuminated several potentially fruitful areas for investigation which could assist the teaching, use, penetration and sustainability of systems ideas in distance based management education in Europe and beyond. In turn this can enhance the contribution of the systems approach to organisational and social sustainability itself.

REFERENCES

Farmer, E., Kornyei, I., and Thomson, A., 1992, The contribution of distance learning to Management Development in Eastern and Central Europe, unpublished paper to the International Organisation Development Association 7th Annual World Conference, December 1992 , Coventry Business School.

B751 1994, Managing Development and Change, The Open University, Milton Keynes.

B882 1990, Creative Management, The Open University, Milton Keynes.

B889 1994, Performance Measurement and Evaluation, The Open University, Milton Keynes.

T245 1995, Managing in Organisations, The Open University, Milton Keynes.

T247 1996, Working with Systems, The Open University, Milton Keynes.

36

APPLICATION OF A DATA MINING SYSTEM AS AN AID TO ORGANISATIONAL LEARNING

Colquhoun-John Ferguson

Department of Mechanical and Manufacturing Engineering
The Quality Centre
University of Paisley
High Street, Paisley
PA1 2BE, United Kingdom

1. INTRODUCTION

The concept of the Learning Organisation has been heralded as the most significant contribution to the future success, and even survival, of organisations in today's global market-place (Senge, 1992). Broadly defined, a learning organisation is one that readily adapts to external and internal influences, by detecting and correcting errors (Argyris & Schön, 1978). It is believed that this can be achieved through a better knowledge and understanding of the system with which it interacts.

At the heart of the learning organisation lies the importance of systems thinking (Nevis, Dibella & Gould, 1995), and implicit within a systems perspective is the discipline of team learning. Learning occurs due to the influence of various factors such as structure, strategy, environment, technology and culture (Weston, 1994). To date, there has been very little research on the influence of technology on organisational learning. The research described in this paper evaluates the technique of 'data mining' as a facilitator for access to corporate knowledge by product design teams, and the subsequent individual and team learning produced by this technique.

The objectives of the research are therefore to: investigate the application of data mining as a means of enabling designers' access; to data and information relevant to their function; identify a set of metrics to measure the change in individual and team learning; analyse the complex processes linking individual learning to that of corporate learning.

2. ORGANISATIONAL LEARNING

Organisations are paying increasing attention to the concept of organisational learning in order that they can increase competitive advantage, innovation and effectiveness

Systems for Sustainability, edited by Stowell *et al.*
Plenum Press, New York, 1997

(Nonaka, 1991; Drucker, 1994). Many practitioners see the significance of this concept as a mark of progress in corporate thought and action, from a resource orientation, to that of human potential (Senge, 1992; Prahalad & Hamel, 1994).

Senge (1992) has described the learning organisation as one which continually tests its experiences and transforms that experience into knowledge—accessible to the whole organisation, and relevant to its purpose. Garvin (1993) also highlights the organisation's ability to learn from experience in his definition of a learning organisation as, "*an organisation skilled at creating, acquiring, and transferring knowledge, and at modifying its behaviour to reflect new knowledge and insights.*"

The basis for learning in any organisation lies with its individual members, and the way they are structured within the organisation. Every organisation is composed of individuals, and the knowledge they possess; the overall knowledge of an organisation however may be less than that of its individuals (Argyris & Schön, 1978). The key lies in the structuring of these individuals into groups/teams, and how these groups access and share knowledge (Shonk, 1992; Katzenbach and Smith, 1993). This paper argues that the individual's view of the system as a whole is of paramount importance to their acquisition and use of knowledge. The importance of the contribution of the individual to the success of a corporation is highlighted by Senge (1992) who writes, "*The organisations that will truly excel in the future are the ones that discover how to tap peoples' commitment and capacity to learn at all levels in an organisation.*"

3. ORGANISATIONS AS KNOWLEDGE SYSTEMS

Checkland and Scholes (1990) state that organisations must think seriously about managing information as a prime resource, and that they would move towards a mode of operation in which self-organising, autonomous groups would be linked in an information network. According to Galliers (1995), the key question in information systems strategy however, which is often overlooked, is determination of the key information requirements to meet individual needs. This paper discusses the information needs of product design teams and focuses on customer feedback, standard parts and form features from existing product as being essential to their function.

Richter (1994) states that knowledge has become the decisive factor for corporate growth. If growth and learning are assumed to be linked, four criteria have been perceived as being important in the organisational learning process. These criteria will be investigated by the research described in this paper: knowledge acquisition - learning occurs when an organisation acquires knowledge, not only from the external environment, but from rearrangement of existing knowledge (Dodgson, 1993); information distribution - sharing of information between different units within the organisation increases learning (Brown and Duguid, 1991); information interpretation—the importance of information or data becoming knowledge before it can affect learning (Huber, 1991) will be tested; organisational memory—the importance of corporate knowledge and learning histories to aid learning, as proposed by Prahalad and Hamel (1994), will also be investigated.

Using these criteria, the organisation can be viewed from a systems perspective, as shown in Figure 1. Figure 1 depicts a model for assimilation of data/information from sources internal and external to the organisation, and their transformation into knowledge.

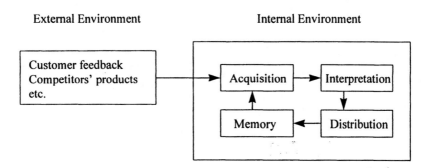

Figure 1. The organisation as a knowledge system.

4. DATA MINING

Many organisations today rely on relational databases and data-server technology to manage ever increasing masses of data. The well-defined structure (of rows and columns) in relational databases, however, restricts the use to which the data contained within will ever be put (Mark, 1996). Data in this format can only really be used to support a basic 'query and display' operation. Ideally, data and information held by a corporation should be used as an aid to a decision support mechanism, instead of mere transaction processing, and this research attempts to analyse the use of 'data mining' to this end. Data mining is the technique by which relationships and patterns in data are identified in large databases (Fayyad and Uthurusamy, 1995). Many organisations are 'data rich', but information which can be derived from these data can very often be 'hidden' in such large databases. Data mining goes beyond automated 'match and retrieval' associated with today's database technology; it is able to address the needs of analysis of data (Fayyad et. al., 1995). The benefit of the technique lies in the fact that the patterns to be searched for, and the models to be extracted are typically subtle and may require significant specific domain knowledge (Fayyad, 1996). In the past, analysis of retrieved data was performed by human analysts, which involved a process of retrieving, displaying and using expert knowledge to reach a decision. With increased volumes of data, a simple query from certain data stores may return substantial matches, making it unfeasible for an analyst to digest the results and reach a quick and correct decision. Data mining however facilitates data retrieval and then presents the data in a way which may improve the user's decision making ability by arguably transforming the data into knowledge.

5. INDUSTRIAL APPLICATION

In this project to date, time has been spent analysing the manufacturing processes of a German corporation involved in the manufacture of pneumatic cylinders. The study resulted in the model shown in Figure 2, which is a representation of processes and information flows within the organisation.

The data/information received by the product development department is restricted in the sense that it is not always in a format which is immediately understandable, and therefore of instant use to designers. Another problem exists in that the sources from which these data come do not allow designers a complete view of the system—in particular, feedback from the customer base. It was perceived therefore that a benefit to the com-

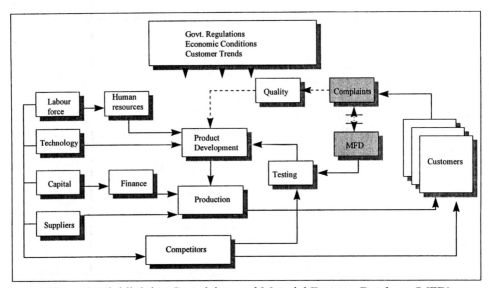

Figure 2 Highlighting Complaints and Material Features Database (MFD)

pany could be achieved by linking customer feedback via a complaints database and product data from the Material Features Database (MFD) to the design function, at the same time allowing testing of the hypothesis that access to these data and information, and proper presentation and analysis of them would increase learning. To this end, the project has reached the stage where it is aimed to identify a set of metrics to measure the effect an artificial intelligence (AI) tool may have on designers' performance.

6. CONCLUSION

Zuboff (1988) warns of the danger in assuming that the informating quality of information technology (IT) is an automatic outcome of the introduction of IT. Furthermore, Dosi (1988) has stated that knowledge is commonly thought to be analogous to technology. The research described in this paper attempts to measure the effect of IT on an organisation by measuring the learning of individuals and teams through the introduction of an AI approach. This paper has suggested that knowledge can only be gleaned from data/information if it is presented in a meaningful way to its users, and proposes that the technique of data mining may provide this mechanism. The research will attempt to 'measure' the importance of technology on organisational learning, by analysing any changes in the performance of product designers. A change in effectiveness of the design function will then be assessed to determine if this has been achieved by an increased awareness of the organisation and its environment as a system. The metric used to measure learning will be based on the five disciplines proposed for individual learning by Senge (1992) of systems thinking, team learning, shared vision, mental models and personal mastery.

REFERENCES

Argyris, C., Schön, D.A., 1978, *Organizational Learning: A Theory of Action Perspective*, Addison-Wesley, Reading, MA

Brown, J.S., Duguid, P., 1991, Organizational learning and communities of practice: Toward a unified view of working, learning and innovation, *Organization Science*, **2**/1, 40–57

Checkland, P.B., Scholes, J., 1990, *Soft Systems Methodology in Action*, Wiley, Chichester

Dosi, G., 1988, *The nature of the innovative process* in Technical Change and Economic Theory, (G. Dosi, ed), Pinter, London: pp.221–238

Dodgson, M., 1993, Organizational learning: A review of some literatures, *Organization Studies*, **14**/3: 375–394

Drucker, P.F., 1994, The theory of the business, *Harvard Business Review*, Sept-Oct. 1994

Fayyad, U.M., 1996, Data mining and knowledge discovery: Making sense out of data, *IEEE Expert Systems*, **Oct. 96**: 20–25

Fayyad, U.M., Uthurusamy, R., 1995, *First International Conference on Knowledge Discovery and Data Mining*, AAAI Press, 1995

Galliers, B., 1995, *Re-orienting information systems strategy: Integrating information systems into business* in Information Systems Provision: The Contribution of Soft Systems Methodology (F.A. Stowell, ed), McGraw-Hill, London: pp.51–74

Huber, G.P., 1991, Organizational learning: The contributing processes and the literatures, *Organization Science*, **2**/1: 88–115

Katzenbach, J., Smith, D., 1993, *The Wisdom of Teams: Creating the High Performance Organization*, Harvard Business School Press, Boston, Mass.

Mark, B., 1996, Data mining - here we go again?, *IEEE Expert Systems*, October 1996: 18–19

Nevis, E.C., DiBella, A.J. and Gould, J.M., 1995, Understanding organizations as learning systems, *Sloan Management Review*, Winter 1995: 73–85

Prahalad, C.K., Hamel, G., 1994, *Competing for the Future*, Harvard Business School Press, MA

Nonaka, I., 1991, The knowledge creating company, *Harvard Business Review*, **69**(6): 96–104

Richter, F-J., 1994, Industrial organizations as knowledge systems, *Systems Practice*, **7**(2): 205–216

Senge, P.M., 1992, *The Fifth Discipline: The Art & Practice of The Learning Organization*, Century Business, London

Shonk, J.H., 1992, *Team Based Organisations*, Business One Irwin Homewood, Illinois

Simoudis, E., 1996, Reality check for data mining', *IEEE Expert Systems*, Oct. 96: 26–33

Weston, D.M., 1994, *Organizational Learning as Strategy*, SRI International, Menlo Park, CA

Zuboff, S., 1988, *In The Age of the Smart Machine*, New York, Basic Books

37

TOWARDS A PROPOSAL TO STUDY THE POLICY MAKING PROCESS AT THE BASIC EDUCATIONAL LEVEL IN COLOMBIA

Nidia Gil

School of Management
University of Lincolnshire and Humberside
Marvell Hall, Hull, HU6 7RT

1. INTRODUCTION

Statistics, indicators and opinions suggest serious and diverse problems of the Basic Educational System (BES) in Colombia. What are exactly the problems, what are their causes and what are their solutions are very difficult and debated questions. Some of the problems that have been mentioned (See Duarte, 1996 and Misión de Ciencia, Educación y Desarrollo, 1994) are the following: policies are not the result of a holistic study of the BES; so they are focused only on particular aspects of the system; policies are defined without a consistent information system to support them; there is not any continuity in policies; the administration of public education is very politicized; the quality of education is very poor, etc. Many of the problems are related to a great extent to formulation, implementation or evaluation of policies, that is to say, to the Policy Making Process (PMP).

This paper is concerned with the definition of a research proposal to study the PMP of BES. It is aimed at two activities: The first one is the formulation of some strategic questions, answers to which will allow the researcher to understand what has been the evolution of the PMP and to propose new mechanisms for process improvement, in the light of experiences in other countries. The second has to do with finding an appropiate methodology to develop the process of enquiry. These two activities are considered in sections 3 and 4 of this paper. Section 2 is a very brief description of the BES, in order to help the reader to understand the current state of the system.

Systems for Sustainability, edited by Stowell *et al.*
Plenum Press, New York, 1997

2. ABOUT THE BES

The BES offers formal education at three levels: Pre-School (composed of three grades); Basic[*] (composed of nine grades[†]); and Media (composed of two grades). Institutions that provide this education service can be public or private. However, most of them are public: 88% of primary schools, 54.3% of secondary schools and 55% of pre-school schools.

The percentage of children covered by the BES has increased over the second half of this century but it has been stemmed during the last fifteen years. For example, primary school coverage went from 50% of potential primary school pupils at the beginning of the second half of this century to 86% in 1980 (Ministerio de Educación Nacional, 1982). After 1980, there was almost no increase in coverage. The increment of coverage is coherent with the policy of expansion of education established in the second half of this century. The big problem with this policy was that it did not take into account the quality of education. Only around 1975 did the Education Department start a program to improve the quality of education. However statistics (CONPES, 1994) show that the quality problem still exists. The so-called inner efficiency of education, measured by promotion, repetition and dropping out rates, is not satisfactory. For example, the repetition rates for the first, third and fifth grades of primary school were 25.5%, 11.5% and 11.7% in 1991 respectively. The dropping out rates were 2.6%, 10.3% and 16.3% for the same grades and year.

The education level of the teachers is very low. For instance, in 1993, only 31% of the primary school teachers had professional qualifications (Ministerio de Educación Nacional, 1995).

Regulations related to personnel administration and educational service financing have not had any continuity. During the 60's and 70's there was an attempt to centralize education management (Laws 111–1960 and 43–1975) but at the same time some regulations (e.g., Decret 1665–1966) tried to decentralized educational service financing. In the last ten years education regulations have concentrated on the decentralization of service. Today it is not very clear what is the state of centralization or decentralization of the BES management.

Regulations of the last few years have been trying to organize the mess. The most important result may be the creation of a Decenal Plan of Education. This plan, formulated during the last year and the beginning of this one, was elaborated in order to give the educational policies the category of a state policy.

3. THE PROCESS OF INQUIRY

Of course there are many systematic questions to formulate about the policy making process surrounding the BES. However, this study is, firstly, concerned to ask some specific questions, the answers to which raise many more questions.

- Who is involved in the PMP of education? If the PMP is understood according to (Lindblom and Woodhouse, 1993) as "the complex set of forces that together produces effects called "policies,"" it is required to define who else has anything to

---

* This level was created by the General Law of Education in 1993.
† Five of them belong to the previously called Primary School and the rest of them to the previously called Secondary School.

do with this complex system. In this particular case, regardless of the responsibility to formulate national policies in education being assigned to the National Educational Department, the power of educational unions and politicians seems to be very strong. An example of this is the role of the unions in the definition of the General Law of Education in 1994.

- What has been the impact of education policies and who has been affected by them? The statistics of quality and efficiency in basic education, and many of the opinions concerning the BES, reveal the existence of serious problems of system performance. Because of that, a study about the impact of these policies which includes the evolution and change in educational policies seems to be necessary.

- In what way are the policies discussed and conceived? This question has to do with the debate process (if it exists) taking place before the formulation of education policies. It includes the analysis of different topics related to the negotiation process: roles, interests and positions of the parties, kind of results obtained and what interests have benefited from these results, etc.

- What is the role of social research in the formulation of policy and monitoring the advance of the implementation of policy? Social research has had a strong influence in countries such as the USA and Great Britain. With respect to the last, Bulmer (1982) says "Research on education is one field in which sociological approaches have had a considerable impact on policy... The findings of studies by Jean Floud, A.H. Halsley and F.M. Martin (1956),...into the social determinants of educational success all exercised a powerful influence upon policy in both primary and secondary education". Affirmations related to the lack of research and information to support education policies, were made by the "Misión de Ciencia, Educación y Desarrollo" in Colombia (Aldana et al, 1995). It leads to the conclusion that the influence of research in education policies has not been so strong. However, is important to see what has been the influence and how to promote it.

What is the legitimacy of the process? Woodward, Edwards and Birkin (1996) mention two views of organisational legitimacy, one of them in the sense of society's assessment of the usefulness of the organisation and its output and the other one in terms of the congruency between the organisation's activities with society's. If the second view is taken in this study, the congruency of BES' activities with society's would be the congruency between the ideal of society and the results of the BES. Besides that, the legitimacy has to be analysed in relation to the parties involved in the PMP, e.g., legitimacy of government, educational unions, private sector, etc.

What is the ideal society defined or projected by education policy? Ball (1990, p.3) says "Policy projects images of an ideal society (education policies project definitions of what counts as education)". Undoubtedly the last Decenal Plan of Education in Colombia reflects the relation between policy and the ideal society. Nevertheless, it is pertinent to see what kind of society is being validated by education policy and how the definition of education has evolved.

4. ABOUT THE SELECTION OF METHODOLOGIES TO DEVELOP THE STUDY

To find one or more answers to the above questions it is necessary to define a framework where all these questions may make sense. For instance it could be possible to use the three levels employed by Ball (1990). These are: ideological, political and economic. One important issue to consider in the selection of these methodologies is to do it in a critical way, being aware of the basic assumptions of the methodologies and the theoretical problems that are involved in using them.

There is not yet enough information to decide what methodology to use, but there are three aspects to consider: Firstly, to find a way to make explicit the power relations influencing the PMP and the interests being served for the policies defined. Secondly, to find a method to evaluate critically all stages of the PMP. Finally, to keep in mind that the experiences of other countries, are only a help to find new ideas. It means that it is not possible to transfer their solutions to the BES in Colombia.

With respect to the second aspect, the study of the stages of PMP has to be done, taking into account that policy making does not proceed step by step. A step by step approach includes: the appearance of some problems on the political agenda, the definition of policy, its implementation and evaluation. Lindblom and Woodhouse (1993, p.10), say that this approach "risks assuming that policy making proceeds through a coherent and rational process" and "Policy Making is, instead, a complex interactive process without beginning or end" (Lindblom and Woodhouse, 1993, P.11). To see the PMP in such a way leads to the analysis of the evolution of the process, trying to find the chain of interactions that explains the current situation, instead of reviewing every policy.

REFERENCES

Ball, S. J., 1990, *Politics and Policy Making in Education. Explorations in Policy Sociology*, 1st ed., Routledge, London & New York.

CONPES, 1994, El Salto Educativo : Documento CONPES 2738 - MEN-DNP:UDS. Colombia.

Duarte, J., 1996, La debilidad del Ministerio de Educación y la Politización de la educación en Colombia: dos problemas a enfrentar en el Plan Decenal, *Coyuntura Social*, 14: 145–167.

Lindblom, C., and Woodhouse, E., 1993, *The Policy-Making Process*, 3rd ed., Prentice Hall, New Jersey.

Ministerio de Educación Nacional, 1982, Estadísticas Educativas (1970–1982), MEN,Colombia.

Ministerio de Educación Nacional, 1995, Unpublished report of MEN - Colombia.

Misión de Ciencia, Educación, 1994, Informe Conjunto : Misión de Ciencia, Educación y Desarrollo, Colombia.

Woodward, D., Edwards, P., and Birkin, F., 1996, Some evidence on executive' views of corporate social responsability and its reporting, Paper presented in the British Academy of Management - Annual Conference 1996.

38

THE CONTRIBUTION OF EVALUATION TO ORGANIZATIONAL LEARNING

Exploding the Myth

Amanda Gregory

Centre for Systems Research
School of Management
Lincoln University Campus
Brayford Pool, Lincoln, LN6 7TS

1. INTRODUCTION

The notion of organizational learning is a popular theme in the evaluation literature (Van der Knaap, 1995; Owen and Lambert, 1995). Whilst, traditionally, this work has been based on a rational-objectivist view, Van der Knaap has recently documented a paradigm shift in evaluation to argumentative-subjectivism. In the light of a discussion of self-producing systems, the argument will be advanced that the shift to argumentative-subjectivism will not promote the effectiveness of evaluation practice. Following a summary review of Stacey's (1992, 1996) work on chaos and creativity, it will be proposed that the roles of 'evaluator as judge', as per rational-objectivism, and 'evaluator as critic', as per argumentative-subjectivism, are redundant.

2. EVALUATION AND ORGANIZATIONAL LEARNING

According to Dodgson (1993), the notion of organizational learning is problematic: 'there is rarely agreement about what learning is and how it occurs'. Van der Knaap (1995) has considered the role that evaluation has to play in promoting learning and proposes three definitions of learning:

- corrective system learning on the basis of feedback;
- learning as cognitive development;
- social learning by means of dialogue and argumentation.

Based on the above, Van der Knaap proposes three corresponding categories of evaluation:

- a feedback mechanism on the effectiveness of policy theories;
- a stimulus configuration reflective policy makers can refer to and learn from;
- a communicative domain in which argumentation and mutual persuasion lead to a social construction of policy theories.

Following his differentiation of three types of learning and evaluation, Van der Knaap goes on to discuss the shift away from rational-objectivism in evaluation towards argumentative-subjectivism. The rational approach, according to Van der Knaap, "...strongly resembles corrective system learning by means of feedback information." (p. 200). The rational-objectivist approach is fundamentally concerned with 'the search for truth' about the effectiveness of a policy or an organization. Van der Knaap contrasts the rational approach with that of the argumentative. The argumentative approach is based on constructivism and, consequently, focuses upon "...the communicative processes between policy actors in 'policy networks' and/or policy advocacy coalitions" (p. 202).

It may be proposed, therefore, that the role of the evaluator has shifted from one of respected expert and supplier of the facts about organizational performance to one of provider of insightful comment and participant in the debate about future organizational policy: "To the policy-making agency, evaluation constitutes 'just another' source of information. If the evaluating body want to influence the outcomes, it has to become an active participant in and influence the social 'arena' or argumentative domain for policy discourse." (p. 205).

As a result of this development in evaluation theory, evaluation practitioners are being urged to take on the role of management critic. But will this promote organizational learning and the effectiveness of evaluation findings? Perhaps the theory of self-producing or autopoietic systems may shed some light on this issue. The argument has been put forth that organizations are self-producing systems. Whilst there has been much controversy over whether organizations can be said to be truly self-producing, it is interesting, even if autopoiesis is simply used in a metaphorical way, to reflect upon how this theory might explain why evaluation studies rarely promote organizational learning.

3. ON THE NATURE OF SELF-PRODUCING SYSTEMS

3.1. Autopoiesis: A Summary

The theory of autopoiesis resulted from Maturana and Varela's (1980) exploration of what distinguishes living systems from non-living and how living systems persist despite changes in structure and components. Maturana and Varela proposed that the fundamental characteristic of living systems is autonomy which is realised through the process of autopoiesis. Given the notion of autonomy, autopoietic systems may be said to produce the components necessary for the maintenance of the autopoietic processes. Hence, an autopoietic system is made up of networks of recurring interactions of the production of component parts. It is this self-produced nature of components which enables the distinction of the autopoietic system from its environmental background.

The autopoietic system is structurally coupled to its environment: it responds to environmental perturbations by producing a feasible set of responses, in such a way as to maintain its autopoietic state, from which the environment selects. When discussing change within the autopoietic system, the crucial distinction between organization and structure must be made. When the organization of an autopoietic system changes, the system takes on a new identity; when the structure changes, the system maintains its identity.

3.2. Culture and Autopoiesis

Robb (1989a) and Gomez and Probst (1989) have advanced the argument that organizational cultures may be said to be autopoietically generated. In establishing this theory, three points are most relevant:

- it is culture which, through the self-production of its component parts of norms and values, distinguishes one organization from another. Robb states that: "If humans come to believe that, through the organization, their perception of the world can be identified with that of their fellows in the organization and that they can realise themselves within the organization and only in that way, then they truly become "components" of it." (p. 249).
- it is culture which bounds the organization with respect to its environment. Gomez and Probst have argued: "The system...is this shared set of beliefs that we call corporate culture and every kind of institutionalization that goes with it. Quite naturally the system's boundaries are very fuzzy; but all members belonging to the system as well as the relevant environment know intuitively where they are." (p. 316)
- the organization's coupling with its environment causes the system to maintain "...its identity in a changing environment by holding invariant its beliefs (organization) while changing everything else about itself (structure)." (p. 316).

The notion that organizations are autopoietic is a contentious one and has resulted in an ongoing debate between Mingers and Robb. Mingers (1989) states that to: "...claim that an Organization or a society *is* autopoietic is to raise contentious ontological claims that in many ways lie at the heart of social theory and its debates between objectivism and subjectivism (Mingers, 1984)." (p. 175).

Mingers goes on to identify three problems with the attribution of the process of autopoiesis to the organization:

- 'if autopoiesis is centrally concerned with the process of production then what, in the organizational setting, is being produced?' (p. 175).
- "Generally, people can choose to belong or not belong to particular institutions and will be members of many at any time. What is it that would constitute the boundaries of such systems?" (pp. 175–176).
- "...how can it be said that such institutions act as unities. Is it not only individual people who can act?" (p. 176).

Robb has responded to the issues raised by Mingers. Whilst Robb agrees with Mingers that: "...humans cannot be seen as components of an autopoietic social system" (p. 344), he adds that: "...it is only those human properties which contribute to the production of the autopoietic system which should be regarded as components." (p. 344).

Secondly, Robb, based on the previous point, takes up Mingers' argument on the definition of boundaries. Robb contends that:

"We can see that the boundary not only divides some whole individuals from others, but also partitions the properties, the actions and thoughts, of those particular individuals who are related to the system. Some actions, those entailed in the self-production of the system, are partitioned from those which are not related to it. Where this boundary lies, what properties of the individual are required for the time being by the system, are determined by the system itself." (pp. 345–346).

Finally, Robb addresses the issue of whether organizations can act. Robb states: "Some modern organizations do appear to me to be much more than a temporary coalition of individuals who act on their own behalf" (p. 346).

In the light of the above debate, Robb (1991) concludes that "Probably the best we can do, then is to talk of "virtual" autopoietic systems, systems which we think behave "as if" they were autopoietic." (p. 218).

The autopoietic metaphor may help to explain why the results of evaluations are commonly not acted upon and fail to promote organizational learning. Robb (1989b) states that: "Intervention, in an attempt to design or adapt such systems by humans, themselves systems of a lower logical order, will be "seen" by the organization simply as a perturbation from its environment which, if it does not serve its autopoiesis, should, and, if the organization is viable, can be dissipated." (p. 248). Hence, an evaluation can only effect the organization fundamentally if organizational actors are involved, claim responsibility for it and it has meaning at their level. For, as Wilkins and Ouchi (1983) state: "...the people of the community come to share a rather complex understanding of their world...which is relatively hidden to the outsider." (p. 469).

So, does this imply the breaking down of the commonly assumed cause-effect relationship between evaluation, learning and improved effectiveness and efficiency? To determine this we need to ascertain what causes autopoietic entities to change. Morgan has also considered this question: "The theory of autopoiesis locates the source of change in random variations occurring *within* the total system. These may stem from random modifications introduced through processes of reproduction, or through the combination of chance interactions and connections that give rise to the development of new system relations." (p. 239).

4. CHAOS THEORY, ORGANIZATIONAL LEARNING, AND EVALUATION

Stacey (1992) has drawn out the implications of random variations and chaos theory for management: "When a system operates in chaos, it is highly sensitive to small changes. It amplifies tiny fluctuations or disturbances throughout the system, but in a complex way that leads to completely different, inherently unpredictable forms of behavior...Clear-cut connections between cause and effect are lost in the unpredictable unfolding of events. At the same time, the behavior of an individual component of a system can have a profound effect on the future of the whole system." (p. 63).

Further, Stacey goes on to state that "...chaos breaks symmetries, and this is an essential step in the emergence of new order. Destruction and creativity are closely related to each other, and continuing creativity requires continuing destruction." (p. 81). It might appear that chaos theory, with its emphasis on destruction, and learning, with its focus on development, are at odds with one another. Stacey, however, argues that there is no contradiction but, instead, a shift from single- to double-loop learning. Single-loop learning is based on a view of "...management as a process of realizing visions through actions planned a long time in advance" (p. 30) whereas double-loop learning does not assume such a stable environment and focuses on the constant questioning and appraisal of events, motives and situations.

So what does all this imply for the practice of evaluation? It appears that the shift from rational-objectivism to argumentative-subjectivism documented by Van der Knaap flounders in the face of self-producing systems theory. From a self-producing systems perspective, as was previously discussed, there is little if any role for the evaluator. The position is little better from a chaos theory perspective.

According to Stacey (1996), organizations consist of a legitimate network and a shadow network. The legitimate network "...consists of links that are either (1) formally and intentionally established by the most powerful members of an organization or (2) established by well-understood, implicit principles that are widely accepted by members of the organization - that is a shared culture or accepted ideology." (p. 24). The shadow network, on the other hand, "...comprises all social and political interactions that are outside the rules strictly prescribed by the legitimate system. It is the arena in which members of an organization pursue their own gain, but also the arena in which they play, create, and prepare innovations." (p. 290). The argumentative form of evaluation documented by Van der Knaap is commonly based on the exposure of the shadow network. An evaluator is very often seen to be astute and aware if (s)he is able to make some pertinent comment about the political activities within the organization. However, from Stacey's perspective, this exposure of political activity is based on the assumption that the shadow network serves only to undermine the legitimate system. Stacey recognises that the shadow network may actually contribute to organizational effectiveness, "...it is primarily the state of the shadow system that determines whether or not an organization operates in the space for creativity at the edge of chaos...For an organization to occupy this space, its shadow system must be in a state of flux behind the stable facade of its legitimate system. The shadow must be working to undermine the legitimate system in acts of creative destruction." (p. 171).

Stacey goes on to differentiate between what he calls ordinary and extraordinary. Stacey claims that the distinction between ordinary and extraordinary management "...coincides with the one between single- and double-loop learning: ordinary management occurs when members of an organization carry out single-loop learning, learning within a constant shared paradigm, and extraordinary management occurs when they switch to double-loop learning, that is, when they alter their shared paradigm or some part of it." (p. 193). This emphasis on the questioning of dominant values and accepted practices by management implies that the 'what' and 'why' questions (double-loop learning) are already being asked in organizations without the involvement of the evaluator operating in argumentative-subjectivist mode.

So does this imply there is no role for the evaluator in organizations any more? If it is accepted that organizations exhibit self-producing systems type characteristics and change by means of flux and transformation then evaluations based on the provision of feedback information seem to be of little worth. Further, the argumentative model of evaluation would not seem to have credence since it, mistakenly according to Stacey's theory, is premised on the bringing to light and resolution of issues residing within the shadow system. Thus, on the basis that organizations exhibit self-producing systems like characteristics, both the evaluator as judge (as per rational-objectivism) and the evaluator as critic (as per argumentative-subjectivism) roles should be seen to be inappropriate in the light of recent developments in creativity and chaos theory. It is time to rethink the role of the evaluator.

5. CONCLUSION

In this paper discussion was made of the shift in evaluation, as documented by Van der Knaap, from rational-objectivism to argumentative-subjectivism. Following a discussion of self-producing systems, it was argued that this shift to argumentative-subjectivism will not promote the effectiveness of evaluation since any recommendations advanced from this perspective would be seen to be perturbations from the system's environment. Furthermore, in the light of Stacey's theory that organizations consist of two networks, the legitimate and the shadow, it was proposed that the argumentative-subjectivism model of evaluation is ineffective since it is assumes that issues in the shadow system should be made explicit and resolved. Finally, it was argued that evaluators should consider the implications of developments in creativity and chaos theory for evaluation theory and practice.

REFERENCES

Van der Knaap, P., 1995, Policy evaluation and learning: feedback, enlightenment or argumentation?, *Evaluation* 1(2): 189–216.

Owen, J. M., and Lambert, F. C., 1995, Roles for evaluation in learning organizations, *Evaluation* 1(2): 237–250.

Dodgson, M., 1993, Organizational learning: a review of some literatures, *Organizations Studies* 14(3): 375–394.

Maturana, H. R., and Varela, F. J., 1980, *Autopoiesis and Cognition: The Realization of the Living*, Reidel Publishing Company, Dordrecht, Holland.

Robb, F. F., 1989a, The application of autopoiesis to social organizations - a comment on John Mingers' "An introduction to autopoiesis: implications and applications", *Systems Practice* 2(3): 343–348.

Robb, F. F., 1989b, The limits to human organization: the emergence of autopoietic systems. In M. C. Jackson, P. Keys and S. Cropper (eds.), *Operational Research and the Social Sciences*, Plenum Press, New York, pp. 247–251.

Robb, F. F., 1991, Accounting - a virtual autopoietic system?, *Systems Practice* 4(3): 215–235.

Gomez, P., and Probst, G. J. B., 1989, Organizational closure in management: a complementary view to contingency approaches, *Cybernetics and Systems* 20: 311–320.

Mingers, J., 1989, An introduction to autopoiesis - implications and applications, *Systems Practice* 2(2): 159–180.

Mingers, J., 1984, Subjectivism and soft systems methodology - a critique. *Journal of Applied Systems Analysis* 11: 85–103.

Wilkins, A. L., and Ouchi, W. G., 1983, Efficient cultures: exploring the relationship between culture and organizational performance, *Administrative Science Quarterly* 28: 468–481.

Stacey, R. D., 1992, *Managing the Unknowable: Strategic Boundaries Between Order and Chaos in Organizations*, Jossey-Bass Publishers, San Francisco.

Stacey, R. D., 1996, *Complexity and Creativity in Organizations*, Berrett-Koehler Publishers, Inc., San Francisco.

39

EXPLORING PARALLELS BETWEEN QUAKER BELIEFS AND SYSTEMS THEORY

Misha Hebel-Holehouse

City University
Department of System Science
Northampton Square
London EC1V 0HB
E-mail: M.Hebel@city.ac.uk

1. INTRODUCTION

The observation that there are parallels between the Religious Society of Friends (Quaker) beliefs and systems concepts originates from research into performance measurement as undertaken in four very different case studies and documented elsewhere (Hebel, 1996). One of these studies looked at the Quaker business method and consequently the Societies decision making process. On the surface the religious faith and practice of Friends (a name often used by Quakers about Quakers) appeared to have little in common with systems thinking and application but this is not so. The two groups share language and concepts—holism, purpose, emergence for instance—and from this it can be argued that given the 300 year sustainability of the Religious Society of Friends, systems thinking may also offer a route to maintaining symmetry at both a range of levels.

2. QUAKER BACKGROUND

It is necessary to start with a brief description of how the Quakers undertake their activities. This is in part due to the different way they practice their religion compared with other Christian groups and also because there is a close link between the manner of worship and the conduct of business.

Quakers are a Christocentric religious group established over 300 years ago as a reaction to the over complex and conflictual churches of the time. The most obvious difference between Quakers and other Christians in worship is the absence of ordained ministers and lack of prearranged liturgy. Places of worship and business are called Meeting Houses, identifiable by location. *Meetings for Worship* are held once or twice weekly in silence. Anyone attending may speak (minister) to the group if they feel so moved to do so. The emphasis is on sharing insights and feelings rather than preaching, hence ministry is not prepared beforehand. Creeds and dogmas are avoided although a book of significant Quaker experiences is updated and republished every thirty to forty years. There is a very practical emphasis which includes holding regular business meetings and active involvement in secular, ecumenical and political activities (Gorman, 1981; 1988; Hubbard, 1985; Allen, 1993).

Business Meetings are conducted in a very similar way to Meeting for Worship in that each one begins with a period of silence, after which the Clerk presents an agenda (Quaker Home Service, 1986). This agenda takes a familiar format - minutes of the last meeting, items of interest or action and other business. It includes items that range from leaking roofs to the spiritual development of the meeting. What is notably different is the response to items, which although passionate at times, rarely includes the non-listening conflict and argument that occurs at other types of business meeting. From the interviews conducted at local and national meetings it appears that opinion is usually voiced thoughtfully and received considerately. Once comment is heard the Clerk attempts to summarise the *sense of the meeting* (Sheeran, 1983) and immediately presents this back for further comment. The process is more like an intellectual argument whereby different views are reconciled by intelligent persuasion. This process sometimes takes a long time. Friends are careful to avoid applying the word consensus to the decision making process as this implies that objectors still exist. If unity cannot be achieved a further period of silence ensues in order to give those involved time to reflect. Sometimes an item is held over to the next meeting for further reflection or for more information to be obtained. Voting is never undertaken and the emphasis is on united decision. Meetings are theocratic rather than democratic (Gorman, 1981).

The benefits of going to a Meeting vary according to the individual. Examples however are the spiritual peace, resulting from a gathered meeting; a comfort derived from sharing time with people one trusts; breathing space in a hectic world; a time to reflect on the happenings of the week; a time to deal with stress (Halliday, 1991). In other words the benefits are not as religiously oriented as one might expect. Another more general appeal of Quakerism is the practicality of their beliefs, especially furthering the interests of human dignity and peace. Simplicity and equality considered vital to their existence (Allen, 1993).

3. DISCUSSION

Table 1 summarises the main parallels between Quakerism and systems thinking. Differences in detail may be observed but in general the table shows many similarities. This semblance may not be as surprising as it first appears. Two key figures in the early development of systems theory had interests in the Quakers. Kenneth Boulding was one of the founders of the Society of General Systems Research (SGSR) in the 1950's and a key influence on the development of core systems ideas. He was much involved with the Quaker community and their peace interests (Hammond, 1996; Boulding, 1956) included a transcendental system in his hierarchy of systems believing that it was inevitable that some questions would have no answers in empiricism. Vickers (1965) on the other hand observed the Quaker business method in action and commented that the time they took was essential because successful decisions are those based on the restructuring of reality and value systems. Perhaps it was the strength of Quaker philosophy, attempting to get the whole picture whilst taking time to consider options and assumptions that helped to form what we recognise as systems thinking today.

Table 1. Summary of parallels between Quaker beliefs and systems philosophy

Concept	Systems	Quaker
Basic Philosophy	Holistic and problem solving - systems are interconnected with purpose and emergent properties - concerned with communication and understanding of different perspectives	That there is that of God in everyone - respect and tolerance for differing perspectives on issues - actions have wider consequences and groups have synergy - simplicity and equality
Structure	Methodologies form basis of systems analysis - tendency for practitioners to prefer or be identified with specific methodologies	Belief system as basis for consequent behaviour and attitudes - could be seen as one of many Christian methodologies
Practice	Primarily reactive, responding to problem situations - overall attempts to improve by intervention - moving towards proactivity by developing concern for sustainability	Primarily proactive in development of spiritual well-being - although origins and many practical activities reactive e.g. response to crisis or hardship - Living by example core idea
Nature	Iterative by use of methodologies and conceptual tools - Secular, theoretical and practical	Reflective by use of silence and consideration of others viewpoints - spiritual, conceptual and practical
Phenomena	Metaphors, paradigms and models major currency of systems thinking - all attempts to convey meaning by example or simulation of reality	Quotes and writings based on real life experiences rather than the Bible for basis of Quaker discipline - wide variety of mediums used to communicate e.g. tapestry, artwork, theatre
Emergence	Fundamental systems idea covering the uniqueness of a system as a collection of interconnected parts.	Readiness to acknowledge added benefit of worshipping and working in a group - Synergy of meetings for worship and business often unexpected in nature

The most apparent similarity between the two ways of thinking is the importance they place on an holistic approach. Living by example is an important part of Quaker ethos (Marsden, 1995). They readily acknowledge that their actions have consequences on others and the environment. They also recognise the need to be as well informed as possible—both factually and spiritually—about a situation of concern. The holistic nature of their belief system is paramount. In systems thinking we are encouraged to look for unintended consequences and to be able to adopt multiple perspectives and methodologies (Flood and Jackson, 1991) in order to provide an appropriate analysis. Quakers also look to gain the bigger picture and encourage an awareness of interconnectedness. Convergence and divergence must necessarily coexist for both philosophies to survive.

Of course it cannot be ignored that Quakerism is a religion and therefore founded on a creed however it is interpreted. From this point it can be argued that doctrine appeals because it gives an 'easy' answer to difficult or apparently unanswerable questions. The belief system provides a structure to either work with or against according to need. The acknowledgement of a Deity can also relieve its participants of responsibility for their actions. Alternatively it gives power to those officials (or Elders in Quaker terms) supporting the framework, possibly also without personal responsibility. The search for management and systems methodologies could also be indicative of a human need for structure and explanation of phenomena. For Quakers, the Bible and Christianity provides a baseline structure to work from, just as the definition of a system and consequent methodologies serve as a starting point for analysis. These basic tenets are constantly reworked by both groups.

Whilst Quakerism is a variation on Christianity it allows the individual control over interpretation and benefit. The results of this are varied and not entirely on a par with mainstream Christian churches. For instance within one meeting there can be as many different definitions of how a meeting 'works' as there are people attending. In fact it is unnecessary to even recognise a Deity in order to be quite welcome at a meeting and benefit from it. Diversity is the norm yet somehow values paradigms are shared. Roles and duties are undertaken but not competed for and can be justified even if contrary to norms if circumstances warrant it.

Probably the most striking aspect of Quaker business meetings—compared with meetings undertaken by other case studies—is the silence and patience evident when decision making. This is especially impressive at British Yearly Meeting, an annual gathering of hundreds of representatives from most Meetings to share concerns and deal with central administration. No individual or matter is treated with more or less consideration. An agreed model of communicating is shared by most Quaker members and attenders although this may vary slightly from Meeting to Meeting or more particularly between countries. This model however has proved robust over many hundreds of years (Oats, 1995) and even when no final decision has apparently been made there is often a sense of moving forward that does not always seem to occur in other business meetings. There also seems a preparedness to adapt the various belief paradigms as the social, cultural and political environment changes. Of course this is a general observation and at times the business method proves inadequate. Periodically, Friends find themselves unable to agree with or accept decisions made and so take action outside the usual paradigm or move on to alternative beliefs.

Systems theory could be perceived as a microcosm of Quaker philosophy, one that is perhaps also prone to convincing itself that its espoused theory and theory in use are the same. Both are very conceptual in nature and this can lead to the development of a pseudo-community (Peck, 1987). For Quakers this can result in the avoidance of overt conflict and in systems it could be argued that pursuit of academic advancement by developing specific methodologies can result in dismissal of old-fashioned but valid theories. Peck, educated in a Quaker school and trained as a psychologist, is particularly concerned with the maintenance and well-being of both individuals and community. He takes a systemic view of community and in *The Different Drum* looks not only at established psychosocial theories of group action but also integrates the spiritual principles of tolerance and love. His argument could be seen as a bridge between Quakerism and systems philosophy.

One of the fundamental differences between systems theory and Quakers is the religious or spiritual nature of Quaker beliefs. This however is not what seems to make the Quaker business method work, but rather a shared set of values and group norms. In other words the ground rules are shared. In fact it can also be argued that one of the reasons systems finds itself in some crisis at present is the persistent search for another methodology, in itself a reductionist activity and fundamentally contrary to essential systems values. Quaker values seem to have a longevity about them. Their structure rests on traditional processes but with the capacity for the organisational change over time. There is stability combined with the flexibility to respond quickly when required, if a crisis or concern requires action there is a good chance there will be some Friends working quietly in the background. The business method isn't just to maintain buildings or fund good works. Many successful businesses have been founded on the same principle—Kays Shoes, Cadbury and Rowntree are examples. There is a tendency even among Friends though to forget that the method requires a certain amount of skill and patience (Halliday, 1991) and handing on the tradition can be made difficult with misunderstandings over the basic assumptions.

4. CONCLUSION

There are many parallels between the two philosophies as well as a few significant differences that could form the basis of sustainability. The main lessons we can learn from Quakerism is the flexibility they exhibit that allows them to retain what is good regardless of how old it is whilst developing new strategies in order to adapt to new challenges in an ever changing sociological environment. Given the similarities between the core tenets systemists may find it beneficial to discard the multiplicity of methodologies that have prevailed over the last ten years, returning to the heart of systems ideas that encourage both tolerance and sustainability.

REFERENCES

Allen, R., 1993, *A Tender Hand*, William Sessions, York

Boulding, K., 1956, General systems theory - a skeleton of science, *Management Science*, **2**:197–208.

Britain Yearly Meeting of the Religious Society of Friends, 1995, *Quaker faith and practice,* Britain Yearly Meeting of the Religious Society of Friends

Flood, R.L., and Jackson, M.C., 1991, *Creative Problem Solving: Total Systems Intervention*, Wiley, Chichester

Gorman, G. H., 1981, *Introducing Quakers*, Quaker Home Service, London

Gorman, G.H., 1988, *The Amazing Fact of Quaker Worship*, Quaker Home Service, London

Halliday R., 1991, *Mind The Oneness*, Quaker Home Service, London

Hammond, D., 1996, *Evaluating the Heritage of GST*, General Systems Bulletin, **XXV**, (1):7–20

Hebel, M., 1996, The impact of value systems on performance measurement, *Systemist, 17(2):64–78*

Hubbard, G., 1985, *Quaker by Convincement*, Quaker Home Service, London

London Yearly Meeting of the Religious Society of Friends, 1960, *Christian faith and practice in the experience of the Society of Friends*

Marsden, L.M., 1995, *The Singing of New Songs*, William Sessions, York

Oats, W.N., 1995, *Values Education*, The Friends' School, North Hobart

Peck, M.S., 1987, *The Different Drum*, Arrow, London

Quaker Home Service, 1986, *Quaker Organisation*, Quaker Home Service, London

Sheeran M.J., 1983, *Beyond Majority Rule*, Philadelphia Yearly Meeting, Pennsylvania

Vickers, G., 1965, *The Art of Judgement*, Chapman and Hall, London (Reprinted 1983 Harper & Row, London)

40

SYSTEMS, CRAFTS, AND SUSTAINABILITY

J. G. Howell and J. G. Gammack

Department of Computing and Information Systems
University of Paisley
Paisley PA1 2BE, Scotland, United Kingdom
Tel: +44 141 848 3301; Fax:+44 141 848 3542
Email: {howe-ci0, gamm-ci0}@paisley.ac.uk

1. INTRODUCTION

Prior to the 1993 UKSS conference at Paisley, in order to better understand the aims of the conference and of the society members, one of the main speakers read the volume of conference proceedings. In his opening address, Owen Taylor (1993) interpreted the domain of systems thinking and practice as being able to offer new and worthwhile insights into varied and complex systems and, in particular, to the environs of Paisley. The Leader of the Town Council envisaged our work (systems practitioners of the UKSS) as being able to appraise holistically the changing systems. Examples of systems were drawn from traditional craft systems such as shipbuilding, car building, thread and cloth making. All of these systems have been reduced to a significantly depleted state with an ensuing effect on employment, wealth and the economic wellbeing of the community of Paisley. Consequent improvements had been noted to other "systems", such as cleaner rivers, reduced pollution, increased leisure hours. Whether these changing systems had, on the whole, proved beneficial to the local communities is difficult to determine. There are different viewpoints and stakeholder interests in play. The contribution of systems thinking to the understanding of complex systems is very real.

Systems thinking provides concepts and methods for dealing with complex issues and scenarios. In the case of the interactions among technological developments, changing organisational and social structures, globalisation and the future of work, economic warfare and quality of life, perhaps only systems thinking can make sense of the potential confusion. With the academic concepts familiar to systemists, along with such tools as systems dynamics, simulation and the other integrating disciplines identified by Senge (Senge, 1994) the systems community is uniquely placed to identify the potential causes of human-scale developments, disasters, successes, tragedies and more specifically those systems which may be approaching a severely depleted state from which any possible future restoration may be impossible. Proactively, systems theory may be able to offer insights into achieving sustainability in systems which stakeholders or other interested parties wish to sustain. The issue of sustainability is of concern to all; not only environmentally with depletion of fish stocks, pollution, global warming and other well documented issues but also the acquisition of skills, jobs dependent on those skills, and learned information. Practical expertise in dynamic and turbulent environments is also an issue of systemic sustainability. We consider this issue with respect to craft skills, which are paradigmatic of the crisis in the complex socio-techno-economic environment which makes incursions on the natural human quality of-life-experience. Following our description and analysis, we consider some of the outcomes, particularly as they impact on educational and systems research strategies.

Our hypothesis is that a systemic understanding is necessary to encompass the complexity inherent in integrating runaway technological expansion with the life patterns of communities. The visionary work of Chermayeff and Alexander (1963) and Chermayeff and Tzonis (1971) implies urgent rethinking of this complexity, as the overthrow of naturally emerging systems of community by essentially economic and privately motivated forces as evidenced daily in passing ways of life. It is simplistic to consider technology just as a neutral invention which may be used for good or ill. Viewing technology, as Chermayeff and Tzonis (1971) do using Suranyi-Unger's definition as: "A composite of technical, psychological and economic concepts ...a social-economic power structure" draws attention to its potential for insidious influence. Only when there is a shared vision of what technology is serving, and when that is rooted in the purposes of implicated humans, can its role be evaluated.

2. SYSTEMS THINKING, SYSTEMS THEORY, AND CRAFTS

In previous times, and still within living memory, the lack of private cars and widespread international communication abilities perforce implied systems of community life based on local interdependencies, shared histories, and the resources of the local land. Complex systems of feedback allowed a stability in the system to emerge, sustainable through periods of famine or plenty. Systems stability is an identifiable property which, in turn, gives rise to the evolution of those 'systems' which together provide for some sustainability. Interventions in stable systems, even well intentioned, can lead to tragedies, by disrupting the balance and holistic integrity of these feedback processes. The tragedy of the Sahel is a famous example (Roberts, 1984), but such systems interventions can be seen closer to home.

One of the programmes in the BBC series *Postcards From The Country* (1996) sensitively depicted life in Kent only a couple of generations ago, where villages had a viable ecosystem based around hop picking and cherry orchards, with a rich diversity of local beers, and distinctive village characteristics. With the incursion of road policies, and non-locally emergent directives to stop farming traditional crops in favour of others, this system has been lost, and many Kentish villages are now undistinguished commuterland homes for non-natives, the beers are fewer, the skills of working with hop-poles are dead or dying, and non-native plants such as rape are an affront to the balance of colours in the garden of England. Similar stories occur in France, with traditional vineyards bulldozed to provide crops convenient for wider markets. The purchasing power of global supermarkets means one vineyard's entire crop is sold, and another's has no market. The associated local expertise in viniculture is not passed on, and is lost.

In the UK, the craft of the dry stone waller almost became extinct about 30 years ago, together with the distinctive sense of locale which derived from the local styles by which regions retained their traditional identity. With people living in the same place for a long time, the natural system of inspection of work by peers and casual neighbours ensured a pride in the job and one's place in the community. Master craftsworkers were brought in from Ireland in the late 1960s (O' Callaghan, 1969), training courses were developed, lore was recorded and shared, and incentives were provided through grants to farmers. The industry is now thriving, and can be well paid as economically, dry stone walls last longer than wooden or steel fences and have numerous other ecological advantages. Without some appropriate analysis, it is not clear why this craft loss has been reversed; this may be simply an emergent phenomenon which we have not yet fully appreciated. To understand the forces which have brought this about a systemic appreciation is required and modelling approaches such as System Dynamics are likely to offer a useful analysis of such scenarios. Many other examples exist. For instance, the recently publicised increase in apprenticeships to some of the traditional shipbuilding crafts within the local environs of Paisley and Glasgow. It is possible to hypothesise about whether these are instances of the same systemic reversal or whether these are simply sporadic instances which might be better understood through other theories, such as chaos theory.

We can cite many other instances of the deleterious effects on traditional patterns of community living wreaked by technological innovation, which includes cars and communication technologies as well as computers. There are literatures available on these themes, as well as treatments explored in artistic and popular cultural forms. Many crafts have died out or dwindled, surviving only in archaic surnames (e.g. Chandler, Smith) and the tricks of the trade, or the knowledge that distinguished a skilled or master craftsperson from a gifted or non-gifted amateur, died then too. With respect to our main theme of sustaining craft skills, the apprenticeship tradition in medieval Europe can be thought of as a form of oral and exemplary transmission of knowledge. To the extent that craft is nonverbally mediated, shallow forms of knowledge representation based on linguistic tokens are inadequate, and present a research challenge to intelligent systems technology. But this, though feasible, may not be desirable. Is it inappropriately romantic to view craft skills as irreducible and worth preserving as a mysterious human ability? Or is the reality that homo faber is an evolutionary vestige, that craft is demeaning, and that purposeless drudgery should be replaced by superior technical knowledge? In the age of knowledge workers, can craftwork systems be delegated to robotic processes ?

In the UK, since the early 1970s many traditional craft systems have significantly depleted, with some approaching extinction. Government initiatives which provided for supportive and sustaining forces such as industrial training boards, skillcentres, the training agency, enterprise companies and so on have failed to sustain a craft heritage. Few new apprenticeship schemes have emerged. To understand this change it is necessary to begin with the evolution of the tradition of craft apprenticeship leading to qualification as a journeyman.

The genealogy of the journeyman can be traced back to the XIth century in Europe, when manual workers and craftsmen joined brotherhoods to help ensure their own survival. Over the following centuries, guilds and professional norms developed before industrialisation and the advent of new construction materials brought a demise to the tradition of the carpenter journeyman from last century onwards. Are there already recognisable forces which may constrain the development of the information technology and information systems journeyman (or person)—long before any possible demise of any underlying and sustainable apprenticeship system?

3. SUSTAINABILITY AND THE INFORMATION SYSTEMS JOURNEYMAN

If organisations are to learn, and if such learning is not to die within one or two generations of rapid change, what structures and strategies can ensure sustainability of craft knowledge? In particular we consider the crafts involved in computing technologies, which, apart from being pervasive, are predicted to form the bulk of jobs in years to come. The institute of employment research in the UK estimates that by the year 2001, nearly 30 percent of all workers will be in data services—for example, gathering, processing, retrieving, or analysing information. We thus begin to examine the issue posed with reference to the apprentice tradition by asking—can there be an IT journeyman?

In computing, the need to "fully exploit changes in technology: client/server and the arrival of object orientation, for example, are accelerating the passing of many traditional skills' sell-by dates". (Hayday, 1996). An IT journeyman then has the *labour of Sisyphus*; just when problems are being resolved and work achieved another technical 'advance' emerges creating new problems (Grint, 1994).

The timescales of technological change are such that specific education in technological fields soon becomes obsolete, and it is unrealistic for anyone to keep abreast of, and professional in, all developments. It is possible to identify and develop within a particular technological niche which allows for some persistence in IT skills, and also allows some stability to be engendered within the particular system for a period. If not, retraining every few years is one possibility, or having a high turnover of young computing staff is another possibly less expensive (in a cursory analysis) one. This sounds pessimistic: identifying the core transferable skills required is surely the basis for vocational education policy. With respect to technical skills, these are likely to be the holistic IS skills which see the potential applications for technologies in systemic contexts, without chasing the details of the latest version of some programming language. The days when someone could be a COBOL programmer for life are gone. (Hayday, 1996). Many organisations have, however, taken the view that DOS or Windows 3.X, a LAN, Lotus Notes and an office suite provide for a stable low-technology development platform and is sufficient for their business purposes, generally. Adding to this, perhaps, one dedicated computer to the outside world for Internet / email activity, and overall there is no need to convert to new operating system interfaces or the newest upgrade of some software package. The business "six pack" (Anderson, 1996) skills are core, the issue is how they impact on human activity, and these are seen as more critical than a refined technical appreciation. Notwithstanding the educational/ training debate, pedagogic constraints require that we should avoid teaching technical skills which may be out of date within the term of an undergraduate or postgraduate course. It is important to be mindful of the 3 or 4 year lead time for undergraduate education in particular. It is a nonsense to focus on providing specific technical training on 'systems' or software packages which enjoy only a short shelf life. We must concentrate on persistent and transferable skills, the knowledgeable and professional employment of these skills and in developing the understanding of the context within which they are employed, for example, the business context. This is very much the domain of IS: Information Systems is not Information Technology.

In his model of the learning organisation Senge (1990, 1993) describes the differences between the *triangle* of organisational architecture, and the *circle* of the deep underlying learning cycle. One corner of the triangle concerns the tools and methods of the day, and changes made in this area of organisations can be short lived. The reflective practice of systems thinking allows increasing awareness of the assumptions upon which such activities are based, and this awareness feeds back into the domain of operational activity. Senge leaves us in no doubt that despite its apparent intangibility, it is the circle that endures, and changes at this level are what really matter.

We view IT as properly located in the triangle of mundane operational tools and methods, and whilst focusing on its undeniable potential to make a difference at this level of organisational activity, it is the field of IS which requires to provide reflection, and to assimilate learning and awareness with regard to its deployment. These are the abstractions and skills which endure, and transfer understanding across fads and nine day wonders, and we find Senge's model highly relevant in distinguishing the two sets of activities involved.

IT reskilling has historically been viewed as a simple problem of developing in people a specific set of skills confined to products, methodologies and techniques. Hayday (1996) has noted that there is more than one dimension; reskilling should be thought of at three fundamentally different levels. *Applied skills*, which are the easiest to learn and are generally the information technology industry norm: they are product- or technique-based, or pertain to a more general category of technology, such as Object Orientation. *Behavioural skills,* which relate to how people act, together with the impact and effect of these actions. Development activities can be used to bring about these changes, and supplemented by practice in a supportive environment. Thirdly, *cognitive skills*, which are arguably the most important in shaping tomorrow's IT department.

Recent work in the UK has recognised that the IT revolution has had an impact on modern apprenticeships. Partly in response to this the *modern apprenticeships* are seen as "the bright hope for the future of British vocational education and training. They combine the virtues of traditional apprenticeships, based on the mutual commitment of employer and apprentice, with all the benefits of National vocational Qualifications, flexibility and more effective ways of learning" (Fennell, 1995). Similar work is underway in Europe and a charter of basic skills is being progressed (Barber, 1995). From early analysis it can be recognised that a unitary model of modern apprenticeships is being structured across all craft domains. Craft systems are human activity systems which differ in nature and context. It is uncertain, in the authors' view, whether this unitary approach to modern apprenticeship structuring will, be as successful as that of the traditional journeyman.

IT can and should be used proactively to gain technological improvement or economic advantage, even while recognising that competitive advantage may not be sustainable (Galliers R, 1993). Today's technological advantage quickly becomes tomorrow's standard working 'platform'. Proactively, IT might encourage new apprenticeships and new ways of doing extant apprenticeships, allowing apprenticeships in fields where "it is hard or impossible to do it in real life, like surgery or learning to fly a plane" (Schank, 1995).

Not only have "recent years witnessed the dramatic decline of the apprentice system in Western economies" (Neale, 1993), but the notion of full employment for a country's workforce may no longer be valid (see Handy, 1989). "Full-timers or insiders will be the new minority" (Pritchett P, 1994). Expectations are of IT skills being essential for most workers who must themselves take responsibility for continually updating their (technical) skills. Constant training, re-training, job-hopping, and even career-hopping, will become the norm ... a labour of Sisyphus. The scenario of part-time temporary working provides an uneasy vision of transitory work and transitory employment "contracts". This transitory and more virtual employment, not centred on building artefacts, may provide for a development environment which does not help develop professional pride, the joy of achievement, and the development of self esteem, personal characteristics, values and beliefs which are axiomatic to the concept of the journeyman.

4. CONCLUSIONS

A systemic approach is required to understand and help analyse the complex socio-economic systems in our culture. Systems thinking offers such tools. These may be applied to offer fresh insights to the reducing and developing ecosystems and to understand what may be perceived as the deleterious effects on some, on one hand, and the beneficial effects on the other hand. Such analysis may help us to take action to sustain those systems which are perceived as important, worthwhile or necessary. Craft systems is such a candidate system; a system which helped develop professional pride and inculcate satisfaction to the apprentice and journeyman alike in "a job well done". It is not clear that modern apprenticeships, including IT "apprenticeships", will provide an adequate development for these nor that the apprenticeship system will remain valid. If valid, IT apprenticeships may not be sustainable if these are built on skills which are constantly out of date. IS apprenticeships which focus on the persistent, sustainable and transferable skills in the use of IT should consider the concept the apprentice journeyman in the developing environment if an IS apprenticeship is developed.

REFERENCES

Bjorn-Anderson , N., and Chatfield, A.,1996, Using IT for creating the 21st century organization *in:Proceedings of the Fifth Annual Conference of Information Systems Development*, Wrycza S. and Zupancic, J. (eds.), Gdansk, Poland, Sept. 24–26.

Barber, L., 1995, EU Report calls for charter of basic skills, *Financial Times*, 22 June.

Chermayeff S and Tzonis A, 1971, Shape of Community: Realization of Human Potential, Penguin Books Ltd., London, UK.

Chermayeff, S., and Alexander, C.,1963, *Community and Privacy: Towards a New Architecture of Humanism*, Doubleday Anchor, USA.

Fennell, E., 1995, Prototypes Prove Their Worth *in: INSIGHT*, summer, Employment Department Information Branch Sheffield, England.

Galliers, R.D., 1993, IT Strategies: Beyond Competitive Advantage *in: Proceedings of the XII Conferenceof the South East Asia Regional Computer Federation.* Pp105–109.

Grint, K., 1994, Sisyphus and the social construction of computer user problems, *Information Systems Journal*, Vol 5, pp3–18.

Handy, C., 1989, *The Age of Unreason*, Arrow Books London.

Hayday, G., 1996, Shifting Hands *in: Business and Technology*, Sept.

Neale, I., 1993, A strategy of engagement: knowledge elicitation for augmentative systems development *in: Systems Science: Addressing Global Issues* (Stowell, F.A., West, D., and Howell, J.G.), Plenum Press, New York.

O' Callaghan, S., 1969, Conversations between the author and the first Irish dry stone waller brought over to Scotland, Glasgow.

Pritchett P, 1994, *New Work Habits for a Changing World* , York, England.

Schank, R., 1995, *in* "New Ways to Learn" by Tom R. Halfhill *in: BYTE*, March.

Senge, P., Ross, R., Roberts, C., Smith, B., Kleiner, A., 1995, *The Fifth Discipline Fieldbook*, Nicholas Brierley Publishing Ltd., London, UK.

Welsh, Louise, 1995, Green Tide rolls out Rich Pickings for a cream of the crop" *in: Herald*, 1.6.95.

41

AUTOPOIESIS

In Search for a Theory of Organisational Change

Jon-Arild Johannessen

Bodø Graduate School of Business
Agder Research Institute and Lillehammer College
Norway

1. INTRODUCTION

By systemic (Bunge, 1983; 1983a; 1985; 1985a) is meant that the parts and the entire structure must be viewed in context. In systemic thinking, the main question is: What is the pattern which combine a given phenomenon or problem? The noticeable thing about patterns is that it is difficult to pinpoint cause and effect. A pattern can metaphorically be regarded as a circle, and a circle has no beginning or end.

The question asked is: In what way can social autopoiesis theory and systemic thinking be used as a means to understand, explain and predicate stability and change in organisations regarded as social systems? This contribution is expressed through postulates and a conceptual model.

2. DEVELOPMENT TOWARDS A MODEL

Autopoiesis means self-producing system. The autopoiesis theory was developed by Maturana and Varela (1980). Luhman introduces the distinction between normatively closed and cognitively open systems at the social level (Luhman, 1975). An autopoietic social system with this distinction is simultaneously closed (normatively) and open (cognitively). The normative and the cognitive are also structurally linked, generating interaction between these two subsystems. A crucial point here is: "closure is a condition for openness" (Luhman, 1986:183). It is among other things the link between the normatively closed and the cognitively open which is Luhman's contribution to the autopoietic theory for social systems The cognitive openness is a form of awareness or knowledge link to the environment of the system. The recursive element is critical for the understanding of the normative element at various recursivity levels.

Systems for Sustainability, edited by Stowell *et al*.
Plenum Press, New York, 1997

Postulate 1: There Will Always Be Tension and Conflict between the Cognitively Open Loop and the Normatively Closed Loop in Social Systems. For the individual system there exists a system-specific normative basis. At a superior recursivity level there is also a normative superstructure in evidence, influencing the normative basis for the subordinate recursivity level. The normative basis at the recursivity level above the individual system-specific normative basis is here called the normative superstructure.

Postulate 2: There Is a Normative Super-Structure in Every Social Field. The study of social systems as autopoietical systems, according to Luhman (1986:186):" is a theory of self-referential systems, to be applied to observing systems as well". This links social auto-poiesis theory to second-order cybernetics, as expressed by Heinz Von Foerster (1981), among others. For the individual researcher it becomes just as much a question of self-observation as observation of the social system. It is self-reflection which Luhman and Foerster bring in as a point. This is also a central point with Bourdieu (Broady, 1991). Luhman (1986:187) says: "To combine these two distinctions (between autopoiesis and observation, and between external observation and self-observation, our inclusion) is one of the unsolved tasks in systems theory". The core of the problem as we see it is that an observer observing a social system constitutes an autopoietical system in his own right, i.e. when we gather information about social systems we cannot avoid collecting information about ourselves. Luhman (1986:188) points out that in order to solve this problem (paradox) a sort of exchange between external observation and self-observation is required. One possible strategy, could be for the observer to make his assumptions, premises and suppositions explicit (the explication principle). The actors will through this process make their norm and value basis explicit for themselves. Ulrich (1983; 1986; 1987; 1988) also directs his attention towards suppositions, the normative content on the part of the observer, and the consequences for the ones affected by the products of a system in the "Critical Systems Heuristic" concept. Ulrich particularly emphasises the question: What should be done? instead of the instrumental question: How is it done? It is Ulrich's position that the freedom of choice is also a type of critical freedom to reflect on ourselves as observers and system designers.

The system-specific normative basis, regardless of its being based on a model-weak foundation (Bråten, 1984), generates an attention focus in the system. They influence and set standards for signals, symbols and the information to be selected, in addition to the expectations on the part of the individual actors in the system. This in turn produces certain experiences in the system, which then reinforce or sustain the system-specific foundation. This is what we here refer to as information capital. If it is so that what we know depends on how we got to know it, a continous examination of explications pertaining to one's own way of thinking becomes essential.

Luhman emphasises communication as the very foundation for social systems, not roles. Luhman's conceptual pairings (normatively closed and cognitively open) make it possible for a social system to be simultaneously self-producing in terms of social norms, and still maintain the capability of learning, through the cognitive openness of the system. Luhman (1990:12) points out: "the concept of autopoietic closure has to be understood as the recursively closed organisation of an open system". The point is the extent to which normative closure and cognitive openness exists in a specific system. It is, according to Luhman (1990: 13), communication which constitutes the evolutionary potential for the construction of systems able to "maintain closure under the condition of openness". It is Ashby's (1968) definition of the cybernetic system which Luhman seems to use as basis for his use of the autopoiesis theory in his study of Germany's legal system: "the legal system is open to cognitive information but closed to normative control" (Luhman, 1990:229). Ashby's (1968:4) expression of the cybernetic system is: "Open to energy but closed to information and control". Even if the system is closed normatively, it does not follow that it is not subject to influences from the outside world. An autopoietical system is open cognitively, and can therefore both influence other systems and at the same time learn and adapt to the outside world.

Postulate 3: Social Systems Are Reproduced through the Maintenance and Development of the Normative Basis. An autopoietic social system is, in other words, both open and closed at the same time. There is openness towards the outside world, starting as internal reflection, redefinition of situations and generation of communication for the purpose of changing the system-specific normative basis. This normative closure is secured by means of a number of mechanisms preventing information and communication from the outside from penetrating the system. Examples of such mechanisms could be: laws, rules, regulations, routines, tribal language, i.e. the concepts, theories and axioms of various professions. In turn these mechanisms can be constituted by standards, i.e. expectations and notions from economic, social, political and cultural systems of the outside world.

Postulate 4: There Is a System-Specific Normative Basis in Every Social System. The epistemological consequence of social autopoeisis theory for a researcher on social systems is that he refers to himself when studying these systems. The researcher must be aware of this self-reference and problematize it. Otherwise the study of social systems will become a self-reference study regardless of method. This makes the subjective element a focal point in the study of social systems. The reflection concerning one's own understanding is important for Luhman. Or according to Geyer and Van der Zouwen (1992:102): "Within a society, all observations are by definition self-observations". One consequence of this is that the observer, the observer's statements and the problem or phenomenon subject to study, are three separate elements subject to evaluation in the study of social systems.

Postulate 5: The Normative Superstructure Impacts the System-Specific Normative Basis in the Social Field. There is not any agreement as to whether social systems can be regarded as autopoietical systems. Luhman (1982; 1986) and Robb (1989; 1989a) argue in favour of the contention that the theory can be adapted to social systems. Maturana (1981), Varela (1979) and Mingers (1989) have more doubt about the fruitfulness of this analogy. This view is that autopoietic processes can be disclosed as parallel processes, not identical, in social systems and organisations. By this we mean that knowledge based on the autopoiesis theory at the cell level with Maturana and Varela can be adapted for the purpose of acquiring knowledge of social processes in organisations regarded as social systems. This we also interpret as Luhman 's point of view (1986:173). Luhman's application of the autopoiesis theory can be used to describe, explain and possibly predicate change or lack of change in social systems. Luhman's autopoiesis understanding is neither a conflict model nor a consensus model, but an evolution model.

3. CONCLUSION

The social autopoietical system is a normatively closed and cognitively open system. In order to describe, explain and predicate stability and change in social systems by

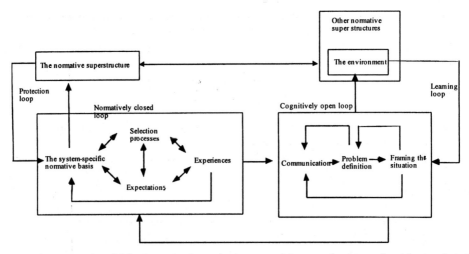

Figure 1. A conceptual model for the study of organisations as social systems by means of social autopoiesis theory and systemic thinking.

means of the autopoiesis theory, I have in this article used an analytical model where the following constructs were in focus: the normative super-structure, the normatively closed loop, the cognitively open loop, the learning loop and the field-protection loop. In addition we have made use of the constructs model-weak and model-strong actors and systems. It is the relationship between all these constructs we consider to be useful in order to describe, explain and predicate stability and change in organisations regarded as social systems by means of the autopoiesis theory. A simplified presentation of the article's contents in order to bring the main message across regarding the change potential for organisations from an autopoietical perspective, is seen in Fig. 2.

	Power systems	Learning systems
Model strong systems	(Internally acting. Little change potential)	(Acting externally. Great change potential)
Model weak systems	Crisis systems (Procedure and rule oriented. Very little change potential)	Epigone systems (Externally seeking. Great change potential)
	Cognitively closed systems (Few system-environment relations)	Cognitively open systems (Many system-environment relations)

Figure 2. Social autopoiesis and system change.

The main message in Figure 2 is that explicit models and cognitively open systems are conducive to learning and have a great change potential. A practical implication is that those who have model power must clarify and make visible the normative basis of their own models, in addition to the models the system is intended to use.

In order to make visible the processes which are operational in changes of autopoietical systems, I have in the analytical model (Figure 1) used the following constructs: the system-specific normative basis, selection processes, expectations, experiences, communication, problem definition, and framing the situation. It is the mechanisms in these processes in addition to the relationship between them I have analysed in this article.

REFERENCES

Ashby, W.R., 1968, Principles of the self-organizing system, in, W. Buckley (ed.). *Modern Systems Research for the Behavioral Scientist*, Aldine, Chicago, Ill.

Broady, D., 1991, *Sociologi och Epistemologi: Om Pierre Bourdieus författerskap och den* historiska epistemologin, HLS Förlag, Stockholm.

Bråten, S., 1984, The third position: Beyond artificial and autopoietic reduction, *Kybernetes*, 13: 157–163.

Bunge, M., 1983, *Exploring the World*, Dordrecht: Reidel.

Bunge, M., 1983a, *Understanding the World*, Dordrecht: Reidel.

Bunge, M., 1985, *Philosophy of Science and Technology*, Part I, Dordrecht: Reidel.

Bunge, M., 1985a, *Philosophy of Science and Technology*, Part II, Dordrecht: Reidel.

Foerster, H.V., 1981, *Observing Systems*, Intersystems Publications, Seaside, Cal.

Geyer, R.F. and Van der Zouwen, 1992, Sociocybernetics, in C.V. Negoita (ed.). *Cybernetics and Applied Systems*, pp. 95–124, Marcel Dekker, New York.

Luhmann, N., 1975, *Sosiologische Aufklärung*, Vol. 1–5, Westdeutcher Verlag, Berlin.

Luhman, N., 1982, The world society as a social system. *International Journal of General Systems*, 8, pp. 131–138.

Luhman, N., 1986, The autopoiesis of social systems, in F. Geyer and J. Van der Zouven, (eds). *Sociocybernetics paradoxes: observation, control and evolution of self-steering systems*, pp.172–192, Sage, London.

Luhman, N., 1990, *Essays on self reference*, Columbia University Press, New York.

Maturana, H., 1981, Autopoiesis, in M. Zeleny, (ed.). *Autopoiesis: a theory of living organization*, pp. 21–23, Elsevier, New York.

Maturana, H.R. and Varela, F.J., 1980, *Autopoiesis and Cognition: The Realization of the Living*, Reidel, Dordrecht.

Mingers, J., 1989, An introduction to autopoiesis: implications and applications, *Systems Practice*, 2 pp. 159–180.

Robb, F., 1989, Cybernetics and supra human autopoetic systems, *Systems Practice*, 2 pp. 47–74.

Robb, F., 1989a, The application of autopoietic systems to social organizations: a comment on John Mingers: an introduction to autopoiesis: implications and applications, *Systems Practice*, 2 pp. 349- 351.

Robb, F., 1992, Are institutions entities of a natural kind? a consideration of the outlook of mankind, in C.V. Negoita (ed.). *Cybernetics and Applied Systems*, pp. 149–163, Marcel Dekker, New York.

Ulrich, W., 1983, *Critical heuristics of social planning: a new approach to practical philosophy*, Haupl, Bern.

Ulrich, W., 1986, Critical Heuristics of Social System Design, *Working Paper 10*, Department of Management Systems and Sciences, University of Hull.

Ulrich, W., 1987, Critical heuristics of social systems design, European Journal of Operational Research, 31, pp. 276–283.

Ulrich, W., 1988, System thinking, systems practice, and practical philosophy: a program for research, *Systems Practice*, 1, pp. 137–163.

Varela, F.G., 1979, *Principles of Biological Autonomy*, Elsevier, New York.

42

SYSTEMS THINKING IN U.K. FILM UNITS

Linda Ludwin and David Wield

Centre for Technology Strategy
Faculty of Technology
The Open University
Walton Hall, Milton Keynes MK7 6AA, United Kingdom

Building on analyses of important learning organization models, we hope to raise a series of issues and questions which need to be addressed as part of the process of developing and strengthening the learning organization concept. One of the authors (Ludwin) is currently undertaking a detailed study of feature film production units to determine whether or not certain commonly agreed learning organization features are present in film units, which operate in environments of radical change. This paper focuses on the relevance of systems thinking issues to film units.

Learning organization theory is developing in response to the climate of increasingly rapid change. This fast evolving environment includes the political, social, economic, technical, cultural, religious, and legal dimensions of change. Learning organization academics and practitioners believe that the most important quality any organization can possess in this kind of setting—more important than the goods it manufactures or the services it delivers—is its ability to learn rapidly both to adapt appropriately and to take proactive steps to set its own agendas for change. Or, to put it another way, the most important competitive advantage any organization can possess is its ability to learn at speed and to capitalise on what it has learned.

We have examined the work of 6 individuals or groups writing on the learning organization: Peter Senge (1990); David Garvin (1993); Dorothy Leonard-Barton (1992); Bob Garratt (1987); Mike Pedler, John Burgoyne & Tom Boydell (1991); and Alan Jones & Chris Hendry (1992). We did this by analysing the intellectual influences on the authors, the learning organization themes they emphasise, the research evidence they present and the implications for action they suggest. These theorists are well respected academics and (in many cases) practitioners who have developed and extended their ideas about learning organizations through consultancy work. Their ideas are widely cited, and they are responsible for current management interest in learning organization ideas. Although the 6 learning organization models differ in important respects, there are a number of activities, attitudes and beliefs which all agree will help organizations to learn. These are:

Systems for Sustainability, edited by Stowell *et al.*
Plenum Press, New York, 1997

- Systems thinking: the ability to see the bigger picture and to think about the interconnections between events and organizations. Systems thinking is a form of holistic thinking;
- The vital ability for organizations to look outside themselves: this enables the organization to understand the world and its current position in it;
- Learning is tied to action. This includes valuing learning through experience, experimentation, innovations and reflection. These approaches are often known as action learning or action research;
- Virtual and transitional learning, including testing solutions and approaches through computer aided and other kinds of modelling techniques, on a project basis (rather than throughout the entire organization) or by setting up demonstration projects outside of the organization;
- Problem solving approaches are important: in particular, the adoption of creative and lateral thinking techniques for problem solving;
- Intellectual property is central to organizational success. This encompasses concepts such as knowledge workers and organizational memory/history;
- Methods for the collection and circulation of 'knowledge' (i.e. information, models, opinions, theories and other intellectual property) throughout the organization must be created, serviced and maintained;
- Reward systems (including non-financial rewards) influence learning;
- Values are central to creating and maintaining a learning organization; for example, learning itself must be seen to be valued;
- Belief that the future can be shaped through the creation and sharing of a generally agreed vision is important;
- Collaborative groupwork is essential for organizational learning;
- The way in which things are done is important: there is an emphasis on process.

Although key theorists agree that these elements are important, little research has so far been undertaken to establish whether or not successful organizations embody these beliefs, practices and methods of working. Furthermore, most of the people who have helped to develop our current ideas about learning organizations had their experiences shaped by close contact with large (1,000 or more employees) companies and through contact with managers in leadership development contexts.

We thought that it would be interesting to examine a more extreme organizational form, the U.K. feature film production unit, to see if the learning organization characteristics mentioned above could be identified in these SMEs which operate in climates of especially rapid change. Are successful film production units learning organizations?

Film production units are very short-lived, typically trading for around 30 weeks. Their unique function is physically to produce the master copy of a film. Their organizational life span typically includes a pre-pre-production period, when the script is developed and finance for the project is put into place; the pre-production period when artistic and technical staff are retained, locations are identified, and sets, scenery and costumes fabricated; the production period when the film is actually shot; and the post-production period, when the film is edited, the sound track is added, and a master print is delivered. Management of a film production unit is similar to project management, although there are special features which distinguish it from other forms of project management.

Ludwin chose research participants in two ways. Firstly, she used existing contacts in the business who are currently working in production management, and who were willing to be interviewed. Secondly, she identified two high grossing and artistically successful British features ('The Crying Game' and 'Four Weddings and a Funeral') and is in process of interviewing managers who were involved in the production of one or the other. All of her participants were, at the time they spoke to her, employed in management roles within film units. As well as asking them to reflect on their experiences in practice, she chose to explore their attitudes to the learning organization features mentioned above and to encourage them to reflect on their experiences whilst producing the case study films.

For this paper, the authors focused on one of the 12 learning organization criteria mentioned above: systems thinking, using a two-part definition of systems thinking articulated in one of the learning organization models, "seeing interrelationships rather than linear cause-effect chains and seeing processes of change rather than snapshots." (Senge, 1990, p. 73)

In evaluating whether or not the people interviewed indicated that systems thinking is applied within film units, we asked ourselves the following questions: Are there special aspects of working in a film unit which influence systems thinking? Did individuals demonstrate an interest in departments other than their own within units? Who owned problems? Did participants consider possible advantages and disadvantages to the entire unit when weighing up issues? Were they aware of inter-connections between their units and other organizations and issues? Did they actively work with others (outside the unit) to achieve mutual benefits?

Because of the transitory nature of units, unit members are compelled to think in systems terms or, at the very least, beyond the boundaries of the unit in which they currently work. They are aware of past units, current units running in parallel with their own, and units which about to be formed. Forthcoming employment depends absolutely on a well honed ability to understand what is going on in the environment beyond one's current unit. An interesting feature of units composed entirely of contract workers is an emphasis on the need for individuals to perform well within their current unit in order to secure their next job. Sue explained, "You're only as good as your last film. You cannot afford to have 'off days' or 'off weeks' or 'off films'. Because people remember it, you know. They don't remember that you've done ten good films and you've had one crappy one. They only remember the last one. It can be very tough."

Within the unit, production office staff feel that they have a particular responsibility to understand the workings of all the other departments. Sue felt this was important: "I try and find out as much as I can about everybody's job and how it works and how the equipment works and what they need and why they need it. And that takes time..." Other unit staff tend to focus on their own jobs and their own departments.

Although each of the managers stressed the collaborative nature of film units, there was little indication that problems were owned by everyone in the unit, or by anyone who felt that he or she could contribute towards a solution. When participants were asked to describe problems in film units, they tended to mention problems which, in their view, belonged to top management.

Peer networks were mentioned by a number of managers. For Bob, "Information is shared amongst peers: it is a way of building up ideas about the deals which can be done and which have been done." Ann talked about a network she found invaluable: "At one stage there were five of us all working in the same capacity when we were line producers, five women, and we would very openly share..." However, Sue warned, "Everyone's very competitive and you don't give away your secrets lightly... If you've got a particularly good way of doing something you certainly wouldn't discuss it with someone who potentially you could be in competition for a job with." Ann shared some of Sue's reservations, commenting when talking about producers' networks that, "it's a more selfishly guarded thing because as a producer you're looking for financial sources and there is still an over-riding feeling, which people can't get rid of, that if somebody else takes up a bit of a grant or a subsidy or a bit of money that's available, that means they won't get it."

Because managers know that they are hired in part for their connections within the industry, it is essential for them to maintain excellent connections with suppliers. Sue made the nature of their contribution clear: "This is where co-ordinators and production managers do a huge amount for the company. The companies are using their credibility and their contacts in order to make this company work, function. Things would cost them a lot more, and they wouldn't get the credit. A lot of the cash flow that they get is down to the contacts that their production team have already."

Managers working in film units know that there are employment issues, practices and problems which extend beyond any particular unit and which are common across the industry. Tim said, when talking about communications structures within units, "...it's a really international thing, you know, the arrangement is very similar everywhere... Most people doing jobs (in British film units) could work on a film unit, you know, in other countries, without being too surprised."

Because each feature film is unique, managers did not consider benchmarking as relevant for them. Pam dismissed benchmarking because, "Each film is so different. You're talking a different budget on each film. If every film was a five million dollar budget, then you might have that (benchmarking)."

Senior managers are very aware of the ways in which relationships must be developed in order to secure funding for units or to enable units to operate in cost effective ways. Ann shared her overview of the sector: "...there are reigning mega-companies that will have satellite companies 'round them...There is a much, much stronger move towards co-producing...The best one (type of arrangement) is with somebody who has another company who has skills that I don't and yet I have skills that he doesn't."

Powerful networks operate within feature film funding structures. For example, Sam had been Fred's external examiner at the Royal School of Art, and also on the Fulbright panel which awarded scholarships to Fred & Paul. Sam introduced both of them to Greg at Channel 4. Greg encouraged them to develop a treatment, and Channel 4 covered the costs of both the initial and the detailed treatments. Greg then funded a short, which Sam's independent production company produced. Greg paid for several drafts of a feature script, finally helping Fred & Paul to pull together a funding package of two million pounds, to which Channel 4 contributed two thirds. The film was produced by Sam's company.

The processes and nature of feature film production attract people who are, at least implicitly, systems thinkers. Anyone who is not able to operate in a universe of complex interrelationships or to grasp processes of change will never progress to another film unit job. However, it is clear that many people limit their systems thinking to certain aspects of their work within the unit. Most interviewees would not describe themselves as systems thinkers, or have had any formal education or training in systems approaches to thinking or problem solving.

Learning organization theorists have suggested that systems thinking is a wholly desirable characteristic. However, in film units, systems thinking can sometimes lead to a situation in which managers deny that film units are organizations. The notion of an almost boundary-less industry is common, and is reflected in Jim's explanation of why benchmarking is not a prevalent management tool in film units: "It doesn't happen because everybody comes out of the same pool and everybody disappears back into the same pool. Everybody's out there in different grades, different stages of the job, and a producer will pull out a production manager and they'll dip into the pool and see who's working 'round at that time, who they (the production manager) can use. So what was the other companies you're measuring against is yourself, really." Ann's comment on benchmarking was, "For a film unit to compare its performance against others, I never quite know whether people see themselves enough as a bonded unit in that way, because they're not distinct, because you get such a cross-over that various films will share the same personnel, you don't have that sense about, 'only this film unit could have done that'." Tim said, "Units don't stay together long enough to ever feel that they have an identity." When Sue was asked whether film units had sets of values, her reply was, "You keep talking about units as if it's a cohesive thing. You're only a unit for a very short period of time. You're talking about individuals who are brought together to make a unit for a short period of time." These managers consider the industry as a whole to be the salient entity to which they relate, not the film units in which they work for such short periods of time.

Such attitudes have led to the industry-wide tolerance of a variety of unsatisfactory management and working practices (relating to health and safety, for example) which are endured by all concerned because unit staff know that they will only have to put up with them for a few weeks. This particular type of systems thinking discourages people from thinking about long term solutions to some very serious problems, it blocks action learning and it prevents reflective practice.

Therefore, preliminary indications are that although an organization may be successful, and although its management and staff may behave in ways identified by theorists as essential to maintaining its status as a learning organization, this is not necessarily a recipe for organizational or personal learning.

REFERENCES

Garratt, B., 1987, *The Learning Organization and the Need for Directors who Think.* Gower, Aldershot.
Garvin, D. A., 1993, Building a learning organization, *Harvard Business Review*, July-August **1993**, pp. 78 - 91.
Jones, A. M. and Hendry, C., 1992, *The Learning Organization: A Review of Literature and Practice*, Human Resource Development Partnership, London.
Leonard-Barton, D, 1992, The factory as a learning laboratory, *Sloan Management Review*, Fall **1992**, pp. 23 - 38.
Pedler, M., Burgoyne, J., Boydell, T, 1991, *The Learning Company: A Strategy for Sustainable Development.* McGraw-Hill, London.
Senge, P., 1990, *The Fifth Discipline*, Doubleday Currency, New York.
References to film industry managers are from the field research notes of Linda Ludwin, Visiting Research Fellow, Centre for Technology Strategy, The Open University. All names have been changed to ensure participant confidentiality. Their current job titles are: Sue: Production Manager/Production Co-ordinator; Pam: Production Co-ordinator; Tim: Line Producer; Sam: Executive Producer; Bob: Line Producer/Production Manager; Fred: Producer/Writer; Ann: Producer; Paul: Director/Writer; Jim: Production Executive; Greg: Production Executive.

43

BRIDGING THE 'OUTPUT-OUTCOME' GAP IN SUSTAINABILITY R AND D

A Fifth Generation R and D 'Punctuated Arena' Model

N. D. MacLeod[1] and A. D. Shulm[2]

[1]CSIRO Tropical Agriculture
St Lucia Q. 4067 Australia
[2]Communication Research Institute of Australia
Hackett, ACT 2602 Australia

1. INTRODUCTION

Research and development (R and D) activities within the agriculture and land resource management domain are increasingly focussed on sustainable use of land and water resources. In Australia, this is occurring within the context of a complex environment characterised by substantial climatic and market uncertainty, poor understanding of fundamental ecosystem processes, conflicts between different land use practices and a recognition of the interests of a wide array of community groups. Traditional research and extension (R,D and E) models based on linear transfer of technology have been criticised as inappropriate to solving such problems, particularly with their focus on output, including technological information and scientific publications, rather than their application or outcome. While R and D specialists may regard this as an *extension* failure, the problems most likely lie at more basic levels, including the relevance of the research questions and the fact that different users of the information are interested in the application of technology regardless of its source (e.g. Jiggins, 1993), or its underlying causal mechanism (Russell and Ison, 1991). The path towards achieving these ideals is increasingly seen to lie within the domain of multidisciplinary and collaborative approaches to R and D problem-solving and communication endeavours (e.g. Jiggins, 1993). However, the performance for *both* generation and adoption of R and D-sourced technologies remains poor and an *output-outcome gap* remains. This performance is reviewed and means to improve it are suggested.

2. FOUR GENERATIONS OF R, D, AND E MODELS

Awareness of the *output-outcome* gap is not new; attempts to increase the relevance of R and D outputs to clients decision-making contexts have generated a progression of four generations of models. Themes underlying this progression are calls for increased I participation' by more constituents, and for R and D enterprises to act more like learning organisations in dealing with the paradoxes of sustainability. However, despite these progressions, the *output-outcome* gap is largely unabated and R and D agencies appear to continue to escalate commitment of resources to unwarranted paths. In our view, these four generations of models have failed to: (a) acknowledge the discontinuous involvement of different constituents over the life of an R and D project; (b) address the moral question of what are good R and D management practices where there are multiple changing constituents; (c) address the pragmatic question of how to minimise unwarranted escalation of resources, while maintaining flexibility with an R and D program to accommodate the unexpected; and (d) provide guidance to research managers for increasing opportunities for negotiating possible outcomes and engaging in reflective organisational learning.

We briefly review these four generations of models and present a fifth generation 'punctuated arena' model for improving the management of R and D.

2.1. First Generation Models of R and D

Linear transfer of technology models (TOT) date largely from the 1950's (Roussel, Saad, and Erickson, 1991) and remain dominant in current R and D practice. R and D specialists typically operate independently from others within the R and D agency (e.g. extension and marketing staff) and from potential clients outside the agencies. Extension of the outputs is usually via independent specialists who seek to package the output into forms that might be useful to the clients. This input typically takes place after the development phase of the R and D, and the R and D staff remain fairly remote from the clients and their context. Despite its continuing use, this model has had limited success in improving R and D outcome performance in the context of sustainable resource management (e.g. Ison, 1993; Jiggins, 1993; Roling, 1992).

2.2. Second Generation Models of R and D

A key feature is an increased dialogue between groups within R and D agencies, extension and marketing professionals and pertinent end-users concerning the aims of specific R and D projects. The models are more consistent with a 'market' or 'client-first' approach. The ensuing dialogue typically places emphasis on both demonstrating the potential relevance of the R and D to clients (science push) and being responsive to client needs (market pull) (Roling, 1992). Participatory R,D and E models of this class typically seek an interactive dialogue between R and D-providers and clients throughout the life of an R and D project. However, this frequently carries an implicit assumption that participation per se will necessarily guarantee successful R,D and E outcomes with limited explicit detail provided of the process by which this occurs (MacLeod and Shulman, 1996). These models have also been of limited success, possibly due to selective filtering of the communication through extension middlemen which preserves the essential linearity of the TOT model and allows R and D staff to continue to focus on what they see as being important (Shulman and Martinek, in press).

2.3. Third Generation Models of R and D

These models commonly recognise the need for partnerships between R and D-providers (including mixed agency teams) and other parties - notably identified clients and the agencies that serve their commercial interests (e.g. agribusiness) to serve multiple needs. A key feature is that they typically involve portfolios of projects and multiple objectives as no single project would meet the interests of all potential stakeholders. Third generation proponents emphasise a need for mutual trust between the parties and their acceptance of the unique contribution that each can make to the R,D and E process (Roussel Saad, and Erickson, 1991). There is some limited evidence (Bellamy and Lowes, in press; Ridge and Cox, in press) of R and D staff, clients and extension specialists forming partnerships that involved problem-solving over time within the context of a project portfolio - although these partnerships appeared to collapse when mutual trust was not present or maintained. Specific evidence of ongoing partnerships addressing sustainable resource issues is sparse. Nevertheless, these models remain consistent with calls for collaborative network structuring of R,D and E organisations to promote flexibility in dynamic environments (Kanter, 1994) and to minimise unnecessary duplication of efforts or unwarranted escalation of commitment of resources (Ross and Staw, 1993).

Our view is that, like the earlier generations, these R,D and E models remain essentially linear in their description of the R,D and E process and too readily assume that participants will be motivated to move towards shared or negotiated objectives. Like involvement in workteams in general (McGrath, 1991; Shulman, 1996), much of the stakeholder involvement within R,D and E is discontinuous and increasingly centred on temporary and often unstable alliances of R and D agencies and stakeholder interests. These are commonly more conflictual than consensual, and involve different episodes of engagement with different stakeholder groups (MacLeod, 1995; MacLeod and Shulman, 1996). Shared objectives can not be guaranteed and multiple agendas, objectives, cultures or reward systems which are in conflict are too readily ignored, including the fact that these are potentially transitory and dynamic. When these various interests and power relationships are explicitly considered, commitment and progress towards common goals are less assured. We believe that these issues represent root causes for many sustainability R,D and E failures (Cox, MacLeod, Ridge, and Shulman, 1996; MacLeod, 1995).

2.4. Fourth Generation Models of R and D

This most recent class places more emphasis on empowering stakeholders within a context that may be represented by a political arena. R,D and E activities are no longer depicted as a set of discrete, rational and systematic acts, but rather comprise a dynamic process involving resolution of conflicting interests, changing alliances and competing world views (e.g. Dunn, Gray and Phillips, in press; Scoones and Thompson, 1994). Moral and ethical questions are more likely to be asked concerning control of the R and D agenda and social or structural changes necessary to genuinely transfer power to stakeholders. Meanings are typically negotiated rather than transmitted between parties and shaped by R and D, institutional, community structures and habits, and in turn, shape those structures with an increased capacity for stakeholders to use R and D-sourced information better and/or do their own research. From the viewpoint of managing R,D and E within a political arena, a major concern becomes understanding the nature and rules of the relevant arena and generating and managing appropriate expectations within the partnerships and alliances therein.

Unfortunately, recognising these issues is, alone, insufficient to prescribe what might constitute good R and D outcome performance or how to achieve such performance. The fourth generation models remain incomplete—commonly ignoring or avoiding difficult questions concerning appropriate communication and management practices for arenas characterised by multiple and changing constituents, or avoiding unwarranted escalation of resources or undue influence from particular stakeholders leading to less integrative outcomes. Importantly, they fail to address the outcome implications of discontinuous involvement of different participants over the life of an R,D and E endeavour. We attempt to do this via a fifth generation R,D and E model.

3. THE PUNCTUATED ARENA MODEL–FIFTH GENERATION R,D AND E

In moving to a fifth generation of model we build upon an arena model (Cunningham and Barawryh, 1993) for addressing the output-outcome gap by emphasising: (a) the opportunities for addressing the gap within changing and punctuated compositions of R,D and E arenas over the life of a project and (b) how these opportunities are also likely to address the moral question of 'what are good outcomes?' The model is pragmatic and consistent with constructionist assumptions underlying an indeterminate learning organisation. Arena Theory suggests that the composition, predisposition, and relative power of different stakeholders will, ultimately, shape the range of possible inputs, outputs and outcomes including the size of the output-outcome gap (MacLeod, 1995). The management of arenas requires skill in activating the interest and engagement of some potential stakeholders and minimising the influence of others throughout the life of a given project. It is also necessary to identify and contrast their power, objectives and available resources and to devise communication and coordination strategies and tactics that are appropriate to meeting project objectives or re-establishing them in a mutually acceptable, or at least recognised, direction. While scientific technical infrastructure and luck are important in affecting the probability of outcomes, the selection and entry of additional stakeholders to the arena and their exits from the arena necessarily changes the distribution of power and rules of engagement. In particular, the addition of stakeholders affects how decisions will be made and how the consequences of those decisions will be managed. Because these consequences can never be known until after the decision has been made (Pfeffer, 1992), how the arena dynamics are managed and changed to deal with these consequences is the major challenge that R and D managers face. These potential effects of changing the dynamics of the arena are importantly overlooked by most of the earlier models.

When the episodicity of R and D is specifically considered, the probability of recognising the composition, context and control structure of an arena will increase. The arena so construed, becomes a 'punctuated' series of arenas which may be both spatially and temporally related. We argue that these recognitions within this punctuated arena model fosters a closing of the output - outcome gap in three ways:

1. It provides an opportunity for reflection within and between arenas. Such reflections, are key indicators of having rational, transparent decision procedures. And in general, the use of rational decision procedures in complex situations, when accompanied with an implementation skill base, has been shown to lead to better outcomes for strategic innovations (Dean and Sharfman, 1996). When built into the episodic nature of R and D, the episodic use of these procedures gives rise to possibilities which can shape subsequent control structures and engagements, including minimising unwarranted escalation of commitment;

2. It provides opportunities for managing other inherent conflicts and unanticipated and unwanted consequences of R and D decisions that are consistent with action

learning and theories of the learning organisation. But unlike the second generation participatory models, managing R and D as punctuated arenas, creates possibilities for using the episodes to utilise the learnings and strategically manage
the involvement of constituents (MacLeod, Shulman and Taylor, 1996);

3. It increases the probability that a moral knowing of what are good outcomes will
be recognised.

Any question of what is good—including what is good R and D performance—is
necessarily a moral one, and R and D scientists have tended to treat morality as a concept
that exists independent of the participants involved. However, under the fourth generation
R and D model, we have argued that ideas do not exist independently of the participants
involved nor can the meanings be completely determined. We draw on Penman's (1994, in
press) development of the implications of this constructionist view for addressing the
question of what is good.

Penman (in press) uses the arguments of Hans-Georg Gadamer and John Shotter,
two twentieth-century authors, that draw on different, but compatible, traditions. Both argue that moral knowledge is about doing. But Shotter expands on this by arguing that it
is something that is about doing with other people. Moral knowing does not exist independently of a social situation, it is brought about within it. It is an understanding that
arises from within the communication and reflecting upon the possible consequences of
the R and D actions. It does not arise within the person but in the interactions of constituents. You cannot reiterate a long list of professional ethics for this form of knowing from;
it emerges from what you **do,** your engagement with others. For Penman this does not
mean researchers and managers can or should avoid retrospective analysis. She extends
Dewey's argument that both participation and reflection are necessary—but that one precludes the other. You cannot be looking back to study antecedents—while looking forward to understand the possibilities—within the same communication process. For
understanding the possibilities of R and D managers to foster good R,D and E performance we need to look forward. In looking forward we are presented with the unfolding of
options and the closing off of others. Thus by using the opportunities for selecting constituents, and then engaging constituents within an arena with reflection within its punctuations, the R and D manager and the participating constituents are in a better position
to recognise and close the (moral) gap between output and outcomes. The above argument has major implications for future research about R,D and E systems. It strongly
suggests that the R and D system researchers and the managers understandings of the
possibilities and constraints for minimising the *output-outcome* gap can best be advanced
by actively engaging in the communicative activity of R and D and not just studying
them at a distance. The episodic nature of R and D teams, documented through participant observation by MacLeod and Shulman, (1996) provides the opportunities for researchers and managers to sequentially act in, and reflect on, R,D and E system
processes. This is, in essence, best practice of good organisational learning (Argyris,
1994).

REFERENCES

Argyris, C., 1994, Good communication that blocks learning, *Harvard Business Rev.* **July-Aug:77–85.** Bellamy,
J.A., and Lowes, D., Decision support for sustainable management of grazing lands, in: *Improving Man-
agement of sustainable R&D Technology Transfer,* Vol. 2. (A.D. Shulman, and R. Price, eds.) Land and
Water Resources Research & Development Corporation, Canberra, in press.

Cox, P.G., MacLeod, N.D., Ridge, P.E., and Shulman, A.D. , 1996, Reengineering agricultural RD&E to support management decision-making : Problems and prospects, *Proc. of 8th Australian Agronomy Conf. Toowoomba,* Aust. Agron. Soc., Melbourne pp. 168–171.

Cunningham, R., and Barawryh, Y.K., 1993, *Wasta: The hidden force in Middle East society,* Praeger, Westport, Connecticut.

Dean, J. W., and Sharfman, M. P., 1996, Does decision process matter?: A study of strategic decision-making, *Academy of management J* **39**:368–396.

Dunn, T., Gray I., and Phillips, E., From personal barriers to community plans: A farm and community planning approach to the extension of sustainable agriculture, in: *Improving Management of sustainable R&D Technology Transfer,* Vol. 2. (A.D. Shulman, and R. Price, eds.) Land and Water Resources Research & Development Corporation, Canberra, in press.

Ison, R.L., 1993, Changing community attitudes, *Rangeland J* **15**(1): 154–166.

Jiggins, J., 1993, From technology transfer to resource management, *Proc. of XVII Int. Grasslands congr., Palmerston North, New Zealand* (February 1993), N.Z. Agron. Soc., pp. 615–22.

Kanter, R.M., 1994, Collaborative advantage, *Harvard Business Rev.* **July-Aug:** 96–108. MacLeod, N.D., 1995, Effective strategies for increasing the suitability and adoption of complex technologies for sustainable grazing land management, LWRRDC-GRDC-RIRDC Project CTC2 Report, CSIRO Division of Tropical Crops and Pastures, St Lucia, Qld. (November 1995).

MacLeod, N.D., and Shulman, A.D., 1996, What is wrong with conventional technology transfer practice for Australian Rangeland R&D?, *Proc. 9th Binennial Conf. Aust. Rangeland Soc., Port Augusta, South Australia* (September 1996), pp. 189–90.

MacLeod, N.D., Shulman, A.D., and Taylor, J.A., 1996, Effective management for R&D projects addressing sustainable rangeland management issues: Resolving complex problems with multiple stakeholders, *Proc. Vth Int. Rangelands Congr. Salt Lake City, Utah* (July 1995), pp. 332–3.

McGrath, J., 1991, Time, interaction and performance: A theory of groups, *Small Group Res.* **22**:147–74.

Penman, R., 1994, Environmental matters and communication, J *of Communication* **21**(3):26–39.

Penman, R., The researcher in communication: The primary research position, in: *Context and Communication Behaviour* (ed. Owen, J.), Context Press, Reno, in press.

Pfeffer, J., 1992, *Management with power politics and influences in organisations,* Harvard Business Press, Boston, Massachusetts.

Ridge, P.E., and Cox, P.G., Market for decision support systems for dryland crop production., in: *Improving Management of Sustainable R&D Technology Transfer,* Vol. 2. (A.D. Shulman, and R. Price, eds.) Land and Water Resources Research & Development Corporation, Canberra, in press.

Roling, N.G., 1992, The emergence of knowledge systems thinking: A changing perception of relationships among innovation, knowledge process and configuration, *Knowledge and Policy* **5**:2–64.

Ross, J., and Staw, B. M., 1993, Organisational escalation and exit: Lessons from the Shoreham nuclear power plant, *Academy of management Rev.* **36**(4):701–32.

Roussel, P., Saad, K., and Erickson, T., 1991, *Third Generation R&D,* Harvard Business School Press, Boston.

Russell, D.B., and Ison, R.L., 1991, The research-development relationship in rangelands: An opportunity for contextual science, *Proc. IVth Int. Rangelands Congr. Montpellier, France* (April 1991), pp. 1047–54.

Scoones, I., and Thomps6n, J., 1994, *Beyond farmer first,* Intermediate Technology Publications, London. pp. 16–32.

Shulman, A.D., 1996, Putting group information technology in its place: Communication and good work group performance, in: *Handbook of Organisation Studies* (S.R. Clegg, C. Handy and W. Nord, eds.), pp. 357–74, Sage Publications, Newbury Park.

Shulman, A.D. and Martinek, T., Managing institutional collaboration in catchment systems research, in: Farming Action: Catchment Reaction (J. Williams, ed.), CSIRO, Canberra, in press.

44

LEARNER-CENTRED EVALUATION OF SYSTEMS, SYSTEMS COURSES, AND FUTURE NEEDS IN SYSTEMS LEARNING

Paul Maiteny[1] and Ray Ison[2]

[1]School of Contemporary Studies
Westminster College, Oxford OX2 9AT
[2]Systems Department
The Open University
Walton Hall, Milton Keynes MK7 6AA

1. CONTEXT

More than 16000 students have learned about systems through supported open learning at the Open University over the last 25 years. This paper reports on a pilot project prompted by a simple question: how do the students and tutors (who are often also ex-students) benefit from systems? It also sought to reflect generally on systems as a discipline and its future development.

Data were gathered, firstly, through SWOT (Strengths, Weaknesses, Opportunities, Threats) analyses of the Open University courses carried out by systems course tutors. 36 responded to the invitation. Focus groups, semi-structured interviews and general discussions with tutors and students then provided more in-depth consideration of issues emerging from the SWOTs. Focus group and interview participants were self-selecting as they were those who responded to invitations. Responses from tutors far exceeded that from students but student input was gained from residential summer school.

As a case study, the findings cannot be widely generalised but they provide an insight, from an Open University perspective, of how systems is perceived, why it is valued and, where it needs to pay closer attention to its own development.

The paper is structured, as closely as possible, around discussants' own words to maintain the user-centred focus.

2. SYSTEMS ADDING VALUE

Both students and tutors value systems for providing skills, methods for structured analysis and problem-solving, and systemic ways of thinking that become second nature

Systems for Sustainability, edited by Stowell *et al.*
Plenum Press, New York, 1997

over time and are helpful in understanding and managing technological and human complexity in various contexts—professional, social and personal. Both aspects are necessary. Methods support systems thinking, but systems thinking is a prerequisite for the systemic use of methods. Tutors insisted in particular that systems is about using systems thinking.

2.1. Systems Thinking: For Empathy and Understanding

Discussants often found it difficult to identify the concrete benefits of systems. Many of the most important are qualitative. For example, respondents recognised that systems thinking improves the capacity to empathise with other people and to recognise the validity of their perspectives. This capacity was considered an enormous asset in problem-solving, negotiation and decision-making:

> "Rather than dismissing something out of hand for no logical reason, (systems) gives you the ability to see that, 'that's not going to work because it'll upset the clerk, from the clerk's point of view'" (student).

Echoing others, one student described how systems had helped her to recognise the assumptions that underpin her, and other people's, habitual ways of seeing. A number of other realisations stemming from this have contributed to substantially reducing stress in her life: that problems are so frequently caused by clashes of assumptions and that they are, therefore, not all her fault; that others feel the same stresses as herself; and that problems never occur independently of their contexts.

Another student expressed this as "an appreciation of doing something systemically"; of "being able to appreciate a whole situation rather than taking just one viewpoint about what the problem really is".

All agreed that systems thinking and practice is invaluable in helping one to stand back and take account of many aspects of a problem rather than to blame one person, perspective or other factor. For many, systems thinking has helped resolve, or come to terms with seemingly intractable problems, including personal and familial, by realising that so much of the complexity is rooted in different, but equally valid viewpoints.

2.2. Systems Language and Concepts: For Legitimising Previous Experience

Some discussants had discovered that they had "…probably thought this way before the courses but didn't realise it - both systemically and systematically". Discovering a framework, language and structure that legitimised their way of thinking (which had sometimes caused difficulties in their formal education) came as a grateful revelation. It also enabled them to articulate and, therefore, to put it into practice more effectively.

Two SWOTs described using systems thinking as a transferable life or social skill that improves everyday interaction. This is one of the most valuable skills that is learned. This learning does not stop at the end of the courses but evolves and becomes more evident over time. This is an important point but one that makes systems benefits still more difficult to pin down. To a substantial degree, such benefits are tacit, systemic and experiential. Systems as a "way of seeing and thinking" is a long-term, active learning process that occurs through engagement in everyday life: "You absorb understandings that become clearer later on". It is more of a process than a product skill which the more instrumentalist discussants also considered to be of immense importance. This is not to say that more tangible, marketable skills are not also important.

2.3. Systems Methods: For Employability

The fact that many of the benefits are hard to measure or "pin down"—especially in the short term—places systems education under pressure in a management and general culture that is oriented towards short-term, readily measurable results and performance indicators.

Discussants, therefore, also value the training that systems provides in concrete transferable skills and methods—in problem-solving and IT use, for example. This enhances employability. The technological content was important for many students. These students also acknowledged, however, that the mere formulaic use of methods could not substitute for systems thinking. The two are complementary and it is possible to use techniques and methods in a non-systems way. Without technical knowledge there can be no product. Nor can you know how to manage it. On the other hand, productivity also depends on skill in managing people. Technical knowledge is not enough on its own.

Systems thinking has helped one student to prototype and modify software packages to meet user needs. This changed the previous practice of basing designs solely on the assumptions of management. The process of prototyping is similar to Soft Systems Methodology: iteration between "conceptual model", "real world", comparison of the two, and subsequent modification to improve congruence between them in a way that is acceptable and relevant.

3. IMPROVING SYSTEMS

3.1. Systems as Discipline

There was consensus on the need for a more rigorous historical and theoretical grounding in the principles of systems in order to contextualise systems thinking and methodologies. This was generally felt to be lacking in UK systems education:

"An element of pure systems theory is needed. If it's not there what are we building all this on?" (tutor).

"Looking at it holistically, the theory's got to be there. The historical helps me understand where I'm at...The practical, problem-solving applications in a work context and broader educational, theoretical understandings need to be balanced. You should learn the basic tools of the trade and then go on to learn more methods and ways of working to expand on the basics. What's lacking is the expansion of the knowledge in Systems" (student).

The importance of theoretical, indeed, experiential grounding was revealed by one student's response to the film Mindwalk (Capra, 1990), based on The Turning Point (Capra, 1982), at a systems summer school. The student, who was relatively 'hard' systems oriented, commented to other students, quite simply, that "if you're serious about systems thinking you have to see that film!".

The film triggered what can be described as a systemic experience of systems thinking which stimulated an understanding quite different, and of a more intense quality, from that which is gleaned from learning methodologies. The latter is a more fragmented and intellectual approach. The experience also undoubtedly improved his understanding of the methodologies and how to use them.

3.2. Systems as Interdiscipline

All discussants wanted to know more about recent developments in systems-oriented thinking and methods, both inside and outside the systems discipline. They know that systems thinking is emerging 'out there', in 'traditional' disciplines and elsewhere. Systemic thinking, often expressed in non-systems language, is increasingly recognised in many areas of science and society as an important and effective way of understanding complexities of relationship, communication and change. We live in an increasingly systems learning society.

Some discussants were concerned that systems, as a discipline, should pay more attention to these developments but that it was relatively out of touch with them. Why else would Ackoff (1995) urge systemists so forcefully to read Capra's The Turning Point: Science, Society and the Rising Culture (1982). Since it was published, this book has been extremely widely read and a core influence on social movements such as environmentalism and the general field of 'holism'.

> "To go on developing this discipline...you'll have to bring in the other bits and pieces, some of which may in fact swallow you - but I don't think one's got to get paranoid about this. And whether you're part of them or they're part of you is something which politics and power will decide. For goodness sake don't forget them because you'll get isolated" (tutor).

Systems can also make 'traditional' disciplines more attractive. One student's interest in biology was stimulated, for example, only when it was approached from a systems perspective. Similar points were made in relation to other disciplines or perspectives:

> "I mean look at the Santa Fe Institute. Every discipline you mentioned is there....and that's where it's all going. It's systems, it's falling off the end of soft systems, and you're in chaos theory and complexity" (tutor).

> "Whatever is a systemic way of thinking, even if it doesn't fit neatly into any one category, is what should be in systems teaching" (student).

In balancing theory with the necessary practical angle, a future strategy would be to investigate how to apply emerging theories, such as chaos and complexity, to management (see, for example, Stacey, 1993). A course on this would be helpful.

With regard to social sciences:

> "We need to widen the overall scope to things that are real; real problems like poverty, health, education, crime. We're saying that it should merge into the social aspect. But that's what they (students) want; that's where they live" (tutor).

> "We've been concentrating on the hard level. Systems can also help with the arts and social sciences. Is it because we're in conflict with the social sciences that they don't accept systems ideas? The whole area of the creative arts and literature (also) needs these understandings" (tutor).

One tutor is currently using, and sees great potential in developing, systems in community and overseas development consultancy.

The mutual benefit to be gained from closer relations and understanding between systems and other disciplines was stressed repeatedly:

"Systems is a great way of helping people in whatever discipline. Just to have a different way of looking at their experience" (tutor).

"Systems is for understanding the world better and doing work better.....It's not a case of teaching systems people the systems of other disciplines but of teaching other disciplines the methodologies of systems" (student).

All discussions confirmed the usefulness of systems thinking and methods, though opinions varied on the necessity of highlighting systems as a distinct discipline, and on whether 'systems' is still the most appropriate label. Subjects such as history, management and systems can be thought of as approaches to understanding; process- rather than subject-disciplines.

Just as there must always be a history of something, so must systems always be applied to something.

This same point underpinned Checkland's (1988) and Naughton's (1981) erosion of the legitimacy of General Systems Theory. Some discussions were taken up with considering the significance of this, and systems in the UK generally. Some tutors felt that they had taken their criticisms too far and this had resulted in systems in the UK focusing on developing methodologies to the exclusion of theories and frameworks in which to locate them. Attention was also focused almost exclusively on management and technology as the relevant domains of systems. On the continent, systems developed in more diverse areas.

"Systems has got bogged down with devising lots of different methodologies. Instead of saying, 'these are the core concepts'. It's as if, 'you can follow this one and you'll be OK' (agreement). The whole secret, to me, is the core ideas. Once you've got them, they're applicable to everything. Why do you need to have this set methodology? Systems talks about taking a holistic view and looking for emergent properties" (tutor).

"The most effective systems that's being used now is...to say 'Look, there's forty methodologies. Use systems thinking, use what you've learnt, use what you know, to just pick and choose - for the particular problem you're looking at, or context'. The strength of Systems is in allowing the lack of structure" (tutor).

In spite of the various arguments about the emphasis that should be given to theory or practice, thinking or methods and so on, the overall feeling from the discussants was that knowledge of systems, in its own right, is still valuable enough to justify its continued existence as a distinct discipline. If it was to be wholly encompassed by other disciplines, who would actually teach systems theory and methods, and where? Varieties of modes of thought and methodology are rarely covered in adequate depth within traditional subject-disciplines. This said, if systems is to survive in its own right, it must re-frame itself in line with new developments in its cultural and intellectual environments.

REFERENCES

Ackoff, R., 1995, Redesigning the future: the new age, *Systems Practice 8, 4.*
Capra, B., 1990, Mindwalk, Atlas Production Company, in association with Mindwalk Productions.

Capra, F., 1982, *The Turning Point: Science, Society and the Rising Culture*, Wildwood House, London.
Checkland, P. B., 1988, Images of systems and systems image, *General Systems* XXXI.
Naughton, J., 1981, Theory and practice in systems research, *Journal of Applied Systems Analysis 8*.
Stacey, R., 1993, Strategy as order emerging from chaos, *Long Range Planning*, **26**, (1), 10–17.

45

THE LEARNING CYCLE–ACTION LEARNING

Learning Organisation

The WL Group 1996[*]

University of Sunderland Business School
St. Peters Campus
Sunderland, Tyne and Wear, SR6 0DD

1. INTRODUCTION

The term 'learning organisation' can mean many things this paper tries to understand learning as a corporate activity and sees it as a strategic issue. In this paper the work is convinced by the Stacey (1993) view of planning. The view that planning to achieve some definable set of objectives on the basis of a static linear cause and effect path is unlikely to bring any profit to a system. That planning as a process to make yourself more comfortable within the world or planning to be something better than you currently are is a laudable activity and the planning process is more beneficial than the plan itself.

Cunningham (1994) suggests that we get wiser through learning from our experiences i.e. thinking about what has happened to us and what we have done. Then trying to understand this by building models of our perceived reality so that we can direct our action in a more precise manner such that we might achieve a more advantageous outcome. Wise people learn from experience so it is imperative for learning organisations to understand this and consider how the organisation as a whole (not just individuals within the organisation) learns from its experience. Two of the current sources of the promulgation of the idea of a learning organisation are IiP based on a (modified) linear cause and effect model of classical management or NVQ which adopts a classic recipe approach (Johnson and Scholes, 1989) where we have a collection of industry specific recipes on how to behave in order to be successful. Both these approaches have drawbacks. This paper adopts a more simple model (the learning cycle) at a macro level and a complex structural model (the Viable Systems Model) for the facilitation of a learning organisation at a micro level.

---

[*] The WL Group are: Penny Marrington: pennym@wkac.ac.uk, 0044(0) 1962 827481; Jerry Meek: jerrym@wkac.ac.uk, 0044(0) 1962 827427; Alfredo Moscardini: alfredo.moscardini@sunderland.ac.uk, 0044(0) 191 5152311; Jim Rowe: jim.rowe@sunderland.ac.uk, 0044(0) 191 5152763.

Systems for Sustainability, edited by Stowell *et al.*
Plenum Press, New York, 1997

The paper suggests that learning is the movement from the being of one thing to the being of another.

Teilhard de Chardin (1959) posits that 'the moment of self reflection is the moment of intelligence.' Systems that can self reflect and self sustain can be viable. All viable systems need to have an inherent formal or informal 'mechanism' for reflection. Many models exist which delineate these ideas, however, the one this paper uses is Kolb's Learning Cycle. This cycle is rooted in an action learning mode, where the learning/doing relationship is key to the process. Reflection (a key aspect of Kolb's cycle) is difficult, and one of the main interventions in reflection is made by the organisation's hierarchy, information being received may well be distorted because of the structure the individual exists in. The best learning often looks chaotic (Cunningham 1994) and hierarchy imposes order. Also an organisations cultural attitude to failure will be important to its attitude to learning and hierarchies are ideally suited to blame allocation rather than learning.

There is clearly a relationship between communication and control and control and geometry. Without communication there cannot be control and without geometry loops cannot be closed. The initial focus of this paper is at university level and the starting point is the Corporate Management Team (CMT). Key to CMT in relation to the above ideas is it's structure. Currently CMT has twenty members. The nearest platonic geometry to CMT (in terms of number) is the icosahedron. This geometry may provide us with an 'ideal' against which we may be able to measure CMT's facility for control and communication as well as creativity and learning.

2. BLOCKS TO A LEARNING ORGANISATION–SYNTEGRITY

We are usually fairly comfortable with our models, however, the moment we have to change our models we become threatened. It takes a great deal of courage to overturn the current model. An organisation that is prepared to upset its old models must be prepared to take its new learning and apply it. It must not get locked into bureaucratic (hierarchical) patterns of behaviour which have a designed-in resistance to change. The danger is that after the initiative is over we go back to our original roles resulting in "abortive excursions" (Greenwood & Hinings, 1988).

Syntegrity is a portmanteau word made up from synergy, tensile and integrity (Beer, 1994). It relates to the connection between the inherent strength of certain geometry's and their ability to facilitate the reverberation of information. The icosahedron is a geometry which has special properties. Its dimensions relate directly to the mathematics of growth. The geometry consists of thirty struts which in an organisational structure would relate to thirty people and twelve nodes relating to interest groups. Each person is a member of two groups as well as being an observer of another. The system allows individuals to work in group sizes that their variety can handle, though information can be circulated around the structure very quickly. The structure naturally includes rather excludes in the way that hierarchies necessarily do. From the Lee[†] experiments at Du Pont, three key issues emerge in the analysis of structure, communication and decision making: Group Dispersion, Relative Centrality and Peripherality. Group dispersion is the sum of the number of steps each person is away from everyone else in the structure. Relative Centrality is the quotient of

---

† The experiments carried out by Walter Lee and Paul Pangaro at Du Pont were based on the work of Alex Bevelas outlined in the Macy Conference of 1952. The source is at present a working paper.

Group Dispersion over the minimal connectivity of the individual and Peripherality is the variance between the relative centrality of the most central member of the structure and the relative centrality of the individual. If one uses these tools to compare a 29 person bifurcating hierarchical structure with a 30 person icosahedron, there is an almost exponential decline in Relative Centrality and the increase in Peripherality through the layers of a hierarchy. One can also show that in a hierarchy the level of dispersion is twice that of an icosahedron. The implications of this are both technical and psychological, however, if we consider the technical, then the potential for errors in mediation, filtration and subjectivism are much increased in a hierarchical structure. This is compounded by the sheer density of the structure which will behave as a high inertia mechanism opposing the 'flow' of information. Though the level of relative centrality is high for the individual at the top of the hierarchy the lower levels appear disadvantaged. This figure reflects the disparity between individuals in their connectedness to the hub of the organisation. The quantity and quality of information will be variable at the different levels. The icosahedron maintains an equity of information flow throughout the structure as long as information is declared. Finally the peripherality of each individual varies in a hierarchical structure such that information will be subject to a great deal more noise for those at the periphery of the structure as compared to the more central individuals. The psychological effects of the disparities are potentially many fold, however, in simplistic terms most people do not feel comfortable if they are either distant from the kernel of activity or if they feel left out.

The implications are that team work and peer reflection will be submerged in a mechanistic template for problem solving or decision making which will provide a more comfortable environment for the individual but will attenuate variety unnecessarily. The University structure is clearly hierarchical with all of the inherent problems outlined above. There is a further difficulty in the functioning of CMT in relation to its role within a viable system. CMT seems to be carrying out roles beyond its variety[‡], audit functions and operational detail appear to swamp the underlying function of strategic development. The next element of the analysis is to consider CMT in relation to a learning model. Beer's Viable Systems Model (VSM) will be used as the model is fundamentally a learning model.

3. VIABLE SYSTEMS MODEL (VSM)

Stafford Beer's model, outlined in Figure 1 can be considered as follows. System 1 is the system which produces and is usually the aspect of the system which gives the whole system its name. System 2 is the part of the system which smoothes out perturbations e.g. bureaucratic mechanisms. System 3 is the part of the system which makes resource bargains with the System 1's and is responsible for resource allocation within the system as a whole. System 3* carries out the audit function within the organisation. System 4 is the aspect of the system which deals with (lives in) the future and therefore research and marketing would normally be considered as System 4 activities. System 5 is responsible for the creation and development of the ethos and culture of the organisation. In simple terms Systems 1, 2 and 3 are concerned with what the systems is doing now whilst Systems 3, 4 and 5 are concerned with what the system will have to do in the future. This makes for a dynamic relationship between Systems 3 and 4 called the 3–4 Ho-

---

‡ Ashby's law of requisite variety states that "Only variety can destroy variety" Ashby 1956.

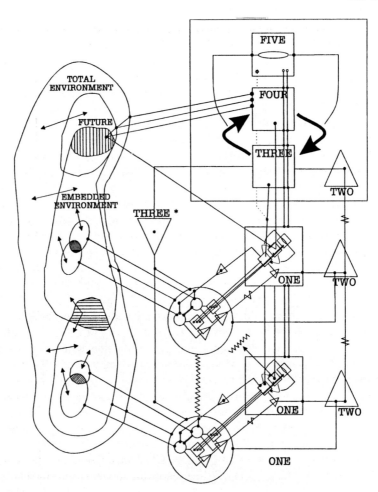

Figure 1. Diagram of the viable systems model.

meostat. It is the role of the 3–4 Homeostat to manage the organisational dichotomy between living in the present and wishing to maintain current processes and changing
(through learning) to ensure survival in the future. The following is a broad outline of
where some of the processes within the University would sit in relation to the VSM.

For the purposes of this work a model is defined as a conceptual framework used to
simplify or consider a complex reality. The model is based on an understanding of cybernetic principles of variety and control, and considers systems as learning entities. The explanation of the various parts can be obtained from Beer (1981). In our example: System
Ones are Schools or programmes, Learning World, Graduate School, Industry Centre.
System Twos are Financial Control Mechanisms, Personnel, Quality, Time Tables (Uni-
versity or School). Student Records, Modular Credit Scheme, Estates. System Threes are
Financial Management - Budgeting, Directorate, School Management Team, Staffing -
Personnel, Finance. System Three* are Internal Audit, Focus Groups, Annual Review Of
Staff Development. System Fours are Corporate Affairs, Vice Chancellor (VC), ProVC,
Planning And Market Research, Equal Opportunities, Academic Freedom Group, Re-

search Committee, Learning Organisation Group. System Five's are VC, ProVC, Board Of Governors. Three-Four Homeostat CMT, School Management Team.

4. PRELIMINARY OBSERVATIONS: THE UNIVERSITY

Drawing from the very basic research done so far the things which militate against CMT acting as the 3–4 Homeostat are the multiplicity of functions it seems to perform. CMT is used as a sounding board, data gathering device, a forum for new ideas, an audit mechanism, a resource bargainer. There is some feeling that the amount of reflection is limited due to the cluttering of the mechanism.

As you move up the structure the view of what CMT is becomes more focused. This is not to suggest that confusion existed elsewhere but that at higher levels of the organisation, whilst the gravity of the problems may be greater the self imposed variety attenuation kicks in. The amount of variety at Systems 1, 3, 4 and 5 becomes progressively reduced and consequently the need for attenuation is increased. There is a feeling that the planning mechanism the University is using is a little out moded. The University plans to do things rather than plans to be something.

The actual structure of CMT will cause high degrees of complexity which can to an extent be quantified. Though the sub-group idea is good there is still the issue of the mass of CMT and the structure of communication i.e. it is one thing to have a circular structure for discussion but the rest of the time the structure is a star.

Communication structures are embedded in the people who take part in the functioning of the University. This mechanism may evolve over time though its ability to adapt is an unknown as well as its actuality. This may lead to the obfuscation of reality and misrepresentation. There is also the difficulty that loss of an individual may cause loss of structure.

For the purposes of this project a simple experiment was carried out. The staff in the School 2 were asked two questions: (a) Do you have an Internal Telephone Directory? (b) If your answer to the first question is 'Yes', how old is the directory? The results (based on 53 responses out of 86 staff). Only 54% of staff have a directory which is less than five years old. Clearly the experiment is somewhat tongue in cheek, however, the Internal Telephone Directory is the only consummate delineation of the University hierarchy (or structure) in everyday use. Bearing in mind that staff turnover in the University runs at approximately 7%. Over a four year period an individual could be blind to a third of the structure. It is interesting to note that a quarter of School 2 staff don't have a directory. The movement towards E-mail as the predominant form of communication has further caused structures and connections within the University to become a function of the individual, this may facilitate innovation on a top down basis as the power resides in the knowledge of the structure but bottom up innovation could well be stifled due to individual blindness to the structures and processes of the University.

5. THE SCHOOLS

Approximately 30% of university employees work within the schools and schools are probably the most obvious System Ones. If we re-focus the VSM at school level we may gain some insight into the potential each school structure has for learning. In brief, all schools run programmes at undergraduate and postgraduate level and should be involved

Table 1. Summary of system four activity at school level

School	School 1	School 2	School 3	School 4	School 5	School 6	School 7	School 8
Academic staff	63	68	55	52	47	47	89	74
Items of activity	79	29	182	156	121	80	52	64
per capita	1.25	0.43	3.31	3.00	2.57	1.70	0.58	0.86
percentage	9.1%	3.1%	24.1%	21.9%	18.8%	12.4%	4.3%	6.3%
External funding	0	10750	86738	0	35700	25750	210024	54800
per capita	£0	£158	£1577	£0	£760	£548	£2360	£741
percentage	0.0%	2.6%	25.7%	0.0%	12.4%	8.9%	38.4%	12.1%
Doctorates	1	0	4	1	3	2	9	1
MPhil's	1	0	0	0	0	1	2	1
per capita[1]	5	0	15	4	13	11	22	4
percentage	6.5%	0.0%	19.9%	5.3%	17.5%	14.6%	30.7%	5.5%
Modules	430	316	318	466	331	243	308	330
per capita	7	5	6	9	7	5	3	4
percentage	14.7%	10.0%	12.5%	19.3%	15.2%	11.2%	7.5%	9.6%
Summation	7.6%	3.9%	20.5%	11.6%	15.9%	11.8%	20.2%	8.4%
Average of % Deviation	-4.9%	-8.6%	8.0%	-0.9%	3.4%	-0.7%	7.7%	-4.1%

[1] x 100

in external work, thus have at least two (or three) system ones. Schools run local timetable systems and other system two functions. Most schools have School Management Teams that allocate resource and make decisions on local spending as far as they can, thus we can assume a system three is in place. However, if we move on to system four and the three-four homeostat we can not be so secure that systems are in general in place. The most common finding when using VSM as a model of a system is that the system two does not work fully and the system four does not exist. The key system four activities in schools are research both subject specific and generic educational and course development. A school needs to learn about its subject and its business and therefore we would expect to see a great deal of research activity and a great deal "teaching and learning" activity (including course development and re-development) in a school with an active system four. If the system two was functioning correctly then this could be measured by the number of times an individual had to intervene in a bureaucratic activity to smooth out a perturbation.

It might useful to see how many research papers are produced (subject specific and educationalist), how much income is generated and how many new programmes are being developed or re-developed per capita in each school. This may give a general indication of system four activity and its relationship with the 3–4 homeostat. The difficulty in evaluating the potential for schools to be viable is the diverse nature of school activity and market positioning. Within the University we have a school which competes with Oxford and a school which may soon be competing with the local FE sector. Table 1 gives an outline of the main system four activities within each school.

The table is based on figures taken from the University's forthcoming research directory, figures produced by the University's Personnel department for May 1996 and the University's administration system. Items of activity are academic papers, books or reviews, the exception to this being in Art where exhibitions are included. This may be a little unfair to Art as counting an exhibition which could mean a great deal of work or many pieces of work as an item of activity might be considered somewhat of an underestimate of value. Doctorates and MPhil's were grouped with PhD's counting double. The per capita figure for PhD's and MPhil's was (x100) simply to make the figure easier to read and compare. All percentages are percentages of per capita figures and therefore the average percentage that schools should aim for is 12.5% (as there are 8 schools). The average of %'s owes much to John Snow's Newsnight performances during government elections or by-elections with his 'poll of polls'. It is simply an average of each schools' average's. The 'Deviation' is a measure of how far each school is from 12.5% which would be the expected norm *all things being equal'*.

Again the analysis is a little tongue in cheek and it would be difficult to draw exacting conclusions without more detailed exploration. However, School 4, School 6 and more so School 5 seem, in general, to have enough system four activity to suggest a learning structure is in place or could be. School 7 and School 3 are over performing which is good locally though it questions the organisation's learning potential when such disparities exist. School 7 has a low variety of modules which may be freeing up time which would have to be devoted to module management. School 8 seems to have a low level of system four activity and particularly research activity. School 2 has a very low level of system four activity with the exception of module variety, which, though high compared to its other system four activities, is still below average.

This analysis brings into question the current model of organisational structure i.e. what does a school look like? If a school is the logical sub-division (academic) of the university then each school should behave as one. Some schools don't seem to be *being schools*.

It may be the case that in a pluralistic market a pluralistic structure is necessary such that whilst a school may a viable system in a particular market an undergraduate programme (standing alone) may be a more appropriate structure for maintaining homeostasis in another market. Rather than subdivision of the university on the basis of size, subdivision on the basis of complexity or viability may provide a more sustainable manageable whole.

6. CONCLUSIONS

Originally this work was not intended to draw conclusions or make recommendations. This work adheres to Russell Lincoln Ackoff's maxim that 'you should never be so arrogant as to assume that you know more about a problem than the people who have it.' However, conclusions were sought and are therefore offered.

It would appear that the University is structured in such a way that would facilitate the development of a learning organisation. The 3/4 homeostat appears to be in place though its structure could be better set up so as to maximise variety and increase the reverberation of information throughout. The system 4 activity is evidenced by such projects as IiP, the graduate school, Learning Development Services, Learning World, New Knowledge, New Learning etc.

System 2 activities are usually a cause for concern in organisations and the University is no exception. The Computerised University Administration system is widely thought of as 'unable to cope' and financial management is not as controlled as it could be. Though these problems are important for the organisation, the main concern here is for learning and so if the system four and the 3/4 homeostat are in place at university level (however well adjusted) then we can move on to consider the next level of recursion, schools.

The schools model of sub-division seems to be *prima facie* a logical one, however, consideration of Table 1 (above) may suggest that questions such as: What should a school look like? What does a school do? If a school does not behave as a school, what should we do? The initial choice seems simplistic i.e. if a school does not fit the University model then close (or merge) it or make it fit. The personal cost in either of these solutions is high and will probably ensure the maintenance of the status quo.

However, there seems to be a need for some form of intervention to consider the structural model most appropriate to the University as it pursues the goal of becoming a learning organisation. This intervention needs to consider both internal and external realities and focus on what the University wants to be as well as what the University wants to do. Otherwise structures will continue to follow people and ephemeral issues, making communication, knowledge retention and therefore learning difficult to maintain other than in a local or personal sense. Coopey (1994), suggests that:

> "People perceiving themselves to be especially disadvantaged might attempt to exercise control by restricting the scope for their tacit knowledge to be translated into objective collective knowledge which, potentially, others could use to control them." (Coopey, 1994)

The disparities in hierarchical power and knowledge access may mitigate against the much needed reverberation of information throughout the University to allow learning in a collective organisational sense to take place. The understanding of what the University wants to be, must consider structure and being in a more rigorous way and inadequate simplifications such as USP, Mission Statements and SWOT need to be deconstructed in the light of real evidence.

REFERENCES

Ashby, W.R. (1956), An Introduction To Cybernetics, Chapman & Hall Ltd.

Beer, S. (1981), The Brain Of The Firm, 2nd edn, Wiley.

Beer, S. (1994), Beyond Dispute

Coopey, J. 'Power, Politics And Ideology', in J. Burgoyne et al (eds) Towards The Learning Company: Concepts And Practices, McGraw Hill.

Cunningham, I. (1994), The Wisdom O Strategic Learning: The Self Managed Learning Solution, McGraw Hill.

De Chardin, Pierre Teilhard. (1959), The Phenomenon Of Man, Collins.

Greenwood, R. & Hinings, C.R. (1988), 'Organisational design types, tracks and the dynamics of strategic change', Organisation Studies 9, 3:293–316.

Johnson, G. & Scholes, K. (1989) Exploring Corporate Strategy, Prentice Hall.

Lee, W, (1992), Why The CEO Choses Not To Listen: Information, Reliability And Decision Making In Corporations, (Working paper)..

Stacey, R.D. (1993), Strategic Management And Organisational Dynamics, Pitman.

46

A CONCEPTUAL FRAMEWORK FOR SELF-ORGANIZATION AND MERGING PROCESSES IN SOCIAL SYSTEMS

Gianfranco Minati,[1] Maria Pietronilla Penna,[1,2] and Eliano Pessa[1,2]

[1]Associazione Italiana per la Ricerca sui Sistemi (AIRS)
viale Jenner 10
20159 Milano, Italy
fax: +39-2-6081122; e-mail: gianfranco.minati@iol.it
[2]Dipartimento di Psicologia
Università di Roma "La Sapienza"
via dei Marsi 78
00185 Roma, Italy
fax: +39-6-4451667; e-mail: pessa@axcasp.caspur.it

1. INTRODUCTION

One of the most important problems to be dealt with when studying organizations and social systems concerns the individuation of their inner structural relationships. These latter appear as particularly difficult to describe when we are in the presence of evolutionary changes, such as the ones which give rise to the emergence of new macroscopic relational structures. This is the case, for instance, when we study growth or crisis phases within business companies, or merging processes between them.

Among the many conceptual frameworks which could be used to deal with the study of these phenomena, there is the one based on the mathematical theory of self-organization, in the form proposed by Prigogine (e.g. Nicolis and Prigogine, 1977) or by Haken (1983). This latter is based, in its simplest form, on the following mathematical entities: 1) a set of evolution equations, describing dynamical changes of system's state variables in time and space, 2) a set of initial and (fixed) boundary conditions for these equations granting both for a spatially homogeneous stationary solution and for infinite spatially nonhomogeneous stationary solutions, 3) a control parameter contained within the equations themselves. The form of evolution equations is chosen in such a way that, when a control parameter crosses a critical value, a bifurcation phenomenon associated with a stability exchange takes place. This means that the critical value divides the interval of possible values of control parameter into two adjacent sub-intervals, one corresponding to the case in which the spatially homogeneous stationary solution is stable, the other corresponding to the case in which one particular spatially nonhomogeneous stationary solution becomes stable.

This rather abstract description works very well for a class of self-organization processes taking place within physical, chemical, and also biological systems (e.g. Mikhailov, 1990; Mikhailov and Loskutov, 1991). It has the advantage of putting into evidence how the formation of structures depends essentially on an equilibrium between two factors: a short-range activation and a long-range inhibition. However, it appears to be too limited when we try to describe some collective processes in social structures, even at the level of animals (such as flocks, swarms, herds, packs, and so on). This happens mainly because the individuals belonging to these structures introduce a further inhibition, on a very short range, in order to preserve their ability as individuals to process information.

The purpose of this paper is to propose a generalization of the traditional framework of the mathematical theory of self-organization processes, able to deal with the description of collective processes and of the relational structures within social systems. This generalization is based on the introduction of three main factors: a very short range inhibition, a middle range activation, and a long range inhibition. We will firstly show, through a simple prototypical example, how the right combination of these three factors can give rise to the formation of flocks, starting from a disordered set of randomly moving elements. Besides, we will list the problems to be solved in order to implement concretely this framework when studying particular social organizations.

2. A SIMPLE PROTOTYPE MODEL FOR DESCRIBING FLOCK'S FORMATION

Let us present here a very simple model to illustrate how the three factors quoted above can combine in order to give rise to flock formation. To this end, we will work in a 2-dimensional space, inhabited by a given number of material points, called "birds", each one of which is moving under the action of a suitable external force. This latter derives from the actions exercised by other birds and acts in such a way as to change the bird velocity. More precisely, if we denote by $x(i)$, $y(i)$ the coordinates of the i-th bird, and by $vx(i)$, $vy(i)$ the components of its velocity, the force exercised on it by the j-th bird will change this velocity if the relative distance r between the two birds (calculated in the usual Euclidean sense) is not greater than a limiting value rc (the maximum interaction range). This change will follow the law:

$$dvx(i)/dt = F(r)[\,x(j) - x(i)]/\,r - kvx(i)$$

$$dvy(i)/dt = F(r)[\,y(j) - y(i)]/\,r - kvy(i)$$

where $F(r)$ is given by:

$$F(r) = -A(r^2 - a^2)\,(r^2 - b^2).$$

A is a suitable amplitude, and the term proportional to v introduces a suitable dynamical friction to prevent velocity changes which are too great.

If we let $a<b$ and we plot $F(r)$ vs r we observe that this function is negative (very short range inhibition) for $-a<r<a$, positive (middle range activation) for $-b<r<-a$ and

$-b>r>a$, whereas it becomes again negative for $-rc<r<-b$ and $rc>r>b$. Of course, $F(r)$ is nil in correspondence to the values a, b, $-a$, $-b$. We have thus two control parameters (a and b), instead of one, as in usual self-organization theory.

It is easy to see, through computer simulation, starting with birds whose initial positions and velocities are randomly chosen, that only a right choice of both parameters gives rise to the formation of flock from disordered bird motions. A numerical example of such a choice is given by $rc=20$, $b=16$, $a=2$, $A=0.0001$, $k=0.2$. We observed, however, that flock formation was favoured when all initial velocities fluctuated around a preselected common velocity.

Looking at this very simple model, it is possible to deduce that a generalization of the traditional framework used to study self-organization processes in social systems needs: 1) the individuation of the two critical parameters a, b defining the influence of very short range inhibition and of middle range activation; 2) the individuation of the frictional forces acting within the system; 3) the individuation of the initial common trend of all individuals belonging to the system under study.

A knowledge of these three aspects lets one build, as a principle, a model of structural relationships underlying collective processes in a social system.

3. IMPLEMENTATION PROBLEMS

When we try to apply the previous scheme to the study of concrete social systems, we encounter a difficulty, due to the fact that, whereas our simple model was defined within ordinary space, in many cases it is not so easy to define the meaning of the word "space" for a social system. Namely there can be many different types of "spaces" and of spatial-like relations. Besides the physical space in which every system is embedded, there is a communication space, in which the distance between two individuals depends on the frequency and the nature of their intercommunications. We can, then, introduce also a relational space in which the mutual distance between a pair of individuals depends on the nature of the relationships holding between them. And, finally, we can introduce even a personal space, in which each individual locates the others according to his cognitive, affective, emotional links.

In each one of these spaces we expect that a different topology will hold. So, we will need a model of activation and inhibition forces in each one of them, together with a set of relationships connecting the spatial-like variables belonging to different "space" types. Once solved the problem of properly defining the concept of "distance" in each one of the spaces previously quoted, we must cope with two important observational problems: 1) how to detect the values of the critical parameters a and b starting from observations?; 2) how to introduce a global description of system's collective processes to be compared with observational data?

As regards the first question, our simple prototypical model suggests considering the "velocities" of the single individuals (suitably defined, once a concept of "distance" has been introduced) as the fundamental dynamical variables. We can then introduce a "velocity field" within the system we are studying by associating with each "point" of the "space" we are considering a particular velocity value as follows. If the point corresponds to the location occupied by a particular individual, the velocity in this point coincides with the one of this individual. Otherwise , if there is no individual, the velocity is zero. Now it is possible to calculate, once velocity field $v(x)$ is defined, its spatial autocorrelation function:

$$C(r) = \Sigma_i \, v(x_i) \, v(x_i + r).$$

If the dynamics of our system are driven by the three factors we introduced before, we should expect, after the initial positive value of $C(0)$, a short interval of negative values of $C(r)$, due to the presence of very short range inhibition. By increasing r, after crossing the zero value, we should find an interval of positive values of $C(r)$ (due to middle range activation), followed again by a second crossing of zero value, and then by a new interval of negative values (due to long range inhibition). After a suitable value of r, $C(r)$ should become nearly zero (owing to the overcoming of maximum interaction range). As a principle, the first zero crossing of $C(r)$ should give an estimate of the parameter a, the second zero crossing an estimate of b, and the value at which $C(r)$ becomes zero an estimate of rc.

Two remarks, however, are needed. The first one is that we should expect that the observation of the first zero crossing be very difficult, if not impossible, for practical reasons. In this case the estimate of a should be made through other methods (including direct observation). The second remark is that, in order to apply this method, we need that the individuals have a non zero velocity. This happens only if the system under study has a dynamical behaviour, induced by external pertubations. This is the case, for instance, when we have merging processes. If, on the contrary, the system is in an equilibrium state, the application of the previous method requires the introduction, by the experimenter, of a suitable perturbation to the system's state. This is a common procedure when we study physical systems. However, its application to social systems raises many epistemological problems which cannot be solved within the limited space of this paper.

As regards the second question, we claim that a global description of a system's collective processes can be obtained by introducing a suitable order parameter. As a principle, we could find it, once the precise form of model's dynamical equations is known, by resorting to some mathematical machinery as the one embodied in Haken's Slaving Principle (Haken, 1983). However, we feel that this procedure is too complicated to be practically implemented when doing observations of concrete social systems. We propose, therefore, two possible alternatives, based on the following considerations: 1) our prototypical model suggests that a good order parameter is given by a suitable measure of the internal coherence, within given space-time intervals, between the dynamical variables associated to the single individuals belonging to the system under study; if we identify these variables with the "velocities", we can introduce the spatial autocorrelation function of the velocities at time t, which is directly proportional to:

$$S(r,t) = \Sigma_i \, v(x_i,t) \, v(x_i + r,t),$$

where $v(x_i,t)$ denotes the velocity value in the location x_i at time t; we will introduce then the temporal autocorrelation function of this quantity, which is directly proportional to:

$$P(\tau) = \Sigma_i \, S(r_i,t) \, S(r_i,t+\tau),$$

and measures the degree of correlation between the different spatial autocorrelations as a function of time delay; then, a good measure of the internal coherence of the internal dynamical variables (the order parameter) is given by the time average of $P(\tau)$ over a suitable observation interval $\Delta\tau$; 2) when a social system behaves as a whole, other candidate order parameters are given by some measures of the external relationships this system as a whole entertains with other systems; they give an indication about the degree to which a system is to be considered as a system and not a collection of isolated elements.

Both choices, of course, can be useful to study quantitatively what happens when two social systems undergo a merging process.

4. CONCLUSION

We show, through a simple prototypical model, how the introduction of three factors (very short range inhibition, middle range activation, long range inhibition) can explain the process of formation of collective behaviours (such as the ones which give rise to a flock) starting from disordered initial motions. These ideas were extended to the study of collective behaviors in social systems. In this regard we introduced suitable quantities to measure the degree of combination among the three factors previously quoted and to define an order parameter able to measure the inner coherence of a given system as a system. The determination of these quantities starting from concrete observations will require a precise specification of the notion of "distance" between individuals within the different "spaces" which could be used to describe the different relationships existing within a social system. This is the main problem to be solved if we want to apply the methods of self-organization theory to the study of concrete systems.

REFERENCES

Haken, H., 1983, *Advanced Synergetics,* Springer, Berlin, Heidelberg, New York.
Mikhailov, A. S., 1990, *Foundations of Synergetics I,* Springer, Berlin, Heidelberg, New York.
Mikhailov, A. S., and Loskutov, A. Yu., 1991, *Foundations of Synergetics II,* Springer, Berlin, Heidelberg, New York.
Nicolis, G., and Prigogine, I., 1977, *Self-Organization in Nonequilibrium Systems,* Wiley, New York.

47

WE'VE SAID IT'S A LEARNING ORGANISATION BUT DOES *IT* KNOW (AND WHAT IS *IT* ANYWAY)?

Joy Murray

New South Wales Department of School Education
Training and Development Directorate
PO Box 423
Rozelle 2039, Australia

1. INTRODUCTION

Most teachers can list the ingredients for effective change and the attributes of a change agent (see for example Miles, Saxl & Lieberman, 1988) and can quote a battery of techniques for reaching agreement about what needs changing. But why is it the results of change programs are so haphazard? Can systems be changed (do systems exist as entities?) or only people? And are they changed or do they change? Recent writing on educational change suggests that the change process is a messy business (Fullan, 1993a; Fullan, 1993b; Fullan 1994). Michael Fullan (1993a:20) talks about the 'New Paradigm of Change' and describes change as a 'Journey not a Blueprint'. The first part of this paper explores some of the territory behind the tools currently used in effecting change, and suggests reasons for why success is somewhat haphazard. The second part of the paper offers an example of an attempt to effect change in a large school system 'to promote schools as learning communities.' (NSW DSE, 1995).

2. THE TERRITORY BEHIND THE TOOLS

2.1. Background

Much of current practice in teacher development dealing with effectiveness and change owes something to the practices of business management. The effective schools movement gained some of its momentum from people like Deal and Kennedy (1982, & Deal 1985) who brought the language and symbolism of corporate culture to the field of education. Since then education has discovered Senge's *Fifth Discipline* (1990) which draws together a collection of what he calls 'component technologies' from a number of

Systems for Sustainability, edited by Stowell *et al.*
Plenum Press, New York, 1997

sources (e.g. 'mental models' from Royal Dutch/Shell) which he suggests are the tools needed to move from the rhetoric of 'learning organisations' to the adoption of the practices which actually create 'learning organisations'. But what fields of study have influenced both business and education and contributed their tools and metaphors to current teacher development practices? Where did they come from? And where are they heading?

2.2. Cybernetics and Systems Thinking

Behind much of the language of business and education reform are the less familiar fields of cybernetics and systems thinking. As Donaldson (1992) says 'cybernetics - as befits a science and an art which is vitally alive - consists of a wide variety of theoretical positions'. Nevertheless the notions of communication, control and circular causal systems are central themes. Cybernetics in the forties and fifties emphasised negative feedback and how systems *maintained* their organisation. Later, what Sluzki (1985) referred to as 'second wave' cybernetics explored positive feedback and how systems *changed* their organisation.

At about the same time the term 'systems thinking' was coined. It came from much the same background as cybernetics and drew on ideas emerging from systems theory proposed in the 1940s by the biologist Ludwig von Bertalanffy (Heylighen & Joslyn, 1995). At the same time as systems theory was being applied in biology, psychology, ecology and quantum physics scientists at the Massachusetts Institute of Technology 'working on the principle of feedback in electronics came to believe that it applied to other systems as well', (Asayesh, 1993).They began applying software developed for mapping electronic systems to other kinds of systems. They talked of single loop learning by the system (maintaining equilibrium through negative feedback) and double loop learning (change through positive feedback). This new field used concepts such as single and double loop learning as metaphors to explore change in organisations.

In the 1980s systems thinking began to be applied to schools as organisations. Asayesh (1993), identified the following principles: each individual is part of the whole and each individual's actions have consequences for the whole; any changes to an organisation are dependent on changes to the system rather than simply to the parts; effective change to the system is dependent on an understanding of how the system works not just at a technical level but also in terms of organisational culture. It requires an examination of values, beliefs and underlying assumptions. Systems thinking employed tools like organisational story telling that served 'to identify the organisation as different from its environment and maintain a shared context of knowledge, skills, and values in the organisation' (Andersen, 1994); and feedback loop diagramming which helped people map out long and short term consequences of actions, (Asayesh, 1993). The approach was further advanced by the work of Senge (1990) where systems thinking was in fact Senge's 'fifth discipline'.

2.3. Second-Order Cybernetics

Over the past fifteen years thinkers in the field of cybernetics, such as Humberto Maturana, Francisco Varela and Ernst von Glasersfeld, have introduced a new dimension to the debate changing the way systems, and communication within and between systems, are described. This new direction they have called 'second-order cybernetics'. Cybernetics and systems thinking assume that the system (reality) can be objectively observed. Second-order cybernetics includes the observer's role in the construction of reality. Reality is not viewed as something 'out there' independent of the observer but as something that an observer describes in language. This requires different ways of looking at *living systems* (e.g. humans), at *systems made up of living systems* (e.g. organisations such as a school) and at *communication* between living systems.

2.3.1. Living Systems. In their book *The Tree of Knowledge* Maturana and Varela (1987:135) discuss the way in which living systems (e.g. people) and the medium in which they operate change congruently (or separate or disintegrate). Briefly Maturana and Varela believe living systems: are structure determined (their structure determines their action in an environment); are informationally closed (they are autonomous and cannot be directly 'caused' or 'instructed' by anything outside); survive by fitting with the outside medium (which includes other living systems); 'fit' (Maturana and Varela call this 'fit' 'structural coupling') or separate or disintegrate; drift in a medium and they and the medium change congruently (or separate or disintegrate), (Efran & Lukens, 1985).

2.3.2. The Observer and the Issue of Objectivity. We are all observers, as observers we each describe *one* domain of reality and what we describe in language (observe) is a product of the activity of our own nervous system. In von Foerster's words 'objectivity is a subject's delusion that observing can be done without him. Invoking objectivity is abrogating responsibility; hence its popularity.' (in Fell & Russell, 1993:15). If we are all observers using language to describe the world an organisation such as a school community is as many different entities as there are people to describe it and each one is equally valid. There is no one 'real' system and there is no 'real' reality by which to compare others. We each experience the system (e.g. school) differently and each person's experience is equally real. Each teacher will therefore *be* in a different school, and the way we experience and act in the milieu of the school will depend on our individual journey through life.

2.3.3. Everything Is Connected to Everything Else. Our journey through life cannot be separated from the life histories of those around us or from the history of the environmental milieu in which we operate. Our history is the history of our recurrent interactions in a medium. As Fell and Russell (1994) point out, each coupling triggers the change which brings about the next possibilities, so the flow of behaviour and the flow of physiology are mutually modulating. Nothing therefore is trivial, everything is connected to everything else, each moment of our lives follows the last and leads to the next. Every encounter, every conversation becomes a part of us. Kandel and Hawkins (1992:60) describe this from a neurobiological perspective: 'Cortical maps are subject to constant modification based on use of the sensory pathways. Since all of us are brought up in somewhat different environments, are exposed to different combinations of stimuli and are likely to exercise our sensory and motor skills in different ways, the architecture of each of our brains will be modified in slightly different ways. This distinctive modification of brain architecture, along with a unique genetic makeup, contributes to the biological basis for the expression of individuality.' In the words of Fell and Russell (1993) 'This means that everything we have ever done together in this world could be a part of who we are and what we do today... We cannot know what the future holds, but we can know that everything we do (or say) contributes significantly to it.'

2.3.4. Communication. Language is part of the medium in which we operate, and communications trigger structural changes in us which make possible different conversations and so on (Kenny and Gardner, 1988: 4), that is, the structure of the living system and the medium change congruently. In Maturana's words 'Languaging is a manner of co-existence, a manner of living together in recursive co-ordinations of consensual actions such that the structure of the participants changes in a manner contingent upon their participation in it' (1978). To Maturana living is a cognitive process, to live is by definition to learn. All that we can do is to contribute to the creation of a milieu in which the learning we want to occur has a good chance of occurring, but we cannot specify exactly what the learning will be.

2.3.5. Cause and Effect. Life is a succession of structural couplings, our structures 'fitting' with the structures around us, and the way of our fitting is determined by our structure rather than *caused* by the medium. Cause and effect are explanations we apply after the event to make sense of our experiences. In life there are no beginnings and ends, no cause and effect, rather a web of interconnectivity stretching back through time and space. This poses great problems for an education system wanting to *cause* specific changes in schools and teaching! However there is nothing in this view that says therefore do nothing. What it says, I think, is: do what you believe in, attempt to create the milieu, but don't expect others to take away what you think it is that you put in!

2.3.6. Organisations: Interactions of Living Systems in a Milieu. '*Structure-determined living systems automatically become organized into interactional systems.* Whenever two or more structurally plastic living systems interact they will begin to co-evolve a closed pattern of interaction. They will form a system… The system is the way that its components fit together. Consequently, there are no systemic processes which create, regulate, or maintain the system: all behaviour of the system derives directly from the interaction of its structure-determined components.' (italics in the original, Dell, 1985). In this view of the world ideas about regulation and system rules which are the foundation of systems thinking are merely the observer's descriptions of the natural course of interactions of living systems in a medium where change occurs spontaneously as we coexist. In fact there is no such thing as *the* system because each observer describes in language *a* system and each system is real. If there is no one system then it is difficult to manipulated a system as an entity, there is no entity to act on, only individuals engaged in co-ontogenic structural drift and no one can directly cause change in another individual. Stacy holds a similar view in connection with educational change: 'successful human organization cannot be the realization of some shared intention formed well ahead of action. Instead, success has to be the discovery of patterns that emerge through actions we take in response to the changing agendas of issues we identify.' (Stacy, 1992:19).

3. EFFECTING CHANGE IN A LARGE EDUCATION SYSTEM

3.1. Introduction

We have 'a habit of seeing "problems", attempting to "fix" them, and then finding that, in a longer time frame and in a wider spatial context, our very "solutions" as often as not make things worse' (Donaldson, 1992). Then what should be done to bring about a desired change? In his discussion of reasons for the failure of reform efforts Fullan (1993a) draws several conclusions including the idea that 'unanticipated changes in the course of any plan or project are guaranteed. They are not abnormal intrusions but part and parcel of the dynamic complexity of present society.' The writings of biologists Maturana and

Varela provide explanations for why this could not be otherwise. If living systems are informationally closed autonomous systems then all change is part of the dynamics of living together and cannot be in any way 'a mistake' or an 'abnormal intrusion'.

The education system cannot *cause* change in teachers, any more than teachers can *cause* specific change in students. Changes that take place are determined by the structure of the living system. The medium (including all acts of communication) acts as a trigger for change but cannot specify what the change will be. Just as change to a living system cannot be specified change to a larger system (made up of living systems) cannot be specified - hence the haphazard 'success' rate of change intervention strategies. Teachers and teacher development personnel will change congruently if there is a fit between living system and medium. If the desired change is in teacher understanding of, for example, the notion of school as learning community then a milieu has to be created in which teachers are able to live and hence learn (as a process of living).

In 1995 an International Advisory Council on the Quality of Public Education in NSW advised that the quality of student learning outcomes could best be improved if action were to 'be taken at all levels to promote schools as learning communities.' (NSW DSE, 1995).

This posed a dilemma. Having read widely in systems thinking, cybernetics and second order cybernetics as well as the literature on change theory it seemed nothing could be done to *impose* such a change. However we could change the milieu. We could also change our approach to teacher development.

3.2. Schools as Learning Communities

First came the writing and distribution to all schools of a discussion paper *Schools as Learning Communities* (NSW DSE, 1995). The Director General, in his foreword, invited 'individuals, professional groups, school staff, school councils and parent groups to explore and discuss the ideas'. This paper was to be used as a focus for personal reflection, staff meetings, and school council meetings. It covered the concept and key features of learning communities. It included an agenda for action. The publication was debated in many schools and school communities.

3.3. Teacher Professional Development

A new concept in teacher development took a little longer—two and a half years in fact—and the steepest learning curve ever experienced by those involved in the creation process out of which the *Certificate of Teaching and Learning* (CTL) was born. CTL had no leader's notes and participant's workbook, no workshops or lectures, no essays to be handed in and no fixed time frame. It required people to work with learning partners or in learning networks. It required participants to choose and work with a mentor. Participants were required to build their own program of study out of the materials provided and choose their own assessor, deciding when and how to be assessed. In essence the learner was to take full responsibility. This program structure, along with the broad ranging and inclusive content, was designed to accommodated the notion of *autonomous learner*.

Of course CTL could not be imposed on teachers. This would have been inconsistent with the beliefs underpinning its development. CTL needed sponsors. Not in monetary terms, but in energy and enthusiasm! The development team introduced CTL wherever they could. In some places whole schools took control and devoured the content. But we live in a changing world and even the best ideas are subject to such things as industry restructuring and changes in government. The NSW Department of School Education underwent a restructure. The framework of ten semi-autonomous regions through which teachers could access CTL disappeared overnight, in its stead 40 districts were created.

Now, twelve months later, those who spent two years of their lives deep in the journey that was the construction of CTL are finding new ways for teachers to access its riches. Several universities have suggested that it become part of a Masters degree. Members of the development team are assessing their new roles and finding different ways of supporting schools in undertaking CTL. New people in positions of influence within the Department are looking at ways of making it available and supporting its implementation. Graduates from the program are spreading the word. Perhaps this is a much slower start than we had anticipated but if the material is good enough and if we have really created an environment in which change can occur, and which teachers want to be part of, then it will survive.

4. CONCLUSION

Since CTL other programs have been constructed using these principles. In line with Maturana and Varela's view of living systems we have accepted the responsibility to provide a milieu in which teachers and those involved in teacher development can coexist. Within that milieu, which includes all forms of communication, we have striven to understand and accommodate the concept of *autonomous learner*. We have (individually) come a long way since being advised to become a learning organisation. In the process of living over the past three years we have learned a great deal. This learning is being reflected in teacher development programs reaching thousands of teachers throughout the government school system. Does *the system* know it's a learning organisation? Is there such a thing as *the system*? The theory outlined above and our own experience, tell us there are many *systems* depending on where you stand, but does that matter? We don't think so. Each of us has no choice but to act out of our personal history, together drifting in a medium through time and space. This co-ontological structural drift (to use Maturana and Varela's term) is, I think, the biological basis for describing teaching (at all levels) as a moral act. It also provides a biological basis for the idea that '[t]he very first place to begin the change process is within ourselves' (Fullan 1993a). In fact it is the only place we can begin and with the development of CTL we hope that is what we have done.

REFERENCES

Andersen, P. B., 1994, The semiotics of auto-poiesis. A catastrophe-theoretic approach, *Cybernetics and Human Knowing* 2(4): 53–55.

Asayesh, G., 1993, Using systems thinking to change systems, *Journal of Staff Development* Fall **14** (4):8–13.

Deal, T., 1985, The symbolism of effective schools, *The Elementary School Journal* **85**(5):601 -620

Deal, T. and Kennedy, A., 1982, *Corporate cultures*, Addison-Wesley, Reading, MA.

Dell, P., 1985, Understanding Bateson and Maturana: Toward a biological foundation for the social sciences, *Journal of Marital and Family Therapy* **11**(1):1–20.

Donaldson, R. E., 1992, Cybernetics and human knowing: One possible prolegomenon, *Cybernetics and Human Knowing* **1**(1):5–9.

Efran, J. and Lukens, M. D., 1985, The world according to Humberto Maturana, *Networker* **May-June** pp. 23–28 & 72–75.

Fell, L. and Russell, D., 1993, *Co-Drifting: The Biology of Living Together*, Unpublished manuscript, Fell, Russell and Associates.

Fell, L. and Russell, D., 1994, Towards a biological explanation of human understanding, *Cybernetics and Human Knowing* 2(4):3–15.

Fullan M., 1993a, *Change Forces: Probing the Depths of Educational Reform*, The Falmer Press, London.

Fullan M., 1993b, Why teachers must become change agents, *Educational Leadership* **March**.

Fullan M., 1994, Turning Systemic Thinking on its Head, Paper prepared for the United States Department of Education, July.

Heylinghen, F. and Joslyn, C., 1995, systems theory, in: *The Cambridge Dictionary of Philosophy*, (R. Audi, ed), pp. 784 - 785, Cambridge University Press, New York.

Kandel, E. R. and Hawkins, R. D., 1992, The biological basis of learning and individuality, *Scientific American* September, pp. 52–61.

Kenny, V. and Gardner, G., 1988, Construction of self-organising systems, *The Irish Journal of Psychology* 9(1):1–24.

Maturana, H., 1978, Biology of language: Epistemology of reality, in: *Psychology and Biology of Language and Thought*, (G.A. Miller and E. Lenneberg, eds) Academic Press, New York, in: C. L. Mendez, F. Coddou, and H. Maturana, 1988, *The Irish Journal of Psychology*, 9(1):144–172.

Maturana, H. R. and Varela, F. J., 1987, *The Tree on Knowledge: The Biological Roots of Human Understanding*, New Science Library, Shambhala, London.

Miles, M. B., Saxl, E. R. and Lieberman, A., 1988, What skills do educational "change agents" need? An empirical view, *Curriculum Inquiry,* 18(2):157–193.

New South Wales Department of School Education, 1995, *Schools as Learning Communities: A discussion paper*, Training and Development Directorate.

Senge, P. M., 1990, *The Fifth Discipline: The Art and Practice of the Learning Organization,* Doubleday/Currency, New York.

Sluzki, C. E., 1985, A minimal map of cybernetics, *Networker*, May-June, p. 26

Stacey, R., 1992, Managing the Unknowable, Jossey-Bass, San Francisco, in: *Change Forces Probing the Depths of Educational Reform,* p19, M. Fullan, 1993, The Falmer Press, London.

48

TIME FOR A NEW LANGUAGE, A NEW DISCOURSE

A Naive Proposition

Elizabeth McMillan Parsons

Systems Department
The Open University
Milton Keynes, MK7 6AA, United Kingdom

1. INTRODUCTION

The thoughts and ideas I put forward in this speculative paper arise out of my initial research on the influence of the new sciences of chaos and complexity on organizational change and transformation. My interest in these and their links to language has been much inspired by the work of Stacey (1993) and, in particular, his reference to the need for a 'new dominant discourse' (pers.comm. 1996).

In this paper I invite you to stand aside from your preoccupations and consider that we belong to a complex, living system that is much more than a biological system of living organisms. A system that is part of an ever increasing eddy of systems, and systems relationships nesting within and radiating around each other. How do we connect and make sense of a world where systems are echoing and resonating to different time frames and different cultures and different technologies? Where activity is driving a dizzying level of change and transformation? A world which Ilya Prigogine describes as 'richer than it is possible to express in any single language' (quoted in Wheatley, 1992). Here lies a significant challenge. How do we describe this world in an attempt to conceptualize, frame and understand it? How do we facilitate understanding of this richness and importantly share it with others? By sharing we also develop and start to continue enriching. By sharing we make new connections and enable the introduction of new ideas, fresh perceptions and novel interpretations. By increasing our connections we introduce more variables and more turbulence and facilitate a personal paradigm shift from near to equilibrium to closer to far from equilibrium. In non chaos language, we increase the possibility that we will energise our creativity and discover some new and exciting, if initially anxiety-provoking, ways of seeing the world. We may enter a chaotic but creative phase.

Systems for Sustainability, edited by Stowell *et al.*
Plenum Press, New York, 1997

2. A NAIVE PROPOSITION

One way to achieve this is to create a fresh system of living language, an elegant vernacular, that reflects the diversity and richness of the world it seeks to interpret and convey. I would suggest that to do so we need to adopt many forms and appeal to many senses. However, in this paper I propose to explore the idea of the need for a new written and a new spoken language, and a new dominant discourse. One that may in turn intertwine with many other forms. This is my naive proposition.

I describe it as 'naive' for two reasons. First in putting forward this proposal I have a strong sense of being very naive in the sense of unknowing or having very little knowledge. This is derived from being very new to systems ideas and systems thinking. However, paradoxically this emboldens me to put forward this proposition. As a novice, I may see very differently. There may be an unexpected value in this.

Secondly, there is a tradition of art known as 'naive'. It describes those artists who owe little or nothing to traditional techniques and training. It is separate from the mainstream, yet is a part of it, and it speaks to everyone. If one thinks of L. S. Lowry, for example, he would portray a bleak industrial landscape full of small 'match stick' humans. The people were dwarfed by the size of the buildings, and often overshadowed by their grimness but still they created a vibrant world of social activity: talking, skating, cycling, being at work or at play. They conveyed a picture of life as perceived by many to be a northern reality but they offered other perceptions and insights and 'his language' or the way he 'spoke' was accessible to all. His work has a universality. The theme of universality is one that resonates with the view of the world espoused by chaos scientists. 'Chaos is the science of the global nature of systems' (Gleick, 1987). If systems are universal, then let us create a language that is universal and speaks to everyone rather like 'naive' art, for I would contend that the dominant scientific discourse does not yet do so.

Senge *et al* (1994) describe the term 'naive realism' as one which philosophers used to describe a rigid and limited view of the world which recognised the 'primacy of the parts and the isolated nature of the self.' This view saw reality as a given entity existing outside our own perceptions, and viewed language as the tool through which this external reality, 'out there', could be described. In this paper 'naive' is not being used in the sense in which the philosophers once held it but as the alternative Senge *et al* go on to describe as follows:

> 'The alternative to "naive realism" is recognising the generative role of the traditions of observation and meaning shared by a community—and that these traditions are all we ever have. When we are confronted by multiple interpretations of the "real world", the alternative to seeking to determine which is "right" is to admit multiple interpretations and to seek those that are most useful for a particular purpose, knowing that there is no ultimately "correct" interpretation. The alternative to seeing language as describing an independent reality is to recognise the power of language that allows us to freshly interpret our experience—and to enable us to bring forth new realities.'

3. PURPOSE

In this context I recognise the reality of 'multiple interpretations' but propose to explore the idea of needing a new discourse that is most useful for a 'particular purpose' in the belief that this may lead to facilitating the emergence of 'new realities'. To provide a structure or a network to facilitate and encourage this I suggest the need for a new 'connectedness'. A connectedness that will enable many different communities within human society to 'talk' to each other. Early developments in chaos science, for example, were disconnected because meteorologists, physicists and mathematicians, did not speak the same language, nor indeed, in many cases did they want to. These isolations delayed the emergence of a significant new way of viewing the world. I would propose that the current interchange between the world of the academic community and the world of the business community is not connected enough. This is counter to the emergence of new ideas and their interpretation into practical realities. Connectedness will help sustain this development. Capra (1996) describes how 'together in language we bring forth our world'. He acknowledges the 'crucial role' that language played in our evolution and how it increased 'our ability to cooperate'. Wheatley (1992) refers to the 'vast web of universal connections' and the need to build strong relationships.

Many insightful ideas whither and vanish. One reason for this is that they are not brought into 'the realm of action' (Morgan, 1993). Academia and business are mutually interdependent, one could not survive without the other and this relationship is intensifying as universities search for more means of funding and businesses look for the newest edge over their competitors. (I use 'business' in a loose sense to describe organizational life with a purpose and thus I refer not only to the business world but the public sector organizations and the higher education organizations themselves.)

Connectedness, therefore is my main purpose, but this has emerged as the result of recognising the need for new terminologies, new language, fresh discourse already identified by others and this in turn has reinforced my belief in the power of sharing ideas, exchanging thoughts, intellectually touching others—connecting. In the following paragraphs I refer to some of those who speak of the importance of language and the need for renewal.

Senge *et al* (1994) further support the importance of the continuing development of language by reminding us that when 'we forget the generative power of language...we develop a level of certainty that robs us of the capacity for wonder, that stifles our ability to see new interpretations and new possibilities for action.' This is a powerful argument for the continuing re-energising of language that underpins the concept of connectedness and which I described earlier in chaos science terms. We are also reminded (Senge *et al*, 1994) that to ignore the generative power of language can result in 'belief systems that become rigid, entrenched, and ultimately self-protective.'

Winograd and Flores (1991) recognise that a 'new way of speaking in turn creates changes in the world we construct.' They give the example of Freud's work and the introduction of such terms as 'ego', 'subconscious' and 'repression'. 'At one level we might say that he recognised and labelled phenomena that had always existed. But the innovation in his language had a major impact on human society.' They refer to Humberto Maturana and observe that he deliberately devised a good deal of new terminology because he realised that 'the old terminology carries within it a pre-understanding that is a trap for new understanding.'

Robert Shaw, a member of the Santa Cruz Dynamical Systems collective has commented that: 'You don't see something until you have the right metaphor to let you perceive it' (quoted in Gleick, 1987). Time for a new language is a theme echoed frequently by Handy (1990) who reminds us in the context of people and organizations that: 'New imagery, signalled by new words, is as important as new theory; indeed new theory without new imagery can go unnoticed.'

4. THE RATIONALISTIC TRADITION AND LANGUAGE

Already in many organizations the turbulence driven by massive technological and economic changes and the fierce nature of global competitiveness and the threat, real or imagined, of an organization's demise, has caused many managers and thereby their organizations to revert to traditional and therefore, familiar behaviours. These behaviours are often rooted in the traditional, rationalistic, Newtonian world view which no longer adequately interprets the world. Charles Handy (1990) talks of organizations and how they have been dominated by the traditional or mechanistic view. People were convinced that there was an explanation for everything and that 'everything should be planned and predicted in a properly ordered world. People were part of a well ordered system. If only they did as they were supposed to do, everything would work fine.' He points out, however, that the old order has failed and that management systems and 'control are breaking down everywhere.'

Senge (1992) in recognizing the powerful influence played by language in the way we perceive the world points out how its structure and development in Western cultures has encouraged linear thinking such that 'we think in linear ways, and we perceive the world linearly'. He points out that this creates real difficulties for managers as they tend to 'confront...complex, dynamic realities with a language designed for simple, static, problems.' Their linear use of language encourages and facilitates traditional, linear thinking.

There are difficulties in introducing new approaches and new concepts heralded by new images and new language. Winograd and Flores (1991) refer to the 'tradition of rationalism and logical empiricism' which 'has been the mainspring of Western science and technology' for centuries and is embodied in the rationalistic tradition of management science. Further this 'rationalistic orientation...is also regarded, perhaps because of the prestige and success that modern science enjoys, as the very paradigm of what it means to think and be intelligent.' Here lies real difficulties. If a new language does not carry overtones or nuances reflective or consonant with the dominant discourse of the rationalist tradition how much credibility will it carry? Yet how does it avoid carrying the unwanted aspects of the 'baggage' of the past?

5. SIGNS OF EMERGENCE

There are some signs of changes taking place in the way organizations think and behave that is demonstrated through their language. As Handy (1990) explains 'Organizations used to be perceived as gigantic pieces of engineering, with largely interchangeable human parts. We talked of structures and their systems, of inputs and outputs, of control devices and of managing them, as if the whole was one large factory. Today the language is not that of engineering but of politics, with talk of cultures and networks, of teams and coalitions, of influence or power rather than control, of leadership not management.' In the newer, more hi-tech organizations in the USA the word 'manager' has begun to disappear. People are not 'managers, they are 'team leaders', 'project heads', 'coordinators' or, 'executives'. The language is significant, once again signalling a change of attitude and a new way of looking at the world.

The world of computing has generated a whole new language—a system of interlocking levels of meaning and complexity of meaning that reflect intensity of involvement. Some levels of the language remain obscure to all but the most involved and it is inevitable that complex layers of meaning and consequent understanding will evolve. The challenge is to ensure that the spirals of language connect from complex design terminology to the words in the 'how to do' manual. Yet Capra (1996) reminds us that computer scientists often rely on old traditional, militaristic, language, derived from the traditional world view, for example, in the use of such terms as 'command', 'escape', 'fail safe' 'target' and so on.

The chaos scientists have demonstrated the need to develop a new language to describe new concepts and ideas and to excite. 'The new science has spawned its own language, an elegant shop talk of *fractals* and *bifurcations* , *intermittencies* and *periodicities*, *folded -towel diffeomorphisms* and *smooth noodle maps"* and the 'chaos scientists sometimes call themselves "believers" or "converts" or "evangelists"'(Gleick, 1987).

6. IS IT ENOUGH?

Is it enough? Does the academic world 'speak' to the 'business' world? Do these worlds 'speak' to all our citizens? Capra (1996) refers to the work of the biologist Maturana and points out that 'the social unity of human societies is based on the exchange of language'. As the world becomes an increasingly more complex and more densely peopled planet then the need for cooperation and understanding, the need for a relevant, 'connecting', language becomes ever more crucial. Some shifts in the use of words is taking place but is it enough if we are to capture new ideas and fresh concepts and so radically shift away from our traditional, mechanistic past?

Is this tradition like Chinese Opera? Years of painful, rigorous training are dedicated to carrying out an elaborate, artificial, ritual that represents but is not, the chaos scientists would argue, real life. Have academics devised an elaborate and complex way of describing the world that uses a language that is not the everyday vernacular and needs an expert to explain, guide and show people how to use it?

Anthony Garrett (1996) is critical of the language of the university business schools and quotes, in this case, the language of a research prospectus, as follows: 'determinants of quality strategy and the role of marketing in affecting the relationship between quality-related positional advantages and business performance' and 'the conceptualisation of strategy and strategic change; the relationship between strategy and values and the role of culture and communication in the management of change.' He comments: 'Where are the vivid images the concrete nouns ? This is abstract to the point of glazing over'.

7. AN INSIGHTFUL EVENT

Fritjof Capra, author of 'The Turning Point' and Ralph Stacey, from the University of Hertfordshire, led a seminar on Self organization and Emergence at the Roffey Park Management Institute on November 1st 1996. The attendees were drawn from public and private sector organizations and the universities. A number of managers and consultants found themselves excited by the concepts and ideas they were hearing but struggling to come to terms with all that they had heard and seen. They described difficulties with the terminology and were working hard to take it all in and re frame so that it fitted within their own knowledge base and intellectual frame of reference. Also, most importantly for them, they also needed to work out the practical implications of what they had been involved in. In other words, how they would use these ideas and how they would 'sell' them to colleagues. Knowing a little of the concepts under discussion and like them excited by their possibilities, I sought to build a simple bridge of understanding between concept and interpretation; between academic dialogue and 'lay' language. It was, I found, possible to go only so far before the language ran out. Even eclectic use of metaphors did not go far enough. It made connecting difficult.

This encounter served to reinforce my view that there were new ideas and concepts which it was difficult to frame and explore further because the words or images to describe them were not readily available and also that a 'new' form of language was needed to serve as a bridge and a connector between the world of the pragmatists and the world of the theorists. Is there a danger that our behaviours are so exclusive and esoteric as to be ultimately reductionist in the new global order that is emerging?

At the same time a number of managers complained that there existed two distinct types of literature. The literature of academic papers and journals and of popular professional or business magazines. However, they felt that the views published in the latter were not respected by the academic community and were considered of minimal value. Is this perhaps another sign of the rule of the scientific rationalist tradition and a further need for us to connect rather better? Are we aware of the differences and of the powerful influences of tradition and its role in our lives? Tradition 'is concealed by its obviousness... It is a way of understanding, a background, within which we interpret and act' (Winograd and Flores, 1991). We are reminded by Dawson (1996) of a tradition where in 'the Anglo-Saxon world we tend to reward people for the great plan or the grand strategy, and to see the implementation of that as a separate and lesser thing.'

8. WHAT NEXT?

Handy (1990) refers to Donald Schon who thirty years ago 'was arguing that creativity, particularly scientific creativity, comes from the "displacement of concepts" - from taking concepts from one field of life and applying them to another in order to bring fresh insights.' This is one way in which a language is re-energized. This argues for a more radical, and energetic interaction between disciplines and not only disciplines but walks of life that extends beyond an exchange of recorded information.

The new scientific ideas derived from chaos and complexity theory encourage us to tolerate and accept paradox, uncertainty and lack of apparent order. Wheatley contends that: 'Information is always spawned out of uncertain, even chaotic circumstances' and that we should welcome it into our organizations and 'ally ourselves with it as a partner'. She warns that we have 'raised the practice of "no surprises" to a high art' and that such behaviour is a 'macabre prescription for self-destruction'.

Again Robert Shaw (quoted in Gleick, 1987) wrote: 'It is hard to break the habit of thinking of things in terms of how big they are and how long they last. But the claim of fractal geometry is that, for some elements of nature, looking for a characteristic scale becomes a distraction. *Hurricane*. By definition, it is a storm of a certain size. But the definition is imposed by people on nature. In reality, atmospheric scientists are realising that tumult in the air forms a continuum, from the gusty swirling of litter on a city street corner to the vast cyclonic systems visible from space. Categories mislead. The ends of the continuum are of a piece with the middle.' Here is a piece of lucid writing with impact that speaks to us all and connects the scientific discourse to the understanding of the everyday person in the street.

A language exists to describe the 'old' world view, but not yet the 'new'. My research into organizations convinces me of the need to develop a new language if we are to discover and create new forms of organizations for the 21st century. A new language—simple, lucid, with vivid images and understandable metaphors is needed. One with immediacy. One that will enrich, elucidate and make more accessible while at the same time taking forward our understanding and perception of the nature of human systems into a new era. A language that will connect together and facilitate the connecting of all living systems and that will more truly reflect the new age we wish to enter. For as Jantsch states (1980): 'In life the issue is not control but dynamic connectedness'(quoted in Wheatley, 1992). I have not here described how this may be achieved but I hope I have made the case for connectedness using language.

REFERENCES

Capra, F., 1996, *The Web of Life*, HarperCollins, London

Dawson, S., 1996, 'Judged on Merit', *People Management*, 8th August 1996.

Garrett, A., 1996, 'A Cuckoo in the Nest', *The Times*, 26th July 1996

Gleick, J., 1987, *Chaos - making a new science,* Abacus, London

Handy, C., 1990, *The Age of Unreason*, Arrow, London

Morgan, G.,1993, *Imaginization - the art of creative management,* Sage, London

Senge, P., 1992, *The Fifth Discipline: the art and practice of the learning organization*, Century Business, London

Senge, P., Kleiner, A., Roberts, C., Ross, R. and Smith, B., 1994, *The Fifth Discipline Fieldbook: strategies and tools for building a learning organization*, Nicholas Brealey, London

Stacey, R., 1993, 'Strategy as order emerging from chaos', *Long Range Planning*, **26** (1): 10–17

Stacey, R., 1996, Pers. comm. 'The Individual and Work', OPUS Conference, 13 July

Wheatley, M., 1992, *Leadership and the New Science*, Berrett-Koehler, San Francisco

Winograd, T. and Flores, F., 1991, *Understanding Computers and Cognition: a foundation for design,* Addison-Wesley, Reading MA

49

TOWARDS INFORMATION SYSTEMS SUSTAINABILITY IN COMMUNITY ORGANISATIONS USING AN ORGANISATIONAL LEARNING APPROACH

Nick Plant

University of the West of England
Frenchay Campus, Coldharbour Lane
Frenchay, Bristol, BS16 1QY, United Kingdom

1. INTRODUCTION

The aim of this paper is to establish the potential utility of a model for improving the sustainability of information systems (IS) in community organisations (COs) in the UK using an organisational learning approach as a complement to an IS strategy perspective.

Some key characteristics of COs and their IS will be summarised, and the research project within which the present study is located will be outlined. A brief review of the development of a sustainability hypothesis, and work on IS strategy in COs, will conclude the scene-setting. An organisational learning approach to interventions aimed at improving sustainability will be described, and the results of early field trials discussed. Conclusions will finally be drawn about the model and the continuing research questions raised.

2. COMMUNITY INFORMATION SYSTEMS

The study which is the subject of this paper is part of a research project on IS in community-based voluntary organisations in the UK. Clear definitions of this diverse and dynamic sector of society are elusive (Handy, 1988), but a working definition is "a small value-based organisation founded on commitment (arising from devotion, compassion, enthusiasm, solidarity, defiance, etc.) and working for a common good or public benefit at a local (typically county or city) level" (Plant, 1996, derived from Paton, 1992).

IS work in COs is particularly challenging given their lack of long-term planning capability, high expectations of IT set against low resource levels, low levels of internal expertise and patchy external IS support. At the same time, COs frequently display continuing resilience and innovative capabilities, are resource efficient, adopt humanistic

Systems for Sustainability, edited by Stowell *et al.*
Plenum Press, New York, 1997

management styles in a highly professional environment, and use a significant amount of IT (Plant, 1996). Research principles adopted in response include: an action research approach derived from the author's background as a practitioner committed to the interplay of action and theory (Zuber-Skerritt, 1992) and a critical systems thinking perspective (Midgley, 1995); a commitment to research outcomes which deliver tangible benefits to CO clients, via practical, usable, accessible tools and techniques; a participative methodology (Schecter, 1991); promoting mutual learning (Elden and Levin, 1991) and a commitment to sustainable knowledge transfer.

Systems thinking is used in this research as a tool for understanding (Checkland and Scholes, 1991), and a community information system is conceptualized as the ensemble of individual IS in a CO, together with their users, owners, procedures, IT infrastructure, management context and allied social/political concerns. Experiential understanding and early fieldwork has led to the hypothesis that IS in COs tend to lack sustainability, and an empirical model for evaluating the extent of sustainability has been proposed. This "sustainability hypothesis" assembles 15 distinct IS factors found to be relevant in the field into three clusters which respectively reflect the degree of success of IS, their life expectancy, and the autonomy of the organisation in IS terms (Plant, 1996). Put in more theoretical terms, the sustainability of an IS in a CO may be regarded as a desirable emergent property of the IS as defined above. Furthermore it has frequently been found during dialogue with stakeholders in COs that this concept resonates strongly with today's consciousness of ecological sustainability and its holistic integration with economic and social sustainability, through the practice of sustainable community development.

Early approaches to improving sustainability focused on the lack of strategic thinking about IS noted in fieldwork and previous experience, encouraged by growing attention to strategic management in the voluntary sector (Barnard and Walker, 1994) and many discussions within the community computing movement about the role and benefits of "IT strategy". A primary task-based model of an end user IS function based on Wilson(1991) was adopted but later rejected, as the simplistic insertion of a missing IS strategy function was seen to be overly rationalistic and unrealistic in the light of the rich mix of social and political issues typical of COs. Notions of emergent strategy, the concept of the flexible information architecture (Galliers, 1993), the use of change management, evaluation and review processes in the IS strategy literature (Earl, 1989; Galliers, 1995), and the notion of applying organisational learning approaches to IS planning (Huysman et al, 1994), show more promise in moving towards a more interpretivist orientation to the research.

3. THE ORGANISATIONAL LEARNING MODEL

A model based on an organisational learning approach (Argyris and Schön, 1996) will now be described, before moving on to discussion of its utility in practice. The model is necessarily simple in order to be easily assimilated by non-IS participants under time pressure, and is shown in diagrammatic form in figure 1. The inner section reflects the dynamism of a learning process, using the classic experiential learning cycle, applied to a series of small, manageable steps, based on the realities of the existing organisational problem situation and the notion of incremental improvement. Clients are prompted to ask repeatedly "What small projects or activities might help bring about improvement, starting now?". Such projects are likely to be many and varied in their nature, reflecting the multifaceted nature of IS practice. They might cover task-oriented objectives such as evaluating technological opportunities within a particular vertical software market, reviewing infor-

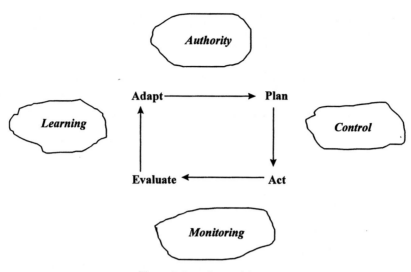

Figure 1. Learning model.

mation requirements in a functional area, staff training needs analysis, or embrace the learning process itself by piloting an IS policy and procedures guide encapsulating good practice.

Overlaid on this dynamic process model, as reflected in the outer section of the diagram, is a more static enabling structure with four components denoting the management framework needed to hold together and generate learning from the project/activity cycle. Three of these are derived directly from the formal system model (Fortune and Peters, 1995) and involve authority (legitimisation of the IS function by management), control (coordination of the ensemble of projects and activities as a whole) and monitoring (a mechanism for evaluating individual projects/activities and overall performance). Overall performance may be measured using criteria derived directly from the sustainability model mentioned earlier. Finally, the fourth outer component, labelled learning, represents -crucially- the need for evaluation outcomes to be managed in such a way as to ensure that new organisational knowledge is always identified and captured as it develops.

In summary, the model embraces structural and process elements coherently, and could be said to represent a learning system. It is also flexible and adaptable to a variety of different problem contexts, and can, furthermore, be operationalised using two straightforward principles, namely the initiation of the learning cycle and the establishment of an infrastructure to support and maintain that cycle. Nevertheless, it was felt that during practical work in participation with CO staff, this model might on its own appear abstruse and overly general. Therefore, as a preface and a complement to the learning model, a simplified strategy model as shown in figure 2 was retained (based on Galliers, 1995) to engage participants with the hard, positivist features of a strategic framework for IS.

4. FIELD TRIALS AND EARLY FINDINGS

An account of early trials of the model will now be provided, and some preliminary findings discussed. A prototype workshop was designed for CO staff, to promote align-

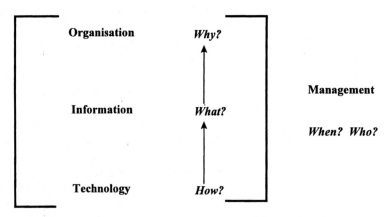

Figure 2. Simplified strategy model.

ment of IS with organisational strategy, and raising awareness about "information strategies". A "sustainable computing" questionnaire was issued to participants in advance, as a consciousness-raising exercise, containing an attitudinal component derived directly from the sustainability hypothesis, and an organisational profiling component based on an operationalised version of the Paton model referred to earlier (Kazi, Paton, and Thomas, 1990). The workshop opened with a brainstorming session, to identify issues and concerns from participants' own organisations. Following a brief presentation of the simplified strategy model and the organisational learning model, small group exercises applied the models to case study organisations, each group of participants looking at an organisation represented by one of its members.

This workshop was run twice, in highly time-constrained circumstances, during the annual conference of a national voluntary sector umbrella organisation, involving participants from COs which run multi-purpose community centres. The major results of these field trials fall loosely into four areas. Firstly, there appeared to be successful transfer of IS awareness, in that participants found it straightforward to categorise brainstorm results according to the Organisation-Information-Technology-Management taxonomy, and readily accepted the rich mix of technical, human and organisational issues that the workshop had intended to communicate. Notions of organisational alignment and integration of IS strategy with mainstream management were also accepted; one participant who, as Director of her organisation was a self-styled "compulsive planner", realised for the first time that it was erroneous to have always left IS management concerns solely to IT-aware junior staff.

Secondly, the learning model was successful in generating ideas for making improvements in IS, in that a diversity of types of projects or activities were identified by the case study groups. Some adopted a highly task-oriented stance and carried out rationalistic top-down IS strategic planning, whereas others took a broader view of the organisation and reviewed the informational needs of external service users in relation to the organisation's aims. Other activities identified included an evaluation of existing IS activities, and a process of integrating IS learning cycles within the organisation's working systems, though the ownership and coordination facets of the model were in some cases perceived as problematic.

Thirdly, an appropriate degree of critical appreciation was apparent, in that the divergent responses mentioned above appeared well suited to the nature of the problem situations represented by the respective case study organisations (Flood and Jackson, 1991). A task-focused example applied to a unitary organisation with relatively few IS resource constraints and relatively formal planning and management processes, whereas a more interpretivist stance was taken by a group whose case study organisation was pluralist, resource-constrained and made up of a divergent range of semi-autonomous projects, each with distinct objectives and values. Furthermore, power, status and control issues emerged unprompted (and in some cases surprisingly vividly) during the workshops, and were readily accepted as appropriate parts of a holistic treatment, though it was observed that an empowerment-based approach to intervention was crucial in order to avoid merely leaving this to chance.

Finally, and more generally, the workshops were felt to be successful in offering, in the words of one participant, a "useful thinking mechanism" to take back to colleagues in their own organisations, in a highly participative atmosphere, involving open dialogue, clear communications and mutual learning.

5. CONCLUSIONS AND FUTURE DIRECTIONS

In conclusion, by returning to the research principles outlined in section 2, the findings will be evaluated, and some outstanding issues identified. It does seem, firstly, that action learning and action research appear to be in harmony using this approach, and critical awareness appeared to be present, though there is no room for complacency that participants' approaches to the case studies appeared methodologically consistent with the problem situations they encountered. Further attention to the surfacing and management of issues of power, conflict and boundary-setting (Ulrich, 1993) is therefore needed.

It also seems that knowledge transfer can occur through the use of the approach that has been described. A participative approach was achieved, with effective communications, and the models were readily accessible to participants, although the abstract features of the learning model require more concrete examples. Tangible benefits appear to have been derived by CO clients, and the strategy model appears to complement the learning model successfully. The extent of self-sufficiency in the crucial tasks of initiating the learning cycle and capturing learning may be problematic, suggesting that external facilitation in these areas may need greater intensity, albeit at some risk to the sustainability of the intervention itself.

A consolidation of the theoretical underpinnings that have been glossed over in the present practice-oriented phase is required, and then the research will move towards intervention focused on intensive development activities using the approach described above as a methodological underpinning. Subject to the further investigations that have been identified, it may be possible in due course to demonstrate sustainability emerging from a systemic process of organisational learning about IS within a CO, with the role of external facilitator limited primarily to that of catalyst for the establishment of endogenous learning.

ACKNOWLEDGMENTS

The author would like to acknowledge with thanks the contribution made to this work by Maria Clarke, in conjunction with whom the prototype workshops were designed and facilitated, and Brian Petheram, for his helpful review comments.

REFERENCES

Argyris, C., and Schön, D.A., 1996, *Organisational Learning II - theory, method, and practice*, Addison-Wesley, Wokingham

Barnard, H., and Walker, P., 1994, *Strategies for success - a self-help guide to strategic planning for voluntary organisations*, NCVO Publications, London

Checkland, P., and Scholes, J., 1991, *Soft Systems Methodology in Action*, Wiley, Chichester

Earl, M., 1989, *Management strategies for information technology*, Prentice Hall, Hemel Hempstead

Elden, M., and Levin, M., 1991, Cogenerative learning - bringing participation into action research, in: *Participatory action research* (W. Foote Whyte, ed.), pp. 127–142, Sage, California

Flood, R. L., and Jackson, M. C. (eds.), 1991, *Critical Systems Thinking - directed readings*, Wiley, Chichester

Fortune, J., and Peters, G., 1995, *Learning from Failure - the systems approach*, John Wiley, Chichester

Galliers, R. D., 1993, Towards a flexible information architecture: integrating business strategies, information systems strategies and business process redesign, *Journal of Information Systems*, **3**: 199–213

Galliers, R.D., 1995, Re-orienting information systems strategy: integrating information systems into the business, in: *Information Systems Provision - the contribution of soft systems methodology* (F.A.Stowell, ed.), pp. 51 - 74, McGraw-Hill, Maidenhead

Handy, C., 1988, *Understanding voluntary organisations*, Penguin, London

Huysman, M.A., Fischer, S., and Heng, S.H., 1994, An organisational learning perspective on information systems planning, *Journal of Strategic Information Systems*, **3**(3): 165–177

Kazi, U., Paton, R. and Thomas, A., 1990, Developing a methodology for an organisational database for the social economy, in: *Supplement to the Proceedings of the 1990 conference of the Association of Voluntary Action Scholars*, pp 153-, Vol. 1

Midgley, G., 1995, What is this thing called CRITICAL systems thinking?, in: *Critical Issues in Systems Theory and Practice* (K. Ellis, A. Gregory, B. Mears-Young and G. Ragsdell, eds.), pp. 61–72, Plenum Press, New York

Paton, R., 1992, The social economy: value-based organisations in the wider society, in: *Issues in Voluntary and Non-profit Management* (J. Batsleer, C. Cornforth, and R. Paton, eds.), pp 3 - 12, Addison-Wesley, Wokingham

Plant, N., 1996 (forthcoming), Sustainable information systems in community organisations, in: *Philosophical and logical aspects of information systems* (R. Winder, S. Probert and I. Beeson, eds.)

Schecter, D., 1991, Participatory research: an emancipatory methodology for systems practice, in: *Systems Thinking in Europe* (M.C.Jackson, G.J.Mansell, R.L.Flood, R.B.Blackham and S.V.E.Probert, eds.), pp 391 - 395, Plenum Press, New York

Ulrich, W., 1993, Some difficulties of ecological thinking, considered from a critical systems perspective: a plea for critical holism, *Systems Practice*, **6**(6): 583–611

Wilson, B., 1991, Information management, in: *Systems Thinking in Europe* (M.C.Jackson, G.J.Mansell, R.L.Flood, R.B.Blackham and S.V.E.Probert, eds.), pp 89 - 97, Plenum Press, New York

Zuber-Skerritt, O., 1992, *Action research in higher education*, Kogan Page, London

50

MULTI-LEVEL MULTI-LOOP ORGANIZATIONAL LEARNING IN THE OPEN UNIVERSITY

Carol Russell and Geoff Peters

The Open University
Walton Hall
Milton Keynes, MK7 6AA

1. INTRODUCTION AND BACKGROUND

The Open University's 'New Directions' programme began in 1993, when the UK higher education funding system was encouraging expansion of student numbers. The University's strategic plan was to expand student numbers from 140 000 to 250 000 by the turn of the century. The plan recognised the need for thematic changes, and for involving all staff in these.

The programme was initiated by the Pro Vice Chancellor for Strategy, with help from the University's Training & Development Manager. It began as a series of workshops which brought together a cross-section of staff, initially chosen at random, to develop and report directly to senior management, visions of what the University would be doing in ten years time — and how we could all start moving towards this. Because some space was allowed for self-organization to follow up the issues raised in these workshops, the activities expanded over the following three years. Several of those involved (mostly volunteers) in the New Directions programme have already published reports describing and reflecting on the various activities (Edwards, Parsons, Peters and Richenburg., 1995; Parsons and Russell, 1995; Russell and Parsons, 1996). New Directions has been about linking learning at the organisational level directly to that at the individual level. Around 500 of the 3500 staff have now take part in one or more of the New Directions activities. Some of the issues raised have been 'mainstreamed', in that they have been taken on board by formal initiatives. Others are still unaddressed.

An earlier analysis (Russell and Peters, 1996) draws on a number of theoretical approaches based on systems thinking. One influence is William Pasmore's observation that, for an organization to respond quickly and effectively to changes in the external environment, everyone in the organization must have 'holographic knowledge'; i.e. a view of the whole (Pasmore, 1995). Another is Dorothy Leonard-Barton's exploration of the management of knowledge assets in knowledge-based organizations. In this she identifies four

Systems for Sustainability, edited by Stowell *et al.*
Plenum Press, New York, 1997

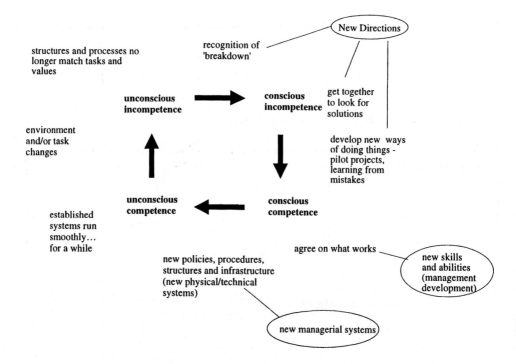

Figure 1. Organizational learning cycle.

levels to organizational learning capability — values; skills and abilities; managerial systems; physical/technical systems. She describes cases of technology-based companies with 'organic learning systems' in which all four levels operate in synergy (Leonard-Barton, 1995). Figure 1 summarises how these can be combined in an organizational analogy of the learning cycle for individuals. The Open University's New Directions activities are seen as a way of moving the organization into and through the 'conscious incompetence' phase — in that it can show where the formal organizational structures are no longer 'competent' for the strategic tasks.

What follows is a further exploration of theories about learning in complex systems — and implications for New Directions activities in the Open University.

2. METHODOLOGY

This analysis is part of an ongoing action research project, in which organizational initiatives are reflected upon by the participants. Previous work identified some of the theories and ideas influencing the New Directions programme. This study first takes note of recent changes in the organization's strategic environment. Then it examines the learning processes in terms of biological systems models, before considering practical options for facilitating learning.

3. RECENT DEVELOPMENTS

Early in 1996, the Open University's strategic environment changed. The Government had withdrawn support for continued expansion of student numbers, and the Open

University's grant funding was significantly lower than had been planned for. This changed the financial climate within the organization. It also changed the nature of the New Directions activities, which began to focus on informing staff about the nature of the financial situation. A New Directions conference in September reviewed three aspects of the University's investment in the future (staff, new technology, student services) and provided a space for staff to discuss the benefits of these investments. Unlike earlier events, the format of the conference was a fairly conventional exercise in internal communications. The Vice Chancellor gave a keynote address. Members of the senior management team, along with others involved in specific projects, formed panels to explain and discuss issues with staff. Invited speakers from other organizations which have undergone change shared their experiences with University staff. There was a little part-time administrative support for planning the event, some facilitation support on the day from Personnel and General Facilities Departments. But the event was structured and driven by a group of staff volunteers on a tiny budget.

Other activities relevant to organizational learning are more formally resourced, and supported by the Personnel Division. There is a career development and staff appraisal scheme. There is a management development programme. Although formally in place, some of these are not wholly embedded in the routine behaviour of the organisation (Open University, 1996). In terms of the Figure 1 model, they have not reached the 'unconscious competence' stage.

4. IDEAS AND MODELS

4.1. Organizations as Organisms

Systems thinking about organizations draws on analogies with biological systems. Figures 2 (a)and (b) show how the development pattern in a biological organism might offer some ideas on organizational learning and development.

4.2. Levels of Learning in Complex Systems

Ralph Stacey (1996) builds up a model of organizational behaviour based on the common properties of all complex systems, whether organisms or organizations. For organizations, he identifies different levels at which learning and change occurs: individual, group, organization, society, ecology.

At each level there are dominant and recessive systems (Figure 3). The dominant pattern is what drives the primary tasks, and determines actions and processes. The recessive patterns are dormant, available but unused, or unshared. Change and learning at all levels involves shifting systems from the recessive to the dominant role. Positive and negative feedback loops operate between the outcomes of the action and the symbol systems. Learning takes place when the recessive system grows, through positive feedback from outcomes, to the point where it becomes dominant. Stacey explains in some detail how this happens in practice at each of the first three levels, and how self-organization at one level creates the next.

The other strand in Stacey's analysis is the need to keep a tension between order and chaos at each level. He describes various strategies for staying at the edge of chaos, for creating space for learning and change without complete shut-down or disintegration.

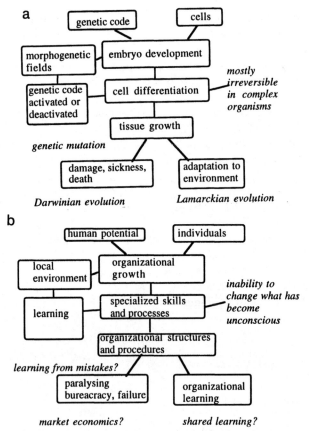

Figure 2. Development in (a) organisms and (b) organizations.

4.3. Evolution and Learning

Stacey's analysis might be interpreted in terms of Darwinian evolution. In other words, learning will be forced through interaction with the external environment and survival/dominance of the fittest. Those parts of the organization (or even whole organizations) that are not fit enough will perish, to be replaced by others from the 'shadow' or 'recessive' system.

However, recent work on the sciences of complexity challenges the simple Darwinian view (Kauffman, 1991, Kauffman and Macready 1995). Stacey notes that every new action by an individual or group changes the 'fitness landscape' in the environment. Individual behaviour changes the environment in a group. Group behaviours affect the whole organization, and organizations influence society.

Kelly (1994) describes how Lamarckian evolution (in which acquired characteristics or learned behaviour are inherited or replicated) works in adaptive self-organising computer simulations. The same may be true of human organizational systems. Individually and organizationally, we can learn from the successes and failures of others, as well as from our own experience.

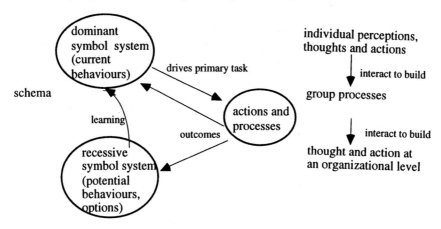

Figure 3. Stacey's model applied to organizational learning.

5. LEARNING IN PRACTICE

Stacey mentions various leadership strategies available to contain anxiety, and thus promote group and organisational learning. This implies that the anxiety is unavoidable, that the whole learning process is necessarily painful. But there are ways of creating an organizational climate which speeds up the learning process for individuals.

Senge, Kleiner, Roberts, Ross and Smith (1994) offer practical suggestions for translating the theory of organizational learning into action. 'Personal mastery' and acknowledging personal values is an important component of making individual learning easier, as are strategies for working with individuals' mental models. There are also processes for understanding and improving team learning, and for developing a shared vision for the whole organization.

The individual learning tools suggested by Senge *et al.(1994),* are very similar to those included in NLP (neurolinguistic programming). A particular benefit of NLP is in developing awareness and understanding of the unconscious processes that can block an individual from considering ideas or from taking action on them (O'Conner and Seymour, 1993). There is scope for using tools and skills such as these to promote a deeper level of organizational learning than that characterised by frequent restructuring, with redundancy and recruitment of staff to suit. People, and the organizations they form, can learn slowly and painfully, or can learn how to learn faster.

6. IMPLICATIONS FOR THE OPEN UNIVERSITY

Stacey's model suggests that New Directions forms a 'shadow' network linking a few members of the senior management team with a varying cross-section of staff. It began when the organization was planning for growth. Resources, especially the spare staff time it relies on to function, are now tighter. However, it has the potential for helping organizational learning.

New Directions could continue to act as an informal communications network to feed ideas between staff and management, without incorporating it into any organizational structures or formal responsibilities. However, it would then not be part of a generally shared schema and would constitute only 'single loop' organizational learning, with no move to unconsciously competent learning. So at times when the learning process is most needed, its resources may dry up.

To achieve double-loop learning (Morgan, 1991), the shared capacity for learning has to change qualitatively. This means that activities and behaviours which have become regular parts of the New Directions programme become formally accepted and resourced. The new communication channels need to be 'hard-wired', so that they operate automatically every time the organization is faced with a new challenge. Similarly, alongside the administrative processes for promoting organizational learning, there needs to be some conscious investment in the development of individual learning skills and tools — so that individuals can make full use of the organizational processes that are available to them. It could be that we already have the capacity to reach this stage.

A further, more open-ended, process of self-organization is also now possible. This might be thought of as 'multi-loop' learning. If the organizational structures can become flexible enough so that individuals automatically form new networks in response to strategic change, then the organization's capability to adapt to its environment will move up to the next level. This would rely not only on individual learning skills, but on a shared acceptance that self-organization works. A staff attitude survey (IFF, 1995) indicates that we may have some way to go towards achieving this.

A final note of caution: The Open University, with around 3500 staff, 7500 associate lecturers and 160 000 students, is undoubtedly a complex system. Stacey's model of the balance between stability and instability has a very practical meaning here. New systems and behaviours have to be introduced without disrupting routine services for students — which often depend on deep-seated 'unconscious competencies' at an individual, group and organizational level. An organic learning system can be nurtured by the internal organizational environment, through resource and information flows. But it cannot be imposed universally, nor engineered in detail.

REFERENCES

Edwards, H., Parsons, P., Peters, G. and Richenburg, K., 1995, Challenging the blame culture—a case study of a mistakes workshop, in Proc. of a workshop on stress and mistake making in the operational workplace 24/10/95, *IEE & Hazards Forum Digest*, 1995/177.

IFF Research Ltd, 1995, The Open University Staff Survey 1994, report circulated internally in The Open University.

Kauffman, S., 1991, 'Antichaos and adaptation', *Scientific American*, August 1991, pp.64–70.

Kauffman, S. and Macready, W., 1995, 'Technological evolution and adaptive organization' 1995 London conference on complexity and strategy, Santa Fe Insititute and The Praxis Group Ltd.

Kelly, K. (1994) *Out of Control: the new biology of machines*, Fourth Estate, London.

Leonard-Barton, D., 1995, *Wellsprings of Knowledge*, Harvard Business School Press.

Morgan, G. (1991) Can organizations learn to learn?. in *Organizations: cases, issues, concepts*, Armson, R & Paton, R., Paul Chapman Publishing in association with The Open University.

O'Conner, J. and Seymour, J., 1993, *Introducing Neurolinguistic Programming: psychological skills for understanding and influencing people*, Harper Collins, London.

Open University, 1996, Investors in People Steering Group, Assessor's Report, internal Open University document IiP/PSG/15/1.

Parsons, M.E. and Russell, C., 1995, 'A programme for organisational change New Directions at The Open University: a case study', *UCoSDA Briefing Paper 14*.

Pasmore, W. A., 1995, *Creating Strategic Change: designing the flexible high-performing organization*, John Wiley, New York.

Russell, C. and Parsons, M.E., 199, 'Putting theory to the test at the OU' *People Management*, 11 Jan 1996.

Russell, C. and Peters, G., 1996, 'Chaos has no plural — a holistic approach to internal communications, self-organization and organizational learning' in *Proc. 40th Annual Meeting of the ISSS*.

Senge, P., Kleiner, A., Roberts, C., Ross, R. and Smith, B., 1994. *The Fifth Discipline Fieldbook: strategies and tools for building a learning organization*, Nicholas Brealey, London.

Stacey, R., 1996, *Complexity and Creativity in Organizations*, Berrett-Koehler, San Fransisco.

51

ORCHESTRATING DISCIPLINE-BASED RESEARCH AND LEARNING

Why, When, and How

Joyce Tait, Dick Morris, and Ray Ison

Systems Group
Technology Faculty
Open University
Walton Hall, Milton Keynes MK7 6AA

1. THE CHANGING NATURE OF RESEARCH AND LEARNING IN UNIVERSITIES

There can be little doubt that the nature of the demands being made on university research and teaching have been changing, particularly over the last ten to fifteen years. We are experiencing increasingly urgent calls for more holistic, interdisciplinary approaches to problems and for greater collaboration and networking between institutions and researchers, nationally and internationally (Hicks and Katz, 1996). This stems from a greater emphasis on practical application of research results.

Research or consultancy work which is loosely referred to as interdisciplinary can take a variety of different forms (Tait, 1987). In some cases, close interaction between two or more established academic disciplines can lead to the emergence of a new discipline, for example the forging of molecular biology from the parent disciplines of physics, chemistry and biology. In cases like these, the new combination establishes its own boundaries and survives and prospers because it becomes a permanent component of the traditional discipline-based academic community. Of greater interest to the systems community are the cases where boundaries are flexible and shifting, where a team approach is adopted to combine several disciplines to give a deeper understanding of an issue and a greater synergy in the solutions than can be achieved from the perspective of a single discipline, and where the issue may not be addressed at all in terms of disciplinary boundaries.

Sustainable development is one of the areas where interdisciplinary approaches of the second type are increasingly being advocated. Sustainability is inherently a systemic concept, relating to a particular perspective on a system that is being managed for some human purpose (Tait, 1996). Taking the example of various agricultural systems, the ques-

Systems for Sustainability, edited by Stowell *et al.*
Plenum Press, New York, 1997

tion of their sustainability could be addressed from a range of human perspectives, depending on how widely the system boundary is drawn (the farm, the region, a trading system involving the supply of inputs and the marketing of outputs), and also from a range of disciplinary perspectives (agronomy, entomology, economics, ecology, sociology, policy). Indeed, it may be more useful to think of sustainability in terms of a process, rather than outcomes, and that process will inevitably be interdisciplinary (Ison, 1990).

Faced with this level of complexity and potential 'messiness', one would expect to see an automatic recourse to systemic approaches to provide the organising principles, the basis for reducing the issue to manageable proportions without imposing any preconceived disciplinary bias (Clayton and Radcliffe, 1996). However, the prevailing impression is that those who, in increasing numbers and often with considerable sums of money at their disposal, are calling for more holistic, interdisciplinary approaches to complex problems, are not aware of this potential in the systems area. Our experience in conducting and evaluating interdisciplinary research projects in the UK, the European Union, Africa and Australia is that each project develops its own intuitive approach to interdisciplinary working, some more successfully than others and there is no overall progress or building up of theory or practical craft knowledge on the subject. Systems, although it has the potential to contribute greatly to issues of sustainable development, is consistently being marginalised.

2. THE FATE OF INTERDISCIPLINARY INITIATIVES IN UNIVERSITIES AND RESEARCH INSTITUTES

2.1. Factors Related to Institutional Power Structures

Consider how interdisciplinary projects and staff fare in our academic institutions. Most of academic life, in teaching and research, still follows the reductionist, discipline-based model. Those with anthropological leanings can observe territory-marking rituals everywhere, with boundaries being patrolled enthusiastically at all levels in university hierarchies and in the bodies set up to administer universities, in research councils, academic journals and professional bodies. Individuals and departments are required to identify themselves within this disciplinary structure—there is no alternative mode of existence.

Where interdisciplinary departments or sub-departments have been set up, they are usually seen as an easy target for cuts and progressive reductions in funding have reinforced the traditional disciplines at the expense of such 'fringe' activities. The common practice of devolving budgets to cost centres based on disciplines means that it is now so time-consuming and contentious to set up cross-departmental initiatives that most people have given up trying to do so.

Performance monitoring in teaching and research is also based on the existing discipline-structure. The disciplinary boundaries for research and teaching quality assessments would have been recognised by academics in the 1950s. The point has been widely made that the Research Assessment Exercise, intentionally or otherwise, is reinforcing the 'gatekeeper' role of the disciplines at the expense of diversity in the academic system, but no realistic alternatives have yet been proposed.

In reporting the results of interdisciplinary research, the most highly-regarded journals accept only papers which are strongly discipline-based. Interdisciplinary journals are regarded as of lower status than others, making it difficult for those who do work in interdisciplinary areas to gain credit for the work that they do. It is also usually impossible to compress the results of an interdisciplinary project into the space requirements of an academic journal because of the need to cover issues from more than one disciplinary perspective and to explain their interactions. One option is to split the work up into its disciplinary components and spread it around which rather defeats the purpose of the integration in the first place. Another option is to write a book, which brings one up against the prejudices of academic publishers who tend to see their market in terms of academic disciplines and who like to give a clear message that a book is highly relevant to a particular sector of this market.

Where interdisciplinary research projects are set up, they are usually co-ordinated by a researcher who does not have sufficient power or status to guide the work of other strictly discipline-based contributors and successful co-ordination comes to mean merely ensuring that the project is completed on time and within budget: little attention is given to ensuring that the whole is greater than the sum of its parts.

The power relationships within universities thus favour the historic discipline-based structure, with some room for new disciplines to arise (as with molecular biology) but with truly interdisciplinary initiatives being marginalised at best and more usually threatened with closure.

A recent paper by Maiteny and Ison (in press) is very relevant to any discussion of the role of systems-based approaches in providing a philosophy and structure for the development of interdisciplinary modes of working. They have analysed the changing nature of systems as a discipline, particularly in the context of the development of the Systems Group at the Open University, noting how Systems was established as a distinct discipline to conform with existing academic structures and came to be regarded as a subject discipline. While it has been relatively successful, its development and the development of the subject as a whole has been hampered by this ambiguous status. It is becoming apparent that regarding systems as just another discipline within the existing academic structure is not leading to fruitful development of the subject.

2.2. Factors Related to Academic Issues of Method and Measurement

Schön (1983) has described the trade-offs that have to be made between rigour and relevance when dealing with complex real-world problems. The discipline-based approach and its underlying reductionist philosophy emphasise the need for rigour and repeatability in measurement, whereas from a systems perspective, with its greater degree of direct relevance to complex practical issues, it is more usual to find that there are no 'right answers' only better answers and worse answers.

The reductionist philosophy also requires that respectable measures should be value-free, whereas systems seeks to recognise explicitly the values of the decision maker(s) which underlie any measure or outcome. These two positions need not be incompatible. Any holistic analysis is likely to need valid discipline-based data as an input to the decision-making process. However, human judgement and values play a very important role at the outset in deciding what to measure; once that decision has been taken, the question of which measurement method to use is relatively value-free. Human judgement also enters into the process again when data from different sources and different measures, qualitative and/or quantitative, are combined or compared in order to reach a decision. Holism and reductionism should be partners, reinforcing each others' benefits, rather than being treated as antagonistic alternatives. However, in most circumstances, reductionism will be treated as the superior approach and given greater weight than a holistic analysis and when quantitative data are combined to give a single indicator, the human values underlying this single figure are usually ignored.

3. ORCHESTRATING DISCIPLINES: A ROLE FOR SYSTEMIC ANALYSIS AND PRACTICE?

While giving full credit to the range of initiatives to develop systemic thinking and philosophy, this paper draws attention to a major gap in these developments - the orchestrating of traditional academic disciplines to provide a holistic contribution to the resolution of complex issues. This challenge is seen as fundamentally different from that addressed by general systems theory, which has sought to develop an over-arching theory applicable to all disciplines and which has not been particularly influential in the UK (Maiteny and Ison, in press).

To satisfy today's needs an approach is needed which recognises the diversity of the potential contained within the academic disciplines and seeks to release this diversity from its current constraining boundaries to enable it to contribute more effectively in a holistic, interdisciplinary context.

Most of those working within the traditional academic disciplines have ignored the systems area. A few have co-opted a limited range of the language of systems - for example in the area of agronomy, a project that involves the development of a mathematical model, even if it remains within the confines of a single discipline, is likely to be referred to as a 'systems approach'. However, given that systems has largely ignored academic disciplines it is hardly surprising that these disciplines see systems ideas as irrelevant to their work. None of the recent influential texts in the systems area gives any indication of the strengths and weaknesses of various disciplines, their role in contributing to different types of issue, or an indication of how they may be integrated (e.g. Eden, Jones and Summs, 1983; Rosenhead, 1989; Checkland and Scholes 1990; Flood and Jackson, 1991). The various systems methods currently in use quite properly show how to avoid imposing a reductionist disciplinary bias at the start of a project. However, they continue to ignore disciplines from that point on.

Some systems advocates have been known to claim in an evangelical manner that the only solution is for all those working in a reductionist mode to change completely their way of thinking and adopt a systems approach to all their work. This kind of preaching, directed at those who are in a dominant institutional power relationship to systems, is unlikely to have much impact.

On the other hand, the suggestion by Jackson that systems should become the handmaiden of the other disciplines (pers. comm., quoted in Maiteny and Ison, in press), while giving an appropriate emphasis to service, implies the wrong kind of power relationship between systems and traditional disciplines. It would not, for example, resolve the problems experienced by co-ordinators of interdisciplinary projects who find that they do not have the authority to impose any particular direction or mode of operation on the research they are co-ordinating.

Systems should therefore have a supra-disciplinary relationship with the rest of the academic community, or at least an interdisciplinary one that gives equality of status,. rather than the present situation where systemic co-ordinators find themselves in an inferior position or alternatively systems is forced into the disciplinary framework as just another discipline.

However, it is also important to recognise that only a limited set of circumstances will justify the extra time and effort required to adopt a holistic approach. The majority of research questions will still be most effectively and efficiently tackled from a reductionist perspective and we should not attempt to take over where a reductionist approach is most appropriate. We also should not suggest that all discipline-based researchers necessarily have to revolutionise their thinking, and we should indicate where disciplines fit into systemic thinking.

A small 'integration unit' in each institution could have the desired effect if it was given the necessary authority and resources to be workable and was able to call on the services of others working in discipline-based departments. A motive would also need to be provided for those working in traditional disciplines to collaborate with others and to develop an understanding of the skills required to do this effectively.

There are some flaws in these suggestions. It is currently very difficult to find staff already trained to work in an interdisciplinary manner to take part in integrated projects, far less to lead them. In addition, most of the theory and craft knowledge on which to base such training has yet to be developed.

Those working in the systems area are ideally placed to respond to the challenges posed by interdisciplinary working. To do so they will need to address more rigorously than they have in the past the questions of why and when a systems approach is justified. The question of how disciplines should be integrated within an overall systemic approach is the most urgent and challenging of all, pointing to the need to develop the philosophical and empirical basis for interdisciplinary working upon which the rest of the edifice can be built.

REFERENCES

Checkland, P. and Scholes, J., 1990, *Soft Systems Methodology in Action*, John Wiley & Sons, Chichester.

Clayton, A.M.H. and Radcliffe, N.J., 1996, *Sustainability: a Systems Approach,* Earthscan Publications Ltd., London.

Eden, C., Jones, S. and Sims, D., 1983, *Messing about in Problems,* Pergamon Press, Oxford.

Flood, R.L. and Jackson, M.C., 1991, *Creative Problem Solving: Total Systems Intervention.* Wiley, Chichester.

Hicks, D.M. and Katz, J.S., 1996, Where is science going?, *Science, Technology & Human Values,* 21(4): 379–406.

Ison, R.L., 1990, *Teaching Threatens Sustainable Agriculture*, Gatekeeper Series, No.21, International Institute for Environment and Development, Sustainable Agriculture Programme, London, 20p.

Maiteny, P.T. and Ison, R.L., (in press), Appreciating systems: critical reflections on the changing nature of systems as a discipline in a systems-learning society. Submitted to *Systems Practice*.

Schön, D.A., 1983, *The Reflective Practitioner: How Professionals Think in Action*, Maurice Temple Smith, London.

Tait, E.J., 1987, Research policy and review 14. Environmental issues and the social sciences, *Environment and Planning A*, **19**: 437–445.

Tait, J. 1996, Sustainable development in agriculture - the need for a systemic approach, *Culture and Agriculture*, in press.

52

A REPORT ON AN ACTION-RESEARCH PROJECT TO STRENGTHEN THE RESEARCH BASE IN PRIMARY AND COMMUNITY CARE

Leroy White[*] and Ann Taket[†]

South Bank University
Faculty of Health and Social Sciences (Erlang House)
103 Borough Road
London SE1 0AA
Telephone: 00–44–171–815–8097/8468; Fax: 00–44–171–815–8099

1. INTRODUCTION

With the drive towards 'evidence-based care' and the desire for a strong R & D base within all parts of the British National Health Service (NHS), there is an increasing need for health-service professionals to acquire a familiarity with, and skills in, health-services research. This paper discusses our programme designed to strengthen the research base in community and primary health care.

As a part of this programme, groups of health-service staff will undertake closely supervised small-scale action-research projects to address issues of service concern. These projects provide a fertile learning environment for the acquisition of health-services research skills. There are a wide range of taught courses in research methods available, however these offer only limited opportunity for acquiring experience in carrying out research and transferring learning into practice, and most are not oriented specifically to the health-services research context. The classic method of research training by carrying out a MPhil or PhD represents a major commitment of time on the part of individuals, and, even if undertaken on a part-time basis, is not an option that is easily open to many health-service professionals. The programme thus offers an addition to the spectrum of training opportunities for the acquisition of health- service research skills, and will complement the provision of taught courses and MPhil and PhD based research training.

In terms of the framework we are adopting (see Figure 1), action-research appears at two different levels. The first of these is that the core team of staff involved in the pro-

[*] Email: whitel@sbu.ac.uk
[†] Email: taketa@vax.sbu.ac.uk

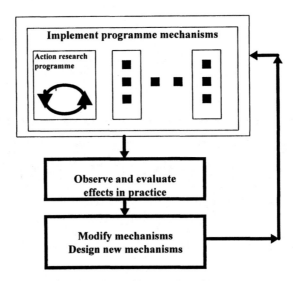

Figure 1. The overall programme framework.

gramme regard ourselves as utilising an action-research approach to develop, evaluate and extend the work of the programme. The second level at which action-research is shaping the programme framework is in terms of the specific health- services research projects arising from the first of the mechanisms identified above, this is discussed in more detail below.

Further benefit is gained by ensuring the relevance of the topic researched. In order to achieve this, the focus of the unit will be an issue of service concern generated from within the student workplace which would benefit from investigation through a small-scale health-services research project. Under supervision, the student (or group of students) undertaking the unit, design a suitable health-services research study to address the chosen issue, and then move on through the stages of data collection and analysis, to writing up a research report and finally exploring the policy recommendations to flow from the research conclusions. This will provide the students with the opportunity for relevant experiential learning. The employing authority will also gain direct R and D benefit in terms of the research report. The projects offer clear benefits in bringing together the experience and expertise of the health-service staff, together with research supervision and support from University staff in order to undertake relevant health-services research, at the same time as providing training to the health-service staff involved. High levels of supervision from the university ensure the quality of the research, so that the outcomes provide policy-relevant results. These projects therefore meet the fulfilment of specific training needs for a group of staff at the same time as addressing a part of the NHS R and D agenda at local level.

The type of research project involved include needs assessment, audit or evaluation, service development and studying the management of change, see Table 1.

A crucial issue for us is the ways in which we work with our clients. Below we set out one of the ways we have worked with them. After a description of this we will illustrate our process further with an example.

Table 1. Examples of projects underway

Evaluation of project aimed at improving access to health services for people with learning disabilities
Development of health education and health promotion resources for British Afro-Caribbeans
Integration of primary and secondary care for the elderly
Evaluation of pilot project on the introduction of clinical supervision for nurses
Outcomes of unsutured second degree perineal tears
Needs assessment for people with learning disabilities

---

2. PANDA: COMBINING PARTICIPATORY RAPID APPRAISAL WITH OPERATIONAL RESEARCH/SYSTEMS METHODS

We have described elsewhere our process for working with groups (White and Taket, 1997; Taket and White, 1996). We have labelled it Participatory Appraisal of Needs and the Development of Action (PANDA), and it was developed from our experiences of the limitations of a number of participatory methodologies, in particular Participatory Rapid Appraisal(PRA). Our main criticism was that some of these processes cannot be used beyond appraisal (White, 1994), i.e. towards analysis, planning, choice and action. Little regard is given to the inherent problems associated with decision-making or planning such as conflict, group interaction and so on (Radford, 1977). No exploration of the inherent uncertainties is taken into account, neither is any conflict of opinions, nor the effects of the interaction of other parties pursuing their own interests (Oakley and Marsden, 1984).

In an earlier paper it was suggested that perhaps the problem structuring methods (psms), or at least parts of them, may be able to make up for this lack of analysis and exploration of options (White, 1994). However, we think it is fairly apparent that one has to be cautious in using psms in this way. The methodologies are quite complex and sophisticated, and it may be difficult to use an psm on its own. Locally elicited information is full of contradictions, anomalies, and differences.

The framework we refer to as PANDA is a response to the criticisms outlined above. Features that are important in the achievement of this are that the framework allows for:

- adopting multiple perspectives (i.e. seek to embrace diversity)
- the affirmation of individuals and difference
- a pluralist stance is used giving voice to individuals and groups
- knowledge and technology are seen as contextual in time and space limiting their transferability
- a group inquiry process i.e. complexity is revealed through group inquiry
- the involvement of a mix of outsiders and insiders
- the use of transparent tools, e.g. diagrams are popular and powerful.
- recognition of the future as uncertain and indeterminate

(Taket and White, 1996; White and Taket, 1997):

In terms of the research projects undertaken in community and primary care, the process by which the overall programme of work is managed is set up as an action-research project itself, with the staff involved in leading the work constituting themselves as an action-research team, with regular meetings for critical reflection and an ongoing programme of evaluation. The PANDA framework is used by the project facilitators/supervisors to help manage the process by which the group works together as an action-research team.

3. CASE STUDY

The case study involves a group of health professionals from different providing agencies, who wish to carry out an Randomised Control Trial (RCT) to investigate an innovative aspect of clinical practice and also to carry out some complimentary qualitative research into some aspects of the practice, specially into patient views and staff attitudes. The group members are very enthusiastic about doing the research but are inexperienced. One of us has been facilitating regular meeting to help them plan and execute the research.

Here we wish to explore how our decisions about appropriate ways to structure the processes involved have been influenced by features of the group dynamics. At a very early stage it became apparent that the group was dominated by two of its members and that the others found it difficult to participate to any extent. Below we describe the sequence of meetings that took place and consequent decisions about how the meetings could be structured to avoid the problem, to facilitate wider participation and to ensure that the group became more productive.

In the initial meeting, which was held in a traditional format, the two dominant members were the only people to volunteer ideas. On questioning the other members, it emerged that there were divisions, previously camouflaged, in the group, about the validity of the alternative form of care under test, and about whether a RCT was an appropriate methodology, in terms of some individuals having strong beliefs that such a methodology would be unethical. At the end of the first meeting, individuals agreed to undertake specific tasks, however these were not undertaken and the facilitator found out about this through individuals phoning him. Individuals were also requesting additional help with some of the tasks. One of the tasks given was for the group to define more clearly the focus of the research (something about which there was no clear agreement in the first meeting).

For the second meeting therefore, it was decided to try a different form of process which would provide individuals with the help they needed, build commitment to getting the tasks done, ensure participation from all group members, and define a focus for the research. The process used was Nominal Group Technique (Delbecq, 1975), which worked well in enabling all group members to participate in framing a focused set of research questions and objectives. Again group members took on tasks to be completed before the next meeting with the facilitator. This included agreeing to meet as a group (without the facilitator) to plan and do the work. However, this unfacilitated meeting was not productive. Again the facilitator was notified by informal contact from one group member. The third meeting was then planned with structured process to compensate for this problem and to provide a more structured framework for organising their work thereafter.

At the beginning of the third meeting, the facilitator acknowledged that he knew about the problems and explained that he wanted to introduce a more tightly structured process to attempt to achieve more productive working. The group agreed that this was a good idea. The next stage was simple brainstorming to identify group tasks, these were divided into four broad areas. The six members of the group were then organised into work teams drawing on Stafford Beer's Team Syntegrity (Beer, 1995) but using the tetrahedron structure (see White, 1996) . This meant that three people were identified to work on each of the four areas, with each person being a member of two work teams. This also meant that no two work areas had the same three people. The next stage was the allocation of group members to the work areas. This was achieved by the group members expressing their preferences for work areas. The final stage involved meetings for each of the for work areas, lasting about ten minutes each, to explore what the tasks were for the work area and to arrange dates to meet. Those not involved in the meeting acted as observers.

At the end of the session the facilitator suggested that they used their regular meeting slots to review the work in progress. This would involve a half hour session for each work area. It was also suggested that for each work area, the three people who were not members of the work team should act as critics in meetings to ensure that tasks are being carried out and to ask reflective questions about assumptions and progress on the work area. Because everyone was involved in each of the work areas in some way, it follows that it is possible to find ideas 'reverberating' (Beer's term) around the group. This is important in that, although an individual may not be a member of a particular work area, it does not necessarily mean that she has no influence on that particular topic. Her involvement, learning and contribution can still be made throughout the study.

4. CONCLUSIONS

In this next section we finish by commenting on some of the aspects of the case study which to us illustrate the value of adopting a framework like PANDA. Firstly, it can be seen that the injection of process into the work helped to stimulate the group to work together and enhanced their capacity to do the research. In other studies we found that this can be further enhanced through using a combination of parts of different methods and techniques, appropriateness of any particular method being judged in terms of its ability to achieve participation with the group concerned.

Another point to emphasise in the discussion is the importance of the features noted earlier of the PANDA framework in dealing with the multi-agency context for the evaluations. Responding adequately to this context was important in helping the activities of the group.

The adoption of an action-research framework allowed the work to be shaped appropriately to respond to changing circumstances, see Figure 2.

Another conclusion which arises from work so far is the usefulness of methods from OR/systems science for group decision-making at various stages, for example, in many of the projects in the programme these have been used to:

- to define the research questions
- to select data required for collection, including relevant outcome variables
- to select relevant research methods
- to plan the execution of the research
- to structure discussion of the interpretation of research data

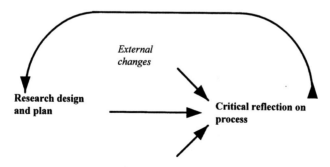

Figure 2. Shaping work according to circumstances.

Thus methods from OR/systems science can be used to enhance the action-research process, this occurred in both the project described above.

Usually the focus of discussion for research takes place in formal meetings. Often it is the case that this type of meeting is not the most productive forum to facilitate full interaction between the different parties involved. Novel ways of working which either supplement or replace the meeting can result in improvement. Managing the group processes using methods drawn from OR and systems science also provide the means for regular critical reflection on the results or decisions produced, providing the means for formative evaluation and forming an important part of the action-research cycle. We have found the use of group processes extremely productive in the multi-agency setting in the development of research projects and their execution. This was certainly the case in the example discussed above.

REFERENCES

Beer, S., 1995, Beyond dispute, Wiley, London

Delbecq, A. L., Van de Ven, A. H. and Gustafson, D. H., 1975, Group Techniques for Program Planning, Scott Foreson, Glenview, Il.

Oakley, P. and Marsden, D., 1984 Approaches to participation in rural development. International Labour Organisation, Geneva.

Radford, 1977 Complex decision problems, Reston, Vancouver.

Taket, A. R. and White, L. A., 1996, Wanted Dead OR Alive, (in press).

White, L. A. 1994, Development options for a rural community in Belize - alternative development and operational research. *Int. Trans. Oper. Res* 1: 453–462.

White, L. A., 1996, Team Syntegrity as a Problem Structuring Method, (in press).

White, L. A. and Taket, A. R. 1997 Participatory Appraisal of Needs and the development of Action, (in press).

53

ENHANCING THE CRITICAL REFLECTION MODE OF TSI

Mandy Brown and Jennifer Wilby

Centre for Systems Studies
Department of Management Systems and Science
University of Hull
63 Salmon Grove
Hull, HU6 7SZ

1. INTRODUCTION

In viewing problem solving as a process of intervention where practitioners can learn about and manage complex interacting issues TSI, as first presented in *Creative Problem Solving* (Flood and Jackson, 1991) and *Solving Problem Solving* (Flood, 1995), employs metaphors, creative thinking, and the knowledge gained from the processes of reflection and critique. Later work has enhanced the critical review mode (Wilby, 1996) which assesses the methodologies, the problem solving mode (Flood and Romm, 1995), and the critical reflection mode which is addressed in this paper.

We begin by describing the critical reflection mode within the existing TSI framework and identifying its constraints in addressing some of the broader issues of reflection in intervention. We then present an enhanced version of the critical reflection mode which draws on later work concerning systemic intervention (Flood, 1996).

2. OVERVIEW OF TSI

Underpinning our discussion is the idea that the process of reflection in TSI is not a linear process but one that operates in a circular, recursive manner throughout the intervention. Before reviewing the existing critical reflection mode we will first revisit the underpinning philosophy, principles, and practice (methodology) of TSI.

2.1. Philosophy of TSI

Two types of organisational activities, technical and social, are addressed by TSI. *Technical activities* relate to organisational processes and design, which address the "how" questions of organisational change and development. This assumes that the end objectives have already been agreed, e.g. how do we efficiently organise processes? Or how do we most effectively design or structure an organisation to achieve a predefined goal? Technical approaches predominantly understand change and development as a linear progression towards a defined solution.

Human activities relate to the "what" issues of organisational culture and the "why" issues of organisational politics. The cultural question addresses the definitions of objectives, the "what" do we do?, and is defined through questions for open and meaningful debate. With this question, an understanding of roles, perspectives, and the potential resolution of differences is gained by the participants. The political question, the "why" are we doing this?, addresses the potentially repressive processes, structures, and cultures present within the problem context.

These four activities of process, design, culture, and politics form a framework which identifies the four core dimensions of an organisation. These dimensions are a key aspect for guiding methodological choice within the process of intervention.

2.2. Principles of TSI

There are four principles underpinning the practice of TSI:

- The *Systemic* principle — viewing the situation taking into account the whole, and implying a form of hierarchy of systems;
- The *Participatory* principle — incorporating the perceptions of people involved and affected by any change process, since to a large extent organisations are what people think;
- The *Reflective* principle — to consider the relationship between different organisational interests, and the possible dominance of favoured intervention approaches, and exploring the practitioner's ability to reflect on their motives and understanding within the intervention;
- The *Emancipatory* principle — a moral justification, where enhancing human freedom is a required management practice. This is grounded in an ethical argument of the human right of inclusion, and an efficiency argument which states that inclusion aids effective design and implementation.

These principles are integrated throughout TSI. The extent to which a methodology, and indeed TSI itself, meets these requirements is crucial when assessing the validity and appropriateness of a TSI intervention.

2.3. The Practice of TSI

TSI operates in three iterative, cyclical, modes: (i) *the Critical Review Mode,* which critically reviews the methods to be incorporated in the problem solving mode, according to their philosophy, principles, and practice; (ii) *the Problem Solving Mode*, which employs the methodologies that have passed through the critical review mode, by matching the organisational context or perceived problem with the most appropriate method; and (iii) *the Critical Reflection Mode*, which reflects upon the adequacy of the problem solving mode. Each of these modes has embedded within it three cyclical phases: (i) creativity, to surface new insights; (ii) choice, to ensure a systemic approach; and (iii) implementation, for purposeful action (Flood, 1995).

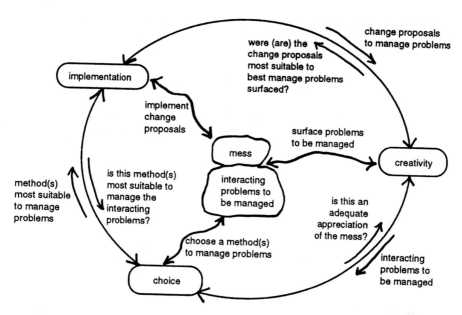

Figure 1. The clockwise (problem solving) and anti-clockwise (critical reflection) cycles (Flood, 1995:32).

3. THE EXISTING CRITICAL REFLECTION MODE

The interaction between the three modes, and the three phases which operate within each of the modes, is illustrated in Figure 1.

3.1. The Criteria of Suitability and Appropriateness

TSI describes the aim of critical reflection as evaluating the intervention in relation to two core questions: was the most *suitable* method used in the circumstances?; and was the output of the chosen method *appropriate* in the circumstances?. Considering these issues is an assessment of the suitability of the methods and gives an enhanced understanding of the utility of the method. The underpinning assumption is that there may be a better way of undertaking the intervention. Three sets of questions are used to guide the problem solver in addressing the central issues of suitability and appropriateness: How? questions which focus on the technical achieving of the output (design); What? questions, which focus on the practical process of the intervention (debating); and, Why? questions which focus on the emancipatory intent of the intervention (disemprisoning). Currently, each of these questions are phrased in sets of 'did', 'should', 'could' and 'would' questions, e.g.: How did the method achieve the output?; How should the method achieve the output?; How could the method achieve better output?; and How would another method achieve better output? These sets of questions are found in detail in Flood (1995, 227–229). In the next sections, the three phases of creativity, choice, and implementation within the current TSI are described.

3.2. Creativity, Choice, and Implementation in the Current Critical Reflection Mode

In the current critical reflection mode the purposes and criteria focus on the activity and outputs generated by the problem solving mode, operating as the reverse of the problem solving mode. Currently the operation of reflection focuses on the phases of implementation, choice and creativity.

3.2.1. Implementation in the Critical Reflection Mode. Reflection on implementation considers choices made for an ongoing intervention. If reflection is on-going, then decisions would be implemented to adjust action. However if reflection occurs post intervention then the new knowledge could be fed into future interventions. Thus this phase must ask:

- Is/are this/these methods and the innovative change proposals it generates(d) most *suitable* given the circumstances?
- Is/are this/these methods and the innovative change proposals it generates(d) most *appropriate* given the circumstances?

Issues arising are: the need to question the use and outputs received from the method; the criteria used; and, the process of implementation itself.

3.2.2. Choice in the Critical Reflection Mode. Reflection on choice considers the operating principles and purpose of i) the chosen methodology; ii) the organisational dimension, e.g. process, design, culture, and politics; iii) the principles of (Flood, 1995); and iv) any wider, relevant, societal debates. Reflecting on the implications of choice, which links the problem details with the methodology(ies) chosen, this phase must ask:

- Is this an adequate *appreciation* of organisational events? Focusing on the need to gain an understanding of the situation and the criteria used for determining whose views are incorporated.
- Is choice capable of leading to the most *suitable* choice of method in the circumstances? Focusing on the need to evaluate TSI's and the practitioner's ability to consider which/whose criteria are utilised.

3.2.3. Creativity in the Critical Reflection Mode. Reflection on creativity attempts to surface the core issues in evaluating appropriateness and suitability of the use of the methods. This uses methods which encourage creative thinking in exploring, via debate, issues of:

- Were/are the change proposals most *suitable* to deal with the problems surfaced? Focusing on investigating the outcome and suitability of the terms/criteria in surfacing the problem's core issues.
- Was/were the method(s) used for creative thinking the most *suitable* one(s) to surface the core problems/issues? Focusing on investigating the creative methods used and the suitability of the terms/criteria of those methods.

In summary the current critical reflection mode considers the suitability and appropriateness of the outputs from the problem solving mode. However, it can be argued that the process of reflection is equally important throughout TSI; and is capable of operating as a separate mode. In Figure 1, the reflective questions to be answered in the current critical reflection mode are related only to the anti-clockwise cycle of the problem solving mode, thereby constraining the mode. However, we view reflection as being autonomous and potentially capable of considering not only all aspects of TSI, but also the broader aspects of the intervention.

Thus, the critical reflection mode can not only address the reflection requirements in an on-going implementation, benefiting current learning (the formative evaluation); but also address the reflection requirements of evaluating a completed implementation where learning is applied to subsequent interventions (the summative evaluation). We will now seek to further enhance the critical reflection mode by addressing some of the discovered constraints.

4. ENHANCING THE CRITICAL REFLECTION MODE

One approach to enhancing our understanding of intervention can be found in the systemic approach to systems interventions (Figure 2) recently developed by Flood (1996). The five layers: purpose, paradigms, practice, principles, and philosophy, relate to the critical reflection mode in that they guide or highlight some of the aspects we should consider when reflecting on our interventions.

The five layers are designed to represent an increasing complexity of information gathered about an intervention, yet each can be shown to be systemic in its own right. For instance:

- the applied methodology may be systemic in terms of its purpose (e.g. the viable systems model is systemic in terms of designing structure), and the reflective criteria of purpose could be appropriateness;

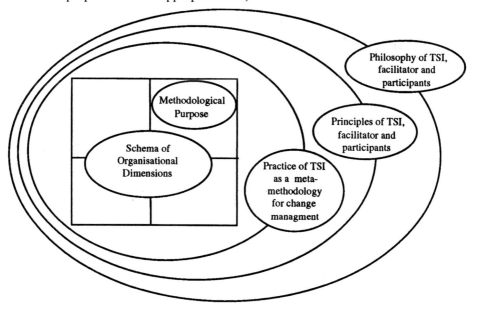

Figure 2. The five levels of systemicity based on Flood (1996).

- the paradigm level is systemic in terms of addressing all four areas of organisation (process, design, culture, and politics), and the reflective criteria of paradigm choice could be suitability;
- the practice of TSI is systemic in terms of managing the change process through the use of the three modes of TSI, and the reflective criteria of management of the change process could be utility;
- the principles are systemic in terms of the application of both TSI principles and the negotiated principles of the facilitator and participants, addressing their honouring in the change process; and,
- the philosophy is systemic in terms of the ideological underpinnings of TSI, the facilitator and participants, and the criteria is the ability to adapt our underpinning ideology and knowledge.

Table 1. The underpinnings of the revised critical reflection mode

Purpose	Is(was) the chosen method's output *appropriate* in the circumstances?
Use of Specific Methodology(ies)	Is(was) the output of the use of the chosen method *appropriate* in terms of its methodological purpose and principles?
Criteria: *Appropriateness*	Specifically, these may be questioned in the form of 'did', 'should', 'could' and 'would' questions (cf. Flood, 1995:228).
Paradigms	Does(did) our creative exploration of the problem situation lead to the most *suitable* problem focus being applied?
Choice of Organisational Paradigm or Dimension	In terms of our understanding of the problem focus, is/was the most *suitable* organisational dimension chosen?
	Given the problem focus(es) is(was) the most *suitable* methodology(ies) chosen, what could other methods add/have added to this context?
Criteria: Suitability	(NB: In allowing for tactical manoeuvring, we may choose (with participants) to address power issues via an alternative structure (Flood and Romm, 1995)).
Practice	Is(was) the outcome of the problem solving mode *useful* for managing change?
TSI's Management Process	Is(was) TSI as a management system the most *useful* tool for managing the intervention process as a whole?
Criteria: Utility	Is(was) TSI's utility as a meta-methodology improved, and in what manner, through reflecting on its use in this intervention?
Principles	Does(did) the intervention *honour* TSI's four core principles of being systemic, enabling meaningful participation, being reflective, and encouraging emancipation?
Adherence to Principles	Does(did) the intervention *honour* the facilitator's stated principles?
Criteria: *Honouring*	Does(did) the intervention *honour* participant's jointly-negotiated principles?
	(NB: We advocate the explicit discussion of the guiding principles of operation for TSI, and the facilitator, and the negotiation of those of the participant.)
Philosophy	Is(was) the philosophy of the individual methodology(ies) *adaptable* to the philosophy of the intervention?
Underpinning Ideology	Is(was) TSI philosophy *adaptable* to the intervention philosophy?
Criteria: *Adaptability*	Is(was) the philosophy adaptable in the light of reflective questioning to the adjustment of our tacit-knowledge?

By employing these five layers, the perceptions gathered can then be assessed in terms of the questions proposed in Table 1 to surface and explore, through debate, our understanding of action and generate options for further action. It is envisaged that through such debate inherent dilemmas and tensions may be openly addressed. Thus, Table 1 represents potential questions to be considered in the course of reflecting on an intervention in terms of issues raised both about the implementation of reflective practice in intervention in general, and TSI specifically. This framework is not a prescriptive approach to reflection, rather it is meant only to assist when considering the various issues that could be swept into a reflective process. Each layer represents an increase in complexity, and together they present an interacting whole which offers perceptions not otherwise available by focusing on individual parts of the reflection.

5. CONCLUSIONS

In this paper we have moved beyond the present constraints of the critical reflection mode which reflects only upon the suitability and appropriateness of the outputs from the problem solving mode. We have further acknowleged the critical reflection mode to be a separate, distinct entity, with a wider field of application, incorporating, as it does, reflection on the other two modes. The five areas of reflective questioning developed in this paper form the basis for the practice of the enhanced critical reflection mode. Specifically, employing these questions in each of the phases produces insights in, e.g.:

- *creativity*—the reflection mode uses the five areas of reflective questioning to surface pertinent issues.
- *choice*—incorporates reflecting not just on the surface issues but also our underlying knowledge which informs our understanding, where re-assessment of our base knowledge impacts future action(s).
- *implementation*—learning and decisions can be either implemented within the current intervention or incorporated within the TSI management framework for use in future interventions. TSI as such aims to be self-generating and developing through the learning cycle inherent within its framework.

In summary, our paper has presented an outline of on-going work on the critical reflection mode. We believe these enhancements will be able to address not only the reflection requirements within an on-going formative evaluation, but also the reflection requirements of a completed summative evaluation.

REFERENCES

Flood, R. L., 1995, *Solving Problem Solving*, Wiley, New York.
Flood, R. L., 1996, Holism and the Social Action 'Problem Solving', Working Paper No. 12, Centre for Systems Studies, University of Hull.
Flood, R. L., and Jackson, M. C., 1991, *Creative Problem Solving: Total Systems Intervention*, Wiley, New York.
Flood, R. L., and Romm, N., 1995, Enhancing the process of methodology choice in Total Systems Intervention (TSI) and improving chances of tackling coercion, *Systems Practice* 8:377–408.
Wilby, J., 1996, Developing TSI: The critical review mode, *Systems Practice* 9:231–261.

54

LIFEWORLD-SYSTEM, JURIDIFICATION, AND CRITICAL ENTREPRENEURSHIP

Annies L. F. Foong,[*] A. E. Ojuka-Onedo, and John C. Oliga

Commerce Department
The University of Papua New Guinea
University P. O. Box 320
National Capital District
Papua, New Guinea

1. INTRODUCTION

The 18th century saw occidental societies celebrate the coming into being of the age of the Enlightenment. With *reason* in science and technology overthrowing magic, myths and blind dogma in religion, modernity was thus born, with all promise for a new world of cultural rationalization and emancipatory progress. But, according to Weber (1976), by late capitalism, the euphoria was over. As the capitalist structures of economic interest and bureaucratic power became dominant, the negative face of rationalization uncloaked itself and the ethical and cultural springs of action began to rot away into the "Iron Cage", with loss of freedom and loss of meaning. It is this seemingly one-sided assimilation and transmutation of ethics and culture into structures of power that Weber perceived as the dilemma of modernity.

But Habermas (1984) disagrees with Weber. He sees it, not as a *dilemma*, a despairing case of mutually exclusive rationalization processes, but instead as the *dialectic* of enlightenment, a redeemable case, with two factors of crucial importance for the possibility of *simultaneous* progress in the structural as well as cultural rationalization process. First, each side contains in its own inner logic universal emancipation possibilities. Second, the development of posttraditional law, particularly in the form of juridification, has come to mediate between culture and power, abetting as well as constraining the latter. The chapter explores these issues, and also whether critical entrepreneurship might not also play a similar mediating role, even if only at the mundane level of everyday practice.

---

[*] Fax: (675) 3–267–187

Systems for Sustainability, edited by Stowell *et al.*
Plenum Press, New York, 1997

2. COLONIZATION: THE EMERGENCE OF NEGATIVE IDEOLOGY

Societies can be conceptualized in many ways. Focussing on the redemptive task, Habermas (1987) proposes that society-as-a-whole (SAAW) be conceptualized in terms of a two-level theory: *the lifeworld*, and *the system*. To reproduce itself, society needs to fulfil the outer and inner needs of its members, both individually, and collectively. The outer needs require *material* reproduction through work (labor). This is the externalist domain of society as a system, comprising the *economy*, and *polity*, with their corresponding delinguistified steering media of *money*, and bureaucratic *power*. The inner needs, on the other hand, require *symbolic* reproduction through communicative interaction processes. This is the internalist domain of society as a lifeworld, comprising three action-coordinating structural components: culture, society (not SAAW), and personality.

Co-ordination of action *consequences* at the system's level leads to *system integration*; while that of action *orientations* at the lifeworld level leads to *social integration*. If these two are balanced, the society-as-a-whole becomes what Habermas (1987, p.152) calls "*systemically stabilized* complexes of action of *socially integrated* groups". Unfortunately, modernity is characterized by failure to achieve this harmonious balance. Increasingly, the lifeworld is systematically undermined by painful transfers of its communicative infrastructures to the system. It is these processes of destructive transfers that Habermas calls the "colonization of the lifeworld", a process paralleling Weber's (1968) "loss of freedom" and "loss of meaning". And it is these sociopathologies that describe the dialectic of enlightenment. That is that, on the one hand, modernity saw man become disenchanted with the premodern, metaphysical beliefs that were not rationally justifiable, such that, with the corrosion of their immunity from rational scrutiny and criticism, *positive ideologies* lost their power to convince. On the other hand, any technical progress seemed to be accompanied by increasing entrapment in Weber's (1976, p.181) "Iron Cage", and with it the emergence of a new form of *negative ideology*, rooted in the rise of an "expert" culture insulated from rational criticism because of its claimed basis in scientific knowledge. Thus, as Habermas (1987, p.355) puts it, "In place of 'false consciousness' [in the form of positive ideology], we today have a fragmented consciousness that blocks enlightenment by the mechanism of reification". It is in these terms that the enigma of modernity has been interpreted as essentially a problem of "instrumental reason", wherein *reason itself* has become modernity's new "imprisoning" force, "sending its 'sentenced' victims to what Adorno (1973) called the 'administered world' ...a prison tunnel without any rational exits whatsoever" (Oliga, 1996, p.220). The new negative ideology, rooted in science and technology, means "technocratic consciousness" and depoliticization of the masses (Horkheimer and Adorno, 1972). "According to Marcuse (1964), [science and] technology [themselves have] become domination, because, by being real, visible force in the technical progress in the material production and ever-widening choice of consumption, their subjugating nature appears no longer oppressive but technically necessary and hence rational. Reason itself has become the [new] vehicle of ideology and alienation. Domination is no longer dependent on political repression; it has become legitimate" (cf. Oliga, 1996, p.100).

3. JURIDIFICATION: A NEW STEERING MEDIUM

Side by side with the process of colonization, there has been another development: the emergence of the postconventional law. In Habermas's view, the nucleus of the mod-

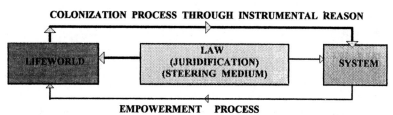

COLONIZATION PROCESS THROUGH INSTRUMENTAL REASON

LIFEWORLD — LAW (JURIDIFICATION) (STEERING MEDIUM) — SYSTEM

EMPOWERMENT PROCESS

Figure 1. Colonization of the Lifeworld by the System Through the Medium of Juridification (Adopted from Morita and Oliga, 1994)   ita

ern state developed in the structures of civil law and public justice. Thus, "the form of posttraditional law embodied a logic of cultural and ethical development that set *coherent* limits as to what could or could not be legitimated. These limits acted as constraints upon the law, even if [the latter was] often used as the medium through which culture and ethics were neutralized and appropriated in the service of power as an instrument of domination and coercion. In modernity, legal structures thus came to mediate between ideas (culture) and interests (power) in *both* directions, …a kind of double-edged sword" (see Oliga, 1996, pp.214–215; Habermas, 1984; Pusey, 1987). As Oliga (1996, p.262) elaborates, "In modernity, *juridification*, the proliferation of law having not only 'regulative', but increasingly 'constitutive' force, takes on the role of a steering medium in the colonization process on the basis of instrumental reason. On the other hand, juridification has also an empowerment effect, enabling the lifeworld to defend or reclaim 'legally' some of its civil rights… Figure [1] illustrates this double role of law: a [dual] medium for the colonization and empowerment of the lifeworld."

4. LANGUAGE AS COMMUNICATIVE ACTION: TOWARDS RATIONAL REDEMPTION OF MODERNITY

In his monumental, 2-volume work, *The Theory of Communicative Action*, Habermas (1984; 1987) has sought to justify his basic argument that efforts toward the rational redemption of modernity are fruitful and feasible, given his thesis that communicative action is *both emancipatory* by its very nature, *and* intrinsically *"originary"* (i.e. having priority) over other modes of language usage. In brief, the argument is as follows. The "originary" basis of communicative action relies on Habermas's (1984) reconstruction of Austin's (1975) distinction between locutionary, illocutionary, and perlocutionary modes of language usage. Through locutionary language usage, the speaker *says something* to be understood; through illocutionary usage, he *acts in saying something*; and through perlocutionary usage, he *brings about something through acting in saying something*. In other words, in locution, the speaker expresses states of affairs. In illocution, he establishes the mode of a sentence, be it a statement, a promise, a command, an avowal , or the like). And, in perlocution, he produces an effect upon the hearer. According to Habermas, while the distinction between locutionary and illocutionary acts is merely analytical, the distinction between these two types of acts, on the one side, and the perlocutionary acts on the other is one where all participants in the former types aim at *direct* mutual understanding in an open manner without any reservation; while in the latter type, at least one participant uses acts of communication to function as a *means* for other pre-conceived purposes (e.g.

to achieve success in instrumental or strategic actions). Thus, perlocutionary acts, by being oriented to *indirect* understanding, cannot be "originary" but only parasitic. The upshot of Habermas's argument is that communicative action, by being originary, is motivated solely by the need for reaching rational understanding and consensus, and hence is intrinsically oriented to the ideals of human emancipation.

The second thesis that communicative action, by its very nature or inner logic, is emancipatory is related to the originary thesis. Here, Habermas (1987) draws upon, and reconstructs Apel's (1976) philosophy of language. Reconstructing Wittgenstein's idea of the language game into the idea of an *ideal* language game, Apel postulates the universal or *transcendental language game*. While Habermas disagrees with Apel's view that language is transcendental in the universal sense, he nevertheless finds Apel's idea that the syntactico-semantical language systems (i.e. the quasi-transcendental aspects of language) may not be independent of their semantico-pragmatic language games (i.e. the quasi-empirical aspects) supportive of his (Habermas's) own argument that modernity represents the flowering of the evolutionary progress of language. Such progress represents our ability to differentiate the three world concepts, namely, "*the*" world of external and objectivated nature, wherein we raise, and if necessary, justify our cognitive claims of *truth*; "*our*" world of norms and morally guided society, wherein we raise, and if necessary, justify our claims of normative, moral, ethical and legal *rightness*, and "*my*" world of internal nature, wherein we raise, and if necessary, justify our expressive claims of *truthfulness* (see Oliga, 1996, pp.239–256). Thus, in a nutshell, the emancipatory nature of communicative action arises in part from language in its originary mode being the medium for coordinating intended human actions for which validity claims are proffered, and which can , if challenged, be defended in terms of truth, rightness and truthfulness.

5. ENTREPRENEURIAL IMPLICATIONS FOR DISPARATE EMANCIPATORY TASKS

In relation to the emancipatory task of redeeming modernity, the cogency of Habermas's arguments for the validity of his theory of communicative action cannot, in our view, be denied. However, the project seems to be Western-centred, and almost wholly focused on occidental societies. Little attention seems to have been paid to the dialectic of enlightenment as it might relate to other societies and cultures. It is for this reason that Oliga (1996, p.293) argued that "insorfar as the legacy of the 'metropolis-periphery' *external, intersocietal* phenomenon, and its continual renewal in new forms of imperialism, continues to structure and restructure both the intersocietal and the *internal, intrasocietal* relations ... the developing countries face a *double* emancipatory problem ... [not only that of internalist *redemption*, but also that of] *rehabilitating* the external coercive forces of domination". It is also for that reason that Morita and Oliga (1997) have argued that different approaches to the emancipatory task may be required for different societal and cultural contexts such as (a) Japan, with still positive ideologies of familism (b) ethnically homogeneous migrant (middleman) groups (EHMGs) such as the overseas Chinese in Southeast Asia, with positive ideologies of "trust" (c) Eastern European countries, ex-USSR satellite countries, and the People's Republic of China, with different social formations and forms of the state (d) Middle Eastern societies, with positive ideologies of religion and (e) New Social Movements (e.g. the women's movement, peace activists, consumer boycotts, etc.) with universalistic principles of morality and ethics (Habermas, 1979; Rasmussen, 1990; White, 1988; Morita and Oliga, 1997). Figure 2 represents these disparate tasks.

SOCIETAL PERSPEC-TIVE DOMINANT IDEOLOGY	INTERNAL	EXTERNAL	BOTH INTERNAL & EXTERNAL
NEGATIVE	* Western World Countries * Australia & New Zealand * Former USSR	* New Social Movements	*Eastern European Countries
POSITIVE	Japan		
BOTH NEGATIVE & POSITIVE	People's Republic of China		* Africa * Asia * Middle East *EHMGs *South & Latin America

Figure 2. The emancipatory tasks for the enigma of modernity (adopted from Morita and Oliga, 1997).

But, who might begin, in practical terms, to spearhead these diverse, daunting emancipatory tasks in each of these disparate societal and cultural contexts? For a number of reasons, we suggest that this be the new, globally emerging "entrepreneur". First, technical progress is itself proceeding neither smoothly nor evenly. There are widespread problems of underdevelopment in developing societies, and recurring problems of socio-economic and political decay in industrially advanced countries. Second, there is the colonization of the lifeworld by the system. For all this, we need all the insightful innovativeness of a self-reflective critical entrepreneur who can engender a holy balance between system's material reproduction and lifeworld's symbolic reproduction. Indeed, other categories of the entrepreneur, such as the *Crusoe entrepreneur*, the *uncertainty-bearing entrepreneur*, the *innovating entrepreneur*, the *arbitrageur-entrepreneur*, and the *culturalist entrepreneur*, may also play the mediating role between culture and power, even if ostensibly they do not appear self-reflectively critical (see Ojuka-Onedo, et al., 1996).

6. CONCLUSION

In examining the enigma of modernity, the chapter suggested that the hitherto untapped, indeed unrecognized, entrepreneurial innovativeness could be looked at as one possible way forward. This would be in line with the growing awareness that the transformational power of the emerging modern entrepreneur offers great hopes for the future of most societies, developing and developed alike; and that we may be already witnessing a paradigm revolution, from the *top-down* wisdom of yester-years to a *bottom-up* entrepreneurship revolution (Berger, 1991; de Soto, 1988; Rosenberg and Birdzell, 1986; Gilder, 1984).

REFERENCES

Austin, J. L.,1975, *How to Do Things with Words*, Harvard University Press, Cambridge, Mass.
Adorno, T. W., 1973, *Negative Dialects*, (trans. by E. B. Ashton), Seabury, New York.
Apel, K. O., 1976, The transcendental conception of language communication and the idea of First Philosophy, in: *The History of Linguistic Thought and Contemporary Linguistics,* (H. Farret, ed.), W. de Gruyter, Berlin.
Berger, B.,1991, Introduction, in: *The Culture of Entrepreneurship*, (B. Berger, ed.), Institute for Contemporary Studies Press, San Francisco, pp.1–12.
De Soto, H., 1988, *The Other Path*, Harper and Row, New York.

Gilder, G.,1984, *The Spirit of Enterprise*, Simon and Schuster, New York.

Habermas, J., 1984, *The Theory of Communicative Action: Reason and the Rationalization of Society,* (Vol.1, trans. by T. McCarthy), Beacon Press, Boston, Mass.

Habermas, J., 1987, The Theory of Communicative Action: Lifeworld and System: A Critique of Functionalist Reason, (Vol. 2, trans. by T. McCarthy), Beacon Press, Boston, Mass.

Horkheimer, M., and Adorno, T. W., 1972, *Dialectic of Enlightenment*, Seabury, New York.

Marcuse, H., 1964, *One Dimensional Man,* Routledge and Kegan Paul, London.

Morita, K., and Oliga, J. C., 1997, The emancipatory tasks for the enigma of modernity, *Entrepreneurship, Innovation, and Change* 6(2), forthcoming.

Ojuka-Onedo, A. E., Foong, A. L. F., and Oliga, J. C.,1996, Entrepreneurship development, ethics, and accounting, *Entrepreneurship, Innovation, and Change* 5(4), forthcoming.

Oliga, J. C.,1996, *Power, Ideology, and Control,* Plenum Press, New York.

Pusey, M., 1987, *Jurgen Habermas*, Ellis Horwood, Chichester, UK.

Rasmussen, D. M., 1990, *Reading Habermas*, Basil Blackwell, Cambridge, UK.

Rosenberg, N., and Birdzell, Jr. L. E.,1986, *How the West Grew Rich: The Economic Transformation of the Industrial World*, Basic Books, New York.

Weber, M., 1968, *Economy and Society: An Outline of Interpretive Sociology*, 3 Vols., with an introduction by G. Roth, and C. Wittich (eds.), Bedminster Press, New York.

Weber, M., 1976, *The Protestant Ethic and the Spirit of Capitalism,* 2nd ed., Allen and Unwin, London.

White, S. K., 1988, *The Recent Work of Jurgen Habermas: Reason, Justice and Modernity*, Cambridge University Press, Cambridge, UK.

55

CRITICAL APPROACHES TO INFORMATION SYSTEMS DEVELOPMENT

Some Practical Implications

Brian Lehaney and Steve Clarke

University of Luton
Park Square, Luton
LU1 3JU, United Kingdom
Tel: 01582 743153; Fax: 01582 743143
Email: Brian.Lehaney@Luton.ac.uk

1. INTRODUCTION

Critical social theory and critical systems thinking have been identified as a theoretical basis for a new approach to information systems development. The objective of this paper is to discuss the practical implications of these theories, in the form of methods or meta-methods, one of the objectives of which is to build critique into the development process.

The relevance of a critical approach to information systems development is outlined. This is followed by a brief critique of the current dominant approaches, showing them to lack an explicit critical framework. The domains of critical social theory, systemic intervention, and action research, are used as the basis for a practical intervention process.

A report is then given of an intervention in which this process has been applied. A critical review of the intervention is undertaken, and further critical assessment invited.

The outcome is a proposed monitoring, feedback and control process for information systems development in which adherence to the key commitments of critical systems thinking may offer benefits to the intervention which are not an explicit part of the current dominant functionalist or interpretivist approaches.

2. A CRITICAL APPROACH TO INFORMATION SYSTEMS DEVELOPMENT

In practice, information systems development relies predominantly on functionalist, structured methods based on the systems development life cycle, although these methods have been challenged to some extent by interpretive, soft methods, such as soft systems methodology (see, for example, Laudon and Laudon, 1996; Kendall, 1989; Kendall and Kendall, 1992; Wetherbe and Vitalari, 1994; Yeates, Shields and Helmy, 1994; Checkland and Haynes, 1994; Stowell and West, 1994). It has been argued that a major shortcoming of both approaches is their failure to be reflective. For example, Flood and Ulrich (1990) categorise hard and soft methods respectively as "non-reflective positivistic and non-reflective interpretivistic".

An approach to computer-based information systems development (CbISD) based on critical theory has been proposed as a possible way forward. For example, Hirschheim and Klein (1989) see functionalism as the "orthodox approach to systems development", and characterise this as means and ends dominated but with little discussion about the ends, since these are taken as given: "there is one reality that is measurable and essentially the same for everyone... the role of the developer is to design systems that model this reality." (Hirschheim and Klein, 1989). But the ends can seldom be assumed to be agreed, and in modelling reality the question of whose reality becomes paramount.

The interpretivist approach attempts to deal with this problem, focusing not on any objective reality, but only socially constructed reality. However: "Because of its relativist stance it is *completely uncritical* of the potential dysfunctional side effects of using particular tools and techniques for information systems development. Different products of systems development are simply viewed as the result of different socially constructed realities." (Hirschheim and Klein, 1989).

There is, therefore, a basis for accepting the theoretical validity of a computer-based information system developed by reference to critical social theory, but questions as to the potential for achieving this in practical terms. It is at this point that developments in critical management science can be used to inform the debate, and derive an interventionist approach.

Critical systems thinking is the branch of Management Science, explicitly underpinned by critical social theory, which aims to overcome these limitations to the functionalist or interpretivist approaches. Its practical implementation is through the meta-methodology of Total Systems Intervention (TSI).

TSI operates through the three modes of problem solving, critical reflection and critical review, and the three phases of creativity, choice and implementation. Such an approach confers many benefits when applied to CbISD (see Clarke, 1995; Clarke and Lehaney, 1995; Lehaney, Martin and Clarke, 1996), of which, in the space given to this paper, the focus will be on the critical aspects. TSI deals with this through the process of critical reflection and through its underlying commitment to emancipation. Critique is required, firstly, in order that the sociological environment in which an intervention is taking place may be understood. Secondly, critique is embodied in the critically reflective nature of TSI, and in the use of TSI for the critical review of available methods. "To reflect upon the dominance of favoured approaches to intervention, demonstrating where the use of one or a few methods dominates, leaving problem solvers with limitations in their ability to effectively tackle the full range of technical and human issues" (Flood, 1994).

The importance of a critical approach to CbISD cannot be over-stressed. CbISD 'problems' are not amenable to engineered solutions, so developing them is not best served by systems development life cycle (SDLC) approaches. The TSI ideology explicitly recognises the part played by both technical and human activities in organisations, and the extent to which human interpretation may in some instances so distort the so called 'real world' that study of the latter may become meaningless.

The TSI approach is to first surface the issues to be addressed, then, having chosen appropriate methodologies to apply to these issues, implement change proposals, the whole taking place within a critically reflective framework.

For the past two years TSI has been used to guide a practical intervention, the details of which are outlined below.

3. ACTION RESEARCH

A major information systems intervention is currently underway using TSI, based on the process shown in Figure 1 (a full account is available from the author). The subject of the inquiry is the student record systems at The University of Luton, and the following provides an outline to support the reasoning behind and success/failure analysis of the intervention to date.

In 1992 the University of Luton piloted an undergraduate modular scheme of study, prior to transfer of the entire undergraduate programme to modular provision from 1993 on. Details of how this change affected the University and the manner in which it has been managed are documented elsewhere (see in particular Clarke and Lehaney, 1995; Clarke and Merchant, 1995).

Throughout the intervention the need to find out about the problem situation by discussion and debate has been more important than the design of solutions. Indeed, the type of problem definition needed as the focus of an information system design effort has proved elusive. The initial solution to the problem was The University of Luton Higher

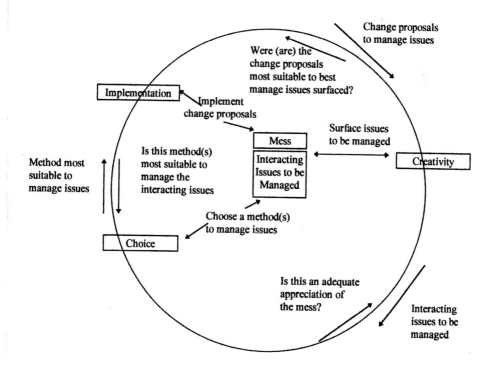

Figure 1. The process of TSI (Flood, 1995).

Education Management Information System (HEMIS), computer software designed to control student records under a modular framework, and provide management information from those records. Now, three years on from the first implementation, an objective has been set by The University to review the whole area of student recording and control in order to make further improvements.

Development of HEMIS to date has taken a structured approach (see Clarke, 1994), and has been seen as a functional system to meet a set of clearly agreed objectives. The current development effort, however, is different, hinging as it does on satisfying the needs of 'users' of the system. Consequently a purely functional view, based on designing a system to solve an agreed problem has proved inadequate, and initially a more interpretivist view was indicated. But the need is for an interpretivist method to determine the 'what' or debate questions of the development, followed by a functionalist approach to the 'how' or design questions, indicating the need to mix methods from the two paradigms.

TSI was therefore used to set the development in a critical, complementarist framework. The users or participants was split into four stakeholder groups: management, academic, administrative and students. The initial intervention has focused on administration, with the other groups to be addressed at a later time. Brainstorming sessions (de Bono, 1977) were held to determine how the problem situation was perceived, as a result of which two parallel investigations were indicated: a review of HEMIS with the aim of improving its functionality, and a review of the perceived needs of a system for student recording and control. The former was set up as a 'hard' project, involving an audit of the HEMIS system taking a functionalist approach. The latter was seen to be a problem situation for which hard methods would prove inadequate, and in the choice phase of TSI the soft method which came out as most relevant and which was therefore chosen was Interactive Planning (IP) (Ackoff, 1981). The two interventions were managed under the TSI framework to give a 'critical complementarist' perspective.

These investigations have been carried out successfully: participants welcomed the opportunity to contribute to these initiatives and the University has accepted and is acting on their findings. In particular, the interactive planning sessions held in the latter part of 1995 through to the beginning of 1996, involving over seventy-five representatives from all the Faculties of the University, have led to a clear perception of the needs in terms of CbISD for the future of student recording.

4. CONCLUSIONS AND CRITIQUE

Arguments about whether to use a hard or soft method, and which hard or soft method to use, in CbISD, seem to offer only a limited perception of most information systems problem situations. A paradigmatic view in which the approaches to development are seen as adhering to different sociological paradigms, gives a richer image. The argument should not be about whether to use this or that methodology, but rather what mix of methodologies best deals with the problem contexts encountered in a given intervention.

Mixing methodologies at a purely methodological level, without reference to underpinning theory, offers an impoverished view of problem situations; a view which can be enhanced by subscribing to the use of a complementarist framework, in which the paradigm problem is acknowledged, and whereby methodologies may be seen as contributing only within a given context. The most comprehensive approach currently in this respect is Total Systems Intervention, underpinned by the theoretical endeavour of critical systems thinking and it is argued that any computer information systems development which is not simply a technological problem will benefit from the use of TSI by comparison to other currently available approaches.

However, such an approach is not without its problems. Firstly, there are those who would deny the view of CbISD as a social domain, seeing it as purely technical, in which case a functionalist approach will seem adequate. A primary difficulty in this case might be seen as the very term 'CbISD', and perhaps a view of the domain as 'human activity-based information systems development' would prove more fruitful. Secondly, assuming a critical social approach is justified, why base it on the work of Habermas (see Clarke, 1997), rather than that of any other critical theorist? Thirdly, the complexity of an intervention of this type cannot be overlooked. TSI is not a simple method to be followed, but a complex approach to the complementarist use of multiple methods, and as such requires extensive learning in order to apply effectively. Finally, the reliance on emancipation begs the question of what to do where coercive forces are at work; or should protagonists of TSI only work in interventions where the conditions for emancipation can be seen to exist?

REFERENCES

Ackoff, R. L., 1981, *Creating the Corporate Future,* Wiley, New York.

Checkland, P. B. and Haynes, M. G., 1994, Varieties of systems thinking: the case of soft systems methodology,. *System Dynamics,* **10**(2–3): 189–197.

Clarke, S. A., 1994, A Strategic Framework for Optimising the Performance of Computerised Information Systems in Higher Education, Masters Dissertation, University of Luton.

Clarke, S. A., 1995, Information Systems Intervention: A Total Systems View, *Adding Value in a Changing World, The Conference of the Operational Research Society,* Springer Verlag, London (in press).

Clarke, S. A., 1997, Critical Approaches to Information Systems Development: A Theoretical Perspective, *Systems for Sustainability: People, Organizations and Environments,* (Forthcoming), Stowell, F. et al (eds.), Plenum, New York.

Clarke, S. A. and Lehaney, B., 1995, Information Systems Strategic Planning: A Model for Implementation in Changing Organisations, *Systems Research* (in press).

Clarke, S. A. and Merchant, K., 1995, A Framework for the Design and Implementation of Distributed Information Systems, *Critical Issues in Systems Theory and Practice,* Ellis, K., Gregory, A., Mears-Young, B. R., and Ragsdell, G. (eds), New York, Plenum: 329–334.

de Bono, E., 1977, *Lateral Thinking,* Pelican Books, Hazell Watson & Viney Ltd, Aylesbury, Bucks. Flood, R. L., 1994, I keep six honest serving men: they taught me all I knew, *System Dynamics,* **10**(2–3): 231–243.

Flood, R. L., 1995, Total Systems Intervention (TSI): A Reconstitution, *Journal of the Operational Research Society,* **46**: 174–191.

Flood, R. L. and Ulrich, W., 1990, Testament to Conversations on Critical Systems Thinking Between Two Systems Practitioners, *Systems Practice,* **3**(1), 7–29.

Hirschheim, R. and Klein, H. K., 1989, Four Paradigms of Information Systems Development, *Communications of the ACM,* **32**(10): 1199–1216.

Kendall, K. E. and Kendall, J. E., 1992, *Systems Analysis and Design,* Prentice Hall, Englewood Cliffs, New Jersey.

Kendall, P. A., 1989, *Introduction to Systems Analysis and Design,* William C. Brown, Dubuque, USA.

Laudon, K. C. and Laudon, J. P., 1996, *Management Information Systems - Organization and Technology,* Prentice Hall, New Jersey.

Lehaney, B., Martin, S., and Clarke, S. A., 1996, Problem Situation Resolution, and the Technical, Practical, and Emancipatory Aspects of Problem Structuring Methods, *Sustainable Peace in the World System, and the Next Evolution of Human Consciousness,* Omni Press, Madison, USA.

Stowell, F. A. and West, D., 1994, 'Soft' systems thinking and information systems: a framework for client-led design, *Information Systems Journal,* **4**(2): 117–127.

Wetherbe, J. C. and Vitalari, N. P., 1994, *Systems Analysis and Design: Best Practices,* West Publishing, St. Paul, MN.

Yeates, D., Shields, M. and Helmy, D., 1994, *Systems Analysis and Design,* Pitman, London.

56

CRITICAL SYSTEMS CRITERIA FOR EVALUATING INTERVENTIONS

Gerald Midgley

Centre for Systems Studies
Department of Management Systems and Sciences
University of Hull
Hull, HU6 7RX, United Kingdom

1. INTRODUCTION

Whether or not any particular intervention can be described as critical or systemic is a matter of judgement. An intervener may claim to be acting critically or systemically, but this claim may be subject to argumentation by others. There can therefore be no absolute definition of what it means to undertake a critical systems intervention. Although this may be the case, it is nevertheless still possible to propose criteria for judging whether an intervention is critical or systemic, around which argumentation can take place. This paper suggests that an actual or proposed intervention may be judged as critical and systemic (or not) on the basis of the view of improvement it takes, the critique that it embodies, and the appropriateness of the methods that it uses. These criteria are derived from the three interdependent themes that form an agenda for Critical Systems Thinking: improvement, critical awareness and methodological pluralism. The three themes have been labelled as such by Midgley (1995a), adapting the different ideas and terminologies of Jackson (1991a), Schecter (1991) and Flood and Jackson (1991a).

As with any debate, different authors have different ideas about the precise meaning of these terms. While the three themes provide a common agenda for discussion, critical systems thinkers continue to learn and refine their systems practice by remaining open to the views of others. I will start the paper by presenting my own understanding of the three themes, and will seek to demonstrate their interdependence. It is these themes that I believe can be used to generate criteria for evaluating claims to being critical and systemic. In this paper, the terms "critical" and "systemic" will be treated as an inseperable pair. This follows Ulrich's (1983) observation that the critical and systems ideas are both inadequate without the other. Critical thinking without system boundaries will inevitably fall into the trap of continual expansion and eventual loss of meaning (as everything can be seen to have a context with which it interacts, questioning becomes infinite). However, systems thinking without the critical idea may result in a "hardening of the boundaries" where destructive assumptions remain unquestioned because the system boundaries are regarded as absolute.

Systems for Sustainability, edited by Stowell *et al.*
Plenum Press, New York, 1997

2. IMPROVEMENT

Let us start with *improvement*. We can say that an improvement has been made when a desired consequence has been realised through intervention, and a *sustainable* improvement has been achieved when this looks like it will last into the indefinite future without the appearance of undesired consequences (or a redefinition of the original consequences as undesirable). The notion of improvement is important for critical systems thinkers because actors are restricted in the number of interventions they can undertake, and must therefore make acts of judgement about what they should do. The extent to which various interventions look like they may or may not bring about improvements, or may bring about improvements that have greater or lesser priority, is a useful criterion for making these judgements.

Of course, we may ask why the pursuit of improvement should be a key criterion for judging whether an intervention is critical and systemic, rather than, say, the creation of beauty, pleasure or spiritual enlightenment. The answer is that, if we value beauty, pleasure or spiritual enlightenment, the creation of these *represents* an improvement. The term "improvement" is general enough to have meaning in relation to almost any value system: it simply indicates a change for the better. According to Rorty (1989), using a term like improvement (or truth, legitimacy, ontology, morality, etc.) suggests a belief in absolute facts or values. Rorty believes that such words are tainted. To talk of improvement is to talk about the attainment of a state that everybody would agree is better. Rorty, along with other writers who have been labelled 'post-modern', have launched a fierce critique of the apparent certainties of the modern world, and the attempt to discredit talk of improvement is central to this critique. Rorty offers a powerful argument, but I part company with him when he says we should *abandon* words like truth, morality and improvement. As you will see in the following section, I believe that we should never universalise understandings of improvement. I wish to retain and revitalise them by making it clear that they only have meaning in relation to the local and temporary contexts in which they are used. To abandon words like truth, morality and improvement is to risk slipping into negativity and inaction. To tear away the modernist certainties surrounding their use and clothe them with an awareness of the frailty of human understanding is to preserve the possibility of positive action while facing the complexities of this head on.

3. CRITICAL AWARENESS

Now, this understanding of improvement is all very well, but we must be able to deal with the thorny issue of who gets to define improvement, and how. We should be aware that definitions of improvement are always both temporary and local (albeit, one would hope, widely informed). Let me explain.

First, improvements are defined locally in the sense that they are defined by a limited set of actors (Churchman, 1970). An improvement is always *an improvement from a particular point of view*. It is possible for an intervention to be seen as an improvement by some actors, but as damaging by others. An example will demonstrate. Logging a stretch of rain forest may bring about an improvement in the eyes of the logging company's employees and those who consume the wood that is generated, but may be considered as damaging by tribal people who are displaced from their ancestral lands, and by conservationists concerned with the preservation of species diversity. As Churchman (1970) says, every improvement assumes boundaries defining what consequences of intervention are to be taken into account, and what are to be ignored or regarded as peripheral. In the above example, the logging will only be seen to bring about an improvement if the displacement of tribal people and the reduction of species diversity are excluded from the boundaries of analysis. Clearly, *what* is included in the boundaries of analysis and *who* conducts this analysis are both vital issues in defining improvement.

Second, improvement is defined temporarily. Even if it there is widespread agreement between all those directly affected by an intervention that it constitutes an improvement, this agreement may not stretch to future generations (Churchman, 1979). The temporary nature of all improvements makes the concept of *sustainable* improvement particularly important: while even sustainable improvements cannot last forever, gearing improvement to long-term stability is essential if future generations are to be accounted for.

If all understandings of improvement are bounded, in the sense that a limited set of actors considering a limited set of variables give rise to them, then the need to be *critical of boundary judgements* is vital. As several authors have pointed out (e.g., Churchman, 1979; Ulrich, 1983; Midgley, 1992a), we cannot avoid making boundary judgements, so the best we can do is seek critical awareness of the limitations they impose. This means questioning two things: the scope of understandings of improvement, and who should participate in their generation. Critique of this nature is not academic, to be carried out in isolation from other aspects of intervention that people engage in on a day to day basis: it is something that needs to be closely interwoven with these. Critical awareness is eminently practical in the sense that it is the only means we have to minimise the domination of interventions by understandings of improvement that are later found to have terrible, unanticipated side-effects, and therefore cease to be viewed as "improvements" at all.

One last thing needs to be said about critical awareness before we move on. If we are to strive to be critical of boundary judgements, both in terms of *what* is taken into account in defining improvement and *who* is involved in the process of definition, then we will inevitably be concerned with the operation of power. On the one hand, power is manifested in acts of judgement about who and what is to be included in, marginalised by, or excluded from the process of developing knowledge and defining improvements. On the other hand, power is manifested in the forms of knowledge that are brought to bear in making acts of judgement (including acts of judgement on issues of inclusion, marginalisation and exclusion). As Foucault (e.g., 1980, 1984) points out (albeit using a different terminology), these two forms of power are interdependent. In the longer term, if we can further develop our theoretical understanding of the operation of power, this should enhance our ability to develop methodological guidelines for practical boundary critique.

To recap, I have argued that the criticality and systemicity of an intervention can be judged according to whether or not it has brought about an improvement, or looks like it might bring one about in the future. However, for an improvement to be adequately defined, there is a need for critical reflection on the boundary judgements that limit what is to be accounted for in an analysis, and who is to conduct that analysis. Hence, the criticality and systemicity of an intervention can also be judged in relation to the adequacy of the boundary critique that frames it. We now have two thirds of the argument in place.

4. METHODOLOGICAL PLURALISM

For the final third, we need to look at how the adequacy of a boundary critique may itself be judged. If we acknowledge that boundary judgements are sometimes made by actors who are seeking to co-operate in looking for the right way forward, then there is a need for reliable methods to foster communication, encourage mutual understanding and provide means for reaching accommodations so that common boundary judgements and understandings of improvement may be accepted. Of course, there may be times when the truth of some matter is disputed, or when it is difficult to make a judgement because there is inadequate information. In such cases, reliable methods are necessary to guide acts of observation. Methods that guide acts of communication and observation are orientated towards the solidification of boundary judgements and thereby the pursuit of improvement.

However, if we also acknowledge that the development of shared understandings may limit critique by smoothing out differences between perspectives that might otherwise have been explored, we see that there is also a need for methods that explore and develop the unique perspectives of individual actors, or which seek out new perspectives. In short, an effective boundary critique is dependent on the possibility of drawing upon a variety of different methods, some revealing or creating different perspectives on the question of improvement, and others supporting mutual understanding and decision-making through the guidance of acts of observation and communication. This use of a multiplicity of methods in a complementary fashion is called *methodological pluralism*. Numerous authors have explored methodological pluralism in Critical Systems Thinking, and several different perspectives have been advanced (see, for example, Jackson and Keys, 1984; Jackson, 1987a,b, 1990, 1991b; Oliga, 1988; Flood, 1989, 1990, 1995; Midgley, 1990, 1992b, 1995a,b; Flood and Jackson, 1991a,b; Flood and Romm, 1996). However, as far as I am aware, the only two authors who have directly related methodological pluralism to the pursuit of critical awareness are Gregory (1992) and Midgley (1992c). We therefore see that methodological pluralism provides the third criterion for judging whether an intervention is critical and systemic.

5. THE INTERDEPENDENCE OF THE THREE CRITERIA

It should already be clear that the three criteria for judging the criticality and systemicity of interventions are interdependent: the possibility of methodological pluralism supports the practice of being critical of system boundaries, which in turn supports the ability of actors to pursue well developed understandings of improvement. However, our appreciation of this interdependence can be further enhanced by demonstrating that it holds when the criteria are discussed in reverse order.

We have seen that there are many possible types of intervention, involving many different types of act (observation, communication, judgement, etc.). A sequence of acts is formalised into a method when it appears possible to make a reasonably reliable prediction of the consequences of the enactment of that sequence: i.e., when it appears that a sequence orientated towards planning will produce useful plans, or a sequence orientated towards modelling will produce a useful model. However, reliability is context dependent: in some contexts the prediction of a particular outcome of the use of a method may hold, but in other contexts it may break down. Of course, it is possible to say something useful about the likely effects of different methods in different contexts (Jackson and Keys, 1984), so we may conclude, as many critical systems thinkers have done, that the ability of actors to act effectively in a variety of different contexts depends on their ability to use a corresponding variety of methods. There is therefore a need for methodological pluralism.

However, defining the context in which actors are acting is not a straight forward matter. Any understanding of context will necessarily be bounded, with some elements included and some excluded from the definition. All definitions of context are also defined *from a particular point of view*. Therefore, critical thinking about the boundaries of *what* is included in an understanding of context, and *who* should be involved in generating that understanding, is crucial (Jackson, 1990). Critical awareness therefore provides a necessary support to methodological pluralism.

Finally, the practice of making critical boundary judgements would be severely limited if the values giving rise to those acts of judgement could not be made explicit and scrutinised. As a number of authors have pointed out, value and boundary judgements are intimately related (Churchman, 1970; Ulrich, 1983; Midgley, 1992a): the boundaries of accepted knowledge define the value judgements that it is possible to make, yet it is value judgements that direct the drawing of boundaries defining accepted knowledge. As I suggested earlier, almost all value systems can be seen as assuming a view of improvement. Therefore, knowing the kind of improvement an intervention is meant to bring about supports the practice of critical reflection on boundary judgements. Having arrived back at the concept of improvement, we could re-enter the argument where it started and show how a given understanding of improvement may need to be subjected to critique. The argument is cyclical.

We see that the three concepts of improvement, critical awareness and methodological pluralism are truly interdependent: none of them could be understood adequately without the other two. It is the three together that provide the necessary criteria for acts of judgement on the criticality and systemicity of interventions.

6. CONCLUSION

In this paper I have argued that criteria are needed to inform acts of judgement about the criticality and systemicity of any particular intervention. I have suggested that these can be derived from an examination of the three themes that form the agenda of Critical Systems Thinking: improvement, critical awareness and methodological pluralism. An actual or proposed intervention may be judged for criticality and systemicity on the basis of the view of improvement it takes, the critique that it embodies, and the appropriateness of the methods that it uses. However, none of these criteria can be understood adequately in isolation: they form an essentially interdependent set. It is only by using them together that adequate acts of judgement on the criticality and systemicity of interventions can be made.

REFERENCES

Churchman, C.W., 1970, Operations research as a profession, *Management Science*, **17**:B37-B53.
Churchman, C.W., 1979, *The Systems Approach and its Enemies*, Basic Books, New York.
Flood, R.L., 1989, Six scenarios for the future of systems 'problem solving', *Systems Practice*, **2**:75–99.
Flood, R.L., 1990, *Liberating Systems Theory*, Plenum, New York.
Flood, R.L., 1995, *Solving Problem Solving*, Wiley, Chichester.
Flood, R.L. and Jackson, M.C., 1991a, *Critical Systems Thinking: Directed Readings*, Wiley, Chichester.
Flood, R.L. and Jackson, M.C., 1991b, *Creative Problem Solving: Total Systems Intervention*, Wiley, Chichester.
Flood, R.L. and Romm, N.R.A., 1996, *Diversity Management: Triple Loop Learning*, Wiley, Chichester.
Foucault, M., 1980, *Power/Knowledge: Selected Interviews and Other Writings, 1972–1977* (C. Gordon, ed.), Harvester, Brighton.
Foucault, M., 1984, What is enlightenment?, in: *The Foucault Reader* (P. Rabinow, ed.), pp. 32–50, Penguin, London.

Gregory, W.J., 1992, Critical Systems Thinking and Pluralism: A New Constellation, Ph.D. Thesis, City University, London.

Jackson, M.C., 1987a, Present positions and future prospects in management science, *Omega*, **15**:455–466.

Jackson, M.C., 1987b, New directions in management science, in: *New Directions in Management Science* (M.C. Jackson and P. Keys, eds.), Gower, Aldershot.

Jackson, M.C., 1990, Beyond a system of systems methodologies, *Journal of the Operational Research Society*, **41**:657–668.

Jackson, M.C., 1991a, The origins and nature of Critical Systems Thinking, *Systems Practice*, **4**:131–149.

Jackson, M.C., 1991b, *Systems Methodology for the Management Sciences,* Plenum, New York.

Jackson, M.C. and Keys, P., 1984, Towards a system of systems methodologies, *Journal of the Operational Research Society*, **35**:473–486.

Midgley, G., 1990, Creative methodology design, *Systemist*, **12**:108–113.

Midgley, G., 1992a, The sacred and profane in Critical Systems Thinking, *Systems Practice*, **5**:5–16.

Midgley, G., 1992b, Pluralism and the legitimation of systems science, *Systems Practice*, **5**:147–172.

Midgley, G., 1992c, Power and languages of co-operation: A critical systems perspective, in: *Sistemica '92: Ira Conferencia Internacional de Trabajo del Instituto Andino de Sistemas (IAS)*, held in Lima, Peru, on 23–28 August 1992.

Midgley, G., 1995a, What is this thing called Critical Systems Thinking? In: *Critical Issues in Systems Theory and Practice* (K. Ellis, A. Gregory, B. Mears-Young, and G. Ragsdell, eds.), Plenum, New York.

Midgley, G., 1995b, Mixing Methods: Developing Systemic Intervention, Centre for Systems Studies Research Memorandum number 9, Centre for Systems Studies, Hull.

Oliga, J.C., 1988, Methodological foundations of systems methodologies, *Systems Practice*, **1**:87–112.

Rorty, R., 1989, *Contingency, Irony, and Solidarity*, Cambridge University Press, Cambridge.

Schecter, D., 1991, Critical Systems Thinking in the 1980s: A connective summary, in: *Critical Systems Thinking: Directed Readings* (R.L. Flood and M.C. Jackson, eds.), Wiley, Chichester.

Ulrich, W., 1983, *Critical Heuristics of Social Planning: A New Approach to Practical Philosophy*, Haupt, Berne.

57

CRITICAL PLURALISM AND MULTIMETHODOLOGY, POST POSTMODERNISM

J. Mingers

Warwick Business School
University of Warwick
Coventy CV4 7AL, United Kingdom

1. INTRODUCTION

Critical Systems Thinking (CST), based on Habermas's theory of knowledge-constitutive interests, has enjoyed a rich period of development during the last decade. I would argue, however, that a number of problems and limitations have now revealed themselves. Some are internal to the approach but, more fundamentally, post-modernism has posed arguments against the the very possibility of a rational, knowledge-based critique. This paper puts forward foundations for the development of a critical pluralism and associated multimethodology in the light of these postmodern challenges. It is developed more in (Mingers, 1997; Mingers and Brocklesby, 1996).

2. THE CHALLENGES FOR CRITICAL PLURALISM

This section will outline the main challenges that have been posed to a critical pluralist philosophy and concomitant multimethodology. Brief rebuttals, responses, or counter-arguments will be given for each challenge, but these are fleshed out in the presentation of the overall approach in Mingers (1997).

2.1. Confusion within the Critical Dimension of Total Systems Intervention/Critical Systems

Challenge: As discussed above, the distinction between critical systems and emancipatory systems raises many problems. In particular, can we really expect any problem solving/management approach that is *critical* towards the status quo to be universally applicable? Surely some groups gain from the status quo and will resist any change?

Systems for Sustainability, edited by Stowell *et al.*
Plenum Press, New York, 1997

Equally, if a critical or multimethodological approach be effective is there anything to stop it being subverted and used oppressively?

Response: We have to accept that genuinely emancipatory approaches will challenge the position of particular actors and thus cannot be universal. As with all tools/artifacts, they can be used inappropriately but should be designed to reduce this as much as possible.

2.2. Loss of Habermas' Knowledge Constitutive Interests (KCI)

Challenge: Criticism of Habermas' KCI make it no longer tenable as a solid foundation for critical systems or multimethodology. This means that it is no longer possible to justify a critical approach from a theoretical basis. We cannot argue that a species-wide interest in emancipation, combined with current distortions in knowledge domains, make an critical approach *necessary*.

Response: In accepting this point, we recognise that critical approaches become weaker. We can only claim that they are desirable, not that they are necessary. This and the previous point focus attention away from the abstract framework onto the onto the person using it, and their commitments, history, and choices.

2.3. Foucault and the Critique of Rationality and Knowledge

Challenge; The work of Foucault, especially, undermines the whole modernist rationalistic enterprise (Brocklesby and Cummings, 1996; Munro, 1996) It shows that *all* knowledge, and indeed rationality itself, is inevitably constituted through and intertwined with the exercise of power. There is no external standpoint from which knowledge can be used to unmask itself.

Response: Whilst Foucault's work does demonstrate the historical and social contextuality of human knowledge, it does not thereby totally destroy the critical potential of knowledge. Foucault himself employed a very systematic and rigorous methodology in his study of historical discourses. He explained his own commitment to rationality (Foucault 1988c), and his own work, I would argue, provides a very good example of the way in which the reflexivity of knowledge may be a beneficial rather than vicous circle.

2.4. Lyotard's Critique of the Grand Metanarrative

Challenge: A related postmodern concern is Lyotard's (1984) critique of the "grand metanarrative" - the idea that there can be some underlying, coherent theory that can be applied to all situations (such as Habermas' critical theory). Within the management science context, this has been endorsed by Taket and White (1993; White and Taket, 1996) who espouse a postmodern position of "pragmatic pluralism".

Response: I have much sympathy with White and Taket's position. Their pragmatic pluralism ends in a very similar practical position to critical pluralism with an emphasis on triangulation, on combining parts of methodologies, and on critical reflection. However I would not accept their denial of theory and their support for 'doing what feels good' as a guiding principle for action. Actions are always the result of choices made, consciously or unconsciously, explicitly or implicitly. But Taket and White's line seems to preclude either an evaluation of actions as being more or less effective or legitimate (e.g. violence or rascism), or an explanation of particular patterns of action in terms of underlying motivations or social situations. In fact, of course, Taket and White make strong prescriptions (e.g., against rascist statements) but it is not clear what justifies this other than their 'feeling good'.

2.5. The Disembodied, Decontextualised, Ungendered Nature of the Subject

Challenge: Traditional critical theory has assumed a universalistic, ahistorical, acultural, disembodied (male) subject (Benhabib, 1992). Such a view of the reasoning subject can no longer be accepted. Critique must be grounded in the actual cultural and political contexts of real people with their individual blends of uniqueness and commonality.

Response: These arguments are accepted and mean that critical pluralism must become embodied and embedded, a microemancipation driven by the commitments of the agent within the constraints and possibilities of a particular, historical and contextual situation.

3. TOWARDS CRITICAL PLURALISM

My response to these challenges is to try to construct a position that is *pluralist* in philosophical and methodological terms, that is *critical* in its stance towards political and social structures, and that utilises a *multimethodological approach*. The context of intervention can be seen as involving three notional systems - an intervention system (IS), a problem-content system (PCS) and an intellectual resources system (IRS). Given this background, what space is there for critical stance and how would such a stance mould one's deployment of multimethodology? I shall aim to construct a position that is in essence Habermasian, but with necessary variants that take on board criticisms of this position.

3.1. Problem-Content System: The Material, Social, and Personal Worlds

Habermas' (1984; 1987) theory of communicative action proposes that communicative utterances raise validity claims concerning *comprehensibility, truth, truthfulness*, and *rightness* with respect to the domains of language, the material world, the personal world and the social world. These may be generalised to suggest that human action (or inaction) in general embodies or expresses relationships to these three worlds—the material, the social, and the personal—plus one medium, language. We must be clear that these distinctions are purely analytical, there are not three separate ontological worlds, nor are they independent of each other. But it is a fruitful way of clarifying the different dimensions of our actions (Midgley 1992). We may analyse these relationships from many perspectives (see Table 1). In particular, we can relate the three worlds both to Foucault's work on knowledge/power and the technologies of the self; and to Habermas's recent approach to discourse ethics.

3.1.1. Power/Knowledge – Technologies of the Self. It has generally been considered that the works of Foucault and Habermas are mutually contradictory, particularly concerning the limits of rationality and the nature of power. However, a number of commentators (Mingers, 1997) have argued that in fact the differences are not that great and that the two

Table 1. Habermas' three worlds and language

	Mode of Interaction	Validity Claims	Form of Science	Power/ Knowledge Technologies	Axiology
Linguistic	We communicate through	Comprehensibility	Semiological	Signification/ Meaning	Expressive-ness
Material	We observe and mould	Truth, possibility	Empirical/ Analytical	Production/ Manipulation	Effectiveness, concern
Social	We participate in and reproduce	Rightness	Sociological/ Cultural	Power/ Conduct	Morality
Personal	We experience and express	Truthfulness	Hermeneutic/ Phenomenological	The Self/ Transformation	Ethicality

are better seen as complementary. Foucault (1988a, p. 26) himself acknowledged that he would have made more progress if he had been aware of the work of the Frankfurt School.

In examining the nature of human experience, Foucault (1988b) categorised four techniques or technologies that apply to our understanding and action: technologies of production that allow us to manipulate objects, technologies of signs that allow us to communicate, technologies of power that control our conduct with respect to others, and technologies of the self that we use for self-transformation. These four technologies relate, in essence, to Habermas' three worlds and to language. Moreover, one of the technologies of self is the concept of "self-examination" - a scrutiny of our thoughts and conscience. Foucault (1988b, p. 46) categorises three types of self-examination - the relation between our thoughts and reality, the relation between our thoughts and rules of conduct, and the relation with our own hidden thoughts. These three correspond almost exactly with Habermas' three validity calims - truth, rightness, and truthfulness.

From the viewpoint of *critical* intervention, Foucault offers many useful insights into the subjugation and suppression of knowledge, the practical mechanisms of power and resistance, and the nature of the individual's constant struggle with the constraints of their own subjectivity. His work shows the necessarily bounded and local nature of critique and emancipation, and that critique should no longer be seen as the discovery of universal and necessary limits, but an exploration of the contingency and plasticity of constraints and boundaries (Foucault, 1988c).

3.1.2. Axiology–That Which Is Good or of Value. The next dimension of importance to all three worlds is that of axiology, i.e., what we value or judge to be right or good. This ultimately provides the criteria by which we evaluate possible actions and make choices. Here, Habermas' (1993a; 1993b) recent work on "discourse ethics" provides a useful framework. Habermas considers that the question "how should I act" differs according to different contexts - the *pragmatic*, the *ethical*, and the *moral*. Pragmatic contexts are those of purposive rational action - situations where we are concerned with the most effective choice of means (given ends) or of ends (given preferences). Ethical questions are deeper, concerning the self-understanding of the individual. They address the Aristotelian, communitarian issues of the nature of the "good life" - that which is important or good for the individual (or the community). Finally, moral questions concern our relations with other people (and possibly nature), our duties and responsibilities, justice, and acceptable norms and practices. Habermas appears to see these three as alternatives, i.e, situations are of one or other type, but from a multimethodology perspective it is more helpful to see these as dimensions, all of which are relevant to any particular situation.

What is Habermas' approach to these issues? First, he accepts that in our fragmented and pluralistic age it is not possible to determine universal and abstract answers to these questions. We cannot specify what everyone must accept. Instead, we can specify procedures to enable people to determine and apply such standards in a rational way. The main principles of the procedure are: first, that it consists of a process of *actual* dialogue and debate by real people. So individuals cannot determine principles in lone monological way, nor can there be imagined or conceptual debates. Second, for standards to become generally accepted they must be such that everyone affected by them would agree that they should be obeyed by all. Third, that in participating in such debates we should make a genuine effort to put ourselves in the place of the other(s). Clearly these are highly idealistic in the sense that they are unlikely to be realised in full in practice. However, they can stand as an ideal towards which we can aim and against which we can judge actual arrangements.

3.2. The Intervention System: The Agent

Any consideration of critical action must begin (and ultimately end) with the actual, embodied and embedded, agent(s) whose choice and action it is. This is because: first, in the light of post-modernism, it is no longer tenable to maintain, with traditional critical theory, the idea of a universal, a-historical, rational (male) subject - the critical analogue to "economic man". Habermas himself has to some extent accepted these points (Habermas 1994), recognising that processes of enlightenment only ever refer to particular individual subjects (rather than an "emancipated society" he refers to "undisabled subjects"); that one cannot specify the future nature of a utopia, only conditions under which it might be generated; and that reason must not wipe out separateness and difference. Second, with multimethodology a particular combination of methodologies is woven together anew each time by a particular agent to meet a unique set of circumstances. This, of necessity, is dependent on the characteristics of the agent—their knowledge, history, relationship to the situation, personality, values and commitments—and so, inevitably brings them centre-stage. Third, I would argue that no critical theory or methodology can, *of itself*, compel its users to employ it critically. No matter what principles or commitments a methodology or framework has, its mechanisms and procedures can be used in antithetical ways. It is, indeed, one of the dilemmas of critical management studies in general that its own methods and knowledge could be used to further oppression rather than emancipation

4. CONCLUSIONS: IMPLICATIONS FOR THE CRITICAL PRACTICE OF MULTIMETHODOLOGY

The starting point for a critical employment of multimethodology must be the real, situated, embodied, activities and desires of actual agents, not abstract theories, frameworks or methodologies themselves. As agents, we find ourselves in a context of an always/already constituted and moralised situation, where all our actions (or inactions) will have effects both on ourselves and on others. We can never be neutral or disinterested. The motivation for action is always *emotional* - desire that the situation be other than it is. That unnecessary and unwanted constraints be broken (*power over*), or that absences and needs be fulfilled (*power to*). This critical moment occurs in the *agonistic* (Foucault 1982, p.222–223) question faced by agents, *what should I/we do?* that continually confronts us in our praxis. We always have to make choices, to act or not to act, to move in this way or that, circumscribed by the apparent constraints and absences of the social and material worlds on the one hand, and our own personal world on the other. We push against these constraints, always testing their immutability by a continual re-appraisal our *appreciation* (understanding how the situation is), our *analysis* (explanation of why the situation is as it is), our *assessment* (exploring the potential for change), and finally our *actions*. The process is renewed through the consequences, both intended and unintended, of our actions both for ourselves and for others.Emancipation will be local, context-dependent, and often very limited, a challenging or transgressing of boundaries, both social and individual

Knowledge, including our methodologies and meta-methodologies, is inevitably linked to power. Knowledge is generally suppressed and distorted, constituted so as to maintain prevailing constraints and structures, yet at the same time, just as with power, it has a positive side for it is knowledge and critical reflection that has the power to assist us in bringing about change. We must recognise that the different methodologies that we might employ are all embedded in their own paradigms, embodying particular and partial views of the world. With critical reflection, we must be aware of the underpoinning paradigm in order to properly appreciate the methodology, but we do not simply accept this. We should always re-interpret the methodology or technique within a critical framework.

Interventions in situations should be made so as to provide the conditions for rationality and discourse, not the final judgements. This should aim towards maximum participation in real, open debate amongst all those affected by decisions; encouragement for participants genuinely to try to put themselves in the place of the other; and discourse about both general norms and agreements as well as their application in particular situations. The actual *process* of critical multimethodology will be a continual cycle of reflection, judgement, and action. It will bring in and knit together methodologies and techniques as seems appropriate to assist action. Such choices depend on both the stage of the intervention and the particular domain of interest at the time as well as the wider context of relationships discussed above.

We must not expect change to come about easily. The social world is constituted and structured through the micro-operation of power, and individually our structural coupling within varied domains is strongly conservative and resistant to change.

REFERENCES

Benhabib, S., 1992, *Situating the Self: Gender, Community and Postmodernism in Contemporary Ethics*, Polity Press, Cambridge.

Brocklesby, J. and Cummings, S., 1996, Foucault plays Habermas: an alternative philosophical underpinning for critical systems thinking, *J. Opl. Res. Soc.* 47(6):741–754.

Foucault, M., 1982, Afterword: The Subject and Power, in: *Foucault: Beyond Structuralism and Hermeneutics*, (H. Dreyfus and P. Rabinow, eds.), pp. 208–226, University of Chicago Press, Chicago.

Foucault, M., 1988a, *Politics, Philosophy, Culture*, Routledge, London.

Foucault, M., 1988b, Technologies of the Self, in: *Technologies of the Self: An Interview with Michel Foucault*, (L. Martin, H. Gutman and P. Hutton, eds.), pp. 16–49, University of Massachusetts Press, Amherst.

Foucault, M., 1988c, What is Enlightenment?, in: *The Foucault Reader*, (P. Rabinow, ed.), pp. 32–50, Penguin, London.

Habermas, J., 1984, *The Theory of Communicative Action Vol. 1: Reason and the Rationalization of Society*, Heinemann, London.

Habermas, J., 1987, *The Theory of Communicative Action Vol. 2: Lifeworld and System: a Critique of Functionalist Reason*, Polity Press, Oxford.

Habermas, J., 1993a, *Justification and Application*, Polity Press, Cambridge.

Habermas, J., 1993b, On the pragmatic, the ethical, and the moral employments of practical reason, in: *Justification and Application*, (J. Habermas, ed.), pp. 1–17, Polity Press, Cambridge.

Habermas, J., 1994, What theories can accomplish - and what they can't, in: *The Past as Future: Jurgen Habermas Interviewed by Michael Haller,* (M. Haller, ed.), pp. 99–120, Polity Press, Cambridge.

Lyotard, J.-F., 1984, *The Postmodern Condition - a Report on Knowledge*, Manchester University Press, Manchester.

Midgley, G., 1992, Pluralism and the legitimation of systems science, *Systems Practice* **5**(2): 147–172.

Mingers, J., 1997, Towards critical pluralism, in: *Multimethodology: the Theory and Practice of Integrating Management Science Methodologies,* (J. Mingers and T. Gill, eds.), pp., Wiley, Chichester.

Mingers, J. and Brocklesby, J., 1996, Multimethodology: towards a framework for critical pluralism, *Systemist* **18**(3):101–132.

Munro, I. (1996). The question of ethics in OR and systems thinking: an exploration of three emancipatory themes. Coventry, Warwick Business School Research Bureau Working Paper 220.

Taket, A. and White, L., 1993, After OR: An Agenda for Postmodernism and Poststructuralism in OR, *J. Opl. Res. Soc.* **44**:9.

White, L. and Taket, A., 1996, Critiquing Multimethodology as Metamethodology: Working Towards Pragmatic Pluralism, in: *Multimethodology: Towards Theory and Practice of Integrating Management Science Methodologies.,* (J. Mingers and A. Gill, eds.), pp., Wiley, Chichester.

58

LANGUAGE IN ITS COMMUNICATIVE ACTION FORM

Mediation of Synchronic and Diachronic Aspects of Language

Keiko Morita

Institute for International Studies
University of Technology
P.O. Box 123 Broadway
NSW 2007, Sydney, Australia
Tel: +61-2-9514-2000; Fax: +61-2-9514-1551

1. ABSTRACT

Habermas argued that reason conceived epistemologically was no longer adequate for the task of illuminating the problem of modernity. Reason, conceived from the perspective of communicative interaction, would emerge as having the potential to redeem modernity from its dilemmas only after a pre-requisite social-linguistic turn had occurred. The focus of discussion in this paper is to connect the synchronic and diachronic modalities of language with Habermas's argument that language in its communicative action form is simultaneously quasi-transcendental and quasi-empirical in terms of the fundamental rules presupposed in linguistic and communicative competencies, and to demonstrate his view that communicative action is the originary mode of language use. The paper also presents an analysis of the Japanese language-in-use, which employ a subtle mediating level, the *honne*, by which the synchronic modality is continually problematised, interpreted and re-interpreted by both speakers and hearers.

2. INTRODUCTION

For Habermas, Reason conceived epistemologically was no longer adequate to the task of illuminating the problem of modernity. A "social-linguistic turn" was necessary whereby Reason, conceived from the perspective of communicative interaction, would emerge as having the potential to redeem modernity from its dilemmas. The rationale for this fundamental paradigm shift is the philosophy of consciousness conceptualizes reason as essentially embedded in, and a reflection of, the subject as a self-centered individual.

Systems for Sustainability, edited by Stowell *et al.*
Plenum Press, New York, 1997

Table 1. Forms of language orientation

Language situation	Language Orientation		
	1. Empirical truth from the observer's perspective	2. Interventionist or strategic success	3. Reaching understanding for participants' coordinated action
Non-social	Theoretical discourse	Instrumental use of language	—
Social	—	Strategic usage of language	Communicative action

The focus of discussion in this paper is to connect the synchronic and diachronic modalities of language with Habermas's argument that language in its communicative action form is simultaneously quasi-transcendental and quasi-empirical in terms of the fundamental rules presupposed in linguistic and communicative competencies, and to demonstrate his view that communicative action is the originary mode of language use. The paper also presents an analysis of the Japanese language-in-use, which employ a subtle mediating level, the *honne*, by which the synchronic modality is continually problematized, interpreted and re-interpreted by both speakers and hearers.

3. SPEECH ACTS, HUMAN ACTIONS, AND COMMUNICATIVE ACTION

As Habermas discusses, language, as a medium of action-co-ordination, is not a unitarist phenomenon. There are linguistic forms that focus only on theoretical discourse, or only on instrumental usage of language, or only on strategic usage of language (Table 1).

Habermas's conviction that efforts towards that end are fruitful in emancipatory terms, that communicative action is originary, and therefore quasi-transcendental in both synchronic and diachronic terms, and emancipatory in social evolutionary terms. For the claim that communicative action is originary, he relies particularly on a reconstruction of Austin's (1975) theory of speech acts in which a distinction is made between locutionary, illocutionary, and perlocutionary forms of language usage. In referring to Austin's distinctions, Habermas (1984, pp. 288–289) summarizes the meaning of those distinctions as follows: (a) "Locutions refer to the content of prepositional sentences... Through locutionary acts the speaker expresses states of affairs; he says something"; (b) "Through illocutionary acts the speaker performs an action in saying something. The illocutionary role establishes the mode of a sentence... employed as a statement, promise, command, avowal, or the like..."; (c) "...through perlocutionary acts the speaker produces an effect upon the hearer. By carrying out a speech act he brings about something in the world". Habermas (1984, p.292–293) builds on Austin's tripartite scheme of speech acts to argue that it is only the illocutionary speech act that is originary. The locutionary speech act means that saying something meaningful is a precondition for an utterance that claims validity for itself, and is open to criticism, counter-criticism, all in the genuine interest of reaching a mutual, rational understanding. Speech act theory thus describes the nature of human beings as speaking and acting subjects.

To reiterate, perlocutionary speech acts are parasitic on the illocutionary, given their opposed aims. Whereas, an illocutionary act is embedded in contexts of interaction intrinsically for purposes of understanding, a perlocutionary act is oriented to success and "thereby instrumentalizes speech acts for purposes that are only contingently related to the meaning of what is said" (Habermas 1984, p. 289). It is in this Austin's distinction between illocutions and perlocutions that Habermas sees the use of language with an orientation to reaching direct understanding based on common convictions as the originary or primary mode of language use. Instrumental use of language for efficient direct intervention in the situation, or letting something to be understood, and strategic use of language for the purpose of efficaciously influencing the decisions of a rational opponent, are all oriented to indirect understanding, and are thus parasitic.

4. MEDIATION OF SYNCHRONIC AND DIACHRONIC MODALITIES OF LANGUAGE

4.1. Introduction

We briefly outline the developments of thought about the synchronic and diachronic nature of language as representing three intellectual phases. In the first phase, the theories of language were underwritten by the philosophy of consciousness, the subject-object perspectives that were pre-occupied with syntactical and semantical than with the pragmatic issues of action orientation. The second phase represented a transition from the philosophy of consciousness to the communicative paradigm; this is the Mead-Durkheim symbolic interactionism phase. The third phase represents a decisive paradigm shift to the philosophy of language.

4.2. Language from the Perspective of the Philosophy of Consciousness: Linguistic Competence

From Chomsky (1957), we get the insight that in learning a language we learn rules that enable us to produce grammatically meaningful sentences. And since language users have creative ability to produce and understand indefinite numbers of new sentences, the grammar of a natural language must be generative, that is capable of allowing users to generate and understand sentences never before encountered. But in syntactical structural terms, only one particular grammar, the transformational grammar, provides an adequate generative power for a natural language. Furthermore, Chomsky argues that natural languages, have underlying structural similarities and that we are therefore born with innate capacities and knowledge of this "universal grammar". Thus, Chomsky makes a contribution to the idea of linguistic competence.

From semiological analysis, Saussure (1959) and Barthes (1967), develop the argument that while language per se represents structural, connotative discourse, speech is manifest, denotative. This distinction is reflected in the anthropological perspectives of the works of, for instance, Levi-Strauss (1972, 1973, 1974) and Godelier (1976), in terms of the distinction between unconscious infrastructures with innate linguistic universals and conscious, contingent linguistic phenomena.

These perspectives are more concerned with language as a medium of meaning and understanding for human beings as speaking subjects than with its more holistic role as a medium of co-ordination for acting subjects. It is in terms of this latter holistic view of language-in-use that the later Wittgenstein made a contribution in his argument that there can be no private language; only public language is possible. In his insightful metaphor, Wittgenstein makes an analogy between using language and playing games. His concept of the "language game" connotes the idea that, in both language and ordinary games, there are sets of rules or conventions that determine what moves are fair or foul in a specific game. On this understanding, it would be unjustified to judge the fairness or foulness of moves in one game by the rules of another game. It is this insight which Apel (1976), "using Wittgenstein against Wittgenstein" (Rasmussen 1990, p.31), transformed into the idea of ideal or transcendental language games; an idea which under Habermas's (1987a) reconstruction sees language, not as idealistically transcendental, but as quasi-transcendental, and hence simultaneously quasi-empirical.

4.3. Transition from the Philosophy of Consciousness to the Philosophy of Language

While the later Wittgenstein can be taken as representing a transition from the philosophy of consciousness to the communicative paradigm, his contribution is best seen more in linguistic than "lifeworld" terms. It is in terms of the latter perspective as a view of society as a whole that the social theory of symbolic interactionism is of crucial relevance. Following Habermas (1987, pp.4–5), we see the work of Mead (1934, 1956) and that of Durkheim (1964, 1976) as of importance. Mead's theory of social psychology seeks to explicate the social constitution of self in terms of symbolically mediated interaction, thus advancing the later Wittgenstein's theory of rule-constitutive language games.

Durkheim's sociology of religion, seeks to articulate the thesis that the foundation of moral rules and moral authority are rooted in the sphere of the sacred, such that moral commands are obeyed, not in response to externally imposed force of sanctions, but in response to an inner conviction that the moral obligations, rules, constraints, in short, norms, have an inherent authority commanding respect. These rules are in contrast to the later Wittgenstein's technical rules of the language game. In this context, one can appreciate the progressive movement in human communicative process from gestures to uni-directional symbols, to reciprocal symbols based on technical rules, and to reciprocal symbols based on moral rules. Durkheim's focus on the sacred foundation of norms and the ritually-preserved fund of communication and solidarity introduces culture as the structural component of the lifeworld, a component missing in Mead's analysis which is restricted only to personality and society. It can be seen that Mead, in referring to symbolically, normatively-guided interaction only in terms of personality and society short-circuited the analysis of culture, the institutionalized and continually renewed background, central stock or fund of values and knowledge from which societal members draw for purposes of socialization in terms of the acquisition of generalized competencies for action (personality), and social integration in terms of legitimations for existing institutions (society). (See Habermas 1987, pp. 119–152 for notions of culture, society, and personality as structural components of the "lifeworld"). Durkheim's phylogenetic focus on culture thus complements Mead's ontogenetic focus on personality and society.

4.4. The Communicative Paradigm

The communicative paradigm marks a paradigm shift from a narrow and abstracted preoccupation with linguistic competence to a more comprehensive view of language as simultaneously synchronic (syntantico-semantical) and diachronic (semantico-pragmatic), or, in other words, quasi-transcendental and quasi-empirical. To justify this view, Habermas builds on the perspectives of linguistic competence, and on the Mead-Durkheim bridging perspectives. Within the new communicative paradigm, Habermas finds,

Austin's work as of significance. Habermas (1970a, 1970b, 1971, 1971b, 1972, 1973a, 1973b, 1979) also reconstructs the historical hermeneutics as represented by the works of Heidegger (1962, 1966), and Gadamer (1975, 1980); the former, following Dilthey (1976) and Husserl (1973), for ontologizing understanding "as a basic feature of human existence"; the latter for taking reaching understanding "as a basic feature of historical life" (Habermas 1984, p.107). While in agreement with the historical hermeneutics intellectual thrust against objectivism, Habermas nevertheless finds it inadequate, because of its failure to mediate the objectivity of historical processes with the motives of those acting within the context of those processes. In essence, he argues that there is a distinction between sensory experience and communicative experience or understanding. While the former is related to perceptible reality immediately, the latter is related to symbolically prestructured reality and to the observable world of events only "mediately" (Habermas 1979, p.9). Thus, the adequacy of our description of observed phenomena may demand causal explanation; whereas, "if, by contrast, the description itself is incomprehensible, we demand an explication that makes clear what the observer meant by his utterance and how the symbolic expression in need of elucidation comes about" (Habermas 1979, p.11). Observation is an experiential act that is verbalized in observational sentences by a speaking subject. To get to what the semantic content of an observational sentence of the speaker requires interpretation by the hearer; and to get to the intentional act of the speaker as an acting subject requires the hearer/interpreter to understand the meaning of the speaker's utterance in a real or virtual context of participants in communication.

Historical hermeneutics is right in seeing language as the necessary medium for the process of interpretation and understanding, the process which depends on symbolically prestructured reality (i.e. the cultural stock of knowledge and normative beliefs). But, by ignoring the causal aspects relating to the perceptible reality, and by naturalizing language as if immune from possible ideological forces, historical hermeneutics shows its limitations in communicative action terms.

In the communicative paradigm, Habermas finds Apel's philosophy of language of tremendous significance (Rasmussen 1990). In seeing the philosophy of language as taking over, from ontology and epistemology, the role of a First Philosophy, Apel (1976, p.32) had this to say, "One could—and, as I think, one should—wonder whether in our day philosophy of language has in fact taken over the role of a First Philosophy which was ascribed (attributed) to Ontology by Aristotle and later claimed for Epistemology of Transcendental Philosophy in the sense of Kant". Apel (1976, p. 57) then proceeds to reconstruct Wittgenstein's idea of the language game into the idea of an ideal language game. In Apel's view, Wittgenstein's idea of the language game is restricted, referring merely to the internal structure of language itself; the proper meaning language usage refers to is the level of competence achieved by the communication community, which in turn depends on the evolutionary stage of a given society's development. From this argument follows Apel's postulation of the "indefinite ideal communicative community" and the "transcendental language game". Habermas disagrees with this view that language is transcendental in the sense that the term describes the universal conditions presupposed in language communication, arguing instead for a quasi-transcendental view.

5. JAPANESE LANGUAGE-IN-USE

There is a belief that the Japanese are extremely sensitive to each other's needs and have a special gift for non-verbal, symbolic communication (Dale 1986, Doi 1973). Verbal transmission is supplemented by intuitive comprehension of what is not said. Communication is visual-symbolic, no less than verbal. They do not trust words and their words are not meant to be trusted. To them sensitivity to what is in a person's mind should make speech superfluous; the use of words evidences a lack of understanding; sympathy and empathy decipher unspoken thoughtless words; verbal skill is for those at arm's length; silence is a sign of honesty and trustworthiness.

Two very commonly used words in Japanese to express these ideas are *honne* and *tatemae*. *Honne* is the inner, subjective thought processes that both speaker and hearer go through to establish what the character of a given speech situation is, might be, or should be. The process problematizes the semantical part of the synchronic level. For the Japanese, that semantical part cannot be taken as given. From *honne*, *tatemae* follows as the verbalization of one's propositional statements or utterance. Because the Japanese are conscious of what other people and the group are thinking, the language has developed a large hedging vocabulary which is "neither yes nor no". Among the most common are "I will have to look into that". Sometimes these mean a tentative "yes" when someone is still doing ground work inquiry and strategy, sounding up influential viewpoints and lining up necessary and needed support. But sometimes they are definite "no" phrased in a roundabout way to avoid hurting the other person's feelings.

Whereas the typical Western model of language usage is predicated mainly on two linguistic levels (the synchronic and the diachronic), the Japanese model has an additional mediating level: the "*honne*ic" level. Taking the model of Western language usage first, we see what Austin (1975), and Habermas (1984, 1987) refer to as two linguistic forms of language usage: (a) the synchronic level of syntactico-semantical language systems; (b) the diachronic level of semantico-pragmatics language games. In the Western model, from the taken-for-granted synchronic level of cultural stock of language as such, one moves directly to the diachronic level in a dichotomous manner between illocutions or perlocutions. The Japanese linguistic model, on the other hand, has in addition a mediating level of *honne* between the synchronic and the diachronic levels. The diachronic level bifurcates into illocutionary *tatemae* and perlocutionary *tatemae*.

When a Japanese has a certain viewpoint and tries to speak it out, he first puts it at the *honne* level and then verbalizes it at the *tatemae* level, the denotative message depending on the particular circumstances of the speech encounter, and not necessarily on the speaker's *honne*. The listener who gets the speaker's *tatemae* language, re-interprets it back to the *honne* level, using of personal intuitive surmises about the speaker's meanings and intentions. The speaker also expects this re-interpretation process reciprocally done by the listener. The Japanese are brought up in this culture, and they automatically go through interpretation/re-interpretation process without even being aware of it. *Honne* draws heavily on the synchronic cultural linguistic stock, not so much as a "given" between the speaker and the hearer, but as a continually interpreted background for most linguistic engagements.

6. CONCLUSION

This paper discussed the connection between the synchronic and diachronic modalities of language with Habermas's arguments. He argues that language in its communicative action form is simultaneously quasi-transcendental and quasi-empirical, and communicative action is the originary mode of language use. The paper also presented the Japanese language-in-use, which employ a subtle mediating level, *honne*, by which the synchronic modality is continually problematized, interpreted and re-interpreted by both speakers and hearers.

REFERENCES

Apel, Karl-Otto, 1976, The transcendental conception of language communication and the idea of a first philosophy, in: *The History of Linguistic Thought and Contemporary Linguistics*, (Farret, H. ed.), W. de Gruyter, Berlin.

Austin, J. L., 1975, *How to Do Rhings with Words*, Harvard University Press, Cambridge, MA.

Barthes, R., 1967, *Elements of Semiology*, Jonathan Cape, London.

Chomsky, A. N., 1957, *Syntactic Structures*, Martinus Nijhoff, The Hague.

Dale, P. N., 1986, *The Myth of Japanese Uniqueness*, Croom Helm, London.

Dilthey, W., 1976, *Selected Writings*, Cambridge University Press, London.

Doi, T., 1973, *The Anatomy of Dependence*, Kodansha International, Tokyo.

Durkheim, E., 1964, *The Rules of Sociological Method*, Free Press, New York.

Durkheim, E., 1976, *The Elementary Forms of Religious Life*, Allen and Unwin, London.

Gadamer, H. G., 1975, Hermeneutics and social science, *Cultural Hermeneutics* 2(4).

Gadamer, H. G., 1980, The universality of the hermeneutical problem, in: *Contemporary Hermeneutics: Hermeneutics as Method, Philosophy, and Critique*, (Bleicher, J. ed.), Routledge and Kegan Paul, London.

Godelier, M., 1976, *Perspectives in Marxist Anthropology*, Cambridge, MA.

Habermas, J., 1970a, On Systematically Distorted Communication, *Inquiry* 13:205–218.

Habermas, J., 1970b, Towards a Theory of Communicative Competence, *Inquiry* 13:360–375.

Habermas, J., 1971, *Towards a Rational Society*, Beacon Press, Boston, MA.

Habermas, J., 1972, *Knowledge and Human Interests*, Heinemann, London.

Habermas, J., 1973a, A postcript to knowledge and human interests, *Philosophy of the Social Sciences* 3:157–189.

Habermas, J., 1973b, *Theory and Practice*, Beacon Press, Boston, MA.

Habermas, J., 1979, *Communication and the Evolution of Society*, Beacon Press, Boston, MA.

Habermas, J., 1984, *The Theory of Communicative Action: Reason and the Rationalization of Society*, Beacon Press, Boston, MA.

Habermas, J., 1987, *The Theory of Communicative Action: Lifeworld and System: A Critique of Functionalist Reason*, Beacon Press, MA.

Heidegger, M., 1962, *Being and Time*, Harper and Row, New York.

Heidegger, M., 1966, *Discourse on Thinking*, Harper and Row, New York.

Husserl, E., 1973, *Experience and Judgment*, Northwestern University Press, Evanston.

Levi-Strauss, C., 1972, *Anthropology*, Penguin, London.

Levi-Strauss, D., 1973, *Totemism*, Penguin, London.

Levi-Strauss, D., 1974, *The Savage Mind*, Weidenfeld and Nicolson, London.

Mead, G. H., 1934, *Mind Self, and Society*, (Morris, C. ed.), University of Chicago, Chicago.

Mead, G. H. 1956, *The Social Psychology of George Herbert Mead*, (Strauss, A. ed.), University of Chicago Press, Chicago.

Rasmussen, D. M., 1990, *Reading Habermas*, Basil Blackwell, Oxford.

Saussure, F. de, 1959, *Course in General Linguistics*, New York.

59

THE IDEA OF EMANCIPATION IN TOTAL SYSTEMS INTERVENTION

An Exploration

P. N. Murthy, V. Sudhir, and U. Supriya

Systems Engineering and Cybernetics Group
Tata Consultancy Services
1-3-10, Coromandal House
Secunderabad - 500 003
Andhra Pradesh, India

1. INTRODUCTION

The framework of Total Systems Intervention (TSI), proposed by Flood and Jackson (1991), has been a subject of intense debate over the past few years. Several comments have been made on issues concerning the theory and practice of this framework. Questions have been raised regarding the classification of problem contexts, the inconsistency between the two phases - creativity and choice, and issues concerning practice (Mingers, 1992; Tsoukas, 1993; Cummings, 1994).

Critical Systems Thinking (CST) which is said to be the underlying philosophy of TSI has also attracted considerable attention. According to Jackson (1990), CST rests on the following principles: (a) critical and social awareness, (b) theoretical and methodological commensurability, and (c) human emancipation. The concept of emancipation is central to CST and TSI (Flood, 1994). While earlier works like Beer's Viable Systems Model attempted to free individuals from the technical barriers (organisational structures), CST proposes liberation of problem solvers and actors from ideological and social barriers.

However, there are several issues pertaining to the commitment to emancipation. Mingers (1992) and Cummings (1994) have pointed out that CST is too idealistic. It is suggested that though emancipation may be ideally desirable, it may not be practically feasible. They have highlighted certain practical difficulties in emancipating the problem solvers and the actors involved a problem situation. This paper attempts to explore the concept of emancipation further. The paper is structured as follows. First, it provides a comparative analysis of the interpretation of the concept in the three works - Habermas' Critical Theory, Ulrich's Critical Systems Heuristics and Flood and Jackson's CST. It then

Systems for Sustainability, edited by Stowell *et al.*
Plenum Press, New York, 1997

explores the comprehensiveness of the present interpretation of emancipation, and in that light comments on the present approach to emancipation.

2. EMANCIPATION IN SYSTEMS LITERATURE

2.1. Critical Theory (CT)

Habermas in his work "Knowledge Constitutive Interests" has argued that creation of knowledge is never value free (Mingers, 1980). It is always obtained to further human interests: (i) a technical interest in prediction and control, and (ii) a practical interest in communication and creation of shared meanings. He has observed that while natural sciences serve the technical interest of human beings, the cultural sciences or hermeneutics serve the communicative interest. In an ideal world, these two domains of knowledge would be sufficient. However, in reality, the norms of the scientific method (instrumental rationality) are illegitimately being applied to the social realm, while communication is distorted by the existing power structures. Therefore, he has proposed that there is a need for an emancipatory interest (in human beings) to safeguard against the distortions in technical and communicative domains. It is suggested that emancipation from power structures that are socially (and materially) imposed and strengthened by knowledge, requires a critical stance, i.e., questioning accepted truths, authorities, and delegitimating traditional power structures. In other words this implies that knowledge acquisition and usage should be critical and self-reflective.

2.2. Critical Systems Heuristics (CSH)

According to Ulrich's CSH (Ulrich, 1983, 1987) people should be free to decide their ends and means (participatory or social planning). This should not be suppressed either physically or due to cognitive limitations (claim of superior knowledge/expertise - positivism). Just because they are not experts in planning they need not blindly or suppressively accept the claim of experts. Ulrich observes that when it comes to boundary judgements there are no experts (the justification breaks-off). It is proposed that emancipation of people from such oppressive structures can come about. In this direction CSH attempts to give heuristic support (power) to the affected groups to question the rationality claims made by experts. Through critical questioning and transferring the problem of justification to the experts, the affected groups can safeguard themselves against the negative impacts of the proposed plans.

2.3. Critical Systems Thinking (CST)

The idea of "emancipation" which is central to CST has been derived from CT. CST emphasises criticality in methodology selection. It appears that CST views methodology selection as taking place in a coercive situation (arising as a result of competing claims made by proponents of methodologies). But, the problem context of TSI may or may not be coercive. CST is primarily committed to the ideological emancipation of the problem solver and increasing the diversity of methodologies. TSI, which is dependent on CST, therefore tends to leave social emancipation to the approaches such as CSH.

The underlying theory of power in CT/CSH/CST emphasise aspects such as power, knowledge, rationality, affected groups. Other dimensions are not considered. Cognitive emancipation is seen as the burst point which can lead to other types of emancipation - material and social. But are these sociological theories of coercive situations appropriate for all types and sizes of systems. Further, CT, CSH and CST assume that if people (weaker groups) are provided with an idea of how they are being dominated, then they could question the dominant forces and through power of argument arrive at a rational and acceptable solution.

3. ADEQUACY OF THE PRESENT INTERPRETATION OF EMANCIPATION

Discussion until now has highlighted two aspects that need attention: (i) the actors to be emancipated, and (ii) the oppressive system from which they have to be emancipated.

3.1. Emancipating the Participants

Mingers (1992) and Cummings (1994) have suggested that an emancipatory approach may not succeed because the dominant participants may not want to employ the approach for the fear of losing their dominance and power. However, no comment is made about the weaker groups. It is assumed that the weaker groups, given a chance, would like to pursue this interest. But, does a coercive situation arise entirely due to imbalance in social and material conditions? Does it not have anything to do with the nature of participants? Are people in a coercive situation willing to be emancipated? For that let us look at the characteristics of participants.

According to Indian philosophical texts, people can be classified into twelve categories based on their character (sattwa, rajas, tamas)[*] and skill/division of labour (knowledge, valour, wealth generation, physical work) (see Table 1). From experience in consultancy practice it has been observed that people with vested interests and those with lack of interest are usually found to operate in coercive situations (see Table 2). Therefore, it is natural that vested groups tend to dominate over the inactive groups. Weaker groups are being dominated because they are willing to be. In such a context emancipation may be meaningless. Emancipation is possible only when an individual has the urge to question existing structures (and the weaker may not always have that). This suggests that understanding the characteristics of participants can be a useful guide for organisational problem solving.

3.2. Emancipation from What?

Mingers (1992) has observed that current emancipatory approaches focus only on the prevalent power structures in a superficial manner. They do not explore how these situations arose in the first place. One such approach has been suggested by Laughlin (Mingers, 1992). According to Laughlin, distortions and the sources of power could be identified from the underlying technical systems.

---

[*] Sattwa: Refers to qualities of intelligence and conservation of energies (harmony, intelligence , enlightenment, peace, and poise); Tamas: refers to qualties of inertia and non-intelligence (inertia of consciousness and force, unintelligent, sloth, and indolence); Rajas: refers to qualities of force and action (Dynamic, vital, restless, passionate, ambitious, driven by desirous longing

Table 1. Profile of participants

	Knowledge	Valour	Productive Activities, Business, Wealth Creators	Perfect Following
Tamas	People who use knowledge for selfish ends and unintelligently (9)	Mafia kind who use their valorous abilities unthinkingly (10)	Create wealth and use it unthinkingly for selfish ends (11)	Unthinking lazy groups who have no interest in work or in life (12)
Rajas	Acharyas, active teachers who go on preaching (5)	Warriors, titans for whom power is main strength (6)	Creators of wealth who are dynamic for its own sake (7)	Trusted, dynamic followers who have to be controlled to get the right behaviour (8)
Sattwa	Seers (1)	Very powerful idea driven leaders (2)	Wise, philanthropic society oriented creators of wealth (3)	Very kind, considerate, but devoted workers with dedication (4)

However, these proposals assume that emancipation would be restricted to the problem context or atmost the organisation in which it is contained. The question that is raised here is should emancipation be restricted to the problem context alone? Actors in a problem situation may be constrained by several systems to which they belong. For example, a manager in a factory belongs to several systems such as family, society apart from the systems in the organisation. In that case, will liberating him from the organisational systems alone help? This raises both practical and theoretical questions. First, will it be possible to emancipate the actors from all the systems? What will be the practical difficulties involved in such an attempt? Where should emancipation start and where should it stop? Second, if emancipation from different systems is considered then is the present conceptualisation of power as an interdependence among knowledge and material status comprehensive enough? In large social systems coercive situations may arise out of material conditions. But, is it so in all the cases? Do they apply to all systems (organisations, families) and societies? Emancipation in family may be different from emancipation in society and organisation. What are the other possible theories that may be more appropriate to these systems? These questions highlight the limitations of focusing only on system and ignoring the participants' characteristics.

3.3. Why Emancipation?

Discussion about CT, CSH and CST highlights another common theme—emancipation of the weaker groups from oppressive structures. But, do only the weaker groups need to be emancipated? and is it required only to fight oppressive forces in a system? For example, if we consider the relationship between a supervisor and a sub-ordinate, we see

Table 2. Type of participants in the problem contexts proposed by Flood and Jackson

	Unitary	Pluralist	Coercive
Mechanical	1, 2, 3, 4 and may be 5, 6, 7, 8	1, 2, 3, 4, 5, 6, 7, 8. This is what we force or make a context to be.	9, 10, 11, 12, 7, and 8. No serious problem for managers
Systemic	1, 2, 3, 4	1, 2, 3, 4, 5, 6, 7, 8. This is the most common context.	9, 10, 11, 12, 7, 8, 4. Managers feel compelled to dictate terms

that work gets affected because the supervisor (a participant) projects his personality on to his context, i.e., his co-workers or assistants (usually treated as sub-ordinates). This may result in concentration of power in the supervisor with the result that he either becomes a dictator or ends up doing most of the work. Here, who is to be emancipated? Should the supervisor not realise that he is the problem in this situation? Emancipation might also provide scope for motivation of individuals from outside the organisational context. This again shows the importance of understanding participants' profile (human aspect) in designing systems. Now let us look at the approach to emancipation.

4. APPROACH TO EMANCIPATION

In all three works—CT, CSH and CST—it appears that criticality is seen as a means to emancipation. This may have certain limitations. Being critical is probably the crudest way to "dissolve" problems. It may be easier to educate the affected groups to be critical of others activities. But, how does one tell the actors to be self-critical (especially those who are introducing the interventions). For criticisms to be taken in a constructive manner, the involved actors must exhibit statesmanship (a participant characteristic). But, can a normal individual adopt such a viewpoint. Moreover, is it not degrading to tell somebody that he needs emancipation? Is it not imposing one's characteristics on to others?

The attempt to emancipate in the above manner may also lead to negative consequences. In the process of emancipating one group by encouraging them to take a critical stance, there is a chance that the other group becomes more closed and tends to defend its position. This does not do away with the imbalance in power. Imbalance in power would always exist which implies that the system would be in a state of turbulence or flux. Additionally, it is also possible that the weaker groups (lethargic ones) may use some of the arguments to their advantage (go on strike, demand more but put in less effort - frequently seen in the Indian context)? So, how does one introduce emancipation in such cases?

Emancipation of actors involved in a problem situation can be seen as an attempt to make participation more meaningful and assist in designing appropriate and acceptable interventions thereby increasing their chances of success. Success of an emancipatory approach, as discussed in this paper, depends on the nature of participants apart from the system. It is suggested that there has to be at least one group (preferably the top) who recognise the need for emancipation and are committed to democratic ideology. They can develop the true potential of the workforce by creating an appropriate environment (through trust). In this respect, participant profile can be a useful guide in identifying the seeds of change. In order to facilitate this change in a least turbulent manner, it may be essential for systems thinking to embrace concepts that appreciate instability, self-organisation, order out of chaos, and not restrict itself to concepts of steady state.

5. CONCLUSION

This paper has argued that the present interpretation of emancipation ignores two aspects: (i) the participant's potential may be constrained not only by the organisational environment but also by several other systems such as family or society to which s/he belongs, and (ii) the inherent characteristics of the participants. Inclusion of these factors, however, raises questions about the level at which emancipation has to start and the domains to which it has to extend. It has also questioned the assumption that criticism and cognitive emancipation would lead to creative conflict and better problem solving. The paper has stressed that a reinterpretation of emancipation, which takes into consideration the profile of participants, will be required.

ACKNOWLEDGMENTS

Dr. Faqir Chand Kohli, Dy.Chairman, Tata Consultancy Services, Mumbai, India.

REFERENCES

Bhagvadgita, Chapter 3, Gunatrya Vibhagayoga, Sri Aurobindo Ashram Publication Department, Pondicherry.

Cummings, S., 1994, An open letter to Total Systems Intervention (TSI) and friends: A postmodern remedy to make everybody feel better, *Systems Practice*, 7(5): 575–587.

Flood, R.L. and M.C. Jackson, 1991, *Creative Problem Solving: Total Systems Intervention*, John Wiley & Sons, Chichester.

Flood, R.L., 1994, I keep six honest serving men: they taught me all I knew, *System Dynamics Review*, **10** (2,3): 231–243.

Jackson, M.C., 1990, The origin and nature of critical systems thinking, *Systems Practice*, **4** (2): 131–149.

Mingers, J., 1980, Towards an appropriate social theory for applied systems thinking: Critical theory and soft systems methodology, *Journal of Applied Systems Analysis*, 7: 41–49.

Mingers, J., 1992, Recent developments in critical management science, *Journal of Operational Research Society*, **43** (1): 1–10.

Tsoukas, H., 1993, The road to emancipation is through organizational development: A critical evaluation of total systems intervention, *Systems Practice*, **6**: 53–70.

Ulrich, W., 1983, *Critical Systems Heuristics of Social Planning: A New Approach to Practical Philosophy*, Paul Haupt, Bern/Stuttgart.

Ulrich, W., 1987, Critical heuristics of social systems design, *European Journal of Operational Research*, 31: 276–283.

60

EXPLORING 'OUR COMMON FUTURE'

Generalised Interests and Specialised Discourses

M. W. J. Spaul

Design and Communications
Anglia Polytechnic University

1. INTRODUCTION

This paper describes the early design thinking and experimentation of a long-term project in sustainability education, prompted by the WCED report on environment and development (World Commission on Environment and Development, 1987) and Agenda 21 of the Rio Summit (United Nations Conference on Environment and Development, 1992). The opportunity for this project was provided by the author's fortuitous involvement in the preparation of two, very different, undergraduate modules: a module on sustainable development, structured around the WCED report, initially intended for a group of planners; and a module which explores the potential of hypertext as a tool for the mass communication of complex ideas, initially intended for a group of multimedia designers. These two projects were brought together by a need to address some of the conceptual difficulties in the WCED conception of sustainable development; in particular, its ambitious multi-disciplinarity. This requirement prompted the question of whether the claimed revolutionary potential of hypertext to promote new, inter-disciplinary ways of thinking (see, e.g., Landow, 1992) could partially fulfill the educational requirements for thinking effectively about sustainable development. In sum, this experiment might be seen as a minor contribution to Chapter 36 of Agenda 21: an attempt to educate students in sustainable development by their reflecting critically on its fundamental assumptions—an interpretation, locally relevant to higher education, of a global need.

The underpinning philosophy for the educational experiment described was derived from critical theory, for several reasons. Firstly, the problems inherent in synthesising genuinely multi-disciplinary modes of thought have been the subject of reflection in critical theory for more than half a century. Secondly, the emphasis in the WCED report and Agenda 21 on citizen participation, and making local sense of proposed global principles, seemed to place its concerns squarely within the late-Habermasian problematic. Thirdly, critical theory itself appears to be re-orienting towards a practical concern with global issues of environment and development (see Habermas, 1996:xlii; Ray, 1993). This experiment is intended to fill the gap between the abstraction of critical theory and the need for a practical orientation in specific cases of environmental decision making; it is intended to make concrete Ulrich's (1993) call for a 'critically heuristic training for citizens' adapted to a highly specific group dealing with a restricted range of problems.

2. THEORETICAL BACKGROUND

2.1. The WCED Concept of Sustainable Development

The initial WCED formulation of the concept of sustainable development is deceptively simple—"meeting the needs of the present without compromising the ability of future generations to meet their own needs" (World Commission on Environment and Development, 1987:43)—but takes on an increasingly revolutionary aspect as its principal tenets are unfolded. At a conservative estimate meeting its requirements involves extensive modifications to the consumption habits of developed nations, a transformation in patterns of world trade in the pursuit of global equity, the growth of patterns of citizen participation in decision-making ambitious by even current western standards, and the development of holistic methods of decision-making combining economic, environmental, political and moral criteria. Whilst the first three of these revolutionary changes are beyond the powers of intervention of the academic (by many orders of magnitude), the last appears to provide a reasonable starting point for enquiry and clarification.

When viewed from the perspective of the literature in critically-inspired approaches to systems thinking (see, e.g., Ulrich, 1994) or planning (see, e.g., Forester, 1989) calls for holistic approaches to decision making (World Commission on Environment and Development, 1987:62–65; United Nations Conference on Environment and Development, 1992, Chapter 8) have a familiar ring - and evoke the theoretical and practical difficulties involved in 'sweeping in' sets of incommensurable factors in decision making. The need for the integration of 'environment and economics' in decision making is, for the WCED, grounded in the fact that they are 'integrated in the workings of the real world'. Our failure to integrate all relevant factors is attributed to 'institutional myopia', which leads to a concentration on single sectors of the economy or isolated frameworks for judgement. Whilst sympathising with the appeal, it is difficult for a critical systems thinker or planner not to see such holistic judgement as standing at the end of a very long road on which different layers of interpretation are peeled from the problems of sustainable development: interpretations of the natural world, technological intervention in it and our perceptions of consequent risk (Beck, 1992); interpretations of science, its findings, and the influence of its institutional structures (Galison and Stump, 1996); interpretations of the self, its needs, and the basis of welfare and economic justice (Nussbaum and Sen, 1993); and, not least, the interpretation of universalist appeals to justice, equity and the common good in a postmodern climate. It is a conception of holistic judgement which makes heavy demands on the cognitive abilities of individuals and the institutions of debate which support them. It places a demand on educational practices which is not well served by existing patterns of disciplinary specialisation (United Nations Conference on Environment and Development, 1992, Chapter 8, 36.5(b)).

The WCED's diagnosis of 'institutional myopia' as the source of one-sided decision making is an ambiguous appeal. If it is interpreted as a cry of frustration with the differentiated structures, specialised roles and expert discourses of modernity, then it is redolent of the Marxist longing for a rational society in which politics and the social division of labour have disappeared (Held, 1987:105–139) - a nostalgic trope which played a major, and not entirely helpful, role in 'previous generation' ecological writings (see, e.g., Bookchin, 1980). The decision making processes envisaged under Agenda 21 are aligned with with the mood of 'new realism' in environmental thinking (Lewis, 1994), with emphasis being placed on the use of existing, but suitably modified, decision making instruments (such as markets and governmental planning procedures). The radical twist to this seemingly conservative stance is that the concrete meaning of 'merging environment and economics' is devolved downwards, through national and local governments, to communities and participating citizens. Thus, the burden of making sense of competing discourses and expertise in environmental debates is transferred from the theoretical sphere (in which no such resolution is possible) to the situated, sense-making activities of citizens acting in their everyday roles. This situation has been described by Giddens (1994:82–91) as one in which reflexive citizens are surrounded by competing authorities, but with no 'super expert' to turn to; a situation which is both liberating and anxiety-provoking. It also provokes the question of what mechanisms of collective will-formation might help citizens to cope with the loss of the kind of final authority once invested in governments supposed to be backed by an omniscient science.

2.2. Critical Theory and Models of Participation

Critical theory has, historically, been centrally concerned with the capacity to synthesise holistic judgements on social practices (see Kellner, 1989:22–35). The dominant contemporary model of citical theory (Habermas, 1984, 1987) locates the source of such holistic judgements in the communicative interaction of socialised individuals raising and responding to varied validity claims. Critical theory retreats to the (fallible and revisable) positing of procedural constraints on the forms of communicative interaction calculated to pursue truth and morally valid norms (Habermas, 1990:43–115). These constraints have provided diagnostic principles for the fairness and validity of extant public policy debates (Fischer and Forester, 1993), and procedural principles for new forms of participatory planning (Renn, Webler and Wiedemann, 1995). A crucial feature of Habermas' model of communicative action is that it is a counterfactual ideal, realised imperfectly in any particular concrete debate: forms of participatory enquiry explicitly based on communicative principles must make some compromises based on limited inclusion and limited duration; real, socialised individuals fall short of the ideal competence required for fair and impartial enquiry. Any practical planning model, such as that required by local decision-making on sustainable development issues, must come to terms with such limitations and—by education and institutional design—seek to raise their threshhold.

A focus on abstract debating and decision making procedures can divert attention from another feature of communicative action: that every enquiry has a substantive subject matter which must also be handled by communicating individuals. Individuals must be competent to discuss the subject at hand; but such standards of competence cannot be imposed from without by any source of authoritative expertise. The participatory planning models of Renn et al include procedures for citizen planners to be briefed by sources of external expertise, to question such expertise, call for supplementary information, etc. - with criteria of relevance being determined from within the group of citizen planners. Ulrich's (1994) 'critical heuristics' and Forester's (1989:150–151) 'communicative distortions' provide tools which help citizen planners to probe the evidence with which they are presented. Habermasian critical theory provides little explicit guidance for the development of such specific competence; but a hint is implicit in his recognition of the need for a 'philosophical' activity which interprets specialised discourses on behalf of everyday communication (Habermas, 1990:17–20). On this account, the differentiation of modern culture into distinct 'value spheres' (using Weber's terminology) brings with it a need for an interpretative activity which can "set in motion the interplay between the cognitive-instrumental, moral-practical, and aesthetic-epxressive dimensions [of modern culture] that have come to a standstill today like a tangled mobile" (Habermas, 1990:19). The allusion is to the interpretative, mediating, deconstructive style of philosophy urged by Rorty (1980) - a style of thought which, with sufficient attention paid to comprehensibility, may be pressed into the service of helping to build cognitive competence.

2.3. Hypertext and Deconstructive Writing

An inter-disciplinary, presuppositionless style of thought and expression has been raised as a possibility by diverse thinkers: the later philosophy of Wittgenstein is inseparable from its fragmentary, self-questioning presentation (Wittgenstein, 1969:17–19); Deleuze and Guattari (1988:1–25) strove to exhibit a style of knowledge organisation freed from disciplinary roots; Landow (1992:120–161) transforms these theoretical models into a manifesto for literary education which frees it from the tyranny of an authoritative canon of great works. Landow's model is based on the availability of hypertext as a technological base; a technology which encourages the form of inter-disciplinary collage, lack of central authority, and easy accessibility required by the critical reader. Although utopian claims for any technology should be treated with caution, the careful use of hypertext as a practical means of presenting competing claims on complex development issues appears worthy of exploration. The emphasis in such experimentation is on the theoretical requirements—mediation between disciplines, deconstructing apparent authority, etc.—rather than the technology.

3. AN EXPERIMENTAL PROGRAMME

The overall structure of development has been partially dictated by the accidents of timetabling and limitations on development time. The sustainability module runs in the first semester of the year, and the hypertext module in the second. Thus a cyclic development was adopted. This involves the collection of experience from teaching sustainability, and then filtering it through design principles abstracted from the hypertext module to produce enhanced teaching materials for the second cycle. Although the students on the hypertext module have no immediate involvement in sustainability issues (apart from any concern they may have as citizens) it is planned to use the development of hypertext materials on sustainability as a running 'real-world example', for teaching purposes.

The experimental programme has begun with the delivery of the first version of the sustainable development module to a small group of planners specialising in leisure and rural development problems in the UK. This initial delivery had to meet the requirement of being a satisfactory and rounded educational experience for those involved as a priority over wholesale experimentation. The strategy adopted has been to explore the WCED concept of sustainable development from, initially, its broadly isolatable strands: environmental limits, such as ozone depletion and global warming; developing alternative technological bases, such as alternative energy sources; models of 'green' economics; development traps and unequal economic relationships; etc. Then environmental and development case studies have been introduced to highlight the conflictual nature and 'incomplete rationality' of real world decision making (the point reached at the time of writing). A gradual transition is then to be made from global to local perspectives. This transition is to be made in parallel with the students researching case studies in their own specialist fields, in preparation for acting as 'expert advisors' to a citizen planning cell comprising the remainder of the students role-playing their 'civilian' social selves (using a participatory planning model drawn from Dienel and Renn, 1995). The expected, indeed the inevitable, outcome is that the fairness and competence required for a consensual debate will, to a considerable degree, be absent. For the students, this experience constitutes a valuable lesson in planning. From the point of view of the experiment, it provides a baseline on the interpretative abilities (set out in 2.1. above) which the students have managed to abstract from readings, taught case studies, and theoretical exposure to the principles of participatory planning. This baseline is intended to feed revised forms of practical role-playing, and the requirements for hypertextual teaching aids.

4. CONCLUDING REMARKS

The experiment described above might be seen as an example of an attempt to find niches of opportunity for critical reflection within an increasingly resource-limited and vocationally strait-jacketed higher education system. It attempts to combine a concern for traditional academic values (a sound philosophical base), a concern for a 'real world' dimension to educational practice which transcends the merely vocational (since the UK is, after all, a signatory to an agreement which makes sustainable development a key part of education), and it also attempts to meet the need of students for experience and qualifications which will help them find employment. It perhaps also raises the question of why such an experiment should have more in common with guerilla warfare than educational planning.

REFERENCES

Beck, U., 1992, *Risk Society*, Sage, London.
Bookchin, M., 1980, *Toward an Ecological Society*, Black Rose Books, Montreal.
Deleuze, G. and Guattari, F., 1988, *A Thousand Plateaus*, Athlone Press, London.
Dienel, P. and Renn, O., 1995, Planning cells: a gate to fractal mediation, in Renn, O., Webler T. and Wiedemann, P. (eds.) *Fairness and Competence in Citizen Participation: Evaluating Models for Environmental Discourse*, Kluwer, London.
Fischer, F. and Forester, J., 1993, *The Argumentative Turn in Policy Analysis and Planning*, UCL Press, London.
Forester, J., 1989, *Planning in the Face of Power*, University of California Press, Berkeley.
Galison, P. and Stump, D., 1996, *The Disunity of Science: Boundaries, Contexts and Power*, Stanford University Press, Stanford.
Habermas, J., 1984, *The Theory of Communicative Action Vol. 1*, Heinemann, London.
Habermas, J., 1987, *The Theory of Communicative Action Vol. 2*, Polity, Cambridge.
Habermas, J., 1990, *Moral Consciousness and Communicative Action*, Polity, Cambridge.
Habermas, J., 1996, *Between Facts and Norms*, Polity Press, Cambridge.
Held, D., 1987, *Models of Democracy*, Polity Press, Cambridge.
Landow, G., 1992, *Hypertext: The Convergence of Contemporary Critical Theory and Technology*, Johns Hopkins University Press, Baltimore.
Lewis, M., 1994, *Green Delusions: An Environmentalist Critique of Radical Environmentalism*, Duke University Press, London.
Nussbaum, M. and Sen, A., 1993, *The Quality of Life*, Oxford University Press, Oxford.
Ray, L., 1993, *Rethinking Critical Theory: Emancipation in the Age of Global Social Movements*, Sage, London.

Renn, O., Webler, T. and Wiedemann, P., 1995, *Fairness and Competence in Citizen Participation: Evaluating Models for Environmental Discourse*, Kluwer, London.

Rorty, R., 1980, *Philosophy and the Mirror of Nature*, Blackwell, Oxford.

Ulrich, W., 1993, Some difficulties of ecological thinking considered from a critical systems perspective: a plea for critical holism, *Systems Practice* 6(6):583–612.

Ulrich, W., 1994, *Critical Heuristics of Social Planning: A New Approach to Practical Philosophy*, John Wiley, Chichester.

United Nations Conference on Environment and Development 1992, *Agenda 21 of the United Nations Conference on Environment and Development*, Rio de Janeiro.

Wittgenstein, L., 1969, *The Blue and Brown Books*, Blackwell, Oxford.

World Commission on Environment and Development, 1987, *Our Common Future*, Oxford University Press, Oxford.

61

SOCIAL AND ORGANISATIONAL LEARNING AND UNLEARNING IN A DIFFERENT KEY

An Introduction to the Principles of Critical Learning Theatre and Dialectical Inquiry

Susan Weil

Head of SOLAR
Nene College of Higher Education

1. INTRODUCTION

This paper explores central concepts and principles associated with my development of two interrelated interventionist methodologies: 'critical learning theatre' (CLT) and 'dialectical inquiry' (DI). These approaches generate critically reflexive organisational learning and 'unlearning' processes and capacity to work with and not against paradox, uncertainty, and ambiguity. These 'grounded in practice' theories have developed from the context of my commitments to organisations working in the service of the public. My concern here is to introduce these processes of collaborative inquiry in order to give renewed meaning to espoused values about social responsibility, social purpose and social outcomes; in ways that transcend narrow understandings of managerialism and efficiency. The learning processes I propose here need to occur at and across boundaries of disciplines, professional groups, organisations and communities. The term 'unlearning' is used to signal my concern to go beyond overly simplistic understandings of learning that derive from positivist and modernist views of the world. Largely instrumental and mechanistic understandings of learning continue to prevail in much of the literature on organisational learning, and in the practices of the public sector. My interest is in "transformative learning". This cannot be understood in terms of mere inputs, processes, outputs and outcomes (see also Argyris and Schon, 1996). The ideas presented here, although not derived from the substantive context of systems theory, are intended to stimulate a dialogue about connections with critical systems thinking, as developed, for example, by Flood and Romm (1996) and Midgley (1992). The concepts and principles will be further developed, differentiated and illustrated in a subsequent paper (Weil, 1997).

Systems for Sustainability, edited by Stowell *et al.*
Plenum Press, New York, 1997

2. KEY CONCEPTS AND PRINCIPLES

2.1. Dilemmas and Live Struggles as the Starting Point

DI and CLT both share as a starting point the 'felt dilemmas' and live struggles brought about by recurring challenges of learning and change. The process of searching for a dilemma on which to work may occur within a group representing a single organisation or in a group comprised of individuals from across different systems. A particular dilemma is selected on the strength of the quality of resonance it generates within the group, and its scope for generating critical reflection on the issues and multi-levelled concerns that connect group members, in terms of their own involvements in learning and change within public service organisations.

2.2. Iterative Cycles of Construction, Deconstruction, and Reconstruction

DI and CLT begin with a live problematic situated in the here and now. The processes then enable the group to extend, in a grounded way, outward from this situatedness in unforeseen directions that have different personal, group, organisational, socio-cultural and socio-political meanings. Cycles of construction, deconstruction and reconstruction evolve. Multiple levels of critique and inquiry reveal patterns in key actors' actions and judgements, which highlight contradictions and paradoxes in their construction of the situation, and ways in which these relate to their espoused assumptions and values about learning and change. Deconstruction begins to reveal ways in which they may be shutting down possibilities for collaborative inquiry; giving rise to recurring and disabling disjunctions across that system. Their complicity in this becomes apparent. An additional focus is the structured search within the group for information and insight about the broader context which is both mediating and being mediated by particular social actors. Therefore, another level of simultaneous exploration and analysis includes competing power relations and cultural norms. The interactions of 'groups of voices' that are both heard and unheard are considered. Dominant and muted processes of sense making, and competing constructions reveal what is at issue and what is not, at a particular point in time, within the context of particular histories and circumstances. The boundaries of the system being constructed, and the consequences of these constructions for giving meaning to the values and social outcomes that *do* connect diverse voices are similarly made the focus for reflexive challenge, as we engage in cycles of deconstruction and reconstruction on different levels, using different modes of discourse (see below).

2.3. Epistemologies of Practice as the Key Focus for Intervention

DI and CLT address a particular dilemma or struggle through a multiplicity of discourses, that helps to reveal, challenge and revise taken-for-granted constructions of the world. These can be understood as 'epistemologies of practice'. Epistemologies of practice are rooted in different ways of knowing—not just conceptual, but for example, expressive, metaphorical and experiential. They are embodied in patterns of interaction, language, and choice. They reveal understandings of the organisational lifeworld that prevail over others and deeply held assumptions about how learning and change happen. More often than not, within public services, at senior level, these are positivist and mechanistic in their orientation. Power, as both a shifting dynamic and a continuity, can shield such key players from the disjunctions that such epistemologies of practice generate between the rhetoric and the peoples' lived experience of an organisation. .However, such matters are often well understood, and become part of the unacknowledged terrain of what remains unspoken. CLT and DI help to bring shielded experiences and processes of managing these disjunctions into view, and illuminate their (often) unintended systemic impacts: for those within, and those benefiting from the organisation. This in turn begins to reveal opportunities for transformative learning, based on the negotiation of meaning and the evolution of connected purposes. At the same time this allows for diversity of interpretation within agreed parameters and makes it possible to take account of different epistemologies of practice exerting pressure from the wider environment.

2.4. The Central Principle of Critique

The focus for critique is not on people, on functions or on tasks, but on the field which binds them. The experience of inquiring collaboratively into the patterns that resist possibilities for unlearning and relearning, no matter how much individuals change, can, in itself begin to create new capacities for unlearning and learning. The focus on the 'live problematic' helps to counterbalance the epistemological panic that can also be felt amongst pragmatists who are new to the terrains of reflexivity, systemicity and social constructionism. Put another way, DI and CLT can be seen to actively cultivate what Foucault (1984) refers to as a, "critical ontology of ourselves", as, "an attitude, an ethos, a philosophical life in which the critique of what we are is at one and the same the historical analysis of the limits that are imposed on us and an experiment in going beyond them".

2.5. Multiple Modes of Dialectical Inquiry

DI and CLT start from a position that construction, deconstruction and reconstruction processes that work merely at the level of the discursive or analytic are severely limited in their capacity to reveal deeply embedded epistemologies of practice. An over-reliance on these shields us from an appreciation of the complex interplay of paradoxes, contradictions, multiple realities, and various processes of meaning making and negotiation that are at play in any social context, and more significantly in any learning or change process. Moreover, the nature of dilemmas faced within the public services demand fresh ways of knowing and seeing that can transcend traditional structures of thought, language and action. These cannot be 'rationally' commanded into place. DI and CLT work actively with what Reason (1994) refers to as an "extended epistemology". This means that the conceptual, the imaginal, the practical, the experiential all become sources for understanding differently what we know and yet what we do not know, and what is at play when we know, think and decide. For example, if we open up the expressive dimension, we can often move into the emotional and experiential source ground that is denied in an analytic rationalist discourse. Exploring dilemmas from different angles, using an extended epistemology, creates the possibility of people taking the risk of living out alternative understandings of themselves in relation to the complex life world of the organisation. DI and CLT help them 'play' with the unknown, in ways that reveal new ways forward. To do this collectively can open up new visions and versions of the 'spaces in between' where alternative patterns of, and possibilities for social and organisational learning can begin to be shaped.

2.6. The 'Space in Between'

These understandings of social and organisational learning, and "unlearning" relate to what Hawkins (1994) refers to as the, "systemic spaces that reside in between". The focus he describes is on, "the patterns that connect the parts; the interfaces, the relationships and contacts between individuals, teams, departments and between the whole organisation and those with whom it relates". CLT and DI begin with a particular dilemma, but then look to, and listen for, the (un)expressed and the (un)experienced which occur in these spaces. New questions begin to be raised about the different kinds of disjunctions that different players—within and at the boundaries of that organisation—may be experiencing in relation to this dilemma. What resistances are being maintained in the systemic spaces being revealed? What patterns repeatedly recur, no matter how much specific individuals change or want to change, and in spite of many structural changes or formal processes of review? CLT and DI therefore place at their core a concern with processes of meaning making as negotiated across these spaces. Such processes inevitably involve issues of identity, culture and power. But the principles of social and organisational learning embedded in CLT and DI systems begin to reveal alternative possibilities for creating a different kind of story that could have greater meaning and impact, in terms of what matters to individuals, to clients, and indeed to managers. But how often, in contrast, do we see managers and consultants engaged in an irreverent and controlling eradication of these dimensions of complexity? I would argue that these, all too prevalent approaches, are derived from positivist understandings of learning and change. Sadly, they often strike at the heart of professional and service effectiveness having the very opposite effect of what is intended. CLT and DI can generate an experiential entry into understanding (conceptually, imaginally and behaviourally) alternative epistemologies of practice, related to learning and change. When disjunctions, ambiguity, paradox and complexity are actively worked with, conscious intent can give way to the emergent potential of new opportunities for making personal and collective meaning of dilemmas, and for inquiry and intervention at and across the boundaries.

2.7. Enacted Social Constructivism and Systemicity

A social construct is an abstraction that aids our analysis and understanding of social phenomena, and which functions as an heuristic device to open up new lines of thought, investigation and action. Systemicity lays emphasis on the notion of an interconnected whole. But how do we begin to transform the perspectives of people caught up in the 'linear archetype' of overly simplistic cause and effect thinking that Mitroff and Linstone (1993) identify as, "inappropriate and outworn images of an earlier age"? CLT and DI encourage individuals to see the parts in relation to the whole, and to see the patterns that connect them, as individuals and as members of different groups (for example, tax payer, citizen, professional and service user) to that whole. These approaches are used to develop the capacity with which to perceive more clearly the processes of disjunction and integration that are at play and which need interrupting if learning and change are to be more than merely cosmetic. What distinguishes CLT and DI are the ways in which they provide opportunities for looking at and experiencing this systemicity and the multiple ways in which meaning is being socially constructed within a complex system, as if for the first time. CLT places greater emphasis on enactment and embodiment, or the living out of multiple positions within that whole. This is supplemented by observer-participants who take roles but also 'chronicle' questions for inquiry, that in turn support the cycles of deconstruction and reconstruction. CLT makes it possible to explore different constructions as influenced by shifting positional, temporal and relational circumstances. I draw on, yet go beyond methods developed in sociodrama (Moreno, 1978; Boal, 1985). DI makes greater use of metaphor, story, and other expressive discourses to go beyond rational posturing. But with their different discursive emphases and dialectics, both CLT and DI tackle the enduring problematic entailed in surfacing epistemologies of practice, captured in the Chinese proverb, "the fish does not know water until it is out of it" (see also, Weil and McGill, 1989; Weil, 1995; Weil, forthcoming). Both processes make it possible to look from new angles at the way different kinds of interventions affect the whole, and create the 'patterns that connect'. Such processes of critical scrutiny inevitably focus on how we include and exclude, disable and enable, mute and un-silence, oppress or suppress different kinds of stories—our own and others, be this intentional or otherwise. When working between different modes—analytical and expressive, imaginal and enacted, collective and personal - unforeseen possibilities for action and choice can open up.

2.8. Situated Reflexivity

Reflection is a key concept in the management and organisational development literature. However, recent critiques of reflection from a gendered perspective place emphasis on the dualisms the literature and much practice perpetuates—thereby recapitulating the traditional positivist disassociation of mind from body, head from heart, self from the environment, theory from practice and thought from action. The emphasis in CLT and DI is on the critically reflexive, the dialectics of organisations and on the contextualisation of dilemmas and 'action choices'. It is not humanistic in its orientation, as it does not see individuals as the sole authors of their experience. Instead, they are seen as dynamically mediating and being mediated by complex biographical and socio-political circumstances. CLT and DI challenge those who prefer to see people as 'resistant to change' to take account of the multiple capacities for agency or resistance that are present within the spaces that connect. As Kosmidou and Usher (1992) argue, "any genuine interest in emancipation, self actualisation, personal and social transformation has to start with recognition of and then a problematisation of those aspects of situatedness". DI and CLT then give meaning to what Kosmidou and Usher go on to argue must be the, "possibility of social actors constructing a bigger story that is open to revision".

2.9. Reflexive Action as Learning; Reflexive Learning as Action

As will be evident, DI and CLT place critique at their centre, but in ways that remain grounded in the requirement to act in socially responsible ways. Moreover, CLT and DI reveal how the requirement to act, simultaneously becomes an opportunity for social and organisational learning in itself. This emphasis can be seen to be complementary to the stance put forward by Flood and Romm (1995). Their work on triple loop learning and diversity management advocates a, "stance of humility towards one's own viewpoints", whereby people can begin to, "consider what processes of knowledge creation may be regarded as allowing maximum inventiveness for people to think alternative relationships to 'the world' while not threatening the rights of others to a viewpoint". As a process, however, CLT and DI keep reflection and action, learning and action, in a dialectical relationship with each other, maintaining a dynamic praxis: as Freire and Horton say, "we make the road by walking" (Bell, Gaventa and Peters, 1990).

3. CONCLUSION

The title of this paper suggested possibilities for processes of social and organisational learning in a different key. Learning processes that are transformative and which go beyond the instrumental, need to engage more than merely our intellect or our rhetoric. As we face more and more that is unknown and not capable of being understood or controlled, we must approach learning and change as relational and improvisational processes. This inevitably entails building cultures that support new forms of collaborative inquiry and action research. DI and CLT begin to offer starting points for these new forms of engagement. Such processes develop respect for that which cannot be controlled or managed, and begin to build capacity for working with the emergent and the unfamiliar. To engage in transformative learning processes creates the possibility of revising and enacting alternative understandings of ourselves and our lifeworlds. This is hard enough in our personal lives. To do so within public service organisations in the 1990s is an altogether riskier business. An explicit assumption of this work is that mechanistic solutions to complex problems of social and organisational learning and change, derived from a positivist view of the world, may generate short term efficiency gains, but they continue to generate major disjunctions in the 'spaces in between' and at the interfaces. These, in turn, contribute to ever escalating social and financial costs, as goodwill amongst dedicated professionals is systematically eradicated, and delusions and illusions of change are perpetuated. The concerns raised here are not dissimilar to those now concerned about the unintended effects of large scale "de-layering" in the name of greater efficiency and effectiveness. These processes have different meanings for individuals and organisations working in the service of the public, but the patterns that connect need to concern us all. This requires methodologies that offer opportunities for social and organisational learning in an altogether different key.

ACKNOWLEDGMENTS

My deep appreciation to the following for their assistance with this paper: Annette Karseras, Gerald Midgley, Norma Romm and Maggi Savin Baden.

REFERENCES

Argyris, C and Schon, D. 1996. *Organisational Learning 2*. Addison Wesley: Reading.

Bell, B., Gaventa, J. and Peters, J. 1990. *We Make the Road by Walking*. Temple University Press, Philadelphia.

Boal, A. 1985 *Theatre of the Oppressed*. Trans. CA and ML McBridge. Theatre Communications Group: New York.

Flood, RL and Romm, N.R. 1995. "Diversity Management: Theory in Action". *Systems Practice*, 8, 4, 469–482.

Flood, RL and Romm, N.R. 1996. *Diversity Management: Triple Loop Learning*. John Wiley: Chichester,.

Foucault, M in Gordon, C (ed.). 1980. *Power/Knowledge: Selected Interviews and Other Writings, 1972–1977*. Harvester: Brighton.

Hawkins, P. 1994. "The Changing View of Learning" in J. Burgoyne *Towards the Learning Company*. McGraw-Hill: London

Kosmidou, C and Usher, R. 1992 "Experiential Learning and the Autonomous Subject: A Critical Approach" in D. Wildemeersch and T. Jansen. *Adult Education, Experiential Learning and Social Change: The Postmodern Challenge*. VTA Groep: Holland

Midgley, Gerald. 1992. "The Sacred and Profane in Critical Systems Thinking". *Systems Practice*, 5, 1, 5–16.

Mitroff, I and H. Linstone. 1993. *The Unbounded Mind: Breaking the Chains of Traditional Business Thinking*. Oxford University Press: Oxford

Moreno, J. 1978. *Who Shall Survive: The Theatre of Spontaneity, Sociometry and the Science of Man*. 3rd ed. Beacon Press: New York

Reason, P. 1994 in N.K. Denzin and Y.S. Lincoln, eds. *Handbook of Qualitative Research*. Sage: London.

Weil, S and McGill, I. eds. 1989. *Making Sense of Experiential Learning: Diversity in Theory and Practice*. SRHE/OU Press: Milton Keynes.

Weil, S. 1995. "Bringing about Cultural Change in Colleges and Universities: The Power and Potential of Story". in S. Weil ed. *Managing Change from the Top of Universities and Colleges: 10 Personal Accounts*. Kogan Page, London.

Weil, S. 1997 forthcoming. "Critical Learning Theatre and Dialectical Inquiry as Social and Organisational Learning and Unlearning In Practice". *Systems Practice,* 10.

62

VIABLE INQUIRY SYSTEMS

Maurice Yolles

Liverpool John Moores University Business School
Liverpool, United Kingdom

1. INTRODUCTION

Systems are organised images of the real world that entail certain principles, and we build systems models because we can attribute to them certain generic characteristics that we believe can help us explain what we perceive as the real world. The idea of the real world being modelled as a system hierarchy composed of networks of organisations seen as semi-autonomous systems is a powerful way of representing what we believe that we see. The theory that is attached to such systems is called viable systems theory.

By *viable* we mean able to maintain a separate (fully or partly autonomous) existence. Viable systems therefore participate in the development of their own futures through self. The theory of viable systems is essentially the theory of networked purposeful semi-autonomous open systems that exist together in a system hierarchy. We say semi-autonomous systems because: (a) fully autonomous systems are difficult if not impossible to find, and (b) semi-autonomous systems are susceptible to both autopoietic (see Mingers, 1995) and cybernetic theory. The latter case is so because fully autonomous systems are autopoietic, and thus cannot have logical relationships with their environment that cybernetic system require (Schwarz, 1996; Yolles, 1997). We can refer to such systems as *holons*. As a consequence, rather than talking about a system hierarchy we can equivalently talk of a hierarchy of holons, or even better a *holarchy*. In general we shall use the terms *holon* and *viable system* interchangeably, as we will *holarchy* and *system hierarchy*.

The idea of viable systems originated with Ashby. It has developed into a powerful cognitive model for inquiry into problem situations through Beer's Viable Systems Model, that seeks to find and correct structural faults in organisations. More recently, the development of work by Schwarz that explores the self-organising behaviour of evolutionary systems, itself sensitive to chaos theory, has contributed to this. Viable systems theory should be seen to subsume general systems theory, and as we shall explain in due course, provides a pathway for methodological complementarism through the creation of viable inquiry systems.

2. THE FUNDAMENTALS OF VIABLE SYSTEMS AND INQUIRY

The work of Beer and Schwarz are fundamental to the development of concepts that we may associate with viable systems and inquiry into the problem situations of organisations. Beer's Viable System Model (e.g. Espejo and Harnden, 1989) has provided the most visible use of the concept of viability. It provides theory that enables a system that is being focused in on to be seen to have what we shall refer to as at least a *metaphorical* cognitive domain that is ultimately responsible for the form of an associated system and its behaviour. It defines the metasystem that is associated with a system, this having a form and associated behaviour (Yolles, 1997). The relationship is defined in terms of a structural model (figure 1) through transmogrify, which may be: (a) seen to be cybernetic, and (b) subject to surprises. The surprises may occur because the relationship between the metasystem and the system can be disturbed due to chaotic perturbations. These disturbances may be the cause for morphogenisis in the system. Further, they may also be the cause for breakdown between the metasystem and the system under conditions of chaos.

This general model can be used to explain the relationship between method and methodology. Both ultimately derive from the cognitive domain that is defined by the paradigm. Methodology is seen as a process of transmogrify, and method is a system domain manifestation that is subject to cybernetic methodological processes.

The work of Schwarz (1994) is particularly important if we are to develop the idea of viable inquiry systems. His work takes on the attributes of chaos and complexity theory as explored for instance by Prigogine and Stengers (1984), Stewart (1989), and by Cohen and Stewart (1994). Fundamental to viable systems is the idea that they are self-organising. Schwarz explains that self-organisation can be seen to occur as a spiral pattern of stable behaviour. It has four successive recurrent phases (table 1) that are shown graphically in figure 2.

A system may drift away from stability by first becoming structurally critical. The view of Minorski (1962, p185) would be that it is criticality in structures that we should be referring to when we see positive feedback occurring, rather than talking about the slightly confusing term of structural stability that has become more popular.

Critical structures magnify perturbations that will contribute towards the definition of a new form for the system. In terms of Schwarzian theory, this works in the following

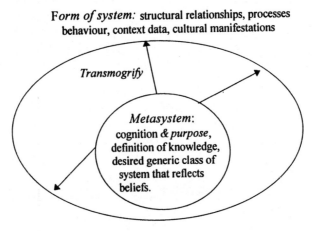

Figure 1. Relationship between system and metasystem (Yolles, 1997).

Table 1. The phases of self-organisation (taken from Schwarz, 1994)

Phase	Steps	Explanation
1 Entropic drift (tropic drift is the general case)	1. Stability 2. Spontaneous entropic drift 3. Tropic drift 4. Increase in tensions	This leads to disorder or more generally to the more probable, to the actualisation of potentialities. It is often the coherent actualisation of the potentialities of the parts of the system that generate tensions and eventually break the global homeostatic or even autopoietic networks that hold all the social agents together.
2 Bifurcation (ALEA: i.e., crisis, random, hazard)	5. Fluctuations 6. Bifurcation 7.0. option 0: decay 7.2. option 1: type 1 (Watzlawick) change	Fluctuations occur internally, or in the environment as noise. Through amplification of fluctuations due to tensions following entropic drift, a discontinuity occurs in the causal sequence of events/behaviour. "Stochastic" selection occurs, influenced by the tensions within a problem situation. The tensions correlate to the amplification of the fluctuations that occur. At this point three options are possible: 7.1, 7.2, or 7.3. Decay represents a process of either destructurising, disorganisation, regression, or extinction of the system. This can be seen as the start of a catastrophe bifurcation. In type 1 the process of change begins with "more of the same" small changes that maintain it current state. However, such changes may be in some way bounded.
3 Metamorphosis	7.2. option 2: type 2 change 8. Complexification	In type 2 change, metamorphosis begins as a local morphogenic event that is amplified within a critical structure to have a macroscopic effect. In the critical structure a new form can arise initiated by the non-linear condition. It is one of many possible bifurcations that could have developed. Complexification can occur during iteration of spiral. Autonomy may develop.
4 Stability	9. Dynamic stability	Occurs through self-regulation and/or existential self-reference.

way. Tensions develop that make the system structurally critical, and thus macroscopically susceptible to small local perturbations. If these occur (as fluctuations), then either the system dies or becomes disorganised (the zero option), or self-organisation occurs and the system regains stability, through morphogenisis. If type 1 change occurs, then the system is capable of further morphogenisis. With type 2 metamorphic change, then a spontaneous alteration in form happens. This occurs when the conditions within the system are

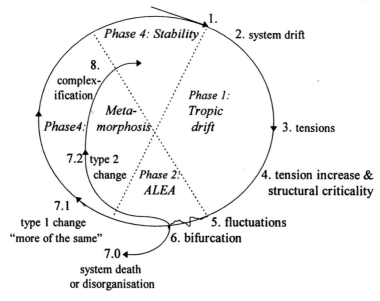

Figure 2. The spiral of self-organisation (Schwarz, 1994).

such that it has reached a bound in its ability to adapt morphogenically with respect to the perturbations from the environment. There are six successive steps involved in the process of metamorphosis: (i) differentiation as a response to tension, (ii) communication/ interaction between differentiated parts, (iii) integration of the parts due to their interaction, (vi) emergence of an encompassing common metalevel, (v) dynamical stabilisation of the whole, (iv) recursion of above to result in more organisational metalevels and their integration (imbrication). The creation of new systemic forms is consistent with unexpected novelty. These are referred to as discontinuous bifurcations that derive from continuous relations. Embedded within the relations that connect with the new form are all the possibilities of innovation that might develop. Unexpected novelty occurs when these possibilities are not predeterminable. New forms are therefore not deterministic, whether or not all the possibilities of form that might develop are known.

3. VIABLE INQUIRY SYSTEMS

Complexity theory (Cohen and Stewart, 1994) is built on chaos theory that itself is built on the theory of dissipative systems (Prigogine, 1976). All of these have as their foundation the notion that viable systems are dynamic and frequently far from equilibrium. It explains how they change and still survive because they are able to maintain stability in their behaviour, even though finding themselves shifting between structural robustness and structurally criticality from time to time. Implicit to the work of Schwarz are a set of propositions (Yolles, 1997) that in the first instance define the mechanisms of viability, but which later are transformable such that they can be used to define Viable Inquiry Systems (VIS).

VISs are triadic. Methodologies, like target coherent situations, are paradigm based, while inquirer operate through weltanschauung. While all offer types of world view, paradigms may be seen as a formalisation of weltanschauung (Yolles, 1996). Thus, the three points of the triad are: (1) methodologies, (2) scoherent ituations (including stakeholder actors), (3) inquirers. The cognitive model of a number of methodologies (like Soft Systems Methodology (Checkland and Scholes, 1990)) already recognise the need to take these attributes into account. However, a more satisfactory formalisation can occur if the points of the triad are considered as orthogonalities in a single frame of reference. For instance, Ulrich (1981) and others (see Jackson, 1992) see VSM as being insensitive to cultural or political attributes of an organisation. However a VIS view can for instance lead us to consider the cultural and political attributes of a situation to be a function of an ideologically driven inquirer. Through VIS we can also see a process of inquiry as, for example, a triad of world views in dynamic conflict that can be appropriately explored.

VIS is seen as a Critical Systems Thinking (CST) approach, involving methodological complementarism (see Midgley, 1995). This explains how we can use a plurality of methodologies together, despite the arguments of the paradigm incommensurabilitists as presented by Burrel and Morgan (1979). Consider for instance the now classical differentiation between hard and soft systems methodologies. From a CST perspective in VIS, they should not be segregated as they tend to be, but can rather be seen as congruent. As we shall explain shortly, they can also fail together. Hard methodologies are defined in terms of tangible things, and are often associated with a high level of structuring. They are also often seen in terms of certainty or probability, thus being deterministic or following a path of rational expectation. Strategy options for intervention are normally rationally determined normally according the criteria that inquirers define within their approaches to inquiry. The selected strategies occur according to predefined criteria, and it is supposed that these criteria will hold in the future. Validation occurs through the deterministic or rational logic used. In contrast to this, soft methodologies involve people and usually suppose that a situation is illstructured and uncertain. Their approach is thus to establish procedures of inquiry that involve stakeholders directly. The degree of stakeholder involvement is an indicator of the softness of the methodology. Soft methodologies tend feed the results of inquiry back to the stakeholders for their validation, and they normally adopt consensus evaluations. In both hard and soft cases, the options generated are implemented, while monitoring and evaluating progress homeostatically. There is also the possibility of behavioural or cognitive methodological change, while inquirers learn about the way in which inquiry and intervention has occurred.

While hard and soft methodologies thus derive from a base of different assumptions, they end up establishing implementation strategies that are quite similar in that they both have an assumption of rational expectation. That is, they expect that if: *(a) their analysis and models are in some way validated, (b) they deduce an intervention strategy consistent with perspectives of the paradigm being used, (c) during implementation of the intervention strategy the specifications are honoured, and (d) that monitoring occurs to ensure that (b) and (c) are validated,* then the result will satisfy the perceived needs of the situation. In situations of chaos, it is this that establishes the weakness of both approaches. Cybernetic principles can themselves fail during chaos when the relationship between metasystemic cognition and system behaviour breaks down. Here, the environment alone drives behaviour subject to Varela's proposition of change being structure determined. Consensus approaches too may become volatile during this time, and shift along with situation contexts.

Intervention strategies will introduce changes into the form and culture of an organisation to different degrees and over different durations. In organisations in which there is a structurally criticality, the cost of a small failure can be very high, even to their survival. What is important, however, is the nature of the criticality. It may be a point criticality that affects only one focus of the organisation, or it might affect a number of foci.

4. CONCLUSION

Viable systems are able to survive through their self-organisational processes despite recurrent structural criticality. Both the cybernetic and Viable System Model work of Beer referred to, and the work of Schwarz also referred to that provides a general model of mophogenic and evolutionary processes in viable systems, provide different attributes of viable systems theory that when taken together with additional theory provides an important and powerful way of explaining systemic behaviour. The concept of viability can be extended to methodological inquiry to arrive at Viable Inquiry Systems (VIS), as indeed it can to other areas like Viable Learning Systems. In VIS we define a triad that couples methodology to a target situation through an inquirer, and is world view centred. The former two each operate through paradigms, while the latter through weltanschauung. Together they provide a more holistic way of looking at situations than simply through methodologies alone. While all three attributes of inquiry are sometimes implicitly included in discussions about methodology, they should be explicitly included as equal partners, and their natures formalised in relation to one another. Critical Systems Thinking is also an important aspect of Viable Inquiry Systems.

5. REFERENCES

Beer, S., 1975, Preface in: Autopoietic Systems. H.M. Maturana, F.G.Varela, (eds.) Biol. Computer Lab. Research Report 9, 4. U. Illinois, Urbana. Reprinted in Maturana, H.M., Varela, F.G., *Autopoiesis and Cognition: The Realisation of the Living*. Reidel, Dordrecht.

Burrell, G., Morgan, G., 1979, *Sociological Paradigms and Organisational Analysis*. Heinemann, London.

Checkland, P., Scholes, J., 1990, *Soft Systems Methodology in Action*. Wiley, New York.

Cohen, J., Stewart, I., 1994, *The Collapse of Chaos: discovering simplicity in a complex world*. Viking, London.

Espejo, R., Harnden, R., 1989, *The Viable System Model: interpretations and applications of Stafford Beer's VSM*. Wiley, Chichester.

Jackson, M.C., 1992, *Systems Methodologies for the Management Sciences*. Plenum, New York.

Midgley, G., 1995, *Mixing Methods: Developing Systemic Intervention*. Research Memorandum No. 9, Centre for Systems Studies, University of Hull.

Mingers, J., 1995, *Self Producing Systems*. Academic Press, New York

Nicholis, G., Prigogine, I., 1989, *Exploring Complexity: An Introduction*. W.H.Freeman, New York.

Prigogine, I., 1976, "Order through fluctuation: self-organisation and social system". In *Evolution and Consciousness: Human Systems in Transition*, E. Jantsch and C.H. Waddington, (eds., 1976). Addison-Wesley, Reading, Mass., USA.

Prigogine, I, Stengers, I.,1984, *Order Out of Chaos: Man's New Dialogue with Nature,* Flamingo, London.

Schwarz, E., 1994 (September), A Transdisciplinary Model for the Emergence, Self-organisation and Evolution of Viable Systems. Presented at the International Information, Systems Architecture and Technology Conference, Technical University of Wroclaw, Szklaska Poreba, Poland.

Schwarz, E., 1996, Private communication.

Stewart, I., 1989, *Does God Play Dice*. Blackwell, Oxford.

Ulrich, W., 1981, A Critique of Pure Cybernetic Reason: The Chilean Experience with Cybernetics, *J. Appl. Sys. Anal.* 8:33.

Yolles, M.I., 1996, Critical Systems Thinking, Paradigms, and the Modelling space, *J. Systems Practice,* 9(3).

Yolles, M.I., 1997, *An Inquiry into Soft Systems*. Pitman Publishing, London. Not yet in print.

63

'INSIDER CONTROL' AND THE EFFECTS ON ECONOMIC SYSTEMS

A Critical Review

Xiaokang Zhao and Wei-hua Jin

Centre for Systems Research
Lincoln School of Management
Lincoln University Campus
University of Lincolnshire and Humberside
Lincoln, LN6 7TS, United Kingdom

1. INTRODUCTION

The purpose of this paper is to discuss the so-called 'insider control' phenomenon and its effects on economic systems, particularly in China. The paper will introduce the concept of the 'insider control' phenomenon and its background, such that a clear view with respect to the derivation of the 'insider control' can be seen. Then, the Chinese case and its impact upon the economic reforms process will be discussed. It is followed by the use of the open-system concept to try to understand the emergence and spread of such a phenomenon, in order to examine the usefulness and plausibility of using Critical Systems Thinking (Jackson, 1991) to guide a systems-based inquiry into ways of solving or dissolving 'insider control'. The importance of this approach is associated with the sustainability of Chinese economic development for the benefit of the Chinese nation and the world as a whole.

2. THE 'INSIDER CONTROL' PHENOMENON

According to Kim and Aoki (1995), 'Insider control' is a phenomenon whereby controlling rights in organisational enterprises are legally or actually seized by management whose interests are then strongly represented in strategic corporate decision-making. Primarily applicable to a phenomenon popular in transitional economies (e.g. the former Soviet Union, East European countries and more recently China), however, this term is actually associated with business managers colluding with shop-floor workers to seek private gains at the expense of the wider organisational system (normally the State suffers the most).

The phenomenon in these countries involved (except for China) share a common background associated with a sudden political change causing a 'power vacuum'. This has led to the insiders, who had acquired many privileges under the old system, seizing the opportunity to expand their influence and becoming the dominant owners of most privatised firms (Frydman, Pistor and Rapaczynski, 1995). Although it may be helpful for us to improve economic efficiency under certain circumstances, 'insider control' normally results in autonomy abuse so as to bring about more benefits to the insiders to the owners' cost. If the reformers cannot deal successfully with the problem of the domination of companies by the interests of the insiders, the emerging microeconomic reforms will be seriously degraded.

3. THE CHINESE 'INSIDER CONTROL' PHENOMENON

The Chinese incremental and experimental approach to the reforms, without enormous turbulence in the society, is completely different from the 'shock therapy' approach in the former Soviet Union and East European countries. The Chinese case of 'insider control', which was not subject to a 'power vacuum' caused by violent changes in the political system, emerged in the process of empowering the management in the three stages of enterprise reform. Perhaps it helps to explain the case by describing briefly the process of the Chinese economic reforms, in particular enterprise reform, since 1978.

The aim of such a reform was to achieve the transition towards a socialist market economy without major disruptions to the Chinese economy. Since 1978, China has been working hard at carrying out the policies of reforms and opening up to the outside world. From then on, China's real GNP has grown by around 10% per year except for a brief contraction in the late 1980's (Bolton, 1995). It was in 1984 that China entered the stage of all-embracing structural reforms of the economy, which focused on revitalising the State-Owned Enterprises (SOEs) because the SOEs represent 46% of industrial output currently, most urban employment, half of all exports, and most large-scale activities in the economy (World Bank, 1995).

The reform of the SOEs was accomplished in three stages (Chen Qingtai, 1995). At the first stage, in order to encourage liberation of the SOEs from the State bureaucratic control and planning, Chinese authorities empowered the SOE managers to retain a percentage of profits and to make limited strategic planning, with the aim of a drive towards market orientation. This was the beginning of decentralised decision-making for the SOEs. Because there were some governmental departments responsible for the operation of the SOEs, it was impossible for the insiders to take full control of the enterprises.

At the second stage, a new Enterprise Law was implemented, which prescribed how the enterprises should be managed and operated. During that period, the main theme was to introduce the Contract Responsibility System and Managerial Responsibility System into the SOEs, since they had worked miracles in the countryside. The aim then was to liberate and empower individual managers to make full use of their potential. The running of the SOEs was assigned to the top manager in charge, confirming that the SOEs should be profit-earning units in themselves rather than relying on the State to organise their material sources and product marketing. It, for the first time, partially separated the operational rights from the ownership of the SOEs. This meant that the managers were freed from many former bureaucratic controls, and many of the government departments in charge of the SOEs were gradually abolished. This, on the one hand, gave the managers more freedom to run the enterprises with more creative entrepreneurship. On the other hand, it created managerial reliance on their subordinates so that they could maximise short-term profitability to meet contractual targets. The insecurity with short-term contracts (normally one to three years) had perhaps pushed the managers to fall into a dangerous trap that was later identified as the 'insider control' phenomenon. Even though overall profitability was greatly improved during that stage, more profit was shared out among the workers than was re-invested back into the business. According to the official statistics, Chinese personal earnings in 1993 accounted for 65.0% of the national GDP, whilst in 1978 it only stood for 50.5% (Statistical Yearbook of China, 1994).

At the third stage, there was concentrated effort to implement further new legislation concerned with the construction of a market-oriented managerial mechanism for the SOEs. This was intended to make a clear distinction between the responsibilities of the government and those of the enterprise managers, in order to have the SOEs run by professional managers without too much outside interference. Prior to this initiative, the SOE managers were chiefly concerned with involvement in sorting out the workers' social welfare, housing, nursery, medical care and so on, while a mayor or a provincial governor was mainly anxious about the running of the SOEs. Because the abolishment of governmental intervention and the empowerment of the enterprise managers occurred almost at the same time, the SOE managers assumed the functions which previously belonged to the State to make decisions and distribute profits without any kind of restriction. That may be the very important reason why the 'insider control' phenomenon has flourished in recent years.

The main theme here had been a conflict for benefits and rights between the enterprise managers and the government. Although the purpose of the economic reforms had been gradual empowerment to emphasise better managerial incentives, Chinese authorities had no experience for how to control the macroeconomy after changing their roles. As a result, the SOEs suffered from the violent shakes between 'hyper-strong external control' and 'hyper-weak external control'.

It will help us to understand the 'insider control' phenomenon by explaining the above two types of external control in more detail. 'Hyper-strong external control' refers to the situation in which the SOEs have no property rights of their own, not even being allowed to act independently as corporations. They can be seen only as enlarged workshops for the 'big company' (the State in China's case). The government has full control of the fate of SOEs, including merging some loss-making SOEs with other profitable ones, changing enterprise managers and so on. The managers are actually 'dummies' with no real power. Under such conditions, the SOE managers have no possibility to obtain control of the enterprises so that 'insider control' could not possibly occur at that time.

'Hyper-weak external control' refers to the situation in which the insiders try to expand their power and influence throughout their management process, both mentally and in action. The insiders want to be free from any form of external controls, such as that of government institutions. Because the insiders do not have, or only have a small part of, the ownership, the results have been that many have put their individual interests above anything else and try to 'transform' the State or societal properties into their own by every possible means. It is in this situation that the 'insider control' phenomenon flourishes with shocking cases of corruption, theft, fraud and criminal offences by the insiders, often collectively. For example, in a factory of about four hundred people in Guangxi Province, more than one hundred people were involved in a serious fraud (Yin, 1996a).

Despite the fact that the Chinese economy has made amazing progress since 1978, little has been questioned about the real cost to the whole society in the long run. It is argued that the economic gains of China came at a very high cost in terms of investment and labour input (World Bank, 1990). Such costs can take the form of low efficiency in utilising materials and capitals, and huge damage to the environment. As Meier (1989) stated, poor productive performance has been the main growth hindrance in many developing economies, and China is no exception. Further growth of the Chinese economy may not be sustained if it occurs without sufficient improvement in efficiency. Hence, we recommend the use of modern systems thinking to analyse and critically reflect upon the economic reform process. This is undertaken with particular reference to the enterprise reform process, so that strategies can be rethought and reformulated with new insights such that sustainability can be injected into the whole economic reform process.

4. A SYSTEMIC VIEW OF THE 'INSIDER CONTROL' PHENOMENON

A useful start can be made by using the concept of Open Systems Theory, first advocated by L. von Bertalanffy (1950). The case of the outsiders and insiders fighting for dominance while not being able to co-operate with each other can be viewed as two closed systems fighting for their own survival without realising their interdependence as open systems. For example, the Chinese government assumes that it is the SOE managers who are responsible for poor productivity, and that if they empower the factory managers, the efficiency of the whole industry will be improved. For fear that managers might abuse their authorities, however, the government still maintain their hold of the appointment power. The managers also imagine that gaining full control of the SOEs will permit them to run it better. Both parties failed to realise and understand the influences of the environment. Actually it is the workers who are the biggest stakeholders because their fate is totally connected with that of the firms. Owing to the incompleteness of the labour market, they cannot easily be re-employed after dismissal. That is just like putting all of the eggs you have into one basket. If the basket fell down, you would have nothing left. Under such a circumstance, the workers tend to force their managers to increase their salary no matter whether the firm goes into the red or not. That is why the more power given to the managers, the greater losses the SOEs have suffered (Yin, 1996b).

For the Chinese SOEs to contribute to the sustainable economic growth in China, both the enterprise management and the bureaucrats must learn the fact that most of the human activity systems are open systems, which permit continuous exchanges with the environment. The workers are not the same as they were, and neither is the culture. The interdependence between the insiders and the outsiders must be viewed as this: freedom without due control is anarchy, while control without freedom means suffocation. Both the insiders and the outsiders must learn to achieve a dynamic homeostasis, which can be realised through finding their own identities and carrying out their own roles, while not trying to live by getting at each other's throat. It is not necessary to list all the essentials of open systems theory such as entropy/negative entropy, structure/ function/ differentiation/ integration, requisite variety, equifinality and systems evolution, and their consequential insights for the Chinese management academics and practitioners to understand more of the 'insider control' phenomenon (Morgan, 1986). This must be done elsewhere. This paper has created a channel to direct the Chinese reformers' attention to the usefulness of modern Western systems thinking, in this case the Open Systems Theory.

When we analyse the 'insider control' phenomenon from a systems point of view, we find that we need to study the inter-relationship between the insiders and outsiders and their relationships with other stakeholders. We also need to study the emergent properties coming out of these inter-relationships. We need to take a holistic view about the 'insider control' phenomenon, i.e. looking at the whole Chinese economic reform process rather than simply dwelling on the phenomenon itself. The insiders and outsiders are both essential elements of the whole process. They are also systems in their own right. Every kind of stakeholder in the above-mentioned problem situations may have different expectation of benefits and interests for their own sakes. From this point of view, we find that Critical Systems thinking, especially its commitment to human emancipation, can be more relevant to us in dealing with the 'insider control' phenomenon in our further study.

5. CONCLUSION

In this paper, we have tried to portray the 'insider control' phenomenon which has been a major hindrance to the Chinese economic reforms and further sustainable development of the economy. More importantly, sustainable economic development in China will not be realised if the enterprise management in particular are only interested in pursuing and fulfilling their technical interest. Our main concern has been the problem exemplified by the 'insider control' phenomenon, i.e. the problem of incapability to deal with an open-system problem situation confronting the present Chinese reformers and the SOE management. The problem may be one of empowerment without real emancipation. By emancipation, we mean that human beings should be allowed to develop their full potential through undistorted communications between each other. In China, people have been used to the idea of finding 'birds of the same feather' while having problems with benefiting from 'birds of different feathers from ours'. Such may be the problem caused by the closed-system approach. Having our doors open to the world, an era of open-system thinking has come. We suggest that it is perhaps high time for the Chinese reformers to seek inspiration from modern Western systems thinking, in particular Critical Systems Thinking. An analysis of the 'insider control' phenomenon is only the beginning of our research into the whole Chinese economic reform process. Bearing in mind the heavy losses incurred by the SOE in recent years, we believe our research will at least add new insight to what is really desired to achieve a sustainable economic reform and sustainable development for China.

6. ACKNOWLEDGMENT

We are greatly indebted to our teacher R. Keith Ellis for his insights and wisdom. Without his help and encouragement, we can not finish this paper. We also want to thank our friend D.P. Dash for his constructive suggestions.

REFERENCES

Bertalanffy, Ludwig von, 1950, The theory of open systems in physics and biology. *Science* **3**: 23–29.
Bolton, P., 1995, Privatisation and the separation of ownership and control: Lessons from Chinese enterprise reform, *Economics of Transition*, **3**: 1–12.

Checkland, P., 1981, *Systems Thinking, Systems Practice*, John Wiley & Sons, Chichester.

Chen, Min, 1995, *Asian Management Systems: Chinese, Japanese and Korean Styles of Business*, Routledge, London.

Chen, Qingtai, 1995, Foreword, in: *Corporate Governance in Transitional Economies: Insider Control and the Role of Banks* (Chinese edition, Aoki and Qian eds.), Chinese Economic Press, Beijing.

Frydman, R., Pistor, K. and Rapaczynski, A., 1995, Corporate governance in an insider-dominated economy: A report on Russia, *Economics of Transition*, **3**: 107–111.

Jackson, M.C., 1991, *Systems Methodology for the Management Sciences*, Plenum Publishing Company, New York.

Kim, Hyung-Ki and Aoki, Masahiko, 1995, English introduction, in: *Corporate Governance in Transitional Economics: Insider Control and the Role of Banks* (Chinese edition, Aoki and Qian eds.), Chinese Economic Press, Beijing.

Meier, Gerald M (ed.), 1989, *Leading Issues in Economic Development*, Oxford University Press, Oxford.

Morgan, G., 1986, *Images of Organisation*, Sage Publication.

Pyke, D. F., 1996, China syndrome *OR/MS Today*, **22**: 24–28.

State Statistic Bureau, 1994, *Statistical Yearbook of China*, China Statistical Press, Beijing.

Stewart, A. M., 1994, *Empowering People*, Pitman Publishing.

World Bank, 1990, *China: Macroeconomic Stability and Industrial Growth under Decentralised Socialism*, Washington, DC.

World Bank, 1995, *Reform of China's State-Owned Enterprises*, a World Bank report, Nov/Dec.

Yin,Yan, 1996a, Collective corruption in a Guangxi SOE, (1996, August 19). *Singtao Electronic Daily*, p. 1.

Yin,Yan, 1996b, China's SOE in red, (1996, August 21). *Singtao Electronic Daily*, p. 1.

64

INVESTIGATIONS ON THE INFLUENCE OF THE GLOBAL SYSTEM OF INSTRUMENTAL CIVILIZATION ON THE GLOBAL ECONOMY AND THE MATHEMATICAL APPROACH FOR SOFT SYSTEMS ANALYSIS AND EVALUATION

Wiktor H. Adamkiewicz

Technical University of Gdańsk
Department of Production Systems Designing
Gdynia Maritime Academy
Department of Basic Engineering Sciences
ul. Powstania Œl¹skiego 10 C/9
81-462 Gdynia, Poland
E-mail: olga@vega.wsm.gdynia.pl

1. INTRODUCTION

In the scale of the whole globe exists a large system as a whole. It may have the designation "The System of Instrumental Civilization" - SIC (Adamkiewicz, 1983; 1995c). One may think that this great universal technical system has a great impact on all the people irrespectively of various divisions which exist among people's groups. It seems that at present, at the end of the 20th century, this impact on people's mentality and their behaviour is not smaller than the impact of gravitation, or also the necessity to use atmospheric oxygen in the process of breathing.

While dealing with the technical problems, it has been generally accepted to divide all people into three groups in respect to the function they perform, that is: designers, producers, and users of products. The aim is to show that the prevailing sphere is the stage of the using of the goods.

I introduced the notion of SIC in order to qualify the relations and their hierarchy among the components of a man's production operation: designing-manufacturing-using. To describe this, I used the simple dependencies of binary mathematical logic. This it not the evidence for truthfulness of the statements. However, the closed loop of logical tautology confirms the correctness of the argument.

The SIC is composed of all devices, tools, engineering structures, and other products made by human beings. This system was self-created by normalisation, typisation and unification activities concerning all products in the global dimensions. This system was caused also by marketing activity, by rapid globalization of markets, by globalization of competitiveness and finances.

Not so long ago it was not the "global system" but only the set of many separated sets of goods. These sets were not connected to each other and meet different needs of different people's groups. These products were produced in small quantities for meeting needs in small regions. The range of qualitative and quantitative satisfying of needs was varied dependings on place, nationality, country, etc.

2. THE SYSTEM OF INSTRUMENTAL CIVILIZATION (Adamkiewicz, 1995C)

The main properties of the SIC system, such as social, economical, organisational and technical are independent of the regional differences. Some differences depend only on external symptoms of technology. The SIC system is still in transformation and develops independently of boundaries. The main problem is the SIC system absorbs more and more resources for its needs, to support its self-existence and for its future development. That problem is perceived only in fragments.

The whole contemporary human activity consists in utilizing various objects while achieving different aims. These objects can be: people and teams of people, animals and plants, materials, energy, information, technical devices, economic and technical systems.

Among these objects technical devices and the systems built on them play a special role. The aim of the existence of these products is to satisfy numerous and new needs generated in social systems. Especially full of technical devices is the productive sphere of human activity. It also refers to the intellectual work.

The avalanche of various equipment serving people devours at increasing rate the material and energy resources of our planet. A natural tendency is, therefore, to create these products in an economical way, which means they are not durable, less reliable and they satisfy the needs in a less effective way. This, in turn, results in the creation of complex, organizational - technical systems which make the utilization of these products more effective.

In all contemporary considerations the sense of the existence of technical products consists in performing certain roles for people. Yet, this is not the case. There are many more kinds of devices which exist only because there are other machines. Therefore, while analysing the problem in this way, one reflects upon all the relations of General Systems only from one side, that is from the people side. The relations that connect that system with people and societies are not only the relations which result from human needs and expectations. A significant part of these relations result from the needs of a technical system. The lack of such an approach has led, for instance, to the situation that people became aware of the ecological threats too late.

In order to make the effective application of the above assumptions let us introduce the following notions: the process of scientific-technical revolution O_R, the system of instrumental civilization SIC, the process of designing P, the system of designing S_P, the process of production W, the system of production S_W, the process of operation E, the system of operation S_E. The systems S_P, S_W, S_E and the processes have already been defined and widely discussed upon in the available bibliography. Let us assume that there exists a certain supersystem consisting of (Adamkiewicz, 1995): U - the set of all technical devices created by man, W - the set of all products which are not devices, but produced by means of devices, L - the set of all people who at the present moment have something to do with devices or products, R_U, R_W, R_L - the set of the relations among the elements in the sets U, W, L; R_{UW}, R_{UL}, R_{WL} - the set of the relations among the elements of the set U, W, L, R_C - the system productive relation.

The environment of this system consists of: N - the set of all natural physical elements existing in the reality, B - the set of all existing biological elements. In the environment the process of intellectual human activity I_i proceeds. System SIC exchanges with the environment: matter (also biomatter), energy (also bioenergy), information (also biological). SIC receives and generates the psychosociological impulses. SIC keeps a constant physical contact with man in a discrete way (through its elements). The psychosocial contact is discrete, but its impact on man is constant. In the system SIC there exist: the general system of designing S_P, the general system of production S_W, the general system of operation S_E.

It results from considerations presented in paper (Adamkiewicz, 1995c) that the system of designing S_P, the system of production S_W and the system of operation S_E are not the result of the partition of the system of Instrumental Civilization S_C into subsystems, since such a partition as it is shown there, does not enable the realisation of the postulate of separation, one of the general postulates of systems engineering. Then it results that the general ("global") system of designing S_P and the general ("global") system of production S_W are the subsystems of the general ("global") system of operation S_E.

Global system of operation is equal to the global system of service's production. It is necessary to have in mind that there are essential differences between the developing Western Countries and other regions of the globe. Only the quantity of the technical goods is comparable. The supply and maintenance systems are completely different. There is also a very interesting technical culture. It is based on special contacts between each other inside social groups. It seems necessary to conduct comparative studies in "developping regions/undeveloped countries" on the influence of innovation processes on: relations to knowledge, relations to innovation, relations to heritage, people mentality, people behaviour inside native society and on relations to strangers, relations to hitherto duties, relations to ethical standards and to religions rights, relations to political, national and other such problems. It is possible to hypothesis that: The general trend of development of human behaviour (Human mind) is the same (now!) all over the world.

3. THE SERVICE FOCUS

It appears that on a world-wide scale, the global system of operation (of using all the goods produced) is the supersystem for the global system of designing (designing all the goods produced) and the global system of production (of manufacturing all the goods). So, it should be presumed that the global system of operation influences the designing and manufacturing of all the goods. This is simply because people use various goods. By using the goods produced, certain tastes, opinions and even mentality of people and the communities are formed. This refers as well to those people who are involved in designing and manufactiring the goods since people use various goods also in the course of the operations process, that is while designing and manufacturing.

The problems of "operation" have been given much attention but usually refers only to the use of the means of operation in the process of production (manufacturing). However, the problem of usage of the goods beyond the production process has not been discussed. Some aspects of this problem have been mentioned only recently while considering the problems within the scope of service focus. This problem has also been considered on a very specific and fragmentary way within the sphere of marketing. Meanwhile for instance, in the USA the service sector represents more than two thirds of America's gross national product (GNP), about 75 percent of the U.S. work force, and as much as 90 percent of new employment (Shaw, 1990).

It is important to be aware of the fact that the goods used are of two kinds: the ones manufactured within professional systems of production and the ones manufactured within the scope of cottage industry. Both kinds of goods are subject to trade turnover and they are used in two ways: in the system ensuring services (i.e. repairs, overhauls, etc), and in the cottage-worker's way.

The relations between those ways of usage and the ways of production are complicated. We can even go deeper into this classification but then the problem will seem to be more complex.

Within the scope of social sciences there are studies on influence of the usage of various goods on development of societies. It refers mainly to information processing and the ways of moving godds and people. These are, however, fragmentary studies relating to individual goods (Hagedoorn, 1995; Hickman, 1990; Hicks, 1988). It is presumed that the global formulation of this problem can lead to achieving some surprising results.

It is worth recalling the example of the problems connected with ecology. Nobody has been able to foresee the extent of devastation in natural environment. Only when the results had been seen with the naked eye, was a relatively serious response made.

Nowadays we observe a rapid globalization process of economies. Financial operations, production, goods turnover, competition are carried out on a world-wide scale. At the same time, national, corporate and regional markets are artificially separated and protected. The economic analyses refer to states, corporations and selected economic branches. There has been observed no generalization attempts.

As a matter of fact, economic development is studied only fragmentarily. And on such principles the economic strategies are built.

The problem in question is not noticed. It may not prove that the lack of appropriate analyses leads to a total surprise and economic difficulties on a world-wide scale.

4. THE INVESTIGATIONS OF THE SIC INFLUENCE ON THE GLOBAL ECONOMY

I dare say, the most important aspect in systems research is the Synergistic Effect evaluation. It is the case with the SIC influence on the global economy. In such studies there are two possible variants: studying the system as a whole and then analysing its components after decomposition of the system, or studying particular components and then their aggregation (summing up) to the whole system. In the second instance the Synergistic Effect may or not may be detected. However, one cannot be sure that the effect in the whole range has been detected because the essence of the Synergistic Effect lies in the additional relations between the components of the system. These are relations which are not revealed in the course of studying individual components. Particular components may also show certain new features, which are not revealed in individual components.

In my view, only in the course of decomposition of the system, can all relations be detected, and among them also those which constitute the Synergistic Effect. Such relations obviously result from certain features of the components. I am of the opinion that direct search for and study of those features is meaningless because they manifest themselves only within the system as a whole causing exactly the Synergistic Effect. We can presume that these features are of a very complex character and depend on all other features of the component. So, those component features that cause the Synergistic Effect within the system can be studied and defined indirectly. The starting point for such studies should be the previous designation of the relations causing the Synergistic Effect.

On the basis of the presented opinions it appears that the key problem in studying the Synergistic Effect is the competence for detecting all possible relations found within the system. In the systems in question, there are many relations. It is not possible to study all relations simultaneously. So, it is very essential to classify the relations property and study them in respect of hierarchy. It is inadvisable to carry out such operations intuitively. The error margin can be too large. On the other hand, it is advisable to use the appropriate mathematical models in order to classify the relations and study them in respect of hierarchy.

Propositions for the prediction of features of a system suggested in this paper are based on three independent ways of investigation (Adamkiewicz, 1983; Barrow, 1991).

1. Are the investigations of real systems in real conditions. Then the first question is a relation between a feature of the whole system and the same feature of the components of the system.

The second and the third are the investigation of possibilities to solve a multicriterion problem, when the components of the problem are not comparable to each other—firstly: its measures are incomparable.

2. Is based on geometrical considerations. If we have a task to investigate many components together it is convenient to describe such a situation as a space with the adequate ("n") number of dimensions. Then the general model is an n-dimensional Riemann's space. Each dimension is suitable to one component, one measure and so on. In this space we can put a tensor. Simplyfying: tensor is a generalized vector situated in n-dimensional space (see: any manual "Riemann's Geometry & Tensor Calculus" or a paper from this field, for instance: Wong, 1943). This tensor may be also n-dimensional. In general if we define a general tensor we do not need to define dimensions. In the next step (if we need) we define the measures' tensors. Without the measures' tensors we may investigate the invariants of our task. The measure tensors make a space very complicated. Euclidean laws of geometry are not convenient to such a space. However, it seems to be the only possibility to describe a multicriterion task in a mode adequate to reality.

3. Is an algebraical one. The mentioned geometrical problem was solved by Albert Einstein on an algebraic way on the basis of the Ricci-Riemann's calculus. It is so called the indexed tensor notation.

The use of enumerated mathematical methods is simple. It is enough to understand the general ideas. We define a general Riemann's tensor adequate to our needs then search (or not) for invariants of the problem. Then we define a measure's tensor and in such a way we will obtain an n-dimensional space of our task in curved co-ordinates. Then we put an adequate simplifying assumptions with this end in view—to receive an n-dimensional space with the Euclidean geometry and, if we need, we put the next presumption—and we receive n-dimensional Euclidean space with rectangular co-ordinates.

Yet, on the basis of each two dimensions we can construct a matrix and we can investigate relations between each two components of our task.

The relations between elements can be arranged by the definitions given in a relations theory but only when we want to make further use of this theory. However, it is not necessary. The relations can be arranged in any way.

The system understood in such a way can be created for any set of elements that we are interested in. The elements can be of material, energy, information or discrete (sets of notions) nature. The most essential problem is the identified relations analysis, their classification and hierarchization from the point of view of a significance test. But in this respect it is better to create some mathematical models for particular set of relations (Wintgen, 1971).

In each system are some processes. The elements of the system take part in those processes by means of the relations connecting them with other elements and the surrounding reality. So, also the relations undergo certain changes. The changes in each relation are arranged as well in a certain process (I assume that everybody understands the process as a state sequence at real time—particular states need not follow continuously—the sequence may also be of a discrete character).

Comparison and hierarchization of relations are possible only when we are able to present them in a combined form. The most convenient form is, in my opinion, to create the matrices for particular sets of relations. The elements of these matrices, in other word the relations, will be the functions dependent on time or the constants.

The point is to form the matrices in which the relations will be seen in an orderly way. The further investigations will be based on a logical analysis. The matrices will be treated as the data boards. Particular matrices will be compared with one another by means of a time axis, which will be common for all the matrices.

Necessary knowledge of particular mathematical branches resolves itself merely into understanding the essence of this branch, in other words into its language. Operational skill is not indispensable.

The procedure was used by the Author for solving some other problems (for instance: Adamkiewicz, 1990a; 1990b, 1995a; 1995b). Practically important results are presented for instance in Adamkiewicz 1995a, 1995b, as a "General Bases for Forming Heuristic Algorithm of Designing". In "Cybernetic Aspects of Technical Objects Investigations" (Adamkiewicz, 1983), (published unfortunately only in Polish), some mathematical tools are presented that can be used in the systems research. I have not come across any considerations of this type in an accessible (for me) bibliography.

REFERENCES

Adamkiewicz, W.H., 1983, *Cybernetyczne aspekty badania obiektów technicznych*, Wydawnictwo Polskiej Akademii Nauk OSSOLINEUM, Wroc³aw.

Adamkiewicz, W.H., 1990a, *The method of aiding the designing of the management systems*. 11th Intern. Cost Engineering Cogress and 6th AFITEP Annual Meeting, Proc. of the 11th AFITEP'90, France, Paris.

Adamkiewicz, W.H., 1990b, *Designing the management system as a set of subsystems of differently oriented aims*. Proc. of the Xth INTERNET'90 World Congress on Project Management - "Management by Projects", Manz-Verlag, Austria, Vienna.

Adamkiewicz, W.H., 1995a, *Some general bases for designing the utilisation system for technical devices*. IMAM'95 - VIIth Congress of the International Maritime Association of Mediterranean. Dubrovnik, (Croatia).

Adamkiewicz W.H., 1995b, *System's models for designing the organisational restructirization of companies during the process of the ownership changes*. Published in: *Critical Issues in Systems Theory and Practice*, Plenum Publishing Corporation, New York (U.S.A.)

Adamkiewicz W.H., 1995c, *The system of Instrumental civilization*. 14th Intern. Congress on Cybernetics, Symposium on Synergistic Effects of Local and Global Developments on our Lives and on our Future. Namur, (Belgique).

Barrow J.D., 1991, *Theories of everything. The Quest for Ultimate Explanation.* Oxford University Press, New York (U.S.A.)

Hagedoorn J. (ed.), 1995, *Technical change and the world economy. Convergence and divergence in technology strategies.* Publ.: Edward Algar Publishing Limited, Aldershot, G.B.

Hickman L.A., 1990, *Technology as a human affair.* McGraw-Hill Publishing Company, (U.S.A.)

Hicks D.A. (ed.), 1988, *Is new technology enough? Making and remaking U.S. basic industries.* American Enterprise Institute for Public Policy Research, Washington D.C. (U.S.A.)

Shaw J.C., 1990, *The service focus. Developping Winning Game Plans for Service Companies.* Dow-Jones-Irwin, Homewood, U.S.A., Illinois.

Wintgen G.J., 1971, *Zur mengentheoretischen Definition und Klassifizierung kybernetischer Systeme.* In:Mathematic und Kybernetik in Oekonomie (III), Humboldt Universitaet zu Berlin.

Wong Y.Ch., 1943, *Some einstein spaces with conformally separable fundanmental tensors*, Trans. Amer. Math. Soc., 53.

65

ADDING STRUCTURE TO THE CULTURAL ANALYSIS OF SSM

Andrew Barnden and Christina Lo

Department of Information Systems
Monash University
Caulfield East, 3135, Australia

1. INTRODUCTION

Information systems practitioners are aware that Soft Systems Methodology (SSM) can help to explicate perceived problems in an organisation. It can also clarify the views held by individuals and groups in that organisation. Once a problematic situation is well understood, proposals for improvement can be developed by the would-be problem solvers, then be put to the organisation for action. SSM is a flexible methodology whose various techniques can be applied to propose improvement in a problematic situation whilst accommodating the varying perceptions of the individuals in that situation.

The methodology is continually changing as a result of learning gained from its use in organisations. Current SSM provides two streams of enquiry; logic-based enquiry and cultural enquiry. The logic-based enquiry processes have been well defined by Checkland and others. (Checkland, 1981; Checkland and Scholes, 1990; Patching, 1990; Wilson, 1984).

The cultural enquiry comprises three analyses: Analyses One, Two and Three. These three analyses concentrate on, respectively, the intervention of would-be problem solvers in the problematic situation, the situation as a 'social system' and, the disposition and exercise of power within the situation. This paper will explore only Analysis Two. Checkland and Scholes (1990) model the social system in a problematic situation as interacting roles (socially recognised positions), norms of behaviour and the values by which role-holders are judged. They based this on Vickers' appreciative system concept and the later interpretation of it by Checkland and Casar (1986). The model as used in SSM gives only a brief definition of roles, norms and values. The interpretation of each has been left up to the user. This paper aims to identify the indicators of culture which are relevant to an understanding of the roles, norms and values of Analysis Two by using some of the established literature on roles, norms and values from the discipline of anthropology.

2. CULTURE IN CONTEXT

Cultural knowledge is difficult to enquire into because there are many hidden assumptions which are not determinable through observing the actions of people. Some of those hidden assumptions relate to the different perceptions people have of any given situation which greatly influence their judgements and decisions about a situation.

The concept of culture originated from the field of anthropology, within which is the socio-cultural stream. It considers the ways in which culture is developed and shaped; unique and different cultures; and how culture can be learned. Culture is an adaptive system where socially transmitted behaviour patterns can occur in human communities in their ecological settings. Such settings that occur in the community include technological, economic and political organisation (Keesing, 1981). Kroeber and Kluckhohn (1952) have found one hundred and sixty-four definitions of culture and have put them into seven categories based on the main emphases in each definition. Each of the emphases stresses a different perspective on culture depending on the situation and the problem being addressed (Hisako, 1988). It is assumed that the concept of an 'organisational culture' is accepted as this is a necessary tenet of SSM. Many of the definitions have implied that 'culture is ubiquitous' and it occurs in all walks of life (Schein, 1990). As information systems represent, support and implement the practices of groups of people, the study of culture is relevant to the information systems analyst.

According to Schein (1990), the analysis of culture should be examined from three perspectives: observable artefacts; values; and basic underlying assumptions. Observable artefacts are the physical tools and material used and displayed in an organisation. Values are the way people feel, think and judge in a given situation. Basic underlying assumptions refer to the unconscious assumptions that are made in the thought processes, feelings, behaviour and perceptions. Elements of these three perspectives are artefacts, languages, myths, beliefs, ideology, rituals, metaphors, stories, symbols and legends.

3. A CULTURAL ANALYSIS FRAMEWORK

From this literature we have synthesized a framework which will provide a theoretical support for the analysis of culture in an organisation. It provides guide-lines for identifying cultural indicators which should be considered in any SSM study. Having used the framework to identify cultural factors, their interpretation in any particular study remains specific to the context of that study.

Language, myth, ritual, ideology, artefacts and stories were extracted as cultural indicators for the framework because of their occurrence in, and significance for organisations. Each of the indicators will be discussed in the context of the roles, norms and values of Analysis Two.

3.1. Language

Language is a symbolic representation of ideas and meanings in a social situation. The three cultural elements of roles, norms and values are expressed in the symbolism of language. A role or social position has a name or label which is a word in our language. That word represents a concept that is the meaning of the role. The concept associated with a word can vary between organisations and even within parts of one organisation, but in its context it references the particular meaning of the word.

Norms are the expected behaviours people must demonstrate when playing a role. Expectations of behaviour are communicated through language and normal behaviour may include the use of particular forms of language. These forms identify a member of the culture.

Values are those particular standards for behaviour by which performance in a role is judged. The skill and appropriateness of the use of particular language forms by a role player is judged relative to the standards for that role and their performance is valued accordingly.

3.2. Myth

A role may have a myth associated with it. Myths recount apocryphal stories or events which have been passed from person to person over time. They reflect the values and ideal-type beliefs generally held about particular roles within an organisation. Those values and beliefs from the myth can have a major effect on the norms of behaviour. As the myth is told, the members of the organisation may recognise the fantasies behind it, yet relate to the essence of the myth and give it credence in their social structure. Revealing the meaning behind myths can reflect the expected nature of the social behaviour of an organisation. As the myth is first told, the beliefs and values of the organisational culture also begin to develop, laying the foundation for the expected behavioural standard. Thus the myth establishes a basis for the standard norms of behaviour.

3.3. Ritual

Ritual has the power to legitimise certain practices and to identify a member's social position within the organisation. It is a set of procedures which people perform repeatedly and not necessarily with deliberate logical justification. It can be seen in the everyday tasks being performed in the same way in an organisation. Each member has their own set of tasks to perform. By knowing what a person's tasks are, one can classify the social position which they hold within the organisation. Ritual repetition gives a sense of certainty and security but may entrench behaviour which may no longer be necessary or even desirable for the organisation.

3.4. Ideology

Ideology 'refers to a collection of ideas and values as to how the social world appears and how it should function' (Alvesson and Berg, 1992). In the case of an organisation, ideology plays the part of providing the guiding or defining ideas and values to every member.

Within each organisation, there are certain sets of behaviours which members must follow. These come from the organisational ideology, often formed by the founder of the organisation. In order to remain with the organisation, members will act accordingly and the organisation expects such behaviour. In addition to the right skills, members are expected to have the right attitude and devotion to the task. Actions which do not accord with the dominant ideology may be perceived as problematic by the mainstream of the organisation.

3.5. Artefacts

There are many different social positions held within an organisation and each social position is required to take on certain tasks. In order to complete the tasks, special tools or equipment are required to perform the tasks efficiently and effectively. Such tools or equipment are the material artefacts which role players need to use. There is always a purpose for using the artefact in a job. In addition, there may be underlying meaning and value behind the artefacts. For example, a secretary has a computer as an artefact. It is a tool which is used every day. The purpose in using the computer is for word processing and other administrative work. However, the underlying reason for using the computer is that the information which the secretary requires to do his work is only available in the computer network. The organisation has standardised and stored all the data in a centralised computer database. Therefore, if the secretary is to survive and continue working in the organisation he must follow the organisational standard and use this artefact.

Artefacts can influence organisational members to act in a certain way, revealing the expected behaviour in a role. Although it might not be immediately obvious what an artefact symbolises nor how it directly affects a role, it usually contains some underlying meaning which is relevant and persistent but not consciously overt. For example, a project manager will use a Gantt chart as an artefact, for a project. In his position he is expected to use tools such as Gantt charts to plan all aspects of the different stages of a project, including human resources, duration of the tasks, technical resources etc. The Gantt chart helps to reinforce what is expected from a project manager, such as giving direction and dividing tasks amongst the members. The project manager uses such artefacts to perform his tasks more efficiently and effectively. Artefacts also have direct influence over the project manager's job performance, causing him to behave in an authoritarian way controlling the progress of the project. It is thus that organisational artefacts can have direct impact on social groups causing them to organise their behaviour and thought in relation to their social position and environment.

Artefacts also have an impact on the values held by an organisation because of their potential for beneficial economic effect on role performance. Members are judged by how well they have used their artefacts to perform their job.

3.6. Stories

The roles people play in an organisation are affected by organisational stories. The stories, as distinct from myths, are important historical events which the organisation values. The valued reputation of a previous manager, recounted in the stories of courageous acts and brilliant strategic decisions may affect the performance of the next incumbent. That person might feel the pressure of the previous manager's reputation and perceive a need to live up to this reputation. This can prevent the new incumbent from doing things their own way because of the stories told about the predecessor.

Stories hold concrete, vivid truths about sequences of historical events. Each of these events has special meanings and values which people can learn from, and use as examples of how they should generally behave in an organisation. They are trusted frameworks of behaviour in cases of a similar situation occurring.

4. SUMMARY

Analysis Two of SSM can be extended by the use of this framework of cultural indicators in assisting examination of roles, norms and values in a given situation. This research has been successful in revealing the principal indicators of organisational culture. It is useful to the analyst in that the indicators allow the for surfacing of underlying mean-

Table 1. Cultural analysis framework

Indicators	Elements		
	Roles	Norms	Values
Language	Do special words denote social positions? Are special words only used by certain social positions?	What are the phrases, jargon, words expected to be used in organisation? What do those words reflect about how they communicate with each other? Why?	Compare the actual usage of language with the expected language use.
Myth	Are there myths associated with the abilities of a specific role?	Are myths prevalent or apparent at any level in the organisation? Can aspects of the myth be seen in peoples' behaviour?	Are value judgements couched in terms of the myth? Compare the implicit behavioural standard of the myth with the actual behaviour.
Ritual	Is certain ritualised behaviour associated with a social position?	Observe the behavioural patterns in the ritual for any organisational significance.	Is the ritual valued to any degree as evidenced by language, deference to ritualists etc?
Ideology	Can any social position or person be recognised as the possessor or guardian of received wisdom?	Are there general ideas/ thoughts which organisation proclaims?	Do the individuals in an organisation exhibit the proclaimed ideology of the organisation?
Artefacts	Are certain artefacts identified with a particular social position?	Are there recognisable artefacts used when performing a role?	Does possession of an artefact confer status or prestige? Are artefacts used as rewards for service?
Stories	Are there stories about a person's position which can affect the next person's social position?	Do stories reflect accepted or expected behaviour?	Are people using the stories' moral as a guide to their job in the organisation?

ings in an organisation's spoken language, artefacts, myths, rituals, ideology and stories. These indicators control an organisation's image, ideas and behaviour, because once the substance of the indicators are passed on to every organisational member, they will use them as a guide for themselves and as a judge of others in how they should act. However there may be many influencing factors that must be considered when being guided by this proposed framework. Its use is situation dependent because not all indicators are relevant in all situations. Novice analysts should not follow this framework blindly but choose that which is relevant in the situation. The extent of the intersubjective understanding of the culture under investigation by the analytical team may thus be enhanced by using the framework. The synthesis of this research appears as a set of proposed questions (Table 1) corresponding to each indicator element. These questions are indicative only.

The main purpose of each indicator is summarised as follows. Language is used to uncover the set of expected behaviours from the words used by organisational members. Myth can expose the beliefs of organisational members. It could hold some truth as to how members act within an organisation. Ritual discovers patterns of behaviour being performed consistently and reveals the reasons behind them. Ideology can portray the image of an organisation and, looking closely at how members help keep the organisation's image, will reveal the expected behaviour of members. Investigation can reveal why, and by whom such ideology is implemented. Artefacts reveal the tokens which both identify and rank role players. The morals in stories can have positive and negative effects on the way members perform their job.

The framework identifies these cultural indicators to reveal their relevance in better understanding of the roles, norms and values within a problematic situation. Each indicator may provide insights into the roles, norms and values so that the underlying meaning of an activity being performed by organisational members can be the better understood by the analyst.

REFERENCES

Alvesson, M and Olof Berg, P., 1992, *Corporate Culture and Organisational Symbolism*, de Gruyter, Berlin, New York.

Checkland, P.B., 1981, *Systems Thinking, Systems Practice*, John Wiley & Sons, Chichester.

Checkland, P.B. and Casar, A., 1986, Vickers' concept of an appreciative system: a systemic account. *Journal of Applied System Analysis.* **13:** 3–17.

Checkland, P.B. and Scholes, J., 1990, *Soft Systems Methodology in Action*, John Wiley & Sons, England.

Hisako, I., 1988, *Theoretica l framework of cross-cultural comparison: Reexamination of Studies on Japanese Communication Pattern,* Thesis(M.A.), Publisher: Michigan State University, Ann Arbor, Michigan.

Kessing, R.M., 1981, Theories of culture, in: *Language Culture and Cognition,* (R. W. Casson ed.) MacMillan Publishing Co. Inc., NewYork.

Kroeber, A. L. and Kluckholn, C., 1952, *Culture, A Critical Review of concepts and Definition,* The Harvard University Press, Massachussets.

Patching, D., 1990, *Practical Soft Systems Analysis,* Pitman Publishing, London.

Schein, E.H., 1990, Organisational Culture, *American Psychologist,* **45**(2):109–119.

Wilson, B., 1984, *Systems: Concepts, Methodologies and Applications*, John Wiley & Sons, Chichester.

66

SYSTEMS THINKING AND GAUGING SUSTAINABLE DEVELOPMENT

Simon Bell[1] and Stephen Morse[2]

[1]Systems Department
Open University
Walton Hall, Milton Keynes, MK7 6AA
[2]School of Development Studies
University of East Anglia
Norwich, NR4 7TJ

1. OVERVIEW

There has been a great deal of interest in how system sustainability can be measured. Assuming that sustainabililty reflects a consistency or improvement in some notion of system 'quality', then an ability to determine how the system 'quality' varies with time should give a handle on the sustainability of the system. System 'quality' can be gauged by the use of indicators such as soil fertility, forest cover and crop yields along with other indicators which reflect Socio-Economic 'quality' (income, employment rates, provision of services etc.) . However, although this approach has been commonly applied to a variety of systems (e.g. the AMOEBA), the problem lies in what indicators to use and how to measure them. Clearly the choice of indicators is critical, and one can find any answer one chooses by selecting a particular group of indicators. Different interest groups will have very different views as to the indicators that need to be included and how these indicators are to be gauged. In short, in studies assessing indicators of sustainability objectivity is a major problem and subjectivity on the part of the researcher should be assumed. In this paper we will review the use of sustainability indicators (SI) in a SI Measurement Tool (SIMT) and provide a theoretical critique of their applicability. The amoeba approach will be discussed and developed, and it will be demonstrated that the problem is essentially one of locating a 'credibility boundary' which any given group of major stakeholders with multiple viewpoints would accept as a key set of SI's for the system. However, the attainability of the 'credibility boundary' may be very low and it may be impossible, and hence the question becomes what level of SI integration is acceptable and yet be achievable. The problems associated with attempting to determine an acceptable and achievable level of SI integration are discussed.

Systems for Sustainability, edited by Stowell *et al.*
Plenum Press, New York, 1997

2. INTRODUCTION AND SYSTEMS BACKGROUND

We are all concerned with wholeness (a thing *is*). Following on from this we are concerned with the continuance or sustainability of the thing (a thing shall *continue* to be). The two idea; of is-ness and continuance of is-ness or sustainability are at the root of this paper and, could be argued to be at the root of the systems movement. But what is a system? For the purposes of this paper we take our definition from Senge (Senge, Ross et al. 1994)

> "A system is a *perceived* whole whose elements "hang together" because they continually affect each other over time and operate toward a common purpose. The word descends from the Greek verb sunistánai, which originally meant: " to cause to stand together". As this origin suggests, *the structure of a system includes the quality of perception with which you, the observer, cause it to stand together*" Emphasis added (p. 90).

So, in discussing systems sustainability we recognise at the outset that the "system" is an artificial devise, arising from our perception (the perception of a stakeholder in the system) and imposed upon some discrete part of reality. We see the system as a wholeness and seek to sustain it into the future. The most important feature of this discussion is that stakeholder perception, subjective and arising from a personal vision which includes all the mental baggage associated with the time/ space/ culture of the stakeholder, is the basis for the understanding of sustainability in any context. We, the stakeholders, define the "system" and define what we consider to be its sustainable features. It is from this core set of definitions and arising assumptions about the nature of the world that this paper arises.

3. THE SUSTAINABILITY BACKGROUND

The term 'sustainability' has become so entrenched into current paradigms of development that it is easy to imagine that the two have always been intertwined. However, this is not the case and the linkage has a relatively recent origin. For example, in 1993 (after the Earth Summit in Rio) we have the following quotation:

> "Sustainable development is an idea whose time has come."(Murdoch, 1993)

Just what comprises 'sustainable development' has been the subject of much debate, and there are almost as many views as there are workers in the field (Pettit and Sarwal, 1993). Indeed, one reason for its wide adoption may be due to it being 'everything to everyone' (O'Riordan, 1988). Problems with definition have dogged the sustainability debate. As a response, some have gone as far as to claim that no formal definition is necessary in order for sustainability to be put into practice (Gibbon, Lake and Stocking, 1995), although presumably one has to have at least a broad vision as to what one is trying to achieve.

It has been suggested that the current drive for sustainability has partly arisen as a response to the growing use of artificial inputs such as pesticides and fertiliser in agriculture since the second World War (Allen and Rajotte, 1990). Sustainable agriculture has become equated with a sort of 'green' or 'organic' approach to food production, and represents a sort of antithesis of 'modern' high-input agricultural systems. Today, 'sustainability' typically incorporates all manner of social, political, cultural and economic dimensions (Gibbon, Lake and Stocking, 1995). Indeed, herein has rested many of the difficulties with sustainability; in order for it to be achievable in practice and not just a rhetorical ideal then it has to be 'measurable', and in order for it to be 'measurable' one has to know what to 'measure' and how. After all, one can prove the same system to be both highly sustainable and unsustainable depending upon the choice of 'sustainability indicators' (SI's), or indeed if the same SI's are measured in different ways!

Nevertheless, in spite of the obvious difficulties the use of SI's has become very widespread (Gibbon, Lake and Stocking, 1995). Organisations currently involved in their development include the Organisation for Economic Cooperation and Development (OECD), United Nations Statistical Office (UNSO), Eurostat, Economic Commission for Europe (ECE), The World Bank, United Nations Environmental Program (UNEP), United Nations Commission on Sustainable Development (CSD), FAO, United Nations Development Program (UNDP), World Resources Institute and International Union for the Conservation of Nature (IUCN). Given this interest, SI's are clearly going to be with us for some time. However, there have been relatively few attempts to tackle the central conundrum of sustainability itself - a multiplicity of views regarding just what is important to 'sustain' and how this should be measured. This diversity of viewpoint is often ignored and instead the SI's refer to the viewpoint of just one group—typically the policy maker. As pointed out by Verbruggen and Kuik (Verbruggen and Kuik, 1991):

"Indicators of sustainable development should take account of the 'integrity' of natural elements and structures, and of the 'diversity' of species and systems."

We feel they should also take account of the diversity of viewpoints *of the same system* that different actors in that system will possess!

4. THE ARISING PREMISES FOR SI DEVELOPMENT

In this Section we build upon this foundation and set out the basic five premises for our analysis:

- Sustainability can provide a qualitative measure of the integrality and wholeness of any given system.
- Subjectivity on the part of the stakeholders in any given system (including researchers) is unavoidable.
- Subjectively derived measures of sustainability are useful if the subjectivity is explicitly accepted and declared at the outset and if the method for deriving the measures are available to a range of stakeholders in the context.
- Measures of sustainability can be valuable aids to planning and forecasting.
- Rapid and participatory tools for developing our thinking and modelling concerning measures of sustainability would be of value to a wide range of stakeholders within development policy.

5. SI AND AMOEBA—A SUGGESTION FOR MULTIPLE VIEWPOINT INDICATORS

Our focus is subjective and systemic but the tool for measuring SIs needs to be practical and useful. The key terms which we have used in defining the tool conform to principles of much contemporary analysis in development studies (e.g. see Chambers, 1992; Cook 1995; Slocum and Thomas-Slayter, 1995). For our purposes it should be *rapid, participatory, qualitative descriptive tool with the potential for prediction.*

1. Identify the stakeholders with multiple views and the system in view. The first point in the development of the SIMT is the establishment of the system to be measured. This would probably arise from a team of stakeholders. Tools for the development of such a team and the means to achieve cohesion and consensus are described elsewhere (e.g. see Thompson and Chudoba, 1994; Thompson 1995; Thompson (report, no date)). The stakeholder group would identify the system to be reviewed with the SIMT being careful in establishing that the system is a system. At this stage the system would probably refer to a task or main issue.

2. Identify the main SIs. SIs are subjective and dependent upon the stakeholder group and the dominant viewpoint of that group. This needs to be affirmed and recognised by the group but following this, in order to achieve a systems wide view of the item under analysis, SI's need to be drawn from a range of areas reflecting a holistic appreciation. SIs should reflect items that need to be balanced in order for the system to be sustained.

3. Identify the band of equilibrium. Measurement of SIs has dogged the literature. The focus of the approach advocated in this paper is to provide a SIMT which can be appreciated by a wide range of stakeholders without prior access to specialised measurement skills. In fact, the entire exercise can be undertaken by the stakeholder group based upon the agreed views and opinions of that group.

4. The development of the amoeba. So far the description given here is remarkable from other work only in that it is based an holistic and systemic approach to the factors which define the sustainability of a project, upon an explicit recognition of the subjectivity of the analysis and the ownership of stakeholders within the context of the analysis as a tool for reflection upon their context. Figure 1 shows the development of the original model into the amoeba. The main function of the amoeba is to provide a relatively instant presentation of the project's state of health in terms of its sustainability.

5. The extension of the amoeba over time. Each time the amoeba is drawn from a project review by stakeholders it gives an indication of the sustainability of a project in a snapshot. Over a period of time the amoeba might be seen to move over the surface of the quadrants with each significant movement being indicated by the SIs.

The resulting amoebic analysis would provide two informing products:

• The overall tendency over time of four major aspects of the project context and,
• A rapid review of what is of importance now in terms of the stakeholder response to the information provided.

The amoebic analysis set over time provides indications of continuance (or sustainability or equilibrium) within a given context from the standpoint of a stakeholder group. Of course other groups might have other ideas and might be candidates for amoebic analysis of their own. In all the analysis would need to lead to informed discussion and action on items agreed to be out of equilibrium. The authors are at present working on a simple to use computerised version of the amoebic simulation. In all, we feel that this would provide a useful group thinking devise for both understanding a projects basic performance

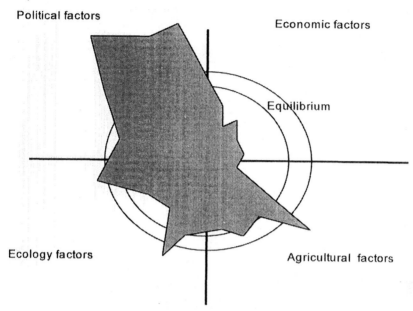

Figure 1. SI amoeba.

and would provide a level playing field between consultants, donors and recipients for discussion and debate concerning ultimate project focus and continuance of positive results.

REFERENCES

Allen, W. and Rajotte, E. G. 1990, The Changing Role of Extension Entomology in the IPM Era. Annual Review of Entomology 35: 379–397.

Chambers, R. 1992, Rural Appraisal: rapid, relaxed and participatory. Institute of Development Studies. Brighton.

Cook, J. 1995, Empowering People for Sustainable Development. In "Managing Sustainable Development in South Africa". (P. Fitzgerald, A. McLennan and B. Munslow. eds.). Oxford University Press, Cape Town.

Gibbon, D., Lake A and Stocking. M. 1995, Sustainable Development: a challenge for agriculture. In "People and Environment". (S. Morse and M. Stocking, eds.). UCL Press: 31–68. London.

Murdoch, J. 1993, "Sustainable Rural Development: towards a research agenda." Geoforum 24: 225–241.

O'Riordan, T. 1988, The Politics of Sustainability. In "Sustainable Environmental Management: principles and practice". (K. Turner, ed.) Pinter. Belhaven.

Senge, P., Ross, R., Smith, B., Roberts, C., et al. 1994, The Fifth Discipline Fieldbook: Strategies and tools for building a learning organisation. Nicholas Brealey. London.

Slocum, R. and Thomas-Slayter B. 1995, Participation, Empowerment and Sustainable Development. In "Power, Process and Participation: tools for change". (R. Slocum, L. Wichhart, D. Rocheleau and B. Thomas-Slayter, eds.). Intermediate Technology Publications. London.

Thompson, J. 1995, User Involvement in mental Health Services: the limits of consumerism, the risks of marginalisation and the need for a critical approach. Research Memorandum No. 8. Centre for Systems Studies, University of Hull. Hull

Thompson, M. (no date), A TeamUp Case Study: agriculture project design. , Team Technologies Inc. Report. Chantilly.

Thompson, M. and Chudoba R. 1994, Case Study Municipal and regional Planning in Northern Bohemia, Czech Republic: a participatory approach. World Bank Report. Washington DC.

Verbruggen, H. and Kuik O. 1991, Indicators of Sustainable Development: an overview. In "In Search of Indicators of Sustainable Development". (O. Kuik and H. Verbruggen, eds.). Kluwer Academic Publishers: 1–6. Dordrecht.

67

AN INVESTIGATION OF HEURISTICS USED IN THE CONSTRUCTION OF CONCEPTUAL MODELS

S. R. Boyle, R. Smith, K. Bluff, and R. B. Watson

School of Computer Science and Software Engineering
Swinburne University of Technology
Hawthorn, Australia 3122

1. INTRODUCTION

Conventional Soft Systems Methodology (SSM) is a seven stage process for tackling real-world problems, most commonly those associated with organisations (Checkland, 1981). The methodology has changed over the years, two recent developments being the recognition that the seven stage logic-driven stream of enquiry is inadequate without also considering the problem situation as a culture (Checkland and Scholes, 1990), and the recognition that the conventional real world/systems thinking world dichotomy may not be helpful (Tsouvalis and Checkland, 1996). The modelling process at the heart of SSM, in which root definitions (RD) are formulated and conceptual models (CM) are derived from them, has also been subjected to greater scrutiny. Among the questions which have been asked are: whether an explicit RD and CM are both necessary (Watson, 1991); the meaning of the logical dependency arrows in CMs (Gregory, 1993); and the nature of the link between the RD and CM (Checkland and Tsouvalis, 1996; Cross and Turk, 1996). This paper is concerned with the last question, and argues that the link between RD and CM is not as mechanical a process as some maintain, and indeed that the way in which experienced SSM practitioners construct CMs from RDs is still poorly understood. Section 2 of the paper sets out some arguments that the RD-CM link is problematic, and the justification for the present research. Section 3 discusses an experimental program to discover the heuristics used by experienced SSM practitioners. Section 4 demonstrates the application of the approach to an SSM "expert" and presents some heuristics for deriving CMs from RDs derived from the analysis. Section 5 summarises the conclusions of the work and future directions.

Systems for Sustainability, edited by Stowell *et al.*
Plenum Press, New York, 1997

2. THE LINK BETWEEN ROOT DEFINITIONS AND CONCEPTUAL MODELS

2.1. Evidence that the Link Is Problematic

Some authors argue that the RD-CM link is close to a technique, a rigorous and un-ambiguous process. Davies and Ledington (1991), for example, describe the process as "mutually adjusting the RD and CM" until there is nothing in the RD which is not covered in the CM and nothing in the CM which does not arise out of the RD. These authors also propose a means of formulating the RD, involving explicit mention of all the main activity verbs, which does indeed make the process almost mechanical, although it has been ar-gued (Checkland and Tsouvalis, 1996; Watson, 1991) that this approach makes one of the pair of RD/CM almost redundant. We would argue, however, that the RD-CM link is problematic, on the following grounds:

- As pointed out by Checkland and Tsouvalis (1996), statements to this effect can be identified in Checkland's seminal writings.
- As argued by Schregenberger (1982) in what was then a radical view, an analyst's experience of the real world, encoded in his/her long-term memory, will deter-mine what sort of CM will be derived from a given RD.
- The "correct" mapping from a RD to a CM can vary between different analysts due to the inherent fuzziness of the English language (Wilson, 1991).
- The CMs produced from the same RD by different analysts will differ due to their different psychological makeups and cultural backgrounds (Mingers, 1990).
- Although deriving a CM from a RD was for a long time believed to be a logical process undertaken "below the line", a number of supporting techniques were adopted by the University of Lancaster in its teaching practices, including the "Formal Systems Model", the five E's, and the DIME (Dependence, Information, Material, Energy) technique (Checkland and Tsouvalis, 1996).
- A classification of the guidelines/heuristics given in the literature for deriving CMs from RDs (Boyle, 1995) found them to be ambiguous, incomplete, stated in the nega-tive case only (proscriptive) and contradictory. In general, the process is taught by means of examples, with the tacit assumption that if the reader sees enough examples they will be able to carry out the mapping themselves. It must be stated that the expe-rience of the authors in teaching SSM casts doubt on the validity of this assumption (Watson, 1991). This classification of heuristics is summarised below.

2.2. Classification of Heuristics Given in the Literature

In a survey of five major instructional monographs and one paper (Checkland, 1981; Checkland and Scholes, 1990; Davies and Ledington, 1991; Patching, 1990; Watson, 1991; Wilson, 1991), the RD-CM mapping was found to be describable by a sequence of six steps:

1. Initial Analysis of RD
2. Activity Identification
3. Adding Monitoring and Control Activities
4. Activity Checking
5. Activity Sequencing (Logical Dependencies)
6. CM Checking

The survey identified 57 distinct heuristics, of which 38 % related to Activity Identification (arguably the central and possibly the easiest step), 21 % related to CM Checking (a broad category, encompassing anything used after CM construction to check for "completeness"), 7 % related to Activity Checking (perhaps this is hard to articulate) and 7 % to Activity Sequencing (perhaps this is considered relatively simple). The heuristics found in the literature are summarised by category and author in Table 1. It should be noted that the final row counts distinct heuristics, i.e. where a heuristic was repeated by authors, it has been counted only ce.

2.3. Objective of the Present Research

Given that the RD-CM link is not a technique based entirely on logic, and that the "correct" CM derived from a single RD will depend on the culture of the analyst, it is of interest to explore the heuristics used by analysts from different cultures. The present research is concerned with the design and trial of a technique, based on the field of knowledge acquisition, to elicit heuristics from SSM practitioners.

3. AN EXPERIMENTAL PROGRAM TO DISCOVER THE HEURISTICS USED BY SSM EXPERTS

3.1. Experimental Design Strategies and Techniques

The range of candidate knowledge acquisition strategies and techniques, drawn mainly from the field of psychology, was surveyed. Strategies include interviewing, observation and protocol analysis. Techniques include process tracing, imposing constraints, simulated scenarios, episodic analogies and analysis of difficult cases (McGraw and Harbison-Briggs, 1989). The strategy of observation was chosen, and within this strategy the techniques of process tracing using retrospective verbalisation, and process tracing using concurrent verbalisation with imposed constraints were selected. Process tracing involves the analysis of verbal and observational data from a domain expert when engaged in problem solving activities. Constraints, such as limited information, help to draw out non-verbal thought processes from the domain expert.

3.2. Technique Used to Analyse the Sessions

To analyse the video taped data, transcripts were created containing all verbal utterances and graphical material, such as CMs, constructed in each session. It was not possible to conduct a full protocol analysis of the data, but rather a technique termed QOC (Questions, Options, Criteria) (MacLean, A, Young, R.M, Bellotti, and V.M.E., and Moran, 1991) was used. Questions could be seen as directing when to use a heuristic, options giving possible alternative actions, and criteria describing under what circumstances an action indicated by a heuristic should or should not be taken. Transcripts were structured into a set of assertions, which are components regarded as substantive. Assertions were referenced as in the following example: (A)S2–112 refers to assertion number 112 recorded during session 2 with subject A.

Table 1. Number of heuristics by author and category

Author(s)	Heuristic Category						
	1. Initial Analysis of RD	2. Activity Identification	3. Monitoring and Control	4. Activity Checking	5. Logical Dependencies	6. CM Checking	Total
Checkland	2	6	–	1	1	6	16
Checkland & Scholes	2	1	4	–	1	1	9
Davies & Ledington	2	4	1	–	1	3	11
Patching	–	4	1	1	1	3	10
Watson	1	8	–	4	–	–	13
Wilson	2	4	–	3	–	8	9
Total	8	22	4	7	4	12	68
							57

3.3. Experimental Design Issues

3.3.1. Selection of Subjects. As this was an exploratory study to develop and trial the experimental design, it was decided that expertise in SSM, rather than cultural background, was the most important criterion for the choice of subjects. However, it was required that subjects have no specific knowledge base of the problem situations posed in the experimental RDs. After some trial runs with four subjects, it was decided to trial the experimental design with two male, caucasian subjects, each of whom had significant practical and teaching experience of SSM. These are denoted as subject A and subject B. Some of the results obtained with subject A are given below.

3.3.2. Construction of RDs. In order to minimise the effects of differences in the subjects' prior knowledge of the problem situation, RDs were constructed in accordance with the following criteria:

- the situation posed in the RD must be in a domain which would be considered common knowledge, and where it is unlikely that the subjects would possess prior domain knowledge;
- the structure of the RDs must be standardised using generally agreed formal structures.

The RD chosen for the Concurrent Verbalisation with Imposed Constraints component of the experiment came from the domain of traditional home life, and is as follows:

"A householder owned and managed system to construct a children's tree-house, out of readily available materials, in a suitable tree on the householder's property to make the recreational activities of the householder's children more enjoyable. The size and design of tree-house must be determined to be safe. Where a council permit is required it must be obtained."

4. TRIAL OF EXPERIMENTAL DESIGN WITH AN SSM EXPERT

4.1. QOC Analysis of Transcripts

A typical QOC diagram, selected from the large number produced, is depicted in Figure 1 (taken from subject A).

4.2. Some Heuristics Derived from the Analysis

Twenty-one heuristics used by subject A were derived from the QOC analysis and from session transcript assertions. Some heuristics pertaining to category 1 (initial analysis of RD) are:

- Identify the main transformation and its main components, inputs and outputs.
- To help identify the main transformation look for the central verb in the RD.
- Create an object diagram from the RD if there are complex relationships in the RD or there is not enough stimulus for ideas to start the CM right away. This is especially helpful for primary task RDs.
- Seek out and explore the implications of "buzz words" in the RD. These are nouns or verbs which, from past experience or logic, imply more activities to be added to the CM at the current level.

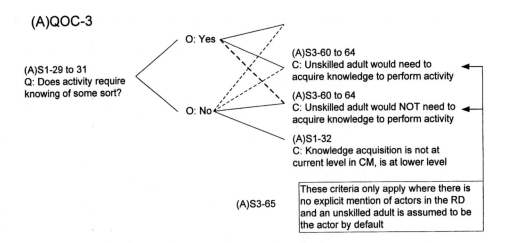

Figure 1. Example of a QOC diagram.

For a fuller discussion of these, and of the heuristics used by subject B, see Boyle (1995).

4.3. Discussion of Heuristics

There were some similarities between the heuristics used by subject A, given above, and subject B. The main RD element both look for during their initial analysis of the RD is the main transformation. This becomes the first activity added to the model. From this they both work backwards adding activities which must logically come before the initial one added. Both subjects are consistent in the application of their own SSM modelling heuristics to different problems. There were however some very significant differences between them. A unique feature of subject A's construction process is the use of an object diagram to help identify the key components in an RD and understand the relationships between them. Subject B does not use any form of diagrammatic cue or aid for analysing the RD. He performs his initial analysis of the RD and then proceeds with the CM construction. An analysis of the heuristics used by subjects A and B revealed that in all categories except 1, initial analysis of RD, there was no duplication of heuristics between the two subjects, i.e. the heuristics identified for one subject were not identified for the other. This is a remarkable outcome, and indicates that although they start the modelling process in similar ways, they employ very different heuristics to complete the process.

5. CONCLUSIONS AND FUTURE DIRECTIONS

This work has reviewed and classified the heuristics for mapping RD to CM reported in the literature and, by means of the experimental program described, extracted a number of previously unreported heuristics. A trial of the experimental design with two SSM experts (results for only one of whom are reported here) with fairly similar cultural backgrounds revealed very significant differences in the heuristics used, which provides evidence in support of the contention that the link between RD and CM is not as mechanical a process as some maintain. Furthermore, the results suggest that even greater variation might be observed in the heuristics used by practitioners from more widely different backgrounds. Future research directions would include an exploration of the effects of cultural background using a greater number of experimental subjects, and an experiment directed at determining whether SSM novices armed with these heuristics produce "better" CMs from RDs than those trained in the conventional "teach by example" format.

REFERENCES

Boyle, S., 1995, An Investigation of Heuristics used in the Construction of Conceptual Models from Root Definitions in the Soft Systems Methodology, unpublished MAppSc Thesis, Swinburne University of Technology (June 1995).

Checkland, P.B., 1981, *Systems Thinking, Systems Practice*, Wiley, Chichester.

Checkland, P.B., and Scholes, J., 1990, *Soft Systems Methodology in Action*, Wiley, Chichester.

Checkland, P., and Tsouvalis, C., 1996, Reflecting on SSM: The Link Between Root Definitions and Conceptual Models, Centre for Systems & Information Sciences, University of Humberside, Working Paper 5/1996.

Cross, R., and Turk, A., 1996, A Means-Ends Perspective for Soft Systems Methodology, in *Learning through Systems Thinking*, Proc. of Australian Systems Conference, Monash University (September 1996).

Davies, L., and Ledington, P., 1991, *Information in Action: Soft Systems Methodology*, Macmillan, Basingstoke.

Gregory, F.H., 1993, Soft systems methodology to information systems: a Wittgensteinian approach, *Journal of Information Systems* 3(3):149–168.

MacLean, A., Young, R.M., Bellotti, V.M.E., and Moran, T.P., 1991, Questions, Options, and Criteria: Elements of Design Space Analysis, *Human-Computer Interaction* 6:201–250.

McGraw, K.L., and Harbison-Briggs, K., 1989, *Knowledge Acquisition: Principles and Guidelines*, Prentice-Hall International, London.

Mingers, J., 1990, The What/How Distinction and Conceptual Models: A Reappraisal, *J. App. Sys. Anal.* 17: 21–28.

Patching, D., 1990, *Practical Soft Systems Analysis*, Pitman, London.

Schregenberger, J., 1982, The Development of Lancaster Soft Systems Methodology: A Review and Some Personal Remarks from a Sympathetic Critic, *J. App. Sys. Anal.* 9: 87–98.

Tsouvalis, C., and Checkland, P., 1996, Reflecting on SSM: The Dividing Line between 'Real World' and 'Systems Thinking World', *Systems Research* 13(1):35–45.

Watson, R.B., 1991, The Nature and Construction of Conceptual Models in Soft Systems Methodology, Dept. of Computer Science, Swinburne University of Technology, Technical Report SIT-CS-14/91.

Wilson, B., 1991, *Systems: Concepts, Methodologies and Applications*, 2nd ed., Wiley, Chichester.

Woodburn, I., 1985, Some Developments in the Building of Conceptual Models, *J. App. Sys. Anal.*, 12: 101–106.

68

FROM SINGLE TO MULTI-PARADIGM SYSTEMS RESEARCH

The Cognitive Constraints

John Brocklesby

Victoria University of Wellington
New Zealand

1. INTRODUCTION

This paper aims to contribute to the growing literature on multimethodology (specifically that which involves combining systems methodologies, in whole or in part, from different paradigms) by briefly examining some of the obstacles that might prevent an agent whose current predilection is to operate within a single paradigm from becoming multimethodology literate. A longer, more detailed, and more fully referenced version of the paper appears in Mingers and Gill (1997). The main theoretical underpinning of the paper is the work on cognition by Maturana and Varela (1980) (hereafter M&V). These authors conceptualise cognition as involved, engaged, activity in the world, and this seems a befitting approach in a discipline which seeks to bring about improvements in the *practical* affairs of organisations and their members. Consideration of M&V's work, which is outlined in the longer paper, but not here, leads to the suggestion that there are four sets of obstacles that may stand in the way of an agent who might otherwise be a candidate to develop the sort of literacy described: developing paradigm awareness, making the commitment to a new or different paradigm, performing effectively in the new paradigm, and moving easily between paradigms. This paper considers these obstacles.

2. BECOMING PARADIGM CONSCIOUS

Because paradigms operate tacitly, people often do not contemplate where they stand in relation to various paradigm categories. An observer, "...cannot observe a cognitive domain by operating in it", as Maturana (1988:61) puts it. Moreover, paradigms are self-contained, each having its own boundaries, vocabularies, and grammars of interaction. So while paradigms provide insight and illumination, they also produce silences around certain issues and themes. The so-called hard systems paradigm, for instance, is silent on the question of plural definitions of problem situations, soft systems is silent on the issue of structured inequalities, and the critical systems paradigm does not provide much help in dealing with complex technical problems. The cognitive closure and partiality of a paradigm, however, is not necessarily a problem. What is a problem is when we fail to recognise this, when we fail to see the paradigm's 'blind spots'. Maturana would view this as a natural consequence of our predilection to operate according to what he refers to as the "objectivity without parentheses" explanatory path (1988:59)—the paradigm 'reflects the way things are'—and because we gradually grow into the paradigm's language we fail to see how it creates a particular way of 'seeing'.

Despite this cognitive closure, clearly there are people who do reflect upon their own and other paradigms. Often this has arisen as a result of some unexpected turn of events—a failure in traditional ways of 'doing things' for example. For some, this has precipitated a switch from one one paradigm to another, and it may explain why many soft and critical systems thinkers were not actually trained in these paradigms. The relocation of these individuals arose out of a disaffection with the dominant paradigm of their initial training and socialisation.

Another circumstance that can trigger paradigm awareness is through an experience in another cognitive domain. In our daily life we populate many different domains, and although these are independent as domains of conversations, they are realised through our bodyhoods, so potentially they influence each other. What happens to us in one, has consequences for our participation in the rest. This is an important point, it being easy to forget that systems people are not just systems people. We all operate in multiple domains, that is, we participate simultaneously in various conversations not only as systems scientists, but also as engineers, economists, mathematicians, quality experts, academics, parents, teachers, managers, community workers, trade unionists, and in a myriad other ways. Thus there is a rich source of interactions that can trigger reflection upon the way we participate as systems scientists. Whenever an agent has an encounter outside a particular domain, it triggers structural changes in him or her. Some of these encounters, in Maturana's terms, will be "orthogonal", i.e. contrary to the 'rules' under which he or she participates as a systems scientist. Upon returning to the systems domain their participation alters, and this, in turn, can trigger structural changes in the domain itself. It is part of the dynamic through which fields like systems are constantly changing.

A third possibility for triggering paradigm awareness is when an external agent requests it. This could take the form of a direct request to reject one paradigm in favour of another, or it could involve some external agent - a teacher or an author perhaps - providing the agent with a contextual framework that allows them to understand where they stand in relation to various paradigm categories. This circumvents the paradigm's cognitive closure thereby bringing it into focus. Examples of such sense-making devices to account for, and locate, various paradigms, include Burrell and Morgan's (1979) well known sociological paradigms, Pepper's (1942) world hypotheses, and, most obviously, the hard/soft/critical framework that is used both here and extensively elsewhere in the systems literature.

3. COMMITTING ONESELF TO A NEW PARADIGM

Becoming aware of one's paradigm alignment may lead one to contemplate the possibility of making the commitment to a new paradigm. Whether or not this eventuates is likely to depend upon the sort of life the agent leads, and the sort of person they are. The take-up of multimethodology, for example, depends very heavily upon an agent's experiential situation. For some—those who have to handle the complete cycle of stages involved in the intervention process, or who have to deal with material, social, *and* personal aspects of problem situations, for example—multimethodology may make a great deal of sense, and the idea may elicit a positive response. For others, it may have little to offer. Equally important in estimating the likely take-up of multimethodology is the agent themselves. Entering a new paradigm, "is an intensely personal process, evolving from not only intellectual but also personal, social, and possibly political transformation..." (Lincoln 1990). If this is so, then we can hardly expect agents to be equally comfortable in all three systems paradigms. The degree of comfort experienced in a paradigm depends, for example, upon the agent's values and beliefs, their personality, and their preferred cognitive style. For example, soft systems pays little heed to the technical rigour that might attract someone of a different disposition to hard systems work. Soft systems, one suspects, is a domain that would suit someone whose emotional preference is to facilitate intersubjective understanding, and who enjoys helping people with divergent viewpoints reach some sort of accommodation. By way of contrast, the critical paradigm almost obliges the agent to have some degree of empathy for the underdog, and (at least in the traditional guise of critical theory), to harbour noble dreams about creating a more equitable society. Here the agent's curiosity is geared towards recovering ideas and thought that have become lost or distorted through power relations. The overall point then, is that if we accept that each paradigm has its own set of explicit and implicit operational premises (values, accepted truths, emotional and political predispositions, etc.), we are forced to admit that journeying between paradigms is not a simple matter.

4. ACTING EFFECTIVELY IN A 'NEW' PARADIGM

Few of our 'lived worlds' in systems have pre-defined bounded environments so effective performance according to the logic of any paradigm requires more than simply learning its set of propositional rules. In soft systems, for example, the propositional knowledge that is required to create rich pictures, produce root definitions, and construct cognitive maps, can be acquired from textbooks. Being effective in this domain, however, involves working directly with people, and responding, often in real-time, to the exigencies of whatever situation develops. Unfortunately these relationship-managing skills are difficult to capture in a propositional format. While SSM is a much vaunted methodology, one could argue that the coupling between the agent and the people involved in the problem situation is a greater critical success factor than is the methodology itself. The propositional content of SSM may be important, but people still have to rely upon their experiences and creativity in defining whatever it is that they have to deal with. These 'ready-to-hand' skills and commonsense understandings have to be learnt somehow, but because "the unmanageable ambiguity of background common sense is left largely at the periphery of the inquiry" (Varela et al. 1991:148), they rarely have chapters assigned to them in textbooks, neither are they regularly discussed at conferences. In relation to SSM, one could argue that there is a distressingly wide gap between what management scientists write about and what they do.

Acquiring propositional knowledge is clearly only the first stage in becoming effective. Generally, this sort of knowledge is sufficient only to get someone started in a task domain (Dreyfus 1996). That which is learnt from teachers/textbooks/journals etc. mainly concentrates on detached uninvolved rule-following behaviour leading to reasoned responses. Typically it lays out ways of decomposing task environments, differentiating commonly occurring situational features, and it produces rules for dealing with these. This is very useful for the novice, but it capitulates in the face of the potentially vast number of situational factors that must be faced, especially when these differ in subtle, nuanced ways. Neither can it provide perspectives for prioritising these, i.e. in deciding what is important and what is not. Competency or proficiency in such circumstances requires active involvement, practice and experience of a large number of cases. Becoming expert, where reasoning gives way to intuition, is even more demanding. This requires a gradual accumulation of a vast number of situational discriminations, associated responses, and acquired feedback on the success or failure of these. Experts, with this sort of experience, know intuitively what needs to be done in a situation and how to do it. They resort to rule-following behaviour and reasoned responses only when things do not turn out as expected.

The concept of enaction or embodied cognition articulated by Varela, Thompson and Rosch (1990), bears upon this issue. Enaction further develops M&V's idea that knowledge is constituted in our actions. As an individual confronts new situations various experiences are gained through thinking, sensing, and moving. This means that the way we experience the world, is very much an active construction involving the whole body. Effective action depends upon having a body with various sensorimotor and orienting capacities that allow an agent to act, perceive, and sense in distinctive ways. If the agent's body has not learned how to orient itself in such a way that the relevant cues are picked up then they run the risk of missing that which others might pick up. Again, I suspect that this is a major critical success factor in soft systems where the agent has to respond expeditiously to the demands of the situation paying due regard to the needs of those involved. The problem is that these sorts of orienting credentials are not easily taught. They grow out of accumulated lived experience of certain kinds of activity. They are entrenched in the day to day experience of acting in the world, and they become entangled in various ways in expert practice.

Operating effectively in a new paradigm, may be said to require both a learning and an unlearning. Indeed, as much training and effort may be required in letting go of established and habitual ways of doing and thinking about things, as is required in learning the new paradigm. In extreme cases, there may be so much intellectual baggage that the odds of someone completing a successful transition are somewhat remote. The choices that people have depend a great deal upon their past experiences. We are all contextually and historically situated actors and our autonomy and freedom to move is often severely constrained. Our thrown-ness, our historical couplings, makes certain decisions and paths for the future unlikely or even impossible, which is why Darwin, for example, despaired of converting any but young uncommitted naturalists to his theory of evolution (see Guba, 1990). Despite this, we can confront and own up to our thrown-ness, and we do achieve some sense of liberation in recognising why this is so, and, in this way, we do broaden our horizons to some extent. By recognising the flow of our thrown-ness, by not just unconsciously accepting it, we may seek to re-direct it to a degree.

5. MOVING EASILY BETWEEN PARADIGMS

Maturana's concept of orthogonal interaction, mentioned earlier, sheds some light on this particular difficulty. When someone interacts outside a particular domain in a way that is different—or *orthogonal* - from what the domain's 'rules' specify—as one would, for example, in moving from hard to soft systems - the interaction triggers structurally determined changes in the individual. The individual then returns to the original domain and participates differently in it. Thus, a hard systems scientist who returns to hard systems practice after having 'discovered' the soft paradigm is not the same person who 'left' the hard paradigm in the first place. It is impossible to remain untouched by this sort of orthogonal interaction, and whether the agent is aware of it or not, there will be practical implications for them, as there will be for the various communities to which they return. Each community will be triggered as a result of the various orthogonal interactions of its members, and will change according to its own structural determination.

6. CONCLUSION

In conclusion, one may claim that the process of transforming an agent who works within a single paradigm into someone who is multimethodology and multiparadigm literate is perhaps an unlikely, although by no means impossible, proposition. For it to happen, a number of obstacles must be overcome. First, the agent must become paradigm conscious. This is difficult because of the cognitive closure of paradigms, and, because the insights accruing out of self-observation are bounded by peoples' experiential situation. Second, the agent must believe that a new paradigm offers them something worth having, and it must fit with their personality, emotional and political predilections. Third, effective performance in a paradigm necessitates learning its commonsense, as well as its propositional, knowledge. This can be difficult if the agent's previous history of structural coupling has not led them to develop, or have the capacity to acquire, the full range of embodied skills that this requires. Even if the agent is capable of learning such skills, appropriate practice and apprenticeship is required, and old habits have to be unlearned. This involves a major resocialisation, and there is no escaping the time and effort that is required. Finally, moving easily between paradigms can also create difficulties.

REFERENCES

Mingers, J. and Gill, A. (eds), 1997, *Multimethodology: Towards the Theory and Practice of Combining Methods,* Wiley, Chichester,

Maturana, H. and Varela, F., 1980, *Autopoiesis and Cognition: The Realisation of the Living.* Reidel, Dordrecht.

Maturana, H., 1988, Reality: The Search for Objectivity or the Quest for a Compelling Argument. *Irish Journal of Psychology* 9, 25–82.

Burrell, G. and Morgan, G., 1979, *Sociological Paradigms and Organisational Analysis.* London, Heinemann,

Pepper, S., 1942, *World Hypotheses: a Study in Evidence.* University of California Press, Berkeley.

Lincoln, Y., 1990, The Making of a Constructivist: A Remembrance of Transformations Past. In *The Paradigm Dialogue.* (E. G. Guba) pp. Sage, Newbury Park.

Varela, F., Thompson, E. and Rosch, E., 1991, *The Embodied Mind - Cognitive Science and Human Experience.* MIT Press, Cambridge, Mass.

Dreyfus, H. L., 1996, The Current Relevance of Merleau-Ponty's Phenomenology of Embodiment. In *Perspectives on Embodiment.* (H. Haber and G. Weiss) pp. Routledge, New York and London.

69

PARTICIPATIVE APPROACHES FOR DEALING WITH COMPLEXITY

A Comparison between Interactive Management and Socio-Technical Systems Theory

A. R. Cardenas,[1] G. Otalora,[1] and F. R. Janes[2]

[1]ITESM, Campus Monterrey
Suc. Correos "J"
Monterrey, N.L. 64 849, Mexico
[2]City University
Northampton Square
London EC1V 0HB, United Kingdom

1. INTRODUCTION

The ability to deal effectively with complexity has become a major focus of systemic methodologies. Among these methodologies, Interactive Management (IM) and Socio-technical Systems Theory (STST), represent two outstanding efforts to address complexity based on an explicit acknowledgement of a participatory/democratic principle. However, these approaches differ significantly in some respects at both the conceptual and the operational levels and, in particular, they differ in terms of the context and nature of the tasks that they propose for dealing with complexity. On the one hand, group work as promoted by STST was initially oriented towards the accomplishment of production activities within an organizational context, an orientation which helps to identify these sociotechnical systems as 'action systems'. On the other hand, IM group work focuses on the development of shared representations of complex situations, as well as on the generation of consensus-based designed solutions for addressing those situations; in this sense, IM group activity could be conceptualized as an 'inquiring system'. In this paper, the similarities and differences between these two approaches provide the basis for a reflection on some conceptual and methodological issues involved in dealing with complexity in terms of the relationship between 'action' and 'inquiry'.

2. ON THE IDEA OF COMPLEXITY

Interactive Management and Sociotechnical Systems Theory share the idea that our times are characterized by increasing complexity and that there is a need to approach this complexity through the means of systems design.

Systems for Sustainability, edited by Stowell *et al.*
Plenum Press, New York, 1997

In the case of STST the idea of complexity is related to the dynamics and uncertainty that characterize organizational environments: "The new environment is called the turbulent field in which large competing organizations, all acting independently in diverse directions, produce unanticipated and dissonant consequences..." (Trist, 1981). On the other hand, the concept of complexity found in the IM literature (Janes, 1995; Warfield, 1994) is described in terms of three interrelated components: situational complexity, cognitive complexity and pluralistic complexity. The three components have in common the connotation of a large amount of variety which needs to be managed, and the last two convey the notion that a human dimension should be part of any account of the concept of complexity: "...any definition of complexity must recognize the sensitivity of the concept to how the human being is viewed" (Warfield, 1994). For the purposes of this paper we will concentrate on this description of complexity as it will be related later to our concept of complex problem solving.

Situational complexity accounts for all the elements involved in a given situation, their relationships and the dynamics of their behaviour through time, as long as they are difficult to grasp for the human mind and are difficult to control. In spite of the fact that this notion of situational complexity incorporates a cognitive component ('difficult to grasp for the human mind'), it is considered that situational complexity takes place independently of any purposeful attempt to change it or to understand it. That is, situational complexity is viewed as the component of complexity which accounts for the 'real world', as opposed to only an intellectual construct of the human mind. In these terms, the STST view of complexity basically emphasizes situational complexity.

Cognitive complexity relates directly to the human mental endeavour involved in any conceptualization of reality, and specifically it refers to "those aspects of our understanding of the situation that make interpretation difficult" (Janes, 1995). Among difficulties involved in interpreting a situation are the limitations of the human mind in perceiving and processing information; and the cultural and psychological factors that influence the way in which meaning is attributed to what is perceived.

Pluralistic complexity introduces a socio-psychological dimension as a part of any serious attempt to understand complexity. By acknowledging that a complex situation may be recognized as such when more than one individual is involved in dealing with the situation, this concept implies that an appreciation of complexity may be reached by shared experience. Pluralistic complexity derives from the problems posed by the diverse individual interpretations of a complex situation (Janes, 1995), together with communication and other social problems involved in human interaction.

Implicit in the concept of complexity is the idea that complex situations are problematic in at least two senses: a) they produce a sense of confusion regarding their interpretation, and b) their perception is associated with a sense of discomfort or dissatisfaction on the part of some human beings.

3. DEALING WITH COMPLEXITY AS A PROBLEM-SOLVING UNDERTAKING

A general conception of problem solving considers it as a purposeful activity aimed at changing a state of dissatisfaction into a state of satisfaction regarding a particular situation. This view of problem solving involves again a human component, whose perceptions and interests define the levels of dissatisfaction/satisfaction; a situation; and a set of activities organized to produce the change from dissatisfaction to satisfaction. In order to accomplish this task three types of changes could be sought: a) changes in the perceptions and/or interests of the human component, b) changes in the situation itself, or c) changes in both.

Concerning complex situations, it is the argument of this paper that problem solving should strive to produce type (c) changes, i.e., changes in perceptions and/or interests, as well as changes in the situation itself, because otherwise problem solving would be covering only a subset of the aspects of complexity mentioned in the preceding section. Changes in perceptions and/or interests would only address cognitive and/or pluralistic complexity, while changes in the situation would only address situational complexity. Because of the dynamic nature of complex situations, complex problem solving cannot be thought of as an activity in which problems are solved once and for all once a satisfactory state is attained. Instead, it is considered as a formally organized, temporary activity through which a situation is improved by a reduction in the initial sense of dissatisfaction that it generated, and by an increase in the ability of those involved in the problem-solving effort to comprehend and manage that situation.

Since complex problem solving requires dealing with both cognitive and pluralistic complexity on the one hand, and with situational complexity on the other, it is proposed that such an effort should involve at least two components: a) inquiry, related to the development of a satisfactory understanding of the situation and the design of appropriate solutions, and therefore mainly devoted to managing cognitive and pluralistic complexity; and b) action, aimed at the implementation of the proposed solutions, and thus directly addressing situational complexity.

Within this framework, IM and STST are related to complex problem solving in terms of their contributions to the inquiry and action components mentioned above. Given the origins and nature of IM it is our view that its contributions are concentrated mainly on the inquiring component of problem solving. On the other hand, even if the original tradition and nature of STST are not related to complex problem solving in general but basically to the task of organizational design, we consider that its emphasis on the design and operationalization of work systems leads to interesting contributions to the understanding and performance of the action component of complex problem solving.

4. THE INQUIRING COMPONENT OF PROBLEM SOLVING

As a basically rational-intellectual activity, inquiry is the component of complex problem solving whose primary aim is to deal with situational complexity through the management of cognitive complexity by helping the human mind to develop satisfactory understanding of situations, and to design appropriate solutions. However, since dealing with complexity normally involves more than one individual (as was stated above), the process of inquiry should also be concerned with managing pluralistic complexity. The answer of IM to these requirements manifests itself in the design of a structured scheme for group activity, in which a formal process of inquiry is conducted on the basis of democratic participation (Warfield and Cardenas, 1994).

Besides the above, and with no consideration of any particular process through which the inquiring activity could be accomplished, it can be argued that at least two dimensions are involved in the type of outcomes that may be expected from such an endeavour:

1. *Cognitive Dimension.* This dimension is related to the aim of managing cognitive complexity, but it also concerns pluralistic complexity since the problem of understanding and arriving at well-designed solutions for a complex situation

should be resolved at the level of a community of problem solvers, that is, the emphasis of the cognitive dimension lies on the intellectual perspectives of all those involved in addressing a situation (cf. the concept of cognitive equilibrium: Warfield, 1991). The outcomes associated with this dimension are the typical outcomes expected from inquiry within the context of a problem-solving activity: clear and satisfactory definitions of the situation (such as a diagnosis or an identification of key issues and their relationships), and proposals for action (such as a system design). On the grounds of a formal theoretical basis (Warfield, 1994), IM responds to the need for variety, parsimony and saliency posed by this cognitive dimension, by providing a facilitated process that enables groups of people to combine a formal language (mathematics) and graphics with their natural language to obtain a better grasp of the situational complexity and to derive considered solutions to deal with it.

2. *Social Dimension.* The social dimension is basically associated with the management of pluralistic complexity, and it derives from all the aspects of inquiry that involve human interaction. Among the social-dimension outcomes that could be expected from the process of inquiry are: the development of mutual understanding and shared meanings; improvement in communication; changes in perspectives and attitudes; consensus; and commitment to action. These kind of outcomes can be very valuable on their own because very often they lead to further changes to the social context in which the problem-solving activity is embedded. There are various specific ways through which IM contributes to the social dimension of the outcomes of inquiry. Among these contributions are: i) specific methods for generating and structuring ideas which allow a group to manage the complexity of their communication and which help them develop a common language; ii) a special emphasis on the learning process that takes place as the activity of inquiry unfolds; and iii) the delineation of the necessary roles, and respect for the balanced participation, of the members of the group.

Besides the considerations mentioned above regarding the contributions of IM to the inquiring process, there are other aspects worth mentioning such as: i) the balance between the technical and behavioural requirements of group work, which is embedded in the various specific methods used for idea generation and structuring; ii) the design of each IM workshop as a part of a global plan for addressing complexity; and iii) the careful and organized documentation of the results, together with management of the information that is produced during the group activity.

Finally, regarding the ultimate outcomes of the inquiring process in general, it should be noted that the cognitive and the social dimensions represent two points of view from which the process can be assessed, and in many cases the outcomes associated with each of them can be regarded, on their own, as 'satisfactory' results of the problem-solving effort. However, even if combined, these outcomes do not contribute to the problem of addressing situational complexity if they are not translated into satisfactory 'action' results.

5. THE ACTION COMPONENT OF PROBLEM SOLVING

The action component of a problem-solving system refers to the implementation of the results of inquiry, which should lead to an actual improvement of the situation that originally initiated the problem-solving effort. The contributions of STST to this task are related to the emphasis it puts on the requirements of a social system to operate in a complex environment, and on the need to approach this endeavour through a participative scheme (Trist and Murray, 1993). In order for the action component of problem-solving to be actually operationalized and attuned to the global effort of the problem-solving system of which it is a part, at least three aspects of its performance should be considered:

1. The relationship between the inquiring and the implementation processes. One particularly relevant issue in the relationship between inquiry and implementation is the difference between inquirers and implementers. In complex situations, it is usual that the people who will be in charge of implementing the solutions do not totally coincide those who participate in the inquiring activity, or else they only participate on a partial basis. This difference stresses the need to ensure a good understanding of the inquiry outcomes and to gain the commitment of the implementers in order to translate outcomes into action successfully. Another kind of problem may arise when the implementers actually participate in the inquiring process but the reality of the implementation is not compatible with the principles that guided the inquiring activity. For example, a participative inquiring process may be followed by an authoritarian implementation setting. This kind of problem is captured in the first sociotechnical design principle, 'compatibility', which states that: "the process of design must be compatible with its objectives" (Cherns, 1976). Also, it is clear that the effectiveness of the implementation process is highly dependent on the perceived effectiveness and legitimacy of the inquiring process.

2. The internal organization and capabilities of the action system. In order for an action system to implement the designed solutions, it should posses the resources, capabilities and power needed to accomplish its task, and should also be able to manage them as needed. The main contributions of STST have been highly concentrated in this area. In particular, STST emphasizes the need to operationalize autonomous viable social systems as the only means to provide for both an appropriate management of situational complexity and an improvement to the quality of work life as an end in itself. These considerations lead to the development of a conceptual framework which emphasizes flexibility and non-hierarchical forms of work organization, as opposed to rigid specifications of the action system: "If we want to implement viable autonomous social systems, the design will not consist of a specification of the final system...; rather, what has to be specified and implemented are the conditions that make it possible for a system of this type to develop." (Herbst, 1974). An example of the sociotechnical design principles directly related to these issues is the principle of Power and Authority: "Those who need equipment, materials, or other resources to carry out their responsibilities should have access to them and authority to command them..." (Cherns, 1987)

3. The social context in which the problem-solving activity is embedded. Since complex problem-solving always implies a boundary judgement about the situation under study and the social system involved in the problem-solving effort, there will be a need to consider the difference between inquirers and implementers on the one hand, and other people affected by the proposed solutions on the other. This difference, besides suggesting some ethical issues, also impinges upon the performance of the implementation process because it identifies social limitations under which the action system should operate.

Another important consideration regarding this action component is that, once enacted into the life of a social system in a complex situation, the implementation process may dissolve to become a part of a larger action system not necessarily concerned with the original purposes of the problem-solving effort. Therefore, in order to be able to learn from, and bring to a closure, the problem-solving activity, its assessment becomes a necessary component of the whole process.

6. CONCLUSION

IM and STST have been used in this paper to illustrate important contributions of their systemic frameworks to the inquiring and action components of complex problem solving. In the terms presented here, each one of these approaches on its own does not seem to constitute a complete complex problem solving system. However, the contributions that they make to the components of this endeavour open up the possibilities of arriving at an integration of concepts and practices in the whole spectrum of complex problem solving.

REFERENCES

Cherns, A., 1976, The principles of sociotechnical design, in: *Sociotechnical Systems: A Source Book* (W. Pasmore and J. Sherwood , eds.), pp. 61–71, University Associates, Inc.

Cherns, A., 1987, Principles of sociotechnical design revisited, *Human Relations* **40**:153 - 161.

Herbst, D. P., 1974, Designing with minimal critical specifications, in: Trist and Murray, 1993, pp. 294–302.

Janes, F.R., 1995, Interactive management: Framework, practice and complexity, in: *Critical Issues in Systems Theory and Practice* (K. Ellis, A. Gregory, B.R. Mears-Young, and G. Ragsdell, eds.), pp. 51–60, Plenum Press, New York.

Trist, E., 1981, QWL and the 80s, in: Trist and Murray, 1993, pp. 338–349.

Trist, E. and Murray, H., eds., 1993, *The Social Engagement of Social Science. Volume II: The Socio-Technical Perspective*, University of Pennsylvania Press, Philadelphia, PA.

Warfield, J.N., 1991, Complexity and cognitive equilibrium: Experimental results and their implication, *Human Systems Management*, **10**: 196–202.

Warfield, J.N., 1994, *A Science of Generic Design*, 2nd ed., Iowa State University Press, Ames, Iowa.

Warfield, J.N., and Cardenas, A.R., 1994, *A Handbook of Interactive Management*, 2nd ed., Iowa State University Press, Ames, Iowa.

70

CVAM

A New Systems Methodology and Systemic Sustainability in an Engineering Company

Jack A. Castle[1] and Shaun A. Spurrell[2]

[1]The School of Operations Management
University of the West of England
[2]Isopad Ltd.

1. INTRODUCTION

This paper describes progress with an action research programme dedicated to the development of a new systems methodology. CVAM was first described in detail by Castle (1995). Firmly placed within the interpretive paradigm it fulfils a particular need in integrating strategy and operational decision making. The literature of operations management urges us to consider trade offs and focused operations, yet only simple algorithms (Slack, Chambers, Harland, Harrison, and Johnston, 1995) and profiles (Hill, 1985) are on offer. CVAM is designed to assist managers with a guide to action in these areas. This paper first presents a brief overview of the new methodology as it stands now, in October 1996. The main findings of the action research carried out earlier in 1996 are then discussed in terms of the contribution they have made to its current state.

2. WHAT IS CVAM?

CVAM (see-vam) is a mnemonic for circumstances, values, activities and means. The methodology develops the idea of an appreciation system graphically explored by Checkland and Casar (1986) from the writings of Geoffrey Vickers. The life of individuals and organisations is seen as an ongoing flux of circumstantial forces (C's), values and viewpoints (V's), activities (A's) and means (M's). Circumstances are those forces acting upon the system under examination that are beyond the control of the actors within the system. CVAM offers a sub-methodology, CIRVE, to address circumstantial time change, and future scenario planning. It argues that this is given inadequate attention by other approaches. It adds to the viewpoint activity concern prominent in SSM (Checkland, 1981), directing attention to means, the resources that are the subject of trade off and focus argu-

Systems for Sustainability, edited by Stowell *et al.*
Plenum Press, New York, 1997

ments. The methodology explores the relationships within this CVAM'ic flux and develops goals as adjustments to relationships to meet individual and organisational needs. It follows the notion of system in soft systemic terms. Unlike SSM, CVAM, does not select a particular viewpoint for modelling, since this precludes trade off analysis, instead the major viewpoints are attenuated to value strands. Each of these is itself envisaged as a CVAM'ic thread or strand of argument. Interactions between the strands may then be considered.

3. THE METHODOLOGY AT OCTOBER 1996

The methodology commences with a "..challenge statement", framed in broad terms by an analysis team, followed by agreement of the boundary to the challenge situation so that circumstantial forces can be identified. The first stage of the methodology, CVAM-STAR requires the systemic un-attenuated (Beer, 1990) collection of information about the C's, A's, V's and M's intrinsic to the scenario. This is achieved using open debate and the collection of evidenced viewpoints, requiring justification, in the case of C's and A's and M's. The collection of V's is an unconstrained exercise in which any view that advances the process may be put forward. The data collected enables the CVAM programme to be planned and located on the CVAM mapping based on three dimensions, time, organisational hierarchy and emergent variety see Castle (1995). CVAM-STAR may be visualised as the first "dip" into the flux as shown in figure 1 below.

In the second stage these viewpoints are entered into the CVAM-VIVA (viewpoints and values) sub-methodology that leads to the identification of the major value (CVAM'ic) strands and their weights as the branches in value trees. This is an enhanced multiple attribute methodology using swing weighting technology. Existing methodologies offer little validation of value tree groupings. Goodwin and Wright (1991) suggest an appropriate approach is that of Keeney and Raiffa (1976). In VIVA the validation of the value strands is accomplished by the construction of strand statements for each strand. These use the verbs in the arguments intrinsic to a strand. The strands are then tested for hierarchical independence. In the third stage the value strands identified are separated and relevant C's, V's, A's and M's from those collected from CVAM-STAR are attached to each strand. This enables an initial testing of each strand's V's, A's and M's versus rele-

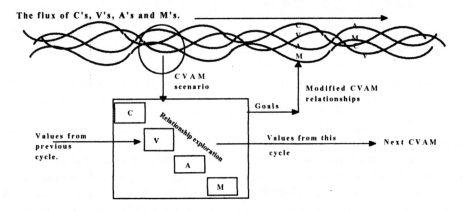

Figure 1. The idea of CVAM as an appreciative system.

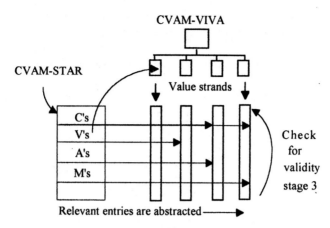

Figure 2. Strand validation.

vant C's for validity. Failure, leads back to the CVAM-VIVA and strand re-construction. In this way considerable emphasis is given to strand formation, validation and testing as a process in strategy formation. These ideas are shown in figure 2.

In the fourth stage validated value strands are subject to "below the line" analysis for sufficiency using CVAM-MRAM. This sub-methodology maps the minimum activities and means required to execute the strand statement (Castle 1995). Comparison of mapped A's and M's with real world entries indicates whether sufficiency has been achieved. Key processes are identified as chains of A's using a process classification guide.

At the fifth stage each strand is examined as a fully furnished CVAM diagonal matrix (Castle 1995). This enables strand domination analysis to be completed. Castle (1995) has proposed that states of C,V,or M domination of activities may exist in any system. The methodology has clear emancipatory potential, as it makes such issues explicit. In the sixth stage focus and trade off issues are resolved by identifying those means and activities that play vital roles in more than one strand. Trade offs are facilitated by completing real world comparison with conceptual trade off diagrams based on value weights from CVAM-VIVA and the relative demands of the technical rationality (Thompson, 1967) intrinsic to the strand.

4. ACTION RESEARCH LESSONS

In the frameworks provided by DePoy and Gitlin (1993) this research is placed in the naturalistic paradigm. It is conducted in a way that allows modifications and improvements to the methodology to unfold from the lived experience of those deploying it. This form of research has been described as co-operative inquiry by Peter Reason writing in Denzin and Lincoln (1994). This study was carried out over the course of one year by Castle and Spurrell (1996). The research took place in a small engineering company Isopad Ltd., in Western England, in which Spurrell is the Engineering Manager. The challenge was concerned with evolving a strategy for marketing a new product for process line heating. The challenge statement was agreed as: ".. understanding the necessary changes required for Isopad to achieve an increase in sales of product A." The analysis team consisted of all of the Senior Management team. Some had little formal managerial training.

In the first stage the CVAM-STAR debate produced results that "...shocked..." some participants. From the viewpoints gathered it was clear that shared values existed about the vital need to improve relationships with key suppliers. Despite the intensity of their feelings, these views had not surfaced at previous conventional gatherings. According to Spurrell, "...the initial CVAM-STAR revealed...the true complexity of the problem...to all of the Senior Management team, and comments were made such as "..I didn't realise that the problem was so complicated...should we really be trying to sell this product line anyway?" He noted that "...the energy, interest and learning exhibited by all of the Senior Managers was exciting to study." Managers did express some confusion over the definitions used and this has been improved by recognising two fundamental types of viewpoint; those that must be justified by real world research (directed or evidenced) and those which are not constrained in any way. Thus views about C's, A's and M's require evidential support, whilst collected V's may be the expression of any opinion that may further the debate. The power of this simple systemic debating methodology has surprised and delighted us.

In stages two, three and four considerable problems with the variety of the challenge were encountered. At the time of the research the method required that all information be gathered for cross correlation analysis into a special worksheet called the CVAM diagonal. The diagonal provided too much variety for cross correlation analysis.

It was at this time that the idea of devising strands of arguments using weighted view points was devised. Spurrell was now able to examine each strand. He noted that "..although the 61 views were grouped into five sets of views, these five sets were then represented by five value strands. It is obvious that using five values rather than 61 views assists when cross correlating values with circumstantial forces, activities and means in the diagonal matrix. This approach within the CVAM methodology is completely new... emerging as a consequence of the action research relationship between Castle and myself." Much useful information on missing and negative cross correlations was noted. Spurrell noted that "...what is apparent is the host of missing activities and means in the real world strand...for example, within the strand labelled, 'build a better distribution system', the activity of monitoring distributor performance is completely missing. If the Senior Management team...hold this view, then the current means and activities are insufficient... this value strand carries the greatest weighting and it is suggested from the analysis that any attempt to implement change should focus on the issues within this strand".

At stage five, Spurrell was also able to complete the analysis of each strand for domination. In this case he concluded that M domination occurred. "Upon analysis, however, the activities which Isopad currently performs are dominated by means. We hold many views about missing activities...we should be scanning the environment for impending circumstantial forces, we should be measuring the performance of our distributors etc., but we do none of these activities because we do not have the means to do so."

It was also clear that the sufficiency methodology, MRAM, used to complete the diagonal needed further refinement. Spurrell needed several attempts to resolve its complexity. It was also apparent that the VIVA methodology needed an improved procedure for the validation of the strand arguments. Since this time Castle has further refined the methodology incorporating increased emphasis on strand validation, using strand statements. Spurrell's conclusion at the completion of this first major application of CVAM was that it had enabled the Company to agree many useful actions to ensure survival and growth in a competitive environment. It was also noted that use of the methodology became second nature to Spurrell, who rapidly developed a mode 2 (Checkland and Scholes, 1990) form of the analysis. In short it appeared to have amended Spurrell's own value systems.

5. CONCLUSIONS

The organisation reports that the methodology did indeed help them evolve a new strategy for the marketing of this product and that it surfaced many new issues that had not been discussed during the strategy formulation process. It was the first time that the issue of supplier relationships had been identified as a critical success factor. It revealed to them that many vital activities were dominated by a lack of resources or the means of progression. These issues have all been formally actioned under the new strategy.

The research demonstrated that CVAM-STAR has surprising power and "enormous" appeal to managers. In this case the Manager's have subsequently used STAR to clarify other complex problems. The problems of dealing with the sheer variety demonstrated by such studies was all too apparent. In this case we needed to re-design attenuating mechanisms with great care. This has been done by introducing the idea of CVAM'ic strands into the methodology. Validation of the strands has been given particular attention. This has helped in the analysis of trade offs in resource allocation. Trade offs are now defined as occurring where activities or means appear in one or more strands. This together with the weightings attached to the strands has allowed the conceptualisation of "trade offs" as trade off diagrams to be made. The research identified user difficulties with the MRAM sub-methodology. This is undergoing re-design.

The action research programme has enabled the methodology to be further refined to the point where these ideas are now under investigation in an expanded action research program involving studies in the leisure industry, telecommunications, and CD manufacture.

REFERENCES

Beer S., 1990, The Heart of Enterprise, John Wiley and Sons, Chichester.

Castle J.A., 1995, The Development of an integrating methodology for Strategic and Operations Management., The Proceedings of the British Academy of Management Annual Conference, Sheffield University, pp 454.

Checkland P.B., 1981, Systems Thinking Systems Practice, Wiley, Chichester.

Checkland P.B., and Casar A., 1986, Vickers' concept of an appreciative system: A systemic account. Journal of Applied Systems Analysis, vol. 13: 4–17.

Checkland P.B., and Scholes J., 1990, Soft Systems Methodology in Action, Wiley, Chichester.

Denzin, N., and Lincoln Y., 1994, Handbook of Qualitative Research, Sage Publications, London.

DePoy E, and Gitlin L., 1993, Introduction to Research, Multiple Strategies for Health and Human Services, Mosby, St. Louis.

Goodwin P., and Wright G., 1991, Decision Analysis for Management Judgement, Wiley, Chichester .

Hill T., 1985, Manufacturing Strategy, Macmillan, Basingstoke.

Keeney R.L., and Raiffa H., 1976, Decisions with Multiple Objectives: Preferences and Value Tradeoffs, Wiley, New York.

Slack N., Chambers S., Harland C., Harrison A., and Johnston R., 1995, Operations Management, Pitman, London.

Spurrell S. A., 1996, An investigation into using a new systems based methodology, CVAM for linking strategic and operations management. Dissertation submitted for the degree of Master of Business Administration. Bristol Business School, The University of the West of England.

Thompson J. D., 1967, Organisations in Action, McGraw Hill, New York.

71

MANAGING CHANGE IS A HUMAN PROCESS WHICH INTERVENTION APPROACHES OFTEN IGNORE

Melvyn Chapman

University of Lincolnshire and Humberside
School of Engineering and Information Technology
Cottingham Road, Hull
email mchapman@humber.ac.uk

1. INTRODUCTION

Successful intervention when managing change is affected by technical, social and personal factors. Whilst the technical aspects of intervention are well covered by methodologies and the social aspects of values are beginning to be covered, the way distorted communications affect change management at the personal and social levels is still at issue (Flood and Jackson, 1991, p.189). Many intervention approaches are primarily technical and are consequently too mechanistic to deal with distorted communications arising out of different worldviews, for example, hard systems methodologies. Structured Systems Analysis and Design Methodology is a typical hard information systems methodology which concentrates on mainly technical aspects and treats information as having meaning only within very limited contexts. Soft systems methodologies, for example, Checkland's Soft Systems Methodology (Checkland, 1981) although incorporating values arising out of different worldviews, does not consider whether the participants, or culture in which they operate, adversely affect the communication process (Flood and Jackson, 1991, p. 188). One problem with both of these approaches is that the content of communications is favoured over the process of communications, with the result that the former maybe derived unequally because the participants possess unequal power. There is no theory within the approaches governing whether the communication process is rationally driven and this allows the charge to be made that non rational factors can distort the communication process. It is suggested here that a more effective approach can be obtained by using management approaches with other methodologies in a complementary manner. Such methodologies should inform participants about the limitations of their own communication and be able to allow adjustment prior to using harder methodologies.

Systems for Sustainability, edited by Stowell *et al.*
Plenum Press, New York, 1997

2. THE NEED FOR COMMUNICATION

A management approach like Schein's Process Consultancy (1969, pp. 21–26) explicitly provides an underlying theory of communication with a view to making it more rational and equal between participants. This has value if organizational structures are seen to be moving away from hierarchical towards networked structures, where individuals are required to have more autonomy and hence where trust between individuals is considered to be of higher importance. Underlying the Process Consultancy approach is a theory of communications which explicitly recognizes that people are not always able to communicate clearly for emotional and other reasons because they either hide information about themselves or are unaware of what they are fully communicating. This may mean for example, that individuals may attempt to dominate a conversation because they fear particular individuals in a group or send contradictory messages by word and action when they imagine that they are being very clear. By concentrating on the communication process, participants are encouraged to reveal to each other the meaning of messages which otherwise may not be understood or clearly appreciated by others. They are also required to feed back to each other constructive comments about what has been revealed or misunderstood in an attempt to improve the quality of communications taking place. In this way participants should appreciate each others point of view more effectively even though there may still be disagreements. Giddens' work on "trust" (Giddens, 1993, pp. 295–303) is significant here because open communications require both personal trust between people and because trust is constitutive of social norms which make up roles. Trust is seen by Giddens to be partly emotionally based (Giddens, 1991, p. 38), insofar as it allows individuals to risk themselves personally and socially, and rational in that they need to be able to express themselves more openly. The very emotional basis for trust also suggests a strong non-rational element which is often considered external to rational debate but where trust is missing it may lead to a distortion of the communication process. Both Giddens and Schein make the point that where trust is less open, communications will suffer and the rationality of the communications will be harder to determine (Giddens, 1993, p. 9 and Schein, 1969, pp. 21–26). Handy also makes the point that where control increases, also implying control over communications, then trust will also decrease (Handy, 1985, pp. 327–329). Control which is required over others will interfere with trust and initiative, where as increasing trust requires the release of control to others. This is exactly what is required in situations of change where networked structures are required at the expense of hierarchical structures. In these situations individuals either separately or in teams are required to operate more flexibly to environmental pressures and to achieve this they have to be able to appreciate the culture they are in rather than operate by fixed rules that restrict initiative. But, as was stated earlier, this is ignored by many hard and soft systems approaches because they tend to take for granted the process of communication taking place between participants. However, these methodologies do not guarantee that different interests will be considered or that commitment will occur. By making explicit communications at the human level there is much more chance that areas of interest will be covered because agendas will be more open to discussion and people can challenge each other as to why they hold certain views rather than be afraid of authority or be intimidated. Where people are blind about any difficulties in communications they have with others then they can be given feedback by them. By encouraging people to disclose information which is hidden about their motivations then people will become more accountable. But if they prefer to restrict information about their true motivations then communications will remain distorted and people will tend to act more in their own interests. These two processes, disclosure and feedback, taken together can help make explicit the factors behind individual or group communications and thus can encourage more negotiation to take place (Schein, 1969, pages 24–25). In this way communication will become more rational because it will operate to principles that are clear to all parties. The theory behind this is that distortion arises out of the confused understanding brought about by what individuals mean when they communicate badly either to themselves or others. Where this process can be made more explicit then communication will be improved, particularly to oneself, and the communication will become more rational. Deliberate confusion occurs in part because people wish to maintain control over others for emotional reasons or social reasons and this of course will continue where the organizational structures support this, as in the case of hierarchy for status reasons. But where the structures are required to change, because the environment also demands more flexible structures, then there is less need to maintain taller hierarchies which tend to restrict communication downwards. This suggests that individuals will therefore be selected who are more willing to learn how to share power with others through having effective communication skills rather than seeking to control others for its own sake. There is therefore a subjective and an objective consideration to this argument insofar as an individual need for security is often served by seeking socially defined status within hierarchical systems but also because such systems require individuals to seek such power in order that they will work effectively. If the individual is also someone who finds it hard to trust others because they are seeking power as a way of compensating for their own weaknesses then their effective contribution will be dysfunctional in an organizational setting which requires more power sharing (and this may also be true in one that is hierarchically based). Major stakeholders often prefer only technical aspects to be discussed because these are mainly concerned with restricting others to a discussion about means rather than ends; which have already been decided. Even with softer methodologies any discussion about whether the ends are wrong might tend to interfere with the status quo.

But this leads to an important question, which is, can methodologies be misused in situations? From the above argument methodologies can be distorted in use even though they are classified as being of a unitary type where everyone is supposed to agree about the goals (as in the case of systems analysis methodologies) but it would normally be expected that at least the major stakeholders will tend to agree. With pluralistic methodologies (e.g. soft systems approaches) where people can reach agreement about the information products by negotiation this is still the case. The reason for this is as stated above, because those in power can reduce the issues to purely technical considerations or restrict the boundary of the study to serve their own interests. The consultant, or anyone making an intervention, can easily mistake a type of methodological approach as being suitable for a situation because they do not question any of the assumptions about the brief they are given by the stakeholders. Such people are often technical experts who work specifically for the major stakeholders and carry this authority into the study. This can be checked out by inviting all of the participants affected by the systems design to consider the nature of the situation they are in and to treat any problems identified already as problematic, but in prior to this they will need to improve their chances for having a rational conversation. Particularly with hard systems methodologies these issues arise but they are often affected because stakeholders can define which areas are off limits by keeping the discussion to a technical domain and by only allowing certain value considerations to intrude such as efficiency.

3. CONCLUSION

We are left with the argument that in order to pursue a more effective intervention it is desirable to consider the individual and group needs and technical aspects of the situation explicitly by using methodological approaches which allow any communication process to be queried. By using complementary methodologies and or approaches it is suggested that change management will be more rationally driven because it is made more explicit to all those involved. Harder and softer approaches like the ones mentioned earlier are able to determine the content of material and even include value considerations, but approaches like Process Consultancy allow participants to consider why they would not even want to consider each others interests by studying their own communication processes. The value of getting participants to study their own communication process means that where it is seen to fail it is exposed as a failure only in itself but there is no value judgement implied about what the communication should be about. It is left to the participants to consider the value of this but it does make explicit where some participants do not recognize or will not accept particular features of communications as being valid. Of course there is no guarantee that individuals will necessarily embark on such a process or will not break off from it, if it becomes difficult or compromising in their eyes. But this is still more rational as a process because it exposes the difficulties for all to see. Power becomes irrational when it appears less accountable, in a Kafkaesque sense, as experienced by those at the bottom of the hierarchy and those without control. But power can only be misused if the communication processes supporting it are allowed to remain distorted. It is only when we can consider each individual and the part they play in the communication processes of an organizational structure that we also can see how they use it or distort it. There are of course other aspects which are not dealt with by such approaches as Process Consultancy which are equally important, such as the skills and personality of the individuals concerned. Even where organizational structures are designed to be less competitive and flatter there will still be people who will prefer to influence and control others through keeping information private. People will also differ as to their abilities to be social and to be dominant and it will be very difficult to equalize these factors even if it is desirable. But what is at issue is not that people have different abilities so much as that a fit should exist between what people are required to do, and want to achieve, and what the organizational requirements should be. If the methodologies we choose do not seriously considered this then we will encourage dysfunctional organizations which state one thing and do another.

REFERENCES

Checkland, P., 1981, *Systems Thinking, Systems Practice*, John Wiley & Sons, Chichester, England.

Flood, R.L., and Jackson, M.C., 1991, *Creative Problem Solving, Total Systems Intervention*, John Wiley & Sons, Chichester, England..

Giddens, A., 1991, *Modernity and Self Identity, Self and Society in the Late Modern Age*, Polity Press, Cambridge, England.

Giddens, A., 1993, The Nature of Modernity in: *The Giddens Reader*, (P. Cassell, ed.) Stanford University Press, Stanford, California.

Handy, C., 1985, *Understanding Organizations*, 3rd ed., Penguin Books Ltd, Middlesex, England.

Schein, E.H., 1969, *Process Consultation: Its Role in Organisation Development,* Addison-Wesley, Reading, Massachusetts.

72

BORN FREE IN AN UNFREE WORLD

A Five-Level Emancipatory Program

Jeremy K. H. Chia,[1] John C. Oliga,[2] and Annies L. F. Foong[2]

[1]Utopia Aire Pte Ltd.
No. 7 Loyang Way
Singapore 508721, Republic of Singapore
Fax: (65) 545-0060
[2]Commerce Department
The University of Papua New Guinea
Box 320, University P. O.
National Capital District
Papua New Guinea
Fax: (675) 3-267-187

1. INTRODUCTION

Modernity, postmodernity, and beyond (who knows ?) are phases of a socially constructed reality, the narratives of which continue unfolding in higher and higher levels of complexity and hostility, as manifested in faster and faster speeds of change. Focussing on contemporary societies, we can discern two distinctive problems. The first relates to a materially conceived world characterized by increasing systemic hypercomplexity, but fraught with the danger of coercive use of power. The second relates to a symbolic world of communicative interaction, but similarly fraught with dangers of strategic deception or ideological distortion or obfuscation. It is through the medium of power (whether in the form of money, or bureaucratic power) that actions for the material reproduction of societies become coordinated for system integration. But there lies the danger of dominative use of power. The problem of coordinating social actions for the symbolic reproduction of society points to the need for social integration through the medium of consensus making via symbolic processes of communication. But again, there lie dangers and problems of deception, distortion or obfuscation. In this chapter we seek to provide an outline of the very daunting task of an emancipatory programme at five levels of recursion, from the most general, lowest resolution level of Habermas's (1972; 1974) interest constitution theory, namely, the Technical, the Practical, and the Emancipatory interests (the TPE model), through Oliga's (1996) Power, Ideology, and Control (the PIC model) to Chia's (1996) three models of the emancipatory task, namely, the Beliefs, Ethics, and Trust (the BET model), the Resources, Vision, and Goals (the RVG model), and the Jobs, People, and Freedom (the JPF model). In a nutshell, the chapter points to an unfortunate situation where individuals are born in this world free and anonymous, but that as this cloak of anonymity is progressively shed, shackles of unfreedom get fastened tighter and tighter.

2. A FIVE-LEVEL EMANCIPATORY PROGRAM

2.1. The Prioritization Rationale

The problematic, characteristic features of our today's world are that we are increasingly facing turbulent and unremitting swirls of unpredictable change, global competitive pressures, and hypercomplexity in our domestic, international, and global transactions and communication.

But, the hope is that we still have faith and confidence in our ability to resolve these problematic issues, not in a "once and for all" manner, but in an on-going process of speaking, acting and interacting. It is in this spirit that we present this chapter on the basic skeleton and broad ideas about this tricky and daunting area of emancipatory programme for the betterment of the human condition.

Although in terms of levels of recursion, Habermas's TPE model is at the lowest level, given its wider generality, we believe that the emancipatory program should begin with the JPF Model at the highest recursion level. Our rationale for this program prioritization is based on the natural, human growth and development from birth to maturity and on. A baby is born free, oblivious of the forces of unfreedom waiting for it ahead as it grows and assumes the mantle of self-identity in society. The emancipatory task should begin at the individual level (striving for an autonomous space), progressively moving to more complex levels: at the organizational (striving for an equitable share among competing goals); the cultural (striving for trust for meaningful interaction and communication); the societal (striving for social transformation of dominative structures and processes); and finally at the human species level (striving for communicative reason, rational social action, and towards ultimate human emancipatory potential). We now turn briefly to these emancipatory models.

2.2. The Jobs, People, and Freedom (JPF) Model

At the highest level of resolution in our schema, the emancipatory program starts with a program of action reflecting the three fundamental human interests: people needing *jobs* (labor), people needing *people* (communicative interaction), and people needing *freedom* (autonomy). Chia's (1996) JPF model is thus the basic form of operationalizing the emancipatory program.

2.3. The Resources, Vision, and Goals (RVG) Model

At the next level of resolution, the emancipatory program translates into Chia's (1996) resources, vision, and goals (RVG). *Resources* refer to a materialist concept where we deal with the natural or an objectivated social world with the instrumental aim of prediction and control (cf. Habermas, 1984; Oliga, 1996). *Vision* is used here in a perceptual sense, and refers to the hermeneutical activity of understanding and interpreting other minds. *Goals* refer to the teleological concept of purposive activity (cf. Habermas, 1984; 1987; Oliga, 1988; 1996).

2.4. The Beliefs, Ethics, and Trust (BET) Model

Habermas (1984) has argued that in speaking and acting, we simultaneously raise a number of validity claims, which are open to criticism by hearers, but which, as speakers, we are prepared to defend in argumentation. For our purpose, three validity claims are particularly relevant: truth/falsity in the theoretical/cognitive domain, normativity right-ness/wrongness in the moral-practical domain, and sincerity/authenticity (truthfulness/un-truthfulness) in the aesthetics domain. Habermas (1984, p.99) elaborates these validity claims as follows: (1) That the statement made is true (or that the existential presupposi-tions of the propositional content mentioned are in fact satisfied); (2) That the speech act is right with respect to the existing normative context (or that the normative context that it is supposed to satisfy is itself legitimate); and (3) That the manifest intention of the speaker is meant as it is expressed.

In Chia's (1996) BET model, *beliefs* correspond to Habermas's validity claim of *truth*, *ethics* corresponds to *rightness*, and *trust* to *sincerity/authenticity*.

2.5. The Power, Ideology, and Control (PIC) Model

In the concluding chapter of his book, *Power, Ideology, and Control*, Oliga (1996) presents his PIC model (p.292). In his words (Oliga, 1996, pp. 291–293): "Our argument in this book is that it is through these two media of *power* and *ideology* that *control* is ex-ercised, leading to social *domination*... Connecting domination and emancipation is our ar-gument that the emacipatory struggle requires educative *enlightenment* against *ideology*, *empowerment* processes against coercive forces of *power*, and *transformative* action against dominative *control*.

2.6. The Technical, the Practical, and the Emancipatory Interests (TPE) Model

Habermas (1972; 1974), in his path-breaking epistemological treatise on knowl-edge and human interests, cogently argued that all human interests, regardless of time (history) and space are exhaustively captured under three categories: the technical inter-est, the practical interest, and the emancipatory interest; and that it is these three basic human interests that drive or motivate our quest for different forms of knowledge. Fur-thermore, he argued that these three basic human interests arise from two fundamental forms of activity, namely, labor (work) and communicative interaction, both of which are again, in spatiotemporal terms, universal and anthropologically invariant to the human species. The technical interest aims at the prediction and control of the natural and the objective social world. The practical interest aims at achieving intersubjective communi-cative understanding. The emancipatory interest seeks to achieve the realization of autonomy from defective actions and utterances stemming from intersubjective/social re-lations of power (cf. Habermas, 1972; 1974; Giddens, 1977; McCarthy, 1978; Oliga, 1988; 1990; 1991a; 1991b; 1996; Laughlin et al., 1981; Chua et al., 1981). Furthermore, the three interests (TPE) reflect three types of interaction, namely "man to nature" for the technical interest, "man to man" for the practical interest, and "man to self" for the emancipatory interest.

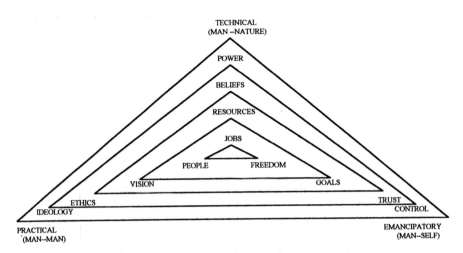

Figure 1. The triangular nesting of emancipatory programs.

3. CONCLUSION

Figure 1 is a diagrammatic representation (and summary) of the nesting of the emancipatory program at different levels of recursion/resolution. The logic of prioritizing the emancipatory tasks from the highest to the lowest program recursion level was argued to make practical sense in development and human learning terms. We grow up by first learning to crawl (a concern with simple issues of jobs, people, and freedom) before we can attempt to run (a concern with the more complex issues of formal discourses and the force of better argumentation).

REFERENCES

Chia, K. H., 1996, Recursive dimensions of the emancipatory program for contemporary societies, *Entrepreneurship, Innovation, and Change* **5**(3):253–262.

Chua, W. F., Laughlin, R. C., Lowe, E. A., and Puxty, A. G., 1981, *Four Perspectives on Accounting Methodology*, Paper presented at the Workshop on Accounting and Methodology, European Institute for Advanced Studies in Management, Brussels.

Flood, R. L., 1993, *Beyond TQM*, Wiley, Chichester, UK.

Flood, R. L., 1995, *Solving Problem Solving*, Wiley, Chichester, UK.

Flood, R. L., and Jackson, M. C., 1991, *Creative Problem Solving: Total Systems Intervention*, Wiley, Chichester, UK.

Giddens, A., 1977, *Studies in Social and Political Theory*, Hutchinson, London.

Habermas, J., 1972, *Knowledge and Human Interests*, (trans. by Shapiro, J.), Heinemann, London.

Habermas, J., 1974, *Theory and Practice*, Heinemann, London.

Habermas, J., 1984, *The Theory of Communicative Action: Reason and the Rationalization of Society*, (Vol. 1, trans. by McCarthy, T.), Beacon Press, Boston, Mass.

Habermas, J., 1987, *The Theory of Communicative Action: Lifeworld and System: A Critique of Functionalist Reason*, (Vol. 2, trans. by McCarthy, T.), Beacon Press, Boston, Mass.

Laughlin, R. C., Lowe, E. A., Puxty, A. G., and Chua, W. F., 1981, *The Function of Subject Makers in the Epistemology and Methodology of Accounting*, Paper presented to the Annual Conference of the Association of University of Teachers in Accounting, Dundee, Scotland.

McCarthy, T., 1978, *The Critical Theory of Jurgen Habermas*, MIT Press, Cambridge, Mass.

Oliga, J. C., 1988, Methodological foundations of systems methodologies, *Systems Practice* 1(1) :87–112.

Oliga, J. C., 1990, Power in organisations: A contingent, relational view, *Systems Practice* 3(5) : 453–477.

Oliga, J. C., 1991a, Conceptions of ideology: An exegesis and critique, *Systems Practice* 4(2):101–129.

Oliga, J. C., 1991b, Methodological foundations of systems methodologies, in: *Critical Systems Thinking: Directed Reading*, (R. L. Flood, and M. C. Jackson, eds.), pp.159–183, Wiley, Chichester, UK.

Oliga, J. C., 1991c, Power-ideology matrix in social systems control, in: *Critical Systems Thinking: Directed Reading*, (R. L. Flood, and M. C. Jackson, eds.), pp.269–286, Wiley, Chichester, UK.

Oliga, J. C., 1996, *Power, Ideology, and Control*, Plenum Press, New York.

Puxty, A. G., Soo, W. F., Lowe, E. A., and Laughlin, R. C., 1980, *Towards Critical-Theoretic Perspective for an Epistemology of Managerial Theory*, Paper presented at the Workshop "Towards an Epistemology of Management Research," Stockholm School of Economics, Stockholm, Sweden.

73

A PRACTICAL PROJECT AT HM PRISON HULL

Total Systems Intervention or Total Systems Failure?

John Clayton and Wendy Gregory

Centre for Systems Studies
Department of Management Systems and Sciences
University of Hull, Hull, HU7 6RX

1. INTRODUCTION

The paper presents an application of the reconstituted version of Total Systems Intervention (called TSI#2 hereafter) in a prison context. Questions are raised about the putative success or failure of the intervention in terms of the principles of TSI#2. The aim of the study was to carry out a practical application of 'Total Systems Intervention' (TSI) (Flood and Jackson, 1991; Flood, 1995), to promote a multi-agency perspective toward support systems for young offenders who find themselves detained in the stark and often hostile environment of an adult prison. Since 1847 it has been recognised in this country that children who break the law should not be treated in the same way as adult offenders (Levenson, 1976). The principles of treating young offenders differently from adults, and endeavouring to educate and reform rather than punish, were granted full statutory force under the Children's Act 1908. Yet it was not until early in 1991 that it was announced by Kenneth Baker, the then Home Secretary, that the practice of remanding 15 and 16 year old youths to prison was to be abolished.

2. HM PRISON HULL

Hull Prison adopted the role of a male local prison and remand centre in 1986, thus catering for a broad divergence of prisoners, all with inconsonant needs. Recently the prison has operated against a background of continuous uncertainty. There have been many policy changes responding to contemporary demands placed on the prison. Since they often came without prior warning, these changes were frequently wanting in terms of prior planning. According to Her Majesty's Chief Inspector of Prisons, Judge Stephen Tumim (Home Office, 1995), juveniles and young offenders up to the age of 20 should not be sent to Hull Prison.

Systems for Sustainability, edited by Stowell *et al.*
Plenum Press, New York, 1997

3. RESEARCH

The project described in this paper was undertaken with an extremely broad remit: Hull Prison's Human Resources Manager was the initial point of contact and introductions to the many agencies and departments who have dealings with young offenders were quickly made. After preliminary introductions, more detailed interview sessions were arranged in which the various stakeholders were given free range to discuss or raise any issues that they felt were appropriate. The aim of the study was to conduct an intervention with practical consequences. It was the intention that the stakeholders—those involved and affected—would be directly involved in the research, and were expected to reap any benefits accrued, either in the form of its outcomes from the process itself. The stages of the project were planned to facilitate the usage of the re-constituted version of TSI (Flood, 1995), with initial interviews designed to elicit the ways that participants viewed their situation. It was intended that a subsequent multi-agency meeting would provide an arena in which participants could begin to grapple with some of the issues identified in the preliminary interviews. Issues are often shrouded by the use of metaphorical descriptions and the next section details the range of metaphors used by participants.

4. METAPHORS

Metaphors are central to the way we think about the world around us (Lakoff and Johnson, 1980). Some people fathom conceptions via the application of imagery more eagerly and effectually than through words, and thus metaphor remains a most appropriate disposition for thinking and communicating. The first of the metaphors used to describe the working environment at HMP Hull demonstrates the belief that all the elements one might require are present, if only they could be brought together and coordinated in an effective manner—in other words: '*working here is like trying to knit fog!*' This metaphor describes an overarching impression of the problems, in which the task of working within the prison system was depicted as one where the individual trying to achieve the objective is the observer and the rolling banks of fog are the elements required to complete the task. The incapacity to 'knit' simultaneously the precise combination of elements essential to the attainment of any objective is further exacerbated by the circumstances echoed in the next metaphor: 'you never know where you stand, they are *continually moving the goal posts!*' Both internal and external agencies used this metaphor in relation to the 'rules and regulations' of the prison. The situation faced is one of not knowing what constitutes a goal. The goal posts are continually moving in response to changes in the policy, personalities, and environment of the prison. Discovering what constitutes the goal posts at any given time is a matter of trial and error, and dogged persistence. In contrast to this imagery, but suggesting some of the same kinds of problems, the third metaphor that was used described working at Hull Prison as akin to '*swimming in treacle*'. This was perhaps the least optimistic of the metaphors utilised. As perceived by an individual faced with the task of working within the prison system, the situation involves him/her (the swimmer) in trying to achieve an objective, and the treacle is the viscous mélange that constitutes the working environment. A vicious circle of events sees the individual in ever thickening treacle with less and less inclination to swim against the viscous tide.

The metaphors used by the participants of the study to describe the problem situation have been outlined - 'knitting fog', 'continually moving goal posts', and 'swimming in treacle'. Attention will now turn to the additional 'political' metaphors we used to aid further understanding. The political metaphor is one of five principal metaphors contained within the scope of organisation and management theory (Flood, 1995) that have been employed as models to aid organisational analysis. When put to use on problem situations, the political metaphor pursues the relationships between individuals and groups as competitive and encompassing the courting of power. There are three contrasting descriptions of the condition of any political situation provided by the industrial relations literature—designated unitary (where goals are common), pluralist (where goals diverge), and coercive (where goals conflict) (Flood and Jackson, 1991). The political metaphor concentrates on three issues through which it is possible to assess the character of a problem situation—issues of interests, conflict, and power—and can be used to analyse the situation at Hull Prison as it was perceived by the researchers.

HMP Hull comprises a number of groups all with their own concerns and interests, but with a mutual focal point which is the security of the prison and the control and care of its inmates. There is a propensity for conflict but there are many points on which agreement is readily made. Also, the conflict inherent in the situation often displays a decidedly positive role. Ultimately, power within the prison rests with the security lobby. However, it is acknowledged that other aspects of prison government directly impact upon security, and this prevents unqualified subjugation of other groups. The relationship between the participants in this situation can therefore be distinguished as of a political character that is pluralist in its complexion.

A second political metaphor that aided reflection was the 'fire fighting' metaphor. We describe it as political since it is inexorably linked to the political metaphor outlined above: whoever has the power will dictate which fires have to be fought on a day-by-day basis. The 'fire fighting' metaphor describes the problem situation at Hull prison as one in which the fires are the individual 'problems' faced and those dealing with these 'problems' are collectively the fire engine and its crew.

Each of these metaphors produced different insights into how the work environment of HM Prison Hull, and specifically the environment of dealing with young offenders, was experienced by the various stakeholders. Having identified these views with the participants, the next stage involved identifying themes that offered potential for action. Some 10 such themes were identified and taken to the multi-agency workshop, where the participant groups rebelled against the very conceptions they had produced and denied that any difficulties of the sort identified for further discussion existed. Following the multi-agency workshop, we were left to ponder what the significant factors were that had prevented the possibility of people moving from their entrenched positions. The next section highlights some of our own reflections on the failure (or not) of TSI in this situation.

5. REFLECTIONS

There are two main areas for reflection on the project: firstly, its status as a piece of research; and, secondly, the extent to which the project adhered to the principles of the methodology (TSI#2).

5.1. Difficulties of Research in Prisons

From the start, establishing an image of an independent agent was problematic. We had the impression that in their eyes being 'an academic' was equivalent to being a 'do-gooder'. Consequently John was perceived as 'for the inmates' and 'anti-establishment' in orientation and a great deal of effort was required when meeting individuals for the first time to allay their fears that the project would unfold to display all the characteristics of a 'witch-hunt'. Although this apprehension was expected, it was nonetheless difficult to surmount in terms of this particular exercise - success in convincing participants that there was no deeply hidden agenda or ulterior motive was limited. Mair (1985) notes that the assumption is often made that there are a number of advantages to be gained from carrying out research into the criminal-justice system from within a government department, such as the Home Office Research and Planning Unit (RPU). The most significant of these advantages is the ease of access to organisations such as the police, prison staff etc., and secondly, the access to unpublished data. However, as Mair quite rightly points out, the advantages cannot be simply taken for granted. The fact that they are extant in methodological terms might be beyond dispute, but in both practical and organisational terms they are 'rather more problematic'. On this occasion access to unpublished data was not an issue. However, access to even the most innocuous of documentation was indeed problematic. This undoubtedly arose from the non official status of the project.

5.2. Principles of TSI#2

TSI#2 has at its foundations four cardinal principles - being systemic, achieving meaningful participation, being reflective, and the goal of enhancing human freedom. In practice, the TSI-user must constantly strive to fulfil these principles in order for the intervention to be considered as a valid use of TSI (Flood, 1995). How did this particular application face up to the principles of TSI?

5.2.1. Being Systemic. Did the project uphold the commitment to study organisational forms as if they were systemic? For all their acknowledgement of the necessity of a holistic approach, and its perceived utility, it was clear that this was nothing more than polite lip service by the stakeholders. The participants betrayed themselves by continuing to display the traditional reductionist thinking that pervades our society, and by their insistence on relieving the 'symptoms' as manifest rather than finding the counteractive cure. So consideration of the 'whole' was left to the researchers.

5.2.2. Achieving Meaningful Participation. Was a sufficient understanding reached to maintain a whole system perspective? A number of difficulties were encountered in achieving the principle of meaningful participation. Fundamental though it is, it proved to be troublesome to incorporate in practice. The work commitments of certain individuals may have compelled them to truncate their involvement. Others appeared to find it necessary to evade participation altogether. The limitations of the restricted time available, and the subsequent lack of access to the inmates, pose a thorny question when it comes to the issue of validity. The sum total of interviews was restricted, and for the most part dictated by circumstance. This led to a situation where individuals captured disproportionate amounts of time and attention. Firstly, this allowed for the possibility of a distortion of the portrayal of the problem situation and, secondly, it restricted the capacity to identify when the interviewees were bending or embellishing the truth, or indeed when they were consciously telling lies - this would have required a far greater depth of detailed knowledge. Finally, we note that it is not possible to force people to participate in a meaningful way. The majority of those representing the outside agencies who attended the multi-agency meeting openly admitted at its conclusion that the only reason they had attended was to 'swap telephone numbers', after 'identifying an agency with a face'. There appeared to be little commitment to attaining meaningful participation.

5.2.3. Being Reflective. The first reflective need is the need to reflect upon the divergent organisational interests and the relationships between them. So the question is: How did they impact upon people and their opportunity to participate in a meaningful way? As with the principle of being systemic, John appeared to be alone on the first of the reflective needs. He was the only one considering the existence of divergent organisational interests. The participants appeared uniformly to agree that they were all working toward the same consensual goal and, therefore, it followed that their interests were also unitary. This seems to fly in the face of the diversity of metaphors used and issues identified. The second need is to reflect upon the precedence of preferred approaches of intervention, and the restrictive nature of the problem solving capability that ensues. What were the preferred approaches and their capabilities in problem solving? The preferred mechanistic approach, combined with an authoritarian style of management is seriously curbing organisational development. Those involved had no genuine intent to pursue the development of the provision of their combined services. Rather what they wanted to consider was the more efficient coordination of that which was already extant. In other words they saw no reason to seriously challenge the accepted way of doing things, the only need they could envisage was one of 'fine tuning' - there remained a belief that the system was essentially sound, and therefore 'development' was unnecessary.

5.2.4. The Goal of Enhancing Human Freedom. There was little or no reflection, and a lack of consideration for the whole, except on John's part. Combined with a doubt as to whether meaningful participation was achieved during the course of the project, and therefore it is impossible to begin to imagine that the fourth principle could have been upheld in the absence of those which precede it.

6. CONCLUSION

The metaphors used by the agencies involved had a number of similarities, but there were also marked differences in their uses. We would speculate that this disparity occurs because of cultural differences and the personality types that the various agencies attract. In addition, some who attended the multi-agency meeting did so with no real intention of participating, leading to what could only be considered as a less than whole system perspective. We would therefore suggest that this particular intervention could only be considered as a valid use of TSI on one count, that in practice the four principles were constantly striven towards by the researchers. Therefore, the minimum requirement to be considered a valid use of TSI was fulfilled. Had all those who made a commitment to participate done so, and access to inmates' and officers' opinions come to pass, and had free access to the prison come to fruition as was pledged, a more fruitful outcome may have been achieved.

Current financial restrictions, and scheduled budget cuts, provide an environment which contains an unrelenting problem of choice. As an organisation that is essentially bureaucratic in its complexion, it is our opinion that HMP Hull is ill-equipped to resolve such a problem. Management practice is reactive and 'solutions' currently in place are resource driven—resources determine policy, managers are given a budget and are expected to do the best job that can be done with it. This has led to a 'coping culture' in which planning is a superfluous and time consuming activity. This and the wide ranging problems expressed by members of the organisation reflect a non-holistic approach and are an indication that the current piecemeal situation is not working. Ultimately the prison management wanted a diagnosis on a plate—a free extension to the current communications survey being undertaken at the prison by outside consultants. Unfortunately, this was not made known until the project's conclusion, had it been surfaced earlier who knows what may have transpired.

REFERENCES

Carvel, J., 1991, Jail remand of youths to be abolished. (1991, February 5). *The Guardian*, p. 4.

Flood, R.L., 1995, *Solving Problem Solving*, Wiley, Chichester.

Flood, R.L., and Jackson, M.C., 1991, *Creative Problem Solving*, Wiley, Chichester.

Home Office, 1995, *HM Prison Hull*, Home Office, London.

Lakoff, G. and Johnson, M., 1980, *Metaphors We Live By*, University of Chicago Press, Chicago

Levenson, H., 1976, Children in prison, National Council for Civil Liberties, Report, **15**.

Mair, G., 1985, Some practical problems of criminal justice research, Home Office Research and Planning Unit, Research Bulletin, **19**.

74

SYSTEMIC REFOCUSING

A Strategy for Sustainability

Peter Dudley and John Hassall

Centre for Systems Studies
University of Hull
Wolverhampton Business School
University of Wolverhampton
Business Designers

The initial formulation of Systemic Refocusing Strategy (SRS) was intended as an attempt to provide the system (at that time through the agency of the strategic decision makers of the system) with a tool for stepping beyond its own boundaries "thinking outside the box". The notion in our initial papers was, that systems were (in general agreement with Checkland (1981)) linguistic devices through which decision makers cognized the world and how, through these devices, systems were able to move toward enhanced self-sustainability. Recursive applications of systemic principles in the work of, for example, Beer (1974; 1985), Bogdanov, (1996) Jantsch (1980), Lovelock (1995a and 1995b) and Prigogine (1980), suggest that systems are not able to exist in an isolated bubble of self-sustainability and, contrary to the precepts of traditional systems theory, the actions of the system can affect its environment in more than a merely trivial way. Therefore systemic decisions regarding self-sustainability (whether through the agency of strategic decision makers or not) must, in some way, be cognizant of the needs of their environment - in short, should its environment collapse, the system cannot survive.

One of the problems in addressing issues of sustainability caused by systems theory, and its view of the world, is the tendency to regard the environment as a unity to be overcome in the struggle for systemic survival. This is apparent in the works of the earliest systems thinkers, e.g. Bertalanffy (1968) or Wiener (1962) and even in the works of what would normally be regarded as pre-systemic thinkers, e.g. Darwin's "Origin of Species" (see Darwin, 1900). This view presents the environment as a source of complexity to which the system must respond to in order to survive (which is correct) and as an essentially robust entity, largely unaffected by the actions of the system (which is not).

When the environment is perceived not as a single mass but, rather, as an interactive agglomeration of individual other systems each as tenuously poised on the brink of existence as the "system in focus", one is forced to accept the fragility of the environment in

Systems for Sustainability, edited by Stowell *et al.*
Plenum Press, New York, 1997

the same manner as one accepts the fragility of the "system in focus". A simple iterative application of the principle of interconnectedness then places the actions of this system in context. Where, in classical theory, the system cannot affect the environment, it can, sometimes catastrophically, affect individual other systems with which it is connected; the actions of the "system in focus" thus affecting the environment as a whole. ("...the butterfly flaps its wings...").

SRS was initially designed as a tool for allowing strategic decision makers to question the assumptions inherent in their decision making processes, with the aim of generating an increased potential for diversity in their responses to the perceived environmental demands made on the system in order to ensure its survival and development. (In the context of the original design, the system was assumed to be some form of organization.) One of the assumptions implicit in SRS was, in accord with Ashby's (1956) notion of "requisite variety", that the greater the variety of responses available to the system in its interaction with the environment the greater its chances of survival. SRS attempted to generate this potential for variety by way of the concrete application of a deconstructive strategy. The motivation was to enhance organizational decision making processes by widening the options open to decision makers. It is now evident that this result was achieved by making decision makers aware of the diversity which surrounded their decision processes per se, by making evident the undecidability of their actions (In this discussion, undecidability in the Derridian sense can be seen as similar to incompleteness in the Goedeliann sense.). In using SRS, decision makers are made aware of the decision environment as being comprised of individual other systems. In SRS the variety of the "system in focus" is enhanced by enhancing its sensitivity to the environment as comprised of individuals rather than its existence as a single unresponsive mass.

This first step in the re-cognizance of the environment as comprised of individual other systems is completely consistent with the search for strategies which enhance long term sustainability. Cognition of the environment not only as the source of complexity confronting the system in focus, but also as any number of equally fragile systems which provide (however difficult it is to perceive in particular circumstances) a greater potential for symbiosis than for confrontation, is completely consistent with the aims and process of SRS.

In this view the environment is not an undifferentiated mass to be overcome but a range of "partners in existence", each individual or group of which has its own needs for survival and makes its own contribution to the survival of all the others. Traditional approaches to systems theory prejudice the extent to which such a view of the environment can be taken since, by their nature, systems approaches define the environment as a function of the system in focus. (As an aside; the argument in the preceding paragraph is interesting in that most systems theorists appear to be realists, tending to question the ability to perceive reality rather than its existence. Thus, restricting what constitutes the environment to what interests the system (the relevant environment), becomes a rationalist sophism which contains potential for its own contradiction.)

The current emphasis on the maintenance of "bio-diversity" seems to support the assertion that complex interconnections of systems are stable in a way that simple systems are not, a notion that is further supported by Lovelock's "Gaia" (see Lovelock, 1995a, 1995b). Simple redundancy (i.e. multiple replication of the *same* process) is an insufficient condition for continued survival in anything but the most mechanical (or mechanistic views of) systems. When one moves beyond the mechanistic to the biological, ecological or social levels simplicity (defined as non-diversity) quickly becomes a pathological state—one need only think of the dangers of a reduced gene pool or the horrors which have, historically, been perpetrated in single party states. Diversity, both logically and, it would increasingly appear, according to contemporary wisdom, is a necessary precondition for sustainability.

The faculty for viewing the environment, or parts of it, as entities with their own rules for survival and, therefore, sustainability, is strictly curtailed. The traditional view of the sustainability of the environment is, necessarily, based in the view that the system in focus has of the conditions of its own survival. What appears to be needed is the ability to broaden the perspective of the system in focus.

As we have shown in our earlier papers (Dudley and Hassall, 1995) SRS provides a possible and practicable approach to this problem through the deconstruction of the normative assumptions the system brings to its perception of itself and, by extension, the rationality it applies in defining its environment. SRS is neither a dialectical method in, for example the manner of Marx or the "dialectical debate" proposed by Checkland (Cheekland, 1981) nor is it an extension of the "polemical employment of boundary judgements" (Flood and Jackson, 1991) suggested by Ulrich (see Flood and Ulrich, 1991; Ulrich, 1991), if it were it would fall foul of the very problem it itself suggests exists in current systems approaches. In the above method(ologie)s the antithetical term is the not us and is, therefore, analogous to the environment in systems approaches. In this manner not only is the thesis, or positive term, of the dialogue a function of the dominant rationality which underpins the dialogue, but so also are the antithesis and the synthesis. The antithetical term may well be diametrically opposed to the positive term. but only on the basis of the standards, values and language within which the thesis was formulated in the first place. It is an intra-paradigmatic opposedness unable to traverse the boundaries of its own, by definition constrained, rationality.

We can also apply the deconstructive strategy of SRS to probe the rationality of our own argument (as developed above) that "the maintenance of "bio-diversity" seems to support the assertion that complex interconnections of systems are stable in a way that simple systems are not". If this is an argument for greater diversity it can certainly be viewed from a number of possible normative perspectives. For example:

1. It is possible to view this from a modernist perspective—the statement represents how the world is described in terms of some sort of "law". It often seems that systems thinkers are striving for this.
2. It might be seen as a pre-religious statement. The world around us has existed for a long time, it appears complex, therefore complexity is necessary for long existence.
3. It could be viewed as a sort of species chauvinism. Human beings are amongst the most adaptable of life forms that we know, a diverse environment yields survival benefits attributable to adaptability, therefore "we would say that wouldn't we".

To argue for sustainability without examining the assumptions behind it could end in difficulties for human beings. Sustaining the planet may be one thing, ourselves another! SRS aims to provide some approach whereby the language and assumptions should be explicitly and emphatically challenged, in particular by recognising that the "systems in focus" can be evanescent in the extreme. And (for example), if we meet another intelligent race which is more adaptable than ourselves, such diversity may look a lot less attractive.

Thus SRS not only satisfies the conditions of diversity generation, i.e. by producing a number of possible interpretations of *the system,* and, therefore, an equal number of possible antitheses, it overcomes the dogma of self implicit in the dialectical method, but, in doing this, also demonstrates a characteristic that we have come to regard as the basis of any critical approach - *it is capable of defeating its own logic.*

REFERENCES

Ashby, W. R., 1956, *An Introduction to Cybernetics,* Chapman and Hall Ltd., London.

Beer, S., 1974, *"Designing Freedom".* Canadian Broadcasting Corporation, Toronto.

Beer, S., 1985, *"Diagnosing the System for Organizations",* Wiley, Chichester.

Bertalanffy, L., von, 1968, *General System Theory: Foundations, Development, Applications,* George Braziller, New York.

Bogdanov, A. A., 1996, *Bogdanov's, Tektology* (P. Dudley, ed.), Centre for Systems Studies Press, Hull.

Checkland, P. B., 1981, *Systems Thinking, Systems Practice,* Wiley, Chichester.

Darwin, C., 1900, The Origin of Species By Means of Natural Selection or the Preservation of Favoured Races in the Struggle for Life, John Murray, London.

Flood, R. L., and Jackson, M. C., 1991, *Creative Problem, solving,* Wiley, Chichester.

Flood, R. L., and Ulrich, W., 1991, Testament to Conversations on Critical Systems Thinking between Two Systems Practitioners, *Critical Systems Thinking: Directed Readings,* (Flood, R. L. and Jackson, M. C., eds.) Wiley, Chichester.

Jantsch, E., 1980, *Self-Organizing Universe: Scientific Implications of the Emerging Paradigm of Evolution,* Pergamon Press, Oxford.

Lovelock, J. E., 1995a, *Gaia: A New Look at Life on Earth,* OUP, Oxford.

Lovelock, J. E., 1995b, *The Ages of Gaia, OUP,* Oxford.

Prigogine, I., 1980, *From Being to Becoming: Time and Complexity in the Physical Sciences,* W. H. Freeman and Company, San Francisco.

Ulrich, W., 1991, Systems Thinking, Systems Practice and Practical Philosophy: A Program of Research, *Critical Systems Thinking: Directed Readings,* (Flood, R. L. and Jackson, M. C., eds.) Wiley, Chichester.

Wiener, N., 1962, *Cybernetics or Control and Communication in the Animal and the Machine,* MIT Press, Cambridge, Mass.

75

CONCERNING COMPUTER-BASED SUPPORT TOOLS FOR THE USER OF THE SOFT SYSTEMS METHODOLOGY

P. J. Dunning-Lewis

The Management School
Lancaster University
United Kingdom

1. INTRODUCTION

Wide interest in, and acceptance for, the using the soft systems methodology (SSM) in the development of information systems (Stowell, 1995; UKSS, 1992; Jayaratna, 1994; Lewis, 1994; Avison and Fitzgerald, 1995; Crowe, Beeby and Gammack, 1996; CCTA, 1993) has greatly increased awareness and use of the methodology. This growth in knowledge of SSM, often obtained through a secondary literature, inevitably leads to a change in the profile of the typical user of the methodology. Many new users will be less concerned with theoretical issues than the immediate, practical benefits that the methodology can provide, have had only limited, if any, supervised experience of the methodology's use and be unaware of theoretical discussions concerning the methodology and its use. This can have benefits (for example, a more daring willingness to experiment and adapt the methodology) but there is also the danger that ideas may be misunderstood, misapplied, employed crudely or inappropriately. New users may also feel at times uncertain in their use of SSM (Moore, 1996)

We are therefore at a point where assumptions of the past no longer hold true and more, perhaps different, assistance needs to be given to the SSM user. Better guidance for non-academic audiences, more detailed guidelines concerning particular techniques, and fully documented exemplar case-studies of SSM are needed. In addition to this we suggest that computer software has an as yet unexploited potential to guide the SSM user and make execution of the methodology easier. We here report on our learning from continuing work to provide computer-based support for the SSM user.

2. DEMONSTRATING THE FEASIBILITY AND UTILITY OF SUPPORT

Like many users of SSM we already make use of computer packages of various kinds when applying SSM, and have experimented with adapting CASE tools created for other purposes. However, our interest in interpretative data analysis (Lewis, 1993a; Lewis, 1993b; Lewis 1993c) has led us to explore the possibility of more tailored software in greater detail. Our research approach has been to try to create demonstrator software to fulfill some perceived needs of the SSM user, and to then try using that software in real-life applications of SSM. The creation of the software allows us to explore the feasibility of support and the use of the created software provides us with insights into practical utility. We recognize of course that since we are not unfamiliar with use of the methodology we cannot claim that the benefits gained in application are necessarily the same as would be gained, for better or worse, by novice users.

We first investigated the feasibility and utility of providing support at the second level (see Lewis, 1994), employing a DBMS package with OLE links to create a support tool that would hold the working documents of an SSM study. This was found to be suitable for archiving finalized working papers, but when used in the course of a study it offered only basic benefits. Furthermore, making amendments to the stored material was inconvenient and the user interface that could be provided was, whilst adequate, not particularly suited to the needs of real projects.

Next, in attempting to provide higher levels of support we followed the same approach as that of Avison and Goldner (1991) and Davenport and Ayers-Hunt (1995) in attempting to code individual modules to support particular SSM techniques. We did not however ascribe to the 'toolkit' approach in that we believe that real benefits only arise from an integrated support tool. The most significant finding from this approach was perhaps that only by linking to commercial software products were we able to produce working papers of the required quality for practical use.

Our current approach is therefore to provide a shell application. This provides a suitable interface for the SSM user, but makes use of any of a number of commercial packages when required. Only for those functional requirements for which professional packages do not exist are coded modules used. Thus when the user needs to create and store records of meetings then a package such as Microsoft's Word will be used to create the actual document, the finished work being then stored by the shell and retrieved as required. When however the manipulation of an interpretative data model is being done then tailored code will be used.

The requirements for this shell software were not specified in advance, but have evolved in response to the needs of a real-world applications of SSM, each function being added as it was required by the study. Among the surprises that came from adopting this approach have been the importance of providing different levels of access and security and the necessity for implementing careful change controls for the stored materials.

3. DIFFICULTIES AND BENEFITS OF SUPPORT FOR SSM

In this work we have necessarily confronted the possible objections to computer-support for the SSM user.

The most easily answered of these is that SSM requires such subtleties of human thought that it can as a process never be automated. Whether or not that assertion is true is somewhat irrelevant to our work, for it has never been the intention to automate the *doing* of SSM, merely to assist the user. Just as a machine can never write a great novel, there is no reason to doubt that word processors make the lives of novelists considerably easier, and may help bring a great novel into being.

Of more weight is that SSM is a methodology rather than a method, and even the original 7 stages model has been superseded (Checkland & Scholes, 1990). It might therefore be argued then that to provide computer-based support for any particular form of the use of SSM would not be useful, since that form, whatever it might be, would only be appropriate to particular problem situations. Our best response to this has been to try to make any support tool flexible enough to be used in whatever way the needs of the situation, and the user, demand. We do not for example make it mandatory for root definitions to be created before an activity model, nor limit the user's freedom to omit particular stages of SSM.

A related though somewhat different point is that regardless of whether or not computer-based support constrains how SSM is applied to the problem situation, it may constrain the user in their application of individual techniques of SSM.

In most cases providing support means some degree of standardization that can restrict thinking and imagination. A good example of this is the creation of rich pictures diagrams where the use of standard symbols could lead to a simple disagreement be represented identically to a major conflict (Lewis, 1992), rich pictures diagrams appearing anonymous and sterile, or misrepresenting the complexity of the problem situation (Kreher, 1993). There is no reason, however, that standardization need be applied in more than the minimum number of occasions, and where it is not contentious. For example, our attempts at support do make use of a standard template for recording expenses and this is not likely to be the cause of disagreement. However, if the user should wish to use some other format for recording such details, store them along with meetings records or omit them entirely then they are free to do so.

There is too the danger that the use of technology may, in itself, be detrimental to the enactment of an SSM study. The technology may be a distraction, act as a barrier to, or slow down the essential social processes of negotiation which are so important in SSM. It may be intimidating or alienating to some of those involved so that full participation is not achieved. And, as Kreher (1993) pointed out in respect to rich picture diagramming, the existence of technological support could distract users from the processes of SSM, and lead to a focus instead purely on the results. The response to these fears must lie with the way in which technological support is provided and introduced. One should of course make the visible face of the technology (the user interface) as natural as possible. Indeed it was the impossibility of doing this that was one of the dissatisfactions that we ourselves had with our first attempts to provide support. But more important will always be the sensitivity of the SSM practitioner to the needs of the study, and if they felt that a support tool could not be actively used with particular involved parties then there is no reason why it should not be represented merely as an aide-memoir for the facilitators during interactions or not publicly used at all. Further, the ubiquity of personal computers is such that few people now feel threatened by such technology and the absence of automated support for SSM is becoming, in itself, obstructive to the conduct of SSM studies. At a time when use of SSM is being advocated (CCTA, 1993) alongside development approaches such as SSADM that do have CASE support it has not gone unrecognized that the availability of automated support is becoming important in practical considerations of whether or not SSM might be used. (Tudor and Tudor, 1995; Avison, Shah and Goldner, 1993).

A final objection is that there exist at present insufficient guidelines on the use of SSM techniques to allow consistency checking or advisory capabilities to be included in any computer-based support. Without such it could be argued that only limited benefits can be obtained from such support. In response to this we would argue that there do exists sufficient theoretical principles and 'craft rules' for some level of guidance to be provided, for example concerning the constitution of system definitions or completeness of modelling. And it is quite possible for the provision of suitable 'help' and 'tutor' functions to assist the novice user; for this one might learn from earlier attempts to create tutoring tools for SSM (Stowell and Stansfield, 1991).

An alternative argument concerning rules is of course that it is sometimes a necessity to break any rules. It is a common experience in SSM studies that it is at times politic to 'go along' with an imperfect, imprecise, technically deficient system definition so that a working relationship can be maintained. To force every detail and assumption to be clarified might lead to confrontations and irrecoverable positions. This relates back to our earlier point that where a support tool can provide guidance it should never be prescriptive; the tool should inform the user of an anomaly rather than classify it as an error.

Against these objections and genuine practical difficulties we should set the possible benefits of providing computer-based support, whilst recognizing that not all of the advantages which are claimed for the integrated case tools (CAiSE) used in mainstream IS design necessarily apply with respect to support for SSM. For example, one of the principal claims for CAiSE is that it should allow systems to be developed more quickly, with lower error probabilities: it is rather doubtful whether this claim could be fruitfully made for support tools for SSM. In the case of very large projects it is conceivable that some time savings might be made, simply because the volume of materials produced and worked with becomes so large. And by handling those volumes more effectively one might expect that a better quality analysis could be achieved. However, to talk of 'lower error probabilities' in terms of a SSM analysis would be inappropriate since it assumes that there is somehow a 'right' answer to be reached; in using SSM one is concerned with reaching agreements over actions. One might after the event decide that such agreements led to actions that were not those that we wished might have been taken, or wish that the processes of negotiation and consultation had led us elsewhere, but this can not be classified as avoidable 'errors'.

Furthermore, it is claimed that the ability to rapidly create models and diagrams of an information system through CAiSE facilitates the ease with which end-users may be involved in the design process, and so enhances users' feelings of ownership and 'buy-in'. With respect to SSM the emphasis is at least as much upon the social processes through which agreement on a diagram is reached as upon the end result of the diagram or model itself. In any design of a support tool then one should be very conscious that if a tool restricts the actual process of modeling then it will be disadvantageous to use it, and that the kind of participation seen as best practice in SSM presents rather more problems than when simple approval of a model 'of the real situation' is required.

Another benefit provided by CAiSE tools is consistency checking of the use of techniques. For example, when creating a relational database design with iCASE the user will be informed if the attribute list for a table does not allow, through foreign keys, for a specified relationship to be implemented. As we have discussed above, we believe that there is certainly some scope for consistency checking of the various artifacts created in SSM. For example, one would wish to ensure that the same set of owners are named in the System Definition and the CATWOE declaration, that the user has named or consciously decided not to name such things as the customers and enactors of a system or that the logical dependencies of an Activity Model are internally consistent. Once again though one should perhaps only ever hope for a support tool that warns of contravention rather than impose compliance to set rules in the way done by mainstream IS CAiSE tools.

4. CONCLUSIONS

In this paper we have described a learning process and some of the lessons learned rather than reach final conclusions. The work so far has convinced us that computer-support can be provided for SSM at the lower levels of support, and that particular benefits accrue from support for those administrative and management activities which are to be found in any real-world use of SSM. We have as yet not achieved such results in the detailed application of SSM techniques that would allow us to claim real benefits there, the major obstacles being technical ones of communications between individual functional modules that prevent the benefits of integrated support being gained. But we have also not discovered any reasons that will in principle prevent such technique support to be better provided in future. By continuing to ground our work in practical experience we believe that further such learning will provide the basis for better support in future.

REFERENCES

Avison, D.E. and Fitzgerald G., 1995, *Information Systems Development: Methodologies, Techniques and Tools*, 2nd ed., McGraw-Hill, London.

Avison, D.E and Goldner, P., 1991, Tools Supporting Soft Systems, in: *Systems Thinking in Europe*, (M.C. Jackson, G.J. Mansell, R.L. Flood, R.B. Blackham and S.V.E. Probert, eds.), pp. 333–338, Plenum Press, New York.

Avison, D.E., Shah, H. U., and Golder, P.A., 1993, Tools for SSM: a justification - a reply to 'critique of two contributions to soft systems methodology', *European Journal of Information Systems* 2 (4): 312–313.

CCTA, 1993, *Applying Soft Systems Methodology to an SSADM Feasibility Study*, HMSO, London.

Checkland, P. and Scholes, J., 1990, *Soft Systems Methodology in Action*, Wiley, Chichester.

Crowe, M., Beeby, R. and Gammack, J., 1996, *Constructing Systems and Information: A Process View*, McGraw-Hill, London.

Davenport, M.S. and Ayers-Hunt, J., 1995, Soft Systems Analysis and Modelling Tool (SSAMT): Computer-Based Support for Conducting Soft Systems Studies, in: *Critical Issues in Systems Theory and Practice* (K.Ellis, A. Gregory, B.R. Mears-Young and G Ragsdell, eds.) pp. 291–295, Plenum Press, New York.

Jayaratna, N., 1994, *Understanding and Evaluating Methodologies*, McGraw-Hill, London.

Kreher, H., 1993, Critique of two contributions to soft systems methodology, *European Journal of Information Systems* 2 (4): 304–308.

Lewis, P. J. 1992, Rich picture building in the soft systems methodology, *European Journal of Information Systems* 1 (5): 351–360.

Lewis, P.J., 1993a, Linking soft systems methodology with data-focused information systems development, *Journal of Information Systems* 3 (3): p. 169–186.

Lewis, P.J., 1993b, Towards an Interpretative Form of Data Analysis for the Soft Systems Methodology, in: *Systems Science: Addressing Global Issues*, (F.A. Stowell, D. West and J. G. Howell, eds.), pp. 391–396, Plenum Press, New York.

Lewis, P.J., 1993c, Identifying Cognitive Categories: the basis for Interpretative Data Analysis within Soft Systems Methodology, *International Journal of Information Management* 13 (5): pp. 373–386.

Lewis, P.J., 1994, *Information Systems Development: Systems Thinking in the field of Information-Systems*, Pitman, London.

Moore, M., 1996, A learning experience with SSM - using Soft Systems Methodology for the first time in primary schools, *OR Insight* 9 (2): 13–20.

Stowell, F.A., 1995, (ed.), *Information Systems Provision: The contribution of Soft Systems Methodology*, McGraw-Hill, Maidenhead.

Stowell, F.A. and Stansfield, M., 1991, A First Step towards the Automation of SSM, in: *Systems Thinking in Europe*, (M.C. Jackson, G.J. Mansell, R.L. Flood, R.B. Blackham and S.V.E. Probert, eds.), pp. 319–325, Plenum Press, New York.

Tudor, D. J. and Tudor, I. J., 1995, *Systems Analysis and Design: A comparison of Structured Methods*, NCC Blackwell, Oxford.

UKSS, 1992, Information Systems Special Edition of The Systemist 14 (3), United Kingdom Systems Society.

76

A TAXONOMY OF HEURISTIC PROBLEM SOLVING

F. J. Garlick and S. Thompson

Department of Information Science
Faculty of Technology
The University of Portsmouth
Milton Campus, Locksway Road
Portsmouth, Hampshire

INTRODUCTION

This paper discusses problem solving and its algorithmic-like properties. In systems literature problem solving is often discussed in relation to its methodological setting - for example, SSM may legitimately be regarded as a problem solving scheme. It is a contention of this paper that five cognitive elemental strategies may be involved in generalised problem solving.

The ideas discussed here arose from studies into how knowledge engineers solved the problem of knowledge elicitation and representation as well as looking at ways to improve the performance of genetic algorithms. These studies were illuminating since the most common situation seemed to be that either no real underlying strategy was employed or at best a minimal one based on chance plus experience. In other words when practitioners were asked what strategy they were using the most common answer was that they *did not know but they could do it anyway*. In general this answer meant that they had solved one problem of significance and this implied that they had solved all problems - a comfortable but flawed logic.

1.1. What Is a Problem?

This question is difficult to answer since the notion of a *problem* is itself vague. However, the following represents a sample of possible meanings for the term.

"Problems are situation related to development or evaluation of the control process." (Ackoff 1962)

(Reitman 1965) proposed a categorisation of problems based on how well one could specify each of two terminal states.

(Simon 1985) proposed that a human being is confronted with a problem when he has accepted a task but does not know how to carry it out.

Systems for Sustainability, edited by Stowell *et al.*
Plenum Press, New York, 1997

"Problems are situations where circumstances confound action and doubt clouds decision." (Bryant 1989)

1.2. A Difference in States?

A common and useful notion is that of a problem being a difference in states (Mayer 1983) - where facts are known and a there is specified outcome. In this sense problem solving is considered as finding an algorithm or transformation that generates the specified outcome. In practice, solving real-world problems may be difficult because:

- The problem may be difficult to formulate
- The problem may be expressible in many equivalent ways
- A given problem may have one, many or no solutions
- If a solution is found we may have no way of showing that it is correct or even optimal

2. ALGORITHMS

An algorithm is a recipe, if the steps are followed, and each step is well defined then we obtain a predictable outcome. However, Harel (1987) comments: "It must be noted, however, that there are no good recipes for devising recipes. Each new algorithm is a challenge for the algorithm designer."

Knuth (1973) attempted to specify the properties that an algorithm must have if it is to actually work. These properties were:

1. *Finiteness*: implies that the algorithm terminates in a finite number of steps, including repetitions.
2. *Definiteness*: implies that each step in the procedure is unambiguously defined. In simple terms this eliminates impossible or vague instructions.
3. *Input/Output*: means simply that we need zero or more inputs and we must have at least one output.
4. *Effectiveness*: implies that each step in the algorithm can be done in a finite time.

2.1. Heuristic Algorithms

The strategies employed to solve many every-day problems are not algorithms in terms of Knuth's metrics, however, human problem solvers, solve complex problems every day but cannot necessarily say how they achieved their solutions. Such *Tacit Knowledge* is better described as *heuristic* or rough, intuitive rules of thumb - *rules of thumb* can be extremely powerful but tend to be problem dependent.

2.2. General Heuristic Algorithms

Analysis of several problem solving schemes or architectures leads to the conclusion that they are themselves constructed from five elemental strategies. The five strategies are a comprehensive and holistic approach to problem solving. The five strategies described below have been represented in other terms (Garlick and Leonard 1993), however, the following framework (Garlick and Wynn 1994) is a simple and more direct description.

Trial and Error (T) may be seen in the search for solutions but with no clear idea as to where to look. In such a scheme there is a high degree of chance as to whether a suitable answer emerges or not

Use of Generic Ideas (G) this is usually the most productive method since ones thinking will be very much in terms of how you or someone else solved similar problems in the past.

Top Down (D) here we break any given problem down into smaller, more manageable problems.

Taking Different Viewpoints (V) in this form one is encouraged to look for other, perhaps novel ways of seeing the same problem.

Identifying Relationships (R) this is a difficult concept in practice and it implies that we search for how elements in the problem domain are related to and affected by each other.

3. A PRECISE DEFINITION?

The following formulation is simple and yet revealing since it illustrates the complexity associated with real-world problem solving and points the way to a better understanding of how one might construct a powerful problem solving architecture.

$$Let\ P = \{problems\} = \{P_1, P_2, ..., P_n\}$$

In practice any given problem, P_n may have many equivalent classes or formulations as follows:

$$P_1 \equiv P_2 \equiv P_3 \equiv P_4 \equiv P_5\ and\ so\ on.$$

Summarising:

$$P_n = \{problems\} = \{R_1, R_2, ..., R_n\}$$

$$PSS = \{problem\_solving\_strategies\} = \{T, G, D, V, R\}$$

$$P\ X\ PSS = \{(problem, strategy)\}X\{problem:P,\ strategy:PSS\}$$

$$S = \{solutions\} = \{S_1, S_2, ..., S_n\}\ for\ a\ given\ problem\ P$$

Using the letters T, G, D, V and R to represent the five basic heuristic algorithms we may speculate that P_1 may be reformulated for example as R_1 or R_2 and we might try *the routes* $\{T\}$, $\{T,R\}$, $\{D,V\}$ or $\{G\}$ in attempts to find a solution. For example solution S may be found after applying $\{T,R\}$ to the R_2 reformulation. The same problem may be reformulated in other ways to yield the same answer but by another route.

The notation $\{T,R\}$, implies a of fusion of the methods *Trial and Error* with *Generic Ideas* where the problem solver is using T and G collaboratively. Clearly this is a difficult process and leads to the conclusion that solving a particular problem may be achieved using just one strategy or a particular fusion of several simultaneously. Mathematically we might express this powerful idea of a fusion or collaboration of strategies as a power set where *problem_solving* is the partial function.

$$Problem\_solving: P \ X \ R(PSS)$$

This fusion of methods may not be easy and problem solvers may revert to using strategies singly or in sequence. Mathematically using the strategies in sequence would be represented by the partial function.

$$Problem\_solving: P \ X \ Seq(PSS)$$

Summarising these two sets and using a simple bracket notation to distinguish the collaborative and serial forms we find that:

$\{T,G,V\}$ means use T, G, and V collaboratively and simultaneously

$[T,G,V]$ means use T then G then V in sequence

4. PROBLEM SOLVING ARCHITECTURES

With these basic ideas it is possible to search for an architecture—a scheme which embodies these ideas in a coherent manner. For example, Soft Systems Methodology (Checkland 1990) is a problem solving architecture because it has all the tools and techniques needed for a thorough analysis of a given human activity system.

4.1. Problem Solving Power

It has always been difficult to compare problem solving architectures. However, using the five basic strategies it is possible to look in detail at an architecture for application of these natural heuristics used singly, in sequence or more powerfully, in a collaborative form. If they are not indeed an essential part of the method, then it can be concluded that the method is weak because it does not *force* a user to work with all the available tools.

5. AN ARTIFICIAL INTELIGENCE PERSPECTIVE

While the scope of this paper is to discuss problem solving in the context of system methodologies it is instructive to examine the attempts to simulate problem solving activities, and agents, from the field of artificial intelligence.

Some of the five strategies discussed above can be identified in the problem solving mechanisms used in AI. *Trial and Error* is obviously the generate and test algorithm used in random walk algorithms (Kauffman 1993). Genetic algorithms (Holland 1975) and inductive systems (Quinlan 1992) such as those used in machine learning employ similar mechanisms but use heuristics to guide the generation process. Case-Based reasoning (Kolodener 1993) use *Generic* ideas—cases from past experience are stored in a Case Base and retrieved with a similarity function matching the problem at hand. Retrieved cases are then adapted to fit new circumstances, used, and stored for future reference. Meta-reasoning or Meta-learning (Chan and Stolfo 1995) system decompose problems into smaller elements in a way similar to *Top-Down* style reasoning. There are no easy analogues to *Taking another Viewpoint* or *Identifying Relationships* in current AI systems. These last two reasoning processes are usually undertaken by humans who select the automatic reasoning methods that seem appropriate.

5.1. An Observation

It is interesting to view the AI tools and observe that, so far anyway, machines are not able to simulate the last two elemental strategies: Viewpoints and Relationships. In contrast, and if one considers SSM, there is at least one phase where attempts are made to directly resolve perceived problems—that is finding *Relevant Systems* related to an issue or primary task. At an elemental level powerful heuristics are at work.

Taking Different Viewpoints (V). Two views of relevant systems are encouraged. The first being that the system is visible in the real-world and the second is that the system is a conceptualisation of something that might exist. In addition, analysts write down many possibilities for the relevant system, each one representing another view of the issue or primary task and therefore leading to further insight into the problem setting.

Use of Generic Ideas (G). During this phase of SSM it is highly likely that one uses ones own past experience of similar settings. This is a very powerful mechanism and so long as one is open-minded, often leads to real innovation and creativity.

Identifying Relationships (R). During this phase good analysts will be mentally seeing links between the various ideas and recognising various themes emerging.

One final point here is that as one works through this element of SSM it is very likely that it begins in a linear fashion trying the strategies *[V,G,R]* one after another but as this proceeds it does seem as if a fusion takes place and one moves into the collaborative strategy scheme *{V,G,R}*.

6. CONCLUSIONS

Our main conclusions are that better problem solving skills result when the five heuristics outlined above are used. Further, we conclude that any methodology that embodies all the above strategies will be inherently more stable and better adapted to real world problems than one that is based on only a partial set of the above five elements. Finally, it is concluded that machine based problem solving might be improved if it were possible to find a mechanism for carrying out the process of taking a new viewpoint or finding relationships. Additionally, it is clear that the five strategies may be used either singly, in sequence or collaboratively—at present it does seem that AI systems are not able to fully address the collaborative processing issue and therefore the practical possibility of simulation of human problem solving is likely to remain a chimera.

REFERENCES

Ackoff, R.L., 1962, *Scientific Method*, John Wiley, New York

Bryant, J., 1989, *Problem management*, John Wiley, Chichester

Brunsson, N., 1988, *The organisation of hypocrisy*, John Wiley, Chichester

Checkland, P.B., and Scholes J, 1990, *Soft Systems Methodology in action*, John Wiley, Chichester

Garlick, F.J., and Leonard, G.L., 1993, *The algorithmic nature of problem solving*, UKSS 3rd International Conference, University of Paisley, Plenum

Garlick, F.J., and Wynn W., 1994, *An Architecture for holistic problem solving*, International Systems Dynamics Conference, University of Stirling

Harel, D, 1987, *Algorithmics - The Spirit of Computing*, Addison-Wesley, Wokingham

Holland, J., 1975, *Adaptations in natural and artificial systems*, University of Michigan Press

Kauffman, S.A., 1993, *The origins of order: Self-organisation & selection in evolution*, Oxford University Press.

Kolodener, J.K., 1993, *Case-Based reasoning*, Morgan Kauffmann Publishers, San Mateo

Knuth, D, 1979, *Fundamental Algorithms 2ed*, Addison-Wesly, Massachusetts

Laird, J.E., and Rosenbloom, P.S., 1994, *The Evolution of SOAR cognitive architecture*, Technical Reports CSE-TR-219–94, University of Michigan

Mayer, R.E., 1983, *Thinking, Problem Solving, Cognition*, WH Freeman, London

Newell, A., and Simon, H.A., 1956, *The Logic Theory Machine: A complex Information processing system,* IRE Transaction on Information Processing, IT:61–98

Reitman, W.R., 1956, *Cognition and thought*, Wiley, Chichester

Simon, H.A., 1985, *Information processing theory of human problem-solving*, Issues in Cognitive Modelling

77

RICH PICTURES

A Counselling Aid

F. J. Garlick and G. L. Leonard

Department of Information Science
Faculty of Technology
The University of Portsmouth, Milton Campus
Locksway Road, Portsmouth, Hampshire

1. INTRODUCTION

It is a maxim when drawing Rich Pictures that one does not look for systems. However, it is common for analysts to draw these pictures by first looking at sub-settings and gradually build the whole picture from these. All this implies that they have some idea as to what constitutes the whole since they often seem to be taking it apart to find out how it functions. Thus it seems we have a dilemma—on the one hand we need to have some view of the whole (at least its purpose) but at the same time we do not want to look for systems as such (which imply a way of fulfilling some purpose).

This paper discuses an extended study with students using Rich Pictures as a means of showing how they view their chosen course - essentially mode two SSM. One of the surprising and interesting features that emerged was that Rich Pictures drawn in this mode almost without exception avoided showing systems as such. Instead they concentrate on several problem themes and either give the reader no idea as to Primary Task or else give a radically different view of what might be described as the Primary Task by the course managers.

An interesting side effect of drawing these picture was the distinct therapeutic effect it had on students, making them more content with their course and the way it was managed. From a systems point of view it does seem to indicate that mode two is a natural way of viewing an organisation and also shows that when an analyst interviews the actors within a system they may unwittingly force them to see the system in an inappropriate or biased manner.

1.1 The Purpose of Study Courses?

Success in any course of study is dependent on many complex, interlocking and interconnecting factors - course content, discipline, integrity, awareness, social roles, stu-

Systems for Sustainability, edited by Stowell *et al.*
Plenum Press, New York, 1997

dent grants, motivation, study skills and so on. It follows that if study courses are to result in success (in its widest sense) for a student then the designers of a course must take an holistic view. Students are much more perceptive than given credit for: Garlick (1992), has shown that most students are well aware of the benefits to be derived in terms of the available resources, the experience of being part of the course and of the totality of outcomes: qualifications, knowledge, confidence, jobs and so on.

Using the Rich Pictures derived in this study it is hard to find evidence that the course content itself motivates and excites students. This is not to say that they have no interest in the content but it does seem that once they have decided on a particular course, it is taken (by them) for granted that the content will be relevant though not necessarily interesting! Curriculum therefore, is a wider idea than simply course content and in this context it is helpful to recall a few apposite remarks (Noonan 1968):

> ...the material gains of learning and earning, sexual possibilities, legal privileges and autonomous strengths - because the adolescent does not know how he will use these things, nor how he will be used by them. Such anxiety and uncertainty promote precipitate actions, withdrawal, anger, inconsistency, depression and euphoria...

2. RICH PICTURES

Rich pictures are an unstructured way of representing organisational and social dynamics and typically contain structural, social, process and role information in an iconoclastic manner. In principle a Rich Pictures is a simple device for describing a given situation as an analysts sees it or perhaps would like to see it. It is common for such pictures to be produced in an interventionist manner - that is the views and opinions of actors within the system are sought and then analysts draw a picture which is a composite of those multiple views. In SSM this form of analysis is known as mode one working.

Alternatively, as we have seen, the actors themselves could draw the pictures either individually or in concert with others - this latter procedure has come to be known as mode two SSM. There are benefits to be gained in both modes of working but it does seem clear that an interactionist approach is more likely to bring about attitude changes because when groups of actors work on a picture they automatically share their viewpoint with others and this in itself is likely to be beneficial.

2.1 Drawing Rich Pictures

Drawing pictures is difficult because one has to find icons to represent functions, structures, roles and so on. However, the pictures shown here express in a condensed way intricate relationships that would require extensive and very high quality prose to expound to the same level of complexity.

2.2. Obtaining Rich Pictures

The pictures included in this paper and the complete set used during the study were obtained as part of the normal work a student does. No special time was set apart and as far as the students were concerned it was just an interesting and enjoyable mechanism for practising a particular Soft Systems technique. This was very useful since it did give the students freedom to express themselves without any pre-conceptions.

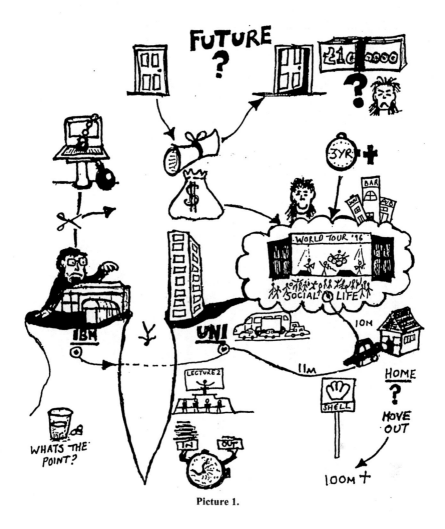

Picture 1.

The majority of students enjoyed the exercise since the method was novel and there was an element of fun as students explained the meaning of their icons to each other. If the pictures are examined it will be seen that the icons are often expressing very complex ideas yet in an obvious manner. It was also observable that a few wanted to work on their own whilst one or two found it impossible to join in. It is easy to speculate as to why some students cannot participate fully but it is legitimate to suggest that they are unwilling to share their view with others because one suspects that they find the process intimidatory.

2.3. Use of Rich Pictures

Once pictures are drawn several mechanism are available for using them, or at least interpreting them. Great care is needed since most staff who might look at these picture are not qualified therapists and therefore must not be too hasty in their interpretations. However the following are possible uses:

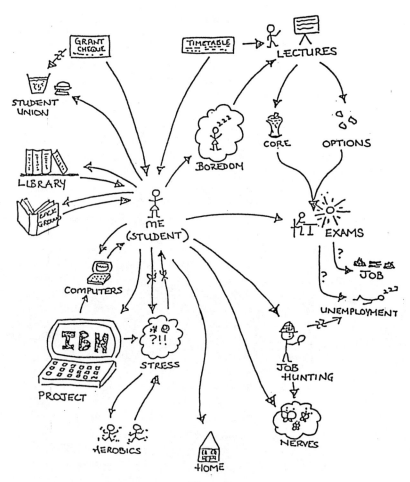

Picture 2.

- *A useful therapy for students to say something about the course and their view of it.*
- *A means of communicating views to both staff and other students.*
- *Say what the course is supposed to be doing as far as the customer is concerned.*
- *Staff may make organisational or other charges to improve the quality of the learning process.*
- *Deepens our understanding of all the elements that go towards making a good course.*
- *Used as a counselling aid in group or on an individual basis.*

2.4. Benefits to Be Derived

By nature students, like everyone else tend to focus on the, shall we say, impoverished parts of their course. It does seem, however that rich pictures have a genuinely beneficial affect. Perhaps the main benefit is aptly described by Job when remonstrating with his comforters.

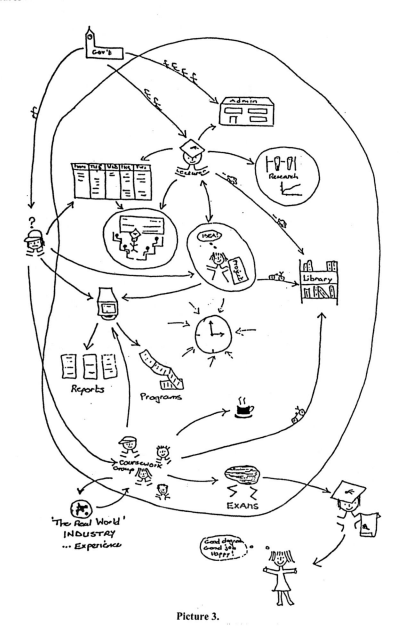

Picture 3.

... do but listen, and let that be the comfort you offer... Job 21v1 (NEB)

This matches the counselling approach of Rogers (1967), in which the client is held *in unconditional positive regard*, and the active listening is therapy itself. The listening in this context is of course enabled by the pictures which avoid the obvious pitfalls of communicating directly with staff. The conversational approach to describing the student's perceptions of the course and its environs can appear confrontational, and will have the effect of reducing critical aspects. As a result the student will feel unheard, even though it is they who have censored the criticisms.

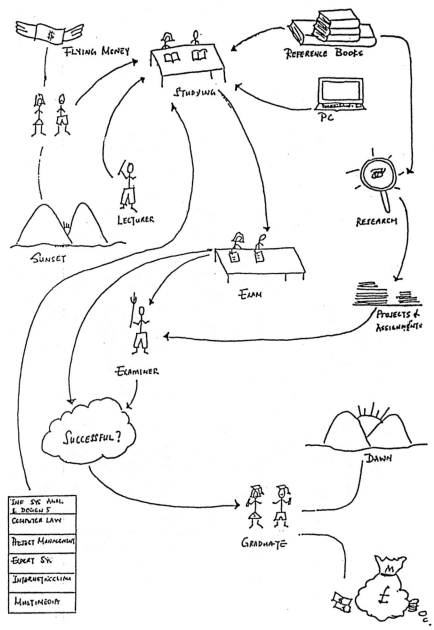

Picture 4.

2.5. Some Observations

It is not appropriate here to analyse in detail each picture, but picture 1 is very unusual in that it shows and effectively names an individual who is shown dropping students into a chasm—it is rare in Rich Pictures to see this and almost always indicates poor social relationships. Also the two doors at the top of the picture seem to be showing that this student is very confused about the future. Picture 2 was drawn by a group but is still typical of the way students see their own world. The pictures used during the study were produced by different groups over several years and yet the issues raised are remarkably stable from year to year

3. CONCLUSIONS

The use of actual course elements as a means of obtaining feedback and acting as a counselling mechanism is appealing and useful since it frees to a certain extent the student to give answers to question that they would like to be asked. It follows that when course leaders see what the concerns of students are they may well be able to alter they way the course runs in order to meet more directly the needs of students. Since the pictures can be regarded as a form of counselling they may have the good effect of reducing the stress level in students and staff alike. In effect we are creating better opportunities for addressing individual student needs within the course.

Finally, these picture point to the fact that mode two may be regarded as an ideal form of drawing Rich Pictures because actors seem to have no compulsion to draw systems as such even when they are told to do so.

REFERENCES

Garlick, FJ., 1992, *Assessing course quality using Repertory Grids*, 4th International conference on assessing quality in Higher Education, University of Twente, Netherlands.
Garlick, FJ., 1991, *Assessing course quality using student generated constructs*, 3rd International conference on assessing quality in Higher Education, Bath.
Checkland, P., and Scholes, J., 1992, *Soft Systems Methodology in action*. Wiley, Chichester.
Ceckland, P., 1981, *Systems Thinking, Systems Practice*, Wiley, Chichester.
Noonan, E., 1986, *Counselling young people*, Routledge, London.
Rogers, C., 1967, *On becoming a person*, Constable, London

78

REFLECTING ON THE USE OF SSM WITHIN HUMBERSIDE TEC

A Special Focus on 'Sustainability'

Giles A. Hindle and Michael C. Jackson

School of Management
Lincoln University Campus
Brayford Pool, Lincoln

1. INTRODUCTION

This paper reports on and examines work involving the use of Soft Systems Methodology (SSM) within Humberside Training and Enterprise Council (TEC). The basic remit of the TEC is to foster economic growth and contribute to the regeneration of the local community it serves. This is to be achieved through strengthening the local 'skill-base' and assisting enterprises to expand and compete effectively. In practice, these objectives translate into a central activity of *contracting*; i.e. a process of developing formal agreements between the TEC and a variety of local training suppliers. The project addressed by this paper sought to inquire into, and develop actions to improve, this process of formulating contracts. As well as a brief description of the project, the paper includes feedback from participants relating to perceived strengths and weaknesses of the methodology. Strengths were seen to be the participative and accessible nature of *rich pictures* together with the overall discipline and action orientation of the methodology. Weaknesses were found with the technical accessibility of *human activity system* modelling and the feasibility of enacting a learning cycle over time within the TEC's normal working practices. The paper goes on to discuss implications of the project for future practice by using the notion of *sustainability* as a guiding focus. Sustainability is taken as being a measure of the methodology's ability to support and maintain a learning process over a long period of time.

2. PROJECT OUTLINE

The formal aims of the project were to improve the effectiveness and efficiency of the TEC contracting process and, synchronously, to enable TEC staff to become more familiar with SSM as a way of tackling ill-structured problem situations. The project team

Systems for Sustainability, edited by Stowell *et al.*
Plenum Press, New York, 1997

Table 1. Structure of the project

Phase	Activities	Group involved
1. Opening day (full day)	introduction to SSM	whole project team
	building rich pictures	in 4 sub-groups
	selecting relevant systems	whole project team
	introduction to modelling	whole project team
2. Group work (over 6 weeks)	modelling relevant systems	each sub-group
3. Work shops (4 ½ days)	modelling relevant systems	each sub-group + facilitators
4. Final day (full day)	presentation of relevant systems	whole project team
	debate regarding action to improve the situation	
5. Future work (ongoing)	action to improve the situation	whole project team
	further iterations of SSM	whole project team
	evaluation of the project	HR and Quality Manager
6. Initial Evaluation (1/2 day)	evaluation of initial facilitated learning process	HR and Quality Manager + facilitators
	evaluation of SSM	

involved around a dozen TEC staff plus two facilitators from The Lincoln School of Management. The TEC group included personnel involved in the contracting process, together with senior management, the Finance Director and the Human Resource and Quality Team.

The study utilised the 'traditional' seven stage form of SSM as described by Checkland (1981), but incorporated *rich pictures* (see Checkland and Scholes 1990) as a technique for structuring and expressing the problem situation (stage 2 of the seven stage version). Also, due to time restrictions, the initial facilitated learning process would involve a single iteration of the learning cycle of SSM. Further iterations, involving the consequences of action taken, were planned by the TEC group, but would take place outside the bounds of the project described here. Table 1 shows the structure of the project in terms of the activities of the TEC staff and facilitators. It has been useful to think of the project as consisting of six *phases*. Also, it is worth noting that the TEC project team was split into four sub-groups of around four participants each in order to enable effective group-work during the production of rich pictures and models.

3. FEEDBACK FROM PHASE 6

The objectives of the initial feedback session with the HR and Quality Manager were to acquire immediate impressions of phases 1 to 4 of the project. Reactions were found to fall within three general categories: (3.1) technical aspects of SSM, (3.2) project management and methodological issues and (3.3) underlying assumptions of the methodology.

3.1. Technical Aspects of SSM

Rich pictures (RPs) proved to be a popular technique with participants and have subsequently been used in other projects within the TEC. "They are good fun and get everyone involved. They are technically easy, and hence *accessible*, and allow everyone's views to be expressed, whatever they are." (HR and Quality Manager). Participants valued expressing aspects of the TEC's contracting process which were of importance to *themselves*, rather than being told to address certain aspects in a prescribed way. This encouraged a broad project as the four groups displayed notably different perspectives on the contracting process and, consequently, tended to pick up on contrasting issues. For example, groups containing senior management tended to concentrate on strategic management issues, whereas HR and Quality staff tended to be more interested in developing contracting skills. Some participants, however, would rather have produced a list of issues in a more traditional fashion. It is unclear whether this was simply due to a reluctance to undertake drawing, evidence of a solution oriented approach to thinking, or a feeling that pictures might not be a serious conceptual tool. The consultancy firm Hoskyns, who have carried out a number of projects with senior management using simulated business games, have suggested that techniques with a light-hearted image work better when participants are dressed casually and are situated in casual surroundings (Young OR Conference, 1996). It was felt that iteration of the drawing process might have improved the use of RPs. Because each group had time to produce only one RP, the pictures tended to be a little scrappy and unconnected. A second or third draft would have enabled groups to look at the situation in more depth and develop their pictures accordingly. Two further developments of rich picturing are also possible: (i) to picture one particular aspect of the situation with a 'specialised' RP (for example, participants could have explored in more detail the TEC's relationship with government bodies) and (ii) to picture the problem situation from an explicit point of view in the same way that *human activity systems* (HAS) apply a particular *Weltanschauung* (for example, participants could have viewed the contracting process from the point of view of its users, or by considering specifically the financial aspects). Specialised RPs might have been more satisfying to participants as pictures of the whole situation tend to lack of detail.

Selecting relevant systems was thought to be an ambiguous step within the methodology as it was not always obvious what to do with an issue once it had been expressed on a RP. Participants felt they needed the experience and technical expertise of the facilitators in order to make the jump between issues raised and relevant HASs to be developed. The modelling aspect of SSM, however, turned out to be even more problematic, especially the CATWOE mnemonic used to help structure the HASs. People felt they would need more time to learn this aspect of SSM and it was clear the TEC didn't warm to what they saw as a technical, disciplined approach. However, the discussion generated by producing root definitions (RD) was felt to be valuable as it allowed groups to clarify their ideas before discussing appropriate action.

3.2. Project Management and Methodological Issues

Conceptualising a project as a process of activity by participants over a period of time, this section of the feedback will describe issues concerning the overall co-ordination of this process and, hence, will relate to the concept of *methodology* and its utility in this project. Throughout the project there was a tendency for participants to suggest problem solutions rather than follow the inquiry process described by the methodology. It was felt by both the facilitators and the HR and Quality staff that this tendency could be the result of (i) a lack of intellectual and group *discipline*, i.e. the extent to which the TEC staff are prepared to *follow* an organised set of principles which *guide* their actions over a period of time (Checkland's notion of a methodology), and (ii) the *logistics* of TEC operations, i.e.

whether the TEC's normal work practices can support an ongoing action research programme. The TEC has a range of on-going problem-solving activities involving a variety of groups and using different methods. These project teams ("working groups") tend to come together to address an issue, then move off to perform their own work and the responsibility for action is given to an individual. These "working groups" rarely revisit issues in the iterative style of SSM because new problems are emerging all the time; the tendency is simply to keep moving on. These features of the TEC's normal work practices, together with constant time pressures for participants, mean the iterative action-reflection approach of SSM is not an approach they would normally be able to take.

Despite these issues of discipline and logistics, participants valued the emphasis on taking action within SSM as the relationship between problem structuring and taking action was seen as important. It was felt that many 'problem solving' approaches (none specified) concentrate on structuring the situation in some way and then leave it at that; there is no requirement within the methods to formulate strategies to improve the situation and take action. This can lead to the feeling that such methods are just about words and ideas, and not part of one's *real work*. Indeed, the feedback suggested that problem-solving methods were still thought of by TEC staff as separate from the day-to-day running of the organisation. They appeared to be thought of as *thinking tools* for meetings and projects rather than as *methodologies* to guide action over a period of time. Facilitation was considered crucial to the success of the project, especially within the technical phases 2 and 3 and the generation of relevant systems at the end of the first day. Participants felt that without the contact with the facilitators, the technical aspects of SSM would have stalled the project and the overall process would have lacked discipline.

3.3. Underlying Assumptions of the Methodology

Phase 1 sought to introduce the nature of organisational decision making implied by SSM, where subjectivity, social relationships and *culture* play an important role. But what impact did this actually have on the participants? The feedback indicated that although participants enjoyed hearing the philosophical background to the methodology, the ideas were new to them and they didn't feel the introduction significantly affected how they actually *used* the methodology. This feedback suggests that participants maintained their own implicit view of social reality and perspective on the situation whilst engaging in the techniques of the methodology. The notion that participants would consciously adopt the *wordview* or paradigm implied by SSM for the duration of the project is therefore not supported in this instance. The implication here is that participants would assess the methodology on its ability to fit into their *worldview* and mode of problem solving rather than the other way around.

4. SPECIAL FOCUS ON SUSTAINABILITY

As stated earlier, this paper will interpret 'sustainability' as being a measure of the methodology's ability to support and maintain a learning process over a long period of time within the TEC. Looking through the feedback, we can see a number of problems for future use of SSM. Firstly, problems with the selection and modelling of HASs are significant for three main reasons; (i) failure by participants to view systems as epistemological devices, "holons" (Checkland 1985), within SSM will negate the selection of relevant systems to aid thinking *about* the problematic situation (*'soft' systems thinking*) and lead to a more traditional or restricted form of thinking; for example, one notable characteristic of system selection from this project was the tendency for participants to favour systems aiming to *resolve* a particular issue within the RP; (ii) with no HAS being *intrinsically* relevant to a problem situation and the methodology being non-prescriptive in the choice of systems, the process of SSM could easily stall at this point; and (iii) the success of projects in general, in terms of their ability to generate learning and desirable improvement, will depend on participants' confidence and creativity when selecting relevant systems. Hoebeke (1994) uses the concept "work system", which he claims maps onto SSM's concept of a HAS, and suggests a number of generic 'work systems' which have been found useful in practice; a technique within SSM could be developed to give some sort of prescriptive help in generating relevant systems, especially for inexperienced participants. We may also want to consider whether some of the more rigorous technical requirements of modelling actually get in the way of more important communicative aspects of the inquiry process, especially with inexperienced participants. For example, success in RPs could be interpreted as facilitating a higher quality, though perhaps less explicit, form of *communication* between participants than simple discussion and could, in effect, provide an opportunity for the group to become more 'self-conscious'. Self-consciousness is this instance refers to the group becoming consciously aware of the ideas and perspectives of the individuals within it.

A strong feature of the feedback concerning project management issues is a concern for the practicalities of completing a process of group inquiry within the TEC. Unless "working groups" within the TEC possess the intellectual and group discipline, together with the necessary logistical support, to perform an explicit piece of action research, it is unclear how a legitimate use of SSM can support future projects. This is a familiar dilemma for management scientists and may be epitomised by questioning whether management science ought to be encouraging problem solving/ organisational inquiry as a *scientific* activity (guided by an explicit intellectual framework and methodology (Checkland, 1985)) or as a *consultancy* style activity ('common sense' eclectic approach utilising a 'toolbox' of techniques). The utility of the notion of methodology as a set of principles which guide action is clearly under question in this project.

A final elementary point concerns the difficulties raised by participants' apparent failure to consciously adopt the underlying assumptions implied by the methodology. Jackson (1991) and Brocklesby (1994, 1995) have discussed the adoption of underlying assumptions from a theoretical and cultural perspective, but their discussions concentrate on the selection and adoption of methodologies by *practitioners*; there now appears to be a need to address the views of *participants*. A participative methodology must be transferred effectively to the individuals constituting the problem solving team. If this is not achieved, the methodology can not be regarded as guiding the process sufficiently. Clearly, this issue is compounded when participants' perspectives on organisational decision making and social reality are incompatible with, or different from, that implied by the methodology. In a worst case scenario participants may reject the approach completely as not making sense within their *worldview*; at best participants may fail to grasp the significance of the techniques. The TEC project has highlighted a number of issues regarding the use of SSM, for a full discussion see Hindle and Jackson (1996).

REFERENCES

Brocklesby, J., 1994, Let the Jury Decide: Assessing the Cultural Feasibility of TSI; *Systems Practice*, 7 :1.

Brocklesby, J., 1995, Intervening in the Cultural Constitution of Systems: Methodological Complementarism and other Visions for Systems Research, *J. Opl. Res. Soc.*, **46**.

Checkland, P.,1981, *Systems Thinking, Systems Practice*, Wiley and Sons, Chichester.

Checkland, P.B., 1985, From optimising to learning: A development of systems thinking for the 1990s; *J. Opl. Res. Soc.*, **36**.

Checkland, P. and Scholes, J., 1990, *Soft Systems Methodology in Action*, Wiley and Sons, Chichester.

Hindle, G.A. and Jackson, M.C., 1996, Reflecting upon an Application of SSM within Humberside TEC: A Special Emphasis on Sustainability; *Working Paper Series,* **13**, Lincoln School of Mgt.

Hoebeck, L., 1994, *Making Work Systems Better: A Practitioner's Reflections*; Wiley and Sons, Chichester.

Jackson, M.C., 1991, *Systems Methodologies for the Management Sciences*; Wiley and Sons, Chichester.

79

THEORY OF ORGANISATIONS

J. Korn

Middlesex University
Bounds Green Road, N11 2NQ

1. INTRODUCTION

An organisation may be described as a collection of interacting objects engaged in the production of a specified outcome. The outcome can be expressed as an ordered arrangement of properties, concrete or abstract and can be referred to as a 'product' for which, in many cases, people are willing to pay. A product is directed towards a user or a receiver which generates the specification for it (Korn, 1996). The operation of an organisation is embedded in that of others: political, social, economic, technological and in the natural environment.

The structure of an organisation can be discerned through product analysis. A product is seen to consist of functional elements and properties (Korn, 1966) leading to the identification of purposive systems each contributing a single, specified property to the product. Product analysis also leads to a hierarchy of purposive systems operating at ascending levels within an organisation. Thus, in general, the primary interest appears to be the production of a specific property which subsequently stipulates the need for the operation of a purposive system, rather than the other way round as happens to be the current practice in systems thinking.

There is a broad range of activities which can be viewed as a pattern of: specification, purposive system, product and user/receiver. These activities take place in the fields which may be recognised as control/computer systems, production systems, political, social, manufacturing and other organisation such as project management. Individuals and groups of animate beings, micro/macroscopic biological organisms also exhibit the kind of activities referred to above.

Many organisations are very much people intensive with fluctuating physical and mental characteristics. People can exhibit will, ambition, emotions, moods, they can be ill and subject to influences external to an organisation.

As a result of complexity implied by the description and of the importance of operation of organisations, the literature is vast. It may approximately be divided into categories dealing with:

1. Human aspects; power, politics, authority, personality, motivation and so on (Huczynski, Buchanan, 1991).

Systems for Sustainability, edited by Stowell *et al.*
Plenum Press, New York, 1997

2. Structure and forms of communication within an organisation (Minzberg, 1979).

3. Viewing an organisation as a metaphor (Morgan, 1986).

4. Systems and problem solving approaches (Checkland, Scholes, 1990, Jackson, 1995).

By and large, the current literature deals with the topic of organisations in a descriptive manner often using vague and ill defined models. It does not really attempt to relate the topic to more fundamental issues rooted in existing knowledge and, as such, has a divisive rather than an integrating effect on the spectrum of knowledge.

This paper intends to introduce briefly a theory of organisations based on empirical content and a symbolism with an inferential structure. In particular, the theory views an organisation as a structured arrangement of purposive systems operating on products and modelled by means of linguistic modelling (Korn, Huss, 1994).

2. DESCRIPTION OF ORGANISATIONS

An organisation is seen as a formal association of purposive systems which, as such, provide a measure of its complexity (Korn, 1995). These are derived from properties which are organised into functional sets. Each set determines the number of purposive systems. Sets themselves can be organised into groups with the corresponding grouping of purposive systems. This hierarchy of functional units of which an organisation is seen to consist, forms a part of its functional structure.

Accordingly, the structure of an organisation formed from objects and their interactions engaged in purposive activities, may be seen in terms of three patterns:

1. Flow of concrete or abstract properties or flow of work (Minzberg, 1979) towards an outcome,

2. Flow of information or informatic properties with meaning (Korn, 1996) required for the production of an outcome,

3. Superimposed mental and physical activities aiding or hindering the flows of properties in 1 and 2.

The first two patterns form the formal part of an organisation, they carry the functional operations within an organisation. The activities within the third pattern are informal and are based on friendship, likes/dislikes, personal interests, emotions, illness, backgrounds etc. Activities within this pattern are peculiar to people, robots do not do them. They can aid the execution of policies and objectives of an organisation and can be a source of initiatives and creative actions. Managers should cultivate an atmosphere to accomodate the activities within the third pattern.

3. SYMBOLIC REPRESENTATION OF AN ORGANISATION

A symbolism representing an organisation should reflect: its structure as suggested by patterns 1. 2., the day to day fluctuation of its operation as in pattern 3 and the dominance of qualitative properties carried by objects and interactions. In linguistic modelling these are taken into account by one and two place statements as the basic constituents carrying graded adjectival and adverbial phrases (Korn, Takats, 1996).

A simple organisation is shown in Fig.1 consisting of a boss and a secretary with the former acting as a purposive system and the latter as its product with two properties to be

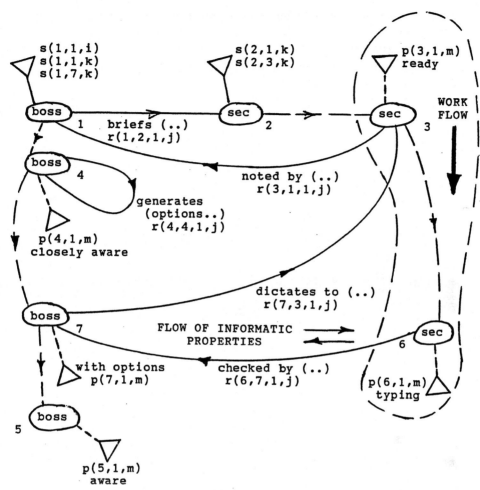

Figure 1.

acquired: 'ready' and 'typing'. The objective of the complete scenario, not shown, is to produce a letter.

The symbols in Fig.1 are interpreted as follows:

s(1,1,i)   boss with (strong, weak) intention to dictate a letter
s(1,1,k)   boss with (strong, medium) need to be satisfied
s(1,7,k)   boss with (strong, medium) sense of happiness
s(2,1,k)   sec with (strong, medium, weak) willingness (ATTITUDE TO JOB)
s(2,3,k)   sec with (50, 30 word/min) typing ability (TRAINING FOR JOB)
r(1,2,1,j)   boss briefs (patiently, impatiently) the sec
r(3,1,1,j)   sec is noted (with attention, absentmindedly) by the boss
r(7,3,1,j)   boss dictates (quickly, slowly) to sec
r(6,7,1,j)   sec is checked (thoroughly) by boss
r(4,4,1,j)   boss generates (options with imagination)

The brackets carry the grades of the adjectival and adverbial phrases. The first grade stands for the outcome to occur with certainty, the others carry decreasing certainty factors (Durkin, 1994). The indexes i, k, j represent the number of grades.

From Fig.1, we can derive the logic relations:

$$s(1,1,j) \rightarrow r(1,2,1,j) \tag{1}$$

$$r(1,2,1,j) \wedge s(2,1,k) \rightarrow p(3,1,m) \tag{2}$$

$$p(7,1,m) \rightarrow r(7,3,1,j) \tag{3}$$

$$r(7,3,1,j) \wedge p(3,1,m) \wedge s(2,3,k) \rightarrow p(6,1,m) \tag{4}$$

and so on for ten relations completing the inferential structure.

Since each grade can be associated with another, the relations can be expanded as the number of indexes vary. This produces a large number of paths along which the outcomes can be reached. For instance, from eq.1

$$s(1,1,1) \rightarrow r(1,2,1,1)$$

$$s(1,1,1) \rightarrow r(1,2,1,2)$$

$$s(1,1,2) \rightarrow r(1,2,1,1)$$

$$s(1,1,2) \rightarrow r(1,2,1,2) \tag{5}$$

A particular path is selected by beliefs asserted about the character or behaviour of an object. For example, we can assert: 'Sec has had a bad day, quarrelled with a friend' which is likely to lead to

$$s(2,1,k) = \text{sec with } (0, 0, 1) \text{ willingness}$$

A particular path is thus selected which is a particular case of the relations eqs.1 4 etc. representing the organisation at a particular instant subject to a chosen set of beliefs. Certainty factors can then be inserted for the antecedents and rules of the relations of this path. For example, eq.2 reads 'If the boss briefs (impatiently) the sec and the sec has a (weak) willingness then the sec with (weak) willingness becomes ready, somewhat irritated' for which we can calculate a certainty factor

$$cf(p(3,1,6)) = 0.27 \tag{6}$$

Eq.6 indicates that the certainty of the sec acquiring the desired property is 0.27, less than 'maybe' on a scale of certainty terms (Durkin, 1994).

If, for example, we believe that next day is a good one for the secretary then $cf(p(3,1,6) = 0.9$.

The selected, particular cases of eqs.1 4 etc. allow the computation of certainty factors for all acquired properties indicated by the dotted flags in Fig.1. This can then show the day to day fluctuation of performance of an organisation i.e. its dynamics. The option possibility indicated in Fig.1 is not discussed here.

REFERENCES

Checkland, P., Scholes, J., 1990, Soft systems methodology in action, J Wiley & Sons, NY.

Durkin, J., 1994, Expert systems, Macmillan Pub.Co, NY.

Huczynski, A., Buchanan, D. A., 1991, Organisational behaviour, Prentice Hall, NY.

Jackson, M. C., 1995, Beyond the fads:systems thinking for managers, Systems Research, v12, n1.

Korn, J., 1996, Domain independent design theory, J. of Eng. Design, v7, n3.

Korn, J., Huss, F., 1994, Linguistic modelling of socio economic systems, Cybernetics and systems, ed.R.Trappl, World Scientific, London.

Korn, J., 1995, Unit of complexity, 11th Complex Systems Meeting, BRE Cardington, 29 November.

Korn, J., Takats, A., 1996, Design of organisations through linguistic modelling, 3rd Int.Congress of Project Eng., Barcelona, 11 14 September.

Minzberg, H., 1979, The structuring of organisations, Prentice Hall, NY.

Morgan, G., 1986, Images of organisation, Sage Publications, Newbury Park, CA, USA.

80

BEYOND FUNCTIONAL DECOMPOSITION IN SOFT SYSTEMS METHODOLOGY

J. Ledington and P. W. J. Ledington

School of Information Systems and Management Science
Griffith University

1. INTRODUCTION AND BACKGROUND

The emergence and development of Soft Systems Methodology (SSM) is well known (Checkland, 1981; Checkland and Scholes, 1990) and has produced a continuing strand of research activity (see for example: Avison and Wood-Harper, 1990; Davies and Ledington, 1991; Lewis, 1994; Stowell, 1995; Wilson, 1984; Wood-Harper, Antill, and Avison, 1985). The research reported in this paper contributes to the research stream by focussing on issues arising in the modelling process within SSM and presents a new approach, termed Decision-Variable Partitioning, to this area of SSM.

Soft Systems Methodology provides a structured approach to making explicit the various meanings associated with a situation through the development and use of human activity system models. Creating such models allows the meanings and the implications of taking those meanings seriously within the situation to be discussed and debated by those involved in, and responsible for, the situation. The aim is to establish a stable definition of the activity supported by these stakeholders in the form of a human activity system model. Soft Systems Methodology appears sound in principle, but in practice it is plagued by a range of issues which limit its usefulness. First, it often appears that activity models are poorly constructed, or at least that they cannot be shown to be readily defensible. The model is central to the SSM approach and therefore any uncertainty or lack of confidence in the model reduces the level of confidence in the overall analysis. Second, it is often difficult to express nuances of meaning within conceptual models, especially for inexperienced users. Third, conceptual models often seem simplistic when compared to the actual situation, which often necessitates the use of multiple models. When, in the extreme, these problems combine users can be faced by a large modelling and comparison effort that creates ambiguous and uncertain results that, in turn, can lead to the rejection of the overall approach. It appears, therefore, that there are problems with the expression of activity systems models in SSM which may limit its acceptance and effectiveness in practical situations

The research theme that this paper begins to explore arises from these practical issues identified above. The theme can be focussed around the question: How can an SSM conceptual model be structured, and expressed other than in the conventional form reported in the research literature? The rest of this paper reports some initial research which has begun to explore this question.

2. A CRITIQUE OF THE MODELLING APPROACH USED IN SSM

The conventional approach to constructing a conceptual model from a root definition in SSM is to identify the activities implied by the Root Definition and then to structure them according to their logical dependence upon each other. The aim is to produce a model that represents the minimum but necessary set of interconnected activities to be the system specified in the root definition. Essentially the process is to partition the overall system as represented by the root definition into the minimal set of subsystems and relationships (activities and logical dependencies). The approach to model development in SSM is therefore consistent with the concept of Functional Decomposition (DeMarco, 1975). SSM provides only limited and informal guidelines for achieving the decomposition, i.e. comparing the model with the root definition and limiting the number of activities to around ten at any one level. The only partitioning enforced for the model is to separate the operative transformation process from the control subsystem which operates upon the transformation process. SSM provides no guidelines for partitioning the transformation process of the system or for determining whether a minimally partitioned set of activities has been established.

Three difficulties can be recognised in the conceptual modelling process. First, real-world problem solving can involve more than one transformation or focus. Often, multiple focuses need to be considered and prioritised yet the process involved in SSM considers each focus separately. The methodology of SSM involves a number of iterations through the cycle of construct, compare, and debate using one transformation statement for each iteration. There is nothing in the methodology that allows a focus on multiple transformations in an iteration.

Second, root definitions often contain secondary transformations. The focus of the secondary transformation is then lost in the conceptual model using the functional decomposition approach because only the primary transformation is functionally decomposed. For example, the root definition "to provide courses to increase technical skills and knowledge for suitably qualified and interested parties, that will be of value to the industry, whilst meeting BTEC approval in a manner that is both efficient and financially viable" (Wood-Harper *et al.*, 1985:57) contains the transformation of unprovided courses to provided courses and the transformation of interested parties (students) with less skills and knowledge to students with more skills and knowledge. In the model that is subsequently produced from this definition, Wood-Harper *et al.* only focus on, and functionally decompose, the transformation relating to courses. The focus on students is lost in their decomposition by being spread over a number of subsystems. Furthermore, it is not clear from the root definition which of the transformations is the primary focus. The prioritising or ordering of the transformations affects the world view. For example, if students are the primary focus then courses can be tailored to meet students' needs whereas if courses are the primary focus and students the secondary focus then students would have to take prearranged courses.

Third, SSM has an underlying assumption that humans socially construct their reality and the power of SSM lies in its ability to make explicit the different views in a situation and to facilitate and record the debate about change. Much real world experience suggests that debate is not always about the primary transformation or focus in a situation but rather about the rules or constraints that govern each transformation. These rules are also socially constructed yet these constraints upon a transformation are not given an explicit focus in SSM. They are not made explicit in the models and are therefore, not available for debate. Some consideration is given to these rules in the environmental constraints but environmental constraints are defined in the methodology as constraints that can be taken as imposed and not open to debate. In the root definition given above, two constraints are placed on the transformation of the provision of courses; the courses must be viable and must be BTEC approved. Similarly, two constraints are placed on students; they must be suitably qualified and they must be interested. Yet, the functional decomposition strategy used in SSM does not allow a focus on these constraints in the model. Furthermore, the constraints are related to the transformation statement. Discussing and debating the constraints in isolation to the transformation or purpose or discussing and debating the purpose in isolation to the constraints does not necessarily lead to a coherent whole. The next section describes a strategy developed to overcome these limitations.

3. DECISION-VARIABLE PARTITIONING (DVP)

Decision-Variable Partitioning (Donaldson and Ledington, 1996) is an approach to managing complex situations using a systems framework by partitioning problems into subsystems in such a way that it allows a focus on a part of the problem in relative isolation to other parts while maintaining a focus on the whole (each transformation). Minimum coupling is achieved by keeping all responses to each decision variable in relation to each transformation in one subsystem of the decomposition thus allowing the modeller to focus on the response to a state of a decision variable in one subsystem.

The process of producing models using DVP results in a decision tree. Figure 1 shows a systems model using DVP that is developed from the root definition given above with the primary transformation assumed to be the provision of courses.

Each transformation is indicated by the iteration decision variable and each constraint on a transformation is indicated by the selection decision variable. The rectangular boxes represent a subsystem to handle all activities (to transform the focus) in response to the state of the decision variable. That is, all responses to each selection or iteration variable are kept in one subsystem thus achieving minimum coupling. The ellipses represent the activities that are placed at the end of each branch of the tree. At each level in the decomposition, a subsystem is added that always must contain at least one activity to determine the state of the decision variable on that level. For example, the activity "Determine if approved" determines the state of the decision variable on that level. The subsystem containing this activity represents all activities in response to the state "For each unprovided course" in relation to the purpose or primary transformation prior to going into the state "If viable"; therefore, this subsystem may contain other activities that are needed that do not depend on viability. Once the decomposition is derived, activities relating to each subsystem can be added at the bottom of each node of the decision tree. For example, all activities that are necessary to transform each student from less skills and knowledge to more skills and knowledge (if qualified and interested) through the provision of courses would be placed at the end of the tree in the subsystem "If interested". Because students is plural in the root definition, a question arises "does the transformation from less skills and knowledge to more skills and knowledge relate to each student (as indicated in the DVP

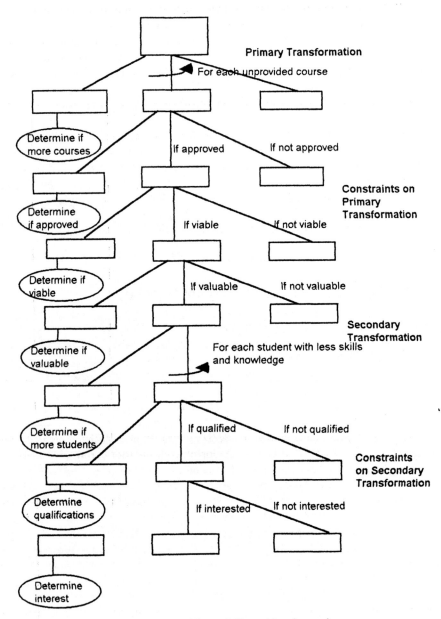

Primary Transformation

For each unprovided course

Determine if
more courses

If approved   If not approved

Constraints on
Primary
Transformation

Determine
if approved

If viable   If not viable

Determine if
viable

If valuable   If not valuable

Secondary
Transformation

Determine if
valuable

For each student with less skills
and knowledge

Determine if
more students

If qualified   If not qualified

Constraints
on Secondary
Transformation

Determine
qualifications

If interested   If not interested

Determine
interest

Figure 1. Decision-variable partitioned example.

model) or group of students?" That is, should there be another iteration level in the decomposition for each group of students between the primary and secondary transformation? This question would have to be clarified as they mean different things.

From this model, it can be seen that prioritising the transformations is important. In this example, students can only be transformed to more skills and knowledge through the prearranged courses because all activities are limited to converting the primary transformation of unprovided courses to provided courses. Changing the world view underlying this particular representation to a focus on students (switching the transformations) would allow more flexibility in how students could be transformed from less skills and knowledge to more skills and knowledge with courses being only one possible method for achieving this end. The model clearly highlights the prioritisation of transformations embedded in this world view and the constraints under which the transformations would be carried out and can suggest and lead to a consideration of alternate world views.

The constraints on a transformation can be of two forms; exclusive or discriminatory. Exclusive constraints state the conditions under which the transformation will be carried out or abandoned. In the above example, all the constraints appear to be exclusive. Courses will only be provided if approved or student knowledge will only be increased if qualified. These constraints dictate whether the activities to transform the focus will be carried out or not. Discriminatory constraints determine which activities will be carried out depending on the state of the constraint. An example would be if different types of students were treated differently. One might wish to distinguish between and create different activities for part-time and full-time students, for example. Discriminatory constraints would not determine whether the transformation would be carried out or not but rather would distinguish the activities to carry out the transformation. A DVP model can be developed by the following process:

1. Identify the transformations deemed relevant.
2. Prioritise the transformations.
3. Determine the constraints deemed relevant for each transformation.
4. Construct the initial structure showing each transformation as an iteration variable in order of priority and each constraint as a selection variable.
5. Add a subsystem at each level of the structure to contain at least one activity to determine the state of the decision variable on that level and the activities specified in the root definition.
6. To the end of each branch of the tree, add the activities.

Once the transformations have been specified and prioritised and the constraints determined for a particular world view, the drawing of the structure of the model is straightforward. The structure can then be used to facilitate adding the activities.

Many accounts of successful SSM studies can be found in the literature, (see for example: Checkland and Scholes, 1990; Davies and Ledington, 1991). Therefore, the question raised by this study is "can the process be improved by the use of an alternate systems representation?"

4. CONCLUSION

We have argued the need for alternative modelling approaches within SSM, and have presented an approach called Decision-Variable Partitioning. It is only in the context of a particular situation at a particular time that one model may be regarded as more useful, valuable, or insightful than another. In the same sense, there is no intrinsic value attached to constructing a model in one way or another. There is no answer to the question of whether a DVP-based model is intrinsically better than a functional decomposition model. However, we have demonstrated that alternative modelling approaches, such as DVP, are possible within SSM and that their use creates different emphases and different areas of attention and insight. Users of SSM may now choose different modelling approaches and this research establishes a significant new direction for the development of SSM.

Having begun to establish that a choice of systems modelling approaches is possible within SSM, the research challenge is to make that choice an informed one. Guidelines for choosing a modelling approach are required. To develop such guidelines requires more experience of applying DVP-based models and a greater understanding of the strengths and weaknesses of both DVP and conventionally-based models. Further, it provides new directions for considering the issues involved in training potential users of SSM and in considering the development of support tools.

REFERENCES

Avison, D. E. and Wood-Harper, A. T., 1990, *Multiview: An Exploration in Information Systems Development*, Blackwell, Oxford.

Checkland, P. B., 1981, *Systems Thinking, Systems Practice*, Wiley, Chichester.

Checkland, P. B. and Scholes, J., 1990, *Soft Systems Methodology in Action*, Wiley, Chichester.

Davies, L. J. and Ledington, P. W. J., 1991, *Information in Action: Soft Systems Methodology*, Macmillan, Basingstoke.

DeMarco, T., 1978, *Structured Analysis and System Specification*, Yourdon Inc., New York.

Donaldson, J. and Ledington, P.W.J., 1996, Decision-variable partitioning: a strategy for decomposing complex problems. Working Paper, School of Information Systems and Management Science, Griffith University.

Ledington, P.W.J. and Donaldson, J., 1995, The adoption and use of soft systems methodology in practice, in: *Systems for the Future*, (W. Hutchinson, S. Metcalf, C. Standing, M. Williams. eds.), pp. 74–83, Edith Cowan University, Perth.

Lewis, P. J., 1994, *Information Systems Development*, Pitman, London.

Stowell, F. A. (ed.), 1995, *Information Systems Provision: The Contribution of Soft Systems Methodology*, McGraw-Hill, London.

Wilson, B., 1984, *Systems, Concepts, Methodologies and Applications*, Wiley, Chichester.

Wood-Harper, A. T., Antill, L., and Avison, D. E., 1985, *Information Systems Definition: The Multiview Approach*. Blackwell, Oxford.

81

COMPLEMENTARITY OF EVALUATION METHODOLOGIES IN THE ORGANIZATION IN COLOMBIA

Clemencia Morales-Montejo

Centre for Systems Research
University of Lincoln Campus
Lincoln, LN6 7TS

1. INTRODUCTION

This paper is about the complementarity of the evaluation methodologies for measuring performance in modern organizations to be more effectively managed in terms of sustainability. The introduction of such methodologies will enable better handling of uncertainty inside and outside the organization.

Colombia began to work in an open market environment in 1993, and then it started to modernize its public organizations accordingly. The Colombian government has been creating mechanisms that enable measurement of performance in organizations in respect of the time taken to achieve objectives, and it is expected to develop evaluation patterns according to the new Colombian Constitution of 1991. There is a specific law for the Modernization of the Public Sector: "Ley 87" and "Directiva Presidencial 02" are concerned with the process of design and implementation of the Internal Control System in the Public Colombian Enterprises.

Colombian organizations need to be more aggressive and adaptable than they are now. They need to develop a greater capacity for learning in order to survive and change the open market environment. The evaluation methodologies should enable the comparison of different organizations both in the same economic sector and also between different sectors. The research will also focus on determining how to integrate in a complementarity way the variety of evaluation approaches with the organizations' usual operating functions.

2. COMPLEMENTARITY OF THE DIFFERENT EVALUATION METHODOLOGIES

The complementarity of evaluation methodologies has gained undenied importance in organizational design and diagnosis. The adequate handling and monitoring of meas-

Table 1.

Evaluation Methodology	View of the Approach	Suggested Systems-Approach	Effectiveness is the organization's ability to
Goal-Based	Machine	Interactive Management	achieve goals
Systems-Resource	Organization as an adaptive	Viable Systems Model	survive and adapt in a dynamic environment
Multi-Actor	Pluralistic System	Soft Systems Methodology	sastify the needs of all involved in its activities
Cultural	Cultural System		generate and perpetuate a culture

ures of performance makes it necessary to introduce swift mechanisms to allow on-going organizational evaluation. In practical terms, there have been certain problems in the design, diagnosis and evaluation of the organizational future because of the use in isolation methodologies that have been used up to date. However, in both practical and theoretical terms, there are problems with the integration of evaluation methodologies which have been used in an isolated manner. It will be argued that the synergy produced by the use of evaluation methodologies in a complementarity can improve the learning opportunity for the organization. Using the methodologies together improves the strengths of the individual methodologies and compensate for the weaknesses.

Analyzing Table 1 as a whole helps to identify four important issues in the complementarity of the different evaluation methodologies: an overview of the methodologies, different ways of viewing the organizations and the suggested systems approaches for conducting each evaluation approach. This analysis has been influenced by Morales (1995).

2.1. An Overview of the Methodologies Explained the Different Methodologies Possible to Use for Evaluation

In a Goal-Based Evaluation Approach, evaluation is based upon the organization's reaching formal, or at least operational, goals.

The Systems Resource-Based Evaluation Approach is based upon the idea that it is impossible to act without causing multiple reactions throughout the organization. The notion of adaptation to the environment and the ability of the organization to survive is very important in this evaluation approach.

The Multi-Actor Approach is a pluralistic approach which recognizes that conflict between actors may occur and evaluates performance in terms of how actors' interests are served.

The Culture Evaluation Approach must judge whether organizational actors are satisfied with the organizational culture and whether the culture provides for opportunities for change.

2.2. Different Ways of Viewing the Organization Explaining the Different Ways of Viewing the Organization to Ensure the Appropriate Form of Evaluation

In a Goal-Based Evaluation Approach organizations are viewed as machines seeking to achieve their goals with the minimum use of resources.

In a Systems Resource-Based Evaluation Approach, the organization is viewed as a complex adaptive system considered as a system of interacting parts.

"The Multi-Actor Evaluation Approach sees organizations as arenas of social action" (Gregory and Jackson, 1991). Each individual has his/her own set of beliefs and values shared through interaction with others.

In a Culture-Based Evaluation Approach the organization is seen as a social system which projects itself onto its members in order to produce a culture or identity.

2.3. The Suggested Systems Approaches for Conducting Each Evaluation Approach Explaining the Suggested Systems Approach for Evaluation Conducting and Monitoring Changes Outside and Inside the Organization

The Goal-Based Evaluation Approach might be helped by the systems-based methodology of Interactive Management. This Interactive Management method provides a process for deciding on objectives and producing an organizational mission and strategy.

Turning to the Systems Resource-Based Evaluation Approach, it seems that the Viable System Model of Beer (1979, 1983, 1985) represents the best model for approaching measures of performance, according to this approach, in the systems thinking tradition.

In a Multi-actor Evaluation Approach and in a Cultural Evaluation Approach some tools of Checkland's Soft Systems Methodology might be used as a model for exploring a problem situation. SSM has been seen by many as an useful tool for managing political and cultural change in organizations (Flood & Jackson 1991) offering the idea that all organizations need to survive and adapt to changing internal or external circumstances.

2.4. Measures of Performance Using the Various Approaches Explaining the Different Organizational Performance Measures for the Different Evaluation Approaches

The definitions of effectiveness, efficacy and efficiency are likely to be employed differently by each evaluation approach. I would use Gregory's (1995) definitions of effectiveness; These do not relate specifically to measurement but to the approaches as a whole.

The Goal Approach must provide the necessary modeling and quantitative techniques that will allow the systems effectiveness to be measured in terms of its stated goals. Gregory said "A form of evaluation based upon the view of the organization as a machine should promote a definition of effectiveness such as: effectiveness is the organization's ability to achieve goals."

The System Resource-Based Evaluation judges effectiveness using concepts such as survival, adaptability, development, growth, flexibility and stability. Gregory stated (1995), "It is logical that a form of organizational evaluation based upon organic principles should adopt a definition of effectiveness such as: effectiveness is the organization's ability to survive and adapt in a dynamic environment."

The multi-actor approach tends to depend upon a consensus of different actors about organizational effectiveness. "Effectiveness is the organization's ability to satisfy the needs of all those parties influenced by and having an influence upon its activities" (Gregory, 1995).

In a Culture-Based Evaluation Approach, evaluation focuses on matters pertinent to individuals and emphasises on communication and relationships. "Effectiveness is the organization's ability to generate and perpetuate a culture which, by enabling those individuals who serve it to reach their potential, enhances its, the organization's, own variety" (Gregory, 1995).

3. CONCLUSION

It is important to use evaluation methodologies in a complementarity way, especially for use in Colombian organizations (commercial, industrial, governmental or social enterprise). In conducting an evaluation there are various issues to be addressed: firstly, what views or perspective on organizations is being adopted and the conditions under which a particular view be taken of the organization for the purpose of evaluation are examined. Secondly, in suggesting the best method for conducting the evaluation, it may be assumed that only systems approaches can deal with the complexity and turbulence faced by modern organizations. Thirdly, it is necessary to discover how to define indicators for each evaluation methodology. Fourthly, whether it is possible to use the different methodologies for evaluation purposes in a complementary way must be considered.

The complementarity use of evaluation methodologies in a complementarist must be the core of the evaluation process allowing the performance measurement of goal, survival potential, stakeholders' satisfaction and culture simultaneously and integrally. The complementarity of evaluation methodologies may be helpful to obtain organizational performance measurements internally and externally. The crucial question is whether the definition of an appropriate set of indicators will generate the basis for an organizational evaluation process and whether they will permit the form of evaluation used in theory to be significant in practice.

4. REFERENCES

Beer, S., 1988, *Diagnosing the System for Organizations,* John Wiley and Sons, Chichester.

Flood, R.L., and Jackson, M.C., 1991, *Creative Problem Solving: -Total Systems Intervention*, John Wiley & Sons, London.

Gregory, A.J., and Jackson, M.C., 1991, Evaluating Organizations: A systems and Contingency Approach, *Systems Practice*, Vol.5. No. 1.

Gregory, A.J, and Jackson, M.C., 1992, Evaluation Methodologies: A System for Use, *J. OPL RES SOC.* Vol 43, No.1, pp 19–28.

Gregory, A.J., 1995, Models in Evaluation: Four Approaches, Second Chapter, *PhD Thesis*, University of Hull.

Morgan, G., 1986, *Images of Organization*, Sage, Beverly Hills, CA.

Morales, C., 1992, Stability Indicators, A Tool for Organizational Planning and Control, *Master of Philosophy Theses*, The University of Aston in Birmingham.

Morales C., 1995, Systems Study of the Scope and Significance of Evaluation Methodologies in the Management of Organizations in Colombia, *Proceedings of the thirty-ninth Annual Meeting International Society for the Systems Sciences*, Free University, Amsterdam.

Warfield J.N., 1990, *A Science of Generic Design: Managing Complexity Through Systems Design,* Intersystems Publications; U.S.A.

82

SPIRALLING INTO THE FUTURE

Graham Paton

The Open University
4 Portwall Lane
Bristol, BS1 6ND
Telephone: 0117 929 9641; G.Paton@open.ac.uk,Internet

1. INTRODUCTION

The terms 'hard' and 'soft' have now become embedded in our discourse and the soft-hard dimension has become accepted as reality. Methodological devices have been positioned along the range, which was now established, from the objective and quantitative at the hard end to the subjective and qualitative at the soft end. But this very image (of a range itself) is problematic. It is useful to arraign methodologies on it for purposes of illuminating their relative strengths and weaknesses. However, it is quite wrong to suppose that any real situation is either hard of soft. All include both elements. Which methodological tools to deploy is a decision which is taken by the human actors in any particular situation. The metaphor of a range has no utility (or is positively dangerous) when applied to the situations-to-be-analysed because it encourages us to think in terms of categorising situations as hard or soft, rather than focusing on understanding both of these aspects of a situation.

2. WHEN IS AN ANALYSIS 'GOOD ENOUGH'?

Does this mean that, in any given situation, we have to apply all methodologies from our range to be effective? Well, in a fundamental way, I think that is precisely the requirement. But in practical terms it isn't quite so daunting. What would be needed is to utilise representative methodologies from each section of the range. You may object to this requirement for a comprehensive approach. I can, myself, see no justification for an argument that situations are either hard or soft, so if that is the basis of your objection we are in fundamental disagreement. But if you would say that, given all situations are a complex intermeshing of both hard and soft issues, nevertheless, in any particular situation it may be more appropriate to adopt either a hard or a soft approach to analysis, then I have more sympathy. This is a particular case of a more general issue facing any analyst, that is deciding when an analysis is good enough. Good enough in terms of depth, breadth, area of

Systems for Sustainability, edited by Stowell *et al.*
Plenum Press, New York, 1997

focus, issues addressed, etc. These considerations arise at all levels of an analysis. There are always trade-offs between the resources available to an analyst and the likely results of a particular piece of analysis. There is need to exercise a firm control of any analysis project; its overall management requires both a good understanding of the resource issues and of the politics and culture of the situation. Deciding whether to undertake hard or soft modelling is a decision which itself requires an understanding of both hard and soft issues!

3. THE SOFT-HARD DIVIDE AND EPISTEMOLOGICAL BARRIERS

So we must, in considering how to undertake any particular analysis, be prepared to employ both hard and soft methodologies. Can we establish one, overall methodology which encompasses both? One possible way to move towards this utopian position is to embed our usual methodological devices within each other. Although initially attractive, this is not easy to do in practice.

Soft within hard does not work. All hard methodologies assume agreed objectives rationality and structure, the existence of which soft methodologies generally deny, at least in principle. Hard within soft could work, but doesn't. It could be because one can perceive any hard methodological device, or (more particularly), modelling as a particularly well-bounded and well-defined instance of the generally more illusive and ill-defined reality we are trying to address. It doesn't work because our currently available softer methodologies are themselves limited and constrained. Checkland's Soft Systems Methodology (SSM), (Checkland, 1981) has been criticised for adopting a managerialist approach which inevitably tends to support the status quo in an organisation. I personally see the methodological mechanism of SSM as powerful and quite unconstrained in this way. But I concede that its language (the role of the client for instance) and, more particularly, the history of its use, both position it in this area. If we are to have a generally applicable soft framework within which to embed hard methodology then it must be free of such stigma. Maybe SSM could be revised to take account of this criticism but the work has not yet been addressed.

Furthermore, present methodologies have tended to be confused unnecessarily by their initial epistemological position. There has been, to stick with SSM, a reluctance by proponents to allow that the intellectual construct, the conceptual model, can legitimately be transposed into a blueprint for design at the will of the actors in a situation. People have (rightly I think) no such difficulties with the decision to implement or realise the results of a hard modelling exercise. This is not to say that there are not significant epistemological differences between existing systems methodologies and between the ontological nature of the models they create and employ. The UK Systems Society has done much to promote the debate about these issues (see, for example, the special IS edition of Systemist, 1992) but more is needed. As Schon has pointed out, and highlights in the title of one of his recent publications (Schon, Donald 1995) 'the new scholarship requires a new epistemology'. There is not space here to pursue this debate in any depth.

4. THE METHODOLOGICAL ARRAY

If, then, we have a complex array of methodological devices available to us, how are we to judge between them? Much of the secondary literature of the Systems movement in the UK over the last six years or so has focused on the ways in which we can compare and contrast the methodological tools on offer. From this activity comes the ability to select appropriate methodological devices in particular situations. Although there work goes beyond merely categorising methodologies, much of Flood and Jackson's work on Liberating Systems Theory (Flood, 1990), Critical Systems Thinking (Flood and Jackson, 1991), and Total Systems Intervention (Flood and Jackson, 1991) provides increasingly sophisticated means of conducting this assessment of which methodology is best in which circumstances. That this work is scholarly and informative is undoubted. However, there are fundamental problems with its practicality.

Firstly, in order to make a realistic choice between methodologies, the practitioner must be conversant with all those under consideration. As all present themselves in a particular form, with a specific and individualistic use of language, gaining a good depth of understanding about them is no trivial task. Yet we are talking of methodologies here; that is of sets of tools and techniques which can be used to create a method to deal with a particular situation. We are not talking of *methods*, *tools*, or *techniques* themselves, where a superficial knowledge may be adequate to allow their application by rote. Using a methodology well requires, by definition, a very good, deep understanding of its strengths and weaknesses.

Secondly, addressing the range of methodologies in this way is anti-systemic. By highlighting the differences between methodologies we create and sustain a reductionist view of these methodologies. The Systems movement, above all else, should address its affairs systemically.

5. A SYSTEMIC ACTION LEARNING CYCLE

My own attempts to make sense of this problem led me to begin to look for some common process, but one in which the criticisms made above would be absent, or at least, less apparent. I came to the conclusion that most existing methodologies founded as they were in the hierarchical organisational thinking of the 60's and 70's, were interventionist in nature. Not surprisingly, (since intervention is the life blood of consultants), they have been well supported by those whose business it is to solve problems for others. In moving towards a means of comparing methodologies I sought some way of moving towards a focus more applicable to the reflective practitioner of the 90's and the need for organisational learning, which looks likely to be so important in the next millennium.

It seems to this author that most methodologies have encapsulated a cycle of activity which leads from some initial alerting event through a thought process to action. Fig 1 is a diagrammatic representation of this process (from Paton 1996).

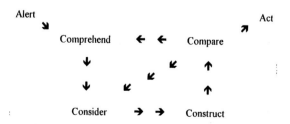

Figure 1. A systemic action learning cycle.

Table 1. Comparison of the elements of a systemic action learning cycle with the stages of soft systems methodology

SALC element	SSM Stage	Remarks
Alert	?	Possibly initial directive from the client
Comprehend	1. The problem unstructured	
	2. The problem structured	
Consider	?	Creating the issue and task list and prioritising it with this element, as does selecting which relevant systems to model
Construct	3. Root definitions	
	4. Conceptual Models	
Compare	5. Compare	
Act	6. Act	In SSM defined as the prerogative of the client

I have attempted to map SSM onto this Systemic Action Learning Cycle, (SALC). The result, (outline below in table 2), is encouraging for two reasons. Firstly it shows that SSM encompasses the cycle very well; I had always felt that SSM was a powerful mechanism which had much wider utility than those who would marginalise it proposed. Secondly, the area where SSM has always seemed weakest to me (in terms of its representation in the classic seven stage Model), that is in the bridging between 'the situation structured' and the 'root definition', is highlighted in the Action Learning Cycle as of particular importance (the action 'consider'). This provides a theoretical base activity for all that SSM work on identifying key issues and tasks and choosing which to work with.

As a contrast from the other end of the methodological range, I have mapped the Open University Hard Systems Approach (HSA), (Open University, 1984), onto the elements of the SALC. Here the constraints on choice of modelling flowing from direct acceptance of organisational goals are highlighted. (See Table 2).

All these comparisons indicate the lack of methodological attention to the act of initiation (SALC's 'Alert') and closure (SALC's 'Act') of the analytical cycle. Yet these acts are of

Table 2. Comparison of the elements of a systemic action learning cycle with the stages of the Open University's hard systems methodology

SALC element	HMA Stage	Remarks
Alert	?	Possibly action by the 'Decision Maker' of within the 'Problem/Opportunity' situation
Comprehend	Problem Perception	
	System Description	
	Identification of Objectives and constraints	
Consider	?	Perhaps 'Routes to Objectives' fits here. In this methodology the stated organisational objectives are taken as given and there is little consideration about what to model; more about how to model.
Construct	Formulating measures of performance	
	Modelling	
Compare	Evaluation	
	Choice of Routes to Objective	
Act	Implementation	Here too an action undertaken by the client

crucial importance if the process of analysis is to be managed effectively. In particular we should consider how to manage multiple cycles of analysis. I see this ongoing cyclic activity as something other than Checkland's flux of events and ideas, (Checkland and Scholes 1990), since Checkland describes discrete events occurring in the course of that flux, whereas I want to emphasise the element of continuity in any particular analysis. Guidance on the conduct of a particular intervention is well evident in the SSM literature. But there is little about management of this as a process over time; what we might term spiral management. Yet the problem for a practitioner, enmeshed in a soft problem's boundary-less domain, is particularly to decide when and how to exit the spiral of iterative analysis.

A series of questions flow from this problem, all relating to the key issue of how to decide when an analysis is good enough for those involved to say it is not necessary to do more. There are two interrelated sets of sub-issues here: resources and definitions. Resource issues are concerned with how many people should be devoted to the analysis task, for how long and to what depth. All these resource issues link directly to definitional issues. The most crucial is that of defining the (necessarily subjective) process by which a judgement about sufficiency of the analysis will be made. Two other questions are of particular importance: The first is where is the knowledge which has been created in the course of the analysis held? The second is what implications does this issue have for methodologies themselves?

The power of systemic analysis is the process whereby a number of actors (analyst, client and many others) become more aware and informed about the situation. It very important to recognise that such knowledge is largely held by people. Therefore where these people go with their knowledge, and what they do with it, at the 'end' of an analysis are both key resource- management issues. Recognising the value of this resource should influence decisions about whether to deploy an organisation's own staff or consultants and about how such knowledge is formalised and transmitted to others. All these issues are at the heart of creating, and sustaining, a learning organisation. Over a decade ago, in closing his work 'The Reflective Practitioner' (Schon, 1983), Schon made a plea that reciprocal reflection-in-action which "some of us do on rare occasions" be made into a dominant pattern of practice. We have moved on to recognise the need for such reflection, but we need to understand the processes at work here far better than we do.

So far as methodologies themselves are concerned, it seems possible to begin to move away from rigid isolationism towards a more congruent representation of the overall cycle of analysis activity. This movement could ease the burden on would-be practitioners and make the central power houses of systemic analysis, the systems modelling activities themselves, more accessible to more people. We need to encourage this movement.

REFERENCES

Checkland, P.B., 1981, Systems Thinking, Systems Practice, Wiley, Chichester.
Checkland, P.B.,and Scholes, J., 1990, Soft Systems Methodology in Action, Wiley, Chichester.
Flood, R. L., 1990, Liberating Systems Theory, Plenum, New York.
Flood, R. L., and Jackson, M. C., (eds), 1991, Critical Systems Thinking: Directed Readings, Wiley, Chichester.
Flood, R. L., and Jackson, M. C., 1991, Creative Problem Solving Total Systems Intervention, Wiley, Chichester.
IS Special Edition, 1992, Systemist, UK Systems Society, Volume 14, No. 3.
The Open University, 1984, The Hard Systems Approach, in Complexity, Management and Change: Applying a Systems Approach, The Open University, Walton Hall, Milton Keynes.
Paton, G., 1996, Systems Analysis - An Action Learning Perspective, in Lessons Learned from the use of Methodologies, Jayaratna, N., & Fitzgerald, B., (eds), Proceedings of the British Computer Society Information Systems Methodologies Specialist Group.

Schon, D. A., 1995, The New Scholarship Requires a New Epistemology, in *Change*, Vol. 27, No.6.
Schon, D. A., 1983, The Reflective Practitioner: how Professionals think in action, Maurice Temple Smith, London.

83

WORKING TOWARDS SUSTAINABILITY THROUGH CREATIVITY

Promotion of Critical Creativity as an Integral Component of Systems Methodologies

Gillian Ragsdell

School of Management
Lincoln University Campus
Brayford Pool, Lincoln LN6 7TS

1. INTRODUCTION

This paper intends to stimulate discussion about the benefits that could emerge from integrating a concept called 'critical creativity' with systems based problem-solving approaches. The premise that has been adopted is that such an integration would be a step towards developing more sustainable systems.

The paper is structured as follows. I start by introducing the link that I have made between sustainability and creativity. The background continues to be set with an outline of the concept of critical creativity. Distinction between critical creativity and creativity *per se* can then be made. Next, Ackoff's (1978) Idealized Design is presented as an example of an approach that implicitly relies on critical creativity for 'successful' application. In the penultimate section it is argued that implicit reliance on critical creativity is not sufficient for interventionists and that Total Systems Intervention (Flood and Jackson, 1991; Flood 1995) can guide a process of critique through which critical creativity is explicitly pursued. A short summary closes the paper.

2. BACKGROUND

2.1. Sustainability and Creativity

Sustainability suggests eternal life. For a system to experience eternal life it must always be deemed to be applicable and valid; not an easy task in a world of accelerating change. Staying 'one step ahead', being proactive rather than reactive, appears to be fun-

Systems for Sustainability, edited by Stowell *et al.*
Plenum Press, New York, 1997

damental to sustainability. Merely responding to the environment is not enough. Likewise, making incremental improvements to systems may prove to be ineffective; quantum leaps are needed. Such quantum leaps may need provoking. Creative thinking is required and creativity enhancing techniques may therefore be usefully employed. While systems thinkers have long recognised the importance of open-mindedness in their activities, creative thinking is not always apparent.

Particularly from the 1980s there have been rapid advancements in the systems movement. Soft Systems Methodology of Checkland (1981), Critical Systems Heuristics of Ulrich (1983) and Total Systems Intervention of Flood and Jackson (1991) are but three recent developments in systems based methodologies. Whilst systems thinking has moved on significantly, an undercurrent of creative thinking has not maintained the same rate of flow. Systems approaches to creativity have been introduced (Rickards, 1985; Csikszent-mihalyi, 1988; Gruber and Davis, 1988) but they do not benefit from the most recent developments in systems thinking—namely that of Critical Systems Thinking. Critical creativity, however, does address the issues of creative thinking in relation to contemporary systems studies.

Bringing these two strands together leads to a suggestion that creativity is pertinent to the process of achieving sustainable systems. It also suggests that the integration of critical creativity with the application of systems based methodologies is a step towards that goal.

2.2. Critical Creativity

I now draw from an understanding of Critical Systems Thinking as I outline the concept of critical creativity in terms of its philosophical foundations, its nature and its principles.

2.2.1. Philosophical Foundations. Being critical in Critical Systems Thinking (see Flood and Jackson, 1991b; Flood and Romm, 1996) involves complementarism, sociological awareness, human well-being and emancipation. These commitments hold significance for creativity. The complementarist standpoint draws attention to the fact that creativity can arise from a number of different origins. It also recognises that approaches for stimulating and enhancing creativity have emerged from a number of schools of thought and that approaches to creativity can yield different outcomes. Sociological awareness in critical creativity encourages increased awareness of the social consequences of using particular creative approaches and any output that is realised. Practitioners of critical creativity are obliged to reflect on societal pressures which participants face. In a similar vein, critical creativity would seek "to achieve for all individuals, working through organisations and in society, the maximum development of their potential" (Flood and Jackson, 1991a, p49).

2.2.2. Nature. To integrate critical creativity into the application of a problem solving framework is to integrate a form of creativity that has a number of core characteristics. First, critical creativity is intended to be practically useful for managers of organisational problems. It does not contradict or confuse the overarching framework but enriches it by reinforcing the original principles. Secondly, critical creativity takes into account ideas developed from many viewpoints and does not attempt to restrict the use of theories. A broad base of knowledge can be drawn from. In doing so, the critically creative process brings a greater possibility of enlightening participants. Critical creativity also creates diversity by encouraging 'quantity' and, finally, allows judgement to be undertaken locally (but with inputs from external parties).

2.2.3. Principles. Four key principles, adopted from the most recent version of TSI (Flood, 1995), underpin critical creativity. The systemic principle asks for an understanding of the 'whole'. Only by gaining an appreciation of the complete scenario (including an appreciation of a large number of creativity enhancing approaches, organisational theories, theories of facilitation as well as the circumstances of intervention) can a practitioner expect to proceed most effectively. The principle of participation reinforces the systemic principle for, only from meaningful involvement by as many parties as possible, can multiple partial views be taken into account. The principle of reflection satisfies the various reflective needs of critical creativity. Amongst these needs is the need to reflect upon the dynamic relationships in the organisation so that parties who may not be able to participate meaningfully can be identified. Thus, the principle of participation is reinforced. Other reflective needs include those in relation to reflecting upon the selection of creativity models and methodologies in order to critically assess their suitability and choose an appropriate facilitation style for a particular context. The three aforementioned principles lead to the wider goal of the pursuit of human freedom. In keeping with Flood's (1993) dialectic, critical creativity attempts to further the emancipation of individuals by encouraging participants to design freedom into their approach, to participate meaningfully in a process of open debate, and to address coercive forces which hinder attempts to free themselves of their mind traps.

Practitioners who intervene, for whatever reason, with a limited toolkit tend to pursue creativity *per se* rather than critical creativity. Their intervention could be limited by the number of creative approaches they are familiar with, their understanding of the intervention situation or their lack of a range of facilitation skills. Such practitioners cannot take the full context of operation into account. Creativity then becomes a 'bolted on' accessory rather than an integral component of the methodology. Consequently, they could constrain creative thinking and suppress quantum leaps.

3. IDEALIZED DESIGN

Idealized Design is an example of a creative, systemic problem solving approach that appears to implicitly recognise its context dependency. An overview of the process is presented. I then highlight the extent to which Idealized Design critically employs creativity. This employment is due more to the intuitive behaviour of practitioners than in response to any methodological guidelines.

3.1. Introduction to Idealized Design

Ackoff's (1978) process of Idealized Design tackles a problem situation with a very strong prospective orientation. The notion of an 'idealized design' is "an explicit statement of what the designers would have now if they could have whatever they wanted" (Ackoff, 1978, p28). When idealized design envelops the process of proactive planning or the solving of complex social system problems, it represents a re/design of a system and its environment. Only two constraints are consciously imposed—that the design be technologically feasible and operationally viable. The product of such a design is an ideal-seeking state or system, rather than an ideal state. With its focus on 'ultimate values' rather than short term objectives and operational strategies, it is suggested that consensus can readily emerge amongst participants.

Creativity is fundamental to the process; it is not just a discrete component as with some approaches. Ackoff (1978) says, "The idealized design process unleashes creativity because it relaxes internally imposed constraints. It sanctions imaginative irreverence for things as they are and encourages exploration of areas previously precluded by self-imposed and culturally imposed taboos." While there is no guarantee of a creative redesign arising solely from pedantic commitment to the steps of the process, there is an explicit removal of assumptions and constraints. There is the prospect of a creative process in which radical and unconventional ideas can flow. 'Quantum leaps' can be made.

3.2. Idealized Design and Critical Creativity

By considering aspects of the contexts in which Idealized Design has proved successful an inherent reflective element has been identified in the process. This reflective element is an implicit reliance on critical creativity. A couple of these aspects are now shared.

3.2.1. Outputs. A useful way to reflect on creative processes is to question their intentions and purposes. More specifically, to ask whether they intend to generate ideas or images. In a similar way that some people associate more readily with text than with diagrams, individuals often find that they have a preference for images or ideas as a medium to express their creativity. An awareness of this preference may improve the application of creative approaches. When examining Idealized Design, it is not obvious whether it is image or idea generating. Indeed it is probably best to think of the process as being founded on the interplay between both intentions. The method does not restrict to either idea or image. The tension created by this interplay may well bring added value to the creative potential of the process but, of greater significance to this discussion, it widens the scope of participants.

3.2.2. Quantum Leaps or Incremental Steps? Another feature of the context in which creative approaches are applied can be surfaced by exploring their anticipated creative potential. Idealized Design has been known to involve senior players from organisations, people who have the power and authority to make radical changes. It has also been applied at the invitation of companies that have been willing and able to take risks. In these circumstances there are few, if any, restrictions to the exercise of the imagination. However, as variations of the original Idealized Design have been developed (Ciccantelli and Magidson, 1993) the process is being more universally practised with stakeholders from different levels of the organisation. Even so, Idealized Design would seem to anticipate quantum leaps in creativity.

Although attention seems to have been paid to the context dependency of Idealized Design so far, its application cannot be 'policed'. Some practitioners may unknowingly try an incompatible match between approach and situation. The guidance provided by TSI could avoid such a mismatch and ensure a successful stimulation of creative thinking.

4. TOTAL SYSTEMS INTERVENTION AND CRITICAL CREATIVITY

The three Modes of TSI (Flood, 1995) have been identified as being capable of providing guidance in the pursuit of critical creativity. Not only could it be used to determine which overarching creative approaches are appropriate to use, as in the case of Idealized Design, but it could also critically assess the practice of creativity components in methodologies. Critical creativity can be effective at various levels of detail. In each of the three Modes of TSI a critique is structured by working through the cyclic phase of Creativity-Choice-Implementation. Each Mode is now outlined. More detail of the operationalisation of critical creativity can be found in Ragsdell (1995a; 1996a).

The purpose of the Critical Review Mode is to critically explore and appraise the candidate approaches allied to creative thinking that could be taken forward into the Problem Solving Mode. Inputs to this Mode can be taken from the wealth of established models, methods and techniques currently available or could conceivably be the practitioners own original contributions. At the level of the methodology, the inputs could include Soft Systems Methodology; at the level of discrete components the input may be the rich picturing stage or the conceptual model development. Outputs will be those models and methodologies which are thought likely to surface creative potential.

The Problem Solving Mode employs the system of creativity approaches put together through the Critical Review Mode. Practitioners are guided into an exploration of the situation in which s/he intends to use a creative approach and a categorisation of the approaches from the previous mode. Bringing together a richly informed impression of the arena for action and a creative categorising tool, enables a choice of the most suitable approach for the circumstance to be made and implemented.

Finally, the Critical Reflection Mode provides an opportunity to reflect on both the adequacies of the approach(es) that was employed and its output. It is a Mode in which future practices of critical creativity can benefit from inquiries concerning whether a more appropriate choice of approach(es) could have been made and whether subsequent outputs were acceptable.

Some may say that the presence of creativity *per se* in a problem solving process is adequate and that the perceived sophistication of a complementary approach to creativity is superfluous to requirements. Case study evidence (Ragsdell, 1996b) has shown this not to be so. Others may say that I am trying to systematise the discipline of creativity. That is not the case. Critical creativity welcomes and works with the diversity of the discipline. The operationalisation of critical creativity is itself underpinned by creativity through the creative phases embraced by TSI.

5. SUMMARY

I started by introducing a complementary approach to creativity on the basis that it benefited from philosophical foundations of contemporary systems studies. Ackoff's (1978) Idealized Design was then recognised as a systemic approach that goes some way towards pursuing critical creativity. Finally, I proposed that the three modes of Total Systems Intervention (Flood, 1995) can provide guidance for the explicit pursuit of critical creativity. In integrating such guidance into systems methodologies more highly original, and therefore more sustainable, systems could emerge.

REFERENCES

Ackoff, R. L., 1978, *The Art of Problem Solving*, Wiley, New York
Checkland, P. B., 1981, *Systems Thinking, Systems Practice*, Wiley, Chichester

Ciccantelli, S. and Magidson, J. 1993, Consumer idealized design: involving consumers in the product development process, *J. Prod. Innov. Manag.* 10, 341–347

Csikszentmihalyi, M., 1988, Society, culture and person: a systems view of creativity, in: *The Nature of Creativity*, (R. Sternberg, ed.) Cambridge University Press

Flood, R. L., 1993, Practising freedom: designing, debating and disemprisoning. *OMEGA*, 21, 7–17

Flood, R. L., 1995, *Solving Problem Solving*, Wiley, Chichester

Flood, R. L., and Jackson, M. C., 1991a, *Total Systems Intervention,* Wiley, Chichester

Flood, R. L., and Jackson, M. C., (eds.), 1991a, *Critical Systems Thinking: Directed Readings,* Wiley, Chichester

Flood, R. L., and Romm, N. R. A., (eds.), 1996, *Critical Systems Thinking: Current Research and Practice*, Plenum, New York

Gruber, H. E., and Davis, S. N. 1988, Inching our way up Mount Olympus: the evolving systems approach to creativity, in: *The Nature of Creativity*, (R. Sternberg, ed.) Cambridge University Press

Ragsdell, G., 1995a, Dealing With Life's "One Offs": Creativity and Problem Solving, in: *Systems Thinking, Government Policy and Decision Making*, (B. Bergvall-Kareborn, ed.), pp 992–1003, International Society for the Systems Sciences

Ragsdell, G., 1996a, Creativity and Problem Solving in: *Critical Systems Thinking - Current Theory and Practice,* (R. L. Flood and N. R. A. Romm, eds.), Plenum, New York (in print)

Ragsdell, G., 1996b, Creative Management of Creative Management, Unpublished PhD Thesis, University of Hull

Rickards, T., 1985, *Stimulating Innovation: A Systems Approach*, Gower, Aldershot

Ulrich, W., 1983, *Critical Heuristics of Social Planning*, Berne, Haupt

84

DIALOGISM

A Bakhtinian Perspective on Communication

Robert Stephens

Faculty of Computer Studies and Maths
University of the West of England
Frenchay, Bristol, BS16 1QY

1. INTRODUCTION

Mikhail Bakhtin has the reputation of one of the greatest theoreticians of literature of the twentieth century. Bakhtin's ideas have also enjoyed some recent influence in post-structural social theory, yet, despite clear similarities, they remain relatively unknown to systems audiences. In this paper some leading concepts of Bakhtin's social philosophy are presented as pertinent to constructivist and linguistically orientated systems thought. Broad affinities exist between Bakhtinian dialogism and the communicative, or second order cybernetics of Bateson (1972), Capra (1983) or von Glasersfeld (1984), as well as some contemporary fields of organizational research, systems thinking and information systems development. In this paper I shall be concerned mainly with the latter, because of a common theme in the concern for the meaning generating properties of linguistic interaction. Firstly, interpretivist criticism of objectivism has made the case that information systems, rather than unproblematically representing the world, are inherently meaningful, open to interpretation and therefore qualitatively different from mechanical systems. Secondly, and in sympathy with this, information systems research is critically concerned with processes of symbolic communication, implying that the information concept, as used in this context, has to be approached in terms of semiotics (Stamper, 1987; Mingers, 1996; Holmqvist, Andersen, Klein, and Posner, 1996). Further, a 'linguistic turn', both in organizational studies (e.g., Morgan, 1986) and information systems research (e.g., Lyytinen, 1985), has encouraged some scholars to adopt language, or language use, for analytical purposes, and even as the analogue for software models (e.g., Winograd and Flores, 1986).

Bakhtin's original contribution, postumously termed 'dialogism' by Holquist (1990), is a challenge to paradigmatic views on human communication. Dialogism is radically opposed to the understanding of human communication as the transfer of an immaterial idea or concept in the 'mind' of one person being *sent* into the mind of another, essentially

Systems for Sustainability, edited by Stowell *et al.*
Plenum Press, New York, 1997

similar person via material signs. It portrays communication as a systemic process in which people occupy different positions in an unending discourse and attempt to influence each other's behaviour in some way. The Bakhtinian view of communication holds that dialogue, which would be impossible or superfluous without differences of perspective between participants, is guaranteed by the fact that each speaker occupies a unique location in space and time. His philosophical orientation therefore, is common to several modern epistemologies that seek to grasp human behaviour through the use made of language, but it is specified by the dialogic concept of language he proposes as fundamental (Holquist, 1990, p.15).

Bakhtin's approach was to concentrate on communication as articulated utterance where the systematicity apparent in language always has to be completed in a community of speakers. The utterance, for Bakhtin, is a border phenomena populating the 'gap' that exists not only between words and the world, but also between speakers, and between what is and what is not said. The utterance is always in response to, and in anticipation of, other utterances, rendering linguistic meanings precarious and incomplete. However, Bakhtin considered language not as an epiphenomena, but as part of the social fabric and an active force in structuring the world. Consequently, dialogism is seen as an agent for change with a predisposition to subvert stability and order.

Communication is increasingly a key theoretical concept in organizational studies, as it is an obvious concern for a growing number of academic and organizational staff engaged with electronic communication technologies. The concept, however, is notoriously resistant to analytical resolution. As Harris (1988) points out, communication is one of those mereticiously perspicuous concepts: everything can be made to seem obvious, but very little is. As an observation word (Ryle, 1990), its use bears affinity to the lack of consensus surrounding the use of the term information (cf, Mingers, 1995; Stamper, 1996). At its extremes communication represents *transmission*, a one way process, and *share*, a common or mutual process (Williams, 1976, p.72). Bakhtin analyses these processes respectively as *monologic* or *univocal* and *dialogic* or *multivocal*, distinguished by the communication item's internal homogeneity or heterogeneity. This contrast is pertinent to styles of organizational information system, and will be pursued in the final section, but first it is necessary to sketch the main contours of Bakhtin's social philosophy.

2. DIALOGISM

It is appropriate to begin by elaborating some basic assumptions. Bakhtin was primarily concerned to examine and conceptualize the forces of flux, change, and difference that he considered to be essential to the social and natural worlds. His ontology was one of a ceaseless battle between the forces of stasis and fixity on the one hand, and movement, change, and creativity on the other: stability and closure are continually threatened and subverted by the forces of multiplicity and openness, a process designated by the overarching concept of 'unfinalizability'. The human condition, in this world, is the 'event of being', characterized by unending self-activity, wherein the 'givenness' of the external world is transformed by an on-going project of meaning-creation or 'architectonics'. So long as the human being *is*, he or she has no choice but to *act*; as it is brutally put, there is 'no alibi' in existence for merely occupying a location in it.

But existence for Bakhtin is properly the event of co-being; it is a vast web of interconnections linking participants in an event whose totality is so immense that no single person can apprehend it. That event manifests itself in the form of a constant, ceaseless creation and exchange of meaning. Having 'no alibi' means having a stake in everything that is experienced, but crucially it means always being in an event. This is the event of being, that is at once unique, connoting perspective and difference, while at the same to being common to others. Dialogism then, is critically focussed upon the relation between the 'I' and the 'other': a relation most economically defined as one in which differences - while remaining different - serve as the building blocks of simultaneity (Holquist, 1990).

An essential feature of dialogue is that it is always 'open-ended', and is characterized by an ongoing conflict of perspectives: because every person is uniquely located in time and space, for any participant in a dialogue there will always be some aspect of the other's perspective that remains unknowable. All meaning is relative in the sense that it comes about only as a result of the relation between two bodies occupying *simultaneous but different space*, where bodies may be thought of as ranging from the immediacy of our physical bodies, to political bodies and to bodies of ideas in general (ideologies).

Dialogism then, is meant to convey the impression of human existence as one of continuing interaction or dialogue with the world, in which the utterance, Bakhtin's basic unit of analysis, continually invokes and animates other voices or speech genres. Utterance is defined simply as a linguistic intervention or a contribution to a dialogue. However, unlike an abstract formulation of language, an utterance is always a link in an unbroken chain of communication, linked both to what precedes it and to what might follow. Bakhtin, therefore like many others, stresses the context sensitivity, or 'embeddedness' of language use. Unusually however, by focussing on the utterance, rather than language *per se*, his idea of context extends beyond the local situation to account for an absent 'other'. He argues that all utterances presuppose other participants, indeed, all communication exists for their sake and is constructed taking into account their projected reactions. The other side of this *addressivity* is *responsivity*. Speech is responsive because it necessarily draws on previous discourse. We respond directly to others' messages, but, even more pervasively, choose our words from previously heard talk. Utterances thus reflect and create one another, and through language's projective and reflective qualities, words take on particular meanings within spheres of activities.

Actual utterances in a dialogue must take into account the (already linguistically shaped) context into which they are directed. Utterance, therefore, is not a completely free act of choice, but is dialogic precisely in the degree to which every aspect of it is a give-and-take between the local need of a particular speaker to communicate a specific meaning, and the global requirements of language as a generalizing system. While there is always room for relative freedom in the utterance, it is always achieved in the face of pre-existing restraints of several kinds. The foremost of these constraints is the fact that an utterance is never *in itself* original, but is always an answer to another utterance that precedes it. It therefore is always conditioned by, and in turn qualifies, the prior utterance to a greater or lesser degree. Formally, this manifests itself in the fact that discourse is segmented not only by words and sentences, but also by protocols that establish the right to contribute to a discourse (cf Bourdieu, 1991). The different ways in which speakers (and writers) indicate appropriate points for others to respond is not only historically contingent and context sensitive, but is always conditioned by the potential response of an other.

3. UNIVOCAL AND DIALOGICAL COMMUNICATION

Many Bakhtinian concepts not discussed here, such as monologic and dialogic understanding, chronotopes, architectonics, speech genres, ventriloquation and heteroglossia, can offer novel insights into the problems faced by systems scholars (see Holquist, 1990; Gardiner, 1992; Dentith, 1995). In the remainder of this paper I shall attempt to develop the idea of univocal and dialogical communication. Wertsch (1991) adopts Bakhtinian theory to argue that communication functions in more than one way: firstly as *univocal*, functioning instructively; and secondly as *dialogical*, functioning to generate new meanings. In the former, the communicative product has a singular and stable meaning, guaranteed by a bounded language. In the latter, however, the communication ceases to be a passive link, but becomes a semiotic space (Wertsch, 1991, p.76), upon which many signification systems converge, interact and interfere with each other. In this context the communicative item functions as a 'thinking device', serving as a prosthesis for the generation of meaning.

The univocal function is fulfilled best when the codes of the speaker and the listener most completely coincide and, consequently, when the communication item has the maximum degree of univocality. This is exemplified by rule bound activities and highly classified domains that are naturally open to architectonic and set-theoretic schemas. Such communication is classed by Bakhtin as 'monologic' because it denies the 'other', and subordinates difference to the hegemony of a single, unified consciousness or perspective. Univocal communication, however, is the special case, and one which is dialogically guided and legitimated. The main structural attribute of the dialogic mode is its 'internal heterogeneity', or the diversity of 'voices' or 'speech genres' at play in the conversational arena.

Bakhtin's concept of dialogism offers some unique insights into inquiry methodologies insofar as they are processes of linguistic engagement. The utterance in the dialogic mode is both the seat of meaning, but more importantly, the point at which different meaning systems converge. In this sense, the utterance is not replete with meaning, but is dialogic itself, as each contribution elicits a set of answering words in the struggle for intelligibility. All linguistic productions therefore, are responsive to, and anticipate, other linguistic productions, which subverts attempts at final definition and completeness.

The distinction between univocal and dialogical communication is pertinent to the debate between objectivist and interpretivist methodological paradigms (Burrell and Morgan, 1979). Wertsch's argument, that dialogic processes are the general case, and that they may occur on both the intra-mental as well as the inter-mental plane, can be readily adopted by the interpretivists, but it thoroughly undermines the rationale of the subject/experimenter relation of objectivism. Moreover, the methodological restriction of semiotic space, apparent in objectivism, can be seen as counter-productive, and possibly the reason why structured methods, despite some recognized utilities, are nearly always supplemented by informal inquiries, critique and discussion.

There is, however, a latency in Bakhtin's theoretical account that interpretivists may not accommodate so comfortably, and the following claims will be of particular interest:

1. that the basic linguistic unit, the utterance, is dialogical, linked to the present, past and future, and by definition always warranting a response;
2. that items in the communicative field can function as thinking devices, and, as a consequence, that linguistic items in communication do not necessarily possess an immediate presence of meaning that can be recovered hermeneutically;
3. that communication involves a proliferation of speech genres and semiotic systems that converge during linguistic exchanges, but these are not interchangeable, or reducible, to others in any straightforward sense; and
4. that reconciling these always involves a further act of *signification*.

What is important about a linguistic form in dialogism is not that there are stable and self-equivalent signals, but that there are always changeable and adaptable signs. This does not deny a systematic character to language, but rather asserts that this systematicity has to be completed, and is always completed in actual language situations. Thus completing the context, which will anyway always be provisional, is not so much a problem of interpretation or of recognizing an invariable meaning, but more a problem of making the context intelligible with available linguistic resources.

REFERENCES

Bateson, G., 1972, *Steps towards an ecology of mind,* Ballantine, New York.

Bourdieu, P., 1991, *Language and symbolic power,* J.B. Thompson, ed, Trans. G. Raymond and M. Adamson, Polity Press, Cambridge, UK.

Burrell, G. and Morgan, G., 1979, *Sociological Paradigms and Organisational Analysis,* Gower Publishing, Aldershot.

Capra, F., 1983, *The turning point: science, society and the rising culture,* Flamingo, London.

Dentith, S., 1995, *Bakhtinian thought: An introductory reader,* Routledge, New York.

Gardiner, M., 1992, *The dialogics of critique: M.M. Bakhtin and the theory of ideology,* Routledge, London.

Harris, R., 1988, *Language, Saussure and Wittgenstein: how to play games with words,* Routledge, London.

Holmqvist, B., Andersen, P.B., Klein, H. and Posner, R., 1996, *Signs of Work: Semiosis and Information Processing in Organizations,* Walter de Gruyter, Berlin.

Holquist, M., 1990, *Dialogism: Bakhtin and his world,* Routledge, London.

Lyytinen, K., 1985, Implications of Theories of Language for Information Systems, *MIS Quarterly,* March 1985: 61–74.

Mingers, J., 1995, Information and meaning: foundations for an intersubjective account, *Info. Systems J.,* **5**: 285–306.

Morgan, G, 1986, *Images of Organization,* Sage, London.

Ryle, G., 1990, *The Concept of Mind,* Penguin Books, London.

Stamper, R., 1996, An information systems profession to meet the challenge of the 2000s, *Systems Practice,* **9** (3): 211–230.

von Glasersfeld, E., 1984, 'An introduction to radical constructivism', in: *The Invented Reality,* P. Watzlawick, ed.,. Norton: New York. pp 17–40.

Wertsch, J.V., 1991, *Voices of the Mind,* Harvester Wheatsheaf, Hemel Hempstead.

Williams, R., 1983, *Keywords,* Flamingo, London.

Winograd, T. and Flores, F., 1986, *Understanding Computers and Cognition: A New Foundation for Design,* Addison-Wesley, Reading, MA.

85

TOTAL SYSTEMS INTERVENTION

Reflections on Achieving Sustainability in a Complex Situation

Lorraine Warren and R. Keith Ellis

School of Management
Lincoln University Campus
Brayford Pool, Lincoln, LN6 7TS, United Kingdom

1. INTRODUCTION

This paper is based on the use of Critical Systems Thinking in a large public sector service organisation, namely West Yorkshire Police (WYP). Both authors were involved in a project which commenced with the expressed need of WYP to improve the effectiveness and efficiency of the Occupational Health Unit (OHU) situated at the Force Headquarters in Wakefield. This need was initially expressed by WYP senior management (who were identified as the problem owners) although it was confirmed by the medical managers of the OHU. More specifically, Total Systems Intervention (TSI) was used to derive a design for the future development and operation of the OHU within WYP. Throughout the application of TSI discussed in this paper, it was necessary to continually be aware of the difficulties associated with achieving sustainable improvement in a problem situation exhibiting a high degree of complexity due to the large number of elements and resulting inter-relationships existing within the system. Although the observed relationships were pluralist (Jackson, 1991) the cultural differences between WYP management and the OHU added to the complexity of the problem situation. Therefore this paper will go on to provide critical reflections on the contribution of TSI to achieving sustainability which may assist with the development of the methodology.

2. PROBLEM SITUATION

The OHU is responsible for providing for providing a wide range of health and welfare services to the workforce of WYP (over 4,000 uniformed and civilian staff). There is also some external provision of similar services, to Wakefield Metropolitan District Council (WMDC) on a revenue learning basis. The OHU is staffed by twelve civilian staff in-

Systems for Sustainability, edited by Stowell *et al.*
Plenum Press, New York, 1997

cluding the Force Medical Officers, the Force Psychologist, Occupational Health Nurses, Welfare Officers and administrators/receptionists. West Yorkshire Police Authority prides itself on the provision of health and welfare services on a scale envied by other police forces. Nationwide, the OHU is seen as a model for internal healthcare provision and the medical staff are active in appropriate national forums. Within WYP at senior management level however, there was a recognition that because there was no long term planning process for the OHU, a lack of direction and purpose had resulted. This project was initiated to address the need for a wide-ranging evaluation and review of the OHU. The methodological process to be employed was explained to the problem owner prior to the start of the intervention process.

3. THE APPLICATION OF TSI

It is beyond the scope of this paper to provide a detailed discussion of TSI. Readers who are interested should refer to Flood and Jackson (1991) and Jackson (1991).

Whilst the OHU is clearly our System of Interest, it was also necessary for us to treat WYP as the containing Wider System. Hence there was a need to include a wide range of stakeholders in a structured Interview Programme designed to provide the fundamental information for the Creativity Phase of TSI. Because of the small number of staff involved, it was possible to interview every member of the OHU. Representatives of key groupings within WYP were selected to include uniformed and civilian staff of both sexes, across the full range of ranks and functions in the Force. In all, over 40 people were interviewed over an eight week period using a standard set of questions. All interviews were tape recorded and then transcribed for analysis.

3.1. Creativity Phase

From the structured Interview Programme we were able to carry out an organisational metaphor analysis (Morgan, 1986). We found that:

- The OHU is an open system to its containing environment; the Wider System, WYP, tended to be the dominant focal point, with the OHU appearing to feel that its survival was threatened;
- The OHU was beset by uncertainty regarding its roles and values (comparative to the Wider System of WYP) and its future; as a result, there was little rational goal seeking and instead, the Task Environment of WYP dominated;
- Conflict and mistrust were inherent in the system;
- There were structural weaknesses in the internal management of the OHU;
- The OHU total environment was both complex and turbulent.

We concluded that the problem situation was dominated by the Culture and Organism metaphors, with the Political metaphor in evidence. The metaphor of the organisation as a Neuro-Cybernetic entity was also present, but weak.

It was clear from our analysis that there was a need to develop a communication forum where stakeholders from WYP and the OHU could produce a design for the future of the OHU.

3.2. Choice Phase

From our initial analysis of the Interview Programme, we drew the following conclusions:

- The system exhibits a high degree of *complexity* due to the large number of elements and resulting inter-relationships existing in the system;
- The inter-relationships were *pluralist* in nature.
- Cultural and Value differences between the OHU and WYP were evident.

These conclusions suggested that we 'place' the OHU problem situation in the complex-pluralist area of the System of Systems Methodologies (Flood and Jackson, 1991) (Jackson, 1991). This led us to select two systems-based methodologies to assist in the development of a design for the future:

- Soft Systems Methodology (Checkland, 1981, 1990);
- Interactive Planning (Ackoff, 1981) (Warfield, 1994).

Although the Neuro-Cybernetic model was relatively weak, we also decided to carry out a diagnosis of the OHU using the Viable System Model (Beer, 1981; 1986).

3.3. Implementation Phase

The selected methodologies were used in accordance with the complementarist principles of TSI. The Viable System Model diagnosis was made in order to assist us in our understanding of the situation which currently existed concerning the management of the OHU. The Soft Systems Methodology and Interactive Planning were used to develop a design for the future.

From the Viable System Model, which was used as a diagnostic tool, it was concluded that the OHU lacked System 5 (Strategy, Policy and Identity), System 4 (Intelligence, Management of Change), System 3 (Internal Audit and Self Reflection), System 2 (Co-ordination systems between functions). System 1 (Implementation) has a high degree of self-regulation, without which the OHU would not function; it was concluded therefore, that the OHU is not a viable system.

For the next stage of the implementation, it was necessary to initiate four separate programmes of activity, reflecting the complexity of the problem situation. We decided that this separation was necessary to enable the stakeholders to focus on problems of a manageable size. Moreover, three issues emerged during the Interview Programme which were of key importance to the stakeholders, yet were outside the remit of the Evaluation and Review: Confidentiality, Performance Indicators and OHU Staff Status and Remuneration. The four programmes were:

1. Soft Systems Methodology and Interactive Planning were used to address Management and Effectiveness issues in an Interactive Workshop involving the majority of those who had participated in the Interview Programme.
   The objectives of this workshop were:

   - To derive a Mission Statement for the OHU
   - To propose a management structure for the OHU
   - To obtain Clarification of OHU roles and services
   - Clarification of reporting lines (internal/external to OHU)
   - To produce Guidelines to resolve issues of conflicting values

2 and 3. Two separate Workshops involving the research team and small working groups selected from the main stakeholder group were held to address the issues of confidentiality and Performance Indicators.
   The expected outputs were:

- A draft outline policy on confidentiality
- A draft set of Performance Indicators for the OHU

4. A formal WYP review of OHU Staff Status and Remuneration was also carried out. The research team were not involved in this review.

4. REVIEW AND CONCLUSION

The expected outcomes of the 'one issue' workshops on confidentiality and Performance Indicators were, by and large, achieved. This was not so for workshops on Management and Effectiveness, where the expected outcomes were not fully achieved, due to:

- The complexity of the problem situation (despite our efforts to simplify it);
- The heterogeneity of the stakeholder group (in terms of values and culture) and their expectations;
- The multi-perspective nature of the problem situation;
- Pressure of time in the workshop.

Perhaps not unexpectedly, using TSI was not without its difficulties, although partial success was achieved. Although space does not permit a full discussion, some difficulties are identified here.

4.1. TSI Process

Those working in the Police Force (uniformed and civilian staff) tend to be highly task-oriented. This resulted in a feeling amongst the stakeholders that the problem formulation stages of the methodologies were 'getting in the way of solving the problem', leading to a tendency to jump ahead to 'solutions'. There was a perception of a 'slow start'. The task oriented nature of the stakeholders assumed that the problem was 'well defined'. However, during the Rich Picture phase of Soft Systems Methodology there was a realisation that they were part of a poorly understood 'mess'. Nevertheless, there was still an inherent desire to jump to a solution which was difficult to control. TSI fails to deal with such behavioural group characteristics, and this in our view is a major weakness of TSI. Because of this feeling and indeed the sheer amount of time involved, not all the stakeholders could attend all the sessions in full. This not only had a negative impact on group dynamics, during the workshops, but also led to *post hoc* attempts by powerful members of the organisation to override the outcome of the Workshops, if they had not been present.

4.2. Methodology

Flood and Jackson (1991) argue that the System of Systems Methodology is fundamental to TSI. However, it is a very broad classification. How many organisational problems, worthy of requiring external consultancy, would not fall into the complex-pluralist area/complex coercive areas? Is the use of TSI/System of Systems Methodologies merely, in part, a rationalisation and justification device for jumping straight to Soft Systems Methodology/Interactive Planning. Is this a criticism of TSI, or merely a fucntion of the lack of methodologies in the complex-pluralist/ complex-coercive area (particularly the latter)? This question became increasingly relevant during this project as it became clearer to us, with the passage of time, that the OHU environment was perhaps less pluralist and more coercive than our initial Interview Programme had suggested (see below).

4.3. Sustainability of TSI

Any serious attempt to use systems-based methodologies to solve highly complex problems requires considerable commitment of time from the stakeholders. In many such situations, it is unlikely that those in senior posts will be able to participate to such an extent, leading to, as in this case, the *post hoc* efforts of senior managers to override the outcome of workshops they could not attend. Thus, a situation which appears at the outset to be complex-pluralist, turns out, with hindsight, to be complex-coercive. Where these circumstances occur, serious doubt is cast on the sustainability of improvements brought about by TSI - and its credibility outside academia. This threat to sustainability casts doubt on the claim that TSI is emancipatory in nature.

We have experienced similar weaknesses with TSI (Ellis and Humphreys, 1995; Ellis, 1996) and such experiences raise doubts with respect to the sustainability of TSI itself.

5. ACKNOWLEDGMENTS

We are indebted to the stakeholders of West Yorkshire Police and the Occupational Health Unit who, by giving freely of their time in the interview programme and participating so actively in the ensuing workshops, made a significant contribution to the development of a design for the future.

We are particularly grateful to the Assistant Chief Constable of West Yorkshire Police, Mr Norman Bettison, MA., MBA., for his encouragement, his participation and his permission to publish this paper.

Any errors or omissions are the responsibility of the authors.

REFERENCES

Ackoff, R.L., 1981, *Creating the Corporate Future*, John Wiley & Sons Ltd, New York.
Beer, S., 1981, *The Brain of the Firm*, John Wiley & Sons Ltd, Chichester.
Beer, S., 1986, *Diagnosing the System for Organisations*, John Wiley & Sons Ltd, Chichester.
Checkland, P.B., 1981, *Systems Thinking, Systems Practice*, John Wiley & Sons Ltd, Chichester.
Checkland, P.B., and Scholes, J., 1990, *Soft Systems Methodology in Action*, John Wiley & Sons Ltd, Chichester.
Ellis, R.K. and Humphreys, A.J., 1995, Total Systems Intervention in Strategic Planning in *Critical Issues in Systems Theory and Practice*, (Keith Ellis, Amanda Gregory, Bridget Mears-Young, and Gillian Ragsdell, eds.) pp.667–672, Plenum, New York.
Flood, R.L., and Jackson, M.C., 1991, *Creative Problem Solving : Total Systems Intervention*, John Wiley & Sons Ltd, Chichester.
Jackson, M.C., 1991, *Systems Methodology for the Management Sciences*, Plenum Publishing, New York.
Morgan, G., 1986, *Images of Organization*, Sage Publications Inc, Newbury Park, Ca.
Warfield, J.N., *1994, A Science of Generic Design : Managing Complexity Through Systems Design* (2e), Iowa State University Press/Ames.

86

RISK MANAGEMENT AND PROJECT FAILURE

Diana White

Systems Department
Open University
Milton Keynes, MK7 6AA

1. INTRODUCTION

Despite the development of numerous techniques designed to estimate and manage project risk a high percentage of all projects end in failure. By reviewing pertinent literature this paper will attempt to catalogue recurrent causes of project failure and identify and evaluate the commonly used techniques for assessing project risk. It will then argue that complex projects are best tackled using a systems approach. Finally, the potential for using the Formal System Model (FSM) (Fortune and Peters, 1995) as a framework for predicting project risk will be examined.

2. PROJECTS AND FAILURE

Projects as considered in this paper, are one-off business ventures that are significant and complex and often involve large sums of money and innovative technology. By their nature these types of project are inextricably linked to people and organisations are full of uncertainty and involve profound risks. In order to maximise the substantial profits and opportunities arising from the successful completion of projects these risks need to be identified, understood and managed.

Organisations often find it difficult to reach agreement over what constitutes project failure because of the very many different viewpoints involved in such complex undertakings; the relevance and appropriateness of the original objectives and because many projects yield profits in spite of failing to meet their objectives.

Much of the literature (Belassi and Tukel, 1996; Fortune and Peters, 1995; Tennant, 1993; Willcocks and Griffiths, 1994) characterises project failure as fulfilling one or more of the following criteria: project not completed on time, project over budget, project outcome inappropriate/unsatisfactory. These characteristics could be described as 'properties' emerging from a project at its highest level of output. They result from the combination of other failures emerging from lower levels in a hierarchy of outputs.

Systems for Sustainability, edited by Stowell *et al.*
Plenum Press, New York, 1997

Table 1. Causes of project failure cited in the literature

Area	Failure type	Literature
Environment	*Failure to:* Manage uncertainty in environment; learn from past experience; take account of the effect of inflation; recognise political influences; view the project from multiple perspectives.	Currie, 1994 Fortune & Peters, 1995 Tennant, 1993 Willcocks & Griffiths, 1994
Context	*Failure to:* Consider complexity; consider context in which project is placed; be fully aware of situation; assess influence of values, beliefs and culture.	Fortune & Peters, 1995 Martinez, 1994 Sauer, 1993 Willcocks & Griffiths, 1994
Objectives	*Failure to:* Identify requirements; formulate clear measures of performance; consider views of end users; produce realistic schedule; produce business plan.	Morris & Hough, 1987 Tennant, 1995 Willcocks & Griffiths, 1994
Control	*Failure to*: Control project; manage team; identify groupthink; gain full commitment of those involved; provide adequate training; abandon project (if necessary) for fear of admitting defeat; measure/monitor progress; establish tracking systems; appreciate that seeking consensus is impossible; manage/overcome resistance to change; put human issues before technical issues; adapt new systems to old ways of working; implement business plan; acknowledge that projects do not follow linear route to completion; overcome end user resistance.	Belassi & Tukel, 1996 Currie, 1994 Fortune & Peters, 1995 Martinez, 1994 Morris & Hough, 1987 Sauer, 1993 Tennant, 1995 Willcocks & Griffiths, 1994
Communications	*Failure to*: Provide effective channels of communication; develop communication plan; communicate benefits of project to staff; halt misleading information.	Belassi & Tukel, 1996 Currie, 1994 Martinez, 1994 Morris & Hough, 1987
Resources	*Failure to*: Supply satisfactory resources; provide adequate/sophisticated technology; ensure reliability of technology; understand underlying technology; provide adequate budget; employ properly qualified staff.	Belassi & Tukel, 1996 Sauer, 1993 Tennant, 1995 Willcocks & Griffiths, 1994

The literature submits that failure to recognise and/or take account of complexity is the main reason why projects fail. Table 1 catalogues further failure types.

Project failure can therefore be regarded as a holistic emergent property arising from the interaction of many elements. In essence, managers must establish clear objectives, provide resources and channels of communications, continually monitor progress whilst being aware of environmental/contextual influences. These elements mirror factors identified by Pinto and Slevin (1987) as being critical to project success.

Table 2. Risk Management techniques

Cash Flow Analysis
Cost Benefit Analysis
Critical Path
Decision Analysis
Decision Trees
Probabilistic Risk Assessment
Reliability Studies
Sensitivity Analysis

Table 3. Project failures identified in the literature mapped onto the FSM

Formal system model	Failures identified in literature
Environment disturbs	*Failure to:* Manage uncertainty; learn from past experience; recognise political influence; take account of the effect of inflation; consider national interests.
Wider system boundary	*Failure to:* Consider effect/views of end users.
Wider system - (places project system in context)	*Failure to:* Consider context; consider values, beliefs, culture which 'surrounds' project; appreciate motives of organisation in which project is placed; consider effect of resistance to change; consider effect of established communication paths; consider effect of company structure, policy, culture and incentives.
Formulates initial design of	*Failure to:* Identify requirements/develop unambiguous objectives; produce business plan; produce realistic schedule; establish tracking systems; formulate clear measures of performance; develop communication plan.
Provides resources and legitimates area of operation	*Failure to:* Supply satisfactory resources; provide adequate/sophisticated technology; provide reliable technology; provide adequate budget; employ/use properly qualified/experienced staff.
Legitimates area of operation	*Failure to:* Adapt new systems to old ways of working; understand underlying technology.
Makes known expectations	*Failure to:* Control project; gain commitment of those involved; make clear that consensus is impossible to achieve; ensure human issues considered before technical issues; communicate benefits of project to staff.
Arrows linking systems/sub-systems and feeding back to wider system/environment (communication channels)	*Failure to:* Provide effective channels of communication; acknowledge projects do not follow liner route to completion; acknowledge project characterised by complexity.
System boundary	*Failure to:* Consider project from different viewpoints - at least from organisation, project team, and end users; trust opinions provided by wider system.
Decision making subsystem	*Failure to:* Assign teams; decide on training needs.
Decides on transformations	*Failure to:* Direct teams.
Provides resources and legitimates operations	*Failure to:* Provide adequate training; define underlying technology.
Makes known expectations	*Failure to:* Control resistance to change.
Transformation subsystems	*Failure to:* Implement business plan.
Provide performance information	*Failure to:* Provide communication channels.
Performance monitoring subsystem	*Failure to:* Measure/monitor progress; identify misleading information; identify groupthink; monitor state of components.
Reports to	*Failure to:* Inform on state of components; report misleading information; report on progress.
Supplies performance information (from system to wider system)	*Failure to:* Report on progress; inform organisation that project should be abandoned if problems insurmountable without fear of admitting defeat.
Attempts to influence environment	*Failure to:* Influence end users; persuade end users to accept change.

3. RISK MANAGEMENT

Most studies suggest that risk should be managed systematically, using analytical and quantitative techniques. It is suggested that the risk process should be tackled in a series of steps or broken down into structures to remove dependencies. Table 2 lists frequently cited techniques.

These techniques tend to be reductionist (White, 1995). Most fail to consider external and contextual factors, the interconnectedness of the different risks involved, and the unanticipated emergent properties that can arise from the combination of components (Willcocks and Griffiths, 1994). Most techniques are also designed to be cost effective and easy to apply, using linear steps that decompose and simplify the risks being assessed. However, these attributes, by their very nature, cause the complexity and high levels of interconnectedness that characterise high risk projects (and which often lead to their failure) to be overlooked.

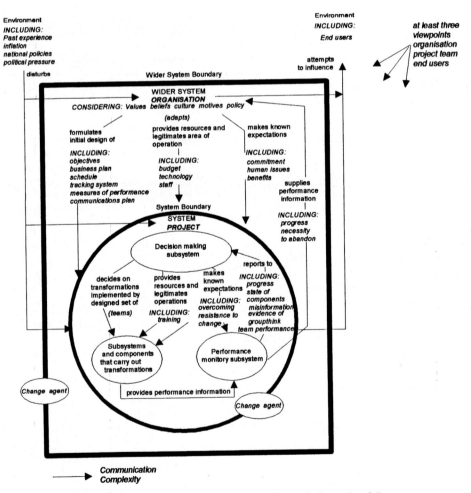

Figure 1. FSM developed to include 'guidelines' for predicting project failures.

4. A SYSTEMS APPROACH TO FAILURE

Studies have shown that problems that are poorly defined, unbounded and dominated by 'soft' complexity are best tackled by the application of systems thinking, that is, by viewing a problem holistically and considering among other things, interconnectedness, boundaries, environment, perspectives and emergence (Fortune and Peters, 1995). It is therefore suggested that project failures could be better understood if they were viewed systemically. Fortune and Peters (1995) have successfully applied the FSM to a wide range of failure situations. These studies have revealed frequently occurring themes that have also been identified in the literature on project failure.

In order to further test the validity of the FSM this paper maps project failures identified in the literature onto the components of the model (See Table 2).

The incorporation of the FSM into the range of risk assessment techniques and its employment as a tool to try and understand risks and anticipate failure in future projects is currently being explored. In this paper a rudimentary attempt is made to develop the model (Figure 1) to incorporate the main failure modes identified in the literature. It is hoped this will result in a more tangible basis for comparison with a detailed description of a proposed project.

In addition, the model illustrated in Figure 1 may be useful as a framework on which to build a model of a proposed project thus allowing project managers to identify all necessary components, investigate communication links and consider multiple perspectives. Further research is underway to ensure all possible significant and recurrent project failure types are identified and incorporated into this prototype model. The framework will then be applied to projects currently being undertaken to test its validity.

REFERENCES

Belassi, W. and Tukel, O. I., 1996, A new framework for determining critical success/failure factors in projects, *International Journal of Project Management* **14(3):** 141–151.

Currie, W., 1994, The strategic management of a large scale IT project in the financial services sector, *New Technology, Work and Employment*, **9(1):**19–29.

Fortune, J. and Peters, G., 1995, *Learning from Failure, The Systems Approach*, John Wiley and Sons, Chichester.

Martinez, E. V., 1994, Avoiding large-scale information systems project failure: The importance of fundamentals, *Project Management Journal*, **25(2):** 17–25.

Morris, P. W. G. and Hough G. H., 1987, *The Anatomy of Major Projects*, John Wiley and Sons, Chichester.

Pinto, J. K. and Slevin, D. P., 1987, Critical success factors in successful project implementation, *IEEE Transaction on Engineering Management*, **EM 34:** 22–27.

Sauer, C., 1993, *Why information systems fail: A case study approach,* Alfred Waller Limited, Henley-on-Thames.

Tennant, D. V., 1993, Avoiding failure in project management, advances in instrumentation and control, *Proceedings of the ISA International Conference and Exhibition,* **48(1):** 675–686.

White, D., 1995, Application of systems thinking to risk management: A review of the literature, *Management Decision,* **33(10):** 35–45.

Willcocks, L. and Griffiths, C., 1994. Predicting risk of failure in large-scale information technology projects, *Technological Forecasting and Social Change,* **47:** 205–228.

87

IMPROVING OUTPUT QUALITY AND MINIMISING BUSINESS RISKS WITH A HOLISTIC APPROACH TO ORGANISATIONAL INFORMATION SYSTEMS DEVELOPMENT

O. J. Akomode

Department of Computing and Information Systems
University of Paisley
Paisley PA1 2BE
Scotland, United Kingdom
Tel: +44-141 848 3327; Fax: +44-141 848 3542
Email: akom-ci0@paisley.ac.uk

1. INTRODUCTION

Improving the quality of products and services in an enterprise is the guide to superior competitiveness. Managers who carry out management functions which can affect the output quality of an enterprise (organisation) often rely on available data/information to make their decisions and to execute other business activities. Information Technology (IT) is capable of offering accurate and timely data/information if suitably integrated into an organisation. This work: (i) proposes a reinforced holistic approach based on 'systems thinking' for developing an IT-based Information System (IS) and discusses its significance for quality improvement and business risks minimisation; (ii) further examines an industrially based project for the design and development of an IT-oriented information infrastructure system for *risk assessment* which employs a holistic approach. Proponents of continuous quality improvement, for example, Deming, Juran, Crosby and Taguchi (TMgt, 1990; Bergman and Klefsjo, 1994) have often referred to quality improvement as a way of managing an organisation (or a business) for growth and profitability as well as mutual benefits to the stakeholders. In the details following, emphasis is laid on a business-led strategy to the development of an information system. The objective of the strategy is to identify key parameters of a business and achieve adequate specifications before attempting to develop an IT-based application. The methodology of 'action research' (AR) is employed as a means for organisational investigation and evaluation of models. Details presented are based on findings from a current industrially oriented project on the *tendering process* in manufacturing management, in which the collaborative establishments are

Systems for Sustainability, edited by Stowell *et al.*
Plenum Press, New York, 1997

Renfrewshire Enterprise, Paisley and Compaq Computer Manufacturing Limited, Bishopton in the West of Scotland. The sections below discuss: (i) a reinforced holistic approach to the development of an IT-based IS; (ii) application of an AR-based method and preliminary results obtained.

2. A REINFORCED HOLISTIC APPROACH TO AN IT-BASED IS

The knowledge or competence to technically manipulate IT without adequate knowledge of long-term business needs for an organisation is likely to lead to inadequate design and development of an IT-based information infrastructure system for that organisation. Conversely, having adequate knowledge of the requirements of an organisation (or a business) with little or no knowledge of how to handle the capabilities offered by IT may equally result in the adoption of inappropriate IT-based information systems. Any such mismatched situations may in turn lead an organisation into a position of competitive stagnation often with disastrous consequences. A *reinforced holistic approach* is proposed as a strategy that draws upon the combined potentials of 'systems thinking' and 'AR methodology', in order to obtained adequate knowledge about an organisation's needs and IT competencies for the design and development of an IT-based information system. The 'systems thinking' component of the above approach implies thinking about the world around us (cf. Checkland, 1981, p.3) and using that idea to develop an IT-based IS to improve output quality at minimum business risks, and doing so by means of the notion 'system'. For a system to continuously work effectively and reliably to achieve its purpose, all components of the system are required to possess the capability for efficiency and effectiveness in order to achieve an adequately combined performance. Similar discussions about the idea of applying a systems approach as a holistic view are advanced by Checkland (1981, pp.3–7) and Parnaby (1995, p.233). Fundamentally, a system embodies an entity (or a single whole) with interdependent elements that work together for the same purpose or goal, in order to display the properties of wholism and not reductionism.

The reinforced holistic approach involves a panoramic and detailed view of an organisation with a focus to determine the organisation's business requirements in conjunction with how to obtain a suitable set of IT components that will fit the business requirements, in order to further enhance management and operational activities. In the ongoing project, both human/business aspect and the IT perspective are considered, including their short and long-term implications before the IT-based model is developed. For example, in developing an IT-based information system for management activities, an 'iterative learning' process of the domain by both the IT-analyst/developer and the organisational experts (or managers) may help in a better understanding of the problem situation. Action research strategy as a subjective way of investigation utilises the notion of a cyclic (or an iterative) learning process. The methodology of AR has been extensively discussed by various experts and commentators (e.g. Lewin, 1946; Susman and Evered, 1978; Hult and Lennung, 1980). Such a cyclic learning philosophy for improving understanding has equally been expressed through phenomenology and hermeneutics (see details in: Winograd and Flores, 1990; Burrell and Morgan, 1994). The organisational investigation and knowledge elicitation process adopted in the ongoing project to obtain the key elements for risk assessment are based on the cyclic learning philosophy advocated by AR strategy. In relation to the design and development of an IT-based IS, AR is capable of strengthening the 'systems thinking' concept of a holistic approach, thereby forming the 'reinforced holistic approach' proposed for: (i) quality improvement and (ii) minimisation of business risks.

3. APPLICATION OF AN AR-BASED METHOD IN RISK ASSESSMENT AND RESULTS OBTAINED

In obtaining appropriate knowledge/data from a domain expert for the design and development of an IT-based information system for an organisation (or a business), an inherent Knowledge Elicitation (KE) 'obstacle' (or difficulty) is often encountered. The inherent obstacle of KE has been extensively discussed by various experts and different methods to overcome the obstacle have been suggested (Feigenbaum, 1984; Gammack and Young, 1985; Neale, 1988). The complex and ill-structured activities often prevalent in organisational management make it an area of human expertise susceptible to KE obstacle. For example, while a 'management' expert may be well talented in his/her domain of expertise, it does not necessarily imply that he/she is an expert in articulating that expertise. The skill may have been acquired by experience in apprenticeship. Consequently, in considering the above obstacle situation for the current project of *Risk Assessment,* the Appreciative Inquiry Method (AIM) has been adopted as a means for *organisational inquiry, learning, documentation and data analysis.* Details about AIM are already available elsewhere (Stowell, West and Fluck, 1991; West, 1995). The method is wholly committed to AR, its epistemology and practical tools are based on Soft Systems Methodology (SSM) (Checkland, 1981; Checkland and Scholes, 1990). A comprehensive application of the method in organisational inquiry involves a three-stage process. For the purpose of demonstrating the application of an AR-based method to obtain organisational needs and to appreciate the domain of investigation with regard to the reinforced holistic approach, a description of the first and the second stage inquiry of the risk assessment project is presented below.

In an initial inquiry session with each respondent at the organisation, a 'systems map' based on a different domain was presented by the knowledge elicitor to illustrate a possible procedure for the 'finding-out and learning' process. The expert (or respondent) was asked to produce a similar 'systems map' based on his/her own view of the domain of investigation. That process was repeated with other participating managers (or respondents) in the same department and within other departments. The elicitor played the role of a *facilitator* during the process. A careful examination of the various maps produced in each section was carried out, away from the venue of the investigation and a *'composite systems map' (CSM)* was developed based on the risk assessment factors identified for Product Quality. The CSM forms a basis for further discussion and investigation. Figure 1 represents an example based on the results obtained in the project. The main elements identified for risk assessment as shown in Figure 1 are: *service and support, reliability, performance, promotion and technology.* These major elements have other associated elements as clearly indicated in the diagram.

At the second inquiry session the data/information already obtained from the previous stage were further explored. During the investigation the various elements of each systems map of the individual respondents (or experts) were grouped or taken as single entities, each representing a separate 'purposeful human activity' (PHA). By using SSM mnemonic termed *CATWOE* as a 'test' (see: Checkland, 1981; Checkland and Scholes, 1990) for each activity, a more detailed 'learning' about each process (or PHA) was carried out at the investigation session. The interviews were recorded by paper and also by tape in some cases. Outside the venue of the investigation the elicitor (or IT-analyst/developer) explicitly described each PHA. Such an activity description usually termed a *Root Definition* (RD) was performed using Soft Systems Methodology. The RD led to the development of a *Conceptual Model* (CM) for evaluation, also as an agenda for further discussion and a basis for extraction of more knowledge/data. An example showing a

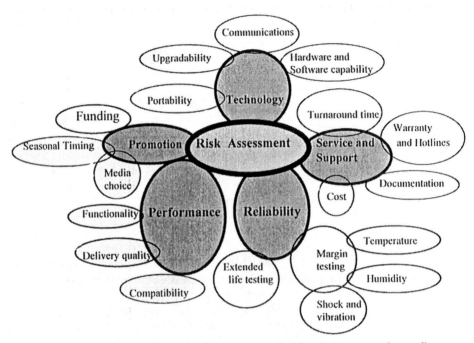

Figure 1. Example of a composite systems map for risk assessment on product quality.

pictorial representation of a CM with a further discussion on the risk assessment domain is available elsewhere (Akomode, Lees and Irgens, 1996).

For the purpose of having an alternative view point towards the reinforced holistic approach for the design and development of an IT-based IS, the CSM shown at Figure 1, may be used to produce a *Cause-Effect* (also referred to as Ishikawa or Fishbone) diagram (Belavendram, 1995, pp.485–7), as shown at Figure 2. Such a diagram with possible 'ex-

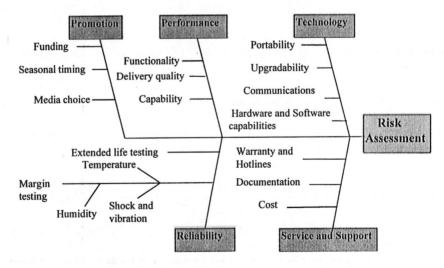

Figure 2. Cause-effect diagram for risk assessment based on figure 1.

tension' may serve as an alternative means to brainstorm and further enhance the investigation/learning process. Also, Figure 2 may serve as a means for linking the identified 'risk elements' with a possible technological perspective.

4. CONCLUSION

The need to continuously satisfy customers' requirements with quality products/services is a better alternative for achieving unrivalled performance and increased profitability. A suitable IS often leads to better performance in management and operations. The proposed reinforced holistic approach for the design and development of an information system is capable of assisting organisational managers and IT-analysts/developers in *creating* better information systems. The situation involves adequate linking of business requirements with essential hardware and software components/specifications of IT through suitable ISs strategies. From the experience gained in the ongoing project, it is believed that the approach advanced with its benefits of group dynamics is capable of helping organisational managers and IT-specialists/researchers to achieve appropriate technology based ISs for: (i) increased output quality; (ii) minimisation of business risks and (iii) better competitive position.

ACKNOWLEDGMENTS

Appreciation and gratitude are offered to Alex Paterson of Renfrewshire Enterprise, Paisley and to the Manufacturing Director, Ian McNair, and other management personnel at Compaq Manufacturing Limited, Bishopton, for their support in the ongoing project.

REFERENCES

Akomode, O. J.; Lees, B.; Irgens, C., 1996, Applying Information Technology to Minimise Risks in Satisfying Organisational Needs. in, *Proceedings of the 2nd International Conference on Design of Information Infrastructure Systems for Manufacturing (DIISM)*, 15–19 September 1996, (eds), Goossenaerts, J; Kimura, F and Wortmann, H., Kaatsheuvel, The Netherlands, pp.15–1 - 15–13.
Belavendram, N., 1995, "Quality by Design", Prentice Hall.
Bergman, B. and Klefsjo, B., 1994, "QUALITY from Customer Needs to Customer Satisfaction", McGraw-Hill.
Burrell, G. and Morgan, G., 1994, "Sociological Paradigms and Organisational Analysis", Ashgate Publishing Ltd.
Checkland, P. B., 1981, "Systems Thinking, Systems Practice", Chichester; Wiley.
Checkland, P. B. and Scholes, J., 1990, "Soft Systems Methodology In Action", Chichester; John Wiley and Sons.
Feigenbaum, E. A., 1984, The Applied Side. in, *Intelligent Systems- The Unprecedented Opportunity*, (eds), Hayes, J. E. and Michie, D., Ellis Horwood, Chichester, pp.37–55.
Gammack, J. G. and Young, R. M., 1985, Psychological Techniques For Eliciting Expert Knowledge. in, *Research and Development In Expert Systems*, (ed.), Bramer, M. A., Cambridge University Press, pp.105–112.
Hult, M. and Lennung, S., 1980, Towards a Definition of Action Research; A Note and Bibliography, *Journal of Management Studies*, Vol.17, pp.241–250.
Lewin, K., 1946, Action Research and Minority Problems. *Journal of Social Issues*, Vol..2, pp.34–46.
Neale, I. M., 1988, "First Generation Expert Systems: a review of knowledge acquisition methodologies", *The Knowledge Engineering Review*, Vol.3, Part 2, pp.105–145.
Parnaby, J., Nov. 1995, Systems Engineering for better engineering. *IEE Review*, pp.233–235.
Stowell, F. A.; West, D. and Fluck, M., 1991, The Appreciative Inquiry Method: an approach to knowledge elicitation as an inquiry system, *Systemist*, Vol.13, No.4, pp.154–65.
Susman, G. I. and Evered, R. D., Dec. 1978, An Assessment of the Scientific Merits of Action Research. *Administrative Science Quarterly*, Vol. 23, pp.582–603.

Traffic Management (TMgt), July 1990, The gurus of Quality, Comments to Quality, Vol. 29, pp.34–9.

West, D., 1995, The Appreciative Inquiry Method: A Systemic Approach to Information Systems Requirements Analysis. in, *Information Systems Provision: The Contribution of Soft Systems Methodology*, (ed.), Stowell, F. A., McGraw-Hill.

Winograd, T. and Flores, F., 1990, "Understanding Computers and Cognition: a new foundation for design", Addison-Wesley.

88

CONSTRUCTING END-USER DESIGN ENVIRONMENTS

Implementing Client-Led Development

Richard B. Beeby, John G. Gammack, and Malcolm K. Crowe

Computing and Information Systems
University of Paisley, Scotland
Tel: +44 141 848 3301; Fax: +44 141 848 3542
Email: {beeb-ci0, gamm-ci0, crowe-ci0}@wpmail.paisley.ac.uk

1. REQUIREMENTS: ONTOLOGY AND PHYLOGENY

The conventional wisdom in the development of software systems is that such systems should be built against a set of requirements that have been captured during the requirements analysis phase of the development life cycle. Textbooks on software engineering describe methods for system design and implementation that are predicated upon the idea that one should not begin to construct a system until one has a detailed (many would say, complete) understanding of what the external behaviour of the system is to be. The investment of considerable effort in the requirements phase, so as to ensure that the requirements have been fully elicited, provides not only the foundation for building the system but also serves as the basis for the contract between system developer and client.

This conventional understanding is no longer a consensus in contemporary thinking on software development. Indeed many elements of it were regarded as simplifications even when first proposed. For example, it has long been acknowledged that the separation of requirements analysis, which produces a description of what the intended system is to do, and design, which produces a description of the mechanisms that will bring the behaviour about, is not as sharp as the early textbooks suggested, and that in practice there must be a number of iterations through these activities, with issues raised during design feeding back into the requirements, and then forward again into design.

This necessity to iterate through the phases of the life cycle led to the practice of requirements-as-contract being publicly attacked in the *Report of the Defence Science Board Task Force in Military Software*, published in September 1987, which questioned that analysis was ever adequate to establish requirements:

Systems for Sustainability, edited by Stowell *et al.*
Plenum Press, New York, 1997

"We believe that users *cannot*, with any amount of effort and wisdom, accurately describe the operational requirements for a substantial software system without testing by real operators in an operational environment, and iteration on the specification. The systems built today are just too complex for the mind of man to foresee all the ramifications purely by the exercise of the analytical imagination."

Explicit in the report and much of the literature since the late 1980s is the importance of building operational models (prototypes) of software systems that can be used to explore various functional aspects of the requirements. Prototyping provides one of the most obvious ways whereby the client can actively participate in this exploration, and models of software development that use prototypes in real operational contexts have been proposed (for one such proposal and a review, see Davies, 1992). However, the use of prototypes in real operational environments produces a dilemma. To invest effort in building a prototype that is useful suggests that the prototype should embody those elements of the system that are best understood, while a significant purpose in building a software prototype is to explore elements that are not yet understood. Evolutionary prototyping involves the progressive implementation and deployment of parts of the system that are well understood as a foundation for the later addition of elements that are not yet defined. This assumes that it is possible to map elements of the requirements onto elements of the design in a way that does not require the redesign of the whole system whenever understanding of a new element of the requirements emerges. Structured methods and object oriented methods have both sought to describe ways of mapping design elements onto elements of the requirements to minimise the effects of change.

Equally significantly for the erosion of the conventional understanding, the social context of software systems has come to be recognised as centrally important in describing and exploring requirements. There has been a movement away from the technical orientation of systems analysis and design approaches. Floyd (1987) called for a "paradigm shift" in software engineering that would bring into the centre of the development process the human uses and contexts that software systems contribute to. A similar shift of focus to computers as tools to support human activity was cogently argued, using biological ideas relating to cognition and perception, by Winograd and Flores (1986). A range of methods have been proposed and explored that promote both techniques to characterise the social and organisational context for a proposed system and to describe the technical data processing functions required (e.g. Mumford, 1983; Wood and Silver, 1989; Avison and Wood-Harper, 1990; Sawyer, 1993).

Co-emerging with this, the whole issue of the nature of requirements (their ontology) was being re-evaluated in the light of process views of software systems. Lehman (1980) had provided an argument that the installation of any software system in a real-world situation alters that situation, and so inevitably leads to change in the views and roles of individuals and groups. A cycle of change is therefore initiated by system deployment which no amount of requirements analysis in advance can anticipate or pre-empt.

The idea that there are a set of characterisable static requirements for a software system is thus undermined and a number of recent publications reject it outright (e.g. Crowe, Beeby and Gammack, 1996; Goguen, 1996). Instead requirements are seen as situated in particular contexts with which they are co-evolving (their phylogeny), and when a new system is deployed it becomes part of this context, which consequentially undergoes a quantum evolutionary leap. This suggests that requirements are rather like scientific theories in revolutionary versus normal science (Kuhn, 1962) or like biological characters in punctuational versus gradual macroevolution (Eldredge and Gould, 1972; Gould and Eldredge, 1979; Stanley, 1979): there is an initial event (system deployment, scientific revolution, invasion of a new adaptive niche) during which there is rapid change, followed by a qualitatively different period of gradual change (system operation, normal science, phyletic evolution). As gradual changes accumulate, components of the evolving system becomes increasingly *burdened* (Riedl, 1977) and the system less adaptable, until the situation again is favourable for a radical change event that starts the process anew. The modern challenge for system development is reminiscent of the adaptive radiation at the end of major geological eras (the most famous following the impact of a large meteorite at the end of the Cretaceous). Macroenvironmental changes and the organisational responses to them are providing a context in which the useful life of systems appears to be greatly reduced in time. So even if requirements could be established by analytic means, the increasing frequency with which systems need to be replaced or modified implies that there is less time available to do so. Making a significant investment in such analysis before work begins is counterproductive if many elements of the requirements have only a short life.

An approach which maximises the coextensiveness in time of the construction of system requirements, the design of system elements, the implementation of the design, and the operation of the reified system would address these issues.

2. THE IMPORTANCE OF CONSTRUCTIVISM

In Crowe, Beeby and Gammack (1996) we discuss a constructivist framework for information systems provision. We pursue the consequences for system development of the idea that systems, organisms, organisations, requirements, and everything we talk about are constructions. We see construction as a process and argue that what is constructed is never static or complete, but evolves.

Kampis (1991) argues that a systems framework which relies on the characterisation of systems in terms of once-and-for-all defined sets of components and relationships will fail to capture the most important aspects of their evolution; for this evolution involves the creation of novel components with consequential new relationships, which render any existing static system descriptions obsolete. His notion of a component-system is a useful basis for modelling evolving situaitons: from this viewpoint it can be recognised that there is no possibility of a predictive theory that will allow developers to anticipate how information systems will evolve, so that methods of system development must take seriously our epistemological limits when confronted with a world that is being constructed even as we attempt to produce formal descriptions of it. Kampis's notion of a component-system involves a sense of construction that encompasses, but is not restricted to, social processes and systems.

For information systems, the important features of the world are socially constructed, and as Giddens (1984) points out, the very attempt to model part of social reality becomes part of that reality (he calls this "a double hermeneutic"). It is not just the introduction of an information system into a workplace that alters that workplace, for the discussions that led to its development involve an ongoing conversation among the participants that involves the negotiation of meanings, concepts, values and so on. As social constructionists such as Shotter (1993) and Harre and Gillett (1994) argue, these very conversations are a significant part of the process by which reality is constructed, so that the process of "exploring" requirements in a deep sense creates them.

Approaches such as participatory design (Schuler and Namioka, 1992), client-led design (Stowell and West, 1994) and user-centric software engineering (DuBellis and

Haapala, 1995) are well placed to exploit this, for they make a more or less explicit attempt not only to ensure that it is the client's construction of the requirements that serves as the basis for the system but also to include the client in the construction of the design.

3. END USER DESIGN ENVIRONMENTS

The idea that this participation is a useful application for computer-supported-cooperative work is not new (see, for example, Kyng, 1991) and is beginning to influence discussion on the kind of functions required in support environments for software development (Winograd, 1995; Gammack and Beeby, 1995). In particular, we believe that design environments need to support the end-user in the development of scenarios and prototypes of various kinds so as to provide opportunities for all participants to construct conceptual structures that can usefully feed into conversations among and between users and professional system developers. Such environments will change organisational culture and ways of working, as well as the nature of the "conversations" by which information systems are created, and are likely to contribute to the acceleration of change processes already alluded to.

The biologically inspired metaphor of an organisation as an adapted whole responding to an uncertain environment is part of the traditional systems-theoretic approach of organisation theory, and the rejection of that tradition in that context has been attributed (Reed, 1992, pages 2–3) to its reliance on, "static conceptions of 'organisation' as distinctive, indeed separable, social units that were constrained, if not determined, by the larger environmental settings in which they operated." In this paper we have argued that the traditional approach to software development for information systems was founded on a number of misconceptions which have been brought into sharp focus by macroenvironmental changes that have led organisations to leaner, more adaptable structures that employ information systems whose usefulness is likely to be of increasingly small duration. We have advocated an approach to information systems requirements that views them as evolving social constructions. We endorse the critique that traditional systems approaches have tended to produce characterisations of entities that are dynamic in terms of the exchange of information and energy with the environment but static in terms of what components they have and how they are related, and note an alternative view of systems that is again biologically inspired. We see a need for computer support to facilitate the evolution of information systems requirements, design, implementation and operation, and have focused, given the current technological state of the art, on end-user design environments as the appropriate medium for this support.

For reasons of space we have been unable to present the arguments that have led us to advocate the points summarised here. Some of these can be found in Crowe, Beeby, and Gammack (1996), and a fuller journal exposition is in preparation.

REFERENCES

Avison, D. E. and Wood-Harper, A. T. 1990 *Multiview: An Exploration in Information Systems Development,* Blackwell, Oxford.

Crowe, M., Beeby, R. and Gammack, J. 1996 *Constructing Systems and Information: A Process View,* McGraw-Hill, London.

Davies, A. M. 1992 Operational prototyping: a new development approach, *IEEE Software* 9(5), 70–79.

DuBellis, M. and Haapala, C. 1995 User-centric software engineering, *IEEE Expert* February, 34–41.

Eldredge, N. and Gould, S. J. 1972 Punctuated equilibria: an alternative to phyletic gradualism, in: *Models in Paleobiology*, (T. J. M. Schopf, editor), Freeman, San Francisco, pages 82–115.

Floyd, C. 1987 Outline of a paradigm change in software engineering, in: *Computers and Democracy: A Scandinavian Challenge*, (G. Bjerknes, P. Ehn, and M. Kyng, editors), Avebury, Aldershot; reprinted in: *Software Engineering Notes* 13(2), 25–38, 1988.

Gammack, J. G. and Beeby, R. 1995 Organisational adaptability: future design structures in distributed environments, in: *Proceedings, SISnet Strategic Information Systems*, Bern University, Bern, pages 1–14.

Giddens, A. 1984 *The Constitution of Society*, Polity Press, Cambridge.

Goguen, J. 1996 Formality and informality in requirements engineering, in: *Proceedings of the International Conference on Requirements Engineering*, IEEE Press CS Press, Los Alamos.

Gould, S. J. and Eldredge, N. 1977 Punctuated equilibria: the tempo and mode of evolution reconsidered, *Paleobiology* 3, 115–151.

Harre, R. and Gillett, G. 1994 *The Discursive Mind*, Sage, London.

Kampis, G. 1991 *Self-Modifying Systems in Biology and Cognitive Science: A New Framework for Dynamics, Information and Complexity*, IFSR International Series on Science and Engineering volume 6, Pergamon Press, Oxford.

Kuhn, T. 1962 *The Structure of Scientific Revolutions*, University of Chicago Press, Chicago.

Kyng, M. 1991 Designing for cooperation: cooperating in design, *Communications of the ACM* 34(12), 65–73.

Lehman, M. M. 1980 Programs, life cycles and program evolution, *Proceedings of the IEEE* 68, 1060–1076; reprinted in: *Program Evolution: Processes of Software Change* (M. M. Lehman and L. A. Belady, editors), Academic Press, London, 1983, pages 393–449.

Mumford, E. 1983 *Designing Human Systems for New Technology: The ETHICS Method*, Manchester Business School Press, Manchester.

Reed, M. 1992 Introduction, in: *Rethinking Organisation: New Directions in Organisation Theory and Analysis*, (M. Reed and M. Hughes, editors), Sage, London, pages 1–16.

Riedl, R. 1977 *Order in Living Organisms*, Wiley, New York.

Sawyer, K. 1993 *OPIUM Handbook*, Topic, Bristol.

Schuler, D. and Namioka, A. (editors) 1992 *Participatory Design: Principles and Practices*, Laurence Erlbaum, Hillsdale.

Shotter, J. 1993 *Conversational Realities: Constructing Life through Language*, Sage, London.

Stanley, S. M. 1979 *Macroevolution: Pattern and Process*, Freeman, San Francisco.

Stowell, F. A. and West, D. 1994 *Client-Led Design: A Systemic Approach to Information Systems Provision*, McGraw-Hill, London.

Winograd, T. and Flores, F. 1986 *Understanding Computers and Cognition: A New Foundation for Design*, Abtex, Norwood.

Winograd, T. 1995 From programming environments to environments for design, *Communications of the ACM* 38(6), 65–74.

Wood, J. and Silver, D. 1989 *Joint Application Design*, Wiley, New York.

89

SOFT SYSTEMS METHODOLOGY

A Metaphor for the Process of Data Analysis

Peter D. C. Bennetts and A. Trevor Wood-Harper

Department of Information Technology
Cheltenham and Gloucester College of Higher Education
PO Box 220, The Park, Cheltenham
Gloucestershire, GL50 2QF, United Kingdom
Department of Mathematics and Computer Science
University of Salford
Salford, M5 4WT, United Kingdom

1. INTRODUCTION

Although early work on methods of data analysis allowed for an interpretative approach, most current texts appear to take a purely positivistic approach. This latter approach can give rise to the following problems. Firstly, there is an expectation that the descriptions agreed represent reality rather than a means of discussing reality. Secondly, different viewpoints cannot always be reconciled or accommodated. Thirdly, objects are thought to have measurable attributes and are seen as existing independently of an observer. Lastly, politics are ignored.

Work in information systems development methodologies and also in software quality assurance has shown that techniques in these contexts benefit from considering the organisation, its culture and politics, as well as being technically appropriate. Checkland (1981) recognises this in his rationale for the Soft Systems Methodology (SSM). The methodology was an encapsulation of the process that Checkland and his colleagues had been following in interventions that they had been involved in over the previous few years. However, Checkland (1981) was aware that the image of SSM was open to misinterpretation as an instrumentalist formula of how to proceed. This was remedied later (Checkland and Scholes, 1990). This later image has been used to model a way of interpreting what actually takes place, both in problem identification (Checkland and Scholes, 1990) and software quality assurance (SQA) (Vidgen, Wood-Harper and Wood, 1993). It is proposed that that model is also useful in the data analysis context.

This paper concerns the description of the process of data analysis, which is a critical area for information systems development (ISD). The paper describes a way of incor-

Systems for Sustainability, edited by Stowell *et al.*
Plenum Press, New York, 1997

porating both the physical and logical aspects of data identification, together with the social and political issues of the organisation. It is important to include these social aspects as many systems have failed in the past because they were not considered (Lyytinen and Hirschheim, 1987).

Little (1993), for example, finds estimates of system failure in the literature running between 25% and 90%. In their major survey of the literature, which examines why information systems fail, Lyytinen and Hirschheim (1987) identify four generic issues. Firstly, the system, as implemented, does not correspond to what was required. Secondly, the system is not forthcoming within time or resource constraints. Thirdly, the system, as implemented, fails to satisfy the users. Lastly, the system does not meet stakeholder expectations.

The incorporation of social issues needs to be based on a systems approach (Checkland, 1981; Hitchman and Bennetts, 1994, 1995; Mitroff & Linstone, 1993). The systems approach is needed as it can incorporate these issues while a science or engineering based approach cannot. Newman (1989) puts it quite strongly when he suggests that it is a myth that organisational issues are not the concern of its information systems professionals. This requirement was recognised by early work but subsequent texts by other authors appear to have taken an approach which ignores this (Hitchman, 1995).

While much interest has been aroused by the problem of incorporating these issues into ISD, very little work has actually focused on the problem of determining the data for a system using an interpretative approach (Hitchman and Bennetts, 1994, 1995). The next section identifies the philosophical implications of recognising the imperative to explicitly include social and political issues in ISD and data analysis in particular.

2. DATA ANALYSIS AS A MEANS OF ENQUIRY

Data analysis and modelling are widely assumed to be 'neutral' or 'value-free'. The analysis 'merely' uncovers an independently existing, objectively true structure of the data in a problem domain. The analysis encapsulates this structure as a conceptual data model. This can be a relational model; an entity-relationship model etc. The model is normally held to describe the real-world precisely. In order to examine the implications of this we need to remember that any general model of organised coherent enquiry is embedded in a paradigm (which includes ontological assumptions, epistemological assumptions, ethical values, a corpus of knowledge, a set of basic concepts and perhaps a mythology) (Ford, 1975; Kuhn, 1970). This is applied through, or operationalised by, a methodology to investigate a particular application area.

In data analysis, the ontology refers to the Universe of Discourse (UoD) being considered, the slice of "reality" being modelled. Similarly, the epistemology refers to the approach for enquiry about what needs to be known. For example, objectivism holds that the contents of the UoD are immutable objects and structures that exist as empirical entities, independently of the observer's appreciation of it. Different opinions concerning this reality must imply human error which can and should be eliminated in principle. If the conflict is unresolved, the integrity of the model is under threat. Subjectivism holds that a data model can do no more than reflect individuals' conventions or perceptions that are subject to negotiated change. A model will be correct if the individuals in an organisation agree that it is. Conflict in this situation is an advantage as it is the only safeguard against misunderstandings and other kinds of errors.

For Lewis (1994), the spectrum of appropriate ontologies runs from realism (there is a commonly experienced external reality with predetermined nature and structure) to nominalism (reality is too complex and confusing to be truly known, different people perceive reality in different ways); and the spectrum of appropriate epistemologies runs from positivism (the world may be investigated by searching for general laws and cause-effect relationships by rational means) to interpretivism (the human world should be understood by examining the way in which the world is understood by individuals).

Hirschheim, Klein and Lyytinen (1995) argue that entity-based approaches to data modelling are positivistic or based on the science paradigm. Lewis (1994) agrees when he suggests that data analysis follows an objectivist approach to enquiry which is characterised by a realist ontology and a positivist epistemology. Hirschheim et al. (1995) further argue that rule-based approaches are essentially subjectivist (nominalist-interpretavist). These then represent the interpretative approaches being sought. It is worth noting that the descriptions of the Functionalist or the Social Relativist in Hirschheim et al. (1995) correspond to Lewis' (1994) Objectivist and Subjectivist approaches respectively. These descriptions are idealised and in practice an organisation will not necessarily follow one approach to the total exclusion of another. This dual approach is recognised by the model developed below.

3. THE USE OF SOFT SYSTEMS METHODOLOGY (SSM)

The model of SSM in Checkland and Scholes (1990) contains both a logic-driven stream (which is primarily concerned with the organised use of systems concepts) and a cultural stream (which focuses on the human, social and political context). Hirschheim et al. (1995) show that the elements of SSM which aim to develop understanding of the problem situation are supported by the Social Relativism paradigm. The approach assumes that no part of the real world can be experienced and understood neutrally. Understanding comes through the development of models of notional systems which are then compared with the real-world. It is the debate implied by the comparison which brings insight and learning. For this to happen, both the logic and culture of the UoD need to be considered. The cultural analysis involves three phases - analysis of the intervention; social systems analysis and political systems analysis. There are four elements to the logic stream in the general methodology context - selecting relevant systems, naming relevant systems, modelling relevant systems and comparing models with perceived reality. For data modelling they can be conceived as - identify the data needs of the organisation, develop a full or partial data model of the organisation, identify the technical requirements of this model and identify the impact of the data model on the organisation.

Vidgen et al. (1993) follow exactly the same argument in the context of SQA. They adapt the classic diagram of Checkland and Scholes (1990) (which was developed in the context of ISD) to identify the four key processes that form the overall development of perceptions of software quality. The argument presented here and the four key processes in data analysis are summarised by the attached diagram (Figure 1).

Checkland & Scholes (1990) recognise that there are various ways of using SSM to resolve problem situations. These range across a spectrum of possibilities, from the formal stage-by-stage application of the methodology (Mode 1) through to an internal mental use of it as a thinking aid (Mode 2). The distinction between these two modes is characterised by Checkland and Scholes in terms of Vickers' "rope" of events and ideas which constitute the flux of daily life. They see Mode 1 as an intervention into the flux from outside, using SSM to structure the enquiry. On the other hand, Mode 2 represents an interaction from within the flux, using SSM to make sense of the experiences. These modes should be

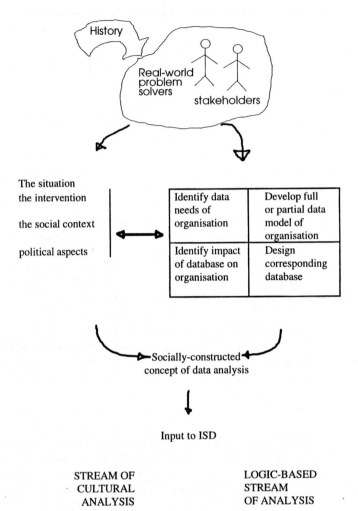

Figure 1. A description of the data analysis process (after Vidgen, Wood-Harper and Wood, 1993).

recognised as ideals. Whenever SSM is used it is actually somewhere between the endpoints of this spectrum. In practice, both modes may be invoked alternately using Mode 1 in formal sessions and Mode 2 when reflecting on that experience to make sense of it. Consequently, SSM might be regarded as a way of describing how data analysis should be performed or, to put it another way, SSM can be regarded as a metaphor for the process of data analysis.

4. CONCLUSIONS

Data analysis is a relatively neglected area despite its importance for ISD and organisations using IS. Data analysis can no longer afford to be purely objectivist; subjectivist approaches also need to be incorporated. A framework which will incorporate this is

Checkland and Scholes' Soft System Methodology. However, the methodology should not be seen from a rigidly objectivist stance and its description of the process of data analysis should be seen as a metaphor for what actually takes place.

5. REFERENCES

Checkland, P.B., 1981, *Systems Thinking, Systems Practice,* John Wiley & Sons, Chichester.

Checkland, P. and Scholes, J., 1990, *Soft Systems Methodology in Action,* Wiley, Chichester.

Ford, J., 1975, *Paradigms and fairy tales - an introduction to the science of meanings,* Vols. 1 & 2, Routledge and Kegan Paul, London.

Hirschheim, R., Klein, H. K. and Lyytinen, K., 1995, *Information Systems Development and Data Modeling - Conceptual and Philosophical Foundations,* Cambridge University Press, Cambridge.

Hitchman, S., 1995, The Development and Evaluation of a Knowledgebase Approach to a Method for the Analysis and Design of Commercial Computer Systems, PhD Thesis, Bristol University.

Hitchman, S. and Bennetts, P.D.C., 1994, The Strategic Use of Data Modelling and Soft Systems Thinking, in: *Information System Methodologies 1994,* (Lissoni, C., Richardson, T., Miles, R., Wood-Harper, T. and Jayaratna, N., eds.), p. 331–336.

Hitchman, S. and Bennetts, P.D.C., 1995, Using Quality Issues in Inquiring Systems to Improve the Understanding and Use of Data Models, in: *Information System Methodologies 1995,* (Jayaratna, N., Miles, R., Merali, Y. and Probert, S., eds.), p. 293–300.

Kuhn, T.S., 1970, *The Structure of Scientific Revolutions* (2nd edition, enlarged), The University of Chicago Press, Chicago.

Lewis, P., 1994, *Information-Systems Development,* Pitman Publishing, London.

Lyytinen, K. and Hirschheim, R., 1987, Information systems failures - a survey and classification of the empirical literature, *Oxford Surveys in Information Technology,* 4: 257–309.

Little, S.E., 1993, The Organizational Context of Systems Development, in: *Human, Organizational and Social Dimensions of Information Systems Development,* (Avison, D., Kendall, J. E., and DeGroes, J. I. eds.), p. 439–454, Elsevier Science Publications B. V.(North Holland).

Newman, M., 1989, Some Fallacies in Information Systems Development, *Int. J. of Information Management,* 9: 127–143.

Vidgen, R., Wood-Harper, T. and Wood, J.R.G., 1993, A Soft Systems Approach to Information Systems Quality, *Scandinavian Journal of Information Systems,* 5: 97–112.

90

BUSINESS ANALYSIS FOR COMPUTING PURPOSES

One Analyst or Two?

David Bustard,[1] Raymond Oakes,[2] and Desmond Vincent[2]

[1]School of Information and Software Engineering
University of Ulster
Coleraine, BT52 1SA
[2]Business Development Service
Northern Ireland Civil Service
Craigantlet Buildings, Stoney Road
Belfast, BT4 3SX, Northern Ireland

1. INTRODUCTION

The goal of any computing-oriented systems analysis technique is (or at least should be) to identify where and how computing facilities can help to sustain the business concerned. Unfortunately, in practice, the analyst, because of his or her strong computing background, will often take it for granted that computing facilities are inherently beneficial and see the problem as one of identifying where such facilities can be used to best effect. Obviously this misses the potential for business improvement. More importantly, however, it can mean that the computing facilities are not adequately motivated by business needs, with detrimental results.

The Northern Ireland Civil Service (NICS) has been addressing this problem for several years by requiring a business analysis to be performed as a basis for any computing development. The favoured technique is SSM - Checkland and Wilson's Soft Systems Methodology (Checkland, 1990; Wilson, 1990). This approach has achieved some success in the NICS and indeed elsewhere (Stowell, 1994; Lewis, 1994; CCTA, 1993). However, the NICS style of application, using separate analysts for business and computing analysis has not been wholly satisfactory. A review of this issue has been prompted by a new release of the computing analysis technique used by the NICS, SSADM, Structured Systems Analysis and Design Method (CCTA, 1995), because it now includes an explicit requirement for some form of business analysis to be performed (specifically, the requirement is that "an explicit Business Activity Model should be included within the scope of an SSADM project"). This paper is essentially concerned with determining how best to meet

Systems for Sustainability, edited by Stowell *et al.*
Plenum Press, New York, 1997

this requirement, taking account of lessons learnt from previous efforts at linking business and computing analysis.

The paper discusses the nature of the problem and includes a consideration of whether or not a computing analyst can or should perform the complete analysis. It also evaluates the various ways in which two analysts might co-operate effectively, in general. The first section examines the joint roles of a business and computing analyst in bringing about system improvement. The second section then looks at particular experiences with combined business and computing analysis within the NICS. A final section outlines possible models of co-operation and gives an indication of the NICS strategy for achieving effective analysis overall.

At the University of Ulster, results from this work are contributing to the development of a general requirements engineering method for software production (Bustard, 1994). One central aspect of this work is the integration of business and computing analysis (Bustard, 1994; Bustard, Oakes and Heslin, 1993; Dobbin and Bustard, 1994). The approach is similar to that of Multiview (Avison and Wood-Harper, 1990), but is aiming for a more integrated linkage between the processes and models involved, and seeks to introduce formal modelling to strengthen that linkage (Bustard and Lundy, 1995 and 1996).

2. BUSINESS ANALYSIS IN A COMPUTING PROJECT

Computing facilities are used, in most cases, as an 'enabling technology'. This means that their primary purpose is to support the performance of tasks in some human activity system—referred to here as the 'business'. By implication, therefore, the main concern should be to first consider how to improve the business and only then examine how computing facilities might enable that improvement, subject to the usual cost-benefit arguments.

This development model suggests two distinct phases of analysis: *business* and *computing*. This is likely to follow naturally from any drive for business improvement but problems can occur when the initial impetus for change is a request for the introduction or modification of a computing facility. Each such change should, in principle, be reviewed in the overall context of the business environment but it is usually impractical to perform a full business analysis each time because of the cost involved. Some approach is required, therefore, which speeds up the process without compromising the underlying concern to ensure that the computing facilities serve a business need.

One way to make progress towards resolving this issue is to appeal to a general model of change. Figure 1, for example, shows a representation of change as a movement from some current unsatisfactory situation to a more desirable target situation, through a number of intermediate steps. An important concept here is that change continues indefinitely; the target situation is progressively redefined but is never actually reached.

Two types of change can be envisaged:

1. *goal-driven*, which focuses on defining the target situation, identifying the necessary changes to improve the current situation, and determining the appropriate steps to bring about change; and

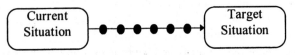

Figure 1. Basic change model.

2. *problem-driven*, which is a reaction to perceived difficulties (or opportunities) in the current situation; improvement is defined as one step towards the target situation; a problem-driven change may also identify uncertainty in goals and so lead indirectly to a goal-driven change.

In relation to the computing-business discussion, the goal-driven case corresponds to change resulting from a general business analysis, where business improvements are identified together with possible computing support. A schedule for phased implementation of related business and computing changes would then be determined. The problem-driven case is where a perceived difficulty arises during phased implementation and needs to be handled within the framework of the overall change plan. This could be a business or a computing issue.

This change process involves two roles: a *business analyst*, who knows how to improve a business, and a *computing analyst*, whose expertise is in determining how best to provide technological support for business functions. When the emphasis is on business improvement then the production of a change definition should be led by a business analyst, bringing in the computing analyst as a specialist to help define precisely *how* a change should be implemented. For a computing specific change, which is the main focus of this paper, the computing analyst and business analyst need to work together to a greater extent. As a computing change is the dominant concern the computing analyst should perhaps have the main responsibility for change management, even though the change must ultimately be business led. What is certain, however, is that the business and computing analysts must collaborate effectively so that each understands the objectives and models of the other and so share a common understanding of the problem situation. The next section summarises the experience of the Northern Ireland Civil Service in addressing the issue of how this combined working should be effected.

3. THE NICS EXPERIENCE

The need for computing change to be tied to business improvement was first recognised in the Northern Ireland Civil Service (NICS) in the mid 1980s. However it was 1990 before formal guidance was issued advising that an analysis of the business should precede any proposal for a major computing development. Such a "Business Analysis", as it was referred to formally, should consider the continued need for the business as well as the effectiveness and efficiency of its operational procedures and organisational structures. Following collaboration between the NICS's central information systems and management consultancy division, the Soft Systems Methodology was recommended as the preferred means for conducting a Business Analysis. Preparatory two day training courses were delivered to NICS Systems Analysts by NICS Business Analysts, who had been using the technique since the mid 1980s. (NICS Business Analysts are skilled in analysing organisational structures, operational procedures, staffing levels, and so on, from a non-computing perspective but would not normally have any computing background.)

Projects were identified to pilot the approach. Initially the Business Analysis was completed separately by a Business Analyst who produced the SSM models and related descriptions, together with recommendations for business improvement. These SSM 'products', and the project as a whole were then handed over to a Systems Analyst. The intention was that the Systems Analyst would use this information to start the SSADM analysis, thereby reducing the need to document the current system and ensuring that any computing development was based on what was needed.

This two stage approach achieved some significant benefits, including the identification and implementation of non-computing improvements, a clearer definition of the scope of any computing development, and a deferment of computing development where appropriate. However, there were also clear operational difficulties. In particular, the Systems Analysts had no sense of ownership of the business analysis products, did not sufficiently understand their implications, and were not sufficiently confident in the application of the models involved. As a result many Systems Analysts largely reverted to their traditional application of SSADM, revisiting some of the clients and users previously interviewed and, in effect, beginning the analysis from the current system. The Business Analysts also contributed to this problem by concentrating too much effort on broad business improvements rather than facilitating the introduction of computing facilities to support the business. The Business Analysts, in effect, tended to perform a full "efficiency review", extending what should have been a short snappy assessment into a full-scale study lasting three months or more.

To overcome these problems, the Business and Systems Analysts were encouraged to work together in multi-disciplinary teams. This meant that Business and Systems Analysts would attend initial fact-finding meetings together and both participate in the development of the SSM models and their translation into SSADM models. This approach succeeded in improving the mutual understanding of SSM and SSADM models and led to the publication of single reports highlighting the potential for business improvement and for computing development to support business needs. However, difficulties still existed. In particular, the Business and Systems Analysts applied different goals to the business analysis. The Business Analysts were eager to bring about organisational and procedural change while the Systems Analysts focused almost exclusively on the introduction of computing systems. Each analyst tended to take a lead in those parts of the study appropriate to their skills and adopt a subservient role at other times, thereby reducing the value of the multi-disciplinary approach. As a result the computing development was not as clearly based on the SSM products as had been hoped and also took too long to perform.

4. ANALYSIS MODELS

SSADM 4+ has effectively forced some resolution of this business-computing analysis problem. Ideally, the business and computing analyst roles should be taken by the same person but it is appreciated that such hybrid skills are currently rare and also hard to develop. For that reason, it is intended to continue, in the short term, using separate analysts where necessary but have them work together where appropriate to help the computing analysts bring their business skills up to the required level. From the previous and current work a number of different analysis models have been identified:

- *Two Phase Model*: a business analysis is performed entirely by a business analyst and the results handed over to a computing analyst who is trained in the use of the models produced;
- *Multi-Disciplinary Model*: a business analysis is performed jointly by a business and computing analyst, both of whom participate equally in the production of business models and their link to computing models;
- *Apprenticeship Model*: as a way of training computing analysts, the business analysis is performed by a computing analyst with the business analyst present throughout, to give direct feedback on the adequacy and effectiveness of both the analysis process and the associated business models;

- *Shadow Review Model*: a business analysis is performed by the computing analyst, with a business analyst reviewing the business models;
- *Hybrid Analyst Model*: the business and computing analysis are both performed by the same person, who is equally skilled in each area, and can ensure a symbiotic relationship between business and computing changes.

As described in the previous section, the NICS have already tried out the Two-Phase and Multi-Disciplinary Model and found that although both bring some benefit, neither is wholly satisfactory. It is the aim of the NICS to move to a position where it can implement the Hybrid Analyst Model. However, there are difficulties with this strategy. Experience has shown that not all analysts are proficient in the use of SSM and fewer in both SSM and SSADM. It is the intention, therefore, to arrive at the Hybrid Analyst Model through a phased approach, via the Apprenticeship and Shadow Review Models.

The NICS has some experience with the Apprenticeship Model and found that many Systems Analysts steeped in SSADM traditions have trouble adapting to the way of thinking needed to perform an effective SSM business analysis. This problem is being addressed by identifying personal characteristics that indicate an aptitude for SSM analysis and training Systems Analysts selectively on this basis. It is also intended that such considerations will be taken into account in future recruitment plans.

5. REFERENCES

Avison, D.E., and Wood-Harper, A.T., 1990, *Multiview: An Exploration of Information Systems Development*, Blackwell Scientific Publishers, Oxford

Bustard, D.W., 1994, Progress towards RACE, a 'soft-centred' requirements definition method, in: *Software Quality and Productivity*, (M. Lee, B-Z. Barta, and P. Juliff, eds.), pp. 29–36, Chapman and Hall, London

Bustard, D.W., Oakes, R., and Heslin, E., 1993, Support for the integrated use of Conceptual and Dataflow Models in requirements specification, in: *Proceedings of Colloquium on Requirements for Software Intensive Systems*, pp. 37–44, DRA Malvern

Bustard, D.W., Dobbin, T.J., and Carey, B.N., 1996, Integrating Soft Systems and Object-Oriented Analysis, *2nd IEEE International Conference on Requirements Engineering*, Colorado Springs, Colorado, pp. 52–59, IEEE Computer Society Press

Bustard, D.W., and Lundy, P.J., 1995, Enhancing Soft Systems Analysis with formal modelling, *2nd IEEE International Requirements Engineering Symposium*, York, pp. 164–171, IEEE Computer Society Press

Bustard, D.W., and Lundy, P.J., 1996, Integrating Process Modelling and Soft Systems Analysis, in: *Methods Integration, Leeds 1996*, (A. Bryant, and L. Semmens, eds.), Springer (electronic Workshops in Computing)

CCTA, 1993, *Applying Soft Systems Methodology to an SSADM Feasibility Study*, HMSO, London

CCTA, 1995, *SSADM 4+*, Blackwell Scientific Publishers, Oxford

Checkland, P., and Scholes, J., 1990, *Soft Systems Methodology in Action*, John Wiley and Sons, Chicester

Dobbin, T.J. and Bustard, D.W., 1994, Combining Soft Systems Methodology and Object-Oriented Analysis: The search for a good fit, in: *Proceedings of the 2nd Conference on Information Systems Methodologies*, Edinburgh, pp. 69–83

Lewis, P.J., 1994, *Informations Systems Development: Systems Thinking in the Field of Information Systems*, Pitman, London

Stowell, F.A. (ed), 1994, *Information Systems Provision: The Contributions of SSM*, McGraw-Hill, Maidenhead

Wilson, B., 1990, *Systems: Concepts, Methodologies and Applications*, 2nd Edition, John Wiley and Sons, Chicester

91

CRITICAL APPROACHES TO INFORMATION SYSTEMS DEVELOPMENT

A Theoretical Perspective

Steve Clarke and Brian Lehaney

University of Luton
Park Square, Luton
LU1 3JU, United Kingdom
Tel: 01582 743136; Fax: 01582 743143; Email: Steve.Clarke@Luton.ac.uk

1. INTRODUCTION

Much has been achieved in information systems development through the methods of systems analysis and systems engineering, but equally much has been written about their shortcomings. Key among these is said to be the functionalist, problem solving perspective from which they are seen to operate, and as a result of which their domain of applicability is seen to be severely limited. The antidote to these approaches has typically been sought from an interpretivist perspective, whereby, it is argued, more pluralistic, complex, human activity problem situations may be addressed. But a criticism consistently levelled at both functionalist and interpretivist approaches is their lack of critical awareness and reflection. This has given rise to a limited exploration of complementarist methods underpinned by critical social theory—or the domain of critical systems thinking.

This paper, after laying a short foundation for the study, develops the theoretical perspective from which the key critical elements may be seen to contribute to a debate addressing information systems development. It reviews the contributions from critical theory which are seen to be relevant to the debate, identifying much of the current work in the critical domain as too narrowly focused. Alternative theoretical underpinnings from critical theory are discussed, providing a basis for practical applications.

2. THE STATUS OF INFORMATION SYSTEMS DEVELOPMENT: FROM FUNCTIONALISM TO CRITIQUE

There can be little argument that many pragmatic approaches to information systems (IS) development rest on functionalist foundations. Concentration is at a technical level,

Systems for Sustainability, edited by Stowell *et al.*
Plenum Press, New York, 1997

with the techniques seen as the series of steps by which the solution can be reached. IS texts almost universally recommend the use of project management techniques in order to build an information system. So, for example, Laudon and Laudon (1996) talk about systems development as "the activities that go into producing an information systems solution to an organisational problem" (p.411); Reynolds (1995) refers to work breakdown structures and information engineering (chapter 9).

Unsurprisingly this adherence to pragmatic problem solving techniques, leads to tensions when the system to be developed requires significant user input.

But, just as systems development texts universally stress the project management, methodological, pragmatic approach to computer-based information systems development (CbISD), so they are equally universal in emphasising the need for discovering the requirements of users. Wetherbe and Vitalari (1994) summarise well the CbISD approach to meeting user requirements in their mapping of user requirements definition on to the systems development life-cycle (p.211). They then proceed to devote a single page (p.213/4) to the subject of how such user requirements are to be determined, citing interviews and questionnaires. This highlights another major problem with CbISD, in that most texts, whilst recognising the need for information to be gathered from the user, offer little or no advice on how this should be done.

Methods derived from the interpretivist paradigm have made significant contributions to the IS development debate in the last twenty years or so (see, for example, Mumford, 1983; Checkland 1989; Avison and Wood-Harper, 1991; Stowell and West, 1994), and offer an alternative to functionalism, but they do so in a completely uncritical way: "Different products of systems development are simply viewed as the result of different socially constructed realities." (Hirschheim and Klein, 1989).

Advancement in the IS domain is being recast as social, rather than 'scientific' (see Clarke, 1995). It can be seen as movement around the sociological paradigms from functionalist in an anti-clockwise direction towards radical humanism (Figure 1). But currently the effort is stalled in the sociology of regulation: functionalist methods based on the systems development life cycle predominate, challenged by ostensibly-interpretive methods

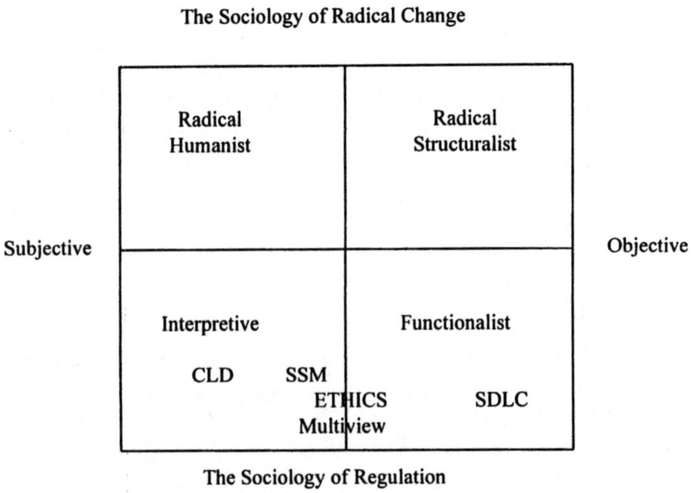

Figure 1. A categorisation of approaches to computer-based information systems development (after Burrell and Morgan, 1979, p.22).

such as soft systems methodology and client led design. Allied to this have been the attempts to combine social and technical approaches, of which ETHICS and Multiview are important examples.

This mirrors practical and theoretical work carried out in the domain of management science, and it is here that a way forward is to be found.

3. INFORMATION SYSTEMS DEVELOPMENT: THE CONTRIBUTION FROM CRITICAL THEORY

An approach informed from the radical humanist paradigm is seen by Hirschheim and Klein (1989) as "hypothetical…in that it has been constructed from theory". They do, however, see theoretical value in an approach based on this paradigm, but question the potential for achieving this in practical terms: "However, while theoretically strong, it is difficult to see how the story actually works in practice. The story is normative without providing clear detail on how it could be implemented." (Hirschheim and Klein, 1989).

But there is a way out of this dilemma. By drawing on developments in critical management science, critical systems thinking (CST), and its practical counterpart, Total Systems Intervention (TSI), offer a critical approach which is both theoretically justified and tested in practice.

CST is founded on the critical theory of Habermas; or, more specifically, his theory of knowledge constitutive interests (Habermas, 1971(a), 1971(b), 1976), in which he sees all human activity as conducted in satisfying three cognitive or knowledge constitutive interests: technical, practical and emancipatory.

A Habermasian perspective sees the functionalist approach to computer-based information systems development (CbISD) as an insufficient basis, serving only the technical interest. Social science is also needed to service the hermeneutic interests of achieving communication and consensus, which Habermas calls 'practical'. In addition, critical science is needed to deal with issues of power and domination, serving the emancipatory interest.

4. CRITICAL SYSTEMS THINKING AND INFORMATION SYSTEMS

Five commitments of CST have been determined (Jackson, 1991), the relationship of which to IS have been investigated by Jackson (1992). Of these, critique and emancipation are key elements in any IS intervention.

Critical Awareness consists of "examining and re-examining taken-for-granted assumptions, together with the conditions which gave rise to them." (Midgley, 1995). The critique of soft systems methodology as regulative and of office systems as purely technical are examples of the value of critical awareness, as is Hirschheim's work viewing IS in social rather than technical terms (Hirschheim and Klein, 1989).

The use of methodology within IS mirrors the problems already encountered in management science, where critical awareness is stifled by the isolationist reliance on one or a limited range of methodologies: "Openness and conciliation between theoretical paradigms is necessary, (but) methodologies (can) do no more than legitimately contribute in areas of specific context." (Flood, 1990).

Critical awareness must be maintained throughout an intervention to examine and re-examine the assumptions made, to inform the choice and mix of methodologies in relation to the changing nature of the problem contexts and the strengths and weaknesses of the available methodologies.

Human Emancipation is seen as necessary in order that the other commitments may be achieved. Certainly, for example, it is difficult to see how the 'taken for granted assumptions' in any systems design can be exposed by critique unless participants feel free to express such critique.

5. ALTERNATIVE THEORETICAL SUPPORT

A major advance in interventionist approaches has been made as a result of the critical stream in management science. From its commencement in the early 1980s to, it could be argued, the present, this development has relied almost entirely on Habermas' theory of knowledge constitutive interests for its theoretical underpinning. There is, however, a wealth of critical theory available to the interventionist, which has been explored recently (see, for example, Midgley, 1995; Brocklesby and Cummings, 1996; Probert, 1996).

In general, the foundation of critical theory is to be found in the work of Kant. Kant's exposure of *a priori* statements shows how an uncritical approach may lead to false consciousness, which a critical approach can expose. A common example in management studies might be the single minded belief that 'business organisations exist to make profit'.

From Kant's original work, a number of key figures have emerged to progress critical theory. Brocklesby and Cummings (1996) refer to a historical development through Hegel to Marx and thereby to the Frankfurt School, the main contributors to which they identify as Horkheimer, Adorno and Marcuse. They conclude that the most important critical thinkers of the late twentieth century are Foucault and Habermas, from whom two alternative theoretical underpinnings to CST may be derived. Probert (1996) queries the exclusion of Benjamin and gives more weight to the work of Adorno.

Whilst it may be seen as justifiable to cast Habermas as currently the most significant critical thinker, the choice of his knowledge constitution theory as a basis for development of a critical approach to organisational studies should be questioned. Habermas' writings are diverse and complex, and a deeper study of them is likely to yield significant findings in this regard. An example of other areas developed by Habermas is his universal pragmatics, in which he argues that communication aimed at reaching an understanding always involves the raising of four validity claims, which may be categorised as comprehensibility, truth, rightness and sincerity. Midgley (1995) has undertaken some initial work to develop these as an alternative basis for a pluralist theory. Truth is seen by Midgley as relating to the objective/external world, and thereby to hard, cybernetic methods; rightness to the normative, social world, and hence soft methods; and sincerity to the subjective, internal world, and cognitive methods such as cognitive mapping and personal construct theory (see Kelly, 1955; Eden, 1988; Eden, 1994).

6. A BASIS FOR FUTURE DEVELOPMENT

In the space of such a short paper it is not possible to develop sufficiently the various lines of thought. However, the important point of issue here is the apparently narrow focus of a critical management science, and thereby a critical approach to IS, based almost solely on the theory of knowledge constitutive interests, and the need to broaden this by investigating more fully the roots of critical theory.

The hard/soft or functionalist/interpretivist debate now seems to offer an impoverished view of the IS world. Information systems are not *per se* computer systems, but are systems of human activity or micro social systems. Consequently, functionalist science or interpretive sociology are an inadequate basis on which to study them. The move to radical humanist approaches seems a fertile way forward, but, for now, the only approaches which have attained any degree of development are those based on the theory of knowledge constitutive interests, under the banner of CST.

REFERENCES

Avison, D. E. and Wood-Harper, A. T., 1991, Conclusions from Action Research: The Multiview Experience, *Systems Thinking in Europe*, Plenum, New York.

Brocklesby, J. and Cummings, S., 1996, Foucault Plays Habermas: An Alternative Philosophical Underpinning for Critical Systems Thinking, *Journal of the Operational Research Society,* 47(6): 741–754.

Burrell, G. and Morgan, G., 1979, *Sociological Paradigms and Organisational Analysis,* Heinemann, London.

Checkland, P. B., 1989, Soft systems methodology, *Human Systems Management,* 8(4): 273–89.

Clarke, S.A., 1995, Information Systems Intervention: A Total Systems View, *Adding Value in a Changing World, The Conference of the Operational Research Society*, Springer Verlag, London (in press).

Eden, C., 1988, Cognitive Mapping, *European Journal of Operational Research,* 36: 1–13.

Eden, C., 1994, Cognitive mapping and problem structuring for system dynamics model building, *System Dynamics,* 10(2–3): 257–276.

Flood, R. L., 1990, Liberating Systems Theory: Toward Critical Systems Thinking, *Human Relations,* 43(1): 49–75.

Habermas, J., 1971a, *Knowledge and Human Interests,* Beacon Press, Boston.

Habermas, J., 1971b, *Toward a Rational Society,* Heinemann, London.

Habermas, J., 1976, On systematically distorted communication, *Inquiry,* 13: 205–218.

Hirschheim, R. and Klein, H. K., 1989, Four Paradigms of Information Systems Development, *Communications of the ACM,* 32(10): 1199–1216.

Jackson, M. C., 1991, Five commitments of critical systems thinking, *Systems Thinking in Europe*, Plenum, New York.

Jackson, M. C., 1992, An Integrated Programme for Critical Thinking in Information Systems Research, *Journal of Information Systems,* 2: 83–95.

Kelly, G. A., 1955, *The Psychology of Personal Constructs,* Weidenfeld and Nicholson, London.

Laudon, K. C. and Laudon, J. P., 1996, *Management Information Systems - Organization and Technology,* Prentice Hall, New Jersey.

Midgley, G., 1995, Mixing Methods: Developing Systemic Intervention, *Hull University Research Memorandum,* No. 9.

Midgley, G., 1995, What is This Thing Called Critical Systems Thinking, *Critical Issues in Systems Theory and Practice,* Ellis, K., Gregory, A., Mears-Young, B. R., and Ragsdell, G. (eds), New York, Plenum, 329–334.

Mumford, E., 1983, Participative Systems Design, *The Computer Journal,* 27(3): 283.

Probert, S. K., 1996, Is Total Systems Intervention Compelling? *Sustainable Peace in the World System, and the Next Evolution of Human Consciousness*, Madison, USA, Omni Press.

Reynolds, G. W., 1995, *Information Systems for Managers,* West Publishing, St. Paul MN.

Stowell, F. A. and West, D., 1994, 'Soft' systems thinking and information systems: a framework for client-led design, *Information Systems Journal,* 4(2): 117–127.

Wetherbe, J. C. and Vitalari, N. P., 1994, *Systems Analysis and Design: Best Practices,* West Publishing, St. Paul MN.

92

MODELLING INFORMATION FLOW FOR IS DEVELOPMENT

Jun-Kang Feng

University of Paisley
High Street, Paisley
Scotland PA1 2BE

1. INTRODUCTION

The information factor in information systems research and information system development is not well understood and its importance fully recognised. Information is by many taken as a synonym of data, information flow is hardly mentioned in the information systems (IS) development literature, such as many well known methodologies for IS development or computer applications development, such as SSADM. My view is that information system research should centre on the concepts of 'information' and 'system'. The latter has been said much more than the former thanks to probably the work of systems thinkers, such as Checkland (1981), Wilson (1984), Stowell and West (1994), and Lewis (1995). Without a good understanding of the information factor, our knowledge about IS will not be balanced and satisfactory. We have encountered enormous difficulties when we try to move from the high level appreciation of a problem domain to the formal specifications of the computer based information systems, which is evidence of the above problem. Thus information should also, just like 'system', have its due position in this game. One issue in the information perspective of information systems development is of information flow, which I believe should play a central role in IS development. Due to the length constraint on papers I will be talking about this issue briefly here.

2. WHAT IS AN 'INFORMATION FLOW'?

When we think about data and information in general and information systems development in particular, there are at least three problems.

1. First, there is a phenomenon of data. That is, humans, probably some other species as well, create, keep, manipulate and use records of whatever we care to record. The problem here is that we should look at how we can structure our records. More generally, we may say how we should view the phenomenon of

people's taking records. In the context of information system, the problem is how to find and specify the structure of the data storage mechanism of the information system. It is a non-trivial task. The structure must be such a necessary and sufficient core of the hard material that the due user of the system should be able to derive information the system is designed to provide from it.

2. Second, we often know something about a situation, we say that we have some information about it. Then we have the problem of how to describe the information. For information systems development, this is a problem of how to accurately express what the due user of the system will be able to derive from the core of the hard material stored in the data storage device of the information system.

3. Third, we somehow get to know something about a situation. We get to know something through knowing something else first. So information can be created, information can flow. Then we have the problem of finding what is created and cascades, and how. In the context of information systems development, this is the problem of revealing the information aspect of the domain of interest in the first place. Only when the dynamic movement of relevant information (It is impossible to reveal all information, as it is unlimited) in a domain is understood and expressed explicitly, can we know which part of the information movement shall be supported by a computer based system and therefore can we specify what information the system shall provide and when and how.

In the context of information system development, the first question is tackled by means of 'data modelling', but the second and the third questions are hardly incorporated. The three questions are concerned with data, information and information flow respectively. They are different but related. The relationships between them appear to be like this: We get to know something about a situation through a chain of information flow; The result of the chain of information flow is information; The physical records of a necessary and sufficient set of facts from which the information in question can be derived are data. Moreover we can observe that in order to answer the first question we have to resolve the second question first, and any convincing and reliable answer to the second question depends on the resolving of the third one. So resolving the third question is the key of the whole business, and it is the problem of information flow.

What is information flow more precisely? It is concerned with how information is created and one piece of information gives rise to another piece of information. Intuitively it is about how we get to know something about one situation through perception and cognition upon a representation of the world or through knowing something about another situation or knowing something else about the same situation. So information flow is actually information creation and cascading. Information flow is unlike data flow. It is not something physical flowing from one place to another.

3. WHY DOES INFORMATION SYSTEMS DEVELOPMENT NEED LOOKING AT 'INFORMATION FLOW'?

I have already touched on this question in the previous section, here I would like to list some more specific reasons.

First, information flow is an indispensable part of any information system. If we take Stowell and West's view (1994), an information system is a notional system regarding the information aspect of a problem domain, then without the creation and cascading of information being explicitly expressed, the notional system does not seem complete. If we use the term 'information system' to refer to just that kind of computer and communication network systems that serve the information needs of human activities, then in their development, we need to know how the human actors get the information they need and how the technology based system will serve as a source of information. Both are an information flow problem, in my view.

For me, there is a second particular reason why information flow needs captured, that is, to fill the gap between the human activity systems' activity model and the formal specifications of the technology based information system. Up till now the best we can do seems to link activity model and DFD directly. But DFD is process centred. Data are treated as the input and outputs of the processes. Moreover data are not structured in their own right. So DFD does not express what one knows about the objects and their relationships/properties. According to our 'infonic' definition of elements of information (which will be explained shortly), DFD does not capture information nor information flow. DFD seem to be merely intuitive representation of the processes and their associated data. IS is about information, so they should be based upon our understanding of information and information flow in the domain that the IS is to serve. I believe what is required is an information perspective of the 'human activity system' (Checkland, 1981). This perspective should explicitly shows the creation and flow of information, the relationship between the information flow and the transformation realised by activities, and the relationship between information of data in a data storage mechanism.

4. HOW CAN AN 'INFORMATION FLOW' BE MODELLED ?

4.1. Information and 'Infon'

The 'material' of information flow is information. So let us look at what information is.

Intuitively, information can be taken as what we know about a situation. To me information is something that *does* exist. We get to know something by sensing a representation of the world, say R, while we are attuned to certain constraint, say C, which is a link between two situations. So we can use $< R, C >$ to denote what we know about a situation through the interaction between R and C. Moreover, attuned to a different constraint, say C', a different representation of the world, say, R', may give the same information as $<R, C>$, so we have $<R, C> = <R', C'>$.

That these two pairs are equal means there is something there in our mind that the two pairs both denote. This is to say, information does seem to exist. Obviously there can be unlimited number of such pairs that give the same information. So we use $[<R, C>]$ to represent all the 'equivalent relations' of $<R, C>$ including the above $<R', C'>$, to mean that 'they give the same items of information'.

For a formal treatment of information, we need a means to describe elements of information. Following Devlin (1991), let us assume that information is made up of discrete elements of whether certain given objects posses certain properties and relationships. These elements can be called 'infon's, and we can use $\ll R, a_1, ..., a_n, t, l, i \gg$ to denote an infon, which means that objects $a_1, ..., a_n$ have or do not have relation R (depending on the Boolean value of i) at time location t and space location l.

Information is higher than objects. The objects involved in an infon are regarded as given, their identification is not regarded as part of 'information modelling'. Infon is concerned with the 'properties/relations' of objects, not objects themselves. From our infonic view data can be seen as a physical representation of R in the $<R, C>$, and the structure of the physical records in a data storage mechanism is just a subtle representation of a set of Rs from which if right Cs are attended to by the user the user will be able to derive the information she wants namely $<R, C>$, with the help of the system probably.

4.2. The Unit of an Information Modelling Formalism

The idea in a nutshell is this: Infons are made true by situations. And situations are distinguished by the infons they make true. Situations can be generalised into situation types through abstraction. Situation types have parameters and types of objects in their structure. Situation types are connected by constraints. Let us denote it using, say, $S_1 \Rightarrow S_2$. S_1 can be termed 1st situation type, and S_2 2nd situation type. When a pair of situation types that are connected are instantiated, that is, facing a R through perception and cognition we find specific values for all the parameters and object types in the structure of the situation types, we obtain infons that are made true by the instance of the 2nd situation type. This is how information is created and flows. Using this idea, for an elementary activity in a 'human activity system' we can have a unit as shown in Figure 1, which describes the relevant situations and their relationships whereby information and its flow can be captured.

The elementary activity the above diagram maps to is 'Select companies for the first visit in a year to find industrial placement opportunities'. This activity can be described by using a number of situations which make some specific infons true.

The embedding situation e refers to the environment and conditions within which the activity takes place. It makes at least one infon true, which is the most relevant element of information the actor must know when she assesses the state of the task to decide what to do next. This element is captured by an infon which means 'It is true that a company has not been selected nor contacted at a time t and location l.'

$$e \models «\neg 1stContacted \wedge \neg Selected, Comp, l,t,1»$$

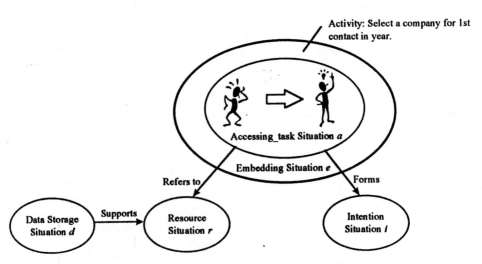

Figure 1. Illustration of the unit of an information modelling formalism.

After the elemental activity is completed, the *embedding situation* changes to *e'*, that is *e* → *e'* and *e'* makes one infon true:

$$e' \models «1stContacted, Comp, l,t^+,1»$$

Notice that t^+ means some time later than t. The *assessing-task situation a* is:

$$a \models «Assesses, Actor, Comp(¬1stContacted, ¬Selected), l,t,1» \wedge «Refers-to, Comp, ,t,1»$$
$$\wedge « Refers-to, Placement, l,t,1»$$

The *assessing-task situation a* refers to some *resource situation r*, which makes either of the two infons true :

$$r \models «Provides, Comp, Placement, l_1, t, 1» \vee « Provides, Comp, Placement, l_2, t^+, 1»$$

The infons the *resource situation r* makes true of can be derived from a *data storage situation d*. The *data storage situation d* must make the following infons true:

$$d \models «Indicates, CompID, Comp, l,t,1» \wedge «Indicates, PlacementID, Placement, l,t,1» \wedge$$
$$«Links, CompID, PlacementID, l,t,1»$$

When she has assessed the situation, the actor is in an *intention situation i* that makes the following infon true:

$$i \models «Of-type, Actor, I(Ain=Comp(¬1stContacted, ¬Selected), out=(Comp(1stContacted)),$$
$$l,t^+,1»$$

The infon above means that the Actor is an object of the type that has an intention to transform the state of a company from neither 'selected' nor '1st' contacted' to '1st' contacted'. After that the action is carried out, and the transformation is completed and the embedding situation will be changed. Then a new activity starts. So it can be seen through modelling information flow, an activity is linked to information that is revealed by the information flow and data that supports the information flow.

5. REFERENCES

Checkland, P., 1981, *Systems Thinking, Systems Practice*, John Wiley & Sons, Chichester.
Devlin, K., 1991, *Logic and Information*, Cambridge University Press, Cambridge.
Lewis, P., 1994, *Information-Systems Development*, Pitman, London.
Stowell, F., and West, D., 1994, *Client-led Design*, McGraw-Hill, London.
Wilson, B., 1984, *Systems: Concepts, Methodologies and Applications*, 2nd edition, John Wiley & Sons, Chichester.

93

SYSTEMS FOR SUSTAINABILITY–OR SUSTAINABILITY FOR SYSTEMS?

J. Gilligan

School of Information Systems
Faculty of Computer Studies and Mathematics
University of the West of England, United Kingdom
Jim.Gilligan@csm.uwe.ac.uk

1. INTRODUCTION

Sustainability demands recognition of diversity. Recognition of diversity means admitting to that which is going on around us. The Systems Movement has too long been engaged in a self-referential discourse on methodologies developed for what have been usefully, if uncritically, defined as 'Information Systems'. Despite attempts to broaden the agenda from the more traditional technical arena into the social realm, Data Processing, Management Information Systems and Requirements Analysis remain at the heart of most Information Systems practice and therefore in much of the associated epistemological and methodological development.

This paper explores one possible future for the Systems movement based on a recognition of diversity in technology and diversity in use. The paper draws on the author's analysis of the nature and language of information, and his current research into the use of emergent communication and information technologies by professional users, in particular the audit profession. By proposing new uses for the words 'Information' and 'System', an alternative view emerges of what Information Systems mean (and *will* mean) to the people who develop and use them. This modified paradigm may be used to make sense of current changes in technology and its use, as well as affecting those who practise or teach the technical, organisational and social contexts and skills of Information Systems.

2. THE NATURE OF INFORMATION

The nature of information is that of an *activity* (Gilligan, 1994) and not as a *product* of information systems. The *convenience* of the word 'information' to describe processed data is not enough to implicitly attribute to that data the means or meaning to *inform* the recipient of such data. Thus however many times we permutate the sorting sequence or selection filters of data for reports generated by Management Information Systems, we remain unsure that what we produce will properly inform those to whom it is provided. Recognition of the gap between processed data and the mythical stuff of information is as well established an idea as M.I.S. itself, though practitioners seem frequently misled by the language of Information Systems into believing that this gap exists because we have failed to properly define what is required by the recipients (Requirements Analysis and 'hard systems' methodologies) or that we and they do not know what is required and in any case the requirement always changes ('soft systems' methodologies). The more profound truth is that we *cannot* produce information, we can merely create the means by which *in-formation* might take place.

As a result of this misunderstanding there has been a constant effort to produce a methodology which would allow processed data to represent information as if it had some substance of its own or indeed was the reality itself. Such efforts are both misleading and counterproductive.

There is a parallel in the field of Artificial Intelligence where the search for the substance of *intelligence* has by some (Barto, Andrew G., Bradtke, Steven J. and Singh, Satinder, 1995) been likened to searching for the Philosopher's Stone. Now they have turned their attention from the mythical *substance* of intelligence to the nature of intelligent *acts*. *'Learning to act'* is a new and more manageable objective for AI researchers: the creation of systems which will *behave* in a way which we might describe as intelligent, rather than containing some mysterious *substance* of intelligence. Once freed from the bonds of linguistic misunderstanding the AI community now finds itself capable of producing useful and productive software, for example, intelligent agents capable of supporting commercial activity on the Internet. For some in the AI community the endlessly complex struggle to define and create the stuff of intelligence was seen, on more careful analysis, to be primarily a linguistic problem. The riddle of intelligence seemed unanswerable, but as Wittgenstein said in the context of a similar analysis of metaphysics: *"The riddle does not exist"* (Wittgenstein, 1953).

3. DIVERSITY OF TECHNOLOGY

Until very recently the Internet has seen no consolidated effort to build a formal structural model of that medium, nor to provide for it a forum for debate towards 'desirable change' (Checkland, 1981). Nevertheless it became and remains perhaps the most powerful computer based Information System in the world. Linked only with the simplest of software tools—typically a browser—professionals and schoolchildren alike may use global search engines to provide themselves with statistics on competitors or images from Jupiter. Imagine, if you will, what the results might have been had we attempted to create such a resource using existing Information Systems methodologies.

The success of the Internet as an information system, apparently by accident, is made clearer each day. With the announcement of Internet II at the time of writing (Peters, 1996) there now exists the material need to meet and apply this new technology with appropriate vision and understanding. The particular concern that Internet II will become "Internet America" must surely require our attention.

It has been the putting in place of networks to allow communication rather than any attempt to provide specific information which has made the Internet a success. By providing the *means to act* in the global environment without concern for requirements analysis or design, allows the user of the Internet to be informed by a body of data and power of analysis vastly greater than anything previously envisioned.

Now that the first generation of those networks are in place, with new and better second generation technology to be established by the early part of the next century, it becomes apparent that the other emergent technologies will form part of this new vision. For example, Computer Supported Co-operative Work, Personal Data Systems and Network Computing are all technologies which will require Internet or Intranet resources if they are to meet only the present requirements of their users. The shift towards those technologies may either be understood or left to evolve by itself. The United States government support for Internet II confirms that it regards the active understanding and development of such technology as fundamental to the future social and economic infrastructure of that country, and we content ourselves with more traditional questions at our peril. Furthermore, as the emerging *global* business world moves towards Network Computing and distributed databases across Intranets, and popular media move towards a full integration of Internet and traditional communications media such as television or newspapers, so the world of bounded traditional systems diminishes. Whether the product is seen to inform or entertain, the integration and therefore the transparency of computer technology as part of everyday life comes ever closer.

4. DIVERSITY OF USE

If Information Systems as an area of study is to be sustainable then we must recognise the diversity of use to which information and communications technology is now being put. Parts of the professional business world in particular have already begun, without the aid of Information Systems professionals, to make use of emergent technologies to redefine and evolve the way in which they work.

Over the last three years, the author has particularly noted the rapid expansion of technological awareness on the part of the audit profession, observing and recording the extensive use of emergent technologies by a profession which may sometimes mistakenly be regarded as more concerned with hindsight, reflection and recording. In analysing these activities and working alongside audit researchers (albeit across the Internet - many of them are in the U.S. and Australia), the author hopes to recognise some of the diverse and sustainable trends within this movement, and through such research draw what conclusions there may be for the Systems community and its own sustainable future.

The use of the Internet by auditors has developed to include the provision of Web sites, mailing lists, videoconferencing and ftp sites created by and between these professionals (Appendix 1). Software packages, technical evaluation, academic research, job vacancies and personal experiences all form part of the utterly informal design which makes up a powerful and global resource for such groups. Auditors see considerable changes to their profession and status coming as a result of recent technological changes. In particular the possibility of remote audit allows a company to have computer systems examined by external auditors at any time and from anywhere. Indeed, to have intelligent agents acting on behalf of the auditors, and capable of investigation or data reconciliation across corporate boundaries and in real time. Together with existing moves towards 'self-audit' (which mirrors the introduction of end-user computing to Information Systems in its impact on the audit profession) there exists the possibility that the audit profession will become technology driven, with a few professionals using sophisticated and intelligent systems to perform much (though by no means all) of the work currently undertaken by armies of manual auditors, or auditors equipped with more traditional computer based systems. The professional consequences of such facilities being put in place are immense, and to ignore the technological opportunity will not ensure the retention of more traditional audit skills. A more comprehensive vision is being actively developed by the audit profession, a vision which sees technology as an integral part of the changes taking place rather than as mere tools to apply to methodologically created solutions.

Similarly, Librarians and Information Scientists have begun a comprehensive discourse among themselves on the potential of new technologies, as well as its capacity to redefine their profession. Among the many issues being discussed, the *current* creation of Digital and Virtual libraries may change the role of the librarian from caretaker to networker, and the consequences of this have by no means been fully debated and thought through by the profession. However one thing is clear, their *awareness of the technology* grows daily and forms an integral and substantial part of that debate.

In both of these professions the embracing of technology as a means to create and understand change contrasts starkly with the sense of technophobia with exists in parts of the present Systems community.

5. TECHNOPHOBIA IN SYSTEMS THINKING, SYSTEMS PRACTICE

For many undergraduates, graduates and professionals, the Information Systems world suggests a world of applied technology. For many it is a surprise to find a Systems Movement whose disengagement with technology is all too apparent, and which finds so little time to discuss that technology. Social, organisational and personal issues prevail leaving the opportunities of technology largely unexplored by the general presumption that technology forms a means to implement solutions which are independent of that technology. Such a view may be based on - and certainly is best suited to - the seventies and eighties when the importance of hardware and software selection was over-emphasised by manufacturers, thus obscuring the more relevant organisational issues. Today the organisational *opportunity* of new technology requires that we become aware of what is possible. To remain distant from the technology in the late nineties is to fail to see the possibilities for change.

In another area of related professional interest, the British Computer Society has chosen to to join with the Engineering Council. This move—whatever the debate around such societies and the merits of this change—has resulted in a requirement for universities to provide a solid foundation of scientific, mathematical and engineering underpinning in order to gain accreditation by the Society. It seems that this professional body still regards the world of Information Systems as more about 'hard' systems engineering than 'soft' systems facilitation.

It may be however that neither soft nor hard systems approaches provide us with the necessary underpinning to understand and develop the emergent technologies. Experience of the Internet suggests that one of the major requirements of such technology is the ability to connect and to see the social and organisational possibilities of connection. One of the strengths of the Systems Movement is precisely this: to see connections, to recognise similarities, common interests, conflicts and dependencies. If the connections between people and organisations become more important than the provision of supposed 'information', then opportunities exist for a new and sustainable vision of Information Systems by academics and practitioners. If this is to take place then the present major weakness of systems thinking and systems practice—that of a deliberately and seriously limited technological vision—must be addressed.

6. THE SYSTEMS MOVEMENT: POSSIBLE FUTURES

While the 1980s saw a shift in interest by academics from the technical to the organisational and social aspects of Information Systems, there remained among them a working concept of the same *kind* of system. In the context of emergent technologies, if the word *Information* requires review then so does the word *System*.

For the concept of 'system' to once again become useful to us it must lose its constraint of boundaries set in time, space and form. 'Systems' must no longer be defined in terms of the relationship between objects and actions (for example, data and process), but rather as the connection across space, time and form between the various parts of representation and reality. In doing so, *learning to act* becomes the purpose of describing the system. The network of connections provides the path through which action can be taken. With such a model Information Systems can assimilate emergent communication technologies, distributed databases, multimedia and so on, recognising in time, space and form the new relationship between representation and reality.

The existing and traditional paradigms of Information Systems as "data and process" or as "social and organisational" may have given birth to the Information Systems community, but it will surely not sustain it in years to come. The widening of our agenda to political, social and personal issues without reference to information technologies will leave us adrift in deep waters while we attempt to create for ourselves and others some acceptable and convincing ground for our place in those debates. In the traditional world of the Systems Movement, it seems that 'the centre cannot hold.' Diversity is replaced by diversion, though some may regard this as a development and not a dilution. Whether it is sustainable is more open to question.

There is a clear role for Systems thinking in the effort to understand and apply new technologies. Just as some within the A.I. community have found new opportunities by abandoning the 'riddle' of the search for intelligence, and now seek to produce systems capable of intelligent acts, so the Information Systems community might find that its own sustainability lies in change, in reassessing what Information Systems means in the light of emergent technologies and organisational change, and working from there towards useful acts in the world.

REFERENCES

Barto, Andrew G., Bradtke, Steven J. and Singh, Satinder P., 1995, Learning to act using real-time dynamic programming, *Artificial Intelligence 72(1–2)*, pp. 81–138.
Checkland, P.B., 1981, Systems Thinking, Systems Practice, John Wiley & Sons, Chichester.
Peters, Paul Evan <paul@cni.org>, 1996, "General information about the Internet II Project", http://www.cni.org/
Gilligan, J., 1994, Patterns on Glass: The Language Games of Information, *Proceedings of the Conference on Philosophical and Logical Aspects of Information Systems, UWE, 1994.*
Wittgenstein, L, 1953, "Philosophical Investigations", Blackwell, Oxford.

APPENDIX 1: AUDIT RESOURCES ON THE WWW

Here are a few of the URLs pointing to Web resources for auditors:

http://www.icaew.org.uk/ ICAEW
http://www.iia.org.uk IIA UK

http://www.gold.net:80/bcs/siggroup/casghme.htm BCS CASG
http://www.bitwise.net/iawww/IAWWW-HOMEPAGE-CM.HTML Internal Audit
    Resources.
http://www.ex.ac.uk/ECU/auditing/welcome.html Software Auditing

94

INFORMATION SYSTEMS METHODOLOGIES

The Problem Rather Than the Solution?

J. B. Hopkins

Anglia Polytechnic University
Chelmsford, Essex CM1 1LL

1. BACKGROUND

For around four decades in this country we have been striving to produce efficient and effective computer-based information systems to serve the needs of organisations in all sectors of our economy. For the last two decades that search for improvements in information systems development (ISD) has looked to the use of methodologies as the most promising vehicle to deliver those improvements.

The contrast between the immense transformations in those two decades in hardware and software products and the largely stillborn efforts at refinement of the systems developers is stark. It should also give us pause for reflection and self-analysis, both as practitioners and as educators/trainers.

We can no longer avoid the uncomfortable conclusion that although we have loyally over this period concentrated on "doing things right" it seems more likely that we have to ask ourselves, as an ISD community, are we "doing the right things"?

This paper explores the sources and roots of these attitudes, questions their validity and current relevance, looks at alternative approaches to ISD and proposes ways of bringing about necessary changes.

2. THE "TRADITIONAL" APPROACH: ITS ROOTS

It is now becoming something of a *cliche* in certain ISD circles to argue that present attitudes to the methods of ISD have their origins in the scientism (and optimism) of the Enlightenment, that age when Western Europe witnessed a heady mixture of both intellectual and social liberation, stimulation and revelation; when, rationality triumphed over what was perceived as myth and superstition.

Clearly there is a persuasive argument that one of the legacies of that exciting period is a fundamental belief in our power to achieve the solutions to problems through the

Systems for Sustainability, edited by Stowell *et al.*
Plenum Press, New York, 1997

painstaking application of orderly, rational and scientific methods. The record of application of such approaches, over the generations, in the fields of science, technology and engineering is a proud one.

Kuhn (1970) traces the development route for these ideas, identifies the inherent features of such developments and, most significantly for our purposes, raises to prominence
the need for researchers "to ask new sorts of questions and to trace different and often less
than cumulative developmental lines for the sciences". He posed a number of fundamental
questions about the nature of "normal science" which we in the ISD community would do
well to consider carefully, if we are to achieve our goal of client satisfaction.

However, in practice, the temptation to transfer these proven methods, along with
their underpinning philosophical foundation, to other fields and other problems has proved
irresistible. Herein lies one of the sources of the current dis-satisfaction and disillusion-
ment with our methodologies. They reflect ways of thinking and doing which are often inappropriate for the problem environment in which they are being applied. The words of
Professor Lou Davis, one of the pioneers of the socio-technical approach, are apt in this
context.

> "No clear objectives concerning roles for men as men are visible, although objectives are
> clearly defined for men as machines." (Davis and Taylor, 1972)

Furthermore, there is observed evidence that, in our education and training approaches within IS, we are re-inforcing these self-same concepts and practices which have
patently failed to satisfy the very wide constituency of interests which comprise the real IS
community - perhaps "diaspora" is a more accurate representation of this group!

3. THE "TRADITIONAL" APPROACH: ITS CONSEQUENCES

The duality identified above concerning the practice of ISD can be taken further. In
practice we are able to identify readily both the successes and failures of the application of
the positivist, rationalist, engineering approaches to ISD.

On the credit side of the ledger we must acknowledge the effectiveness of the structured, disciplined, goal-oriented methods in the whole area of transaction processing systems such as payroll, invoicing and stock recording. These applications are broadly
characterised by agreed objectives, clearly-stated and well-understood rules for processing
and a defined set of outputs (sometimes embodied in statutes).

Set against these undoubted successes we have the unwelcome record of complaint,
frustration and disappointed expectations of those clients who were promised information
provision to support their decision- making. They were assured that it would be tailored to
their **practical and professional** needs in that it would be available where, when and in a
form which they chose.

It is in the second area that the Enlightenment inheritance has had the most perni-
cious effect. We have employed the same approaches and methods in the two disparate application areas, confident in the belief that what demonstrably works in the one area will,
of course, work in the other.

"Computer systems design, although it has been with us for only a comparatively
short period of time, appeared to become structured and formalised very quickly. It was
associated with a problem solving philosophy which was accepted uncritically by most
systems designers. The philosophy saw the design of computer systems as a technical

process directed at solving problems which were defined in technical terms." (Mumford, 1983).

It is from this beginning that our obsessive pursuit of the ideal, universal methodology has grown. As Schon has noted "professional activity consists in instrumental problem-solving made rigorous by the application of scientific theory and technique." (Schon, 1983). The "silver bullet" has pre-occupied us since the 1970s to the exclusion of a more eclectic approach which takes account of the range of other disciplines which have an impact on ISD.

One of the consequences is an ingrained approach to ISD which, as well as lacking relevance to the shifting needs of the clients, contains a core non-sustainability in the sense that it fails to provide a consistent platform on which to build systems capable of sufficiently rapid adaptation in the dynamic environment of modern organisations.

"The moral here is that both systems objectives and the final system need to be adaptive. Objectives that, once set, are never revised may merely enable an organisation to tackle today's problems on the basis of yesterday's obsolete needs. Rigid technical systems which cannot be adapted to changing human needs will produce an alienated workforce." (Mumford, 1983)

4. OUR UNIVERSITY CURRICULA: THEIR PHILOSOPHY AND CONTENT

Observations over a period of 20 years in higher education in the UK leads the author to the conclusion that, far from introducing gradual changes and improvements in the education and training of entrants to the information systems profession, our pedagogical approach in fact reinforces the very mindset which militates against any such progress.

Historically, our curricula grew from computer science, were seen initially as subsets of mathematics and engineering and incorporated all the positivist attitudes prevalent in those disciplines. Although in more recent times the curricula have been amended to reflect a growing understanding of the complexities associated with organisational analysis there remains a strong goal-oriented undertow within our thinking.

Checkland picked up this theme when he stated that

"From the 1960s to the 1980s....organisations are conceptualised as goal-seeking machines and information systems are there to enable the information needs associated with organisational goals to be met." (Checkland and Scholes, 1990)

Evidence for these claims can be found in the specifications provided by, say, the British Computer Society, for syllabi to which prospective accredited courses should conform. The recommendations are deeply grounded in the rationalist worldview which perceives problems as capable of solution **if only we can reduce them to their component elements**.

Our experience at Anglia supports the above assertions. Attempts to develop courses which place emphasis on the uncertain, unknown (and unknowable?) and "messy" nature of so many organisational IS problem situations have been, at worst, dismissed by colleagues as trivial. At best, they regard them as falling into some peripheral category of topic seen as broadening, of general interest but not of central concern to either the students or their future employers.

On the other side of this debate we encounter students who react appreciatively to these "unconventional" perspectives, recognising in them a reality which accords with their experience of life and of work. In particular, our mature students are most enthusiastic in their welcome. There is also some evidence growing to indicate that employers are now beginning to question the previously received wisdom regarding ISD methods and are applying more a rigorous analysis of the causes of dis-satisfaction with their ISD.

In this movement the combined impact of the work of authors like Checkland, Mumford and Schon on the one hand, and of Peters and Handy on the other is serving to influence thinking and gradually engender a re-consideration of ideas. It is to be hoped that this review will be translated into practice over time and that we, in higher education will be in a position to assist in the achievement of better outcomes and results in ISD.

5. A CRITIQUE OF BOTH PRACTICE AND TRAINING

The woeful record of practitioners in the field, as demonstrated in the continuing series of surveys pointing to a less-than-satisfied client group, should prompt a continuing introspection on the part of all the partners to the process of ISD.

There is **some** indication that this process is under way. However, there also appears to be a strong rearguard action in the continuance of the search for an "improved" methodology. Its proponents continue to argue forcefully that the problems which confront us in ISD are primarily susceptible to engineered solutions **if only we were more proficient in our methods**.

One influential facet of this tendency is the direction taken in the training of practitioners (both within and outside their organisations). Various pressures are cited to justify the rigidly instrumental thinking which pervades this area. It is usual to hear that operational requirements inevitably lead to such a philosophy; that management are not prepared to accept a different approach and that, ultimately, we have to adopt "efficient" training methods. The result is a perpetuation of the blinkered goal-seeking thinking which then becomes translated into the methodological straitjackets which continue to undermine our chances of progress and success in ISD.

We find ourselves in a closed-loop system of thinking and practice where the imperatives of deadlines and budgets are supreme and unarguable, notwithstanding the poor record of such a stance in practice.

6. A WAY FORWARD

It would be easy to arrive at the conclusion that, because of the all-pervasive impact of the rationalist position and its apparent continued ascendency, there is little purpose to be served in persisting in a struggle to open up and democratise the process of ISD even though the existing process manifestly demands improvement.

Such a counsel of despair does not allow for the patient and painstaking work already carried out (and still succeeding in gaining acceptance and approval) in academia and in practice to demonstrate that wider participation in ISD does in fact contribute to greater chances of success in implementation. The work of, for example, Mumford, Checkland, Flood and Jackson in the UK, of Ehn, Kyng and Bjerknes in Scandinavia, of Ackoff, Churchman and Greenbaum in the USA and of other (perhaps) less celebrated researcher/practitioners in many countries testify to the determination, spirit and creativity of proponents of this approach.

Given these examples within practice it falls to those of us in the academic community to endeavour to prepare the next generation of practitioners in such a way that they can pursue theses goals in the face of what will certainly continue to be strong opposition.

Within our curriculum development we must incorporate, at least, an alternative perspective to the "engineering" view. We must argue forcefully against colleagues who adopt the "vocational" stance, claiming as they do that "nothing will change and we must prepare our graduates for the 'real world'". Central to the philosophy of participative design is the tenet that different stakeholders in the ISD process have different views and interpretations of this 'real world'and that each of these must be valued, understood and if at all possible, accommodated. Therein lies the difficulty and the challenge; to ignore this is to avoid the obstacle but also to miss the point.

We have a duty to our students to alert them to the complexities, inconsistencies and anomalies of the organisational environments in which they will find themselves. We fail in that project if we persist in giving the impression that it is possible, through a goal-oriented, reductionist approach, to simplify and then solve the problems inherent in IS.

We have a wider duty to the cause of successful and sustainable information systems provision in ridding our profession of its obsessive and self-satisfied adherence to a development philosophy which is failing our clients.

Information systems are too important to our organisations and to our society to allow them to continue to be hamstrung by such blinkered views.

REFERENCES

Checkland, P.B., and Scholes, J., 1990, *Soft Systems Methodology in Action*, John Wiley and Sons, Chichester.
Davis, L., and Taylor, J., 1972 *The Design of Jobs*, Penguin Books, Harmondsworth.
Kuhn, T.S., 1970, *The Structure of Scientific Revolutions*, University of Chicago Press, London.
Mumford, E., 1983, *Designing Human Systems*, Manchester Business School, Manchester.
Schon, D.A., 1983, *The Reflective Practitioner: how professionals think in action*, Basic books, New York.

95

REASONING ABOUT SOFTWARE SYSTEM DESIGN WITH SSM

Peter Kokol

University of Maribor–FERI
Centre for Medical Informatics
Smetanova 17, 62000 Maribor, Slovenia

1. INTRODUCTION

The very rapid development of hardware results in unthinkable new possibilities generating a great demand for very complex information systems (IS). Unfortunately current software design technology was not able to cope with such enormous demand and consequently the software crisis emerged. It appears that following symptoms of the crisis are the most evident: SS do not meet users needs and expectations; SS are not portable or optimised; SS are to costly, to late or incomplete; they are complex, error prone, fail to operate; are user unfriendly etc. Recent research (Brynjolfsson 1993) shows that many recent software systems suffer from same symptoms, meaning that the software crisis is not yet completed.

Numerous development methods, based on the variety of paradigms (Agresti 1996), have been proposed over the years. Of these few were successfully applied in the real world applications. As a consequence new approaches both generic and more specific have been proposed and old approaches has been adopted and extended to meet the changing needs.

Despite many advantages of new software design paradigms (Kokol, Zumer, Debeljak and Stok 1996; Kokol, Stiglic and Zumer 1995; Zave and Jackson 1993) it is unreasonable to rely on only one paradigm, because the tools and techniques for one set of circumstances need not be appropriate for others. Various solutions based on reuse, metadesign and modelling of software design paradigms were proposed in the manner to enable more flexible design in different design situations.

Another recent software design paradigm, which can be seen as a generalisation of above approaches, is method engineering (»Method Engineering«, 1996). Method engineering (ME) is a very promising, but at the same time very young paradigm, and consequently not yet very well defined. Because of it's encouraging features we decided to analyse the possible application of method engineering in our future IS design adventures. In this manner we need to clarify some points about method engineering and the aim of

Systems for Sustainability, edited by Stowell *et al.*
Plenum Press, New York, 1997

this paper is to present how the Checklands Soft System Methodology (SSM) (Checkland and Scholes 1990) has been used in the accomplishment of this task.

2. METHOD ENGINEERING

Since their introduction various life cycle models and specific supporting techniques have played an important role in building software systems. More recently the topic of software processes have received increased attention in software community. A SS design approach called "Evolution of Software Processes" (Bruno 1995; Conradi, Fernstorm and Fuggeta 1993; Davis 1995; Madhavji and Penedo 1993) is based on the emerging view that software processes—like software—also need to be evolved lest they become obsolete. The aim of the evolution is to fulfil the needs of the people who perform the process and the developmental and organisational goals to be achieved. Another recent software design paradigm, that can be seen as a generalisation of software process evolution, is method engineering. While there is a great overlapping of method engineering and process evolution activities, there is also an important divergence—process evolution is oriented more toward the improvement of existing processes and method engineering more toward the construction of new methods, where processes can be seen as the representation of methods in specific design situations (Sutton, Heimbigner and Osterweil 1995).

3. REASONING ABOUT METHOD ENGINEERING

The SSM as described in Checkland and Scholes (1990) has been used in the process of reasoning about method engineering. As a starting point to root definition construction we used the definition of engineering found in McGraw Hill Encyclopaedia of Science and Technology where the engineering is defined (Parker 1989) as:

the art of directing the great sources of power in nature for the use and the convenience of people. The engineering design is concerned with the creation of systems, devices and processes useful to, and sought by society.

Following above definition we can define the method engineering as:

the art of directing the great power of computers in means of software design methods for the use and the convenience of people. The method engineering design is thereafter concerned with the creation of software design methods and processes useful to, and sought by society.

But this definition outlines just the output of the method engineering process and not its inputs and actions to be taken to achieve the desired outputs. Using the SSM "framework root definition" a system to do X by Y in order to achieve Z we can imagine possible Ys, Zs and inputs shown in Table 1. and Xs (transformations) presented in Table 2. According to the product they generate we grouped similar transformations and constructed a high level common conceptual model shown in figure 1.

The idea of process is to be seen as fundamental to software development. But as Davis (Davis 1995) correctly observes there is about every ten years that the software community redefines "the problem" by shifting its focus from product issues to process issues (i.e. from structured programming language to structured analysis; from data encapsulation to Maturity Model; etc.) and the same can be argued for method engineering - the

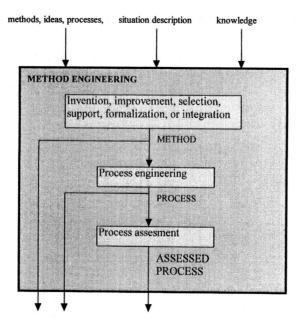

Figure 1. The high level common conceptual model representing the method engineering process.

software design process has become product for method engineering which can be regarded as a process. Thereafter it is best not to concentrate on process or product but on both and to advance (Davis 1995) on the notation of duality (the very good example is the successful use of the dual nature of light in physics).

Using the principle of duality outlined in the preceding paragraph, and the conceptual model from figure 1 as a basis we have been able to define the following common root definition:

The method engineering is a process in which an idea about a "new" methodology and underlying process is transformed into an assessed process using integration, adoption, automation, etc., according to the situation in which the process should be applied,

Table 1. Possible inputs, Ys and Zs defining the method engineering

Inputs
    the description of the design situation including the system to be designed
    knowledge about: design methodologies, approaches, paradigms; engineering; management; evaluation;
        metamodeling etc.
    ideas about possible methods and processes to be used in the given situation, existing methods, etc.
Ys
    system theory, management theory
    metamodeling
    method automation
    assessment, evaluation and selection
    maturity models, standards
Zs
    to design more successful software systems in short to resolve the software crisis
    to construct more successful SS design methods and processes
    better life for all

Table 2. Possible Xs (transformations) defining method engineering

Transformation	From	To
Invention	Idea	New method or process
Improvement	Existing method(s)	Improved method
Selection	Existing methods	"The best" method
Support	Existing method(s)	Computer supported method
Formalization	Existing method	Formalised method
Integration	Existing methods	Integrated methods
Assessment	Existing process	Assessed process
Representation	Existing method	Process (method representation)

using the knowledge about design methodologies, methods, paradigms, etc., with the aim of introducing of better design methods and processes and in the manner to design more successful information systems.

4. CONCLUSION

The aim of this paper was to introduce the use of SSM in the reasoning about information system design approaches. The study showed that a systemic approach can be very useful also in a more unconventional information system design application. The results of the study revealed that with the use of method engineering many IS, like the one presented in the paper, design weaknesses can be solved and as a consequence more successful information systems can be designed.

REFERENCES

Agresti, W. W., 1986, *New Paradigms for Software Development*, IEEE CS Press, New York.

Brynjolfsson, E., 1993, The Productivity Paradox of Information Technology, *Communications of the ACM*, **36**(12):66–77.

Checkland, P., and Scholes, J., 1990, *Soft Systems Methodology in Action*. John Willey & Sons, Chichester.

Conradi, R., Fernstorm, C., and Fuggeta, A., 1993, A Conceptual Framework for Evolving Software Processes, *ACM Software Engineering Notes* **18**(3):26–35.

Davis, M. J., 1995, Process and Product: Dichotomy or Duality? *ACM Software Engineering Notes* **20**(2):17–18.

Kokol, P., Stiglic, B., and Zumer, V., 1995, Metaparadigm: a soft and situation oriented MIS design approach, *International Journal of Bio-Medical Computing* **39**:243 - 256.

Kokol, P., Zumer V., Debeljak, M., Stok, B., 1996, Computer Supported Two Level Information System Design, *Cybernetics and Systems* **27**:265–277.

Madhavji, N. H., and Penedo, M. H., 1993, Evolution of Software Processes. *IEEE Trans. Soft. Eng.* 19(11):whole issue.

Parker, S., 1989, *McGraw - Hill Concise Encyclopaedia of Science and Technology*, McGraw-Hill, New York.

Sutton, M. S., Heimbigner, D., and Osterweil, L. J., 1995, APPL/A: A Language for Software Process Programming, *ACM Trans. Soft. Eng. Meth.* ,4:221:286.

Zave, P, Jackson, M. A., 1993, Conjunction and Composition, *TOSEM* 2:379–411.

96

BRIDGING THE GAP BETWEEN IS DEFINITION AND IS SPECIFICATION

R. Lander, S. McRobb, and F. A. Stowell

Department of Computer and Information Science
De Montfort University Milton Keynes
Hammerwood Gate, Kents Hill, MK7 6HP
Tel: 01908 695511; Fax: 01908 834948
Email: rlander@dmu.ac.uk, smcrobb@dmu.ac.uk, fstowell@dmu.ac.uk

1. APPROACHES IN IS—A MEASURE OF SUCCESS?

Fitzgerald (1996) gives a useful overview of the benefits claimed for Information Systems Development Methodologies (ISDMs) which encompassing structured and Object-Oriented (OO) approaches and the problems associated with their use. Humphreys (1989) found that only 3% of companies in the United States could be said to have achieved a level of IS process maturity such that systems were developed using formal documented processes. Yourdon (1992) comments on the majority of software development organisations found in the initial level of maturity "...one where anarchy prevails... where programmers consider themselves to be creative artists". Taylor and Moynihan (1996) suggest reasons for non-use of methods and highlight one case where an informal approach was highly practical—analysts knew the application areas well, designers were skilled in the use of development tools and communication between all parties was rated excellent.

The use of ISDMs is consistently seen as problematic by practitioners. Assumptions underlying ISDMs are those of "rational" technicist problem solving with a nod in the direction of Simon's "satisficing" concept of decision making. However, the process of IS development is more appropriately characterised by uncertainty and conflict (Robey, Farow and Franz, 1989), with cycles of learning and communication between participants.

In contrast to ISDMs, approaches developed within IS, such as Soft Systems Methodology (SSM), have achieved a measure of success. Stowell (1995) edits a collection of papers highlighting the contribution of soft systems thinking to IS. Ideas from soft systems thinking have also been taken up by CS practitioners and attempts made to incorporate these as a front end to ISDMs, for example, the CCTA's COMPACT methodology.

In addition to CS and IS work in this area there is current research on application of Soft OR and systems dynamics to software development (Lane, 1994). There is a general

Systems for Sustainability, edited by Stowell *et al.*
Plenum Press, New York, 1997

recognition of the need for work building on the success of soft systems approaches within the technical specification phases of information systems development.

In SSM, requirements for change are produced as the end result of a learning cycle. The success of SSM lies in its "rich and realistic approach to learning and change" (Dahlbom and Mathiassen 1993), but the methodology is criticised as difficult to plan and manage and requiring substantial expertise from practitioners. SSM's hermeneutic perspective privileges *processes of creation* over products created. This leads practitioners back to the humanities and social sciences for theories to provide a sound conceptual base for the methodology and for conceptual tools to make sense of what happens in the systems development process. ISDMs lack this theoretical base, an issue we expand on in our discussion of object oriented methods below.

2. WHAT IS TO BE GAINED BY LINKING INTERPRETIVIST PROBLEM DEFINITION TO "HARD" ISDM?

ISDMs require a more successful approach to problem definition than is presently offered, and a link with soft systems methods offers a way out of this difficulty. SSM has been the most usual choice for authors who have considered the problem (Avison and Wood-Harper, 1990; Stowell, 1985; Mingers, 1988; Prior, 1990; Lewis, 1993; Savage and Mingers, 1996; Liang, West and Stowell, 1996; Stowell and Mingers, 1997). Given the successes cited earlier, we see no reason to depart from this reliance. The first question to examine is the extent to which such a link is feasible.

2.1. Feasibility of a Link

We could as well ask why it might *not* be feasible to move from soft problem appreciation to hard system specification. The familiar objection is that soft methods belong to the "interpretive" quartile of Burrel and Morgan's (1979) typology of social science paradigms, while hard methods (systems engineering and the range of methodologies derived from it - in practice, virtually all ISDMs), belong to the "functionalist" quartile (e.g. Mingers, 1988). They are therefore based on conflicting ontological and epistemological assumptions. Other objections have been based on more practical grounds; this point is discussed below.

However, the validity of objections on philosophical grounds is not beyond question. Probert (1996) examined in some detail the philosophical antecedents of both hard and soft information systems methodologies, and found the conflict not to be irreconcilable. He concluded (following Haack, 1993) that both schools have epistemological roots in *empirical foundationalism*, characterised by derivation of some beliefs from others held to be true beyond question. Soft and hard methods differ only in the type of beliefs held as basic. For soft methods, these are experiential beliefs derived from the subject's current conscious state; for hard methods they are "extrinsic" beliefs about the external world. Both could gain from a mutual cross-referencing, given "the truth-indicative nature of *bona fide* subjective judgements", and "the ineliminably subjective nature of objective judgements" (Probert, 1996).

A corresponding point was made by Lewis (1993), who examined the possibility of linking SSM specifically to data-focused methods of IS development. The latter's positivistic roots in computer programming-oriented concepts was seen as a problem, leading to the common assumption that data analysis has an objectivist basis. But Lewis argued this is illusory, and in practice there is an ineluctable core of subjectivity which is simply not recognised by practitioners. A link was therefore theoretically feasible.

Mingers (1995) discusses earlier attempts (e.g. Stowell, 1985) to use SSM in conjunction with structured data flow diagrams, and found there were technical problems in converting a conceptual model to a DFD, due to mismatches in the information captured in each diagram.

These technical difficulties raise the question of selecting an ISD method whose tools are sympathetic to the conceptual demands of soft approaches.

2.2. OOA: A Sympathetic ISDM?

This question will be determined largely by whether adherence to the underlying concept of a "learning cycle" for participants in the problem situation remains possible, and whether the rich appreciation of the problem situation (multiple viewpoints or *weltanschauungen* which are a principal outcome of soft methods) can be preserved through analysis, design and implementation activities.

Several attempts have already been made. Multiview (Avison and Wood-Harper, 1990) was an early pioneer, with the traditional software life-cycle providing an overarching framework. Other exemplars include: data flow diagrams (e.g. Stowell, 1985; Mingers, 1988; Prior, 1990), data-focused methods—with OO seen as a subset of these—(Lewis, 1993), Jackson System Development (Savage & Mingers, 1996) and OO (Liang, West & Stowell, 1996). To date most authors have concluded that further work needs to be done to achieve a good fit, but the path is promising.

There are a number of reasons to consider an OO method as the hard partner, including their recent growth in popularity. Many organisations are switching to OO development methods. This must be put in context of our earlier observation that most organisations still admit they use no method at all, nevertheless OO methods are likely to be a feature of software development for some time to come.

Some aspects of an OO model are particularly resonant for an interpretivist. The concept of an object as encapsulating data and behaviour within a single package holds considerable promise of being derivable from a conceptual (or activity) model. Initial experience shows that it can in fact be fairly straightforward to identify objects from a conceptual model, and to make a preliminary identification of operations (Liang, West and Stowell, 1996). An emphasis on iteration in the development life-cycle and liberal use of prototyping also have positive resonance for interpretivists. While not in themselves a consequence of the OO "paradigm" OO models do appear to support iteration well. This is due to the use of a single, progressively more detailed, but otherwise coherent model throughout the life-cycle. This contrasts favourably with the abrupt switches between models so characteristic of structured methods.

Researchers on both sides of the IS / CS divide have been working on a possible bridge between SSM and OO. Liang, West & Stowell (1996) tackled the extent to which a soft approach can remedy a perceived weakness in OOA: identification and selection of relevant objects from the problem domain. Meanwhile, from the CS side (e.g. Cook & Daniels, 1994; Graham, 1994) have also identified the identification of "relevant" objects as a specific problem area, and some (e.g. Dobbin and Bustard,1994) have investigated the compatibility of OO methods with SSM.

3. APPROACHES TO INTEGRATION

3.1. What Is the Need That Is to Be Met?

Miles (1988) identified three possible strategies for linking interpretivism to an ISDM. Of these, two have been explored by others: *grafting*, also described as front-end-ing the ISDM with SSM (this is how Multiview works) and *embedding* (explored by, e.g., Savage and Mingers, 1996). We choose to investigate the third option, that of creating a new meta-framework to embrace both SSM and ISDM, for the simple reason that we believe it has been given insufficient attention to date. The initial task is to consider the requirements for a framework to enable integration of interpretivist and hard ISDMs.

It may help first to distinguish two categories of existing approach. One defines at the outset who is to *decide* what; for example, "hard" ISDMs deriving from the structured school, best typified by SSADM. The second defines who is to *do* what. The best example is the Scandinavian participatory design (PD) school (e.g. Floyd, 1993; Bødker, Grønbaek, and Kyng, 1993; Kyng, 1995), which drew much of its inspiration from the workplace democracy movement (Howarth, 1984). Clement and Van den Besselar (1993) studied a number of PD projects and found that many had achieved significant success, and on a wide range of criteria including increased consciousness by workers of the social implications of information technology for them (Clement and Van den Besselar, 1993). In PD approaches there is an emphasis on assigning responsibility to the eventual users for significant parts of the overall design. Moreover, there is a recognition that success in design involves creating representations of work practice, thus rendering tacit knowledge explicit. These are very positive features of this school, but we feel that they still do not go far enough.

During every project it is necessary to address questions of who has decision making power, and who should carry out particular activities. But both the process and the outcome of these decisions will depend on the specific features of the problem situation. It is thus inappropriate to define in advance which individuals (or even which roles) should have responsibility for specific parts of the overall design process. An *appreciative* approach encourages all stakeholders to improve their understanding of the entire problem situation. This can even be taken as its sole aim, with IS development only one of many possible, but contingent, consequences of such an improved understanding.

The need, then, is to identify, at a meta-level, elements and themes which may need to be addressed during the appreciative learning cycle, whenever computer system development is a possible outcome. This constitutes the requirements for a meta-level framework, capable in principle of guiding the integration of a project which begins in "soft" problem appreciation activity and leads on to "hard" computer system specification, design and implementation. We propose that such a framework must embrace and organise methods to:

 a. identify all stakeholders
 b. expose power relationships among stakeholders
 c. capture and express multiple viewpoints on the problem situation, held by the stakeholders (and their wider *weltanschauungen*)
 d. maintain quality of debate among the stakeholders, both regarding these viewpoints, and also about desirable and feasible change
 e. preserve the richness of problem appreciation through later activities (too often during IS specification, design and implementation, the tools of the method en-

force closure of design possibilities before participants are ready - i.e. before an appreciation has developed. Ideally, a possibility once identified should remain possible until the stakeholders are ready to give it up)

f. enable forwards and backwards traceability through later models.

4. CLD: A POSSIBLE FRAMEWORK FOR MIXING INTERPRETIVISM AND OO

Client Led Design (Stowell and West, 1994) offers a possible framework, which, with suitable development, could meet the need identified above. The CLD framework is based explicitly on the thought of Vickers and Checkland, in particular Vickers' notion of the "appreciative system" (Checkland and Casar, 1986). Represented graphically as a model with five phases, there is nevertheless no intention that the "phases" of CLD should be followed sequentially. CLD is not implemented by a "waterfall" lifecycle. Some enhancements to CLD are required and these will form the basis of the accompanying presentation which,we believe, may be sufficient to enable it to meet the requirements stated above for a meta-level framework to integrate soft problem appreciation with an OOA methodology for IS specification and development.

REFERENCES

Avison, D. and Wood-Harper, A. T., 1990, *Multiview: An Exploration in Information Systems Development*, Blackwell, Oxford.

Avison, D. E. and Fitzgerald, G., 1995, *Information Systems Development: Methodologies, Techniques and Tools*, 2nd ed, Blackwell Scientific Publications, Oxford.

Bjornestad, S., 1994, "A research program for object-orientation". *European Journal of Information Systems,* **3** (1):13–27.

Bødker, S., Grønbaek, K. and Kyng, M., 1993, "Cooperative design: techniques and experiences from the Scandinavian scene", in: *Participatory Design: Principles and Practices* (A. Namioka and D. Shuler, eds.), Lawrence Erlbaum, Hillsdale, N. J.

Burrel, G. & Morgan, G., 1979, *Sociological Paradigms and Organisational Analysis*, Heinemann, London.

Checkland, P. and Scholes, J., 1990, *Soft Systems Methodology in Action*, Wiley, Chichester

Checkland, P., 1995, "Soft Systems Methodology and its relevance to the development of Information Systems", in: *Information Systems Provision: the contribution of Soft Systems Methodology*, (F. A. Stowell, ed), McGraw-Hill, Maidenhead.

Checkland, P. and Casar, A., 1986, "Vickers' concept of an appreciative system: a systemic account", *Journal of Applied Systems Analysis,* **13**:109–15.

Clement, A. and Van den Besselar, P., 1993, "A retrospective look at participatory projects", *CACM,* **36** (4):29–37.

Coad, P. and Yourdon, E., 1990, *Object-Oriented Analysis,* 2nd ed, Yourdon Press / Prentice-Hall International, Englewood Cliffs.

Cook, S. and Daniels, J., 1994, *Designing Object-Oriented Systems: object-oriented modelling with Syntropy*, Prentice-Hall International, Hemel Hempstead.

Dahlbom, B. & Mathiassen, L., 1993, *Computers in Context: The Philosophy and Practice of Systems Design*, NCC Blackwell, Oxford.

De Raadt, J. D. R., 1989, "Multi-modal System Design: a concern for the issues that matter", *Systems Research,* **6** (1):17–25.

Dobbin, T. J. and Bustard, D. W., 1994, "Combining soft systems methodology and object-oriented analysis: the search for a good fit", *Proceedings of the 2nd Information Systems Methodologies Conference,* August 1994, Edinburgh,.

Fitzgerald, B., 1996, "Formalized systems development methodologies: a critical perspective", *Information Systems Journal,* **6**, 3–23.

Flood, R. L. and Jackson, M. C., 1991, *Critical Systems Thinking: Directed Readings*, Wiley, Chichester.

Floyd, C., 1993, "STEPS: A methodical approach to participatory design", *CACM,* **36** (4):83.

Graham, I., 1994, *Object-Oriented Methods*, 2nd ed, Addison-Wesley, Wokingham.

Haack, S., 1993, *Evidence and Enquiry*, Blackwell, Oxford.

Howarth, S., 1984, *The Way People Work*, OUP, Oxford.

Humphreys, W., 1989, *Managing the Software Process*, Addison Wesley, Reading, MA.

Kyng, M., 1995, "Making Representations Work", *CACM,* **38** (9):46–55.

Lane, D. C., 1994, "With a little help from our friends: how system dynamics and soft OR can learn from each other", *System Dynamics Review,* **10** (2–3):101–134.

Levin, M., 1996, "The quest for quality in participatory inquiry: a critical reflection on validity", *Forum One: Action Research and Critical Systems Thinking,* Hull University, April 1996.

Lewis, P. J., 1993, "Linking soft systems methodology with data-focused information system development", *Journal of Information Systems,* **3,** 169–186.

Mingers, J., 1988, "Comparing conceptual models and data flow diagrams", *The Computer Journal,* **31** (4):376–9.

Mingers, J., 1995, "Using soft systems methodology in the design of information systems", in: *Information Systems Provision: the contribution of Soft Systems Methodology* (F. A. Stowell, ed), McGraw-Hill, Maidenhead.

Mingers, J. and Stowell, F. A. (eds) 1997, *Information Systems: an Emerging Discipline?* McGraw Hill, Maidenhead (in press)

Prior, R., 1990, "Deriving data flow diagrams from a 'soft systems' conceptual model", *Systemist,* **12** (2):65–75.

Probert, 1996, "The metaphysical foundations of soft and hard information systems methodologies", UK Operational Research Society Conference 1995

Probert, S. K., 1997, "The Actuality of Information Systems", in: *The Discipline of Information Systems,* (F. A. Stowell and J. Mingers, eds).

Robey, D., Farow, D. L. and Franz, C. R., 1989, "Group Process and Conflict in Systems Development", *Management Science,* **15** (10):1172–1191.

Rumbaugh, J., Blaha, M., Premerlani, W., Eddy, F. and Lorensen, W., 1991, *Object-Oriented Modeling and Design,* Prentice-Hall International, Englewood Cliffs.

Savage, A. and Mingers, J., 1996, "A framework for linking soft systems methodology and Jackson System Development", *Information Systems Journal,* **6,** 109–129.

Stowell, F. A. (ed), 1995, *Information Systems Provision*, McGraw-Hill, Maidenhead.

Stowell, F. A., 1985, "Experience with soft systems methodology and data analysis", *Information Technology Training,* May 1985:48–50.

Stowell, F. A. and West, D. (eds), 1994, *Client-Led Design*, McGraw-Hill, Maidenhead.

Taylor, M. J. and Moynihan, E., 1996, "The Evolution of systems methodologies and why they are sometimes not used", Research Paper, Liverpool John Moores University.

West, D., Liang, Y. and Stowell, F. A., 1996, "Identifying, selecting and specifying objects in object-oriented analysis: an interpretivist approach", *Proceedings of the 1st UKAIS Conference,* Cranfield, April 1996.

Yourdon, E., 1992, *The Decline and Fall of the American Programmer*, Yourdon Press, Englewood Cliffs.

97

THE POSSIBILITY OF LINKING SSM WITH OBJECT-ORIENTED INFORMATION SYSTEMS DEVELOPMENT

Ying Liang

Department of Computing and Information Systems
University of Paisley
High Street, Paisley PA1 2BE, United Kingdom

1. INTRODUCTION

Many object-oriented methods such as OMT (Object Modelling Technique) (Rumbaugh, Blaha, Premerlani, Eddy, and Lorensen, 1991), OOSE (Object-Oriented Software Engineering) (Jacobson, Christerson, Jonsson, and Overgaard, 1992), Booch (1994) have been created and can be used in object-oriented information systems development. These methods are hard system methods which address the 'hard' system thinking. This means that they focus on only describing the things and information that exist in a problem situation and specify them as objects to object models. Similar to conventional information systems methods, object-oriented methods have also lack of an activity of appreciating and understanding a real-world problem situation before building an object model for the problem and describing a boundary of an information system in the development. The lack is thought harmful both to individual development projects and to the evolution of methods and many projects have failed because their requirements were inadequately explored and described (Jackson, 1995). In order to overcome the lack, appreciating and understanding a real-world problem situation in a human environment should be emphasised and added as a special activity to the process of development. As Cook and Daniels suggest (1994), a "soft" approach may benefit the identification and abstraction of objects from messy and complex problem situations. SSM (Soft System Methodology) (Checkland and Scholes, 1993) is such an approach that concentrates on purposeful human activities in the problem by reflecting about the real world using systems concepts, within the human environment and the needs of an organisation. In this paper, we discuss the possibility of linking SSM with object-oriented information systems development by focusing on four essential modelling principles addressed by object-oriented methods and considering how a conceptual model can be used to build an object model.

Systems for Sustainability, edited by Stowell *et al.*
Plenum Press, New York, 1997

2. THE OBJECT MODEL

Object-oriented development is thought of as "a new way of thinking about software based on abstractions that exist in the real world" (Rumbaugh *et al*, 1991). Object-oriented methods used for supporting such development normally build an object model by analysing a problem statement. Basically, the object model encompasses four essential modelling principles in object-oriented information systems development: *abstraction, encapsulation, inheritance* and *polymorphism*. Objects are basic components in the object model and each *object* is "an abstraction of something in a problem situation, reflecting the capabilities of a system to keep information about it, interact with it, or both" (Coad and Yourdon, 1991). Object-oriented methods often take a problem statement as a starting point of object-oriented information systems development and provide a declarative specification (i.e., an object model) of the behaviour of an information system based on objects. The objects that have common characteristics are then recognised from the statement and then specified as a *class* in the object model. That is, a class is a set of objects that have common attributes and operations. For example, "book", "library member" and "librarian" may be abstracted from a library statement and specified as real-world objects and classes that have attributes such as "ISBN", "membership number" and "staff number", in an object model of a library system.

A process of building an object model usually includes: (1) identify individual objects and group them into classes; (2) identify object attributes and add them to the objects (e.g., "book" (ISBN, title, author, and publisher), "library member" (membership number, name, and address) and "librarian" (staff number, name, and address)); (3) link the objects together using their relationships (e.g., a member *borrows* a book); (4) identify object operations and then add them to the objects (e.g., "library member" *borrows, returns* and *reserves one or more books*); (5) identify inheritance of objects and classes (e.g., a superclass "person" is created that contains two common attributes (i.e., name and address) of two subclasses "library member" and "librarian"). An example of the object model built by the process is shown in Figure 1 using the OMT notation (Rumbaugh *et al*, 1991).

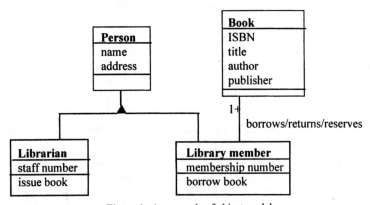

Figure 1. An example of object models.

3. ABSTRACTION

Rumbaugh *et al* (1991) defined that abstraction is the selective examination of certain aspects of a problem and the goal of abstraction is to isolate those aspects that are important for some purpose and suppress those aspects that are unimportant. We think that *abstraction* is a principle for identifying important things from a real-world problem situation and specify them as real-world objects in an object model. Many object-oriented methods available, e.g., OMT (Rumbaugh *et al,* 1991), often concentrate on abstracting the existing things and information which are explicitly described in a problem statement as real-world objects and classes by considering the nouns in the statement. However, in reality, a noun in a statement may not represent a significant thing in a situation. Two different nouns may represent the same thing in the same situation. The same noun may be interpreted differently by different people for different purposes. In addition, a thing may consist of, or imply, other things, e.g., a library consists of books and a book implies the author(s) and the publisher.

In order to capture really important things in a situation rather than considering only nouns in a problem statement, we suggest to add an activity of appreciating and understanding the knowledge about a problem situation to the process of object-oriented information systems development. In this new activity, the analyst is required to use SSM to construct a conceptual model of a problem situation based on appreciating and understanding the content of the situation within the human environment. The conceptual model represents purposeful human activities in the situation and forms an accommodation which different parts in the organisation are prepared to go along with. Then the analyst can identify real-world objects based on the conceptual model by focusing on purposeful human activities and the roles who are responsible for performing the activities in the organisation. To do this, the analyst can ask the questions such as "who fulfills each activity in the model?" and "what does the activity act on?". For example, if we have used SSM to produce a conceptual model of a library system, as shown in Figure 2, *"librarian"* and *"library member"* that are responsible for performing activities 1–8 in Figure 2 can be recognised and specified as real-world objects by asking the questions. Another real-world object *"book"* is also identified as it is acted on by activities 3, 4, 6, and 7.

4. ENCAPSULATION

An object is an encapsulation of data (i.e., attributes) and operations in an object model. Booch (1994) defined that *encapsulation* is a principle that hides the internal detail of an object from other objects and other objects are not aware of this internal detail. For example, the values of attributes (i.e., membership number, name, and address) of object "library member" in Figure 1 are invisible to other objects "librarian" and "book" in an object model of a library system. Other objects have to communicate with "library member" in order to get such detail. Objects may contain attributes or operations or both which represent their characteristics in a real-world problem situation. After real-world objects have been recognised, the attributes and operations of the objects can be also identified based on the conceptual model by (i) finding the information which each activity can access or provide and specifying the information as the attributes of the object that fulfills the activity; and (ii) specifying each activity fulfilled by a real-world object as an operation within that object. In this way, the attributes and operations which can be encapsulated into "librarian", "library member" and "book" are identified using the conceptual model shown in Figure 2, as listed in Table 1.

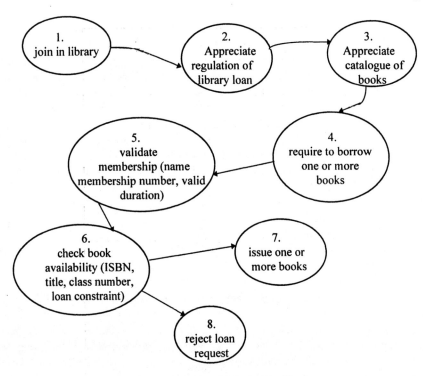

Figure 2. An example of a conceptual model for a library system.

5. INHERITANCE

Inheritance is a principle used to construct a hierarchy of abstractions in which a subclass inherits the definitions of one or more superclass (Booch, 1994), such as "librarian" inherits the attributes of "person" in the example shown in Figure 1. The conceptual model can also help to identify inheritance structure for the object model. For example, the conceptual model shown in figure 2 shows that there is a human activity "appreciate

Table 1. Real-world objects and classes and their attributes and operations

Real-world object	Attributes	Operations
library member	membership number name valid duration	join in library, appreciate regulations of library loan appreciate catalogue of books require to borrow one or more books
librarian		appreciate regulations of library loan validate membership check book availability issue one or more books reject loan request
book	ISBN title class number loan constraints	

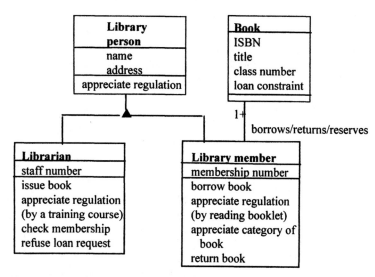

Figure 3. An object model of a library system built based on the conceptual model.

regulations of library loan" which both real-world objects and classes "librarian" and "library member" are responsible for performing. A superclass "library person" that fulfills the activity can be recognised and specified in the object model, and then "librarian" and "library member" become the subclasses of "library person" in the object model. This means that the two subclasses inherit the activity from the superclass "library person", as illustrated in Figure 3.

6. POLYMORPHISM

Polymorphism is a principle which means that different objects in an object model may fulfill the same operation differently for different purposes. Such an operation is *polymorphic*. Polymorphic operations can be identified also based on the conceptual model by examining the purposeful human activities. For each activity in the model, we can ask the questions such as: (i) how is it fulfilled in the organisation for a specific purpose? and (ii) if more than one person needs to perform the same activity in the organisation, do they do it in the same way or different ways? For example, by detailing the activity 2 in the conceptual model shown in Figure 2, we find that the librarian appreciates the regulations of library loan by attending a training course while the library member does the same thing by reading a booklet. This means that the same activity "appreciates the regulations of library loan" done by both librarian and library member is implemented in two different ways. In an object model, such an activity should be specified as a polymorphic operation within objects and classes, as shown in Figure 3.

7. CONCLUSION

This paper discusses how a conceptual model can be used as a medium of appreciating and understanding a real-world problem situation, so that an object model can be built to reflect a real-world problem situation using object-oriented methods based on the conceptual model. A simple example is also shown in the paper in order to demonstrate our ideas in the discussion. The discussion and example illustrate that it is quite possible to use the conceptual model as a vehicle in object-oriented information systems development for abstracting real-world objects from a real-world problem situation and organising the objects into an object model by addressing encapsulation, inheritance and polymorphism principles. However, the ideas shown in the paper are our initial thoughts and needed to be further enriched and completed. More exercises of linking SSM with object-oriented information systems development are also needed to be done in order to confirm the benefit of the link in future. Then a formalised approach which can support such a link should be further developed.

8. REFERENCES

Booch, G., 1994, *Object-Oriented Analysis and Design with Applications*, Benjamin Cummings Publishing Company, CA.

Checkland, P.B., and Scholes, J., 1993, *Soft Systems Methodology in Action*, Wiley, Chichester.

Coad, P., and Yourdon, E., 1991, *Object-Oriented Analysis*, Prentice Hall, Englewood Cliffs, New Jersey.

Cook J., and Daniels, S. J., 1994, *Designing Object Systems: Object Modelling with Syntropy*, Prentice Hall, Englewood Cliffs, New Jersey.

Embley, D.W., Kurtz, B.D., and Woodfield, S.N., 1992, *Object-Oriented System Analysis: A Model-Driven Approach*, Prentice Hall, Englewood Cliffs, New Jersey.

Jackson, M., 1995, *Software Requirements and Specifications*, Addison-Wesley, Wokingham.

Jacobson, I., Christerson, M., Jonsson, P., and Overgaard, G., 1992, *Object-Oriented Software Engineering*, Addison-Wesley, Wokingham.

Rumbaugh, J., Blaha, J., Premerlani, M., Eddy, F., and Lorensen, W., 1991, *Object-Oriented Modelling and Design*, Prentice Hall, Englewood Cliffs, New Jersey.

98

INFORMATION, SYSTEMS, AND DASEIN

Yasmin Merali

Warwick Business School
University of Warwick
Coventry CV4 7AL, United Kingdom

1. INTRODUCTION

Work on the role of information systems and IT in competitive advantage is often aligned to strategic positioning models and industry structure analysis of competitive strategy (Porter and Millar, 1985). Latterly the resource-based view of the firm (Peteraf, 1993) has emerged as a counterpoint to industry structure analyses of competitive strategy, and is accompanied by research focusing on the importance of core competence management (Hamel and Prahalad, 1994) and organisational learning (Senge, 1990) in the competitive context. Deriving from the more recent literature and based on the twin premise that:

1. the sustainability of an organisation operating in dynamic competitive environments is influenced by the ability of that organisation to respond effectively to new behaviours and opportunities presented by that environment, and that
2. organisational learning is key to developing "appropriate responses" in this context.

This paper deals with the role of information systems in enabling organisational learning and the development of the essential organisational "sense of being" and "appropriateness" in a dynamic context.

Using a precise definition of information, the paper introduces a typology of information systems and examines the individual information system types in terms of their ability to impact on:

- formal and informal communication,
- individual and societal perception formulation,
- organisational learning and the diffusion of knowledge, and
- the development of *Dasein*.

2. A DEFINITION OF INFORMATION

For the purpose of clarity of discourse, it is important to work with a precise definition of information. In this paper information is defined as "An abstract concept which,

Systems for Sustainability, edited by Stowell *et al.*
Plenum Press, New York, 1997

when received by an individual, gives new form to that individual's perception" (Merali and Frearson, 1995). The important contention of this definition is that information can not have a being if it isn't received and internalised by a human being. The term "latent information" is used to refer to that which would become information on receipt by a human being (Stonier, 1990).

3. A TYPOLOGY OF INFORMATION SYSTEMS

The typology for information infrastructures is based on earlier work (Merali, 1995; Merali and McGee, 1995), and identifies three types of infrastructure as characterised by distinct organisational *Weltanshchauungen* for IT-dependent information systems, namely: *Function Orientated Systems, Process Orientated Systems, and Purpose Orientated Systems.*

The dominant features of the three types are illustrated in Figure 1 and outlined below.

3.1. Function Oriented Systems

These systems are designed predominantly with a business function in mind. The case for the relevance of these systems rests entirely on what the business is *supposed* to do, and how it is *supposed* to do it, based on formal statements of functional criteria. The design mindset is geared towards efficient data processing.

3.2. Process Oriented Systems

These systems are designed to support a *business* process in its entirety. In this context, the term "business process" incorporates all that is accomplished up to and including the de-

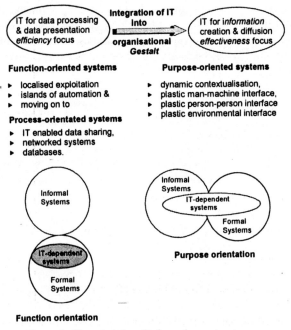

Figure 1. Characteristics of information system types.

livery of the final product and/or service to the end customer (Hammer, 1990). Consequently such systems are designed to support cross-functional activities and multi-disciplinary teams. The case for the relevance of these systems is based on the satisfaction of process output criteria (which are measured in terms of things like product cycle times, number of defects, transaction volumes and customer service levels). As typified by Hammer's examples, the information system specification is usually focused on the provision and collection of data to support efficient formal process management. The design mindset is attuned to the efficacious and efficient delivery of the end product/service (Merali, 1995).

3.3. Purpose Oriented Systems

Purpose Oriented Systems are systems that are designed to support human beings who exist within organisations, and to enable them to develop an organisational existence where "doing the appropriate thing" is dictated not by what Argyris and Schon refer to as the *Espoused Theory* of the organisation, but is attuned to the emergent *Theory in Use* (Argyris and Schon, 1978). The concept of *Purpose Oriented Systems* is developed further in the next section.

4. ORGANISATIONAL IMPACT OF THE THREE TYPES OF INFORMATION SYSTEMS

The characteristics associated with each type of system have a profound impact on organisational capabilities. This impact is mediated by the effect of the system type on organisational learning, communication, information processes and knowledge diffusion.

4.1. The Impact of Function Oriented Systems

As shown elsewhere (Merali, 1995) *Function Oriented Systems* are designed to support what Argyris and Schon refer to as the *Espoused Theory* of the organisation, rather than the *Theory in Use* (Argyris and Schon, 1978). Consequently they will support formal communication to an extent specified by the functional specification, but will be poor at enabling informal communication between individuals. Hence, given that organisational knowledge is communicated via human interaction (through discourse and shared action), *Function Oriented Systems* are, at best, capable of promoting adaptive learning rather than generative learning. The design emphasis for such systems is one of efficient data processing rather than one of communication, and consequently the role of these systems in the development of new organisational perceptions is limited. The information system is conceived as a tool for conscious and rational deployment to create a specified data collation in order to service an explicit pre-defined function.

4.2. The Impact of Process Oriented Systems

Because they allow integration of data across functional boundaries, and enable communication within and between multi-disciplinary teams, *Process Oriented Systems* are better in terms of the scope of communication supported. However, the system design is essentially geared towards enhancing *process* efficacy and efficiency, communication support is primarily for the support of explicit, prescribed, formal data exchange, and the system does not become transparent to the user.

Typically *Process Oriented Systems* make data available to enable efficacious and effective process execution. They are not designed to enable individuals to engage in generative discourse. It is more likely that any learning that takes place in this context is largely attributable to the organised team-based human interaction (which encompasses formal and informal communication) and is not a direct result of the information system.

4.3. The Impact of Purpose Oriented Systems

In the context of learning organisations and core competence development, the significance of human *being* is paramount. The relationship between the individual sense of being and organisational being and performance is the subject of many writers on organisational capability, behaviour and performance (see for example Hamel and Prahalad, 1994; Kanter, 1984). In this section some ideas of human *being* as invoked in Heidegger's concept of *Dasein* or, literally, "being there" (Heidegger, 1962) are employed to explore the concept of *Purpose Orientated Systems*.

4.3.1. Ontic Transcendence. The notion of what Dreyfus (1991) translates as "ontic transcendence" is important in understanding the limitations of *Function* and *Process* oriented *Systems* and in elucidating the concept of *Purpose Oriented Systems*.

Function and *Process Oriented Systems* limit the possibilities of ontic transcendence. These systems have a fixed articulation of what they are supposed to do and how they are supposed to be used. Their specification is based on snapshot views of what the *Espoused Theory* demands and there is little *discourse* about the significance of these systems. The design of these systems is predicated on the implementation of subject-object distinctions, and is "closed" to alteration by mere human *being*.

As explained by Dreyfus (in Magee, 1987) Heidegger uses the word *clearing* for human *being* as an openness to things in a situation. We are in a shared *clearing* in which entities can be encountered. According to him, it is the understanding of being in a shared public clearing that makes possible the individual activity of *clearing*. Hence, *Dasein* has an *attunement* -a wholeness of being which includes its context. In the case of *Purpose Oriented Systems*, the *significance* of the information system is dynamic -the information system makes sense in the context of whatever use it is put to. Heidegger refers to this as the *referential totality of significance*.

As indicated in Figure 1, there are two practical considerations related to the embodiment of this concept.

Firstly, the realisation of such systems is only possible when the use of IT becomes integrated into the organisational *Gestalt*. The dominant organisational *Weltanschauung* in such a scenario would be one where IT-based systems are used *transparently* in human existence in the wider organisational context. The concept of transparency is key to the definition of *Purpose Oriented Systems* as it makes it easier for the *referential totality of significance* of the system to be realised.

Secondly, the implementation of such systems demands plastic interfaces. The term "plastic interface" is employed to connote dynamic, context-sensitive, user-tailored interfaces, enabling the information system to be *to hand* contiguously for formal and informal communication. Whilst currently there is a dearth of examples of such interfaces, the technological development trajectory promises a realisation of this concept presently.

4.3.2. Embodiment of Time. As described earlier, the conceptualisation of *Function oriented Systems* and *Process Oriented Systems* is in terms of precisely defined, discrete (in terms of timing, function and process) behaviour specification circumscribed by the *Espoused Theory*. In other words these systems serve an institutionalised specification. The conceptualisation of *Purpose Oriented Systems* on the other hand is in terms of human existence and endeavour in the context of the dynamic *Theory in Use*. The conceptualisation of these systems encompasses IT-dependent and non-IT-dependent informing capabilities, and the *significance* of the information system is dynamically *realised* by the employment of the system.

4.3.3. Authenticity. The literature on learning organisations (see Senge, 1990, for example) underlines the importance of personal authenticity in the organisational context. By the nature of their conception (based on the directive, *Espoused Theory*) and design (validated against discrete input/process/output models) *Function Oriented Systems and Process Oriented Systems* minimise the scope for innovative uses of the system capabilities. Rather, their form dictates process and function execution to the humans that interact with them. It is conceivable that not only do such systems fail to promote authenticity, they actually embody "technicity"—the attempt of modern man to dominate the earth by controlling beings that are considered as objects. *Purpose Oriented Systems* on the other hand are open to realisation of significance by the individual and hence it is argued that they support authenticity. The potential of *Purpose Oriented Systems* to enhance the authenticity of individuals who not only operate in the context but are *of* the context is significant but it can only be realised in the organisational climate of individual empowerment and shared vision.

5. CONCLUSION

The definition of information introduced earlier in this paper is attuned to the concept of human *being* "embodying time". According to this definition information is that which "gives new form" to an individual's perception. The way that *Function Oriented Systems* and *Process Oriented Systems* are conceptualised makes them impoverished in terms of their capability to generate new perceptions. This is because they are grounded in embodying the formal organisational perception articulated by *Espoused Theory*. Innovation comes from *Theory in Use*. In terms of developing *Dasein*, information systems should:

- be open to the realisation of Heidegger's *referential totality of* (their) *significance*,
- support individual authenticity, and
- be changing in time to maintain attunement in their context.

The concept of *Purpose Oriented Systems* was introduced to explore the significance of these aspects. The term "Purpose Oriented" was not chosen to reflect the notion of considered rational goal orientation. Rather, it was chosen to reflect the notion of *Dasein* pressing into new possibilities, that is, the notion of sensemaking in the context of "that for the sake of which" *being* is directed at any given time. The characterisation of such systems as having open, plastic interfaces (complementing the notion of *clearing* discussed earlier) to enable discovery of new perceptions which are not circumscribed by the *Espoused Theory* is key to the effective use of information systems within the dynamic context of the learning organisation.

REFERENCES

Argyris, C. and Schon, D., 1978, *Organisational Learning: A Theory of Action Perspective*, Addison-Wesley, Reading, Massachusetts.

Dreyfus, H. L., 1991 *Being-in-the-World*, MIT Press, New Baskerville.

Hamel, G. and Prahalad, C., 1994, *Competing for the Future*, Harvard Business School Press, Boston.

Hammer, M., 1990, Re-Engineering Work, Don't Automate, Obliterate, *Harvard Business Review*, July-Aug **1990**: 104–112.

Heidegger, M., 1962 *Being and Time*, (translated by Macquarrie, J. and Robinson, E.), Harper & Row, New York.

Kanter, R. M., 1984, *The Change Masters: Corporate Entrepreneurs at Work*, Allen & Unwin, London.

Magee, B., 1987, *The Great Philosophers*, p. 245–277, Oxford University Press, Oxford.

Merali, Y. and Frearson, N., 1995, Information and Realisation, unpublished Research Note, Warwick Business School.

Merali, Y., 1995, Information Systems: Assembling the Gestalt, unpublished working paper, Warwick Business School.

Merali, Y. and McGee, J., 1995, Getting Change From The Firm's IT Investments: Informing Infrastructures and Core Competence Management, paper given at the 15th Annual Strategic Management Society Conference, Mexico City, (October 1995).

Peteraf, M. A., 1993, The cornerstones of competitive advantage: a resource-based view, *Strategic Management Journal*, **14**: 179–191.

Porter, M. E. and Millar, V.E., 1985, How information gives you competitive advantage, *Harvard Business Review*, July-Aug **1985**: 149–160

Senge, P., 1992, *The Fifth Discipline: the Art and Practice of the Learning Organisation*, Century Business, London.,

Stonier, T 1990, *Information and the Internal Structure of the Universe*, Springer-Verlag., Berlin.

99

A CRITICAL ANALYSIS OF THE THESIS THAT SYSTEMS ARE SUBJECTIVE CONSTRUCTS

Stephen K. Probert

Department of Computer Science
Birkbeck College
University of London
Malet Street
London, WC1E 7HX
United Kingdom
Tel: +44 171 631 6717; Fax: +44 171 631 6727
Email: skp@dcs.bbk.ac.uk

1. INTRODUCTION

In information systems (IS) projects, it may well be a sensible strategy to treat the computer as a "black box", if this results in an increase in systems practitioners' abilities to design new information systems with greater freedom than would otherwise be the case, but it will be argued that treating information systems as subjective constructs tends to trivialise the importance of crucial, technical aspects of such systems. Furthermore, IS projects (at any rate) generally have economic objectives, and many (if not most) other systems projects are highly constrained by economic considerations—both in terms of objectives and resources. Treating information systems as subjective constructs leads to a tendency to deny (or ignore) the importance of these crucial aspects of most IS projects. It can be argued that the same is true for (virtually) all projects aimed at improving socio-technical systems. It will be concluded that socio-technical systems are best treated as being actual wholes (containing both social and technical components).

2. INFORMATION SYSTEMS AS CONTAINING BOTH SOCIAL AND TECHNICAL ASPECTS

Recently, there has been an increasing tendency to treat information systems as, by and large, subjective "constructs". This approach is largely a product of the Soft Systems Methodology (SSM) advocates (e.g. Checkland, 1981; Checkland and Scholes, 1990; Lewis, 1994). But information systems are not purely subjective constructs—they have ob-

Systems for Sustainability, edited by Stowell *et al.*
Plenum Press, New York, 1997

jective features such as processors, storage media, etc. (i.e. hardware); there is a good reason why these features should not be construed as "ultimately unknowable external reality" to use Lewis's (1994, p. 179) phrase. To do so would give these features an almost magical unintelligibility—and may give practitioners a feeling of powerlessness in the face of the unknown (and, on a subjectivist's view, the unknowable). The use of subjectivist terminology reduces the technical aspects of information systems to that of being mere noumena, and consequently denies their intelligibility. Moreover, it is worth noting that some advocates of the often-supposed intellectual basis (phenomenology) for such a manoeuvre do not seem to support such an endeavour. Husserl (who championed phenomenology) himself thought that to trivialise objective realities by (discursively) rendering them as "social constructs" was a wholly illegitimate move, "...[T]here is a certain disadvantage involved in saying, 'there is only absolute consciousness', as if one wished to say: all other being is only seeming... This would, of course, be *fundamentally false*. The objects of nature are evidently true objects. Their being is true being... It is fundamentally false to apply to such being a standard other [than] the one it itself requires in accordance with its category and to discredit something because it is 'constituted' or rooted in consciousness." (Husserl, cited in Bernet, Kern and Marbach, p. 57). So if we wish to understand the technical aspects of information systems then, according to Husserl, we should accord these features "true being", i.e. we should accept that they exist ("in themselves").

2.1. Philosophical and Empirical Critiques of Subjectivism

At a more fundamental level, treating information systems as subjective constructs is certainly to fall into the trap of all subjectivist philosophy; the trap of needing to pose unintelligible "worlds (i.e. noumena) behind" the apparent world (i.e. phenomena), "He who interprets by searching behind the phenomenal world for a world-in-itself (*Welt an sich*) which forms its foundation and support, acts mistakenly like someone who wants to find in the riddle the reflection of a being which lies behind it, a being mirrored in the riddle, in which it is contained." (Adorno, 1977, p. 127). As well as being philosophically (highly) problematical the subjectivist's view does not accord well with many recent empirical studies, which indicate that the social and technical aspects of information systems are actually intertwined. One symptom of this can be exemplified by the fact that, in many organisations, the (old) "information technology (IT) = possible solution" formula has given way to an "IT = possible opportunity" formula, "The increasing tendency for organizations to privilege innovation over efficiency...places a particular stress upon the human qualities of flexibility and creativity which even the 'impersonal machinery'... of IT hardware cannot yet provide." (Scarbrough and Corbett, 1992, p. 19). The end result of the shift in emphasis concerning the role of IT (from "solution" to "enabler") has two important implications for our understanding of work in IS. Firstly, the role of people as utilisers (rather than users) of information systems is enhanced; secondly, it becomes more difficult to set a clear boundary between people and the IT with which they interact, "...[T]echnology and organization are not ontologically separate categories, but rather mirror reflections of a mutual interchange of knowledge, meanings and political interests." (Scarbrough and Corbett, 1992, p. 157). Such a view actually requires that a new, more appropriate (but inevitably more complex), theory of the role that technology plays in shaping the culture of organisations (and vice versa) is employed. As Scarbrough and Corbett note, "...[T]he relationship between technology and organization is neither one of 'impacts' [of IT] nor of 'choice' [made by managers] *per se*. Rather, technology and organization are closely intertwined through flows of knowledge and ideas which transcend the individual organization but which find expression in, and are reinforced by, political interests and agendas at the organizational level." (Scarbrough and Corbett, 1992, p. 157).

2.2. "Hard" and "Soft" Systems Approaches?

If Scarbrough and Corbett are even approximately right, then it would seem *prima facie* that simplistic distinctions between "hard" ("objectivist") and "soft" (subjectivist) systems approaches to IS development will not be adequate forms of conceptualisation for IS development and utilisation—two notions which themselves may be much more intertwined than is often acknowledged (see e.g. Fitzgerald, 1990; Paul, 1995). As Gardner (*et al.*) argue, the need now is for "tailorable" systems to be put in place; in such systems the concepts of 'developer' and 'user' (and 'technology' and 'organisation') are increasingly blurred, "A computer system is tailorable if it provides a user with control over its operation. This means a user should be able to regulate or operate the system, thus providing ultimate power to direct or manipulate a system's behaviour... A control is understood to be a device or interface widget that enables a user to regulate or operate a system and provides the user with the power to direct or determine its state." (Gardner, *et al.*, 1995, p. 187). Such considerations from the world of IS practice have important implications for systems concepts also. A "binary opposition" view of the distinction between "objectivism" and subjectivism is surely inappropriate when the "objects" in the research area contain such intertwinings between technical and social aspects; the tailorability of an IS is surely an emergent property of the possibilities (and the constraints) created by definite technical "configurations", and the actual social arrangements, pertaining in the situation. Adorno (1973a; 1973b; 1978; 1982) conducted research into the relationship between subjects and objects; he argued that a legitimate separation between subjects and objects can be made, but generally this distinction is not made in an appropriate manner, "The separation of subject and object is both real and illusory. True, because in the cognitive realm it serves to express the real separation, the dichotomy of the human condition, a coercive development. False, because the resulting separation must not be hypostatised, not magically transformed into an invariant." (Adorno, 1978, pp. 498–499). The separation between subject and object is, on this view, a feature of economic (rather than ontological) reality; this view is explained in further detail below.

3. SUBJECTIVITY AND CRITIQUE

Adorno considers that "the subject" makes possible the idea of critique—of a critical interpretation of the world (or a part of it, such as an actual socio-technical system). But the concept of 'the subject' is an intellectual construction—an abstraction—derived from (and not prior to) actual, real, living individuals, "It is evident that the abstract concept of the transcendental subject—its thought forms, their unity, and the original productivity of consciousness—presupposes what it promises to bring about: actual, live individuals." (Adorno, 1978, p. 500). It should be noted that this is a Nietzschean argument (e.g. Nietzsche, 1956, pp. 178–180), and this debt is acknowledged by Adorno (1982). Although we can treat the subject as real (or "standing in for" real, live individuals) in Adorno's view the subject does not "make the world up" (this is often termed 'constructivism'—Adorno uses the term 'constitute' instead of 'construct'), "While our images of perceived reality may very well be *Gestalten* [*Weltanschaunngen* - in SSM jargon], the world in which we live is not; it is constituted differently than out of mere images of perception." (Adorno, 1977, p. 126). However, Adorno does not argue for a return to "vulgar objectivism", because this would deny the possibility of a critical interpretation of the actual circumstances. The world is certainly "real enough", but what we see is always mediated by concepts (although we may not be aware of this all of the time), "What must be eliminated is the illusion that ... the totality of consciousness, is the world, and not the self-contemplation of knowledge. The last thing the critique of epistemology ... is supposed to do is proclaim unmediated objectivism." (Adorno, 1982, p. 27). In the earlier quotation (above) concerning "perceived reality", what Adorno means by 'constituted differently' is that the world is, to a large extent, determined by economic realities, which he sometimes refers to using the term 'exchange', "The living human individual, as he is forced to act in the role for which he has been marked internally as well, is the *homo oeconomicus* incarnate, closer to the transcendental subject than to the living individual for which he immediately cannot but take himself... What shows up in the doctrine of the transcendental subject is the priority of the relations—abstractly rational ones, detached from the human individuals and their relationships - that have their model in exchange. If the exchange form is the standard social structure, its rationality constitutes people; what they are for themselves, what they seem to be for themselves, is secondary." (Adorno, 1978, p. 501).

3.1. Systems Analysis and Economic Reality

For Adorno (as for IS professionals) the world of economic activity is very real, and an increasing (managerial) demand is placed on IS professionals to economically justify their activities, "Somebody pays for what analysts and designers deliver. New systems have to be justified by the benefits that they deliver. It is easy to use terms like "the users" and "user management"...and forget that they are subtitles for "the customer"." (Yeates, Shields and Helmy, 1994, p. 2). In fact, the systems analyst should be seen not purely as some sort of enquiring transcendental subject, but as an economically-constituted actuality. Adorno argued that critique is only possible if some status is given to the subject who can become critically aware of these sort of circumstances. Therefore Adorno preserves a critical role for the subject; moreover, a role which transcends the "binary oppositional" approaches of "positivism" and "interpretivism", "To use the strength of the subject to break through the fallacy of constitutive subjectivity... Stringently to transcend the official separation of pure philosophy and the substantive or formally scientific realm..." (Adorno, 1973b, p. xx). At the very least, the economic activities which generate systems development projects have a key determining role on the analysts' foci of attention in the project; systems analysts do not generate knowledge purely in the interest of advancing science (a point which "computer scientists" might like to take note of!).

3.2. Critical Systems Analysis

Dialectically conceived, subjectivity is that which allows us to develop a critical interpretation of events (organisations, information systems, etc.), but it is not responsible for the precise forms these things actually take, i.e. subjects do not "make them up", but they may criticise such things, "Dialectically conceived "subjectivity" is historically formed and yet not reducible to historical determinations; historical subjectivity is reconstructed from the framework of reflective critique in that the limits of constitutive synthesis establish the range of possible experience. Only in such reflective reconstruction of the genesis of subjectivity is it possible to distinguish between real possibilities and those modes of appearance that are but abstract illusions...So conceived, the dialectical notion of subjectivity is a fundamental category of critical reason. In reflective reconstructions of self-formation processes, it is possible to show the pseudo-necessity of socially unnecessary motives and to thereby promote a reversal of consciousness that can dissolve the causality of these objective illusions." (Schroyer, 1973, pp. xii-xiii). Consequently, subjectivity can help us to free our thoughts from purely economic considerations (should we so wish), such that we can conceive of critical alternatives to the actual current arrangements; i.e. we may critically analyze (but not "mentally construct" in an arbitrary manner) actual socio-technical systems. In this respect, it seems reasonable to suggest that the systems with which the systems movement as a whole is concerned with are generally best conceived as socio-technical systems, and as such they can best be conceived of as being actual wholes (systems).

4. CONCLUSION

The tendency to treat systems as being subjective constructs has been critically analyzed. IS projects (at any rate) generally have economic objectives, and many (if not most) other systems projects are highly constrained by economic considerations—both in terms of objectives and resources. Treating information systems as subjective constructs leads to a tendency to deny (or ignore) the importance of these crucial aspects of most IS projects - at least in the literature! However, an ineliminable (dialectical) element of subjectivity, in both systems research and practice, provides us with a basis for the development of critical interpretations of the socio-technical systems that are actually being studied/analyzed both by practitioners and researchers. Work is in progress (by the author) to develop guidelines for the employment of critical (dialectical) subjectivity in systems research and systems practice.

REFERENCES

Adorno, T. W., 1973a, *The Jargon of Authenticity*, Routledge, London.
Adorno, T. W., 1973b, *Negative Dialectics*, Routledge, London.
Adorno, T. W., 1977, The actuality of philosophy, *Telos* 31: 120–133.
Adorno, T. W., 1978, Subject and object, in: *The Essential Frankfurt School Reader* (A. Arato and E. Gebhardt, eds.), pp. 497–511, Blackwell, Oxford.
Adorno, T. W., 1982, *Against Epistemology: A Metacritique*, Blackwell, Oxford.
Bernet, R., Kern, I., and Marbach, E., 1993, *An Introduction to Husserlian Phenomenology*, Northwestern University Press, Evanston.
Checkland, P., 1981, *Systems Thinking, Systems Practice*, Wiley, Chichester.
Checkland, P., and Scholes, J., 1990, *Soft Systems Methodology in Action*, Wiley, Chichester
Fitzgerald, G., 1990, Achieving flexible information systems: the case for improved analysis, Jnl. of Inf. Tech. 5: 5–11.
Gardner, L. A., Paul, R. J., and Patel, N., 1995, Moving beyond the fixed point theorem with Tailorable information systems, in: *Proceedings of the 3rd European Conference on Information Systems, Athens/Greece, June 1–3 1995* (G. Doukidis, B. Galliers, T. Jelassi, H. Krcmar and F. Land, eds.), pp. 183–192.
Lewis, P., 1994, *Information-Systems Development*, Pitman, London.
Nietzsche, F., 1956, *The Birth of Tragedy and the Genealogy of Morals*, Doubleday, New York.
Paul, R. J., 1995, An O.R. view of information systems development, in: *Operational Research Tutorial Papers 1995* (M. Lawrence and C. Wilsdon, eds.), pp. 46–56, Operational Research Society, Birmingham.

Rorty, R., 1980, *Philosophy and the Mirror of Nature*, Oxford University Press, Oxford.
Scarbrough, H., and Corbett, J. M., 1992, *Technology and Organization: Power, Meaning and Design*, Routledge, London.
Schroyer, T., 1973, Foreword, in: T. Adorno, *The Jargon of Authenticity*, pp. vii-xvii, Routledge, London.
Yeates, D., Shields, M., and Helmy, D., 1994, *Systems Analysis and Design*, Pitman, London.

100

A SYSTEMS APPROACH TO STRATEGIC IS INTEGRATION

K. A. Reynolds, A. J. S. Thethi, and C. E. R. Wainwright

The CIM Institute
Cranfield University
Cranfield, Bedfordshire, MK43 0AL

1. SUMMARY

This paper considers strategic Information System (IS) integration from a systems perspective. First it considers the changing role of Information Technology (IT) over the last two decades from localised technologies to process wide IS integration. A discussion of the limitations of systems methodologies follows. This discusses the use of systems modelling to aid IS integration. The paper then proposes a decision based mechanism which evaluates information flows in the business process from a holistic perspective. This mechanism consists of three modules: Audit, Assessment and Suggestion which identify information bottlenecks and appraise possible IT investments from operational, strategic and financial viewpoints.

2. INTRODUCTION

Within the last two decades, the role of Information Technology (IT) in organisations has shifted from one of operational gain to one of strategic benefit. Initially IT was owned at a department level and its investment was justified using labour cost reduction estimates and the time required to payback the original investment cost. As Personal Computer (PC) performance and capability improved, the use of IT significantly improved efficiency levels, however within organisations the lack of an integrated approach often reduced the effectiveness of these technological investments.

At this time, organisational reform initiatives such as Business Process Re-engineering (BPR) argued that IT should be used to re-design and improve the business processes instead of supporting ineffective and out-dated processes (Davenport, 1993). This process approach required widespread commitment and understanding across the organisation. Information systems integration was usually troublesome and time consuming as it required a high degree of data consistency and reliability. This was especially difficult considering

Systems for Sustainability, edited by Stowell *et al.*
Plenum Press, New York, 1997

the comprehensive nature of these new technologies and the lack of ownership and control at a local level. The benefit of process orientated IT investments was also difficult to evaluate. Intangible strategic benefits were difficult to quantify, so investment appraisal relied on local financial evaluation techniques such as payback and discounted cash flows. The risk of failure associated with these IT investments and their respective integration was also high, hence organisation's were reluctant to release the full potential of information systems.

Another influence was the contradictory nature of IT expenditure in organisations. Whilst other divisional budgets were reducing costs, the IT expenditure per employee increased. This often led to discussions of the necessity to keep all IT in-house, especially considering the increased investment required and the accelerated pace of technology. Subsequently, many large organisations out-sourced large portions of their IT departments. Hence, the integration of information systems within the organisation has become increasingly difficult given its alternative roles of strategic importance and operational improvement. This is usually combined with the reduced ownership and control as information systems are often enterprise wide and large portions may be out-sourced external to the organisation. The consideration of these factors suggested the utilisation of a systems approach to evaluate the strategic integration of information systems.

3. A SYSTEMS APPROACH

The term 'system' is often used in different contexts and by different disciplines causing much confusion in the process. Aktas defines a system as *"an organised collection of people, machines, procedures, documents, data, or any other entities such that they interact with each other as well as with their environment to reach a pre-defined goal"* (Aktas, 1987, p.1). This definition is typical of the systems engineering or hard system methodologies domain where a system and its objectives are clearly defined. Here, models of alternative systems are first developed and tested using criteria which relates to the system's objectives. Conversely, soft systems are associated with ill-defined problems and often those involving human activity where the process of enquiry is seen as the system (Checkland, 1990).

Hard System Methodologies (HSM's) were developed in the early 1970's in response to the lengthy and costly failures occurring in information system development. These methods concentrated on the approach used to design an information system. Despite the changing focus from software development to IT procurement and integration, these methods are still popular within industry today (Baines, Small and Colquhoun, 1996).

The most common HSM's include Structured Systems Analysis and Design Method (SSADM), Structured Analysis and Design Technique/Integrated Computer Aided Manufacturing Definition (SADT/IDEF). These modelling techniques are used to create functional requirement specifications which define the information requirements of an organisation. SSADM and IDEF assume a top down approach. A high level diagram depicts the entire system. This then allows gradual and controlled development of increasing detail at lower levels. One of the major constraints of these techniques is the rigid structure they impose on the process. The process is split into activities and its respective inputs and outputs. This description can often ignore the flexibility issues and emergent properties of the holistic process.

Another limitation of these modelling techniques is their static nature. They only present the situation at one point in time and from one viewpoint, therefore models have to be regularly updated to remain useful. These models cannot readily adapt to changes in the business environment as it requires time to produce an extensive description. An information system will require a large quantity of these models each containing detailed information. Computer Aided Software Engineering (CASE) tools can be used to ease the repetition as they automate the modelling process making modifications easier. Unfortunately, any modifications can escalate through the modelling hierarchy causing unintentional amendments.

In response to some of these limitations, Checkland proposed his Soft Systems Methodology (SSM) for information system development (1981;1990). He argued that the structured approach of HSM was appropriate for man-made systems where boundaries and objectives were well defined, however most systems were far more complex in practice and so a broader and more adaptive methodology was required. When used in the information system domain, the SSM would determine what information the organisation requires before using HSM's to determine how this information is to be presented.

Although Checkland's SSM presents an eloquent solution, in reality his methodologies are rarely used for information system development. A recent survey found only 4% of 88 manufacturing enterprises had encountered SSM and a second survey of 22 manufacturing enterprises using modelling techniques found only 5% used SSM, in comparison to 37% using Data Flow Diagrams (DFD) and 20% using SSADM techniques (Baines et al., 1996). It could be argued that these are engineering environments and therefore likely to persist with HSM's, however a survey of SSM users listed one of its problems as difficulty in connecting SSM to information systems (Mingers and Taylor, 1991).

4. THE INFORMATION INTEGRATION MECHANISM

Consequently an information integration mechanism is proposed (Figure 1). This combines the structured domain of HSM with the adaptive nature and multiple viewpoints of SSM. It seeks to highlight the most appropriate information integration opportunities for IT investment based on impact to information throughput and the effect the investment will have on the financial performance indicators. Hence, it is a valuable tool for all organisations who need to target focused areas of the process for investment, yet want the benefits to impact the whole business.

Any new IT investment has to be integrated across the business process, therefore its effectiveness is dependent on the legacy systems already in place. Two IT investment projects may be incompatible or mutually exclusive. Within HSM, the cumulative effect of several IT projects would be a difficult scenario to model. Whereas this mechanism allows the simulation of the process and an adaptive approach instead of a static, snap-shot approach. This mechanism considers the IT constraints and identifies the best use of the IT budget from strategic, operational and financial viewpoints. This is particularly useful to organisation's with little process knowledge who cannot easily assess the importance of new technologies to their organisation. Often IT suppliers are left to explain the benefits and costs of each system, whereas this mechanism allows an objective suggestion based on various scenarios of the investment's effect on the whole business.

The mechanism comprises of three modules which have synergical benefit but also have their own objectives. A software tool has been created to validate the mechanism. This is to be used in industrial case studies where the IS environment is to be modelled and an optimum solution for IT investment proposed. The modules which make up the mechanism are explained in greater detail below.

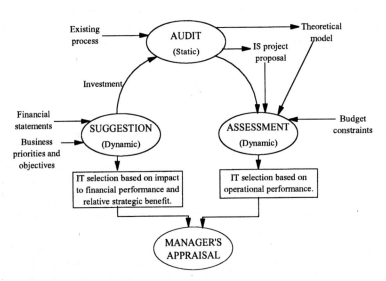

Figure 1. A conceptual model of the information integration mechanism.

4.1. The Audit Module

The Audit module is used to describe the existing situation of the information flows within the business process. A generic process model is used as the main template. An organisation uses this as a base and can expand or reduce the number of activities within the process according to their own characteristics, for example sales and purchasing may be two separate departments in one organisation or just one in another. The arrival and service rate of each information flow in the process are inputted into the Audit Module. The mechanism can then calculate the information throughput, wait time and resource utilisation of the process using queuing theory techniques. This creates a profile of the steady state condition of the existing process.

4.2. The Assessment Module

This module uses the framework created in the Audit module to simulate the dynamic, current situation. The aim is to target investment opportunities which will benefit the whole organisation. It is a rule based simulation which examines the method of information transfer between different information systems and business activities. The existing process is compared to an ideal theoretical process model. Using sensitivity analysis, the information bottlenecks can be identified. IS project proposals can then be assessed through simulation to determine the effect of individual or sets of IS projects on the operational performance of the organisation.

4.3. The Suggestion Module

The Suggestion Module evaluates the implications of new investments based on the IS project scenarios created in the Assessment Module. The operational improvements calculated for each scenario such as resource utilisation and throughput are linked with the organisations financial indicators such as gearing, cash flow, sales revenue and Return on Investment (ROI). The mechanism then suggests the optimum selection of IS projects based on the organisation's priorities and budget constraints, thus providing a useful mechanism for investment appraisal.

5. CONCLUSIONS

The Information Integration Mechanism is a useful technique for organisations seeking to achieve holistic benefits from IT investments. It combines operation research techniques and accounting principles to evaluate the merit of technological investment on an organisation. This mechanism uses a systems approach whilst seeking to avoid some of the limitations associated with systems modelling. Unlike HSM it has been developed for the strategic integration of IS. It uses simulation techniques to provide a dynamic analysis of processes instead of static models. SSM tends not to be used for information system development as users have expressed difficulties in connecting to IS, although its use in broad, ill-defined situations is acknowledged. This mechanism examines the process at an information flow level whilst considering the business objectives of the whole organisation. This mechanism is particularly useful when assessing IT investments from different viewpoints.

REFERENCES

Aktas, A.Z., 1987, *Structured Analysis and Design of Information Systems*, Prentice-Hall Inc. Englewood Cliffs.

Baines, R.W., Small, C.A. and Colquhoun, G.J., 1996, Modelling methods in the manufacturing change process, in: *Advances In Manufacturing Technology*, Proceedings of the Twelfth National Conference on Manufacturing Research, University of Bath, September 1996,(A.N. Bramley, A.R. Mileham and G.W. Owen, eds.) pp 91–95, University of Bath, UK.

Checkland, P., 1981, *Systems Thinking, Systems Practice*, John Wiley and Sons Inc., Chichester, UK.

Checkland, P and Scholes, J., 1990, *Soft Systems Methodology in Action*, John Wiley and Sons Inc., Chichester, UK.

Davenport, T.H., 1993, *Process Innovation: Re-engineering Work through Information Technology*, Harvard Business School Press, Boston, Massachusetts, USA.

Mingers, J. And Taylor, S. 1991, The Use of Soft Systems Methodology in Practice - A Survey of Potential Users (Part 2), Working Paper No. 19, Warwick Business School Research Bureau, Warwick University, Coventry, UK.

101

INFORMATION WITHIN THE (HUMAN) SYSTEM

Some Implication for Information Systems Concept

Antonín Rosický

Department of System Analysis
University of Economics, Prague
Winston Churchill Sguare 4
130 67 Praha 3, Czech republic
e-mail: rosicky@vse.cz

1. INTRODUCTION

The present days are usually called an "information society" on the one side and "turbulent times" on the other. We live and manage business activities "in chaos" despite being aware of the value of information and taking advantage of the vast power of modern information technology. Why is it like this if information is "negentropy" and its wealth removes uncertainties, reduces chaos and gives order?

The same problems—perhaps in a differently formulated form—emerge on the lower level of business life: Professionals from the information systems domain reflect on the failures of IS (Lyytinen 1988) and desire better methods of design. Businessmen think about the efficiency of used information technology and reduce massive investments to IT (Earl, 1992). Also managers search for radical ways of working. perhaps re-engineering represents the major stream among them. Hammer and Champy (1993, p. 38) base re-engineering on four terms: "Fundamental", "Radical", "Dramatic" and "Processes".

Let us consider only the partial success of "more sophisticated and better structured" methodologies and the fact, that the main reason of IS failures is mentioned by Lyytinen (1988). Such dramatic change of our thought about information systems could be useful for fundamental improvements to IS. It seems that "getting to the roots of things"—to the information process within business organizations, to the nature of information itself—presents a feasible way.

2. INFORMATION WITHIN SYSTEMS

The information is an extraordinary phenomenon not just in its importance, but also in a range of meaning which is covered by its concept: From the previously mentioned

Systems for Sustainability, edited by Stowell *et al.*
Plenum Press, New York, 1997

negentropy and property (or a miracle?) of reality and genetic information of living systems on the one side, through empiric data taken in well structured databases and message transmitted by TV, to human knowledge on the other... It seems that the major stumbling block lies in two basic significances that are complementary to one another:

- *Information as a basic feature* of a system. In this sense information determines systems organization and we create its recognized image - information about system. Organization, determined in this way isn't an "order", that we can distinguish and use as a framework for building our models.
- *Information as meaning* of its receiver. In this sense information emerges as a relationship between systems or between a system and its some elements. In human systems the meaning of information evolves by interpretations upon a recognized image and the knowledge of a receiver and becomes evident as its behavior.

Similarly Stonier (1990, p. 17) regards information as a *property of universe*, and argues: *In contrast to physical information, there exists human information which includes information created, interpreted, organized or transmitted by human beings.*

Our major concern is with human information but a concept of "meaningful information" is wider. In this conception information is understood as a view of its receiver, who recognizes its environment from the position of his shared purposes or intentions. The concept of information has a character of a relation between the recognized system and a recognizing element. In other words: Meaningful information isn't an objective "internal" information of the system, but it is a purposefully recognized image of its internal information—it is an external "information about system".

3. INFORMATION AND ADAPTABILITY

We needn't accept Stonier's concept of "information as a property of the universe" but it is not possible to doubt that genetic information is the internal information of living systems. The basic purpose of living systems is the survival (of system as the species) and these systems adapt to the external environment—changes genetic (proper internal) information through the process of evolution. Meaningful information presents an outside impetus for the living system (receiver). Systems behavior as a suitable response results from the meaning which the system assigns to this impetus (see fig. 1).

It seems suitable to mention some important conditions necessary for systems evolution, known from biology (Fleger 1994). Four of them, validated on a general level, are interesting for our topic:

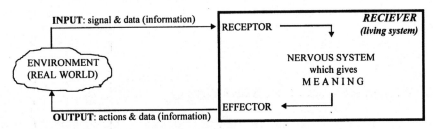

Figure 1. Information in system's interaction with its environment and selforganization.

- The variety of a system (systems elements) which results in the possibility of different responses to the same input impetus in various ways in the end.
- Nondeterministic character of a system, that is founded on accidental or uncertain behavior of systems elements. In other words: The ambiguity and uncertainty inside a system is necessary.
- The evolution is opportunistic and the adaptation to present conditions leads to systems improvement and it hasn't the ability to optimize.
- Evolution doesn't signify a progress and system improvement, it is only the result of systems adjustment to its environment.

In conclusion we can say that the adaptable system must be fit to respond to the same input impetus in various ways. In other words: The possibility to interpret the same information in different and individual ways is necessary for systems adaptability. A higher scope for individual interpretation offers a better opportunity for adaptability.

Considering the hierarchy of systems complexity (Boulding, 1956) meaningful information emerges with open systems. Systems on a higher level interact more with their environment—they are more dependent on information on the one side, but they have wider possibilities of behavior on the other. These systems have better "nervous systems" that involves better recognition of the environment and have wider framework for their behavior.

4. HUMAN INFORMATION

The phenomena of a human considered from a systems viewpoint presents very high complexity, which is given by a mind and a consciousness. From our view we stress two important aspects:

- Humans are "animal symbolicus"—they have the ability of abstract thought and use symbols for the expression of information.
- Human beings are intentional—their activities, including cognition and the acquisition or creation of information is a token of their intentions (an effort to be objective is the particular intention).

If we take information in management and business into account, we always consider meaningful information, presented through particular characters, usually there are terms of some language but gestures and other signs of nonverbal communication are important for interpersonal communication... Those characters, that carry meaning and (or) information are data conveyed by, physical signals. To obtain or better to create information we must go to the higher levels of mental processes of interpretation (Liebenau and Backhouse, 1990). Nevertheless the physical world of used signals isn't the same as the system (real or abstract) depicted by these data. Human cognition lies between recognized systems on the one side and signals, data and information on the other (see fig. 2).

Figure 2. Information as a product of human cognition and interpretation.

Despite often-mentioned differences between data and (human or meaningful) information they are considered only as an academic discussion not only by technologically oriented "designers of IS", but by most managers too. Let us point out the idea of Peter Drucker (1989, p. 209): *Information is data endowed with relevance and purpose. Converting data into information thus requires knowledge.*

5. INFORMATION, KNOWLEDGE, AND RATIONALITY

Also Stonier, when noticing human information, argues: *The term "information" includes "data" on the one hand, and "knowledge", "insight" and "wisdom" on the other. A datum is a small chunk of information. Usually the term information is thought of as organized data, or "facts" organized into coherent pattern.*

The question of converting data into information leads us into the middle of intricate interpretation processes refining human knowledge through mental activities in a recognized context, including particular intentions of an interpreting person. Let us note that human interpretation includes both aspects: semantic which covers the content of signs (ontological cognition) and pragmatic, that assigns the function and the value (teleological). The conceptual character of our knowledge is based on intentionality which is a purely human affair and is narrowly connected with the ability to use mother tongue. Nevertheless we cannot separate human knowledge as a "content of suitable organized memory" from mental processes. Similarly it isn't possible to reduce human mental processes to a logic reasoning or an inference, they cover other ways of thinking as intuition, creating of analogies, evaluating etc. Also human knowledge covers the whole and dynamic framework of knowledge, some procedures, strictly and more loosely formed rules and successfully used patterns of problem solving...

Individual knowledge systems arise or better evolves through the learning process and together with the process of interpretation create closed loop (see fig. 3). Human knowledge is individual, but strongly depends upon the shared culture within society, business organization etc. Winograd and Flores (1986) argue, that "human knowledge is neither subjective nor objective", but it is principally important that they are individual.

An extraordinarily complex system of human knowledge is original and it is not possible to substitute it by sophisticated and formalized procedures (Ennals, 1991, p. 19–31). For a human being knowledge is not less important than data and its individuality is the presupposition for adaptability of social systems.

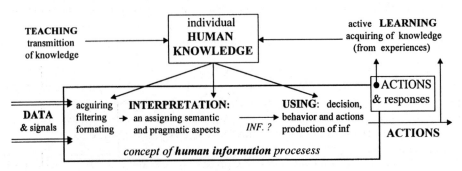

Figure 3. Relationship between information and knowledge through learning.

The interpretation narrowly corresponds with human rationality, including its limits. The positivistic thought reduces rationality to the "procedural rationality" (Simon, 1979) and puts stress on the techniques of problem solving that defines the "information needs" afterward. Those "successful or optimal" procedures are described by (mostly deterministic) models of universal use, that have the character of Stonier's "coherent pattern" mentioned above. The process of interpretation doesn't require knowledge that is included within the used model. Problem solving is reduced to acquiring "correct empirical data" (and pressing buttons of computers).

Nevertheless rationality is a wider affair with more complementary aspects. Herbert Simon defines the substantive rationality (Simon, 1979):

> Behavior is substantively rational, when is appropriate to the achievement of given goals within the limits imposed by given conditions and constraints. Notice that by this definition, the rationality of behavior depends upon the actor, in only a single respect—his goals.

In other words rationality unfolds from individual intentions, defines problems and assigns suitable solving procedures that demarcate the content of used database (see Ackoff, 1989). However rationality isn't an objective matter, but it is the result of individual intentions, knowledge, values and thoughts... Therefore a provision of MIS (IS/IT) asks urguent questions: "Who has created models and programs being used, what values and intentions he has shared and what knowledge he has held". And also "to what extend the user shares these value, intentions and knowledge". Similar questions lead to the concept of individual authenticity and possibilities to decide and to act freely or in different ways and to the adaptability of the whole organization. In these context let us remember F.A. Hayek (1979) that strongly warns against the rationalism.

6. (UNCERTAIN) CONCLUSIONS

The themes mentioned above immediately refer to the conception of information systems within (business) organization. The novelty and fantastic possibilities of modern IT results in prevailing consideration of IS as the same computer based IS (IS/IT). These information systems are designed as artifacts, which are built as a business commodity, which considers human (managers) not as individual interpreters of information, but as anonymous "users" or "clients". Those concept of IS gives unsuspected wings to rationalistic influence upon an organization and opens problems of adaptability of business organizations in the end (which substitutes an ability to react quickly). The concept of IS/IT has two "advantages": It allows designers to use means derived from traditional engineering methods (Crowe, 1993) and it apparently relieves managers of responsibility for the information.

However the information interpreted through individual knowledge is the essential feature not only for a human himself, but for whole organizations (Rosický, 1995). The "understanding information" influencing organizational culture, learning and structure supports basic properties of organizations and their success in business management too. To accept the concept "human information" and consider "its uncertainty as the opportunity" (advantage) results in the concept of a social character of an information system. The wider and more subtle concept of IS as a human matter using (and strongly influenced by) artificial components is more suitable but it gives rise to some problems: We must rather provide and develop than design IS, including managerial knowledge and skills. This approach overtakes the traditional consideration and it demands systems thinking (Stowell, 1993) and individual responsibility of both the IS designers and managers.

If we consider failures of IS/IT (Lyytinen, Hirschheim,1987) the necessity of the radical new concept of information systems which accepts character of human information within an organitazions seems evident. New professions and role of "information" or "hybrid" managers are narrowly connected with the ideas, mentioned in this article.

REFERENCES

Ackoff, R., 1989, From data to Wisdom, in: *Journal of Applied Systems Analysis*, 19, pp. 3–10.

Boulding, K., 1956, General System Theory - The Skeleton of Science, *Management Sciences,* pp. 197–208.

Crowe, M.K., 1993, Engineering Systems, *System Sciences: Addressing Global Issue* (Stowell, West, Howell, eds.), Plenum Press, New York.

Drucker, P., 1989, *The New Realities*, Harper & Row, New York.

Earl, J.M., 1992, Putting IT in its place: a polemic for the nineties, *Journal of Inf. Technology*, No7:100–108.

Ennals, R., 1991, *Artificial Intelligence and Human Institutions*, Springer-Verlag, London.

Flegr, J. 1994, *Mechanismy mikrorevoluce* , Karolinum

Hayek, F.A., 1979, *Law, Legislation and Liberty*, Routlidge, London (Czech: Academia, Praha 1991.

Hammer, M. and Champy, J., 1993, *Re-engineering the Corporation: A Manifesto for Business*, Revolution, Harper Colins, New York (Czech: Management Press, 1995).

Liebenau, J. and Backhouse, J., 1990, *Understanding Information*, London, MacMillan, 1990.

Lyytinen, K., Hirschheim, R., 1987, Information Systems Failures: a surveyand classification of empirical literature, *Oxford Surveys in Information Technology*, 4, 1987.

Rosický, A., 1995, Information for Management and Organization, in: *Interdisciplinary Information Management Talks 95*, Oldenburg, Wien.

Simon, H.A., 1979, From Substantive to Procedural Rationality, *Philosophy and Economic Theory* (Hahn, F. and Mollis, M., eds.), Oxford University Press,Oxford, p. 65–86.

Stonier, T, 1990, *Information and the Internal Structure of the Universe*, Springer-Verlag, London.Stowell, F.A., 1993, Information Systems and Systems Sciences, *Systems Sciences: Addresing Global Issues*, (Stowell, West, Howell, eds.) Plenum Press, New York.

Winograd, T. and Flores, F, 1986, Understanding Computers and Cognition, Ablex Pub. Norwood, NJ.

102

INFORMATION SYSTEMS DEVELOPMENT

Gurmak Singh and Kate Gilbert

Wolverhampton Business School
University of Wolverhampton
Shropshire Campus
Shifnal Road, Priorslee
Telford, TF2 9NT

1. INTRODUCTION

Cognitive Psychology has gained a strong influence in the design of Information Systems. However, systems are still being designed using traditional, scientific methods. These methods provide a singular approach to design of these systems. In this paper we present a dual approach to developing Information Systems. The approach differentiates between the need for customised and flexible-adaptive Information System. The resulting framework encompasses cognitive styles and strategies from the field of Psychology.

The gulf between the designers and users of information systems was recognised over twenty years ago. There was strong evidence that designers operated with a task- and technology- centred approach in the development of information systems (Blackler and Brown, 1986), and developed systems to suit their own cognitive styles rather than those of the users. It is this lack of attention to the differences in the ways humans operate, differences both from machines and from one another, that is a major contributory factor in the under-performance of information systems (Clegg, 1989). This typically and traditionally scientific approach was designed to create systems for rational and objective user and tended to ignore other characteristics, such as, subjectivity, creativity, flexibility and adaptability.

Designers are not able to produce information systems to match the human information-processing models of the users. There are two main reasons for this. The field of cognitive psychology has not yet developed sufficiently, and no specific tools, techniques or methodologies are available to the designers of information systems. Presently, systems designers have to infer the psychological attributes of the users, and so tend to make assumptions that people think in the same way as they do. However this approach, apparently objective but actually subjective, promotes a systems development that does not offer advantages to the user, and creates an additional burden for the designer. Researchers have not been able use individual personality characteristics as a consistent and reliable predictor of individual behaviour. Rather, behaviour appears, to a large degree, to

Systems for Sustainability, edited by Stowell *et al.*
Plenum Press, New York, 1997

be determined by characteristics of the task in which the individual is involved (Chervany, 1978). This has led to researchers in the field of human-computer interaction directing their attention towards gaining deeper understanding of the user-task environment. A major focus of this research has to be in analysing how the user acquires, processes and categorises information while performing the task.

Information Systems need to be built to achieve a fit between the user's cognitive style and the information-processing constraints of the task. Information Systems have to be developed using the cognitive styles and strategies employed by users within their task environment.

2. COGNITIVE STYLES

Using evidence collected from subjecting individuals to different problem solving situations, Witkin (1962) established differences in individuals' information-processing behaviours. He concluded that individuals prefer, and will tend to use, their own information-processing behaviour patterns even when faced with totally different problems. This phenomenon he referred to as preferred cognitive style. Cognitive styles are defined as high level heuristics that enabled individuals to organise and control behaviours across a wide variety of situations.

In recent years, research to identify the range of cognitive styles has produced over twenty-two dimensions on which styles differ (Haynes and Allinson, 1994). However, not all of these impact on information systems. Benbasat (1978) identified three dimensions of cognitive styles that have a major impact on the design of information systems. These are field independence and field dependence, cognitive complexity and simplicity and analytic-holistic. These are defined as follows (each continuum is explained in terms of one polarity so that the opposite may be inferred:

- Field independence - dependence
- Field independence - this individual shows an ability to distinguish items from the background, is not distracted by elements in the environment, and prefers to divide tasks into smaller sub-tasks.
- Cognitive complexity and simplicity
- Cognitive complexity - involves process in differentiation, fineness of discrimination and integration and the rules used to combine data.
- Analytic - holistic

The analytic individual prefers quantitative information, presented in the form of graphs, charts, tables, etc.; uses means-end problem-solving strategy, and develops frameworks and fits information into them.

3. COGNITIVE STRATEGIES

Challenges to Witkin's theory on cognitive styles has come from Messick (1976) and Streufert and Nagomi (1989). They suggest that some individuals, depending on the problem and its environment, might combine styles to construct a unique and temporary framework to solve the immediate problem. Cognitive psychologists such as Messick identified two levels; cognitive styles and cognitive strategies. Cognitive strategies were defined as a circumstantial and transient function of problem-solving, being dependent on task environment. This two level approach was supported by Kogan (1980) and Robertson

(1985), who also differentiated between style and strategy. They argued that cognitive styles produce consistent behaviours across a wide range of problem situations, whereas strategies are specific and essentially represent the somewhat conscious decisions individuals make in coping with cognitive tasks.

4. IMPACT ON THE DESIGN OF INFORMATION SYSTEMS

Cognitive styles can have important implications for task design. Mason and Mitroff (1973) were the first to stress the significance of end-user characteristics in the design of Information Systems. Robertson (1985) illustrates that much of the recent work on human-computer interaction assumes a universal human information-processing system. Robertson suggests that an exciting development may be to design systems that allow human operators to select from a variety of different operating modes, each designed to match a particular type of human cognitive strategy. This view is taken up by Olsen (1993) who proposes malleable interfaces under the control of the users, thus allowing them to select according to their preferences. Having only a restricted number of operating environments, based upon the most commonly used cognitive styles of the users would be the most attractive option. This would make it realistic and feasible to develop tools and techniques to identify users cognitive styles.

Information Systems need to be developed at two levels. There is a need both for customised information systems based on cognitive styles of the users and adaptive-flexible information system based on cognitive strategies. These two levels should thus be combined to form one optimal information system.

5. CUSTOMISED INFORMATION SYSTEMS

Systems that have been customised according to the users cognitive styles offer many benefits. The users are able to learn the system quicker, are able to navigate the system more efficiently and are more likely to use the system. The system is more efficient as unnecessary elements are not included.

There are elements of these cognitive styles, such as preferences for modes of presentation, that can aid the development of the information systems. There is a need to identify these elements for each user and use them to develop a cognitive psychological profile. A variety of methods for identification may be needed ranging from the subjective (interviewing) to the objective (Psychological tests). Once the cognitive profile has been identified the designer has to structure the data sources available to suit the psychological profile of the user. This profile will give indications on how data is to be summarised, aggregated, categorised and visually presented, plus the amount of information usage and the information load (Bergstrom, 1995).

The major arguments of information systems designers against customised Information Systems stem from the need to have flexibility. There are likely to be many users of the same system, and the problem task can be revised continuously, this will cause major problems for the inflexible customised systems. These factors require information systems to be flexible and adaptable to task environment.

6. FLEXIBLE AND ADAPTIVE INFORMATION SYSTEMS

In the development of flexible and adaptable information systems, cognitive strategies have to become the important factor. Cognitive strategies adopted by the user are dependent on the task context and influenced by working group membership. Task analysis, offers a limited set of techniques and methods for identifying the strength and interplay of these factors. The task analysis needs to be oriented towards the users needs, and may thus use a range of "subjective" or participative techniques such as interviewing, meetings and seminars. These can be complemented by prototyping-iterative methodologies offering a way forward in establishing how the users will use the system, how tasks will be performed and helping in carrying out information requirements and information structuring.

Information processing models of the user will differ depending on the amount of information available and at speed at which it needs to be processed. The user will adopt a strategy that requires minimum cognition and trade-offs will be made during decision making. When the user is confronted with complex problems with many alternatives, simplifying (heuristic) strategy will be selected. Prior task knowledge also needs to be considered in designing flexible-adaptive system. Users will also modify the strategies depending on social context in their working environment.

Methodologies to design IS have begun to move from a scientific analysis approach to a more problem-oriented user approach. The scientific approach generally involves breaking down large complex systems into their constituent parts to aid further analysis and development. The approaches have now moved to a greater inclusion of user requirements; and, in many cases, users' cognitive (information Processing) styles, to some degree, form part of the Information Systems. These iterative-prototyping methodologies have incorporated the user's task environment, but need to formally recognise the need to include analysis of the human information processing model.

Prototyping methodologies are moving closer to meeting the user requirements in developing the IS. Rapid Application Design encourages user involvement at management and operational level. This methodology is able to intrinsically able to capture user task environment by Joint Application Design workshops. To design a more customised IS the methodology needs to incorporate cognitive profiles of the users. Cognitive psychologists and IS designers need to work together in developing tools to capture the user's psychological profile.

Majority of the tools and techniques available are designed to capture the information requirements of the user and to aid structuring of information sources. Set of tools need to be developed to capture cognitive profiles of the user.

Information Systems need to be developed which operate in accordance with the user's information processing model. The user will be able to switch between operating modes as the task environment changes.

7. CONCLUSIONS

Much of the current research attention seems to focus on HCI theory or tools or problem-oriented ideas, with less concern for methodology. Development of user interfaces is the process where the discipline is put into practice. .

Information System designers want to get past the analysis stage fast and get on to the more understood coding, testing and evaluation. More attention needs to be devoted to the early stages to produce a more effective and usable system.

Some of the end-user cognitive styles are implicit part of the Information Requirements analysis. These will not produce Information Systems that will better utilised by the user. Today most of these processes are still ad hoc, resulting in quality that varies with the experience of the developers. More formal methods need to be employed. Information

Systems methodologies need to recognise the need to incorporate cognitive profiles of the users in the design process.

Cognitive styles represent only some of the characteristics of Information Systems. An equal amount of attention needs to be paid to organisational context (Mason an Mitroff, 1973), user characteristics (intellectual ability, attitudes etc.) and problem solving environments (social environment). Multiple approaches need to be used to design systems; varying from 'top-down' strategic business requirements to 'bottom-up' user profiles and problem environments. Major long-term research will bring about new theories and major breakthroughs that change the way we think about problems. Smaller-scale research projects are also needed to find solutions, often low technology solutions, to pragmatic problems.

REFERENCES

Bergstrom, F., 1995, Information Input Overload, Does it Exist? Research at Organism level and Group Level, *Behavioural Science*, **40**:56–75.

Blackler, F. and Brown, C., 1986, Alternative Models to Guide the Design and Introduction of the New Information Technologies, *Journal of Occupational Psychology*, **59**: 287–313.

Benbasat, I. and Taylor, R., 1978, The Impact of Cognitive Styles on Information Systems Design, *MIS Quarterly*, **2**: No 2.

Card S.K., 1983, *The Psychology of Human-Computer Interaction*, Erlbaum, New Jersey.

Chervany, N. and Dickson, G., 1978, On the Validity of the Analytic-Heuristic Instrument Utilized in 'The Minnesota Experiments': A Reply, *Management Science*, **24**:1091–1092.

Clegg, C., Ravden, S., Corbett, M., and Johnson, G., 1989, Allocating function in computer aided manufacturing: a review and a new method, *Behaviour and IT*, **8**:175–190.

Haynes and Allinson, 1994, Cognitive Styles and its relevance for Management Practice, *British Journal of Management*, **5**:53–71.

Kogan, N., 1980, Cognitive Styles and Reading Performance, *Bulletin of Orton Society*.

Mason, R., and Mirtoff, I., 1973, A Program of Research on Management Information Systems, *Management Science*, **19**: 475–487.

Messick, S., 1976, *Personality consistencies in cognition and creativity: Individuality in Learning*, Jossey-Bass, San Francisco.

Olsen, D., 1993, Research Direction for User Interface Software Tool, *Behaviour and IT*, **12**.

Robertson, I., 1985, Human Information-Processing Strategies and Styles, *Behaviour and Information Technology*, **4**:19–29.

Streufert, S. and Nagomi, G., 1989, Cognitive Style and Complexity: Implications for I/O Psychology, in: *International Review of Industrial and Organizational Psychology, (*C.L. Cooper and I. Robertson, eds.), Wiley, Chichester.

Witkin, H., 1962, *Psychological differentiation*, John Wiley and Sons, New York.

103

MODELLING THE DISCHARGE DECISION-MAKING PROCESS IN THE DOMAIN OF MENTAL HEALTH CARE

Susan Anne Smith

Department of Computing and Information Systems
University of Paisley
Paisley PA1 2BE

1. INTRODUCTION

The aim of the research is to model complex, subjective and 'messy' problem situations, such as the discharge decision-making process in the domain of Mental Health Care, as a first step towards the computer simulation of the models in the development of an IT based decision support system.

In this paper the use of the Appreciative Inquiry Method (AIM) to produce models of the discharge decision process in the domain of Mental Health Care is described and illustrated. The use of these models as a valuable learning exercise for the researcher and the experts and as a basis for the future development of an IT based decision support aid is discussed.

1.1. The Discharge Decision

The Mental Health Act (1983) in England and Wales and the Mental Health (Scotland) Act (1984) in Scotland makes provision for the hospitalisation and treatment of individuals judged to be suffering from a mental disorder. When deciding if a patient should be discharged the Responsible Medical Officer (RMO) consults the various professionals who comprise the multidisciplinary team (MDT) which is responsible for the decision making process such as nursing staff, including the Community Psychiatric Nurse (CPN), Social Workers and sometimes Occupational Therapists and Psychologists. It is recognised that the practice of the act has to be balanced against the individual's civil liberty rights (Carson, 1990). The decision making is complex as it is a result of MDT decision making and it results from an assessment of a mixture of rules (derived from the Mental Health Acts) and 'personal' knowledge gained from professional judgement resulting from previous experience.

Systems for Sustainability, edited by Stowell *et al.*
Plenum Press, New York, 1997

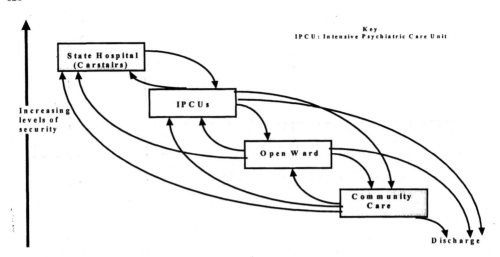

Figure 1. The possible progression levels in mental health care in Scotland.

After consultation with the other members of the MDT if the RMO decides that the patient should be discharged then a discharge plan or Care Programme is formulated to assess the services and care the patient will need in the community. However the decision may be to move the patient to a ward with less security, such as an Open Ward, prior to discharge or to move him to a ward with more security, such as the State Hospital, if the patient is particularly violent. The patient may move through the different levels of security and care until ultimately he/she is discharged into Community Care.

Figure 1 shows the possible levels of progression of a patient in the domain of Mental Health Care system in Scotland.

2. NATURE OF THE RESEARCH

The aim of the research was to model the discharge decision and, when all those involved were happy that the model was a reasonable representation of the decision-making process, then the resulting model was used as a way of thinking about the potential use of IT to help manage and structure this complex decision. The modelling of the discharge decision process was carried out by using an appropriate method of inquiry, namely AIM (West, 1990, 1995).

This method emphasises exploration and learning on the part of all those involved as a way of building up a rich appreciation of the domain, as it represents an attempt to operationalise Vickers' notion of appreciation (Vickers, 1965). The method is seen as useful as it focuses upon learning about the whole domain out of which may come the elicitation of information about decision making within the domain.

The different phases of AIM, carried out with each expert, lead to a learning process about the domain and the method itself for both the researcher and the experts. Using AIM, models of the discharge decision process were developed and taken back to the experts for group discussion, 'validation and as a learning experience for the experts and the researcher. The researcher then considered the potential use of IT to support this model in

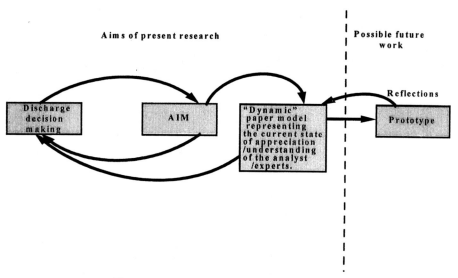

Figure 2. Diagram to show the aims of the research.

the future development of a prototype decision support aid. These processes are outlined in Figure 2.

The aims of the research were:

1. For the researcher and the experts to 'learn' about the domain of Mental Health and through this process of reflection find out about the discharge decision;
2. To develop a model of the discharge decision process to show the issues, relationships and roles involved in the way that the discharge is decided;
3. That as a representation of the overall decision making the model can be used to help formalise and standardise this process;
4. That the model could be used as a foundation for discussion between the experts;
5. To consider the possible use of the 'validated' model in the development of an IT based tool to support the decision making process; and
6. To consider the lessons learnt from the research and the potential application of these identified lessons in any future research.

3. THE MODELLING PROCESS AT LEVERNDALE AND GARTNAVEL ROYAL HOSPITALS

The research was carried out in the form of two case studies at Leverndale and Gartnavel Royal Hospitals over a twelve month period. RMOs and Nurses at Leverndale Hospital and RMOs, Nurses, CPNs and Social Workers at Gartnavel Royal Hospital, working in the IPCUs, were interviewed by the researcher.

The first interviews using AIM were conducted with the RMOs at Leverndale Hospital, who are the psychiatrists who are ultimately responsible for the discharge decision at that hospital. The first phase involves the 'client' in developing a systems map of their

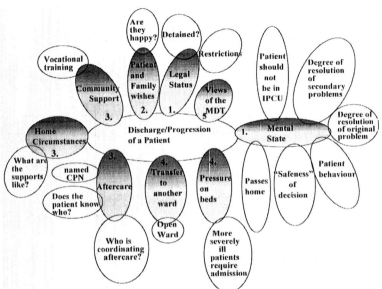

Figure 3. A composite systems map derived from the individual systems maps of RMOs working in IPCU at Leverndale Hospital, Glasgow.

perception of the area of interest (Stowell, West and Fluck, 1991; West, 1995). Composite Maps were then developed which encapsulated the components from the psychiatrists' individual maps. Figure 3 shows the Composite Map developed from the individual maps of the RMOs at Leverndale.

The composite maps were then taken back to each of the psychiatrists for comment, discussion and where necessary further development. Through this discussion the original concepts of the individual systems maps were grouped together and 'validated' by the different psychiatrists as offering an acceptable and useful way of looking at the area of concern at this stage of the project. For the Composite Map in Figure 3 five main areas were identified: the patient's mental state; the patient's or relative's wishes; home circumstances which include community support; resources which includes pressure on beds and transfer to other hospitals; and the views of the MDT.

Each grouping was considered in terms of the overall activity represented in the named group. This was achieved by the psychiatrists considering each grouping as a Transformation and supplying the details necessary to enable the researcher to develop a strict description of the activity in the form of a Root Definition (RD) (Checkland, 1981; Checkland and Scholes, 1990; West, 1995). The RDs were then developed as Conceptual Models (CMs) which are used as the basis for a more detailed discussion about the domain.

Different members of the MDT have their own specialist areas of interest and it was hoped that by gradually building up a picture of the whole domain a greater awareness by all those involved (researcher and clients) of the decision-making process and the complex interaction of the many factors involved could be achieved. The RMOs were interviewed first as those who are likely to have the most complete picture of the discharge decision making process as they have the ultimate responsibility for this process. Then the nursing staff at Leverndale Hospital were interviewed as they tend to look at their own specialist area within the overall decision process. The lessons learnt by the researcher from this study were then used during the interviews at Gartnavel Royal Hospital. Similar to the study at Leverndale Hospital, in Gartnavel Royal Hospital the RMOs were interviewed first and then the nurses, CPNs and the Social Workers.

In both of the studies individual CMs of the domain were developed and 'validated' by each expert and a single CM for all the experts was drawn by the researcher. The model was then taken back to the experts to be used as a basis for group discussion, debate and 'validation'. On 'validation' the researcher then considered how IT could be used to support this model in future developments.

4. LESSONS LEARNT BY THE EXPERTS AND THE RESEARCHER

The process of inquiry, using AIM, has lead to the experts and the researcher learning, using the modelling process, about the domain and AIM itself. This learning has identified problems and questions which have to be addressed. Some of the lessons learnt and the questions identified will now be outlined.

4.1. Learning about the Domain of Mental Health Care and the Discharge Decision Process

The experts and the researcher have learnt about the roles, responsibilities and issues involved in the domain of Mental Health Care and the decision-making process within that domain. Each member of the MDT has their own area of responsibility and they may not have been aware of the functions of the other team members previously.

During the field studies using AIM the researcher became an 'expert' in the chosen domain as the learning process involved in the process of inquiry, with all of the experts, lead to an overall understanding by the researcher.

4.2. Learning about AIM

The researcher, and to a lesser extent the experts, learnt about the method of inquiry AIM. Each phase of AIM lead to a learning cycle for everyone involved. Some of the lessons learnt about this method were:

1. The CMs became very complex and had to be explained to the expert by the researcher during Phase III of AIM. The complexity of the models lead to the development of hierarchical conceptual models (Wilson, 1984).
2. Arranging interviews with the experts was very difficult as they were all very busy and this lead to the field studies taking longer than was expected originally.

To maintain the rigour of the method each interview was recorded and then transcribed onto paper. This was a very lengthy and time consuming process.

5. USING IT TO SUPPORT THE MODEL?

The aim of the process of inquiry was to try to make sense of the complexity and multidisciplinary nature of the decision-making process. The researcher developed a model of the discharge and then considered what IT support for this model might look like.

IT could be used to support the inquiry process as a decision-making prompt rather than to provide answers. Isenmann (1993) argues that "the solving of wicked problems requires the development of a structured view of the problem and its solutions. This requires a discourse among the participants, where issues are brought up and disputed, and argumentations are constructed in defense of or against the different positions. This process should lead to better founded solutions, where more aspects have been taken into consideration." The experts could use the model to formalise and reflect on the decision-making process as a prompt to decision-making where the experts are made aware of the issues and complexity involved in the process.

6. COLLABORATORS

The staff working in the Intensive Psychiatric Care Units (IPCUs) at Leverndale Hospital and Gartnavel Royal Hospital have taken part in the field study phase of the project.

REFERENCES

Carson, D., 1990, *Risk-taking in Mental Disorder; Analyses, Policies and Practical Strategies*, SLE Publications LTD., Chichester.

Checkland, P.B., 1981, *Systems Thinking, Systems Practice*, Wiley, Chichester.

Checkland, P.B. and Scholes, J., 1990, *Soft Systems Methodology in Action*, Wiley, Chichester

HMSO Mental Health (Scotland) Act 1984, Chapter 36, HMSO, London.

Isenmann, S., 1993, How to deal with wicked problems using a new type of information system, in: *Systems Science: Addressing Global Issues*, (F.A. Stowell, D. West and J.G. Howell, eds.), pp. 367–372, Plenum Press, New York.

Stowell, F.A. and West, D., 1990, The contribution of systems ideas during the process of knowledge elicitation, in: *Systems Prospects: the Next Ten Years of Systems Research*, (R.L. Flood, M.C. Jackson and P. Keys, eds.), pp. 329–334, Plenum Press, New York.

Stowell, F.A., West, D. and Fluck, M., 1991, The appreciative inquiry method: an approach to knowledge elicitation based upon the notion of knowledge elicitation as an inquiring system, *Systemist* 13: 4: 154–165.

Vickers, G., 1965, *The Art of Judgement*, Harper and Row Ltd., London.

West, D., 1990, 'Appreciation', 'expertise' and knowledge elicitation - the relevance of Vickers' ideas to the design of expert systems', *Journal of Applied Systems Analysis*, 17: 71–78.

West, D., 1995, The appreciative inquiry method: a systemic approach to information system, in: *Information Systems Provision: The contribution of Soft Systems Methodology*, (Stowell, F.A., ed.), pp. 140–158, McGraw-Hill.

Wilson, B., 1984, *Systems: Concepts, Methodologies and Applications*, Chichester, Wiley.

104

THE ROLE OF DIAGRAMS IN INFORMATION SYSTEMS ANALYSIS

Daune West

Department of Computing and Information Systems
University of Paisley, Scotland

1. INTRODUCTION

Diagrams play an important but often overlooked role in the process of information systems analysis (ISA). The type of diagrams that feature predominantly in traditional computer systems analysis is that of some form of data flow diagram that is an integral part of a structured computer systems analysis and design method. In this paper the roles of modelling and diagrams during the ISA process are explored. It is suggested that an awareness of the implications of diagrams and diagramming techniques is especially important where the ISA approach adopted emphasises the need to learn about the domain and problem situation as a precursor to analysis and the consideration of possible technical components. In the next section a brief review of the argument for adopting an ISA approach that supports problem appreciation is offered as a context for discussing the use of diagrams in ISA.

2. INFORMATION SYSTEMS ANALYSIS

The distinction between computer systems analysis and information systems analysis is as much an epistemological one as a reflection of the developments in information technology (Stowell and West, 1994, p. 4). The term 'computer systems analysis' is used here to describe the traditional approach to the design of computer systems to improve the performance of the business organisation. By comparison, the term 'information systems analysis' is used here to signify the exploration of the wider implications of information and the effects that a computer-based information system might have upon the organisation. Whilst the former concept relies upon and enforces a datalogical and, arguably, technological perspective, the latter places emphasis upon learning about the way in which information is utilised in the organisation. The subjective nature of information means that a rich description of the situation needs to be built up over time by means of a process of exploration and learning. Only when those within the situation are content that a thorough

Systems for Sustainability, edited by Stowell *et al.*
Plenum Press, New York, 1997

understanding of the situation and its difficulties has been gained can potential solutions and the appropriate use of information technology to support those solution be discussed. Such an approach places emphasis upon the need for the information systems analyst to be able to engender a process of inquiry through which a growing appreciation of the situation can be gained. Models and diagrams play an important role in the process of appreciation.

3. DIAGRAMS AND MODELLING

It is difficult to separate the concepts of model and diagram. For the purpose of this paper, modelling will be taken to be the wider activity of exploring, abstracting and representing one's understanding of a situation of concern whilst diagrams are viewed as being a particular expression of some model of a situation, and one which graphically represents someone's interests.

Wilson offers a useful definition of models which will be adopted here since it emphasises the idea of a model being the product of someone's ideas about a situation:

> "A model is the explicit interpretation of one's understanding of a situation, or merely of one's ideas about the situation. It can be expressed in mathematics, symbols or words, but it is essentially a description of entities and the relationships between them. It may be prescriptive or illustrative, but above all, it must be useful" (Wilson, B., 1991. p.11).

This considered definition can be compared with the type of description we find in the more traditional approaches to modelling to be found in computer systems analysis texts. For example, if we look at Yeates, Sheilds, and Helmy's description of modelling (1994) we see the more specific computer technology related and prescriptive description that is popular in systems analysis texts:

"Modelling refers to the use of graphic models which are employed wherever possible, in place of narrative text, to provide clear and unambiguous information about the system. They are produced to represent both the current system and data structure, and the required system and data structure. They enable detailed investigation to be made of the requirements and the design before money is spent in actually producing the system" (p.112).

It is tempting to suggest, from looking at the literature, that in computer systems analysis modelling is seen as being a natural skill which does not warrant any more discussion than, say, the process of interviewing. However, much time seems to be spent on modelling with relatively little thought as to what it is that happens when we model. The example given above from Yeates et al. is interesting in that it states that modelling brings about 'unambiguous information about the system', the implication being, of course, that (i) an ability to be unambiguous is possible and (ii) that some system of interest can be taken as given. The view of the process being undertaken is data driven and, therefore, a third implication is that a datalogical perspective will provide a useful and appropriate medium through which to describe the situation. The assumptions here are in conflict, on a number of grounds, with the arguments set out above, namely, the need to distinguish between computer systems analysis and information systems analysis and Wilson's description of modelling. (Whilst Yeates et al. have been used to draw out the points above, their work is taken as being an example of the many structured systems analysis approaches taught and practised).

The argument put forward above concerning the need to facilitate a process of appreciation amongst all those involved in the situation of interest makes the concept of 'unambiguous information about the system' impossible. Understanding and appreciation are products of individual (and group) interpretation, their attempts to make sense of the world and to explain and share their meanings: there can be nothing unambiguous about appreciation since it is a continuous process, and one which is difficult to represent although aspects of the state and process of appreciation may be captured, in part, by various representations (e.g. the use of diagrams, tape recordings, minutes to meetings). The idea of 'the system' as being taken as given is also alien to the process of information systems analysis as described in section 2 above since the process of exploration and problem appreciation is a precursor to trying to identify any possible system of interest: in other words the system is not there to be identified and analysed but through the process of analysis and investigation some system of interest may be determined. Information systems analysis, then, begins a process prior to that of traditional computer systems analysis of the sort represented by Yeates et al. and involves a considerable amount of time being spent in trying to make sense of the situation before considerations of such things as data and the possible use of technology (West, 1991, p.277). It may be that Yeates et al. were focusing on the later stages of what we might call problem specification and yet if this is so they give no attention to the earlier stages of problem appreciation. Another area for concern is the datalogical approach that lies at the heart of Yeates et al.'s description. Whilst this approach is popular there is no recognition that in taking the flow of data to be the way of describing a situation aspects of the situation cannot be taken into account. Furthermore, the approach adopted will dictate the sort of modelling that takes place.

A final area of conflict lies in the idea of a model. In Yeates et al.'s' description it would appear that there is little concern as to the implications of the type of model and the process of abstraction. It would appear that the model, or graphical representation (diagram) is considered as a (neutral) tool which is used to represent various aspects of 'the system'. No discussion of the problems of diagramming, assumptions underlying the diagrams used, the way that diagrams may distort, direct, or promote a view or concept is offered. As with their reference to 'the system', diagrams seem to be taken as given. However, given the nature of models as described by Wilson and the fact that they are produced by someone, it is important to consider the implications of any diagram we use in terms of assumptions underlying the diagram's conventions, our purpose and intent in producing the diagram, and the way in which the production of the diagram 'feeds back' into our cycle of appreciation.

4. DIAGRAMMING

The argument offered here is that diagrams are a graphical representation of an abstraction of some 'reality' (and as such represent someone's view). In this sense they are a model of some situation of concern. But by their very nature they are a simplification of our reality which is coloured by our way of looking at and feeling about our world. Vickers' notion of appreciation (1965) offers a useful way of considering the continuous process as we seek to make sense of our world. The role of judgements in this sense-making activity, and the 'readinesses' they promote, provides us with a rich image of the way in which we develop our personal interests, our view of 'reality' and, of course, abstract from this reality. It is worthwhile considering diagramming in the light of this process: a diagram can be argued to be a representation (abstraction) of a modelling process (abstraction) of our interest in and perception of a situation (appreciation). Consequently, the question of the 'validity' of any diagram (see Checkland, 1995, for a discussion of the validity of models in soft systems practice), becomes a different issue to that of diagrams that have been developed out of the tradition of conventional computing systems analysis in that what we end up with can only be seen as something which may be useful to someone for some particular purpose (i.e. to record an understanding, to illustrate and communicate ideas to others, to promote understanding through simulation, to facilitate discussion); they are not diagrams of 'the system'.

Given the nature of modelling and diagrams, then, it becomes important to ask questions of the diagrams we use and the purpose to which we intend to put them. In asking such questions we have the opportunity to become more aware of our process of abstraction and the implications of diagramming. Questions we might ask are as follows:

4.1. Why Use Diagrams?

We use diagrams for a number of reasons: they enable us to place some form of structure on the complexity surrounding us; they allow us to identify aspects of our view of a situation long enough for us to inspect and consider our view; they offer us the opportunity to explore and 'play' with the situation described, and consequently, our ideas of it; their production can help us ask questions of our understanding and show areas of uncertainty.

4.2. How Do We Use Diagrams?

We use diagrams to help us clarify our thinking by giving us a way of 'putting things down on paper' and thereby give us an opportunity to illustrate and communicate our ideas to others: ideas that can be confirmed or challenged by others. We may use diagrams to allow us some insight into possible behaviour of a situation by methods of simulation, or attempt to define structure and/or process as a prerequisite for design.

4.3. What Are the Dangers of Diagrams?

A number of 'dangers' surround diagrams such as: the complexity or lack of clarity regarding the conventions of diagrams. Lack of knowledge of conventions and their application lead to the development (often unconsciously) of hybrids which are unlikely to be as rigorous as the original diagram that was developed to meet a specific need. There is a problem that we develop a familiarity with particular diagramming techniques and these are then used and re-used without due consideration of the task in hand. The problem of level of resolution at which we abstract is a serious one in that we need to be able to represent a situation at a useful and consistent level of detail. There is a danger that even though we are aware that a diagram is only an abstraction of our understanding, others may take the diagram as a representation of reality, or worse - of reality itself.

4.4. What Results Can Be Expected from Different Diagrams?

If we are to utilise available diagramming techniques to the full we need to have an understanding of the intended purpose of any technique. For example, has a diagram convention been developed to help illustrate aspects of structure of process, or, perhaps, climate? This three-way classification may be useful in helping us select useful diagramming approaches. Alternatively, we might use a different method of classification such as distinguishing between the types of model proposed by Ackoff and added to by Wilson (1991) or adopting a classification based upon the identification of datalogical and infological approaches.

5. THE NEED FOR AND NATURE OF AWARENESS

In addition to the awareness that we seek by posing questions such as those outlined above, it is worthwhile considering the potential of 'blindnesses' that are in place alongside 'readinesses'. Some interesting ideas about the problems of blindness can be found in Winograd and Flores (1986) in their reference to the work of Heidegger. The problems of 'blindness' can be considered in the following ways:

1. when we model we are concerned with identifying objects (or entities) and the relationship that we may assign between them. This, as Wilson's definition of a model states, is a central aspect of what we do when modelling and representing some situation. However, this concentration on objects and their relationships with one another, though experience proves to be a useful strategy, is, nevertheless, a constraining factor and as such may limit our successful use and development of the model.
2. the tools and techniques which we use in the modelling process may themselves create blindness in that they make us think in certain ways. Moreover, their strong images and the habits they engender may prevent us thinking in different and novel ways.
3. our personal experience and interpretation may lead us to 'see' some objects and 'relationships' and not others. This point reminds us that the process of seeing what is 'relevant' (i.e. the product of Vickers' 'readinesses'), means that it is difficult for us to consider and develop new relevances.

Heidegger does not give us a method for overcoming these blindnesses. Instead, he advises that we should consider them as being natural and, therefore, we need to ensure that we are aware of the constraints that such blindness creates. Of course, our problem then becomes that of being aware of the blindness of our awareness!

6. CONCLUSIONS

If we take together the definitions we have of modelling and the notions of blindness and readinesses then we may begin to assemble a number of issues relevant to the investigation and appropriate use of diagrams in information systems analysis. For example, we need to consider:

- the underlying assumptions and interests we may assign to a diagram
- the conventions and constraints of a diagram
- the origins of a diagram
- the reasons for selecting a particular diagram
- the purpose of a diagram (in producing it and then in the way that we use it)
- the content of a diagram (what we include and what we exclude - including levels of resolution).

Our view of the world and the way in which we attempt to make sense of it plays an important role in the way that we approach the process of modelling and the use of diagrams as the discussion of Yeates et al's proposal suggests. For example, if we 'assume that the social world is composed of relatively concrete empirical artefacts and relationships which can be identified, studied and measured through approaches derived from the natural sciences' (Burrell and Morgan, 1979, p. 26), then, defensibly, we treat modelling and diagramming as a process of representing what is 'out there'. Consequently, it is important for the systems analyst to be aware of their own epistemology and to ensure that the modelling and diagramming process is consistent with that epistemology. For the information systems analyst (as distinguished from the computer systems analyst in section 2 above), it is important that in using diagrams an awareness of their strengths weaknesses, the assumptions and theories upon which they are based , their characteristics and the implications of adopting the diagram are considered.

REFERENCES

Burrell, G. and Morgan, G., 1979, *Sociological Paradigms and Organisational Analysis*, Gower, Aldershot.

Checkland, P.B., 1995, Model validation in soft systems practice, *Systems Research*, 12(1):47–54

Stowell, F.A. and West, D., 1994, *Client-led Design: A Systemic Approach to Information Systems Definition*, McGraw-Hill, London.

Vickers, G., 1965, *The Art of Judgement,: A Study of Policy Making*, Chapman and Hall, London.

West, D., Towards a subjective knowledge elicitation methodology for the development of expert systems, unpublished PhD dissertation, Portsmouth Polytechnic.

Wilson, B., 1991, *Systems: Concepts, Methodologies , and Applications*, (2nd edit.), Wiley, Chichester.

Winograd, T. and Flores, F., 1986, *Understanding Computers and Cognition: A New Foundation for Design*, Ablex Publishing Corporation, New Jersey.

Yeates, D., Sheilds, M. and Helmy, D., 1994, *Systems Analysis and Design*, Pitman Publishing, London.

105

DEVELOPING FIRMER GROUNDS FOR CLIENT-LED DESIGN OF INFORMATION SYSTEMS

S. Xia

Department of Computer and Information Sciences
De Montfort University
Kents Hill, Milton Keynes, MK7 6HP, United Kingdom

1. INTRODUCTION

The design and development of modern information systems requires the use of both soft systems methods and hard systems techniques in an integrated manner. This paper is an attempt as the first step to incorporate some concepts developed in Automated Modelling work (Xia & Smith, 1996) into the approach of the client-led design of modern information systems (Stowell & West, 1994). In particular it intends to apply the automated modelling framework to substantiate the interpretivist philosophy (Stowell, 1996), which was adopted in the client-led design approach. This framework is basically concerned with relating and considering all the relevant issues surrounding the design and use of an information system, which include environment and boundary, decision-making rules, designer's expertise, application, design, and general observation. Some of these issues are complementary to others and some are in direct conflict. A design of an information system will be a result of an overall consideration and compromise of these issues. Strictly speaking this automated modelling approach is still very much rationalistic in the sense that it still applies the activities of decomposition, quantification and then composition in its underlying problem solving process. However the reference model, based on which the activities are applied, is built at a much lower level than that adopted by the rationalistic or posivitist tradition of design. As a result this makes it easier to carry out the client-led design and closer to the interpretivist philosophy. The primary motivation of this work is to stir discussion on some concepts, rather than to reach any conclusions.

2. CONTEXT

Organisations are becoming more complex in scale and more efficient in operation due to the increase in competition (Laudon & Laudon, 1996). They are also becoming

Systems for Sustainability, edited by Stowell *et al.*
Plenum Press, New York, 1997

more dynamic and flexible due to rapid changes in business environment, resources and market demand. Utilising information technologies to keep up with changes and make correct decisions all the time in a short space of time is the key for organisation survival. Among many technologies, information systems and communications are arguably two most important information technologies for modern organisations.

An information system can be defined crudely as an interrelated collection of coherent computer-based decision supporting and making tools. It is normally employed by organisations with complex businesses and its functions include collection, extraction, manipulation, and presentation of useful information in support of decision-making for organisations.

Organisations are under constant changes. These changes gradually become more fundamental, not only in organisational structures but also in operational procedures. They can include some changes of basic references which used to be regarded as a long term commitment like ownership of an organisation. Performance measurements can change from making as much profit as possible to being more efficient and environment friendly. All these changes make it essential for organisations to use information systems to help decision-making. They also have serious implications on design of information systems, which will need to include less assumptions and consider more fundamental issues. As a result of this design, information systems will demonstrate at least three characteristics. Firstly they will be a combination of soft and hard systems, including finance, manufacture and production, and sales and marketing. Secondly they will be hybrid systems with incorporation of operation-level systems, knowledge-level systems and management level systems. Finally they will integrate strategic thinking and low-level day-to-day running, performing qualitative thinking and quantitative processing in a mixed manner.

3. DESIGN OF INFORMATION SYSTEMS

The traditional design of information systems has been heavily governed by the rationalistic or positivist tradition of thinking. This tradition of thinking regards decision-making as a collection of three separate activities, task decomposition, sub-task and sub-decision quantification, and sub-decision composition. Task decomposition is an activity of breaking a large task into smaller ones which will be easier to complete. The solutions to these smaller tasks in the form of sub-decisions are acquired at the stage of quantification. Decision composition is an activity of combining sub-decisions into a whole decision. This approach has worked well in the past because organisations involved were relatively small-scale, stable and reasonably independent. The central role that information systems played in these organisations was a table or dictionary in which a decision to a task could be looked up. However modern organisations tend to be large-scale, constantly re-structuring and highly interactive with related organisations and markets. It is therefore very difficult to use the traditional design to develop new information systems for modern organisations.

4. CLIENT-LED DESIGN AND ITS TECHNICAL IMPLICATION

The client-led design is a new design methodology for large-scale modern organisations. This new methodology attempts to transfer to clients the ownership of design, development, implementation and subsequent applications of information systems. Clients are the focus of all activities. The client-led design places clients and application at the fore-front and takes a global view to decision making. As a result it is possible to incorporate changes and interactions into a framework and give an overall consideration to all important issues. In contrast the traditional rationalistic design took a local view to decision making. Clients played a passive role and in some situation even had to adjust to limitation of the design and implementation.

The issues addressed in the client-led design are more fundamental than in the traditional rationalistic design. This has many technical implications. First it takes a model-based representation rather than a look-up table one. Second it tends to use real organisations and their structures as a reference model rather than an abstracted after much simplification and specialisation. Third all basic terms of reference and any underlying assumptions will be declared explicitly and will be represented as an integral part of an organisational model. Finally the concept of parsimony is introduced as a design criterion, that is to make decisions on a right amount of information.

5. DEVELOPING FIRMER GROUNDS FOR THE CLIENT-LED DESIGN

A good basis for the client-led design of an information system is the incorporation of people, organisation and environment. In more technical terms the client-led design must take into account the environment, organisational structures and rules governing their functions, designers and their expertise, users, and applications. In order to be successful in practice, this design methodology must consider the following elements and resolve them properly:

- Environment: this refers to the boundary of an information system. Anything outside this environment is irrelevant.
- Decision-making rules: these are applicable knowledge of the environment.
- Designer's expertise: this specifies the principles and laws that must be applied.
- General observation: this lists the constraints that a design must satisfy.
- Application: this is the purpose for development of an information system and can contain information on relevant perspective, approximation, assumption and even important phenomena, variables, and parameters.
- Design: this is the resulting specification.

With a framework of these elements behind the client-led design, information systems so designed will satisfy the criterion that clients and applications will be the real focus of all activities. They are also more likely to use the right amount of information and make the right decision. Moreover they have the capacity to accommodate more easily any changes in terms of reference and performance assessment like the changes of tax or organisational regulations.

6. DISCUSSION

This work is only a first step to study the underlying issues behind the client-led design of information systems. There is no intention to draw any conclusions at this stage. What we hope to achieve is to point to a few issues for discussion and see whether it is sensible or possible to approach design of modern information systems in a new way. This new way will surely be a way of incorporating people, organisations, and environments into one system.

REFERENCES

Laudon, K.C. and Laudon, J.P., 1996, *Management information systems: organisation and technology*, Prentice-Hall, New Jersey.

Stowell, F. A. and West, D., 1994, *Client-led Design: A Systemic Approach to Information Systems Definition*, McGraw-Hill, Maidenhead.

Stowell, F.A., 1996, Departmental seminar on The Systems Epistemology and Information Systems, Department of Computer and Information Sciences, De Montfort University, March 1996.

Xia, S. and Smith, N., 1996, Automated modelling: a discussion and review, in Journal of Knowledge Engineering Review, 11(2): 137–60.

106

COMPETITIVE SYSTEMS—SEDUCING CICERO

Graeme Altmann and Gordon Boyce

Faculty of Business and Law
Deakin University
Geelong, Victoria, Australia
email altmann@deakin.edu.au

1. INTRODUCTION

Information technology (IT) and information systems (IS) have become the new catalyst of competition; changing ways of doing business, streamlining work practices, and improving the quality of product and services. While innovative organisations are adept at recognising new opportunities and capitalising on available technology, others impulsively act without understanding the complexities and risks. IS and IT have become the high priestess of managers—tempting, tantalising and seducing them into believing that competitive advantage is theirs for the taking. Yet the achievement of sustainable competitive success through IS remains one of the most elusive of all business goals. Achieving operational excellence through the use of IT can be real and substantial, but for many managers the challenge of confronting new technologies is daunting, and few even begin to see the possibilities for innovative applications of systems within their organisations.

In this fast changing world, it might be asked, "Can IT deliver sustainable competitive advantage, and if it can, do contemporary managers understand how to use systems to seize competitive advantage over rival firms?" This paper examines the type and nature of competitive systems being applied in a cross-section of Australian organisations, in which participants outlined the extent to which their organisations were successfully using IT in the competitive arena, and discussed key issues and factors that continue to either drive or hinder competitive IT initiatives. The application of systems thinking, using Soft Systems Methodology, was considered as a way in which organisations may capitalise on the competitive potential of available technology, and IS.

2. COMPETITIVE ADVANTAGE THROUGH INFORMATION TECHNOLOGY

Given the widespread use of IS, some researchers question the extent to which such systems can deliver a long-term competitive advantage. For example, a study of thirty

Systems for Sustainability, edited by Stowell *et al.*
Plenum Press, New York, 1997

firms commonly cited as classic examples of strategic uses of IT has found that not all of these firms could be touted as sustained winners (Kettinger *et al*, 1994). Today, this scepticism continues and there are suggestions that opportunities for achieving *sustained* competitive advantage through early use of IT may be more difficult than originally thought. For example, a recent survey of managers found that only 28% of managers believed that IT "held the key to competitive advantage for their companies." Two years earlier, 57% of managers surveyed had thought that IT provided the key (Maglitta, 1995).

The IT literature is replete with competitive IT success stories. Certainly, these encourage all organisations to endeavour to make better use of IT. Yet there is a vast difference between *wanting to use* IT in a more competitive way and *knowing how* to use IT to achieve competitive advantage. Four particular problem areas must be addressed to enable firms to realise the competitive potential of IS:

- a lack of an integrated approach to thinking and planning for IS within organisations, leading to poor strategic vision and failure to capitalise on available opportunities;
- a lack of ability to deal with complexity, risk, and uncertainty;
- a failure to look beyond mere technology for solutions; and
- a lack of IT leadership within organisations, and management complacency.

Benjamin, Rockart, Scott-Morton and Wyman (1984) argue that an "entrepreneurial attitude" on the part of senior management, including the holding of a view that IS are central to business operations and an important strategic weapon, is important to enable a firm to exploit IT opportunities. Building on this view, Munro and Huff (1985) identify two key factors in IS strategy formulation: "sensing where the opportunities lie, and providing the leadership required in bringing information technology to bear on those opportunities". They contend that strategic IS opportunities are more likely to emerge from issue-driven organisations (where the driving forces of action include problems, emergencies, opportunities, questions, decisions), rather than technology-driven (where the organisation devotes considerable resources to scanning for new technological developments) or opportunistic (where neither technology nor issues drive the acquisition of new technology) organisations.

Lado and Wilson (1994) have outlined four types of competencies that affect competitive sustainability. These are described as managerial competencies, input-based competencies, transformation-based competencies, and output-based competencies. It is only those competencies that are not readily substitutable that can provide sustainable competitive advantage. These include managerial competencies such as strategic vision; transformation-based competencies such as organisational culture, innovation and entrepreneurship; and output-based competencies such as reputation and customer loyalty. Input-based competencies, such as the physical resources of information technology and people, are substitutable so therefore sustainable competitive advantage is less likely to accrue.

Clearly, competitive success through the application of IS/IT is achievable, given an appropriate organisational culture, including its approach to IS/IT. In an endeavour to identify the key types of competitive systems used in business and the factors driving the development and use of these systems, the authors sought the views and perceptions of system users and managers in a broad cross-section of Australian organisations.

3. COMPETITIVE SYSTEMS IN AUSTRALIAN BUSINESS

A survey of Australian managers was conducted in 1996 to identify the nature of competitive systems used in their organisations. The managers in the survey group were participants in a distance-learning MBA program. All held full-time positions of responsibility within their organisations, they were typically aged in their mid-thirties, and had an average of nine years experience in using IS/IT.

The research instrument used was a questionnaire consisting of twenty-five questions, several of which were open-ended in nature, adding to the richness of the answers and providing additional data for analysis. Three of the questions related to the use of competitive systems and are reported in this paper. They elicited responses on the strategic role of IS in the organisation, competitive opportunities for using IT, and issues affecting the management of IS. Questionnaires were sent to 200 managers with 93 valid questionnaires returned—a response rate of 46.5 percent.

3.1. Results

3.1.1. Dependence on IS/IT and Technological Leadership. The majority of respondents (83.9%) indicated that IS/IT was either vital (43%) or important (40.9%) to their organisations. Only 12.9% thought that IS/IT was of average importance and 3.2% that it was not important. A majority of respondents (51.1%) believed that their organisations had technological leadership rather than lagged other firms in their industries. The full distribution of answers is shown in Figure 1.

3.1.2. Classification of Strategic Systems. Asked to identify key systems that provide strategic or competitive benefits to their organisations, 82.8% of survey respondents were able to describe such systems. Respondents classified these systems according to the competitive or strategic benefits that the systems provide as shown in Table 1. Note that figures show the percentage of organisations using each type of generic system—naturally, organisations can and do use several types.

3.1.3. Trends in the Use of Strategic Systems. A review of the competitive systems described by the respondents revealed a number of recurring themes:

- a desire and continuing need to support further cost efficiencies;
- the necessity to further improve work practices;
- the need to provide continuing and higher levels of customer service;
- the desire to improve identification of market opportunities;
- the need to provide easier access to and a wider sharing of information across the business;

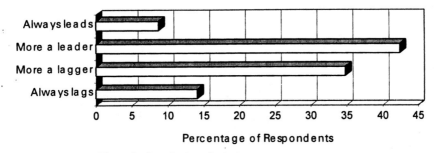

Figure 1. Organisations displaying technological leadership.

Table 1. Classification of strategic systems

Systems that provide management with strategic information	57.1%
Systems that provide innovative processing or analysis of data	39.0
Systems that link the organisation to customers/ suppliers	37.7
Systems that allow sharing of strategic information	26.0
Systems based on new or innovative uses of technology	24.7

- a continual search for smart technologies that can change ways of doing business; and
- trying to achieve greater levels of cooperation along the supply chain.

IS/IT was widely seen as a vital element in improving organisational effectiveness and competitiveness. The IS/IT knowledge of managers is evident, and most were able to highlight strategic and competitive systems that are used to support and drive their businesses. However, results suggest that system sophistication varies greatly and reflects vastly different levels of IS/IT infrastructure and maturity. Competitive systems were widely seen as having changed the roles and work practices of managers and system users, but respondents noted that the *potential* for the use of competitive systems in their organisations is largely unrealised.

4. SYSTEMS THINKING FOR INFORMATION SYSTEMS

Addressing these concerns is now a prime issue, and organisations must take a *entrepreneurial attitude* to IS/IT. Organisations must become IS-issue-driven, not technology-driven, and must capitalise on the non-substitutable systems competencies available to them. Chu (1995) suggests that there remains "a need for a systematic and consistent model for *conceiving* strategic information systems" (emphasis added).

Systems thinking can play an important role in breaking this impasse by *supporting organisational understanding and learning* and relating the everyday activities carried out within an organisation to its larger vision, mission, values, and goals. Systems thinking allows people to look at an organisation in an open and holistic way and review how the business interacts with its environment at every level. Senge (1996) notes that, in applying the systems approach to a problem, "resolutions come from thinking about how one deals with complexity .... when a group of people collectively recognise that nobody has the answer, it transforms the quality of that organization in a remarkable way."

Soft Systems Methodology (SSM), originally developed by Checkland (1981) and further developed by Checkland and Scholes (1990) and others, is a well-developed approach to systems thinking that can be used to explore strategic IS opportunities and foster organisational learning. The methodology is explicitly holistic, and recognises that different players may have different views about the aims, objectives, and purposes of the organisation, these being influenced by social and personal contexts, and individual experiences and values. These individual, social, cultural, and 'values' issues are explicitly dealt with in the context of the strategic planning exercise, Checkland (1981) suggesting that it may be necessary to "pause and reflect" during the initial stages of thinking, when dealing with expression of the problem situation, and to temper peoples' "over-urgent desire for action". SSM does not seek technological solutions to problem situations, but *systemic* solutions, which may be aided by the application of technology. It involves an iterative process of thinking about problem situations, developing 'rich pictures' and 'root definitions' of the situation, building conceptual models of relevant human activity systems, comparing models with the real world, and taking action to modify the real world situation.

Many other approaches used within organisations to examine IS operations and uncover strategic and competitive opportunities set out to solve an *existing* problem or, at best, improve an *existing* situation. In contrast, SSM sets out in the first instance to *learn* about the existing system and to generate potential *new views* of it. SSM is designed to generate possibilities for *change*. The process emphasises thinking about the system in the way it should be, *then* considering the existing system as it is and making appropriate changes. Therefore, it does not suffer by 'carrying the baggage' of an existing system. Checkland (1981) points out that conceptual modelling in a systems thinking mode is done quite apart from any single perception of reality, as opposed to trying to model an *existing* system. It also allows for the consideration of the most interesting questions, including the purpose and meaning of desired (*then* current) information flows. Checkland describes one of the primary aims of SSM as being the generation of "radical thought" (*ibid*). In this sense, SSM has been shown to be particularly capable of "making the transition from present to future" (Galliers, 1992). This approach may result in a very different perception of the problem to be solved, and consequently a very different solution.

5. CONCLUSIONS

IT can provide opportunities for competitive advantage but IT must be regarded simply as the infrastructure that supports innovation and entrepreneurship. As Duffy and Matheson (1994) point out, "for IT to be used to maximum advantage, senior executives and business managers need to view information technology differently than it is viewed today...it is the capability offered by the information technology infrastructure as a whole that is the key to adaptability, hence survival, not the power of the individual pieces."

The issue of how strategic systems are conceived has not been adequately dealt with in the IS/IT literature. Organisations are too often seen to be investing in technology without adequately addressing issues pertaining to the *management* of information and how information can be used as an asset for the achievement of competitive advantage. The managers participating in the survey reported in this paper have indicated an understanding of the role of IS in developing new competitive applications but they continue to be frustrated by a lack of systematic and systemic approaches that can be used to highlight competitive possibilities. SSM can be used to stimulate action and empower managers to challenge traditional ways of thinking in their organisations. The best managers are now looking beyond technology and highlighting the competencies that are the real drivers of competitive success.

Perhaps the managers of the future should look to the lessons of the past. The great Roman orator M. Tullius Cicero has been described as a man who was an "eternal optimist" but "[t]here is no doubt that he was [also] easily deceived" (Clark, 1962). Optimism remains a characteristic of the best leaders, but like Cicero, many managers are still being deceived by the promise of easily won competitive gains through using IT. Research continues to show that sustainable competitive gains are possible, but strategic goals cannot be reached without first generating possibilities for change, accumulating knowledge, encouraging innovation and fostering IT leadership.

REFERENCES

Benjamin, R. I., Rockart, J. F., Scott-Morton, M. S., and Wyman, J., 1984, Information technology: a strategic opportunity, *Sloan Management Review*, **25**(3): 3–10.

Checkland, P., 1981, *Systems Thinking, Systems Practice*, John Wiley & Sons, Chichester.

Checkland, P., and Scholes, J., 1990, *Soft Systems Methodology in Action*, John Wiley & Sons, Chichester.

Chu, P. C., 1995, Conceiving strategic systems. *Journal of Systems Management*, **46**(4):36–41.

Clark, A. C., 1962, Cicero, *Encyclopaedia Britannica* (Vol. 5), William Benton, Chicago.

Duffy, J., and Matheson, K., 1994, The need for flexible technologies, *CMA Magazine*, **68**: 9–12.

Galliers, R., 1992, Soft systems scenarios, and the planning and development of information systems, *Systemist*, **14**(3):146–159.

Kettinger, W. J., Grover, V., Guha, S., and Segars, A. H., 1994, Strategic information systems revisited: A study in sustainability and performance, *MIS Quarterly*, **18**(1):31–58.

Lado, A. A., and Wilson, M. C., 1994, Human resource systems and sustained competitive advantage: A competency-based perspective, *Academy of Management Review*, **19**(4): 699–727.

Maglitta, J., 1995, Anxious allies, *Computerworld*, **29**:5–9.

Munro, M. C., and Huff, S. L., 1985, Information technology and corporate strategy, *Business Quarterly*, **50**(1):18–24.

Senge, P., 1996, Systems thinking, *Executive Excellence*, **13**(1):15–16.

107

A SYSTEM-STRUCTURAL VIEW OF RELATIONSHIP MARKETING ANALYSIS

Ahmed Beloucif

Aberdeen Business School
The Robert Gordon University
Hilton Place
Aberdeen AB24 4FP, Scotland
Tel: (01224) 283741; Fax: (01224) 283809

1. INTRODUCTION

The aim of this paper is to produce a theoretical framework of relationship marketing analysis from a system perspective. Based on the previous work (Beloucif, 1995), it is an attempt to identify the major dimensions of auditor-client relationship.

2. THE BACKGROUND OF THE STUDY

Explaining behaviour within a social system can be classified as the *system-structural perspective* (Ruckert and Walker,1987). According to Van de Ven ,1976; Nauman and Lincoln, 1984; Zeithaml and Zeithaml, 1984 and Leimberg, 1989, this perspective, which is widespread within both organisation theory and marketing literature, holds that a social system can be examined by exploring the interrelationships among its environment, its relationship structure and process, and its outcomes.

Generally speaking, different types of system structure and processes are judged to be best suited to certain environment situations. Therefore, different systems adopt different internal structure and process. It has been argued that the merit attributed to the fitness between the system's internal characteristics and its environment helps determine the nature of its performance outcomes (Van de Ven and Astley, 1981).

Using the system-perspective, it is believed that many researchers have gone this way to examine relationships (i) between autonomous organisations (Frazier, 1983; Dwyer et al., 1985; Anchrol et al., 1988) and (ii) between individuals at different levels within a single organisation (Zey-ferrel, 1981; Astley and Van de Ven,1983; Ruekert and Walker,1987). This present paper shares the same view and believes that the perspective is also useful for understanding auditor-client relationships. Therefore, this paper will outline the major dimensions of the conceptual framework describing the interactions be-

Systems for Sustainability, edited by Stowell *et al.*
Plenum Press, New York, 1997

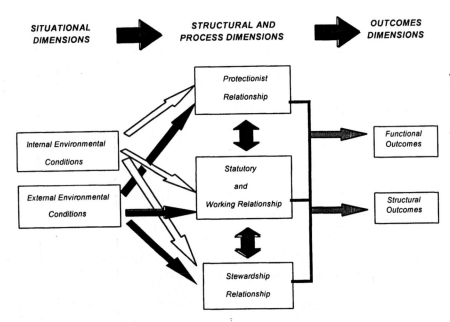

Figure 1. Major dimensions of auditor-client framework.

tween auditors and their clients on the basis of a system-perspective. This paper shows three types of interrelationships (protectionist relationship, stewardship relationship, and statutory and working relationships.)

3. ENVIRONMENTAL SITUATION ANALYSIS

It describes the context in which interaction between auditors and clients takes place. It also includes two dimensions, internal environmental conditions and external environmental conditions. The intervening variables in the internal environment emerging from the analysis are; audit opinion, audit work, self-interest, accounting techniques, opinion shopping, going concern, expectation gap, dependency and ethical guidance etc. For instance, dependency can be seen as exchange between "audit opinion" and audit fees. The client (management) needs to show that they are taking care of the money of their shareholders. The management works towards maintaining the shareholders confidence. This can be shown through the audit opinion expressed by the auditors. In the same time, auditors need work to remain in business. Therefore, auditor audit the company accounts and receive in return an audit fee from the management. This interaction shows the dependency of both of them. It is to note that the internal variables have an influence on the structure and the process of audit-client relationships (protectionist relationship, stewardship and, statutory and working relationship).

The intervening variable in the external environment are; audit regulations, competition, self-regulation and the third parties (banks, creditors, investors, stock exchange, politicians, academics, analysts etc.)

4. STRUCTURAL AND PROCESS ANALYSIS

The two sets of situational dimensions (internal and external environments) combine to influence the ways auditors, shareholders, management and third parties (government, DTI, Stock Exchange, regulators, investors, creditors, banks, stockbroking firms, analysts, etc.) interact. The structure and process dimensions of interactions can be divided into:

1. Protectionist Relationship: (Auditor–Shareholders)
2. Stewardship Relationship: (Management–Shareholders)
3. Statutory and Working relationship: (Auditor–Client)

4.1. Protectionist Relationship

It derives from the fact the auditors are theoretically appointed by the shareholders to protect their interests in the company, i.e., Auditors are paid by the shareholders to check upon the management and protect them from wrongdoing and frauds. In practice, the shareholders are less involved with auditors as the management do.

The *protectionist relationship*, i.e., the interaction between auditors and shareholders has not seen the debate in the City. But, there is a general understanding of making the information available and easy accessible to it through the stock exchange and internet. However, there has been no studies or suggestions on how to make auditors communicate with the shareholders and investors apart from the audit annual report or the audit interim report. However, companies faced a difficult task in steering course between *compliance* with the complex rules and meeting the legitimate demands of analysts for information. A study carried out by Lamb (1996), showed that companies believed the meetings were the most valuable *form of communication* with *investors* at which a wide range of topics and future prospects could be discussed. There are two types of meetings:

1. General meetings held for a wider audience from a range of stockbroking firms and institutional investors;
2. Special meetings held for an individual or small group from one organisation.

Although special meetings are viewed as being more important and more valuable to the companies, they are also more risky for a regulatory standpoint. The less formal, more friendly atmosphere which often surrounds such meetings can lead easily to the unintentional release of price sensitive information. To achieve equal access to information for all users, it has been suggested that details records of all meetings held between investments analysts and directors of quoted companies should be disseminated to market as soon as possible after the meeting using the stock exchange's Regulatory News Service and the Internet. Moreover, a greater use of the Operating and Financial Review should be encouraged to increase the available published information.

4.2. Stewardship Relationship

It involves the management and the shareholders. On the basis of the annual report the shareholders judge the management performance, i.e., it reflects whether the management is taking care of the money of the company's owners (shareholders).

The interaction between management and shareholders, (*stewardship relationship*), has been argued by a number of people. A survey published by ICAS research committee based on 500 of UK's largest companies of their perceptions of the meeting held by companies for analysts and fund managers, it confirms such meetings are firmly established part of the companies investors relations programmes (Lamb, 1996).

4.3. Statutory and Working Relationahip

It is a legal requirement. Under UK company law all limited companies are required to have their financial statements audited by qualified accountants who must report whether or not the statements show a true and fair view. Then, the owners of the company, investors and other interested parties will draw their own conclusions and act accordingly.

The relationship between auditor and client involves formal and informal working rules in preparing the accounts, agreeing about the accounting techniques and the influence of one member on the other. Moreover, it deals with the conflict resolution mechanisms when formal rules or informal influence fails.

From the study of auditor client-relationship five dimensions emerged and are as follows: rapport, capabilities, working relationship, problem solving and commitment. Adding to this, the auditor-client relationship goes through three main stages:

1. Developing relationship: "tell the client what are you good at"
2. Building Relationship: "do what you are good at"
3. Long-term Relationship: "support what you are good at"

5. THE OUTCOME DIMENSIONS ANALYSIS

The results of interactions (i) auditor-shareholders, (ii) management-shareholders and (iii) auditor-client reflect the final components of the system analysis framework.

The outcome dimensions related to statutory and working relationship can be subdivided into (1) functional outcome dimensions and (2) structural outcome dimensions.

The functional outcomes includes the degree of involvement (cooperation) in audit task by auditors, achieving a common goal, i.e., mutual satisfaction, compromise and so on. As functional output dimensions, compromise emerged as important issue. It derives from a mutual understanding and mutual background. Compromise as a dimension describes a situation in which both dyads (auditor and management) have a mutual understanding and background, which lead them to cooperate and reach an acceptable solution without jeopardising the integrity of the auditors (conflict of interest) or showing any danger or bringing the management under scrutiny.

If the public discontent continue, the accountancy profession as self-regulated will lose its privilege to a Government Office which will oversee all audit function. In meanwhile, changes are needed. Reforms within the company (client) are: i) management should respond to the shareholders interests not its own interests, ii) audit committee should be formed, iii) a review of internal management control should be in place and iv) auditors should express their view on the company going concern. In the other hand, reforms within the audit firms are: i) audit firms should be registered as limited liability, ii) their partnership model requires a change and iii) they should disclose their account to the public.

6. CONCLUSION

In the present paper Auditor-Client Framework has been outlined. This framework seeks to identify input dimensions related to environmental conditions, which have influ-

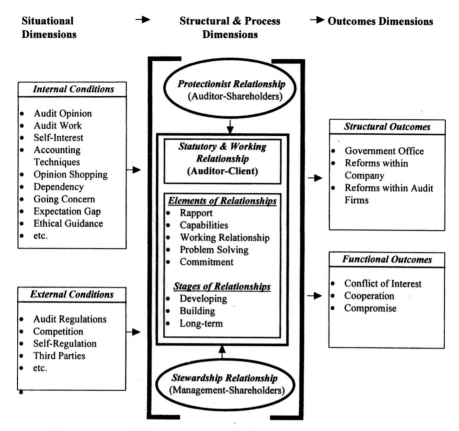

Figure 2. Conceptual framework of auditor–client relationship: a system-perspective.

ence on the structure and process of a particular relationship such as the interaction between auditor and their clients. As results of these influences, output dimensions were identified. Two other relationships (protectionist relationship and stewardship relationship) were also outlined but not examined in details.

The framework still in its exploratory stage and needs to encompass further details when the other two relationships are examined in depth. Nevertheless, it is an attempt to show that previous models using system- perspective are plausible for auditor–client relationship. It has the merit to show as well that the relationship structure and its environment determine the nature of its performance outcomes.

REFERENCES

Achrol, R.S., Reve, T., and Stern, L.W., 1988, Environmental Determinants of Marketing Decision Making Uncertainty in Marketing Channels, *Journal of Marketing Research*. 25:36–50.

Astley, W.G and Van De Ven, A.H., 1983, Central Perspectives and Debates in Organizations Theory, *Administrative Science Quaterly*, 28:245–273.

Beloucif, A.,1995, An Integrated Approach of Analysis, in "Critical Issues in Systems Theory and Practice", (eds) K. Ellis et al. Plenum Press, New York, pp.433–437.

Dwyer, F.R and Welsh, M.A., 1985, Environmental relationships of the internal political economy of marketing channels, *Journal of Marketing Research.* 22:397–414.

Frazier, G.L., 1983, Interorganizational Exchange Behavior in Marketing Channels: A Broadened Perspective, *Journal of Marketing,* 47:68–78.

Glaser, B., and Strauss, A.,1967, "The Discovery of Grounded Theory", Aldine, Chicago.

Lamb, A, 1996, Touching question of compliance, *The Times,* February 1, p.28.

Leimberg, S.R., 1989, Utilizing a "System" Approach to Buy-Sell Planning, *Trusts & Estates*, vol.128, No.5, pp.14–22.

Naumann, E and Lincoln, D.J., 1989, Systems theory Approach to Conducting Industrial Marketing Research, *Journal of Business Research*, vol.19, No.2, pp.151–154.

Ruckert, R.B and Walker, O.C.,1987, Marketing's Interaction with Other Functional Units: A Conceptual Framework and Emperical Evidence, *Journal of Marketing*, 51:1–19.

Van De Ven, A.H., 1976, On the Nature, Formation, and Maintenance of Relationships Among Organisations, *Academy of Management Review*, October, pp.24–36.

Van De Ven, A.H and Astley, W.G., 1981, Mapping the field to Create a Dyanamic Perspective on Organization Design and Behavior, *in* A.H Van de Ven and W.F. Joyce, (eds.) *Perspectives on Organizations Design and Behavior,* John Wiley & Sons, Inc. New York.

Zeithaml, C.P and Zeithaml, V.A., 1984, Environmental Management, *Journal of Marketing*, 48:46–53.

Zey-Ferrel, M., 1981, Criticisms of the Dominant Perspective on Organization, *Sociological Quarterly*, (Spring), 22:181–205.

108

A SYSTEMIC FRAMEWORK FOR SUSTAINABILITY OF PERFORMANCE IN OPERATIONS MANAGEMENT

Alan Fowler

Department of Management Studies
University of Newcastle Upon Tyne
United Kingdom

1. A SYSTEMIC VIEW OF OPERATIONS

Contemporary Operations Management, whether in the manufacturing or service sectors, is ultimately concerned with the processing of input resources to create value-added outputs. Its performance is ultimately measured in terms of cost, quality, variety and delivery. At its highest level a systemic perspective of Operations may be depicted as shown in Figure 1. Operations is thereby seen to be located in the primary value-chain, at the core of the business, and is potentially subject to several uncontrolled external disturbances arising from the business environment. The role of strategic objective formulation and its associated control implications are also presented schematically in Figure 2.

The traditional view of Operations was that it needed to be buffered against such disturbances by the insertion, at critical locations in the system, of stock, inventory and work in progress. Functional buffering was also provided by contiguous departmental functions such as Purchasing, Human Resourse Management (HRM) and Marketing. More recently, pressures of commercial life have dictated that in order to remain lean, agile and competitive these traditional buffers should be removed and Operations subjected to the full rigours of environmental turbulence (Slack, Chambers, Harland, Harrison and Johnston, 1995). Such changes in perspective are encapsulated by Just-In-Time (JIT) and supply chain management concepts with clear implications for the relationships and systemic boundaries between Operations and other departments both internal and external to the organisation. Consequently the boundary of Operations can be thought of as encroaching on, and even subsuming, many of the activities traditionally associated with other functional departments. The existence of this extended boundary is also indicated in Figure 1.

Also considered are the feedback linkages which transform the core processes from a set of linear sequences into a network of interactive, closed loop, circular processes. The main feedback would traditionally occur from the customer through the marketing and

Systems for Sustainability, edited by Stowell *et al.*
Plenum Press, New York, 1997

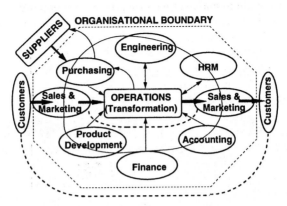

Figure 1. Operations as a system.

sales interface and hence, hopefully, into Product development and Operations. However, additional feedbacks, directly from Sales to Operations and Product-Development may also be envisaged. The advantage of incorporating such direct linkages is that time-delays and attenuation or distortion in the communications process may be mitigated with salutary effects on performance throughout the system.

Finally it may be noted in Figure 1 that the suppliers, traditionally external to the organisation's system boundary, are also included in an additional closed loop comprising information/material flow processes which extend outside of the organisational boundaries. This reflects recognition of the increasingly important role of the supply-chain and the potential for deriving competitive advantage from its effective management (Lamming, 1993). However, the basis upon which these external functions are incorporated into the system may prove more complicated than is the case for internal functions, a point which is taken up later in this paper.

The final point concerning this networked, multivariable model of the customer-focused value-chain is that it must be treated as a dynamic system. Time delays are inevitable in the various physical and informational processes depicted. The system therefore exists in a state of perpetual change and due to the existence of feedback is always, in ac-

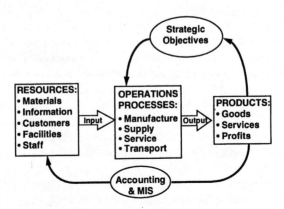

Figure 2. Strategy and control.

cordance with the principle of classical feedback theory, potentially subject to dynamic instability. Furthermore it must be recognised that in practice, many of the elements in the system will display non-linear characteristics in terms of the relationships between their inputs and outputs.

While the consequences of these effects may arguably be understood within the local domain of a particular function, the overall systemic implications in such closed-loop systems can be highly unpredictable and even counterintuitive. These complications are compounded by the long time-constants often experienced in management systems. This means that effects often materialise at some location in the system, remote from the point of initiation and displaced in time, often by months, possibly by years. As a result, causality and cause-effect sequences may be very difficult to trace.

It is in this sense that the discipline of systems-thinking and its supporting tools of dynamic-modelling, control systems theory and simulation become essential factors in contemporary Operations Management.

2. CONTROLLING THE TRANSFORMATION PROCESS

A closed-loop control perspective of Operations may usefully be visualised by reference to Figure 2. The system's inputs are categorised either as transformable resources or transforming resources. The transformable resources are typically materials, information, finance and people. This broad range of inputs accommodates a generic set of processes which include manufacturing, supply, services and transport. These produce a range of outputs including goods, services and profit.

Feedback is shown to occur through two primary routes. Revenue generated in the output block flows back to feed the resourcing block on the input side, through the medium of the accounting function. Information flows similarly occur which could, for example, lead to developments in the technology used or to motivational changes affecting selection, morale and performance of the people employed. Information relating to outputs also affects the attractiveness of the business with respect to investment prospects, value of the company, credit-worthiness, capability for securing favourable supply terms etc. Formal and informal management information systems facilitate these respective linkages. The upper feedback loop accommodates the process of Operations-strategy formulation and implementation, thereby encapsulating the circular relationship between strategy formulation and implementation. This reflects the concepts of Hayes and Wheelwright (1984) who showed that good Operations Management could lead, as well as be led by, business strategy.

Hence it is seen that Operations must be seen as a dynamic network of closed loops within loops, permeated by delays and nonlinearities to produce a system which is complex and therefore potentially subject to counterintuitive dynamic behaviour.

3. THE ROLE OF SIMULATION IN OPERATIONS STRATEGY

Simulation in production and operations management traditionally implies the discrete-event approach involving queues and servers, with probabilistic distributions for arrival and service times. These are a powerful aid to, for example, problems of detailed factory layout design. However, at a strategic level, where there is a need to gain an overall, holistic and systemic view, there has recently occurred a surge of interest in continuous system simulation with its emphasis on aggregated variables, process flows and state-variable integration (Spurr, Layzell, Jennison and Richards, 1993). Several simulation products now exist which are specifically formulated for application in a business context, being primarily aimed at Business Process Reengineering (BPR) and similar applications. These tools potentially present a very useful mechanism for modelling, analysing and synthesising Operations with other aspects of the business (Fowler, 1995). A typical example is therefore presented below featuring the topical issue of supply-chain management.

3.1. Supply Chain Dynamics

Concepts such as Porter's value chain and value system analysis, in the strategic management context, and JIT, lean production concepts arising in the production and operations context, find a natural and integrative expression in the subject content of supply chain management. The value-adding process, as perceived and paid for by the customer, may transcend several organisational boundaries. From this holistic perspective what matters most is the achievement of an effective and efficient process overall. However, where boundaries exist there is always a danger of suboptimisation. BPR, for example, aims to eliminate the adverse effects of functional boundaries with respect to process flow within the organisation (Hammer and Champy, 1990). However, it may prove more difficult to achieve this objective when working across not just internal functional boundaries but company boundaries also.

For example JIT has been criticised on the charge that it merely reduces internal inventory held at the expense of the supplier (Lamming, 1993). In other words inventory has not been eliminated, simply displaced, thereby becoming someone else's problem. If this is the case, the net gain is substantially reduced and the aim should be to improve the total process, not just part of it.

The potential for problems is further extended if a significant change in operating conditions is encountered. For example, it may not be apparent to those involved in outlets near to the customer that dynamically, the consequence of their actions may have disproportionate consequences for those located further upstream in the supply chain. Forrester (1958) recognised this situation almost forty years ago in his seminal work on systems dynamics theory. However it remains questionable as to how far this realisation has permeated into collective managerial consciousness. Arguably, the current emphasis on tight

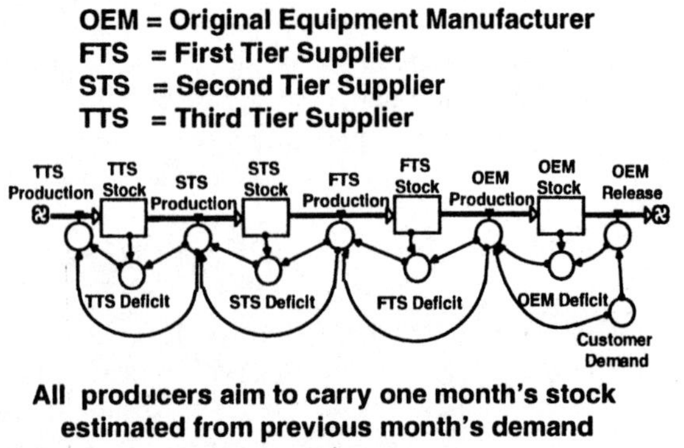
OEM = Original Equipment Manufacturer
FTS = First Tier Supplier
STS = Second Tier Supplier
TTS = Third Tier Supplier
TTS Production
TTS Stock
STS Production
STS Stock
FTS Production
FTS Stock
OEM Production
OEM Stock
OEM Release
TTS Deficit
STS Deficit
FTS Deficit
OEM Deficit
Customer Demand
All producers aim to carry one month's stock estimated from previous month's demand

Figure 3. Four-tier supply-chain.

control, minimal stock, lean productions and cross company co-operation should bring these issues much more sharply into focus than at any time in the past and the full potential of systems-theory may prove highly advantageous in helping to solve associated problems in this area.

For example, Figure 3 depicts a typical four-tier supply chain in which production rates and stock control policy follow a simple heuristic in which production, at each stage, is geared to demand during the previous month. Production control policy thereby aims to ensure sufficient stock is carried at each stage to match one month's demand based on last month's consumption. This is a good approximation to actual production policy in many cases (Slack et. al., 1995).

However, even this apparently rational and innocent looking system can display dynamic behaviour which may, to many, appear surprising. While everything works well under steady-state equilibrium conditions a relatively modest change in customer demand produces an intriguing set of dynamic responses as displayed in the simulation result shown in Figure 4. Significant swings in production occur and these are amplified the further we move back down the supply-chain. It is also apparent that the transients do not subside until four months after the initial disturbance occurred. Although the OEM can cope reasonably well with the change, the impact on suppliers is potentially disastrous. It is readily shown, for example by refining the simulation model, that inclusion of the production and transport delays which inevitably occur in practice, make matters even worse than those depicted in Figure 4.

Viewed holistically, this arrangement is clearly unsatisfactory. A solution is required which takes account of all systemic linkages in order to produce a process which genuinely increases efficiency, reduces cost, and therefore affords better value to the customer whilst simultaneously providing improved margins for all the production stages. Clearly the need for a systemic view is demonstrated and once again it is seen that this need arises primarily as a result of the paradigm shift from a static, or equilibrium view of the system, to one which is wholly dynamic.

4. CONCLUSIONS

Operations, in one form or other, is at the heart of the value-adding activities undertaken by virtually all organisations. Operations interacts with, and arguably subsumes, key

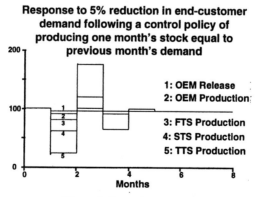

Figure 4. Dynamic responses.

aspects of most other functions. However, to become more fully integrated into the strategic framework of organisational thinking it is increasingly necessary to adopt a more holistic and systemic treatment of the subject.

A natural extension of the systemic perspective, when taken in this context, is the application of continuous-system simulation methods. This involves modelling aggregated state-variables to acquire a strategic overview of operational dynamics which naturally unfold when the system is subjected to uncontrolled disturbances arising in the environment.

Control is also presented as an important dimension affecting the sustainability of operational performance. Control philosophies including feedback and feedforward, MRP, JIT and Supply-chain management may be considered within the linked systems-thinking and simulation framework. Systems design may thereby proceed in a flexible and relatively risk-free environment.

It is concluded that Operations Management and its associated control and information systems, can significantly benefit from a complete opening up to, and re-evaluation by, open systems thinking and continuous-system simulation.

REFERENCES

Forrester, J.W., 1958, Industrial Dynamics: A Major Breakthrough for Decision Makers, *Harvard Business Review* 36 (4):37–66.

Fowler, A., 1995, Simulation As a Management Tool in Strategic Analysis And Decision Making, *Proceedings of 7th European Simulation Symposium*, Erlangen, Oct. 26–28, 1995, p.553–557, Society For Computer Simulation, Ghent.

Hammer, M. and Champy, J., 1993, *Reengineering the Corporation, A Manifesto for Business Revolution*, Nicholas Brealey, London.

Hayes, R.H. and Wheelwright, S.C., 1984, *Resoring our Competitive Edge*, Wiley, Chichester.

Lamming, R., 1993, *Beyond Partnerships: Strategies For Innovation and Lean Supply*, Prentice Hall, London

Slack, N., Chambers, S., Harland, C., Harrison A. and Johnson, R., 1995, *Operations Management*, Pitman, London.

Spurr, K., Layzell, P., Jennison, L. and Richards, N., 1993, *Software Assistance for Business Re-engineering*, Wiley, Chichester.

109

INTEGRATING KNOWLEDGE FOR INNOVATION

Jon-Arild Johannessen,[1,2] Jens Otto Dolva,[1] and Bjørn Olsen[1]

[1]Bodø Graduate School of Business
Agder Research Foundation, Norway
[2]Lillehammer College
Norway

1. INTRODUCTION

The focus on knowledge as a productive resource for innovation, economic growth, in addition to the productivity of the knowledge workers, has received increasing attention during the 90s. The persons who have discussed this theme extensively have been, among others, Toffler (1990), Reich (1991), Quinn (1992), Drucker (1993), Archibagi & Michie (1995) in addition to Nonaka & Takeuchi (1995) and Barton (1995). Clear research findings from , among others, Von Hippel (1988:5) indicate that companies performing innovative activities display greater earning power than companies which do not innovate. Furthermore research (European Commission, 1995, table 29: 26) indicates a correlation leading up to a conclusion that smaller companies are more dependent on external sources to develop innovation, than larger companies.

The concept of the regional innovation centres is developed (in this paper) to promote the interaction and structural couplings between the elements in the regional innovation system. The purpose of this paper is to develop an analytical framework for this interaction and structural coupling to promote the development from a potensially to an actually regional system of innovation.

Regional innovation systems comprise the same elements as in the national innovation system, only in a smaller geographical area. Even if the necessary elements are in evidence to the extent that a regional innovation system could be said to be existing, that would not constitute an adequate basis for operative status on the part of the innovation system. There have to be additional structural links, securing interaction and co-ordination in the regional innovation system. This leads to a conceptual distinction between the actual and potential innovation systems, both regional and national. The purpose of this conceptual distinction is to present structural terms required if national and regional innovation systems are to promote innovative behaviour at the company level.

Systems for Sustainability, edited by Stowell *et al.*
Plenum Press, New York, 1997

2. DEVELOPMENT TOWARDS A MODEL FOR REGIONAL INNOVATION CENTRES

For an actual national innovation system investment in the knowledge-based infrastructure is critical for the development of innovation activity at the company level (World Bank ,1991; OECD,1992). In this context the OECD report also emphasises that a critical factor to success and innovation is the existence of a link between technological knowledge accumulation, company-internal learning processes and institutional strength. In other words, it is knowledge integration which is being stressed.

The variables appearing as important in this context are the following:

- The public support system
- National financing systems (bank, insurance etc.)
- R & D environments
- Technological /economic competence
- Organisational competence
- International competence

It is important that the link between companies and the knowledge capital, also is linked towards a network of international knowledge institutions in order to maximise the innovation potential in the individual companies. It is further crucial that a "scanning" system functions satisfactorily, making companies continually updated on national and international affairs of critical importance in the local context. The strong upheavals and radical innovations in the market and in technology require a "scanning" system and structural links which SME is not in the position to gain access to, neither in an initiation phase nor later (European Commission, 1995). It is structural links and scanner systems (scanning institutions)we try to bring forth through the idea of regional innovation centres (Compare figure 1). The purpose of these scanning institutions is to insure:

- Global thinking and local innovation
- Quick response to market changes
- Market flexibility
- The development of a culture for innovation of SME in the local context
- Continuos updating on international trends, with regards to "image and design", which can be critical for market penetration.
- Organisational learning based on the global input.
- The development of knowledge-based infrastructures locally, but linked globally.

It is the systemic nature (Johannessen, 1996; 1997) which is focused on in national and regional innovation systems. This appears clearly from the following excerpt from OECD (1992:22): "National systems of innovation involve a set of networks linked in such a way that the creation and diffusion of technology and its transformation into commercial products depends as much on the vitality of the whole set of relationships as on the individual performance of any given element of the system". The systemic nature of national and regional innovation systems means that the focus both in research and policy implication should be on the system of relations and the coupling structure to the relations, not the elements constituting a national and regional innovation system.

The idea in figure 1 is that there is a tight structural coupling between all the elements of the model, and furthermore the organisation is coupled to regional innovation centres with scanning and diffusion functions towards needs/wishes of the local SME. Re-

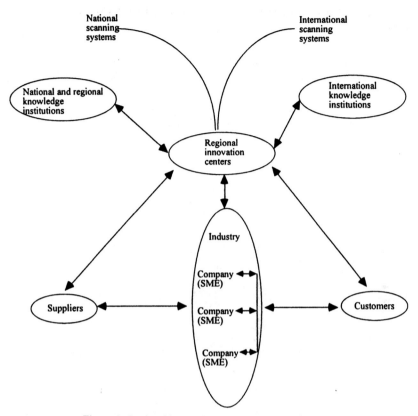

Figure 1. Regional innovation centres: The innovative bee.

gional innovation centres is meant to function as information selection filters and local receiver competence centres for the SME (Eliasson, 1996; Cohen & Levinthal, 1989).

The model can be seen as a transfer of experience from, among others, the Emilia Romagna region in Italy (Bellini, 1990; Bianchi & Giordani, 1993), in addition to the experiences from Baden-Wurtenberg (Morgan, 1992). (NB. While the innovation system in Emilia-Romagna is based on SME, the innovation system in Baden-Wurtenberg is based on large companies).

We have in fig.1, also integrated the system elements by David & Foray (1994) denoted as central for innovation activities.

Integration of R & D activities in the region with experience-based knowledge in companies, is regarded as critical for the development and reinforcement of innovation processes in companies (see Bianchi & Giordani, 1993). Rhetorically expressed, there is in the R & D sector either too much R and too little D, or little R and much D, while new business establishment and innovation activity as a result of the institutional R &D are inadequate. We believe, on the basis of the previous analysis, that a lot of the answer to this is found in the lack of knowledge integration, structural links and a poorly developed "scanning" system.

3. REGIONAL INNOVATION CENTRES: THE IMPORTANCE OF KNOWLEDGE INTEGRATION

Increased innovation activity as a result of integration and co-ordination of knowledge, which is a focal point for regional innovation centres, has been documented in several international studies:

- Between the supplier and the company this has been documented by Lundavall (1988) ; Andersen (1992); Håkansson (1989).
- Between companies in the same line of business this has been documented by Von Hippel (1988), Schrader (1991), De Bresson & Amesse (1991).
- Between National innovation systems and line of business this has been documented by Carlson (1992).
- Between national innovation systems and regional service centres this has been documented by Freeeman (1987).
- Between regional service centres and line of business this has been documented by Freeman (1987) and Malerba (1991).
- Between regional service centres and international R & D this has been documented by Hagedorn & Shakenrad (1990).
- Between company and customers this document is represented with Von Hippel (1986); European Commision (1995, table 30: 26) and Craig (1995).

The model (fig. 1) incorporates these results in the coupling structure, where the regional innovation centers constitutes a knowledge-based intermediary scanning institution, or what OECD refers to as "intermediate structures".

Instead of developing direct contacts between SME and knowledge workers, the OECD report (1993) argues in favour of developing "intermediary structures", supposed to function as knowledge brokers in a structurally linked network. Fig. 1 is a continued development of the idea from the OECD report, ingrained in our concept regional innovation centres.

One important consequence of the idea of national and regional innovation systems, is that the innovation activities depend more on a system of relations between the elements than of the efficiency of the individual elements. It is around this part-total understanding that policy implications should be focused, i.e. contexts and patterns between company-internal, company-external and national and regional innovation systems should be subject to contextual considerations, both in terms of organising such links, knowledge development and knowledge integration in these structural links. Experiences from USA show up to a 40% productivity increase for companies in command of this type of knowledge integration (Henderson, 1994). The same tendencies have also been pointed out in Japan (Nonaka & Takeuchi, 1995).

The knowledge diversity which will exist in regional innovation centres makes it possible for SME to exploit important complementary advantages of which the individual SME is not in total command. These examples of complementary access may generate and use ideas which the individual SME can take advantage of in their internal innovation processes.

CONCLUSION: THEORETICAL IMPLICATIONS

An important point in the concepts national and regional innovation systems is the emphasis on interactive learning processes. In this context it is the interaction between in-

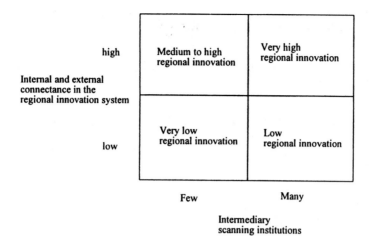

Figure 2. Connectance and scanning institutions.

ternal and external knowledge sources in SME which is supposed to be the driving forces in the innovation process. It is the exchange of information between the internal knowledge base and external knowledge bases localised in various types of knowledge institutions, which is supposed to have impact on innovation activities in the individual SME. It is this very link between the market knowledge of the companies, knowledge about customer needs and desires on the one hand and the intimacy between companies and knowledge institutions, which is pointed out as important mechanisms in the perspective on national and regional innovation systems. It is both the identification and development of the possibilities for continuos innovation processes, in addition to the identification and development of innovative potential which is implicit in a closer link between companies and national and regional knowledge institutions. The communication of knowledge and the transfer of competence between the various sources is regarded as a central element in this concept. How the various links are developed is in this context regarded as particularly important as a trigger of innovation activities in SME. It is, however, only the explicit knowledge which immediately can be transferred between the various systems. The tacit or skill-based knowledge can less easily be transferred. It is conceivable that the tacit knowledge is in fact the element which starts off the continuous innovation processes in the individual companies, while the preconditions for this sequence of events taking place will be the existence of structural links with high degree og connectance in the regional and national innovation system.

Regional innovation centres can be one mechanism securing innovative routines in the individual companies. The role of the regional innovation centres, in this context, might also be knowledge brokers and information "scanners" in the international environment, in terms of technological and organisational innovations, in addition to transferring this competence to the respective SME. The role as information "scanners" will be increasingly important if the tendency towards globalization of the economy and the concentration of R & D activities to the home bases of big companies is strengthened. In this way the field of institutional inertia, likely to come in conflict with innovative ideas, can be circumvented. If we capitalise on established institutions as vehicles for the promotion of innovative activities in the companies, factors for power, social relationships, norms, and value systems may function as institutional brakes, more likely to hinder than to further, innovative activity in the companies. This could be an explanatory factor of how companies to such a limited extent establish contact with the knowledge institutions related to innovation, as shown by several studies.

REFERENCES

Andersen, E.S. (1992). Approaching national Systems of innovation from the production and linkage structure. In B. Lundvall (Ed.). Towards a new Approach, Pinter, London.

Archibugi, D. & J. Michie (1995). Technology and Innovation: An Introduction, Cambridge Journal of Economics, 19: 1–4.

Barton, D.L. (1995). Wellsprings of Knowledge: Building and Sustaining the Sources of Innovation, Harvard Business School Press, Boston, MASS.

Bellini, N. et.al. (1990). The industrial policy of Emilian Romagna: The business service centres. In R.Leonard & R. Nanetti (eds.). The Regions and European Integration: The case of Emilia-Romagna, p. 171–186, Pinter, London.

Bianchi, D. & Giordani, M.G. (1993). Innovation Policy at the local and National Levels: The case of Emilia- Romagna, European Planning Studies, 1, 1: 25–41.

Carlsson, B. (1992). Technological Systems and Economic Development Potential: Four Swedish case studies: Paper presented at the conference of the international Joseph A. Schumpeter Society, Kyoto, August

Cohen, W.M. & Lewinthal, D.A. (1989). Innovation and Learning the two faces of R&D, Economic Journal, 99: 569–596.

Craig, T. (1995). Achieving Innovation Through Bureaucracy: Lessons from the japanese Brewing Industry, California Management Review, vol. 38, no. 1: 8–37.

David, P. & Foray, D. (1994). Accessing and Expanding the Science and Technology Base, OECD, DSTI/TIP, nr. 4.

De Bresson, C. & Amesse, F. (1991). Networks of Innovation: A review and introduction to the issue, Research Policy, Vol. 20: 363–379.

Drucker, P.F. (1993). "Post-capitalist Society," Butterworth Heineman, New York.

Eliasson, G. (1996). Spillovers integrated production and the theory of the firm, Journal of Evolutionary Economics, 6 (2): 125–140.

European Commission, (1995). Green paper on innovation, Brussel.

Freeman, C. (1987). Technology, Policy and Economic Performance: lessons from Japan, Pinter, London.

Hagedorn, J. & Schakenrad, J. (1990). Inter-firm partnership and co-operative strategies in core technologies. In C. Freeman & L. Soete (eds.). New Explorations in the Economics of Technological Change, Pinter, London.

Håkansson, H. (1989). Cooperative Technological Behaviour. Co-operation and networks, Routledge, London.

Johannessen, J-A. (1996). Systemics Applied to the Study of Organizational Fields: Developing a Systemic Research Strategy for Organizational Fields. Kybernetes, vol. 25, 1: 33–51

Johannessen, J-A. (1997). Aspects of causal processes: A Systemic view, Kybernetes, Vol. 26 (1) (Forthcoming).

Lundvall, B. Å. (1988). Innovation as an interactive process: from user-producer interaction Economic Theory, Pinter, London.

Malerba, F. (1991). Italy: The National System of Innovation, Mimeo, CESPRI, Bocconi, University Milano.

Nonaka, I. & Takeuchi, H. (1995). The Knowledge Creating Company, Oxford University Press, Oxford.

OECD, (1992). Technology and the Economy: The Key Relationships, Paris, OECD.

OECD, (1993). Small and Mediumsized Enterprises, Technology and Competitiveness,

Paris, OECD.

Quinn, J.B. (1992). "Intelligent Enterprise", The Free Press, New York.

Reich, R.B. (1991). The Work of Nations, Alfred A. Knop, New York.

Schrader, S. (1991). Information transfer between firms: Cooperation through information trading, Research Policy, vol. 20: 153–170.

Toffler, A. (1990). Powershift: Knowledge, Wealth and Violence at the Edge of the 21 st. Century, Bantam Books, New York.

Von Hippel, E. (1986). Lead-users: A source of new Product Concepts, Management Science, Vol. 32, no. 7: 791–805.

Von Hippel, E. (1988). The Sources of Innovation, Oxford University Press, Oxford.

World Bank, (1991). World Development Report, Oxford University Press, New York.

110

SYSTEMS OF INNOVATION

Jon-Arild Johannessen,[1,2] Jens Otto Dolva,[1] and Bjørn Olsen[1]

[1]Bodø Graduate School of Business
Agder Research Foundation, Norway
[2]Lillehammer College
Norway

1. INTRODUCTION

Schumpeter's view of the conditions for developing innovation changed from a very early view (Schumpeter, 1934) of the entrepreneur as the motor of innovation processes, to a later notion (Schumpeter, 1942), where he strongly emphasised the collective process constituted by the R & D activities. Through the concept national innovation systems, Lundvall (1988; 1992) and Nelson (1993), among others, further developed Schumpeter's view of innovation as an interactive process. Our contribution in this article is also at the collective level, but contrary to Lundvall and Nelson, we do not view the collective pre-requisites which have to exist in the individual company in order for innovation processes to occur. It is systemst working in an interactive process which will constitute our focus of attention.

2. THE PATTERNS WHICH COMBINE INNOVATION PROCESSES

An analytical scheme for the understanding of innovation as an evolutionary process is shown in figure 1.

We find support for an analytical scheme of this kind with Schumpeter (1934), Kirtzner (1976; 1985), Nelson & Winter (1982) and Winter (1987).

Routine-based behaviour in systems and social fields functions as a conservative mechanism in relation to innovation activities, and "the economic paradigm" (see Anderson, 1994: 46), "the technological paradigm", "the technological trajectories" (see Dosi & Orsenigo, 1988), "technological regime" (Nelson & Winter, 1982) or a "the techno-economic paradigm" (see Freeman & Perez, 1988), which keeps the economic system in a state of stable equilibrium, and dominate the technical and managerial decisions in this phase.

Exovation is a concept used by Clark & Staunton (1989). By exovation is understood the prerequisites required by the organisation in order for it to take advantage of the

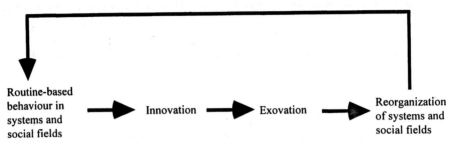

Figure 1. Analytical scheme: innovation.

innovation potential. Exovation focuses on the processes which are required to induce the removal of the old in order for the new to thrive and grow.

The transition from routine-based behaviour to innovation in the individual companies constitutes periods of experimenting, testing and search for e.g. new production methods, new markets, new production processes, new organisational structures, new products and raw materials. For the individual company and the social fields this means periods with great political tension, where routine-based behaviour is directly juxtaposed and compared with innovative behaviour. In this period of transition, control and stabilising mechanisms will be prominent instruments (see Boyer, 1988:67–95) both in the individual company, in social fields and in social systems in general. It is in this transition phase that competitive openings appear and are filled with innovative entrepreneurs while old competitive regulations change character. In Dosi's (1988a:221–239) article the four conditions for innovation can be linked to this phase (see table 1). We put these prerequisites in connection with the consequences for the individual company and possible policy implication in table 1.

Innovation and exovation are parallel phenomena. If the one operates without the other no development will take place in the long run. On the other hand one could function without the other in certain fields, geographically or trade-wise. Some geographical fields can be exposed to exovation without simultaneous innovation in the field. These areas will thus feel the economic and social consequences most strongly, as the new is not simultaneously breaking through.

Table 1. Innovation: prerequisites, consequences and policy implications

Prerequisites	System consequences	Policy-implications
Accepting uncertainty	Less routine- based behaviour	Developing attitudes which reward and accept "error"
Sensitivity towards technological possibilities	Experimental orientation	Developing an innovation strategy where new products will be a part of the company´s portfolio
Extensive searching activity	Network activities	Formalizing contact with regional, national and international R&D institutions
Learning through application and performance	Knowledge creation and knowledge integration in the company	Developing internal and external learning systems for the companies

The more systems and social fields are internationalised organised and globalized, the more far-reaching are the consequences for systems not continuously subject to innovation, as there will always be on-going innovation and exovation processes in a global context, and the consequences of these processes are more strongly felt locally in a global economy.

3. CLASSIFICATION OF INNOVATION

Basically there are two types of innovations: product and process innovations. These are not mutually preclusive, but depend on each other in a major degree. Process innovations can furthermore be divided into organisation and technology, where by organisation is meant new market organisation and new internal company organisation. By technology is here meant artifacts. We have omitted these distinctions in figure 2, in order not to increase the complexity in the figure. In practical contexts these distinctions will however be of great importance.

Innovations can also be seen as incremental, i.e. small step-by -step improvements, or radical, i.e. something qualitatively new. Incremental- and radical-innovations can also be autonomous, i.e. what is new can be kept separate, or systemic, i.e. the new is dependent on changes taking place in the process/product linked to the new product or process. One example of autonomous innovation is "snowboard". One example of systemic innovation is IBM's OS/2, which presupposed change in other systems in the value chain. Figure 2 offers a schematic depiction of these distinctions and some presumed consequences. Systemic innovations are, among other things, described by Jagger & Miles (1991), Fleck (1993) and Kodama (1992). The importance of various types of organisation forms for various types of innovations (autonomous and systemic) has been discussed by Chesbrough & Teece etc. (1996). The right side of the figure gives no indications as to the types of reorganisation of systems and social fields which can conceivably be envisaged as the result of product- and process innovations.

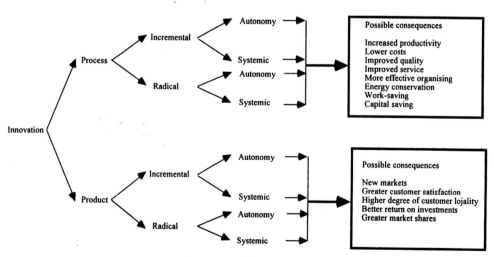

Figure 2. Classification of innovation.

4. THE CIRCULAR MODEL OF INNOVATION

Kirtzner's (1985:12) view is that the entrepreneur engages in a continuos innovative process in the market and thus: "fuels a tendency toward equilibrium". But if this continuos renewal process is carried out internally in existing companies, with the emphasis on continuous innovations, this will bring about a process jeopardising market equilibrium and thus fuel(ling) a tendency towards dis-equilibrium, as new combinations will continuously destabilize the market. Put in another way, an innovation being brought to the market will destabilize monopoly rents from previous innovations in the same area, and thus disturb the equilibrium. If innovations are constantly occurring, the market will also be in a constant state of disequilibrium. To prevent imitation in order to sustain monopoly rents is essential for any company. This puts the company in the position to cover the costs of one innovation by cashing in extra benefits from this for a time, and it is time which is the main point of figure 3.

It is, among other things, these two contrasting tendencies which generate the dynamics of the economy. In this perspective the entrepreneur and the innovator become opposite poles in the economic dynamics. While the entrepreneur pushes the accelerator towards the state of equilibrium, the innovator does the same towards dynamic states of disequilibrium. Figure 3 indicates these two conflicting tendencies in the economy.

Innovation activities is in this way understood as the shock waves which are constantly trimming the economy and sustaining the economic dynamics.

CONCLUSION

Innovation is supposed to be a major element in economic growth, and secure an improved competitive position for the companies. Innovation research is a fundamental study

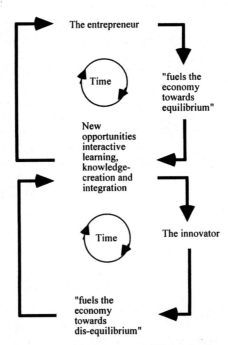

Figure 3. The entrepreneur and the innovator as different functions in the economy.

of change processes, knowledge development and knowledge integration, for the purpose of generating new combinations. To uncover critical innovation factors hindering/promoting change processes, knowledge development and knowledge integration is thus regarded as essential in innovation research. Knowledge is to a great extent a result of interactive learning processes at various system levels. How these learning processes can be improved is thus essential for innovation.

While the linear model focuses on explicit knowledge, the circular model (also denoted as the co-operation model, the interactive model and the cyclical model) emphasises a system of relations between the following entities: R & D activities, structural links, tacit knowledge, interactive learning, the cultural context, social processes, national and regional innovation systems and customer and supplier relations (see Lundvall, 1992; Campagni, 1991:8).

It is the emphasis on a variety of knowledge types, and the links between them which is regarded as the most valuable resource in the circular model, and learning is regarded as the most important process. This is also the basic idea in the circular innovation model (see Lundvall & Johnson, 1994). Another dominant feature pertaining to the circular innovation model is the store set by collaboration, as opposed to the emphasis on competition (see Lundvall & Johnson, 1994:26; You & Wilkinson, 1994: 265).

The circular innovation model observes the connection between organisational, technological, and environmental factors (see OECD, 1992; Smith, 1994; Klein & Rosenberg, 1986; Dosi, 1988; Malerba, 1992). The model presupposes that innovation processes vary from company to company, and that there is a pattern of interactive processes which generates innovation activity in the companies.

The circular model is based on theoretical assumptions for a more evolutionary economic theory (see Jacobsen 1992; Metcalfe, 1995:25–46) and knowledge derived from new economic growth theories (see Scott, 1989). In the circular model R & D activities are not seen as the primary process generating innovations, but rather as part of a bigger system of relations among various elements: market contact, design, financial opportunities, the possibilities of linking the company to external knowledge systems, the use of information and communication technology, management skills, company culture, network activities and the regional and national innovation system (see Smith, 1994: 7–8; Klein & Rosenberg, 1986).

The research policy implications of the circular model will be that the emphasis on research must turn more toward relations between elements generating innovation systems at various system levels, in order to disclose patterns hindering/promoting innovation in social systems. To achieve this goal several methods must be applied in the same research project or at least research program, e.g. statistical investigations, hypothesis testing, longitudinal studies, comparative studies and more angles of incidence based on action research. By using an interdisciplinary approach simultaneously, we may find ourselves in a position to disclose the system of relations between elements constituting a pattern which hinders/promotes innovation.

REFERENCES

Boyer, R. (1988). Technical change and the theory of regulation. In Dosi, G., Freeman, C., Nelson, R., Silverberg, G. & Soete, L (Ed.).: 221–239. Technical Change and Economic Theory, Pinter, London.

Camagni, R. (Ed.). (1991). Innovation networks: spatial perspective, Belhaven Press, London.

Chesbrough, H.W. & D.J. Teece (1996). When is Virtual Virtuous? Organizing for innovation, Harvard Business Review, Jan-Feb.

Clark, P. & Staunton, N. (1989). Innovation in technology and organization, Routledge, London.

Dosi, G. (1988). Sources, procedures and microeconomic effect of innovation, Journal of Economic Litterature, Vol. 36: 1126–71.

Dosi, G. (1988a). The nature of the innovative process. In Dosi, G., Freeman, C., Nelson, R., Silverberg, G. & Soete, L (Ed.).: 221–239. Technical Change and Economic Theory, Pinter, London.

Dosi, G. & Orsenigo, L. (1988). Co-ordination and transformation: An overview of structures, behaviors and change in evolutionary environments. In Dosi, G., Freeman, C., Nelson, R., Silverberg, G. & Soete, L (Ed.).: 13–38. Technical Change and Economic Theory, Pinter, London.

Fleck, J. (1993). Configurations crystalling contingency, The international journal of Human factors in manufacturing, Vol. 3, no. 1: 15–36.

Freeman, C. & Perez, C. (1988). Structural Crisis of adjustment, business cycles and investment behaviour. In Dosi, G., Freeman, C., Nelson, R., Silverberg, G. & Soete, L (Ed.).: 38–67. Technical Change and Economic Theory, Pinter, London.

Jagger, N.S.B. & I.D. Miles (1991). New telematic services in Europe. In Freeman, C. M.Sharp & W. Walker (Ed.). Technology and the Future of Europe, Pinter, London.

Jacobsen, R. (1992). The Austian School of Strategy, Academy of Management Review, 17, 4: 782–807.

Kirzner, I.M. (1976). On the method of Austrian economics. In E.G. Dolan (Ed.). The foundation of modern Austrian economics, 40–51, Sheed & Ward, Kansas City, MO.

Kirzner, I.M. (1985). Discovery and the Capitalist Process, University of Chicago Press, Chicago.

Klein, S. & Rosenberg, N. (1986). An Overview of innovation. In R.Landan & N. Rosenberg (Ed.). The positive sum strategy, National Academy Press, Washington.

Kodama, F. (1992). Japans unique capacity to innovate: technology fusion and its international implications. In T.S. Arrison, C.F. Bergsten, E.M. Graham & M.C. Harris (Ed.). Japans growing technological capability: Implications for the US economy, National Academy Press, Washington DC.

Lundvall, B.Å. (1988). Innovation as an interactive process from User-producer interaction to the national system of innovation, In G. Dosi, C.Freeman, R.Nelson, G. Silverberg & L. Soete (Ed.),349–370. Technical Change and Economic Theory, Pinter, London.

Lundvall, B.Å. (Ed.). (1992). National Systems of Innovation, Pinter, London.

Lundvall, B.Å. & B.Johnson (1994). The Learning economy, Journal of industry studies, 1, 2: 23–42.

Malerba, F. (1992). The Organization of the innovative process. In N. Rosenberg; R. Landan & D. Mowery (Ed.). Technology and the Wealth of Nations, s. 247–280, Stanford University Press, Stanford.

Metcalfe, J.S. (1995). Technology systems and technology policy in an evolutionary framework, Cambridge Journal of Economics, 19: 25–46.

Nelson, R. R. (Ed.). (1993). National Innovation Systems, Oxford University Press, Oxford.

Nelson, R.R. & S.G. Winter (1982). An Evolutionary Theory of Economic Change, Harvard University Press, Cambridge, Mass.

OECD, (1992). Technology and the Economy: The Key Relationships, Paris, OECD.

Schumpeter, J. (1934). The theory of economic development, Harvard University Press, Cambridge: Mass.

Schumpeter, J.A. (1942). Capitalism, Socialism and Democracy, Unwin, London.

Scott, M.F. (1989). A new View of Economic Growth, Clarendon Press, Oxford.

Smith, K. (1994). New direction in research and technology policy: Identifying the key issues, STEP rapport, nr. 1, Oslo.

Winter, S.G. (1987). Natural Selection and Evolution. I J. Eatwell, M. Milgate & P. Newman (Ed.). Vol.3: 614–617. The New Palgrave: A Dictionary of Economics, 4 vols, Macmillan, London.

You, J.L. & F. Wilkinson (1994). Competition and Co-operation: Toward understanding industrial districs, Review of Political Economy, 6,3: 259–278.

111

A SYSTEMS PERSPECTIVE OF THE EXTENDED ENTERPRISE

G. P. Nelder, P. A. Lowenthal, P. J. and Sackett

The CIM Institute, SIMS
Cranfield University
Cranfield, MK43 0AL, United Kingdom

1. FUTURE MANUFACTURING TRENDS

Recent reports have identified a number of imperatives that will have a profound effect on the system of manufacturing during the next century (Iaccoca Institute, 1991; Browne, Sackett and Wortmann, 1992). These include the globalisation of markets, the preclusion of any one organisation possessing singularly all the required know-how, mass customisation, reduced product life cycles, and the requirement for environmentally benign products and processes. In addition, the emphasis on sustainability and the need to focus on actions to preserve the reserves of natural resources and to decrease the level of pollution to the greatest possible extent, presupposes development activities between industry, governments and research institutions (Browne et al. 1992; Krause and Kind, 1996) This will not be a linear process with clearly-delimited sequences and automatic follow-on, but rather a system of interactions, between different players whose experience, knowledge and know-how are mutually reinforcing and cumulative. As a result, more and more importance is attached in practice to mechanisms which aid the interaction (co-operation) between entities within a network.

2. A SYSTEM OF MANUFACTURING

The Extended Enterprise has been advanced as an inter-enterprise system of manufacturing (Browne et al. 1992; O'Neill and Sackett, 1994). Realisation of the Extended Enterprise is enabled by different entities with different core functionalities that are able to act efficiently, effectively, and in concert for the purpose of providing a customer-defined product/service. At the same time it is recognised that these plug-compatible entities will have to take responsibility for any environmental impact arising from the product during its life-time, and any environmental effects arising from any manufacturing, disassembly, disposal or refurbishment processes during the product's life in effect, responsibility is extended beyond that of providing a finished product (Browne, 1995).

Systems for Sustainability, edited by Stowell *et al.*
Plenum Press, New York, 1997

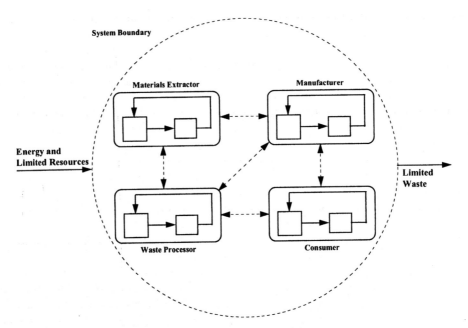

Figure 1. A viable sustainable industrial system.

This system of manufacturing clearly characterises the Type II Industrial Ecosystem from the typology identified by Jelinski, Graedel, Laudise, McCall, and Patel (1992), Figure 1. In the Type II system, energy and "limited" resources flow into a transformation cycle made up of a number of ecosystem components with limited waste flow occurring as an output. This is brought about through the concerted action of Type II entities whose waste outputs are transformed by waste processors to be used by other system components; it exemplifies a viable sustainable system.

The Extended Enterprise has been distinguished from the traditional hierarchical command structure and the open market models (Busby and Fan, 1993). The differentiating characteristic is the nature of the relationship between the organisations of the Extended Enterprise. Browne et al. (1992), emphasise that, "The ability to integrate the activities of a number of entities to produce and sell manufactured products profitably will depend on the relationship of these entities and the communication that passes between them". Busby and Fan (1993) point out that the relationship is of a duration "...that greatly exceeds the lead times associated with specific transactions. Furthermore, the prospect of repeat business discourages attempts to seek narrow, short-term advantage. This persistence means that they can build channels between themselves through which information and knowledge can pass...". The idea of the Extended Enterprise is that reliable proprietary information and knowledge (Ring and Van de Ven, 1992) can be exchanged by entities on a non-commercial basis (Busby and Fan, 1993). A co-operating entity (customer) can provide process expertise to another (supplier) without explicitly selling it, simply because they know that in a long-term relationship both parties will ultimately reap the benefits from greater efficiency.

Crucially, this inter-organisational communication addresses the exchange of firms' unique core-competence knowledge. Given the value of such know-how and expertise it is essential that the inter-entity relationship permits organisations to confidently engage in co-operative activities. In this, respect a number of characteristics need to exist for the relationship to occur, including cultural, organisational, regulatory, technological, and process characteristics. However, by far the most important determinant of co-operation enabling organisations to work together, is of trust (Smith, Carroll and Ashford, 1995). As Ring and Van de Ven (1992) observe, the more frequently that an organisation transacts with other organisations, the more its wealth of knowledge increases regarding the predictability or reliability of others. Thus, entities forming an Extended Enterprise are confidently able to configure themselves for the purpose of providing further customer-defined products.

Bessant (1994) recognises the value of networks of organisations in general, in that they "...behave as a single large firm with all the implications for flexible response, close contact with customers, manageable scale, innovation...". And as Browne (1995) observes in describing the Extended Enterprise, the ability to tap into a network allows for speed of response and innovation. This sharing of know-how and expertise permits firms through the process of continuous improvement, to provide "prosumer" products (Madu, Kuei, and Winokur, 1995). In particular, Porter and van der Linde (1995) note that "...where both companies and consumers are very attuned to environmental concerns, innovation is not uncommon". The adoption of a viable sustainable environmental philosophy necessitates organisations effectively utilising the "4Rs" -recycle, reuse, reduce and redesign, where the knowledge and information received are transformed into the development of complementary, viable business strategies and plans. Furthermore, this ability to share such knowledge without fear of losing control, serves as an avenue to improve "eco-feedback" between Extended Enterprise entities by helping them to respond more efficiently to changes and improvements.

The potential for inter-enterprise competitive advantage arises from the vision and opportunity in co-operating and effectively co-ordinating activities. The authors believe that the resulting synergistic and emergent property of this system of manufacturing is enterprise agility.

3. CLOSING THE LOOP

Co-operation between the Milton Keynes Borough Council, Milton Keynes householders, local institutions, associations and industry provides an example of an Extended Enterprise. Since 1990 the Milton Keynes Borough Council has run a domestic recycling scheme second to none in the United Kingdom. The UK Government's Environmental Protection Act of 1990 required every local authority to recycle 25 per cent of domestic refuse by the year 2000 and led the Council to rethink radically its then current policy. It was this which led the Council to embark upon a major recycling initiative and invite Milton Keynes householders to participate voluntarily in the Door to Door Recycling Collection Scheme. Plysu plc, an international plastic packaging company whose Head Office is located at Woburn Sands, Milton Keynes, initially became involved in the Door to Door Recycling Collection Scheme when the Milton Keynes City Council asked local companies to supply plastic boxes free of charge in which household waste could be collected. As another local company was willing to supply the raw material, Plysu's household division agreed to manufacture the boxes. Further participation in this Extended Enterprise is observable: the Milton Keynes Materials Recycling Facility (MK-MRF) is run in conjunction with C.R.O.P. Limited, a company of charitable status which additionally provides an environmental education service to local schools, businesses and the community. A number of other industrial firms base their production on the processed post-consumer waste.

The commercial viability of this Extended Enterprise is dependent on its ability to provide processed post-consumer materials of the best possible quality to satisfy market demand. To this end, targeted household waste is collected which includes glass, mixed cans, paper and plastics. Subsequent streaming of the waste takes place at the MK-MRF. By far the more interesting is the plastics fraction, in particular high density polyethylene (HDPE), a material used extensively in the packaging industry because of, amongst other characteristics, its light density. Plastics in general are perceived by the public to be a major "pollutant" of the environment as it is the more visible -its' light-weight properties allow it to blow around freely in the wind.

The scheme has gained momentum over the last few years as more households join. As a consequence it became necessary for the MK-MRF to build a larger facility to include the separation of mixed plastics. At this point Plysu's interest in the scheme increased and they took a proactive step to influence the streaming of the plastic and thus obtain a higher quality material. This opportunity enabled Plysu to gain commercially from the relationship and to uphold its environmental and moral responsibility. The company's objective is to use 25 per cent post-consumer HDPE as a raw material within the foreseeable future so as to reduce the amount of virgin HDPE in its plastic products, although it is willing to take as much as the MK-MRF can supply. A conventional product life cycle can be utilised to illustrate the transformation of HDPE within this Extended Enterprise, Figure 2.

The co-operative arrangement established between Milton Keynes Borough Council and Plysu resulted in Plysu installing and commissioning a plastic separation facility within the MK-MRF at their own cost. Sharing of know-how and expertise led to changes in the design and building of the MK-MRF to location the latest technology and water-storage tanks. The automated process removes HDPE packaging from the mixed plastics which includes a high proportion of milk containers, fabric softener and laundry liquid bottles. During the

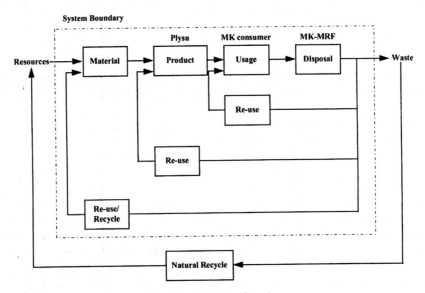

Figure 2. A product life cycle.

washing process limited cleaning agents are required, as the residual fabric conditioner in the containers provide the necessary functionality, anti-foaming agents are however required. The streamed HDPE is dried, flaked and bailed at the MK-MRF ready to be transported to Plysu. On arrival at Plysu, further streaming takes place to transform the flaked HDPE into pelletised HDPE suitable for the manufacture of plastic products and containers. Depolymerisation of mixed plastics is a further option available to close the loop and remake new products, although this is not commercially available at the moment. Any labels attached to the vessels are also removed during the washing process and are collected and subsequently re-used by another entity of the Extended Enterprise.

It is not inconceivable that the milk container bought within a Milton Keynes supermarket by a Milton Keynes consumer, is collected and streamed at the MK-MRF to be subsequently re-cycled by Plysu into further HDPE products, and to be resold in Milton Keynes supermarkets.

4. CONCLUSION

Through a case study example we have mapped and described a system of manufacturing advanced as the Extended Enterprise. This particular enterprise extends through industrial organisations, non-profit orgnaisations, and consumers. The authors have demonstrated its applicability through the utilisation of a conventional product life cycle.

ACKNOWLEDGMENTS

The authors would like to thank the following: Brian Haigh, Technical Director, Plysu plc, Woburn Sands, Milton Keynes, UK and Dawn Kupczyk, C.R.O.P. Limited, MK-MRF, Milton Keynes, UK for the substantial contribution to the content presented; The European Commission support for the BRITE EURAM, Fundamental Research Programme, "AMBITE", Project Nr. 7094.

REFERENCES

Bessant, J., 1994, Towards Total Integrated Manufacturing, *International Journal of Production Economics*, **34**(3):237–252.

Browne, J., 1995, The Extended Enterprise - Manufacturing and The Value Chain, *Balanced Automation Systems* (L. Camarinha-Matos, and H. Afsarmanesh, eds.), pp5–16, Chapman and Hall, London.

Browne, J., Sackett, P., and Wortmann, H., 1992, *The System of Manufacturing: A prospective study*. DGXII of the Commission for the European Communities, Brussels.

Busby, J.S., and Fan, I.-S., 1993, The extended manufacturing enterprise: its nature and its needs, *International Journal of Technology Management*, Special Issue on Manufacturing Technology Diffusion, Implementation and Management, **8**(3/4/5):294–308.

Iaccoca Institute, 1991, *21st Century Manufacturing Enterprise Strategy*. Bethlehem, PA, Lehigh University, USA.

Jelinski, L.W., Graedel, T.E., Laudise, W.D., McCall, D.W., and Patel, K.N., 1992, Industrial Ecology: Concepts and Approaches, *Proceedings of the National Academy of Sciences*, **89**:793–797.

Krause, F.-L., and Kind, C., 1995, Potentials of information technology for life-cycle-orientated product and process development, in: *Life-Cycle Modelling for Innovative Products and Processes*, (F.-L. Krause, and H. Jansen, eds.), pp.14–27, Chapman and Hall, London.

Madu, C.N., Kuei, C.-h., and Winokur, D., 1995, Environmental Quality Planning, *Futures*, **27**(8):839–856.

O'Neill, H. and Sackett, P., 1994, The Extended Manufacturing Enterprise Paradigm, *Management Decision* **32**(8):42–49.

Porter, M.E., and van der Linde, C., 1995, Green and Competitive: Ending the Stalemate, *Harvard Business Review*, (**Sep/Oct**):120–134.

Ring, P.S. and Van de Ven, A.H., 1992, Structuring Cooperative Relationships Between Organizations, *Strategic Management Journal*, **13**(7):483–498.

Smith, K.G., Carroll, S.J. and Ashford, S.J., 1995, Intra- and Interorganizational Cooperation: Toward a Research Agenda, *Academy of Management Journal*, **38**(1):7–23.

112

THE DIVERSITY, MYSTERIES, AND DILEMMAS OF TOTAL QUALITY MANAGEMENT

John C. Oliga, Annies L. F. Foong, and A. E. Ojuka-Onedo

Commerce Department
The University of Papua New Guinea
Box 320, University P. O.
National Capital District
Papua, New Guinea
Fax: (675) 3-267-187

1. INTRODUCTION

The notion of Quality Management (QM), and its later version Total Quality Management (TQM), has been conceived in a diverse number of ways, which can, however, be presently grouped under two paradigms: the empiricist paradigm, associated with orthodox, quality *gurus* (e.g., Deming, and others); and the critical hermeneutics paradigm, associated particularly with the name of Flood (1993). It is from this latter paradigm that this paper takes its point of departure, suggesting that yet a third paradigm, the communicative action paradigm, be brought to bear on the intellectual and social-practical arena of TQM. There is a vast amount of detail about specific approaches to TQM. Obviously, it would not be within the scope of a paper of this length to delve into those details. In light of this, the next section provides only a brief outline of the rationale guiding the structure of the discussion. This is followed by a brief examination of each of the three mentioned paradigms.

2. THE RATIONALE UNDERLYING THE DISCUSSION

Taking each paradigm in turn, the discussion focuses on two key issues thought to be of particular significance to an understanding of TQM: (a) what are the broad paradigmatic assumptions that underwrite quality producers' worldviews about the nature, meaning, or purpose of quality? and (b) what is the nature of the relationships between producers (P), consumers/customers (C), and quality (Q)? Finally, the paper poses the question: how serious are we, or have we been, about trying to ponder over the "physi-

Systems for Sustainability, edited by Stowell *et al.*
Plenum Press, New York, 1997

ological" significance of the three "anatomical" parts of the catchword, TQM? This enormous question is about *the diversity*, *mysteries*, and *dilemmas* of TQM.

3. THE PARADIGMS UNDERWRITING CURRENT TQM POSITIONS

3.1. The Empiricist Paradigm (the Philosophy of Objectivism)

We owe much of the evolution of quality ideas to a number of quality "gurus": Shewhart (1931), Deming (1966; 1982; 1986), Juran (1964; 1980; 1982; 1988a, b), Crosby (1979; 1981; 1984), Shingo (1986), Taguchi (1976; 1982; 1985; 1986), Ishikawa (1976; 1984), Hoshin (1986), Feigenbaum (1986), and Imai (1991). All these writers belong to the *empiricist paradigm*, where the world of external and objectivated social nature is presupposed to be made up of hard, relatively immutable structures or mechanisms, whose existence is restricted to only what is observable and hence independent of individual consciousness. Epistemologically, all valid knowledge is taken to be only empirical (experiential) knowledge grounded in the explanation and prediction of observable phenomena, and therefore theory-neutral and value-free. Thus, the human subject, in relation to the object of observation, is a passive recipient, whose mind is like a mirror, reflecting whatever is observed or discovered to exist. It is this philosophy of objectivism that emphasizes the object-subject focus. Within this paradigm, other influential contributors to quality ideas include, inter alia, the International Organisation for Standards (ISO, incorporating the British Standards and the European Standards), Drucker (1985; 1992), Bendell (1988), and Besterfield (1990).

The following are some of their typical, orthodox, objectivistic definitional ideas about quality: (i) 'quality is a predictable degree of uniformity and dependability, at low cost and suited to the market' (Deming, 1982); (ii) 'quality is fitness for use' (Juran, 1980, 1988a); (iii) 'quality is conformance to requirements' (Crosby, 1979, 1984); (iv) 'quality is the (minimum) loss imparted by the product to society from the time the product is shipped' (Taguchi, 1986); (v) 'quality is in its essence a way of managing the organisation' (Feigenbaum, 1986); and (vi) 'quality is the totality of features and characteristics of a product, service or process, which bear on its ability to satisfy a given end; from the customer's view point' (British Standards definition).

Some of the major contributions to quality ideas include: (i) Deming's 'statistical process control (SPC)', and 'plan, do, check, and act (PDCA) cycle'; (ii) Juran's philosophy of 'plan, control, and improve (PCI) triology', (iii) Crosby's 'five absolutes of TQM', his 'quality improvement (QI) program', his 'quality maturity grid', 'make certain program', 'quality vaccine (QV)', and his advocacy for 'QI through worker participation', and 'zero defect (ZD)'; (iv) Shingo's 'poka-yoke' ('mistake-proof' or 'defect = 0'); (v) Taguchi's philosophy of 'build quality into design', his 'prototyping method', and 'quadratic loss function'; (vi) Ishikawa's philosophy of 'company-wide quality (CWQ)', and his 'fishbone diagrams, control charts and graphs, histograms, Pareto charts, and quality control circles (QCCs)'; (vii) Feigenbaum's philosophy of 'total quality control (TQC)', 'cultural sensitivity', and 'TQC in value chain' (suppliers-producers-customers); (viii) Imai and the Kaizen Institute's philosophy of 'Kaizen mentality', and the '3-level quality chain' (upstream-midstream-downstream); (ix) the ISO's philosophy of 'international quality standards', and 'international accreditation system'.

The next issue we wish to consider is the view presupposed in this paradigm regarding the reason or motive for according importance to the activity of providing quality as an object of value. It does seem that the empiricist common view is that of seeing quality as a competitive advantage under market exchange conditions in which the marginalist economics of Robinson Crusoe are played out. The Crusoe pedlars of quality are abstract, isolated, utility-maximizing individuals endowed with given tastes, skills, and resources, making rational decisions in conditions of scarcity (cf. Clarke, 1982; Ojuka-Onedo, et al., 1996). As is obvious from the above definitions and contributions, the idea of any serious debate or dialogue with consumers of quality "to find out" their needs is conspicuous by its absence. Action co-ordination between producers and consumers is left to the "hidden hand" which functionally intermeshes *action consequences* through the "delinguistified" steering media of money and power (cf. Habermas, 1987; Oliga, 1996). The relationship between the producer of quality (P), the consumer/customer(C), and quality(Q) can be depicted as follows:

$$C \longrightarrow P \longrightarrow Q,$$

where P owns Q, and C is a mere accident, whose human identity as a social actor is irrelevant, except as an institutional element in a given mode of production.

3.2. The Critical Hermeneutics Paradigm (the Philosophy of Consciousness)

Flood (1993) is perhaps the one who has made the most significant contribution to the evolution of quality ideas within critical hermeneutics, an interpretivist paradigm with an onto-epistemological commitment for understanding the social world through the dialectical mediation of interpretive (subjectivist) and explanatory (objectivist) approaches in the form of ideology critique, the aim being the freeing of human emancipatory potential. In commenting on Flood's contribution, Oliga (1996, p.14) had this to say, "The total and complementarist view of TQM as entailing the need for *design, debate and disimprisonment* (the 3Ds) lifts TQM from the popular but miserably impoverished view of it as merely another marketing gimmick dressed in the new seductive dress fashionable since the late 1980s. Flood's three 'Ds' are essentially an innovative, homomorphic transformation of Habermas's [1971] three human interests (the technical, the practical, and the emancipatory)". Ackoff (1992) is another contributor here. He advocates serious critical reflection on TQM theory and practice, instead of the current, widespread thinking which, in his view, is shallow, misguided and downright wrong. In anticipation of the next, communicative action paradigm, critical hermeneutics, grounded as it is on the subject-centred epistemology (philosophy) of consciousness, is subject to the critique that it conceptualizes reason as essentially embedded in, and a reflection of, the subject as a self-centred individual. Such reason is subject-trapped and therefore necessarily instrumental or strategic, implying a preoccupation with ego-centric issues of subject-object, rather than with the subject-subject basis of action co-ordination (Habermas, 1984; 1987). The relationship between quality (Q), producers (P) and consumers (C) of quality can thus be depicted as follows:

$$Q \longrightarrow P \longrightarrow C,$$

where P takes Q as merely a means of strategically achieving egoistic success over the rational opponent, C.

3.3. The Communicative Action Paradigm (the Philosophy of Language)

Building on Habermas's (1984; 1987) *Theory of Communicative Action*, Oliga (1994) seeks to situate TQM within the philosophy of language, such that any communicatively achieved agreement through intersubjective dialogue between producers and consumers of quality is motivated solely by the need to achieve a rational consensus, "[which] cannot be imposed by either party, whether instrumentally... or strategically..." (Habermas, 1984, p.287). In this attitude, quality can be seen as the consequence of joint efforts towards individual freedom and collective autonomy. The relationship between producers (P) and consumers (C) of quality (Q) now becomes:

where P and C rationally seek to harmonize their action orientations, without any reservation or strategic preconceptions, on the basis of *criticizable validity claims of truth, rightness, and truthfulness*(cf. Habermas, 1987; Oliga, 1996). And the enormous, and practically intractable problematic issues of diversity, mysteries, and dilemmas in TQM can now be faced, not with a sense of despair, nor with the motive of taking one-sided advantages of the situation, but with the conviction that the game being played out is grounded in symmetry of chances in dialogue, reciprocity in terms of equal distribution of

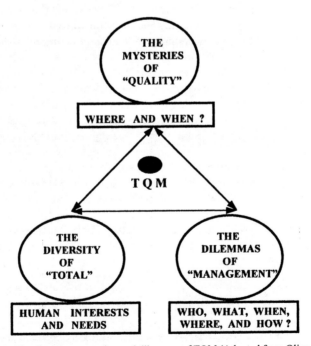

Figure 1. The diversity, mysteries, and dilemmas of TQM (Adopted from Oliga, 1994).

opportunities, and the norms of generalizable interests (Habermas, 1979; Rasmussen, 1990; White, 1988; Oliga, 1996, p.288).

4. THE DIVERSITY, MYSTERIES, AND DILEMMAS OF TQM

Starting from the notion of "Total" in TQM, the paper argues that this embraces the Habermasian idea of three human interests, the actual contents of which in the real world, can be exceedingly *diverse* in terms of the interpretations of co-operating "producers" of quality as to what constitutes a "total" set of relevant inputs. Similarly, the meaning of "quality" to "consumers" becomes difficult for producers to anticipate and interpret, given that in the real world different consumers/customers may take different positions about the quality offered (i.e., accepted, not accepted, or not-yet-decided), in terms of the Habermasian criticizable validity claims of truth, rightness, and truthfulness. Thus, these potentially differing critical positions render the notion "Quality" one shrouded in real problematic *mysteries* (Ackoff, 1992). Notwithstanding these real problems of interpreting diversity in "Total", and unravelling the mysteries in "Quality", management must still make practical decisions for everyday on-going action in situations fraught with real possibilities for disagreements at all levels of human and social action. There lie the real *dilemmas* of "Management" in TQM. Figure 1 represents these ideas.

5. CONCLUSION

The paper has briefly traced the evolution of quality ideas, from the pioneering work of quality "gurus" working within the empiricist paradigm, to endeavors within the philosophy of consciousness, and finally to the philosophy of language. Within the communicative action paradigm, the real problematic issues of diversity, mysteries, and dilemma in TQM were seen, not as a case of despair, but as offering challenges toward progress in human emancipation.

REFERENCES

Ackoff, R. L., 1992, *Beyond Total Quality Management,* A Public Lecture at the opening of the Centre for Systems Studies, University of Hull, UK.

Bendell, T., 1988, *The Quality Gurus. What can They do for Your Company?* Department of Trade and Industry, United Kingdom.

Besterfield, D. H., 1990, *Quality Control,* Prentice-Hall, London.

Clarke, S., 1982, *Marx, Marginalism, and Modern Sociology: From Adam Smith to Max Weber,* The Macmillan Press, London.

Crosby, P. B., 1979, *Quality is Free,* Mentor, New York.

Crosby, P. B., 1981, *The Art of Getting Your Own Sweet Way,* McGraw-Hill, New York.

Crosby, P. B., 1984, *Quality Without Tears,* McGraw-Hill, New York.

Deming, E. W., 1966, *Some Theory of Sampling,* Wiley, New York.

Deming, E. W., 1982, *Quality, Productivity and Competitive Position,* MIT, Cambridge, MA.

Deming, E. W., 1986, *Out of the Crisis,* MIT, Cambridge, MA.

Drucker, P. F., 1985, *Innovation and Entrepreneurship: Practice and Principles,* Heinemann, London.

Drucker, P. F., 1992, *Managing for the Future,* Butterworth-Heinemann, Oxford.

Feigenbaum, A. V., 1986, *Total Quality Control,* McGraw-Hill, New York.

Habermas, J., 1971, *Knowledge and Human Interests,* Beacon Press, Boston, Mass.

Habermas, J., 1979, What is universal pragmatics? in: *Communication and the Evolution of Society,* (J. Habermas, ed.), (trans. by T. McCarthy), Heinemann, London, pp.1–68.

Habermas, J., 1984, *The Theory of Communicative Action: Reason and the Rationalization of Society,* (Vol.1, trans. by McCarthy, T.), Beacon Press, Boston, Mass.

Habermas, J., 1987, *The Theory of Communicative Action: Lifeworld and System: A Critique of Functionalist Reason*, (Vol. 2, trans. by McCarthy, T.), Beacon Press, Boston, Mass.

Imai, M., 1991, *Kaizen (Ky'zen): The Key to Japan's Competitive Success*, McGraw-Hill, New York.

Ishikawa, K., 1976, *Guide to Quality Control*, Asian Productivity Organisation, Tokyo.

Ishikawa, K., 1984, Quality and standardisation: Progress for economic success, *Quality Progress* **1:** 16–20.

Juran, J. M., 1964, *Managerial Breakthrough*, McGraw-Hill, New York.

Juran, J. M., 1980, *Quality Planning and Analysis*, McGraw-Hill, New York.

Juran, J. M., 1982, *Upper Management and Quality*, Juran Institute, New York.

Juran, J. M., 1988a, *Juran on Planning for Quality*, Free Press, New York.

Juran, J. M., 1988b, *Quality Control Handbook*, McGraw-Hill, New York.

Ojuka-Onedo, A. E., Foong, A. L. F., and Oliga, J. C., 1996, Entrepreneurship development, ethics, and accounting, *Entrepreneurship, Innovation, and Change* **5**(4):323–381.

Oliga, J. C., 1994, *The Diversity, Mysteries, and Dilemmas of Total Quality Management (TQM)*, Public Lecture delivered at the University of Papua New Guinea, National Capital District, Papua New Guinea, September 21.

Oliga, J. C., 1996, *Power, Ideology, and Control,* Plenum Press, New York.

Rasmussen, D. M., 1990, *Reading Habermas,* Basil Blackwell, Cambridge, UK.

Shewhart, W. A., 1931, *Economic Control of Quality of Manufactured Products*, Van Nostrand, New York.

Shingo, S., 1986, *Zero Quality Control: Source Inspection and the Poka-Yoke System*, Productivity Press, Cambridge, MA.

Taguchi, G., 1976, *Experimental Designs*, (Vols. 1 and 2 in Japanese), Maruzen, Tokyo.

Taguchi, G., 1982, *Design and Design of Experiments*, Annual Meeting of the American Association for the Advancement of Science, Washington, DC.

Taguchi, G., 1985, *What is Total Quality Control? The Japanese Way*, Prentice-Hall, Englewood Cliffs, N J.

Taguchi, G., 1986, *Introduction to Quality Engineering: Designing Quality into Products and Processes*, Kraus, New York.

White, S. K., 1988, *The Recent Work of Jurgen Habermas: Reason, Justice and Modernity*, Cambridge University Press, Cambridge, UK.

113

WORKING TOGETHER

R&D Partnering in the New Zealand Dairy Sector

M. S. Paine and M. E. Wedderburn

NZ Pastoral Agricultural Research Institute Ltd.
P.O. Box 3089
Hamilton, New Zealand

1. INTRODUCTION

Successful commercialisation of R&D outcomes depends primarily on an evolving partnership between science and commercial agencies. An ex post analysis of the CIDR technology identifies the significance of R&D partnerships in development programmes. A second case study uses an action research methodology to extend understanding of the partnering process in relation to resource management issues. Insights are reported in [] following each narrative.

2. THE DILEMMA OF TECHNOLOGY: THE CIDR

Controlled Intravaginal Drug Release (CIDR) is a silicone device impregnated with progesterone to regulate the cycling of breeding livestock, particularly dairy cows. An outline of CIDR development is analysed in terms of R&D partnerships. Data about the way partnerships evolved in the CIDR case were gathered using semi-structured interviews with 18 key informants. The interviews averaged 2 hours, each transcript generating about 15,000 words of text. Interview data was supplemented with secondary material gathered from dairy sector journals, science papers and conference proceedings. Each secondary data source was exhaustively searched for articles relating to CIDR from 1986, the year of commercial release, to 1996. Text data was analysed using NUD.IST™ rev. 3. This computer based programme was used when coding and comparing online transcripts and offline secondary data following Grounded Theory (Glaser, 1978).

2.1. The Need for CIDR in Farm Practice

High performing seasonal supply farms in NZ have cows pregnant for about 280 days. Bovines cycle every 21 days following a 40 day post calving recovery, leaving the

Systems for Sustainability, edited by Stowell *et al.*
Plenum Press, New York, 1997

NZ farmer with 2 natural cycles to maintain an annual balance between feed management and milk yields. Costs from not getting cows in calve every 365 days include later calving (ie. the system is out of balance with the annual cycle) and more empties (cows without calves and therefore non-yielding). Development of the CIDR provided farmers with a means of synchronising the cycling of their herds, to achieve a compressed pattern of calving. This study investigates how different agencies actively contributed to CIDR development success.

2.2. A Changing Continuity of Partnerships to Develop the CIDR

The technical parentage of CIDR evolved from polymer engineering, organic chemistry and controlled release of hormones. New Zealand was among a number of developed countries evaluating devices for the controlled release of hormones in farm animals during the 1970's. A variety of hormone release devices similar to CIDR were available. Welch (Ruakura based reproductive physiologist) was dissatisfied with a number of attributes in these devices and set about the task of formulating an alternative device that used naturally occurring hormones while minimising animal trauma. Welch contacted Millar (a leading plastics fabricator) with examples of the available synchrony technology. Millar was intrigued by the problem of releasing hormone from a polymer based device. The dominant design problems included shaping a device with appropriate hormone release properties and manufacturing at an economic rate and scale of production. [During this initial development phase disparate professions share an interest and begin a shared design process.]

Welch's membership of the Controlled Release Society provided international contacts in medical research that linked Welch with a polymer engineer who had developed a prototype with the attributes sought by Welch and Millar. Accessing the polymer enabled Welch and Millar to concentrate on refining the device shape. CIDR developers offset many of the dye cast testing expenses by piggy-backing on a project that was solving a problem in another factory product. By the early 1980's a commercial device was released for sheep and goats. At that time the high value of goats cashflowed many of the trials required to refine the product for successfully synchronised dairy cows. By the mid 1980's (10 years after Welch's initial idea) a number of changes in company ownership and personnel altered the emphasis in the programme. A new manager with development and marketing experience led the division, and a leading dairy reproduction researcher, now headed the research programme. In 6 months (1987) the pair had joined forces with the NZ dairy sector consultancy network to position the product in the management system of farmers. Agreement was reached whereby the fabricator held the patent rights on the shape of the device, royalties were paid to Ruakura acknowledging their R&D contribution, and the consultancy company held the sole distribution rights to veterinarians who administer the device to New Zealand animals. [The CIDR programme had progressed from an idea to a shared practice among professions through networking for access to resources, and sharing development roles that aligned with the sector infrastructure.]

The plastics fabricator faced problems manufacturing pharmaceutical products. Its core business did not equip the company to deal with drug registration procedures, or the laboratory techniques necessary to develop and test products. Collaboration with Ruakura was adequate for registration within NZ, but entering the international arena was a greater challenge. Efforts to partner with a large drug manufacturer failed, stalling entry to USA markets. The contingency plan developed a number of smaller international markets using local agencies in a partnering process similar to the NZ situation. Marketing efforts depended on evidence of significant economic gains in field trials. From 1987 to 1992 farmer experience with the CIDR provided feedback to researchers, resulting in a suite of programmes for use in different classes of stock. The CIDR is now common place in New Zealand dairy farming after 20 years of effort in R&D, manufacturing and farming. Furthermore, CIDR opens a technical door to many new technologies in coming years. [Partnering professions need to understand the routines of their partners to share practices. When this understanding needs to cross scale and distance barriers it is difficult to succeed. R&D partnering continues because of the need to continuously improve the CIDR.]

2.3. Strategic R&D Partnering

Development of the CIDR technology used a partnering process to evolve one man's idea into common practice. Dependence and respect among diverse professions formed around a shared need. This shared need was in turn fostered by a vision of synchrony practice that was communicated among the professions. Various professional practices entered, interacted, and in some cases left the programme over time. Practices develop skills to interact with each other, and perform competently in their professional capacity.

CIDR technology is more than a material artefact. The CIDR device emerged from the efforts of an evolving practice. This practice is observed as an expanding social network, that develops and modifies its tools, and evolves a specialised language (jargon) that various professions share over time. Investors in science invest in practices, that have clients and professions working to clearly define problems and take collective action. These activities involve implicit (routines) and explicit (reflections on) action. An individual's innovative thinking may initiate an evolution in practice, but linkages among professions ensures a practice remains when individuals and organisations change over time. Practices emerge and perform in environments which influence their development. Vertically integrated infrastructures accelerate the construction and use of new materials, networks and concepts.

Partnering processes depend on respect for allied professions, as evidenced by farming, science, policy, farm management and veterinarian practitioners in the case of CIDR. All members benefit from working together. When a practice confronts a problem beyond its capability to act it acquires essential skills by introducing new members. A sequence of internal interactions develops competence in the practice to perform as desired. Collaborative interaction is influenced by the extent that perspectives are shared about the problem. Professions may share different perspectives, but they have a capacity to interpret and accommodate these differences in their shared practice.

We need to observe these professions in action to improve our understanding of technology management as collaboration. In particular, we are searching for an understanding that enables the development of general principles for improving collaboration in R&D.

3. SHARING THE PROBLEM OF SUSTAINABLE FARMING

Our second case is not about 1 specific technology, but rather the development and mixing of technologies in a group process to design sustainable dairy farm practice. This case, using groups to develop sustainable farm practice, observed professions in action to understand how they interact and build a common future.

3.1. Set-up

A Dairy Farmers Divisional Chairman (Jim) spent a frustrating 6 months trying to progress a problem of targeting sector technology development to satisfy consumer needs with farm system and environmental vigilance. An agricultural scientist (Liz) suggested a partnership approach to address the problem rather than a linear technology transfer programme. Partnering involved action from farmers that developed and implemented guidelines for sustainable farming using a collective learning process.

Though Liz asked more of Jim than he initially expected, he reacted positively to the offer. They were both aware of the risks they incurred using a joint proposal. There was no precedent to follow. The task of funding was more demanding, and the expectations of other interested parties was further delayed. Jim and Liz had limited professional exchanges—Liz's ability as a scientist and communicator was largely taken at face value. Both experienced excitement about the opportunity, and fear about designing a project that deals with such a pertinent but complex subject. They were frank with each other about their concerns and decided to use an extension researcher to help with the programme design. The final design combined farming guidelines and study groups using intensively monitored dairy and sheep & beef farm systems.

[The people had a past working background with a problem that they realised was more than they could handle alone. They invested a large amount of time and emotional effort on the problem because they were driven by an ethical motive. The programme evolved because the people owned an idea and were prepared to work on building a shared vision. Risks and unknown events confronted all parties, not the least being a new form of dependence on each other requiring trust to perform joint activities. The people were flexible in their outlooks and plans to accommodate new ideas.]

3.2. Growing Pains

Jim and Liz shared a vision that required the involvement of others who had yet to grasp their intent. Jim's farming colleagues are practical people who expect to see tangible results from his efforts. Liz worked on funding agencies with similar pragmatic expectations, "what product will come out of this investment?" They found the concept of developing sustainable farm practice by collectively learning was viewed as ambiguous, obscure and full of jargon by the agencies on whom they depended. Political and financial support would only come when these people clearly identified desirable outcomes and how the proposal would achieve these. Producing tangible guidelines is a simple task, but fostering a process that uses them in farm practice is a more difficult proposition. Liz and Jim were committed to using a 'problem solving' approach to foster collective learning in the groups. Describing the process is not difficult, but predicting the outcome in terms of a process that can transfer to other groups required continual lobbying. After many proposal revisions the funding was secured through a contract for joint contributions from farmers and a purchaser of public good science.

Included in the group was a regional council worker with responsibility for resource management. His initial stance on resource condition clashed with farmer views on production as the priority. The farmers expressed fear their decision autonomy would erode with this position. The professionals in the group came to realise accessing farmer knowledge required skills in questioning and listening. When professionals met on farmers' terms they developed an increasing respect for farmer knowledge. It was routine for farmers to discuss, integrate and resolve intergenerational and production goals in the paddock.

In turn farmers were more relaxed with the professionals who made an effort to grasp what was involved in practical farming. The debate about the Regional Council provoked further reflection on the group process, to combine the local knowledge of farmers with the various sources of professional knowledge, to collectively design and operate sustainable farm practice. After several meetings discussions extended to review the performance of various group roles. All were concerned with the time required to make progress on the group process. This exercise achieved an explicit agreement about goal priorities and the process for goal achievement.

[Timing is critical to optimise the benefit of actions. Jim was initially criticised by his peers for moving slowly on the initial intent to produce guidelines. Taking a decision to grow a project requires persistence amid opposition. When dealing with complex problems the critical tasks (like developing a collective learning process) are difficult to communicate to the uninitiated. Appropriate funding is critical when expanding the options for action. Science must respect farming knowledge. This respect does not undermine the science knowledge system, it appropriates it through informed interaction with productive sector knowledge systems. Honest intentions are required among all parties to develop and use knowledge collectively. Locating collective activities in the productive sector requires new skills among science workers, but reduces the burden on farmers to translate the information coming from different sources and apply it to their specific needs. Evaluation is central to developing a process that is transferable to other groups. When many groups come together they start with a simple shared language to build terms and concepts over time. Open debate helps clarify direction and build respect for the diverse outlooks in the group.]

3.3. Positive Patterns

The group has been meeting for a year and is taking stock of its achievements. Jim is pleased with the development and use of scales and recording systems in group activities. In particular, actions to manage pasture pugging by stock during the wet winter, and understanding nutrient cycling effect on farm performance and resource status. Farmers are refining their conventional recording systems for fertiliser and weighing of stock as they strive to align their farm practice with the condition of their resource. Liz notes the level of questioning and thinking has changed as the group makes more use of modelling tools to develop their dairy systems. Jim considers thinking and action are inseparable in farming. He refers to the way farmers preferentially treated stock after weights from the livestock recording system were compared to target weights for their class of stock. Similarly, farmer records of pasture programme were run through the farm simulation model 'Udder' to compare longterm economic outcomes for different scenarios. They agree that tangible evidence of changes can be tabled in terms of technical development and collective learning abilities but insufficient time has passed to demonstrate the economic achievements of the project. Conflict between resource management and farm production goals declined, and eventually resolved into emerging best management practices.

[Commercialising R&D to address problems with complex systems requires access to relevant tools like computer models and experienced people to use these tools in a group context. Trust builds among participants as evidence of shared values accumulate, usually as services rendered among members in the group. The collective learning process draws on a variety of technologies and techniques to construct sustainable farm practice. The process simultaneously refines the environmental ethics guiding group action, according them priority so they become the code of ethics shared by all members.]

We conclude with a general frame for strategically managing technology.

4. MANAGING TECHNOLOGY AS AN INTERPLAY OF PRACTICES

The above cases generate a coherent view of technology management when analysed using a theoretical model that links science and commerce. Gremmen (1993) claims practices follow an evolutionary pattern of interaction. Gremmen places action, not knowledge, as the central shared aspect of science and commerce. A mix of professions will co-ordinate a sequence of their collective actions to achieve shared goals and satisfy their clients' needs. These professions use their social networks, concepts and material tools to perform these actions. Knowledge is only one aspect of action, yet action is the phenomena shared by professional groups to develop a practice.

Professions work together in a practice because they depend on each other for resources and results. This dependence is influenced by professional perceptions of exposure to risk. To share some activities may often demand considerable trust among the professions when science and industry have a limited shared work history. The evolution of practice will also depend on the conflict among professional goals. The sustainability study groups resolved their conflicting goals by searching for and formulating a higher shared goal that served to represent the critical elements of their specific professional goals.

Investment in science is so dependent on the nature of interaction among professionals we are surprised it has received such scant attention by researchers, management strategists or policy analysts. The second case involves a process of documenting change in group actions and group reflection to underpin the transfer of learning experiences among groups who confront similar problems.

In conclusion, a new understanding of professional practice is required to progress the use of science and technology in New Zealand business. This in turn requires some clarity about the way professional groups work together to build a common improved future for research and commerce. Interactive skills among professions evolve as they perform shared tasks. Working together will change the nature of relationships among professionals. As goals, concepts, language and tools are shared among professions in common work, a new sense of shared identity will emerge. This creates a new practice that enhances the relevance of professional groups to client needs, that in turn interweaves scientific work with commercial activity.

REFERENCES

Glaser, B., 1978, *Theoretical Sensitivity. Advances in the Methodology of Grounded Theory*, Sociology Press, California.

Gremmen, B. 1993, *The Mystery of the Practical Use of Scientific Knowledge*, published PhD Thesis, Twente University, The Netherlands.

114

STAKEHOLDERS' PERCEPTIONS OF A BUSINESS PROCESS REENGINEERING PROJECT

Weniubel Ratana Trihajuwidjajani, Peter Marshall, and Judy McKay

School of Information Systems
Curtin University of Technology
Western Australia

1. INTRODUCTION

Over the past twenty years business environment has changed dramatically. Modern organisations are now faced with the increasing strain of global competition, globalisation of markets, shorter business cycles and technological and political changes. This new business climate has almost 'forced' organisations to find new ways, techniques and methodologies to help enhance business performance. Amongst the many business concepts which exists today, Business Process Reengineering (BPR) is said to be *the* business concept of the 1990s (Carr and Johansson, 1995). Although this claim may seem somewhat of an overstatement, there can be little disagreement that in a relatively short period of time, BPR has generated large amounts of interest within the business community (Rigby, 1993), and has spawned a very substantial literature. The majority of these case studies in the BPR literature were reported from the perspectives of the academics and some consultants who performed the post-hoc investigations on BPR projects. Hence there has been very little work stemming directly from the perspectives of the BPR participants. In recognising these issues, research using the case study methodology was conducted on a large government organisation in Western Australia in order to determine the appropriateness and relevance of some of the recurrent and salient theoretical issues in practice. This paper reports on qualitative research undertaken as a "reality check" of these issues from the perceptions of the people who were involved in and affected by the BPR project.

2. THE ESSENCE OF BUSINESS PROCESS REENGINEERING

The origins of BPR is still considered to be somewhat controversial. Some suggests that the seeds of BPR stemmed from the Total Quality Management philosophies (Carr and Johansson, 1995) which was then developed further and introduced as "business proc-

Systems for Sustainability, edited by Stowell *et al.*
Plenum Press, New York, 1997

ess reengineering" by Hammer in 1990, whereas some believe it is nothing more than a clever sales pitch for old ideas which can be traced back to the late nineteenth century (Rigby, 1993). Irrespective of the precise origins of BPR, it can be said with a great deal of certainty that BPR should not be considered as a singular concept but rather, should be number of business concepts packaged as one (Earl and Khan, 1994).

The most commonly cited definition of BPR is that of Hammer and Champy (1993, p.32) who write that BPR involves "the fundamental rethinking and radical redesign of business processes to achieve dramatic improvements in critical, contemporary measures of performance, such as cost, quality, services and speed". There are basically four key elements in this definition. The word fundamental suggests that unlike many business concepts, BPR requires organisations to examine the basic purpose of their business (Talwar, 1993). The *radical* nature of the BPR implies that organisations need to be willing to completely reconstruct both their way of working and thinking in order to achieve the dramatic and "quantum" improvements in performance which BPR often promises (Hammer and Champy, 1993, p. 33). Finally, BPR involves organisations to be process focused, and this focus almost "forces" organisations to take account of their customers, both internal and external (Carr and Johansson, 1995).

2.1. Review of the BPR Literature

For the purpose of the research, BPR literature was examined in order to extract the seminal and significant emergent themes that were present in the extensive literature on BPR. In all, seventy six articles on BPR, which were judged by the researchers to be 'quality' articles, were reviewed in detail to arrive at a set of major themes that were both repeated often and seemed to be of significant concern to the majority of the authors on BPR.

A great number of themes were mentioned in the articles. These are discussed at length in Trihajuwidjajani (1995). However, given the confines of this paper, only three will be given any detailed consideration. These are listed below:

Theme 1   Motivations for undertaking BPR projects
Theme 2   The communication process during a BPR intervention
Theme 3   The outcomes of BPR projects

After the above themes were identified, it was realised that the majority of the articles reviewed tended to report information written from the perspectives of academics who carried out post-hoc investigations of BPR projects, by senior executives who led the intervention, or by consultants who conducted the BPR project. Hence there was an obvious lack of information on BPR written from the perspectives of people at middle or lower level management of organisations who were actually affected by the BPR project. It was these considerations that ultimately lead to the formulation of the research questions:

1. What are the perceptions of employees who experienced the BPR project? the consultants who facilitated the BPR intervention?
2. In what ways do these perceptions match the important themes that are predominant in the BPR literature?

As seen in the above research question, it was a major concern in this research to capture the *perceptions* of the people. Theoreticians may write about what they regard as important in BPR, but of key concern in this research was the elicitation of people's feelings, beliefs, understandings and interpretations about their experiences of BPR, that is, the 'truth' from each individual's perspective. This research also attempted to compare and contrast these perceptions with the collective wisdom of writers on BPR.

3. THE RESEARCH PROJECT

From the articulation of the research objectives, an interpretivistic, single case study was chosen as the appropriate research methodology in this context. The taxonomies put forward by Galliers (1991) and Shanks et al. (1993) propose that, *inter alia*, the case study method is suitable for exploratory research, theory building and studying an organisation. This is illustrated in table 1.

Given the nature of the research questions, it was implied that qualitative data (dealing with words, concepts and meanings) rather than quantitative data (dealing with numbers and measurements) should be collected. The data collection techniques used were semi-structured interviews, questionnaire and the examination of documentation from both the participants of the organisation and the consultants involved. In addition to these techniques, recommended by Yin (1994) with regards to the conduct of the case study research, a questionnaire was also used to gather data from a slightly larger number of participants. By using convenience sampling, a large amount of data was collected from two of the consultants and five participants of the various levels of the organisation.

To arrive at the findings, this research used a qualitative content analysis to assist in drawing conclusions from the collected interview and questionnaire data. Qualitative content analysis is a way of classifying and organising textual data, leading to analysis according to meanings attributed to categorised chunks of text (Minichiello *et al.,* 1990). Conclusions were then drawn on the basis of the meanings derived from the data. It should also be mentioned that an independent expert was used to confirm the researcher's approach to data analysis.

3.1. The Case

This case study research involved a review of a BPR project undertaken within a large government agency in Western Australia by a local consulting firm some months previously. Prior to the change process, the consulting firm's assessment revealed that this organisation had an excessively bureaucratic structure which caused several internal problems such as the obvious interdepartmental rivalry and ineffective business operations. In addition, the organisation suffered due to their ineffective use of information technology, a lack of planning and low staff morale. The consultants also found that the organisation had a lack of customer focus. This problem can be detrimental for any organisation operating in today's highly competitive environment. In response to some of these internal problems and increasingly vociferous complaints from a number of prominent stakeholders, the Western Australian government introduced an Act which implied major changes to the operation of the organisation and hence precipitated the reengineering project.

The BPR project aimed at reengineering the organisation's current state so that it could excel in providing services for its customers while also having internal efficiency and effectiveness so that it could successfully operate in the current economic and political environment. To achieve these goals, the consulting firm reengineered the organisation mostly at a strategic level, which involved implementing a new vision, mission, planning

Table 1. Extracts from the taxonomies of Galliers (1991) and Shanks et al. (1993)

	Theorem Proof	Laboratory Experiment	Field Experiment	Case Study	Survey	Future Research	Simulation	Subjective / Argumentative	Descriptive / Interpretive	Action Research
Galliers 1992										
Group / organisation	N	possible	Y	Y	Y	Y	Y	Y	Y	Y
Methodology	N	N	Y	Y	Y	N	Y	Y	Y	Y
Theory Building	N	N	N	Y	Y	Y	Y	Y	Y	Y
Shanks et al 1993										
Exploratory	N	N	N	Y	maybe				Y	Y

activities at all levels of the organisation and a new structure which changed the old traditional "stovepipe" structure that they had (Obolensky, 1994) into a set of business units which related to the type of service provision rather than the departmental discipline. This process involved shifting the organisation's business philosophy from being a traditional public organisation to a more commercially oriented organisation.

4. FINDINGS

The findings from the analysis of the data enabled several conclusions to be drawn about the three themes identified earlier.

Theme 1: The Motivations for Undertaking a BPR Project

Both the interview and the questionnaire data suggest that there was a general agreement amongst the employees that the main objectives for the BPR project for this case was the political motives which the government had at the time of the change. The second major motivator for the change was the internal inefficiencies. Several participants said that the organisation had never assessed their operations, hence whenever problems arose, they would only take action to ameliorate the problems without really assessing the cause of the problems. The majority of the participants believed that this internal problem stemmed from the highly bureaucratic structure of the organisation prior to the BPR project. Interestingly, these internal problems which were not seen as the main driver for change by internal employees, but were viewed by the consultants as the major motivator for change. The consultants felt that since the organisation suffered so much internal inefficiencies, it tended to dwell on this rather than focusing their operations on outcomes. Since focusing on outcomes involves the organisation to be customer focused, the consultants believed that the organisation needed to place much more attention on customer needs rather than on the individual tasks that each department has to perform.

Theme 2: The Communication Process during the BPR Intervention

In terms of the communication process during the project, both the employees and the consultants saw communication as a vital element in any BPR intervention. However, in this particular project, all the employees felt that there had been a definite lack of communication during the change process, in particular, 'two-way' communication. The majority of the employees felt that this lack of communication from the drivers of the project (the core team, the CEO, senior level management and the consultants) led to the discomfort, uncertainty, stress and anxiety which all the participants felt.

By contrast, the consultants did not generally perceive a lack of communication during the BPR project. The consultants said that it was a part of their methodology to ensure that most of the communication process was performed by members of the organisation in order to maximise their feelings of involvement, understandings of the change and hence their commitment to the project. The consultants also stated that "it doesn't matter how much communication went on during a project, it can never be enough".

As the literature also sees communication as an important factor which can influence BPR success, the researchers were curious whether it was dangerous to leave the responsibility for communication to the internal members of the organisation. The consultants' response was that they had ways to assess the sponsor's communication skills and commitment to the project, and hence it was fairly safe to leave this important function to the project team members.

Theme 3: The Outcomes of BPR Projects

Generally, the employees felt that the project had been a success. However, even though they admitted that they have seen improvements, they still expressed the great dissatisfaction and discontent about the whole change process. Several employees mentioned that the negative impacts of the change did not just affect their work life, but also their personal life. Hence the researcher felt that the employees' perceptions suggested that the human aspects of change should not be overlooked. This is a significant finding. Their perception confirms the literature's point that a change process will often involve pain, it is rarely a smooth and painless journey.

5. CONCLUSION

Elden and Chisholm (1993) said that theory should not only serve to inform practice but practice should also serve to inform theory. Hence the researcher believes that if exploratory research like this can suggest that in practice, actors do sometimes present different priorities on aspects of BPR, it may also be worthwhile to investigate further these difference in priorities of the local actors who experienced and were directly affected by the change process itself. Hence if the perceptions of the BPR practitioners were considered in the literature, it could perhaps improve BPR conduct. As mentioned earlier, the literature review performed for this research revealed that there was plenty of 'How-to do-BPR' literature and literature entailing consultants' experiences in BPR. The researchers hence believe that it is time to increase the amount of serious analytical research which can hopefully inform BPR practitioners in the various aspects of BPR interventions.

REFERENCES

Carr, D. K. and Johansson, H. J., 1995, Best practices in reengineering what works and what doesn't in the reengineering process. McGraw-Hill, Inc., U.S.A.

Earl, M. and Khan, B., 1994, How new is business process redesign? *European Management Journal*, **12**(1): 20–30.

Elden, M. and Chisholm, R.F. ,1993, Emerging varieties of action research: introduction to the special issues. *Human Relations*, **46**(2):121–142.

Galliers, R.D., 1991, Choosing appropriate information systems research approaches: a revised taxonomy, in: Contemporary approaches and emergent traditions, *Information Systems Research*, (H.E. Nissen, H.K. Klein and R. Hirschheim, eds.), pp. 327–345, Elsevier Science B.V.,North Holland,, Amsterdam.

Hammer, M. and Champy, J., 1993, Reengineering the corporation: a manifesto for business revolution. Nicholas Brealey Publishing, London.

Hammer, M., 1990, Reengineering work: don't automate, obliterate. *Harvard Business Review*, (July/August 1990), pp. 104–112.

Minichiello,.V., Aroni, R., Timewell, E. and Alexander, L., 1990, In depth interviewing: researching people. Longman Cheshire, Australia

Obolensky, N., 1994, Practical business reengineering. Kogan-Page, London.

Rigby, D. ,1993, The secret history of process reengineering. *Planning Review*, **21**(2):24–27.

Shanks, G., Rouse, A. and Arnott, D., 1993, A review of approaches to research and scholarship in information systems. *Proceedings of the Fourth Australian Conference on Information Systems*, University of Queensland, Brisbane, Queensland **1993**: 29–44.

Talwar, R. ,1993, Business re-engineering- a strategy- driven approach. Long Range Planning, **26**(6): 22–40.

Trihajuwidjajani, W. R., 1995, A review of stakeholders perceptions of a business process reengineering project, An unpublished honours dissertations, Curtin University of Technology, School of Information Systems, Western Australia.

Yin, R.K., 1994, Case study research: designs and methods. (2nd ed.), Sage Publications, California, USA.

115

EXPANSION OF THE SYSTEM BOUNDARY

A Case Study of the Influence of a Multinational Organisation on a Middle Market Supplier

J. T. Wilton and L. R. P. Reavill

Department of Systems Science
City University
Northampton Square, London, EC1V 0HP

1. INTRODUCTION

In an era of unprecedented change throughout the global economy, how can the pressures faced by Medium sized suppliers to the large multinationals be overcome in order to exploit the opportunities that also exist? What approaches have they taken, and should they take in the future, to satisfy and exceed their customers expectations? To what extent can a systemic approach assist SMEs in interpreting the complex environment that they are now working in?

In recent years, throughout the business world, the pace of change has accelerated. However, not only has it speeded up but it is perceived to have much broader social and business implications for the future. When looking at the views put forward by various writers and business leaders, they each have their own way of describing what is meant by this state of flux. Opinions an evidence from Fortune International's *Welcome to the Revolution* (Stewart, 1993) and Rosabeth Moss Kanter's *New Corporate Olympics* (Moss Kanter, 1989) suggest that organisations need to adapt, to make orders of magnitude change, and to do this rapidly. It appears that an organisation's position in the market will increasingly rely on its ability to embrace the continuing pressures and complexity brought upon it by the changing environment, and counter the threats and exploit the opportunities which these many changes bring.

2. MULTINATIONALS AND THEIR SUPPLIERS

In order to explore the influence that multinationals have on their middle market suppliers, it is necessary to understand the forces affecting the business environment. In defining the 'Middle Market', it is categorised as those organisations with between £5m-

Systems for Sustainability, edited by Stowell *et al.*
Plenum Press, New York, 1997

£200m turnover per annum (Coopers & Lybrand, 1996). The underlying forces affecting the pressure for change in organisations and customer-supplier relationships have been widely documented, for example (Stewart,1993; Tapscott and Caston, 1994). Moss Kanter points out that, "Globalizing markets, instantaneous communications, travel at the speed of sound, political realignments, changing demographics, technological transformations in both products and production, corporate alliances, flattening organisations—all these and more are challenging the structure of the corporation. The once very rigid and unbreach-able boundaries of business are fading in the face of change."(Moss Kanter, 1991, page 151).

For Western multinational organisations these forces have led to major change pro-grammes being initiated in order to remain competitive. One of the biggest challenges to-day is the ability to cope with market demand. Moss Kanter (1989) likens their goals to 'Giants learning to dance'. This was highlighted in a Harvard Business Review survey (Moss Kanter, 1991), containing 12,000 responses, from managers from around the world. In a question aimed at the large companies of more than 10,000 employees, 70% had un-dergone major restructuring; 45% had gone through a merger, divestiture or acquisition; 36% had reduced employees and 45% had expanded internationally. However, in compa-nies of less than 500 employees, the results were considerably less at 54%, 18%, 16%, and 15% respectively.

As the multinationals strive to become flexible and enhance their own efficiency and productivity, they have adopted and initiated many programmes, from Total Quality through to Business Process Re-engineering. In addition they have consolidated many of their activities to concentrate on their strategic 'core competencies' (Hamel and Praha-lad,1995). Consequently, they have sought to reduce non-value adding activities, often re-sulting in divestitures and downsizing. This in turn has increased the demand for service and contracting companies. Evidence to suggest this transition is supported by the 3i re-port (1994) and Magnet (1994). The 3i report found, in a survey of 210 organisations with a mean turnover of over £86m, that 72.4% of them had actively contracted out services; 92.4% felt that their actions were advantageous, and 84.2% believed that there was still scope for expansion. The clear benefits for selected core suppliers is an increase in busi-ness and revenues.

3. A SYSTEMS APPROACH

As highlighted in the Harvard Business Review survey (Moss Kanter,1991) the mid-dle market organisations are also adapting to the changing environment albeit at a reduced rate. Yet while they are certainly affected by the forces of change in their own right, they are also being pressed into changes through the actions of their customers.

Indeed the middle market suppliers are facing increased pressure to adapt and com-ply to new and higher standards of operation. Not only do they need to be nationally if not internationally price competitive, but also offer more innovative products and services whilst consistently aiming to reducing their costs. This was recognised by J.Welsh, CEO of General Electric, when he remarked: "If you can't meet a world standard of quality at the world's best price, you're not even in the game." (Sterman, 1993, page 45)

Yet if the suppliers are to gain the maximum benefit from this transition and remain profitable, then they will also have to understand the complexities that it will entail. As more business is contracted out and the prospect of working alongside other such suppli-ers also increases, middle market suppliers can no longer afford to maintain an insular view of their business position or the change programmes that they initiate. Instead they will have to understand and embrace the wider system of interest with regard to the industry that they are in.

With resources often already tied up and the flexibility limited within the middle markets, it is argued that they would benefit from adopting a more systemic approach. As such, it is interpreted as being: "an approach to a problem which takes a broad view, which tries to take all aspects into account, which concentrates on interactions between different parts of the problem." (Checkland, 1995). In a previous paper, (Wilton and Reavill, 1996) the authors examined the issues faced by a middle market supplier using a systemic approach. A variety of systems tools were used to interpret what the organisation was faced with. The circumstances were assessed using a metaphor based approach. As the complexity was primarily soft and the key problems involved human motivation and resistance to change, Soft Systems Methodology (SSM) was adopted. Whilst this was helpful, it did not entirely resolve the problems. The analysis highlighted the need for the supplier to take a wider view of the environment and system of interest since so many factors were affected by its customer's intentions and other suppliers.

It is argued, through the observations of the case study, that middle market suppliers can be slower to adapt to the forces of change than either the large multinationals or recently formed start-ups. It is the middle markets that seem to be struggling most with the impact of the changing environment. Factors such as their history, management styles, the lengths of service of their staff, and the age of the operating systems all affect their dynamism, flexibility and openness to the changing environment. Consequently, their economic potential is not being fully exploited. The issue is compounded since the middle markets can no longer wait for change initiatives to percolate down to them. Increasingly this sector has to create and offer new alternatives to cope with changing demands of their customers if they are to remain competitive.

4. A CASE STUDY OF A MIDDLE MARKET SUPPLIER

The case study in point is of a middle market organisation that the authors have already worked with (Wilton and Reavill, 1996). It is an example that highlights some of the actions that have been taken in response to client demands and the changes put upon them, whilst it also provides an insight into the complexities that such an organisation faces.

The organisation is a UK based print and communications holdings group founded 45 years ago with a prevalent conservative culture. It has a turnover of £20m per annum, with 260 employees and predominantly serves the non-production supply side of the automotive industry, throughout Europe, with printed matter and data management services. Over the last five years the company has gone through a considerable amount of turmoil and change. They include a management buy-out; acquisitions; a Total Quality initiative; process improvement projects; international expansion; development of closer links with its primary customer (a world-wide automotive producer undergoing its own restructuring programme) and improvement initiatives set by its principal customer.

Though the supplier has understood the need for improving its own internal processes through exploiting new technology, it has had to consider the changes taking place in its customer's restructuring programme and work in conjunction with it. The pressure is also on the company to place the same standards on its own suppliers in order that the quality remains high throughout the whole supply process. Added to this is the complication that some second tier suppliers for certain projects are themselves multinationals, for example the paper mills and some IT service firms. How the company intends to achieve this and exploit this opportunity, remains one of the primary tasks of the management team.

Additionally, whilst it has obtained the coveted position of a first tier supplier, its role as one varies according to the projects carried out. In some circumstances it plays a primary role in co-ordinating whole projects and other suppliers, whilst for others it reverses its role and supplies another project co-ordinators. With other projects, its staff are located within the customers offices on a full-time basis. The effect is "...the blurring of external boundaries is happening faster." (Moss Kanter, 1991, page 162) between the suppliers and the customers. It is this phenomenon which leads the authors to argue that the boundary for the system of interest needs to be expanded.

5. EXPANSION OF THE SYSTEM OF INTEREST BOUNDARY

Whilst the middle market suppliers are currently benefiting from an increase in revenues (Coopers & Lybrand, 1996), they are also faced with the necessity of linking their strategies and change programmes to those of their customers. In effect the multinationals, in their quest to become more nimble, are moving towards generating a networked organisation of partnerships and alliances (Snow, Miles, and Coleman,1992). Charles Handy views this development using descriptions such as the Shamrock, Federal and 'inverted do'nut' organisational structures (Handy, 1990). Tom Peters noted from the Harvard Business Review world survey (Moss Kanter, 1991) that there appeared, at the time, to be more rhetoric than reality. However he highlights "that the 'borderless' idea represents a fundamental paradigm shift in our conception of the modern organisation. We are moving from a 'Pre-Copernican' business world, where the individual company is at the centre of the universe to a far more fluid 'Post-Copernican' environment, where each company is but one point in an extended network of equals. Given the enormity of this shift, the fact that today the rhetoric of partnership outstrips the reality is really no surprise. After all, not so long ago, we didn't even have the rhetoric!" (Peters, 1991, page 98)

With the reality catching up with the rhetoric, the complexity of understanding and operating in such an environment becomes more difficult. As the links between the customers and suppliers grow closer, it is still the multinational customer that can exercise its power in the direction it believes is beneficial, leaving supplier to either comply with them or look elsewhere for business. This suggests a more coercive relationship better represented by a prison metaphor. If the middle market suppliers are to overcome this they will have to become considerably more flexible and innovative in their dealings with such customers.

As a consequence, the middle market supplier should no longer view its situation in isolation but as part of the system between the other suppliers and their multinational customer. It is proposed that an orbital approach be taken to expand this understanding and perspective of the system of interest and its boundary. The model highlights the relationships in the form of suppliers orbiting a customer's field of influence, whilst the extent of their inter-relationship is determined by their distance from each other. As external boundaries diminish, the distances between some suppliers and customers become negligible. The interpretation of such relationships is that the supplier's operations are closely, if not inextricably, linked to that of its customer. At the same time, however, these suppliers will have their own suppliers orbiting their spheres of influence. However, unlike the planetary metaphor that this is based on, secondary suppliers are not necessarily smaller than their clients. The authors stress the need for suppliers to see where they are placed in relation to the wider system of interest and their multinational customer in order to interpret how strong the influencing forces are. The concept of using an orbital model is to force the observer to extend his perspectives of the situation beyond that of the organisation's own boundaries and include both the customer's and other supplier's systems of interest. In taking this approach a more holistic perspective can be attained. The benefits of taking such an approach, will be the ability for middle market organisations to adapt to the changing business environment whilst benefiting from the opportunities that arise.

6. CONCLUSION

The relationship between the customer and its suppliers is changing as is the overall business environment. With the level of complexity increasing and the organisational boundaries blurring, it is argued that a systems approach be adopted to understand and interpret the situation holistically. In addition, as the implications of the changing environment affect all aspects of the supply system, it is proposed that to cover all the relevant issues faced by middle market organisations today, the boundary of the system of interest should be expanded to include both the customer and other suppliers.

REFERENCES

Checkland, P.,1993, *Systems Thinking, Systems Practice* (John Wiley & Sons, Chichester).

Coopers and Lybrand 1996, *Middle Market Barometer - a focus on competitiveness,* (1996, Spring).

CSC Index 1994, *State of Reengineering Report - Executive Summary.*

Handy, C., 1990, *The Age of Unreason,* (Arrow Books, London).

Hamel, G., Prahalad, C.K., 1994, *Competing for the Future - Breakthrough strategies for seizing control of your industry and creating the markets of tomorrow.* Harvard Business School Press.

Magnet M., 1994, The New Golden Rule in Business *Fortune International,* Feb. 21: 28–32.

Moss Kanter, R., 1989, *When Giants Learn to Dance,* Routledge, New York.

Moss Kanter, R., 1991, Transcending Business Boundaries: 12,000 World Managers view Change, *Harvard Business Review,* May-June 1991: 151–164.

Peters, T., 1991, The Boundaries of Business: Commentaries from the experts, *Harvard Business Review,* Sept.-Oct. 1991: 93–101.

3i Report, 1994, *plc UK: A Focus on Corporate Trends* January 1994.

Ray, M. and Rinzler, A. [Eds.] 1993, *The New Paradigm in Business - Emerging Strategies for Leadership and Organizational Change* The Putman Group, New York.

Snow C.C., Miles R.E., Coleman Jr., H., (1992) Managing 21st Century Network Organizations, in: *Managing Change,* 2nd Edition, 1993 (C. Mabey and B. Mayon-White, eds.), pp.20–34 Paul Chapman Publishing, London.

Sterman, S., 1993, Are You as Good as the Best in the World?, *Fortune International,* Dec.13: 45–46.

Stewart, T. A., 1993, Welcome to the Revolution, *Fortune International,* Dec.13: 32–38.

Tapscott, D and Caston, A., 1993, *Paradigm Shift: The New Promise of Information Technology* McGraw-Hill, New York.

Wilton, J.T. and Reavill, L.R.P., 1996 How Systems tools and Methodologies can assist with Process Oriented change within Small to Medium sized Enterprises (SMEs) in the UK - A Case Study, in: *Proceedings of the Fortieth Annual Meeting of the International Society for the Systems Sciences* (J.M.Wilby, ed.), pp.563 - 574.

116

AN HOLISTIC MODEL FOR CHANGE MANAGEMENT

George Allan

Department of Information Science
University of Portsmouth
Milton Campus, Southsea
Hampshire PO4 8JF, United Kingdom
Tele: +44 (0)1705-844034; Fax: +44 (0)1705-844006
E-mail: allangw@sis.port.ac.uk, Mobile: 0802-811374

1. INTRODUCTION

There is a growing consensus that any healthy organisation does not stand still but develops and grows. This means change in terms of organisational development (Luthians, 1989) or as problem solving (Wilson, 1984). Change to any established system or way-of-life is perceived as a traumatic experience. The causes of change are not the subject of this paper but we are concerned here with changes that affect daily life within a system. The raison d'être of proper management of the changes to any situation is to preserve sustainability within the overall organisation. As Senn (1990) puts it, today's challenge is to achieve success in a changing world. The following text adopts a systemic view of change and proposes an holistic approach to change management. The background research recognises that any proposal for active change within an established system must provide due cognizance of the human resource as the most influential factor which will both help and hinder the proposed change. Mullins (1996) sees change as an inescapable part of both social and organisational life. Emergent properties of attempts at change are discussed and an holistic model for change management is put forward. This new model is systematic in its thoroughness but systemic in its considerations of the work environment into which any change is proposed. It is also systemic in its approach to an hierarchical system of management of proposed changes. Types and media of communications play an important role in the change management model and emphasis is placed on proper interfaces between stakeholders.

2. ACTIVE CHANGE

If change means improvement to business processes in support of company mission, then this can be regarded as sustaining or improving the position of the company within

Systems for Sustainability, edited by Stowell *et al.*
Plenum Press, New York, 1997

the market place. In this context, change and the proper management of change can be regarded as preserving the sustainability within the overall organisation. Change can also have a detrimental effect if not handled or managed correctly. To this end the proposed change should be regarded in the context of a whole system, and this paper therefore proposes a model which takes an holistic approach to the management of change. Thus change should be seen as holistic, not in isolation. Stair (1992) discusses a linear approach for organisational change and then moves to IS planning. There is a whole debate as to the similarities and differences between control and managing. Control can mean authority, a narrow view dictating decisions taken in isolation which ultimately could well lead to things going wrong. This is often to be seen in a past-orientated culture (Trompenaars, 1993). Control can mean feedback to stay on course, using plans to monitor progress. This is the meaning that will be used here. This paper deals with how to control or manage changes in Information Systems (IS).

3. CHANGE MANAGEMENT

A *change agent* is that person or group who appears to cause the change to happen in the work environment. This could be seen as the person who requested the change in the first place or the person overseeing the change mechanism. It will not necessarily be the engineer who performs the actual mechanics of the change. It is very important to manage changes and not "just let them happen" as any change to an IS configuration can have a potentially adverse affect on the whole system. *Change management* is a disciplined system for planning, implementing, monitoring, controlling and reporting/recording configuration changes. This management will involve the process of helping End Users adapt to the impact of IS implementation in their work environment. One of the most important objectives of change management is to preserve the sustainability of the changing organisation.

4. OBJECTIVES OF CHANGE MANAGEMENT

The first objective of change management is to implement only necessary and acceptable changes. A second objective is to "manage" these changes in such a way as to ensure that service levels are not impaired by the change activity; to ensure that system changes are implemented with the minimum or acceptable levels of risk both at unit level and to the whole system. Another objective of change management is to record change at unit level and document interfaces at system level, and preserve the currency of the overall objectives, the activities and tasks of the system in question. A further important objective is to communicate the impending change, its effects and benefits, to all relevant personnel. In the following model for managing change it will be seen that communication to all stakeholders is a very important and inherent part.

5. A METHOD FOR CHANGE CONTROL

If change is not well handled an emergent property is resistance. This resistance is often based on a black-box attitude to IS leading to low self-confidence born of a feeling of self-inability within a new technology. This can result in a perceived threat to job security. The 're-

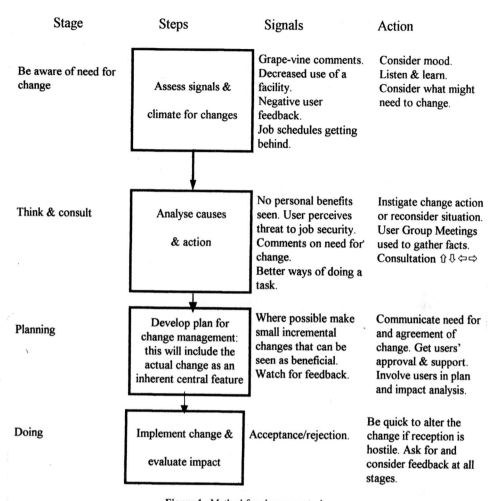

Figure 1. Method for change control.

sistance' is an emergent property because the resultant feelings within personnel go far beyond the actual difference(s) caused by the change. Emergence is discussed in more detail by Checkland (1984) in considering differences between the old system and the new.

Figure 1 considers a method for change control. Notice the systemic nature of the steps in the above model. The steps contain verbs to do with people actions. The signals are all to do with the human aspect and all actions are people-oriented.

It cannot be emphasised enough that any proposal for active change within an established system must provide due cognisance of the human resource as the most influential factor which will both help and hinder any proposed change. Changes can only be understood and actioned by people, and thus carried into the organisational administration (Harrington, 1991). Individuals are the organisation and change affects individuals' perception of their environment, therefore interfaces between stakeholders are essential.

Let us now consider a plan for change management as in figure 2.

It is essential to establish a climate of harmony and trust when managing changes meaningfully (Hochstrasser and Griffiths, 1991), thus creating a proactive culture. On a

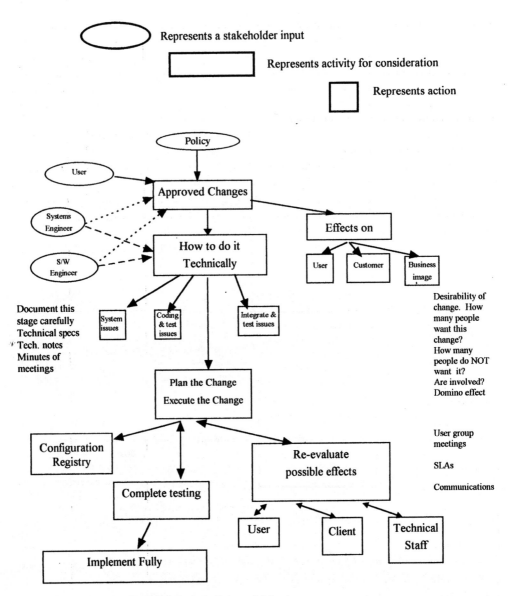

Figure 2. An holistic model for change management.

question of trust, Collins, Miller, Spielman and Wherry (1994) when discussing the soft-ware process from creation to implementation describe this as a social process involving human participants who want and need different things from the process. This should be born in mind at all times. Notice that 'people' are important in the model - the user, the customer, even the software engineer, the system's engineer, the configuration registry, the client, the technical people - these are all stakeholders.

The essence of the model is in developing a plan for change management. Once the policy makers have approved the changes in essence, then the users, the systems engineer and the software people must be involved from the very beginning. The effects of the change must be ascertained, the effects on the user, the customer and the business image. If approved, the next question is how to do it technically, and for this we must consult the systems issues, software issues, any integration issues, as well as documenting carefully the technical specifications. An important question at this stage is the desirability of the change, how many people actually want this change and how many do not; who are the people involved, and consider any likely domino effect of the change. This is where communications to all stakeholders is essential.

Moving on to the plan for the change the people involved here would include the configuration registry in any system and a re-evaluation of the possible effects of the change by the user group. Consider service level agreements, and again communication with the users, the client and the technical people. Once the plan has been agreed, this plan should be completely tested before even considering the implementation. It is not the subject of this paper to outline how changes are to be implemented, only to give a model, a holistic model, for change management.

ACKNOWLEDGMENT

My grateful thanks to Dr. David Anderson of Portsmouth University, England, for his continued support during the preparation of this paper.

BIBLIOGRAPHY

Checkland, P. B., 1984, *Systems Thinking, Systems Practice*, Wiley, Chichester.
Collins, W. R., Miller, K. W., Spielman, B. J., and Wherry, P., 1994, How good is good enough *Communications of ACM* 37(1):81–91.
Faitlough, G., 1993, A systems approach to social innovation, in: *Systems Science Addressing Global Issues*, (F. A. Stowell, D. West, and J. G. Howell, eds.),pp. 289–294 Plenum Press, New York.
Harrington, J., 1991, *Organisational structure and information technology*, Prentice-Hall, New York.
Hershey, G. L., and Kizzier, D. L., 1992, *Planning and Implementing End User Information Systems*, South-Western Publishing Co., Cincinnati, Ohio.
Hochstrasser, B., and Griffiths, C., 1991, *Controlling I.T. Investment*, Chapman & Hall, London.
Jackson, M. C., 1991, *Systems Methodology for the Management Sciences*, Plenum, New York.
Luthians, F., 1989, *Organisational Behaviour*, McGraw-Hill, London.
Mullins, L. J., 1996, *Management and Organisational Behaviour*, Pitman, London.
Senn, J. A. S., 1990, *Information Systems in Management*, Wadsworths, Belmont, California.
Stair, R. M., 1992, *Principles of Information Systems*, Boyd & Frazer, Denver, Mass.
Trompenaars, F., 1993, *Riding the waves of culture*, Brealey, London.
Wilson, B., 1984 *Systems: Concepts, Methodologies and Applications*, 2nd ed., Wiley, Chichester.

117

A SYSTEMIC APPROACH TO ORGANIZATIONAL ROLE AND THE MANAGEMENT OF CHANGE

Robert French and Peter Simpson

Bristol Business School
University of the West of England

1. INTRODUCTION

This paper describes an action research project undertaken over the period of one year with the senior management group of a Civil Service organization. Like much of the UK Public Sector in recent years, this organization has experienced a period of radical change, including restructuring, delayering, and projected staff cuts of approximately 20%. The challenge has been to manage the transition from a traditional bureaucracy to a new organizational form (Cravens, Piercy and Shipp, 1996).

One of the consequences of the fast pace of change has been a series of role re-definitions, following or promoting restructuring, and a consequent blurring of role relations. This research project was established to investigate the contribution that could be made to managing the change by focusing on organizational role.

Our approach has been to work with managers' experience of role and relationships in the workplace. Our work can be located within the fields of Group Relations (Colman and Geller, 1985; Gillette and McCollom, 1990; Trist and Sofer, 1959) and Socio-Technical Systems (Miller, 1993; Emery and Trist, 1969; Miller and Rice, 1967). In particular we combine systemic thinking and psychodynamic theory (see, for example, Hirschhorn, 1988; Lawrence, 1979; Menzies-Lyth, 1988 and 1989; Obholzer and Zagier Roberts, 1994; Trist and Murray, 1990).

This paper will describe the insights gained from undertaking four activities: (i) one-to-one work on role with the chief executive; (ii) individual interviews with all eleven members of the senior management team; (iii) developmental work on role with a sub-group of senior managers; (iv) exploration with the whole senior management group on the way in which the experience of "representation" affects their work.

2. THE PROJECT

This is a case study of an organization in transition. For most of this century the organization has operated as a traditional bureaucracy, characterised by clarity of roles, lines

Systems for Sustainability, edited by Stowell *et al.*
Plenum Press, New York, 1997

of authority and communication, and rules for the settlement of disputes. However, external pressures for improved effectiveness with less resource have necessitated a search for radical changes. Prevailing organizational wisdom suggests new organizational structures that have fewer layers, are more flexible and responsive, and are based on empowered teams and individuals with the expertise to modify and develop ways of working in response to changing circumstances and demands.

We became involved with this organization twelve months after a major restructuring had been initiated. At this point, the presenting problem amongst the senior managers was that of role confusion. It was our hypothesis that the bureaucratic concept of role, based on a clear description of tasks and procedures for reporting within a well-defined hierarchy, was no longer adequate. In the more complex organizational form that was developing, managers needed to find new ways of managing.

The Chief Executive was the primary sponsor of this project, and was himself experiencing particular difficulties in defining his role at a manageable level, as pressures and demands came from all directions, along with advice about what he should and should not be doing.

2.1. One-to-One Work on Role with the Chief Executive

The work undertaken was based on a process entitled *Organizational Role Analysis* (Lawrence, 1979; Quine and Hutton, 1992; Reed, 1976). This involved a series of eight, monthly sessions of approximately two hours. The aim was to work with the Chief Executive "to make a bridge between his consciousness of his experience and the realities of the institution" (Reed, 1976: 96).

Thus, rather than starting with a list of activities in the form of a job description, we sought, through reflection upon particular issues, hopes, problems, or stresses, to frame and reframe his understanding of his role within the changing organization. This involved paying particular attention to the aim of the organization and working relations with others, both internal (other senior managers, senior civil servants, staff) and external (clients, the public, MPs, etc.).

2.2. Individual Interviews with the Senior Management Team

We were interested in the possibility of working with this different concept of role more widely within senior management. The Chief Executive appeared to be very comfortable with the ideas and able to work with them readily. Would the same be true of others? In order to explore this question and to get a broader picture of the problems that were being experienced in role, we interviewed the other senior managers. Each interview lasted approximately two hours. The aim was to work together to explore the manager's image of his role (they were all men) in relation to the organization and the wider system.

These interviews revealed the wide diversity within the senior management team in understanding the nature and importance of role and of its relation to authority. It also became clear just how strongly conceptualisations of role influence and are in turn influenced by the culture of the organization.

2.3. Work on Role with a Sub-Group of Senior Management

The largest operational area in the organization involved five of the eleven senior managers. The interviews indicated the existence of a number of differences that appeared to cause specific difficulties for these five in clarifying their roles and role relations within the senior management group. These included differences in function, history, perceptions, and size, and in the fact that four out of five members of this sub-group were not included in the strategic management group, which included all other senior managers and was seen to influence major strategic decisions.

We worked with the group for a day, on the theme of "Managing Oneself in Role". The day was designed to provide this group of senior managers with the opportunity to explore their shared and different perceptions and experiences of working in role.

2.4. The Experience of "Representation" in the Senior Management Group

As the project progressed, we found ourselves paying increasing attention to the relationship between the senior managers' roles and the complex management structure which comprised a range of formal and informal groupings, sub-groupings, and steering groups. It appeared to us that a critical difficulty within the emerging organizational structure was linked to what we saw as the "representational" dimension of role.

In contrast to a bureaucratic organisation, where role definition and clarity are externally imposed, there exists in the new organizational forms greater potential for confusion in knowing what role an individual is taking in a particular interaction. We designed and facilitated a workshop, with the primary aim of enabling senior management collectively to experience and reflect upon the practice of representation in the context of the senior management structure.

3. WHAT DID THE FOCUS ON ROLE REVEAL?

The focus on organizational role proved to be effective in two ways. Firstly, in revealing the patterns of interaction and perception among senior managers. Secondly, in helping senior managers to see the possibilities inherent in developing new ways of working in role.

3.1. The Patterns of Interaction and Perception

The early interviews and meetings presented us with a view of an organisation dominated by what approximated to "basic assumption mentality" (Bion, 1961; Pines, 1985), where the primary task is obscured by emotional states arising from anxiety. At the level of system, the experience of senior managers was of separation and division. This was most clearly captured in the notion of a "patch", a relatively "closed system" where the "Senior Manager is squire of his domain". What had once been functional, at a time when boundaries were carefully policed and impermeable except with appropriate rigorous authorization, had become dysfunctional because for these senior managers their primary focus had shifted to the whole organization.

There was also evidence of the counter-tendency, Bion's "work" mentality. Individuals who welcomed the changed and changing nature of the system demonstrated the desire to get to grips with the new, broader concepts of role and system and the new forms of representation that these require. However, the general role confusion had supported a culture of distrust, expressed in terms of micro-political manoeuvring, with gossip and rumour as the dominant mode of communication, and negative competition over resources and access to power. Interactions tended to occur at the level of *person* not *role*.

These dynamics may always have existed within the organization, but the nature of control within a bureaucracy would have been sufficient to ensure that the required organizational tasks were undertaken despite these potential problems. However, within the new organizational form the control of rules, procedures and lines of accountability are neither explicit nor enforced from above. The primary source of organizational control comes from the ability of organizational members to maintain for themselves an attention to the task. We found some support for the contention that this may be achieved by working constantly at the experience of role in oneself and in others, as it is revealed in action and interaction.

3.2. New Ways of Working in Role

The critical shift that we saw occurring for some of the managers was a decreasing dependence upon clear job descriptions and a growing awareness that role can be utilised as a method to access authority in a range of situations. Working with role in this way helped managers to make judgements about priorities within the system. Within the new organizational forms they need to be able to make these judgements for themselves moment by moment, meeting by meeting, in contrast to bureaucratic organization where stability is a design feature. The dynamic nature of role became clearer for some, leading to an awareness that priorities could and would change over time, and in relation to different tasks and contexts.

Work on the relatedness of role and system enabled a growing sense that the ranking of roles—i.e. the level of emotional identification with different aspects of one's role—needed to be addressed, both individually and collectively. Historically, the perception of managerial priorities had involved a hierarchy which placed Divisional management at the top, followed by Functional and, finally, Corporate responsibility. In the new organizational form a new ranking of senior management responsibilities needed to emerge, giving primary importance to the Corporate, followed by responsibilities at Functional and Divisional levels. However, working this out in practice is not straightforward. For example, is it always possible for a corporate decision to be taken by a divisional manager in a manner that fully acknowledges both divisional and organizational responsibilities? A systemic approach to organizational role directs attention to the importance of managerial judgement but this does not mean that the judgement will be easy to make.

This relates to the most difficult area of work, for us as well as for the managers, on the representational dimension of role. It is our proposition that in any interaction an awareness of who each party is representing will facilitate more effective work on the task. However, the nature of the new organizational forms is such that all managers have a complex array of roles. The discussion above has indicated that it can be difficult enough to decide for oneself which role takes priority within a particular situation. How possible is it also to establish clarity in relation to others? In the limited work that we were able to undertake on this issue, we observed the achievement of a greater level of clarity in working on two specific strategic tasks as a result of conscious attention to the representative membership within working groups. However, some managers appeared to find aspects of this process threatening or difficult to appreciate. As a consequence, some chose deliberately to avoid giving attention to issues of representation in the latter part of the workshop on this theme. It appears to us that this is an aspect of organizational experience that is currently under-theorised and requires more work.

4. CONCLUSION

The project has shown how experience in role can be used both to make sense of and to work with change in relation to system and task. If the understanding of role and role relations does not develop to keep pace with change, the authority of management within the organization may become overly dependent upon interpersonal relationships, and structures may evolve that are founded on basic assumption mentality despite the appearance of being task-related.

REFERENCES

Bion, W.R., 1961, *Experiences in Groups*.Tavistock Publications. London:

Colman, A.D. and Geller, M.H., 1985, *Group Relations Reader 2*. Washington: A.K. Rice Institute.

Cravens, D.W., Piercy, N.F. and Shipp, S.H., 1996, "New Organizational Forms for Competing in Highly Dynamic Environments: the Network Paradigm", *British Journal of Management*, vol. 7: 203–218.

Emery, F.E. and Trist, E.L., 1969, Socio-Technical Systems reprinted in F.E. Emery (ed.) *Systems Thinking*. Penguin, Harmondsworth.

Gillette, J. and McCollom, M., 1990, *Groups in Context* Reading, Addison Wesley, Massachusetts

Hirschhorn, L., 1988, *The Workplace Within: The Psychodynamics of Organizational Life*, The MIT Press: London.

Lawrence, W.G., 1979, "A Concept for Today: The Management of Oneself in Role" in W.G. Lawrence (ed.) *Exploring Individual and Organizational Boundaries: A Tavistock Open Systems Approach*, John Wiley and Sons. Chichester.

Menzies Lyth, I.E.P., 1988, *Containing Anxiety in Institutions: Selected Essays, Volume 1* ,.Free Association Books, London.

Menzies Lyth, I.E.P., 1989, *The Dynamics of the Social: Selected Essays, Volume 2*. Free Association Books, London:

Miller, E.J., 1993, *From Dependence to Autonomy. Studies in Organization and Change*. Free Association Books, London:

Miller, E.J. and Rice, A.K., 1967, *Systems of Organization* London: John Wiley.

Obholzer, A. and Zagier Roberts, V. (eds), 1994, *The Unconscious at Work*. Routledge, London.

Pines, M. (ed.), 1985. *Bion and Group Psychotherapy*, Routledge and Kegan Paul, London.

Quine C. and Hutton, J.M., 1992, *Finding, Making and Taking the Role of Head*. An edited version of a presentation to the East Midlands Nine Consortium of LEAs Initial Seminar on Headteacher Mentoring on 16 January 1992.

Reed, B.D., 1976, Organizational Role Analysis in C.L. Cooper (ed.) *Developing Social Skills in Managers: Advances in Group Training*. MacMillan Press.

Trist, E.L. and Murray, H. (eds), 1990, *The Social Engagement of Social Science, Volume 1* , Free Association Press, London.

Trist, E.L. and Sofer, C., 1959, *Exploration in Group Relations*, Leicester University Press, Leicester.

118

HIGH PERFORMANCE TEAMS AND THEIR DEVELOPMENT

L. R. P. Reavill

Department of Systems Science
City University
Northampton Square, London EC1V 0HB

1. INTRODUCTION

Trends towards the use of less hierarchical structures in organisations have been evident in the 1990s. Moss-Kanter (1984) has advocated empowerment, commercial organisations have de-layered in search of cost savings, and matrix, project and team based methods of organising staff have been examined. The increasingly competitive environment has put pressure on organisations to reduce the number of their employees, and to obtain the best performance from those that remain. This would-be maximisation of effectiveness has heightened interest in the mechanisms of group performance, and the means of achieving synergy with groups which will enhance the efforts of the individual members of the group, and also achieve more than the sum of their parts.

Differentiation of the performance of the "group" and the "team" has also engaged the attention of writers on management. The perception is that if a group can be made to work as a team, enhanced performance will be obtained. The group is merely a collection of individuals assembled to perform a task, but the perception of the team is of a highly efficient and well coordinated machine with all the components committed to the team objective. Thus achieving the characteristics of the team, or what Hilarie Owen calls "teamness" (Owen, 1996), is a worthwhile objective for any organisation.

Team metaphors are popular in management writing, particularly those concerning football. The need for "a level playing field" for commercial competition is pressed on governments, employees are urged to "play as a team", and "keep an eye on the ball", and the problem of "moving the goal posts" is often encountered. The author was drawn into these analogies on one occasion to the extent of finding possible virtue in less commendable football practices, such as "getting the retaliation in first".

2. A TENTATIVE BEGINNING

In 1995, the author and a colleague started to consider the possibility that there was much to be gained by examining the operative mechanisms, training methods, and per-

Systems for Sustainability, edited by Stowell *et al.*
Plenum Press, New York, 1997

sonal interactions, of sports teams; and their possible application to competitive commercial organisations. Association football (soccer), cricket, and rugby football were considered. Football, particularly soccer, was the preferred area, and some initial discussions took place with Premier Division clubs.

Consideration of teams in other competitive sports suggests that investigation would be less fruitful. It could be argued that the Davis Cup tennis competition is a team competition, but each match is played as four games of singles and one of doubles. The team can be as few as three players. Only the doubles game would provide any indicators of "teamness". In squash matches the competition is between teams of five players, all performing as individuals, and the same very individual contribution is made by runners and swimmers arranged in relay teams. Ryder Cup golf competitions are also an aggregate of individual performances. The rowing eight, (plus cox), might present an interesting example of a highly coordinated team with a focused objective, and netball, basketball, hockey and many other team sports might be considered. It appears that only sports which involve teams of a dozen or so players have sufficient complexity of individual interaction to be worthy of investigation.

A successful sports team may not be composed entirely of "star" players. Clearly, the greater the talents of the individual players, the more likely that the team will triumph. However, other factors such as the extent to which the skills of the players complement one another, the development of the willingness of each player to put the good of the team before his or her own advantage, and training to obtain good coordination, are very important. Indeed, a team of "stars" might suffer ego problems, and be deficient in what Adair (1979) has termed "team maintenance" skills. In another area, that of music, the best string quartets are formed by teams of excellent instrumentalists who do not have quite the phenomenal individual skills to become international soloists. When international instrumental soloists play in string quartets, their individualism, plus perhaps their inability to spent many hours practising and performing together, may not produce a superlative performance.

Thus the value of a study of team performance may well be in the insight it might give to why a group of individuals of any level of talent perform to a standard which is better, equal to, or worse than that which would be expected from the aggregate of their individual abilities. This is the extent to which the group shows synergy (or anti-synergy, if such a term is permitted). Given an understanding of the process which is occurring in the amalgamation of the group members into a team, improvements could be made in the performance of any team, regardless of the talent of the individual members.

More recently, the author has commenced an examination of a car racing team. Here, more complex issues such as the technical development of the vehicle, and the contribution of the support team are germane to the outcome, and the driving "team" may be no more than a pair of highly skilled and highly competitive individuals.

3. LITERATURE BACKGROUND

Blake and Mouton (1964) have demonstrated the personal and task elements of leadership, and Adair (1979) showed that leaders must take into consideration task, personal needs, and team maintenance elements. Belbin identified the team roles which were needed if the team were to function successfully, first with an eight role model (Belbin, 1981), subsequently extended to nine (Belbin, 1993). Belbin found that the model he had developed in the "experimental" conditions of Henley Management College required modification when he applied it in the work-place. Also few work-groups have the luxury of developing their own leader, in most instances the leader is appointed by higher management. Consideration of the work of Maslow (1943) suggests that the personal needs of team members must be addressed, and Herzberg (1959) shows the importance of the growth and motivating factors of the job content. Stafford Beer (1994) has proposed a complex model of team member inter-relationships ("Team Syntegrity"), and emphasised the importance of the "shared information that had changed them into purposive individuals".

4. TOP FLIGHT TEAMS

Hilarie Owen (1996) has recently made a highly significant contribution to this subject with her two year study of the selection, training, and team building procedures of the RAF Red Arrows aerobatic display team. Space limitation does not permit a full analysis of her in-depth study, but a brief summary of the key points will be given.

The Red Arrows have nine pilots, one of whom is the leader. The rest, though they may have different RAF ranks, are of equal status. They stay three years in the team, three new pilots being introduced each year. Applicants to join the team are experienced RAF pilots with excellent flying skills, and from these a short list of nine is prepared by senior officers. However, the selection of the three new pilots is made by the existing team, following a week of flying tests and social interaction. Each year, the partly changed team trains during the winter, and creates a new air display which is performed some 200 times world-wide during the summer. There is a travelling support team of 20, a base support team of 40, and an administration team. Precision high-speed flying is akin to "driving down the outside lane of the motorway with eight other cars, all doing 200 miles per hour, bumper to bumper, knowing that no one would do anything silly, each relying on the other to do their job".

Owen (1996) analyses the factors in the development of this "top flight" team which enable them to perform to such a high standard. These include for the team: 1) objectives and goals; 2) openness and confrontation; 3) regular reviews; 4) support and trust; 5) clear procedures; 6) standards of performance; 7) personal development; 8) inter-group relations; 9) reward system; and 10) centred leadership. For the team members, they include: 1) personal goals and vision; 2) self esteem and assertive communication; 3) values and focus; 4) self awareness and confidence; 5) innovation and involvement; 6) personal standards and individual achievement; 7) growth and fulfilment; 8) social needs and skills; 9) pride and commitment; and 10) consistency and balanced roles. She links the individual team factor with the similar numbered team member factor, and in number order, to give a new model for team development which she calls the "Synergy Chain Process". Owen (1996) argues that the introduction of the same approach would be beneficial to the development of high-performing senior management teams in commercial organisations. Case studies of her application of the method to such organisations are given.

5. CRITIQUE OF THE CONCEPT OF TOP FLIGHT TEAMS

A strong case is made for the value of the Red Arrows methods. Evidence of the application of these principles to commercial organisations is compelling. Those with practical experience of managing teams in the commercial world would find no difficulty in appreciating the value of the factors Owen (1996) has identified.

Even so, there are some aspects of the Red Arrows example which might limit its applicability. The objective of their activity is simple and easily defined, (if complex and difficult to achieve in practice), i.e. to provide a spectacular flying display of the highest quality. This objective is understood by the team members, and they are fully committed to it. Owen (1996) argues that achievement of this ideal state would deliver many advantages to commercial top teams, and cites case studies demonstrating that working toward a full understanding and commitment works wonders for commercial top team performance. However, in a commercial organisation, the objective (or strategy) may be more complex or not totally clear, and there may not be consensus in the senior management team. Owen might argue that in such a case, resolution of this situation is a major priority.

The provenance of the team members is very specific in the Red Arrows. Potential team members have already demonstrated excellent standards of education, skill and character to be considered. Commissions in the RAF, and subsequent promotion to the rank of Flight Lieutenant or Squadron Leader, are achieved only by capability and good performance. However, this implies that the pool of potential Red Arrow pilots will have very similar characteristics. Peas in a pod may not be identical, but there is a high level of similarity. The selection process adds to the similarity by using skill tests and allowing the current team to have the final say in the selection. This delivers the high degree of compatibility which is clearly important for such a team, but it does suggest the possibility of cloning. Owen (1996) shows, using Belbin's eight role model, (Belbin, 1981), a significant change in profile in subsequent Red Arrow teams, although six of the nine members were the same. Even so, *company worker, teamworker,* and *shaper* scored high in both teams studied, respectively: 1, 2=, and 4 in the first team, and 2, 3, and 1 in the second team. Top management teams also include "high quality" individuals, but their education, training and experience would be different: financial, commercial, technical etc. The analogy is "mixed vegetables", rather than peas. In potential team compatibility, the Red Arrows have a flying start.

The last concern is what could be called the personal/team objective differential. The specific situation of Red Arrow pilots generates a remarkable congruence of personal and team objectives. The rewards of success: personal satisfaction, pride and more, are available to the team members primarily from the success of the team. Despite the suggestion that aerobatic flying is not dangerous to a team member because of the skill of, and trust in, the other members of the team, the risk of individual poor performance is obvious: criticism, departure from the team (one example is quoted), or a serious accident. The only competition in the Red Arrows is to improve individual precision of performance, for the overall benefit of the team. In top management teams, the competitive element is still present, and it may benefit an individual to put his or her personal objectives ahead of those of the team. For example, directors have been known to attempt to out-shine colleagues when the post of managing director falls vacant. Elimination of the political element in top management teams is difficult. The Red Arrows provide an example where it appears to have been eliminated.

6. DISCUSSION

The Red Arrows represent a "working model" of the ideal team building procedure. Can this be generalised for the complex operations of organisational top teams? The Red Arrows system is highly ordered; the procedures established and tested; the changes regular and premeditated. Owen used the 8 role Belbin model for analysis, as Belbin's revised model was unpublished at the time of the study. Belbin (1993) included a ninth role, (specialist), as a consequence of his application of his original model in the workplace. In top management teams, a number of specialisations are needed; in the Red Arrows, a single specialisation, albeit at a high level of performance. The author has shown (Reavill, 1996), that in high performing project teams, team membership may need to change to accommodate different specialisations as required by the progress of the project, but not with the regularity of the Red Arrows pilot changes. There is a similarity, as the new pilots import new ideas, but no new techniques. A key feature of the Red Arrows team is openness, good communication, and shared information. This correlates with Stafford Beer's model (Beer, 1994) in which the group is converted to a team, or "infoset", by shared knowledge of the objective, shared information, etc. Owen's "Synergy Chain" parallels Beer's "Team Syntegrity".

Another serious problem surfaces when the resources supporting the Red Arrows are considered. The high-tech jet aircraft, the engineering support crews, and the cost of top rate RAF officers are not perhaps the most significant feature. Many managing directors would be delighted to have one hundredth of the training time for their top team. The implication of the study is that it might pay them to find such time.

7. CONCLUSION

The study of the Red Arrows has provided illumination on the high standards of team development that can be achieved in real conditions, but it is argued that the conditions are close to ideal. It may be difficult to translate the principles to the less ideal and more complex conditions of top teams in other areas, although examples have been given of their beneficial application in workplace situations, (Owen, 1996). What would now be helpful is the expansion of the investigation to established team activity where there is greater complexity of objective; divergence of team member talent; differentiation of personal and team objectives; and more limited availability of resources. It is suggested that the study of sports teams discussed earlier in this paper could provide a suitable extended model.

REFERENCES

Adair, J., 1979 *Action Centred Leadership,* Gower, London.
Beer, S., 1994 *Beyond Dispute: The Invention of Team Syntegrity,* Wiley, Chichester.
Belbin, R.M., 1981 *Management Teams: Why they Succeed or Fail,* Butterworth, London.
Belbin, R.M., 1993 *Team Roles at Work* Butterworth-Heineman, London.
Blake, R.B., and Mouton, J.S., 1964 *The Managerial Grid* Gulf,
Herzberg, F.W., Mausner, B. and Snyderman, B.B., 1959 *The Motivation to Work,* Chapman and Hall.
Maslow, A.H., 1943 "A Theory of Human Motivation" *Psychological Review,* volume 50, July, pp. 370–96
Moss-Kanter, R., 1984 *The Change Masters,* George Allan and Unwin, London.
Owen, H., 1996 *Creating Top Flight Teams,* Kogan Page, London.
Reavill, L.R.P., 1995 "Team Management for High Technology Projects", *Management of Technology Conference,* Aston University, April, pp. 535–37.

119

A CONSIDERATION OF TEAM DEVELOPMENT LIFE CYCLES USING BEHAVIOURAL PARADIGM MODELS AND COMMUNICATION ANALYSIS

Roger Stewart

School of Information Systems
Kingston University
Penrhyn Road
Kingston upon Thames
Surrey KT1 2EE

1. INTRODUCTION

Many organisations are adopting structural forms, such as Flat, Federalist or Decentralised in order to be more reactive to market conditions and more efficient in their operations. An integral part of these structural changes is the creation of teams whose effectiveness is perceived to be a critical part of the efficiency of the organisation as a whole. The understanding of team behaviour is therefore an important part in the restructuring and management of the process of change.

This paper addresses a particular aspect of team behaviour, that of the Team Development Cycle. This cycle demonstrates that teams do not form spontaneously into high performing cohesive units, but rather undergo a developmental process with observable stages. A consideration of these maturation stages using behavioural models and sociometric techniques enables a better understanding of why some teams fail and others succeed. These models have been developed as a result of naturalistic research using psychological theories, sociological techniques, soft systems and failure analyses within a selection of organisations, for example Stewart (1994).

2. LIFE CYCLES

An assumption has been made that a Team is a particular form of group characterised by close co-operation and high cohesiveness. This does not ignore the fact that teams are composed of individuals, but that a common purpose exists, either imposed

Systems for Sustainability, edited by Stowell *et al.*
Plenum Press, New York, 1997

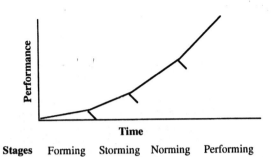

Stages   Forming   Storming   Norming   Performing

Figure 1. Group development life cycle.

from outside or developed internally. Teams, as in groups, do not form spontaneously into high performing cohesive units, rather they undergo a developmental process. Many models of group formation, such as Homans (1951) and Gibson, Ivancevich and Donnelly (1994) have been proposed. Arguably the most commonly used model is that of Tuckman and Jensen (1977) which describes the stages of Forming, Storming, Norming, Performing and Adjourning and shown in figure 1.

At the *Forming* stage the set of individuals have yet to become a cohesive group. They are finding out what their individual backgrounds and capabilities are and formal patterns of authority and responsibility are generally adhered to. This stage is characterised by politeness. During the *Storming* phase individuals try to reconcile their own and group goals, find and establish the methods of handling conflict within the group. At the *Norming* stage the norms and rules of behaviour are established and the roles of individuals are confirmed. This may be the same as the formal roles or the establishment of new ones. The *Performing* stage is achieved when the group has formed as an entity and the prime consideration is achieving its goals. The fifth stage of *Adjourning* is not considered within this paper, however it is important in the context of rapid change and transient teams.

These maturation stages of group development are now considered in the context of behavioural models of teams and their associated communication patterns.

The models described below are examples of emergent counter-productive behaviour exhibited during the stages of team development. Teams that are successful have adopted conscious strategies in order to avoid the pitfalls portrayed in the models. The complete model consists of four components: behavioural descriptions; associated communications patterns; underlying theories and possible causes. For the purposes of this paper only the first two components are used. The first component describes the actual behaviour of the team and the second component describes the communication patterns exhibited by the team. A graphical example of communication patterns, a sociogram, is shown in figure 2.

The communication patterns associated with the behavioural models have been established in research by the author using the Netmap computer package of Alta Analytic Ltd. Figure 2 is an example pattern with the inner circle showing inter-team communication links between individuals and the outer groups showing intra-team communication links between individuals. Different types of sociograms can be produced showing agreed communications (where both parties agree on the incidence/importance of the communication), disagreed communications, and emergent groupings of people corresponding to the informal groupings of individuals in normal operation.

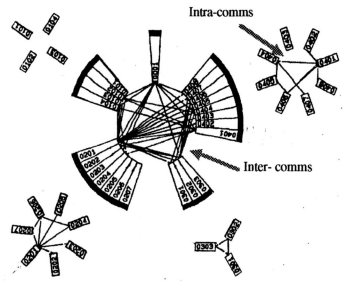

Figure 2. Example Sociogram.

The different maturation stages identified are necessary for all groups to go through in order to develop their efficiency and cohesiveness. At any stage the group can fail to develop to the next stage, or extreme cases, disintegrate. The following behavioural models are examples where groups have failed to develop their full potential as teams.

3. ANOMIC REACTION MODEL

This is an example of where a group at the *Forming* stage has failed to develop into a team, the initial operation has been unsuccessful with the result that the team has fragmented or been dismantled. This can be due to a combination of reasons such as, insufficient time available for team bonding, incorrect choice of team members and unclear goaling.

3.1. Behavioural Description

The team has been formed with the members coming from different areas of the organisation. There is a degree of uncertainty as to exactly what they are meant to be doing and the scope of their authority. This manifests itself in a continuous checking of work and decisions, both internally within the team and with other areas of the company. The level of communication of team members with previous formal and informal networks is high, showing a propensity to discuss previous activities. There is a reluctance to let drop past 'favoured' activities and a possible low commitment to, or understanding of, the new tasks. There is not yet a full identification with the new team, nor an understanding of how this new appointment may serve an individual member's long term needs.

3.2. Communication Patterns

There is a high incidence of inter-team communication to higher levels of authority, other teams or previous teams and departments. The high level of intra-team communications generally follows the formal structure of the team and there is the strong probability of formal chains of communication. Informal groups within the team tend to be formed only when team members are previously acquainted, however there will be a high incidence of informal groups that contain external people. There is a low level of disagreement on the frequency or importance of intra-team communication and the presence of some isolated individuals who do not communicate with anyone.

4. INTERCON MODEL

The *Storming* stage of team development occurs when the team has been operating for a short period and its roles and responsibilities are clearer. Individuals are in the process of reconciling their individual and group goals.

4.1. Behavioural Description

Individuals are establishing the formal and informal positions within the team and bonding between individuals is evident. The methods by which the team as a whole takes decisions are being established. Team members are establishing their identities and strengthening or rejecting individuals in their formal roles. 'Expert' and transient leaders are starting to be apparent and informal alliances are being formed. This stage is characterised by the conflict that occurs and the strategies, overt and covert, that individuals and the team adopt to overcome the conflict. If a team does not formalise these strategies it will never develop its performance and in the case of a major problem or decision at a later time it will not achieve consensus decision-making and indeed may disintegrate.

4.2. Communication Patterns

A lower level of inter-team communications is shown which tend to be on role or task required lines. There is a high level of intra-team communications with some notable exceptions by a small number of members who appear to be isolated by choice or by estrangement to the team. The high level of disagreed communications indicates the conflict between the team members. Isolates at this stage will tend to be ignored at later stages of team development. The team may be split into a number of smaller informal groups that reflect internal power struggles.

5. TEAM CULT MODEL

This model may be seen at the *Norming* stage of team development and covers the period in which the team has developed as an entity and is performing normally. Members have been assimilated and old links to previous work areas have changed or decayed and new links established. The roles, responsibilities and authority of members have been clearly defined and strategies for handling conflict have been established.

5.1. Behavioural Description

This model examines the relationship of individuals to the team. Intra-team norms, work and social patterns have stabilised. A tightly knit society has developed with a 'clan' type of operation of close working ties and personal connections within the team and to other teams. A strong or charismatic leader may have arisen, with pressure on members to conform to the team. A team developed in this form can cause dissatisfaction and indeed some form of cognitive dissonance to individual members. Other problems may surface as a result of the formation of a strong team. For example, 'deindividuation' may cause a lack of self-recognition, 'groupthink' and 'group polarisation' may run counter to an individual member's strongly held attitudes and beliefs. This can lead to disassociation from the team or indeed 'reactance' or rebellion. The end result is an inefficient fragmented team.

5.2. Communication Patterns

Some inter-team communications can be seen. These are probably on the lines of the formal organisation structure. The majority of communications will be intra-team and agreed. Those disagreed communications may form linked isolates or dyads indicating team fragmentation. True isolates will need further investigation. There will be a high incidence of internal communications.

6. TEAM PRIMACY MODEL

This model may be evident during the *Performing* stage of team development. and occurs when the team is well established and has been operating successfully for a period of time. There is strong cohesion in the team coupled with a high self-belief which can lead in certain circumstances to the estrangement of the team from the organisation.

6.1. Behavioural Description

This model examines the relationship of the team to the organisation. The team has developed a strong identity, self-belief and self-importance bordering upon arrogance. It is very clear on how to run its activities successfully, the resources it should have, how it should be structured and demands the authority to define its own boundaries of operation. It perceives as interference hierarchical and lateral organisation attempts to control its activities by setting detailed objectives, goals and budgetary limits in areas where the team believes it knows best. The team feels that it does not have the power to follow its own strategies and is not being given the support or recognition warranted. This leads to some stormy external relationships. The belief of the team is that its activities are of prime importance to the success of the organisation, and hence a 'primacy' or pre-eminent status should be attributed. The result of not obtaining this status is an alienation of the team to the organisation. This team alienation is demonstrated by a resentment to the way in which the team is forced to operate and frustration at the way in which they are required to apply their skills and knowledge without the discretion and autonomy they expect. The end product is an estrangement of the team to the organisation and from the senior management's perspective, counter-productive behaviour.

6.2. Communication Patterns

There is a widespread pattern of agreed intra-team communication, indicating the strong cohesion of the team. This may follow the formal organisation pattern, however the team may have adopted their own agreed informal organisation. There is a very low incidence of isolates and the team is strongly integrated. There is little intra-team disagreed communication, however, some individuals may have a high volume of inter-team disagreed communications reflecting conflict with the organisation. Gatekeepers of information may be in evidence.

7. CONCLUSIONS

The development of team models and associated communication patterns reflecting emergent counter-productive behaviour has been applied to a group development life cycle and proved useful in explaining why some groups fail to develop into high performing teams. If the problems highlighted by the models are addressed by strategies and actions to counteract the inherent dangers shown in the stages of team development, the possibility of success is substantially improved.

REFERENCES

Gibson, J. L., Ivancevich. J. M., and Donnelley, J. H., 1994, 8th ed., *Organizations: Behaviour, Structure, Processes*, Irwin, Mass.

Homans, G., 1951, *The Human Group*, Routledge & Kegan Paul, London.

Stewart, R. W., 1994, Behaviour and Communication Analysis of command and control teams, *Journal of Naval Science*, **20**: 164–174.

Tuckman, B. W., Jensen, M. A., 1977, Stages of small group development revisited, *Group and Organisation Studies*, **2**:419–427.

INDEX